LIVING
THROUGH
LOSS

FOUNDATIONS OF
SOCIAL WORK KNOWLEDGE

FOUNDATIONS OF SOCIAL WORK KNOWLEDGE
Frederic G. Reamer, Series Editor

Social work has a unique history, purpose, perspective, and method. The primary purpose of this series is to articulate these distinct qualities and to define and explore the ideas, concepts, and skills that together constitute social work's intellectual foundations and boundaries and its emerging issues and concerns.

To accomplish this goal, the series will publish a cohesive collection of books that address both the core knowledge of the profession and its newly emerging topics. The core is defined by the evolving consensus, as primarily reflected in the Council of Social Work Education's Educational Policy Statement, concerning what courses accredited social work education programs must include in their curricula. The series will be characterized by an emphasis on the widely embraced ecological perspective; attention to issues concerning direct and indirect practice; and emphasis on cultural diversity and multiculturalism, social justice, oppression, populations at risk, and social work values and ethics. The series will have a dual focus on practice traditions and emerging issues and concepts.

A complete series list follows the index.

LIVING THROUGH LOSS

Interventions Across the Life Span

Nancy R. Hooyman

Betty J. Kramer

COLUMBIA UNIVERSITY PRESS

New York

Columbia University Press
Publishers Since 1893
New York Chichester, West Sussex

Library of Congress Cataloging-in-Publication Data
Hooyman, Nancy R.
Living through loss : interventions across the life span / Nancy R. Hooyman,
Betty J. Kramer.
p. cm. — (Foundations of social work knowledge)
Includes bibliographical references and index.
ISBN 978-0-231-12246-7 (cloth : alk. paper)—
ISBN 978-0-231-12247-4 (pbk. : alk. paper)
1. Grief. 2. Bereavement. 3. Loss (Psychology) 4. Counceling. 5. Social service.
I. Kramer, Betty J. II. Title. III. Series.
BF575.G7H66 2005
155.9'3—dc22
2005050738

∞

Columbia University Press books are printed on permanent and
durable acid-free paper.
Printed in the United States of America

In memory of my son Chris, my husband Gene, my parents, my brother Tom, and my friend and mentor Naomi Gottlieb; and in celebration of my family: Mani, Kevin, and his partner, Athena (Nancy)

In memory of my sister Barbara, my brother Jimmy, my father, my grandparents, and the deceased elders and their family members who have shared their journey with me. I would also like to dedicate this book to all living beings who are suffering and to all those who seek to alleviate that suffering; and in celebration of my family: Jim, Jenner, and Clariel (Betty)

CONTENTS

PREFACE

THIS BOOK, like good social work practice, is an interweaving of the professional and the personal. We were motivated to write this book because based on our teaching, practice, and scholarship, we recognized a growing need in the profession. Although social work professionals work daily with persons grieving loss, they often are inadequately prepared to address both their own and their clients' losses. The relatively limited research is striking given the centrality of loss in the lives of most social work clients. We also were motivated by our own personal experiences of loss, which have profoundly shaped our view of the world, our relationships, and ourselves. A theme throughout this book is that loss is universal, pervasive, and a daily occurrence in our lives. We are no different from any of you who have confronted losses of separation, divorce, unemployment, adoption, abandonment, illness, and death. What does distinguish us is our particular configuration of losses and how we have confronted them and integrated them into our lives. We share our losses with you not because they are out of the ordinary or deserving of your sympathy but because in this book we are trying to integrate the personal and the professional. As we discuss various aspects of grief and loss in the succeeding chapters, we occasionally illustrate theoretical points through our own losses. We believe that we learn mutually from each other rather than from a hierarchy of student/teacher, author/reader, and therapist/client. We are stepping outside our roles of professionalism and authority to show how we have dealt with loss and grief in our lives. Throughout this book, we inject our personal stories into theory and research. We live in a society that denies or pushes death away, acknowledging it briefly with three to five days of bereavement leave and then expecting the bereaved to be able to move on quickly. Few other rituals exist for other types of loss, such as divorce or unemployment. In contrast, we suggest that as social work professionals, we will be more effective at helping our clients deal with loss if we are able to personalize loss. As you discuss this book with your students and colleagues, you can also bring a depth and richness to the dialogue by sharing your losses and how you have chosen to address them. Our personal and professional lives are inextricably intertwined when dealing with grief and loss, the most common and yet the most mysterious of life's lessons.

ix

We began writing this book before the events of September 11, 2001, and we have been shaped by what we learned from this tragedy. This day brought all of us emotionally close to these unexpected deaths, which affected large numbers of people, and reminded us of our own mortality and vulnerability. Images of the World Trade Center falling, burned bodies, jammed phone lines from families calling loved ones in New York City to check their safety, and the daily *New York Times* photos and stories about the deceased are seared forever in our minds. We now live daily with not only the trauma of the deaths but also the loss of security for our government, our country, and our world as we once knew it. Yet such a tragic loss still can produce life-enhancing experiences, as witnessed by the outpouring of support from New Yorkers and people around the world and the memorials established to honor the victims. By living through loss, we can find a deeper understanding of ourselves, our lives, and how we choose to live them.

Our Personal Reflections

Before I went to graduate school, I had been reasonably protected from major loss, even though an unspoken loss had always hung heavily around my family. My father's first wife died in childbirth, and he grieved deeply for four years before remarrying. Vague references were made to her death and that of the unborn child, and we would periodically visit her grave but would never talk openly about her. I knew that there was a locked trunk in the attic where my father kept some of her cherished possessions, and my mother would periodically cry about its presence, wishing that he "would just get rid of those things." The legacy of loss and the accompanying sadness were ever present but never openly discussed. Three of my grandparents died before I was born, and my memory of my paternal grandmother's death when I was six focuses largely on my new shoes and the abundance of desserts. Like many young adults, I had dealt with the loss of first loves and a broken engagement. But none of these earlier losses prepared me for the first tragic loss in my life when I was in graduate school: a drunk driver's hit-and-run death of my brother Tom. I watched helplessly as my parents struggled with their grief, at a time when health care providers, ministers, and other helping professionals had little skill or knowledge about how to support bereaved parents. In fact, the main advice my parents received was to get over it as quickly as possible.

Although they lived nine and eighteen years, respectively, after his death, my mother and father never reached what some theorists have called "recovery" or "adaptation," or what we define in chapter 2 as integration of the loss. Their grief was always present, looming large, and sadness surrounded them. My parents tried to escape the pain by leaving the church that failed them when they most needed healing care, moving from the family home, traveling, and distracting themselves with various social activities. Just as silence surrounded the death of my father's first wife, an even greater silence shrouded my brother's death, despite my best attempts as a social work student to reminisce, talk about feelings, or try to find meaning in my brother's death. If the Mothers Against Drunk Drivers (MADD) organization had existed then, my mother would have had an outlet for her anger and distress. Instead, no one ever mentioned Tom's name. Memories of my parents' pain and sadness are still with me. I tried to be the strong one, offering them support, but I received little support as a sibling. Years later, my sadness over my brother's death emerged in counseling.

Next came my parents' deaths, both from pancreatic cancer. Because they died when I was in my twenties and thirties, these deaths were somewhat "off time," when I also was beginning my academic career and busy with two small boys. As a gerontologist, I was intellectually prepared for their deaths; yet nothing prepared me for the lonely feeling of being an orphan without siblings, especially on holidays, which intensified my awareness of having no family of origin. The moment of realizing that one is an orphan forever changes one's life.

Nothing in my life—and little in our culture—prepared me for the death of my best friend and university colleague, Naomi Gottlieb, who was killed in Prague by a tram. Because we had shared so much over the years, I lost my closest confidante, someone in whom I confided even more than my husband. In our society, however, the death of a best friend often is disenfranchised, evoking little expression of sympathy. Her family viewed me as "just a friend," even though our relationship was probably closer than that of many relatives. In addition, as dean, I was expected to be strong, "handle" arrangements for her son and sister, and honor her publicly with our school's memorial service. There was neither time nor support for me to grieve.

Because of my brother's accidental death, I had always feared something happening to one of our children: two birth sons and an adopted daughter. I vividly recalled how my parents' lives had been shattered and changed after my brother's death. The thought of losing one of our children was unbearable to me. But it was always present, since I had a son who thrived on high-risk adventures: white-water kayaking, bicycle racing, and mountain and rock climbing. I had imagined and feared his death numerous times, especially when he was late in calling after coming off a mountain glacier or out of a raging river. Fortunately, we had been able to talk about my fear and assure each other of our love. Yet because of my fears and images of his death, I immediately knew why a Rainier mountaineering guide was at our door at 9:30 on a June Saturday night. The worst thing that could happen had happened: our beloved son who had everything going for him—a loving girlfriend, success as a Stanford undergraduate, a new summer job in outdoor education with youth—and who had celebrated his twenty-first birthday on the mountain, fell to his death while guiding on Mount McKinley. Winds of more than eighty miles per hour had blown him off the mountain while he was trying to help a client who had slipped. For one indescribable week, we waited until he was found, two thousand feet below, on the edge of a crevasse.

I wondered whether I could go on and then realized that I must do so for the sake of my older son, daughter, and husband. But for many days, simply getting out of bed was an act of courage. I was so deep in my grief that I was ineffective at supporting my family. We all coexisted in a blur of constant loving and well-intentioned visitors, an abundance of food for which we lacked the appetite, the media wanting our stories, making plans for a memorial service while still holding on to the thread of a hope that he miraculously would have survived the week of high winds, snow, and ice. Since the day the ranger called from Alaska to tell me that "we've found Chris," I have read hundreds of grief books, written a journal, spent hours with a grief and loss counselor, talked and walked with friends and then talked and walked some more, raged at the gods for letting this happen, gone numbly through holidays, attended a mothers' support group, and gradually, slowly, almost imperceptibly discovered meaning, purpose, joy, and laughter in my reconfigured life. Writing this book is part of my ongoing "meaning making" of this most painful of losses.

Eight months after my son's death, my husband was diagnosed with stage 4 colon cancer and told that he had three months to live. I raged at the unfairness of it all, wondering how much more we were expected to endure. Like many parents, my husband and I grieved our son differently, unable to bear the pain in each other's face. We turned more to friends and relatives for support than to each other, escaping each other's pain through our work and our two children. We would alternate between holding each other and then screaming at the unfairness of it. Faced with my husband's death, we experienced moments of intense sadness, intimacy, closeness, and connection before his surgery. And then my husband of twenty-nine years, the man whom I loved deeply, left the hospital and never returned home to his family. For this abandonment and loss, I have only questions. I have no answers, only hunches that I have been able to glean from talking to friends, reading his journal after he died, and rearranging the pieces of our marriage. Perhaps it was a way of escaping the pain of grief on my face, mirroring his and too much to bear. Perhaps it was a way to run away from our home of seventeen years filled with memories. My older son once said, "Dad died for all of us the day Chris died." Perhaps it was hope, nurtured by naturopaths, to try to start a new life and relationships as a way to defy the cancer and the odds and miraculously get well. Perhaps it was his anger—at God, at me, at mountain climbers, at doctors who misdiagnosed his cancer as an ulcer and then later told him that it was too late, that nothing could be done to extend his life. Probably it was a mixture of all these feelings and many that I will never know. Even before he died, I was rapidly thrust into another unanticipated loss through separation—single parenting and needing to manage as if I were a widow. Five years later, I can only conclude that we all were "acting crazy" in our grief.

These losses are not unique to me. In fact, when I read or hear of other tragic events, I often think that I have not had to endure as much as others. I have walked, talked, e-mailed and written, cried and laughed with other parents whose child died. Loving friends who are a blessing in our lives surround my daughter, son, and me. I have talked with other men and women whose partners changed dramatically with a diagnosis of terminal illness, leaving them in search of a magical cure. I do well on a daily basis. I was an effective dean and now thrive in my teaching and scholarship, have many friends, and a loving son and daughter. But there still are moments when grief, despair, and intense sadness overwhelm me, and I wonder how I can keep going on. There still are mornings when it is hard to get out of bed and face the life that is now reality. But these moments come less often, are less intense, and are of shorter duration.

A small reminder can trigger tears, but the tears do not last as long nor is my sobbing as deep. Holidays, vacations, and birthdays remain challenges to try to create new memories and traditions for our small family: on a daily basis for my daughter and me, and then with my son and his girlfriend across the country in New York City. I fear something happening to my son or daughter and wonder how I then could survive. But life does go on, challenging us, urging us forward, patiently waiting for us when we are stuck, affirming past loves, and providing new loves and opportunities to learn and grow. My son, my daughter, and I each are different people than we were before my son's and husband's deaths. I would much prefer to have them alive and physically present in my life. But that is not what life has given me. And so I value the new person I am becoming—one who is stronger and more empathic, open, tolerant, passionate, and loving and better able to take risks. Since nothing else is as horrifying to me as losing a child, I am less afraid and calmer; I have survived what I consider to be the worst thing that a parent can experience. I know what is most important in life. I try never to end a conversation without expressing appreciation or love for the other person.

I like myself better as a person now, even though I would give anything not to have had to go through the process that created the new me. My hope is that what I have learned through both my research and my personal losses has translated into a book that will be helpful to each of you, the readers who are embarking on this journey with us of "living through loss" across the life span.

NANCY R. HOOYMAN

WHEN I first joined the faculty at the School of Social Work at the University of Wisconsin at Madison more than a decade ago, I was asked: "What would you like to teach?" Without hesitation, I chose courses on grief and on social work practice with older adults. As a gerontological social worker with years of experience in various settings (hospitals, nursing homes, and community-based agencies), I had had many experiences that informed the development of these courses. A course on grief that I had taken in the 1970s focused primarily on grief associated with death. In contrast, I wanted my course to address more broadly the many and varied forms of grief that social workers confront in their practice. I also wanted the course to be relevant to students in a wide variety of concentrations, such as aging, health, disabilities, children, youth, families, and mental health. I adopted a life-span perspective to examine losses common at different phases of the life course, the developmental issues and needs that affect grief, and developmentally appropriate interventions. Without a text that synthesized the relevant research, theory, and practice, the class readings were vast and comprehensive but unsatisfactory. This book is designed to close this gap and serve as a resource for students and faculty as well as practitioners confronting losses for which they may be inadequately prepared.

I ask my students on the first day of my grief course to explain why they are taking it and what they hope to learn, and on the last day of class, I ask them to describe what they have learned. Some of the reasons that students take my course are

> They have been caught off guard by a client's grief and have not known how to respond.
> They do not know how to cope with their clients' deaths.
> They have experienced so many traumatic losses that they find it difficult to help clients with similar losses.
> They want to learn how to intervene, what to say, and what to do with the bereaved.
> They want to prepare themselves for their own future losses.

My students' comments often have moved me to tears. They describe being more aware of how their losses influence their professional practice, being less afraid of death, being better at implementing interventions, and being more helpful to and at peace with the bereaved. Many students describe synchronistic events during the semester at which they were called on to practice the skills taught in class for responding to loss. Through this process, I have become more convinced of the need to use knowledge and skills to prepare social workers to competently address both personal and professional grief.

I become even more aware of the inadequate preparation of social workers and other professionals when I find friends and colleagues who have experienced incompetent and even harmful responses from their coworkers. For example, one social worker in a large urban hospital was expecting a baby and planning to be on maternity leave during the summer, but instead her baby died soon after being born. When she returned to work after taking the summer off to mourn, several coworkers, who did not know about her baby's death, asked about her new baby. Told of her baby's death, these helping professionals simply walked away. Their discomfort with grief and death prevented them from being able to look her in the eye, to help her, or to express their deep regret and sympathy. The baby of another friend, an emergency room social worker, died just hours after birth. He shared his anger and frustration at his professional colleagues' lack of support. What made it even worse was that their discomfort was so evident that he had to support their emotional reaction to his own baby's death. After a month of not receiving any support from his social work colleagues, he and his wife decided to leave the country for a while to seek solace within themselves. These examples reflect the consequences of living in a death-denying society and the inadequate preparation of social and health care providers to address the needs of the bereaved.

In my professional life, I also have been deeply moved by the tremendous resilience of my older clients, many of whom were dying. One African American woman always welcomed me into her home with open arms. She had endured many profound losses, including the death of her son, her husband, and all her siblings. Yet she was fully engaged in her church activities and embraced the troubled youth in her community by caring for them as if they were her own. She reflects some of the attributes of resilience described in chapter 3.

Going to work in a nursing home one afternoon, I found one of my "favorite" residents, Mrs. S., lying in bed, moaning, and crying out in pain. She told me that the nurses were not answering her call. I discovered that she had had a stroke and had fallen and broken her hip. I insisted that the nurses treat her pain and stood by her bedside feeling helpless to comfort her. But then a calm came over me when I realized that all I needed to do was to "be present." I sensed that she did not want to be alone, so I stood silently beside her bed. In the silence, I recalled that Mrs. S. was deeply religious and loved music. When I asked her if she would like me to sing, she nodded yes. As I sang an old spiritual familiar to her, she smiled at me, continued to cry softly, and then began singing along. Mrs. S. died that night, and I felt privileged that she allowed me to be with her during her last day. Experiences like these have convinced me of the need to be an advocate to improve end-of-life care and to help fill the spiritual, emotional, physical, and psychological needs of the dying and their families.

Like many of you, I have had many losses throughout my life. My earliest memory (at age two) is the death of my baby sister Barbara from sudden infant death syndrome (SIDS). When my sister and I were rushed to a neighbor's apartment, we could only watch from their window what was taking place at our house. I remember feeling confusion and fear, since we did not know where our sister had gone or what had happened to her. Six months later, my sister and I visited the same grandparents whom we had visited just before Barbara's death. We ran from room to room asking, "Where is she?" "Where is she?" We thought that somehow we had left our sister at their house, since we could not find her at home. Overcome by their grief, our parents did not know how to include us in our sister's death.

When I was thirteen, my mother underwent a life-threatening surgery to repair a brain aneurysm. I remember standing by her bedside, watching help-lessly as my normally stoic father wept when we said good-bye to my mother. We were told that the outcome of this very serious operation was uncertain. I felt respected to be informed about the realities of her condition and was grateful to my parents for their honesty. Although my mother did die during the surgery, she came back to life after undergoing a profound and life-changing near-death experience that she shared with us years later. During her lengthy recovery period, I distracted myself from my grief by busying myself with household responsibilities, taking care of my younger siblings, and cooking and cleaning. Given our different developmental phases, each family member grieved differ-ently about both our fear of our mother's dying and the losses entailed by her long period of incapacity.

When my parents divorced in my teen years, my siblings' grief responses var-ied tremendously. The divorce was especially difficult for my younger brothers, who identified more closely with our father, their only male role model. A sub-sequent challenge facing our family was the leukemia diagnosis of my brother Jimmy at age fourteen.

My family and I experienced a roller coaster of emotions as we attempted to address his medical needs (including selling our home and possessions to pay for his medical care and moving across the country to get the "best" care available) and deal with our profound grief and fear. It was especially difficult to watch him suffer during his treatments and to see my mother and siblings struggle with their own response to Jimmy's illness and their unmet needs. Jimmy's resilience and growth touched me deeply. Before his death, this sixteen-year-old boy asked to speak privately with each one of his five siblings. He assured me that he was not afraid, told me not to be afraid, and shared his hopes for me. I felt that I was in the presence of a wise spiritual being. After his death, he visited one of my sisters in a dream, who was having what I now recognize as complicated grief. Her problematic grief symptoms evaporated, however, after her dream about him, when he assured her that he was happy and at peace.

On September 18, 1997, my older sister called very early in the morning to tell me that our father, a long-distance truck driver, had been found dead by a state trooper. My father's semi had traveled off the highway for quite a distance before crashing into an embankment, probably because he had fallen asleep with the cruise set at seventy. The suddenness of his death intensified our grief, and how family members variously grieved his death reflects the determinants of grief highlighted in chapter 3 (kind of loss, age, gender, individual and social capacities, developmental phase of life, and the prior and current relationships).

My own grief response was relatively uncomplicated because of the synchronicity of events that had preceded his death. Although I did not see my father regularly, he phoned and surprised me one week before his death, asking if he could drive up to Madison to visit us, see his grandson, and meet for the first time his six-month-old granddaughter. I was thrilled to spend time with him and astonished by the quality of our conversations, since he typically expressed his love by inquiring about the condition of my car or other practical matters. For reasons unknown at the time, our conversations were more meaningful than usual as he voiced his regrets about placing his father in a skilled nursing facility, his grief over his mother's death, and his beliefs about an afterlife. The next day we drove around the countryside, because my father loved to see hills and valleys stretched across the land. We climbed a tall tower at a state park to take in the natural beauty. At the top of the tower, I took a photo of my father holding my daughter. After the camera shutter clicked, the camera died. Suspecting that this was significant, I paused and paid careful attention to the moment. Ten days later at his memorial service, that beautiful photo of my father and daughter was displayed. In a dream soon after his death, I was having a wonderful time playing with my father in a toy store. I had never seen him as happy in life as I did in that dream. Somehow, this whole experience felt orderly, which comforted me and initially lessened my grief.

The experience of my dad's death also heightened my empathy for bereaved middle-aged adults who are juggling numerous responsibilities. As a mother of two young children with a demanding academic position, I had little time to dwell on my father's death. The effects of this became apparent during my grief class, when I broke into tears upon hearing the song "No Time to Cry," by Iris DeMent. This song is about a woman in midlife whose father has died, but she is too busy working and caring for her children to grieve. I then realized that I had been carrying intense grief just below the surface. I used this experience to illustrate to my students how grief that is not addressed may surface at inopportune times (e.g., when teaching a class). This happened to be a teachable moment, but if I had been with a client, my grief would have prevented me from attending to her needs. I hope that our discussion of self-awareness in chapter 14 will encourage you to reflect on and acknowledge your own grief that may lie below the surface.

Not long after my father's death, I received a call that my only living brother had been diagnosed with a large brain tumor. What was most striking about my initial grief response was my absolute numbness and shock, making it very difficult to drive the seventy-five miles to meet him at the hospital. Unable to concentrate, I remember tightly gripping the steering wheel as a way to "hold on." The doctor who found the tumor explained that surgery was required, and in making his referral, he cautioned us that there were three types of surgeons:

1. Those who were compassionate but not necessarily skilled.
2. Those who were highly skilled but not necessarily compassionate.
3. Those who were both compassionate and skilled but were few and far between.

As I listened to the surgeon's matter-of-fact assessment of the training and skills of surgeons, I was disappointed in our acceptance of a medical educational system that does not require or expect health care providers to be compassionate communicators and technically skilled clinicians. We were referred to the second kind of physician (good with the scalpel but not with his bedside manner). From our perspective as family members of a surgical patient, the hospital environment felt cold, sterile, and uninviting. Nurses came and went, busy with their tasks, not seeming to notice our tears or difficulties, and physicians were difficult to track down for progress reports. Nevertheless, the surgery was successful, and my brother has recovered beautifully. This experience heightened my desire to engage in research and education that will challenge the culture and improve the quality of interdisciplinary health care and care of the dying in America.

Other loss experiences include my grandmother's neurological disorder that took her life and prevented me from knowing her, and the death of my pen pal of many years: my dearly beloved grandfather. Since I was with my mother at my grandfather's death, I was comforted by the peaceful look on his face and his freedom from suffering. But I still miss him and grieve that my children never knew him. Disenfranchised grief from other unspeakable losses has strengthened my empathy and compassion for others. Because of my experience with loss and grief, I realize that none of us may fully appreciate the loss experienced by our family, friends, colleagues, acquaintances, and clients but that we must be open and sensitive to these possibilities.

My experiences with loss are an important part of who I am and have taught me many lessons. I have learned to be open and honest with children about life and death and to include them in my grief. I have learned not to take anything for granted. My children know that they can never leave the house or go to bed angry and that we treat each parting with respect because we do not know when death or some other event might dramatically change our lives. Compelled to confront my own mortality through my many experiences with loss, I have completely embraced death as an inevitable transition and have lost all fear of it. Accordingly, my priorities have shifted. I am more interested in my spiritual development and being a compassionate, kind, and loving presence for others than in impressing them with material or intellectual accomplishments. I am also more aware of and committed to improving end-of-life care for the dying and their families. I hope that this book will help you, the reader, be less afraid of death and other losses and that the interventions it describes will help you alleviate your clients' grief. May you cultivate the ability to have an open heart in the midst of the suffering in your personal and professional lives and compassionately tend to your own grief.

BETTY J. KRAMER

ACKNOWLEGMENTS

THIS BOOK grew out of our personal experiences with loss; our losses of friends, colleagues, and family members; and our professional commitment to prepare social workers to work effectively with individuals, families, and communities grieving loss across the life span. The questions and concerns of the bereaved have made the need for this book clear to us and sustained us when other work and family demands interfered with writing. We are grateful for what we have learned from the bereaved, the students in our classes, and colleagues.

We greatly appreciate the support of numerous colleagues and friends who encouraged us to write this book. Our special thanks go to Cynthia Tomik, University of Washington, and Dr. Virginia Richardson, Ohio State University, for their insightful reviews of drafts of the manuscript, and Lynn Carrigan, who eagerly awaits this book for her course on multicultural and multigenerational approaches to healing grief/loss at the University of Washington's School of Social Work. Their external validation assured us that this book would indeed contribute to the profession. Don Armstrong, the director of Aging and Disability Services, Jewish Family Service, provided information about Jewish traditions surrounding death and grief.

I specifically want to acknowledge Rick Reamer, a professor at the School of Social Work, Rhode Island College, and the special editor of the Social Work Series, and the late John Michel, who was a senior editor at Columbia University Press, both of whom gave me the courage and freedom to change plans and write this book and who were supportive throughout the long writing process.

My special appreciation goes to my son, Kevin, who shows increasing wisdom and empathy to others who experience major losses, and to my daughter, Mani, who taught me about what is important to children who grieve. I will always cherish my friends and colleagues at the University of Washington and across the country who have listened sensitively and openly during my intense periods of grief and supported my personal and professional growth through the process of living through loss.

NRH

I, TOO, am grateful to all those who provided constructive reviews of manuscript drafts and to the editors at Columbia University Press.

I wish to acknowledge my students who have convinced me of the need for this text through their enthusiastic desire to gain the knowledge and skills necessary to respond to their and their clients' pain resulting from traumatic events, difficult life experiences, and a variety of social problems. I am encouraged by witnessing these students' compassion, caring, and commitment. Many of them have chosen their work in order to teach other professionals culturally relevant and developmentally appropriate strategies for addressing grief.

I express my deepest gratitude and affection to my mother, Marge Collins; my sisters, Margie, Barbara, Janet, and Mary; and my brothers, Buddy and Jimmy, for their great influence on my understanding of grief, loss, resilience, growth, caring, and love. My most valued and important source of support is my partner, Jim. Without his tireless encouragement and willingness to be fully engaged in virtually all the responsibilities associated with raising a family and running a household, I would not have been able to carry out my academic activities. My children, Jenner and Clariel, have been incredibly patient with my demanding work schedule and allow me to cherish the very rich quality time we spend together.

Finally, I wish to express my deepest appreciation to Domo Geshe Rinpoche, my spiritual teacher.

BJK

LIVING
THROUGH
LOSS

Introduction

THIS IS a book of questions, not answers. It is about the inexplicable, the mysterious, and the universal nature of mortality and other loss experiences. Death, loss, pain, and grief are pervasive and inevitable aspects of the human experience. They touch all of us in different ways, times, and cultures. As we confront the mystery of loss, we are faced with questions about who we are and why we are here. Whether social workers or clients, each of us must deal with the issues of meaning and purpose in our lives, in our own ways and in our own time.

This is a book of sadness and joy, despair and hope, darkness and light, profoundness and simplicity, good-byes and hellos. It is written primarily for social workers and other human service professionals but also for anyone who has loved and experienced loss. It is for those who are committed to living life fully, no matter what challenges life offers them. This is a book for those who are the searchers, the seekers, and the doubters, those who are willing to ask the hard questions and struggle with the ambiguity of the answers when trying to make meaning of life (meaning making). It is for those committed to the journey and adventure of life, even at its darkest points. This book is for all of us who have ever wondered "why bad things happen to good people" (Kushner 1985). This book does not attempt to answer this question but instead recognizes the many types and meanings of loss and the inevitability of unanswered questions.

Although we have immersed ourselves in the literature, drawn on our and others' life experiences, and suggested interventions that may be helpful to those who are grieving, we do not consider ourselves "experts." Indeed, often our clients are the "experts" who teach us the most about life and death, loss and grief. Instead, we join you, the reader, on this journey—learning as we wrote and rewrote this book over three years, continuing to learn more each day, making numerous revisions, and now offering you our insights and guidelines. We did so knowing that you too can offer much to us. Our hope is that this book will lead to reflection and dialogue among you and your colleagues, family members, friends, and clients.

The Pervasiveness of Grief and Loss

Although we typically refer to grief and loss, the more appropriate term in many ways is loss and grief, since loss precedes the grief. Regardless of the order, grief and the pain of loss are universal human experiences that every person repeatedly encounters, although the meaning and rituals of grieving vary tremendously by culture. Loss is produced by an event that is perceived to be negative by the individuals involved and results in long-term changes to their social situations, relationships, and patterns of thought and emotion. Even perceived positive changes, such as a career move, relocation, or retirement, may evoke feelings of loss and grief (Bozarth 1994).

Losses can be physical or symbolic, but they always result in a deprivation of some kind; in essence, we no longer have someone or something that we used to have. Physical loss is something tangible that becomes unavailable. The clearest example is death: the permanent and total absence of someone we love. Symbolic loss refers to a change in one's psychological experience of social interaction, such as the loss of status and colleagues as a result of a job demotion or the loss of a couples-oriented social network after a partner's death (Rando 1988). Losing someone we love or our health or job is like losing part of ourselves. To be human and alive means to absorb loss each day. The grief that follows most losses is not a disease or illness that can be cured. Instead, it is the price people pay for love and commitment to one another. Grief is a natural reaction to loss, and loss is a necessary and natural part of existence (Viorst 1986). Through the grief process, which entails searching for meaning, we need to learn how to live in this altered world.

Major losses are the most personal and emotional happenings that we experience (Harvey 1996). Such losses never really leave our consciousness, greatly affect our lives, and create a sense of lack of control, although we still are able to choose how to respond to loss. Most of us think of death as a major loss, but its magnitude depends on our earlier relationship with the person who has died. For example, a divorce after thirty years of marriage may be more devastating than the death of a distant relative. Our initial responses to a major loss include numbness, shock, denial, and perhaps the wish not to be alive. Life's greatest and most grievous losses disconnect us from ourselves but also provide opportunities to create more connections with ourselves and others, live more deeply, and find greater meaning in our lives (Bozarth 1994). Whether or not a loss is major is a highly individual matter, based on the nature of the relationship, and varying with culture and religious/philosophical beliefs. (The impact of culture on grieving is discussed more fully in chapters 1 and 3.) In other words, the degree of loss is not a hierarchy, since its magnitude varies with a person's life experiences, culture, and social relationships.

Life is continuous change. Change in itself—whether positive or negative— always contains loss and learning to let go, although not all losses precipitate a grief response. Such a response depends on a wide range of personal, family, and community capabilities and the degree of attachment to the lost person or object. Moreover, grief affects not only the individual but also the family system, communities (e.g., school shootings mourned by the community), and, in some cases, the nation or world, as occurred with the attacks on the World Trade Center. The tragedy of September 11, 2001, created a ripple of complex losses: the immediate ones of death, as well as the longer-term ones of a sense of safety and security, such as the ability—previously taken for granted—to greet arriving passengers at the airport gate or to watch a loved one depart on a plane. In effect, that day changed our world and worldviews forever, creating cumulative effects of secondary losses across time.

Loss reverberates both across and within generations. The multigenerational legacies of loss in our own families, communities, and cultures are powerful. Consider that most adults who were alive when President John F. Kennedy was assassinated can remember in great detail how they heard about his death, where they were at the time, and how they felt. Nearly fifty years later, his death still affects our country. Similarly, future generations will experience and re-experience the losses created by the events of September 11. Both family systems and communities feel losses across generations, such as the legacy of the Columbine High School's shootings on schools or the death of a child or sexual violence within families. The multiple traumatic losses of the December 26, 2004, tsunami will reverberate across Southeast Asian cultures, families, and communities for decades.

Some people think that they have never grieved if they have not experienced the death of a family member or friend. But we are grievers a thousand times over in our lives (Rando 1988). We all are subject to many "little deaths" and the subsequent lessons they teach us, including giving up our impossible expectations of others and ourselves (Kübler-Ross 1969; Kübler-Ross and Kessler 2001; Viorst 1986). Grief is "like a neighbor, who always lives next door, no matter where or how we lie, no matter how we try to move away" (Tatelbaum 1980:8; also see Becvar 1997). "Life is good-bye" because it means having and holding and then giving up what we love the most; we gradually shift from surviving to thriving and experiencing "life is hello"—ready to meet the new and unknown, to change with time, and to receive new and different gifts in our lives (Bozarth 1994).

Losing someone we love through death, divorce, or separation; our health and mobility; our birth or foster parents; or our job all are similar to losing part of ourselves: the self before the loss. In addition, each loss typically has cumulative and secondary consequences, reverberating across generations and social systems. When we experience multiple related losses, we tend to "regrieve" our earlier losses at a later point, although from a different perspective (Oltjenbruns 1998). For example, after a partner's death or divorce, we may experience the secondary loss of friends, income, in-laws, and other extended family members, and we may regrieve losses experienced in our childhood. The death of a child often results in the later loss of friendship networks and the marital or partner relationship, with each of those losses intensifying the pain from the child's death.

The Nature of Loss

Loss always contains some ambiguity, even when it is anticipated, such as a relocation or divorce. Part of this ambiguity is being able to hold the opposing ideas of absence and presence in our minds at the same time, to live concurrently with joy and sorrow. We learn that we can live with sadness and grief as well as with joy and grief. Life and death each require the other, and without both, neither would be a meaningful concept. When we experience loss, we can no longer maintain the illusion of being inviolable or believe in an omnipotent rescuer. By asking "why me," we must face our own mortality and the apparent meaninglessness of life. We must find a personal solution to be able to engage in life again. As we grapple with our losses, we not only must acknowledge grief as a constant companion, regardless of the amount of time that has passed, but also learn once again to open ourselves to joy as well as sadness as part of our reality (Becvar 2001). Paradoxically, the process of living and grieving makes the strongest demand on individuals when they feel most exhausted and overwhelmed (Leick and Davidsen-Nielsen 1996).

In a society that tends to deny and fear death, we often feel uncomfortable talking about grief and loss, wanting to avoid the pain and the darkness. As Becvar wrote, death is "the horse on the dining room table," the "elephant in the living room," and the one life transition that everyone experiences but few want to discuss (2001:4). Even so, death and life, pain and joy are interconnected. Paradoxically, the only thing permanent about our life is its impermanence. Even in the midst of the intense pain of loss, we can enrich our life by acknowledging and living in the awareness of our own mortality. As reflected in the title of our book, *Living Through Loss*, the process of searching for meaning can be life changing. Such awareness and such questions encourage us to live in a more vital and honest manner, which, over the long term, will change the way we relate to others and to our lives. In turn, this process will prepare us for handling our own future pain and losses of life.

When we confront loss, we are challenged to create meaning where none seems to exist. This intensely personal process means weaving an entirely new picture and story about ourselves, our world, and what it means to live. Loss through death, for example, marks the end of one chapter and signifies the beginning of a new one in our lives. As such, it can open doors to greater awareness, sensitivity, compassion, and even wisdom. As Theodore Roethke implied in his poem "Dark Time" (1966), it is only in the darkness that the eye sees clearly. Despite feelings of powerlessness and despair, we have choices to make regarding how we will live in a now dramatically altered context. Paradoxically, when we lose someone we love, we may also lose our fear of death and whatever it represents, feeling a freedom that we once thought impossible (Becvar 1997). For example, parents who earlier lost a child tend to fear their own dying less than do those who have not lost a child. In fact, some bereaved parents welcome death as a way of reuniting them with their lost child (Klass 1999).

Loss Through Death

Death is the only type of loss that can never be recovered; it is loss forever. In the most basic terms, dead is dead (Miller and Omarzu 1998). Even if one believes that life continues in some form beyond death, there still is the absence of a physical presence to adjust to. We miss the touch, the smell, the smile, the hug, the tone of voice, the laugh, and the lightness, even while we hold these senses in our memories. Becvar (2001) suggested that perhaps we must speak of death in order to understand fully what it means to be in the presence of grief. And to speak of death is to enter the realm of the supreme mystery, that of the unanswerable questions. But in a society that seeks ready answers and solutions to questions, many of us remain uncomfortable with the unanswered questions, the lack of control, and the feelings of powerlessness initially inherent in loss through death.

Loss Not Related to Death

Although this book deals largely with the grief and loss entailed by death, it also is relevant to interventions with persons who are grieving a loss not related to death. Grief is pervasive and affects our clients of all ages in a wide range of practice settings: children who have been separated from their birth parents through adoption or foster home placement; older adults who must leave their longtime homes and neighborhoods; immigrant families who have lost their country; and individuals and their families who are coping with chronic physical or mental illness or a history of sexual violence. We briefly review several of these types of losses here and then cover them in more depth in later chapters.

Sigmund Freud (1917) deemed the two great wellsprings of mental health as being love and work. Accordingly, the loss of a job can have wide-ranging repercussions on individuals' self-concept and identity, their families, and their larger social networks of friends and relatives (Harvey 1998). The long-term impact varies with the personal and social resources available to the unemployed person (e.g., counseling, extensive networks) and how he or she uses those resources to cope with the loss (e.g., the unemployed person is highly motivated to use his or her social networks and finds a new job or becomes chronically unemployed). In the current tight economy, many people of all ages are faced with long-term unemployment and the inability to find a job congruent with their skills and background. In this instance, losses are multiplied many times over: loss of income, status, self-identity, and perhaps even one's home.

Chronic physical and mental illness and disability create numerous losses for both the person with disabilities and his or her caregivers. The parents of a child with disabilities immediately face the loss of a long-awaited "normal" baby and their ideal of what their child was to be. They suddenly have to live with something unexpected and, as parents, accept what is unacceptable. They face the loss of what they had defined as rewarding parenthood (although they may later redefine what is rewarding from raising a child with disabilities). Their grief is long term, or what is termed *chronic sorrow*, since they constantly face adjustments throughout the child's life and grieve at each milestone (e.g., birthdays, school graduations) when they reflect on "what might have been" (C. Brown 1999; Roos 2002). Their grief is unending and is associated with the living, not with the deceased. They may also face financial losses through the actual costs and lost opportunities of caring for their child. In response to their losses, they may feel disillusionment, aloneness, and vulnerability, and perceive life as unjust and unfair and their family as disrupted.

Adults with a chronic illness or disability (e.g., burns, spinal/brain injury, Alzheimer's and other types of dementia) lose not only control over their body and independence but also physically intimate, sexual, or romantic relationships. For them, everyday relationships are central to understanding the meaning of loss if they feel dependent on others and are unable to develop relationships of interdependence or reciprocity (Harvey 1998). When illness or injury occurs, at any time during life, a person's self-image of competence is replaced by a new self-image as a patient whom others treat objectively. Life-threatening accidents, such as the late actor Christopher Reeve's spinal cord injury when he was thrown from his horse, profoundly change a person's sense of self.

Dreams also are lost in job loss, infertility, illness and disability, sexual assault and domestic violence, and separation or divorce. When a dream has been lost, something inside a person has been lost, too. When a dream dies, a sense of potential dies too, so individuals must search inside themselves for the seeds of another dream (Bozarth 1994:109). Divorce or separation requires letting go of these dreams along with all that was invested in the relationship, by dissolving other ties, relationships, family structures, and previous roles. We may also have to abandon our dreams as a result of a loss of place through moving or not being able to afford a home; this loss can occur throughout life, for the child whose parents are homeless, for the wife who flees an abusive situation, and for the older adult who must move to an assisted-living facility or nursing home. Place defines our sense of space, how we feel in that space, and it adds predictability to life. Consider the emotional connotation of being able to "go home," no matter what phase of life we are in. Losing the space that is "home" throws us psychologically off base, making it even more difficult to deal with the secondary losses associated with the loss of physical space.

Some of us have undoubtedly experienced a loss that others dismiss lightly or quickly: the loss of a pet, a favorite object, a job, a friend to AIDS, or our first love as a teenager. We may recall feeling misunderstood or dismissed when we shared what for us was painful, only to have someone respond by telling us "the greatest loss is . . ." or "think how fortunate you are that . . ." To imply that any type of loss is greater than another is to overlook the complex, intensely personalized nature of loss and its various meanings based on our family history and rules, personalities, past experiences, and cultural beliefs and value systems—in sum, the essence of who we are. It also overlooks how we choose to react to our loss. Each of us, despite our feelings of despair and powerlessness, can choose how we interpret our losses, give them meaning, and incorporate them into the core of who we are and who we will become. Even when we find new ways to understand and live life as meaningful, the changes in our belief systems and behaviors continue to reverberate throughout the other systems in which we live: our families, neighborhoods, communities, and workplaces.

The Nature of Grief

People grieve because they have lost someone or something to which they were closely attached. In most instances, there has been affinity and attachment before the loss (Leick and Davidsen-Nielsen 1996). Joy, light, and love may have preceded the pain, sadness, and darkness. This pattern of "good" followed by "bad" is not universal, however, since an adult child may grieve the death of a parent who was abusive, neglectful, or absent; a wife may mourn her divorce from an emotionally distant husband; or a widower may grieve his wife's death after years of exhausting caregiving. Despite any limits of their past relationships, many adults still feel an attachment—even if negative—and thus feel loss, perhaps combined with some elements of relief.

Although we may fear it, *grief* is the normal psychological, social, and physical reaction to a loss. It is experienced through our feelings, thoughts, and attitudes; our behavior with others; and our health and bodily symptoms (Rando 1988). Intensely personal, our grief is based on our own perception of the loss. It is not necessary for us to have the loss recognized or validated by others for us to feel grief, although the lack of social validation may intensify our loneliness. Accordingly, no two people grieve in the same way. Well-meaning friends and professionals may try to reassure us by telling us our grief will end in six months, a year, five years. But a fixed timetable or sequence of stages does not exist (Hagman 2001). Indeed, some losses are so profound and life changing that the grief never completely ends, with its intensity, acuteness, and form ebbing and flowing over time. In such instances, "getting over it" may not be possible or desirable. Instead, once we have lost, we always live to varying degrees in the presence of grief (Klass 1996a, 1999). Nor can the process of healing be hurried or magically speeded up, even as we may implore others to do "something," "anything," to remove the hurt. To grieve requires a great deal of time, energy, and attention. There is no simple formula or escape through drugs, alcohol, isolation, or anger. As implied by this book's title, each of us must be permitted to struggle to come to terms with loss in a way that works for us. The journey of grieving is toward learning to accept and live with loss, not closure. This journey—the various phases and challenges inherent in the grief process—is discussed in chapter 2.

Disenfranchised Grief

The concept of *disenfranchised grief* refers to grief that persons experience when they incur a loss that is not or cannot be openly acknowledged, publicly mourned, or socially supported. For example, people who are in a relationship that is not publicly recognized or socially sanctioned—such as a gay, lesbian, or bisexual relationship; cohabitation; extramarital affair; or a relationship with a former spouse or past lover—may grieve the loss of the relationship through death, divorce, or separation but not receive support from family members, friends, or coworkers (Doka 1989b). The bereaved is disenfranchised from the role of griever when others do not acknowledge the loss, such as a prenatal or perinatal death and the loss of a beloved pet, and among families of persons with mental disabilities, Alzheimer's, or other types of dementia. The reality of the loss may not be socially validated, such as the "social death" of a person who is comatose, the "psychological death" of an individual who is brain-dead, and the "psychosocial death" in which the person has dramatically changed, whether through dementia, stroke, mental illness, or alcoholism. In other words, the person who previously existed is now perceived as dead by loved ones, even as they continue their physical care of him or her (Doka 1989b:6).

Disenfranchised grief can intensify feelings of anger, guilt, powerlessness, and ambivalence. In fact, the very nature of disenfranchised grief precludes social support; although individuals have undergone an intense loss, they may not be given time off from work, have the opportunity to verbalize the loss, or receive the expressions of sympathy and support characteristic of the death of a socially sanctioned relationship. Every society has rules for or norms of grieving that attempt to specify who, when, where, how, how long, and for whom people should grieve. These grieving rules are often codified in personnel policies regarding bereavement leave. For example, someone experiencing a loss that is not publicly or legally recognized, such as a young man whose partner has died of AIDS, generally cannot use bereavement leave to attend any rituals or to begin to work through his grief. The various types of disenfranchised grief in each developmental life phase are discussed more fully in later chapters.

Social Workers' Understanding of Grief and Loss

Ideally, all human beings should understand the processes of grief and loss. Unfortunately, many will never have the time, space, freedom, or support to do so because their lives are dominated by loss, pain, poverty, and death. Social workers and other health care professionals, however, regardless of the type of their practice or age group, must take time to acquire such understanding. Social workers, in particular, often work closely with individuals and families who are grieving a loss, whether in a child welfare setting, hospital, hospice, assisted-living facility, refugee center, urban school, or homeless shelter. They need to under-stand that grief is an inevitable and ever present part of their practice. They should take note of earlier losses and how they were resolved, since past losses can complicate the grief process by intensifying both the emotional and the physical reaction to recent losses (McCandless and Connor 1997).

In addition, social workers and other human service professionals must acknowledge the nature and centrality of loss and subsequent grief in their own personal lives, as well as in the lives of their clients and in their role as professional helpers. When we accept grief as a given, at least at some level, we then can search more productively for meaning for those whom we wish to help. Yet we also must recognize that facing and overcoming the fear of loss as well as dealing with tragedy are not things we can *do for* our clients (Becvar 2001:192). Grief is hard, painful work that no one can do for anyone else. But we can and must do this for ourselves, including constructing a belief system that can give us meaning and a safe context in which to facilitate our clients' journey of grief and healing.

Because death and loss are so often feared or denied in our society, social work professionals must first acknowledge that all of us have a finite lifetime. The harder task is then to become comfortable with the fact that "each of us ultimately must die," to cognitively and affectively confront and accept the inevitability of one's own death. As Worden observed, "If loss is not adequately resolved in the counselor's life, it can be an impediment to a meaningful and helpful intervention. If it has been adequately integrated, then the counselor can be more helpful" (1991:134). Our comfort with our mortality varies with what we bring from our family of origin, our family history, and our culture's rules and norms. We all receive a variety of messages, both implicit and explicit, about whether death is to be considered an uninvited stranger or a welcome guest (Becvar 1997, 2001). Becoming conscious of those messages is the first step toward working with those who are grieving. Professional helpers must acknowledge explicitly the pain that others feel while at the same time recognizing the potential to reclaim joy.

Despite the centrality of loss for most clients of social workers, few social work practice texts or courses adequately address issues of loss and grief (Kramer 1998; Kramer, Pacourek, and Hovland-Scafe 2003). Although social work's role in end-of-life care and thus in death and dying has become more important, little has been written specifically for social workers about individual, family, and community responses to different types of loss across the life span. Our hope for you, our readers, is that this book will deepen your self-awareness and knowledge, increase your ability to help both yourself and others through grieving, and point to other resources that can assist you in your work. While the bereaved person is the one who must engage in the hard and painful process of grief, social workers with the appropriate knowledge, skills, values, and resources can avoid providing misinformation, imposing unrealistic and inappropriate expectations, or using ineffective interventions that only intensify feelings of pain, confusion, and anger. Given the universal nature of loss, the traditional hierarchy of and the boundary between professional and client are less relevant. Rather, it is our clients who are our true teachers in learning about and understanding the meaning of loss as they show us the many facets of the emotions of grief.

Underlying Themes of This Book

The issues or themes that underlie our approach to grief and loss that we discuss throughout this book are the following:

• Grieving is an extremely *complex, ambiguous,* and *individualized experience* with physical, emotional, and spiritual dimensions. Different people grieve in very different ways. Although there is no right or wrong way to grieve, there are empirical examples of complicated grieving. Accordingly, there is no "cookbook" or linear approach that professionals can use with persons confronted with loss.

• Appreciation of *cultural diversity and norms* regarding loss, rituals, and cultural constructions of grieving is important in order for professionals to understand the meaning of loss for different groups of people across the life span. *Cultural competency* is essential when working with diverse populations who have their own norms about how to grieve. We distinguish cultural competency from *cultural appropriateness* (i.e., being sensitive to cultural norms, values, and beliefs) and *cultural access* (providing information and services in ways that break down barriers created by language, institutionalized discrimination, etc.). In this text, cultural competency refers to the preparation of service providers to value diversity, to be able to engage in cultural self-assessment, to be aware of the dynamics of interacting cultures, and to adapt their service to reflect their clients' culture and traditions. When possible, we include examples of cultural norms and variations throughout the text and examine them in detail in chapter 1. The absence of evidence-based interventions for diverse populations is inexcusable.

• There is a wide variation in what is considered *normal* or *healthy grieving.* For example, what was once considered pathological, like a continuing attachment to the deceased, is now viewed as normal. Indeed, what is considered "normal," "complicated," or "pathological" changes over time and with different social-cultural contexts. Accordingly, we have tried to avoid using the words *pathological, resolved,* or *normal grief.* But because those concepts are so deeply rooted in early grief-work theories, we sometimes have had to use them in our discussion of theoretical perspectives. Within the overarching concept of grief are different types of grief that have clinical significance, such as disenfranchised grief, discussed in chapter 1, and chronic sorrow, described in chapter 7.

• The value of taking account of the *larger social and physical environment.* What is considered a loss may vary markedly for an adolescent in a low-income community terrorized by violence, a single mother struggling to maintain her family as she flees an abusive situation, or an upper-middle-class parent of a child with learning disabilities and extensive resources. This larger environment affects the individual and social capabilities that he or she can bring to the grief process.

• The necessity of recognizing how the *developmental phase of life* interacts with and is complicated by grief and loss. For example, the loss of one's job through retirement at age seventy has a meaning very different from that of the layoff of a single mom in her forties from a high-tech company. Whether losses are developmentally on time (e.g., death of a partner in her eighties) or off time (e.g., the death of a partner in his twenties) also affects the grieving process. The *accumulation of loss* during a lifetime magnifies the grief with each loss, especially in old age. Each chapter that discusses loss at different phases of life—childhood, adolescence, young adulthood, middle adulthood, and old age—is organized according to that phase's customary developmental processes and tasks. The recommended interventions therefore need to be developmentally appropriate and are organized by each phase of life.

• *Evidence-based interventions* work more effectively with bereaved individuals. Such interventions are presented in chapters 5, 7, 9, 11, and 13, following our discussion of losses characteristic of different phases of life. We tried to include only evidence-based interventions, but we need more empirical evaluations of interventions with bereaved individuals, and we lack such interventions for different cultural and ethnic minorities. Because of the unevenness in the intervention literature, the interventions are not always targeted to the types of losses discussed in these chapters. Usually, however, we suggest interventions for each of the types of loss covered in the life-span chapters.

• Most people are *resilient* and through loss or adversity experience psychological growth, development, and well-being (Fredriksen-Goldsen 2006; Fredriksen-Goldsen and Hooyman 2003). Such abilities emerge in individuals, families, cultures, and communities and interact with and modify the relationship between adversity (e.g., loss) and physical and mental well-being. In contrast to intrapersonal models of grief, we emphasize social and cultural capabilities as moderating variables. The concept of resilience resonates with social work's strengths perspective and the ecological model of person and environment.

Overview and Summary

In this book's review and discussion of the literature and its recognition of the many types and meanings of loss, we discuss how developmental tasks intersect with only some of the most common losses throughout life. We hope that organizing the chapters according to developmental considerations, individual, family, community, cultural capabilities, and resilient outcomes, along with discussing interventions, is useful to your clinical work and research. At the same time, the gaps in research—especially the lack of evidence-based interventions related to grief and loss, particularly for diverse populations—prevent our exploring them fully in each developmental phase.

Throughout this book, the word *partner* refers to a spouse in a heterosexual marriage or a life partner in either a homosexual relationship or a heterosexual, nonmarried relationship. This definition recognizes and honors the diversity of intimate committed relationships. Accordingly, *widow* and *widower* represent all sorts of partner relationships, not just legally married couples. The words *wife* and *husband* are used when the research findings are based on only husband/ wife samples, not gays and lesbians or heterosexual partners in a committed relationship.

Chapter 1 defines grief, loss, mourning, and bereavement; reviews the major theoretical perspectives of grief and loss; and describes some cultural variations in the experience of grief and loss. Chapter 2 analyzes the dynamics, phases, and challenges of the grief process; discusses the distinctions between healthy grieving and complicated mourning; defines disenfranchised grief; and examines the various manifestations of grief. In chapter 3 we look at the factors influencing the nature of the grief, including the type of loss, personal capabilities such as spirituality and meaning making, gender and age, and family, community, and cultural capabilities or strengths. We present a resilience model to conceptualize assessing the grieving individual's abilities or strengths and how the adversity of loss affects his or her mental and physical well-being (Fredriksen-Goldsen 2006). The losses often experienced at different times of life are examined in the chapters on childhood (4), adolescence (6), young adulthood (8), middle age (10), and old age (12). These losses include the death of child, parent, or partner; those experienced in adoption and foster care; caregiving for an older adult or child with physical or mental disabilities; and sexual violence. A chapter on the appropriate grief intervention immediately follows each chapter on a different type of loss. The intervention chapters (5, 7, 9, 11, and 13) analyze the existing evidence about which methods are most effective for which populations and suggest future directions in both practice and research. Since working with the bereaved inevitably raises issues about our own mortality as well as past losses, we look briefly at self-care for the professional in chapter 14.

1

Theoretical Perspectives on Grief

GRIEVING IN response to loss is universal among human cultures; it is described in works of literature from ancient times to the present day and throughout the contemporary world in scientific and nonscientific accounts (Archer 1999; Rosenblatt 2001). According to Parkes, "There is something that all who suffer a major loss have in common and the word 'grief' does have a universal meaning that transcends culture" (2001:35). An anthropological study of seventy-eight different cultures found grief expressed through tears, anger, personal disorganization, lamentation, depressed affect, and difficulty in engaging in normal activities (Rosenblatt, Walsh, and Jackson 1976). Although grief appears to be universal, there is no universal theory of grief that applies to all people (Rosenblatt 1993), because grief is a complex, highly individualized phenomenon with a wide range of what is considered "normal" in different social and cultural environments (Lund 1989; Parkes 1972, 1996; Raphael 1984; Sanders 1998; Zisook and Schucter 1986). Despite such wide variation, much of the research on grief and loss takes an ethnocentric perspective, without considering how culture and religious or philosophical convictions influence grief and loss experiences and professional assessment and interventions.

Cultural norms and variations help determine how grief is expressed, especially in the rituals that surround grieving. The relationship with the deceased and notions of deviant grieving also are culturally constructed. In fact, Rosenblatt (2001) maintains that as it is socially and culturally constructed, grief is malleable, since how we grieve is affected by cultural norms. Most definitions of grief in response to loss, however, follow a cross-cultural norm. Cross-cultural views conceptualize grief as a nonlinear process without an end point. Although it typically becomes less intense, it can be restimulated to its initial intensity throughout the process (Cowles 1996). The early theoretical perspectives, which are reviewed in this chapter, did not take account of cultural variations in the grief process.

This chapter begins by defining the key concepts used throughout the text. We then discuss how culture affects the grief process and provide a review of the primary theoretical perspectives on grief that influence interventions. Finally, we compare the classic psychodynamic model of grief work with a postmodern, social constructionist perspective.

Definitions of Terms

Grief is defined as the physical, psychological, and social reaction to the loss of something or someone important to us. Grief represents the particular reactions that a person experiences while in a state of loss or bereavement (Sanders 1998). Grief may be manifested in physiological changes (e.g., loss of appetite or insomnia); emotions of sorrow, distress, or guilt; and socially through family and other interpersonal relationships. Grieving is the price we pay for being able to love the way we do; it is not an illness or pathology (Fleming and Bélanger 2001). In grief, people lose an essential part of what has become their inner experience of themselves and their assumptive world. They therefore must change their ideas about identity to match the new reality emerging from the loss and incorporate these changes into a new assumptive world (Archer 1999; Doka 2000a). The word *grief* comes from the Latin word *gravis*, meaning "heavy." Think how often we refer to someone's carrying a heavy burden of grief. Griev*ing* implies the movement from being injured or burdened to bearing or carrying on, making choices, and, ultimately, healing. When we grieve, we may move from being acted upon or passive to taking action and making choices. Grieving pertains to not only the way that we survive a loss but also the way that we act or choose to learn to live more fully and creatively, to go into the deepest part of ourselves, and to redefine ourselves. It takes courage to grieve fully and deeply, to feel the pain and face the unfamiliar (Doka 2000a; Tatelbaum 1980).

Although there is something basically human in grieving, a simple biological or developmental process does not control or shape how people grieve a loss, how long they grieve, or the meanings they ascribe to the loss (Rosenblatt 2001). Grief has a pervasive quality, which affects a person's whole being. It is experienced psychologically and cognitively through painful feelings, thoughts, and attitudes; socially through behavior with others; and physiologically through health and bodily symptoms (Rando 1988). When we grieve, every aspect of our lives is thrown out of balance (Tatelbaum 1980). Intensely personal, our grief is based on our own individual perspective on the loss.

What is important is the meaning to us of that loss. It is not necessary for the loss to be recognized or validated by others for us to experience grief. Accordingly, no two people grieve in the same way. Each person's grief process differs in intensity, duration, and time to resolution (Kagawa-Singer 1998). Although stage theories of grief are now generally rejected (Klass 1996, 1999; Walter 2003), a constellation of feelings typically accompanies a significant loss. These are fear, including the fear of expressing one's feelings, numbness and shock, dread, anxiety, guilt, anger, rage, and intense sadness.

While grief is the normal response to loss, not every loss gives rise to grief. In some situations, a bond of attachment is absent, for example, divorce or widowhood from a bad marriage or after a long, difficult period of caregiving for a partner/spouse. In such instances, relief may be the primary emotional response, at least initially. Some people may suppress, compartmentalize, or refuse to acknowledge their grief. The early research on grief labeled such responses as pathological, but more recent critiques of "grief work" recognize that responses to loss vary widely and that pathology is culturally constructed (Corless 2001; Moos 1995; Murray 2001; Neimeyer and Mahoney 1995; Rosenblatt 1993). In fact, some people who have lost a loved one through death or divorce may adopt a stoic style, try to appear "strong," and not grieve publicly. But the lack of visible grief does not mean that their grief is denied, suppressed, or abnormal. Instead, their type of emotional constellation permits attachment without giving rise to grief. Other people are better able to incorporate their loss into an existing worldview in terms of God's will or that "bad things happen, even to good people" and nothing can be done about them. For example, those who have strongly held conservative religious beliefs may accept the death as a sign of God's omnipotence and visibly show few signs of grief (Klass 1999).

No matter what the nature or the cause of a loss, guilt may manifest itself through either feelings of self-doubt and responsibility for one's actions or inactions ("if only") or accepting others' blame and judgment. Unfortunately, some bereaved individuals may try to deal with guilt by blaming everyone and everything for what has happened, a process that can lead to isolation and rejection by others. A complicating factor is that secondary feelings—rage, guilt, and sadness over their primary feelings of rage, guilt, and sadness—can get in the way of expressing primary feelings. Those who are grieving may need the support of a professional or friend to separate secondary from primary feelings.

Guilt is most likely to be salient in instances of suicide or sudden death, when people had no chance to say good-bye or felt they could have done something different to prevent the loss, or when things have been left unsaid. But many people have no guilt associated with a death, usually when people have communicated and resolved conflicts as they emerged. Nothing has been left unsaid. Some families may agree that they will not go to bed or leave the house without saying good-bye or without resolving their anger, because they recognize that they might not wake up or return to resolve it. Other people need years of counseling to help them say good-bye after a loved one's death and to alleviate their guilt.

Bereavement is the objective situation of having lost someone significant (e.g., being deprived) and the overall adaptation to loss (Parkes 1972; Sanders 1998; Stroebe and Schut 2001a). It usually refers to loss through death, although we can be bereaved through other types of losses, such as the loss of relationships through divorce, separation, or disruption.

Mourning, a term often used interchangeably with grief, is a cultural and social rather than a psychological process (Weiss 1998). Mourning is typically associated with loss through death, but a person can be in mourning over the loss of a relationship, dream, home, job, or country. Mourning is defined as "the social expressions or acts expressive of grief that are shaped by the practices of a given society or cultural group" (Stroebe et al. 2001:61). It consists of the conscious and unconscious adaptive process that gradually reframes the psychological ties that bind us to a loved one or an object and help us find a new balance in our lives changed by the loss. In fact, mourning can lead to a new mastery over our lives (Tatelbaum 1980). There is no right or wrong, good or bad way to grieve or mourn. To imply otherwise to ourselves or other mourners is to do a tremendous disservice to the intensely personal journey of grief. Although we later define pathological, complicated, and chronic grieving, we strongly urge caution when using the term *pathological*. For example, what was once considered pathological or abnormal, such as maintaining a bond with the deceased, is now considered normal and healthy (Klass 1996, 1999). This illustrates the inherent limitations of most definitions, which are culturally bound, subjective, and susceptible to changing over time.

Cultural Variations

The early theoretical perspectives on grief generally did not take account of cultural differences. Although grief appears to be universal, it has variations in different cultures. As Klass found (1999), the universal is experienced within a culturally defined reality. Shukria Alilmi Raad, an Afghan Muslim, wrote at her husband's death, "No matter how different we look, what kind of religion we practice, or which direction our faith takes us, we all have two things in common in this world: life and death. We have no control over death" (1998:47). Mourning is also influenced by cultural variations. Each culture has its own extrinsic and intrinsic beliefs, values, expressions, expectations, ceremonies, and rituals to give meaning to their individual and collective loss, especially through illness or death. As the bereaved try to make sense out of the deaths in their lives, cultural and social contexts shape the answers to their questions: What does death mean? What does life mean? What did this person mean to me and this community? What does my life mean now that this person is dead? (Benoliel 1994; Parkes, Laungani, and Young 1997). The cultural context of the individual and community modifies the perception of and interpersonal and intrapersonal responses to the grieving process, in effect, determining whether we will be beaten down by loss or emerge more resilient (Klass 1999; Rosenblatt 1993; Shapiro 1994). For example, in Western cultures, we tend to expect individuals to recover from grief quickly; in fact, we may have more tolerance for recovery from physical illness than from an emotional wound. Friends, coworkers, and even family members may urge us to "get over it," be strong, keep busy, and move on with life. Independence and autonomy are highly valued in mainstream American culture, in which grieving is seen as interfering with daily routines.

Most Americans are uncomfortable around others' sadness and tears and so want a quick solution to grief. In our culture, pain is seen as something that can and should be avoided, instead of being viewed as an inescapable part of being human. We should not assume that Western concepts of grief, such as depression and anxiety, apply universally. People from other cultures understand and categorize their experiences differently in the context of their beliefs about the origins of events, the nature of the person who has died, the appropriate way to behave, and the meaning of loss (Rosenblatt 1993).

In life crises, people are likely to return to their cultural values and beliefs, which they may not use in their daily lives but now help them make sense of their world or bring meaning to guide their behavior (Kagawa-Singer 1998). What may appear to outsiders to be discordant beliefs may be normal for a particular culture. For example, although crying appears to be a universal response, the Balinese do not cry but instead put on a smooth, unruffled, even happy exterior as though they are not bereaved. They do so because they believe that the gods will not heed their prayers if they are not calm (Rosenblatt 1993, 2001). Culture also strongly influences the structure and content of language. Language, in turn, subtly configures the experience of death and bereavement. For instance, the Spanish translation of the word *grief* is *afflicion*, or affliction. This implies suffering from an outside source and a passive experience; it contrasts markedly with the English meaning of grief in reaction to loss that affects a person's whole physical, emotional, psychological, spiritual, and social being; is internal; and has a potentially active connotation (e.g., to act to overcome our grief) (Neimeyer and Keesee 1998).

Every culture has expectations about how strongly we should grieve and how much we should distance ourselves from grief, and we move between these expectations over time (Parkes 1972; Rosenblatt 2000). Cultural variations are particularly noticeable with regard to how loss through death is understood. Beliefs about death, including the possibility of future reunion with the dead, the meaning of various forms of emotion following a death, and what to say to oneself and others following a death also are culturally defined (Rosenblatt 2001). For example, the Ilafuk, a Pacific atoll people, distinguish losses that are inevitable or justified (e.g., dying naturally in old age) from those that are illegitimate frustrations, especially those caused by and preventable by others (e.g., accidents caused by others). Different losses call for different self-talk about the loss, behaviors, and expressions of feelings and others' responses. After a good cry, the bereaved Ilafuk are expected to return to ordinary functioning and forget the person who has died. By contrast, among Egyptian slum dwellers, a major loss is expected to cause years of muted depression, suffering, and bereavement. By Western standards, the contrasting behaviors of the smiling Balinese, the composed Ilafuk, and the mute Egyptian mother all might be viewed as pathological. The somatization of grief—presenting emotional distress in the form of physical complaints such as weakness, discomfort, and physical pain—is more common in other cultures than it is in the United States. For example, *men*, a Chinese term for something pressing on the heart and chest, may be interpreted in Western culture as heartbreaking (Rosenblatt 1993).

Instead of expressing emotion, Buddhists try to focus on their belief in karma and reincarnation and the predetermination of their current life by good or bad deeds in their past lives. The deceased is viewed as moving toward enlightenment while survivors continue their bonds with him or her. A mourning period of forty-nine days, during which the mourners wear black clothes and armbands, is prescribed. A special ceremony is held on the seventh day after the funeral and is then repeated every seven days for seven weeks. The anniversary of the death and two special memorials (March and September) are set aside for surviving family members to pay their respects at grave sites (Lee 1991; Rosenblatt 2001).

Latino families place a high value on interdependence, and they regard the loss of a family member as a threat to the family's future and that may lead to extreme anxiety. They may express their grief in seizure-like behavior and hysterics diagnosed as "ataques," with some bereaved persons fainting, feeling nauseated, vomiting, or experiencing other physical symptoms. Bereaved men, however, who are influenced by *machismo*, may try to suppress their feelings. After the deceased is buried, both men and women are expected to accept the death and be strong; as Roman Catholics, they believe that the spirit of the dead person needs reassurance from the living in order to find peace in his or her after-life (Juarbe 1996; Younoszai 1993).

Wide cultural variations exist in the rituals and ceremonies preceding and following a death, including those of ethnic minority cultures in the United States. For example, traditional African American funerals containing vestiges from West Africa can still be found in the rural South, whereas funeral customs among African Americans in northern cities, especially in the middle and upper-middle classes, tend to resemble those of the dominant majority (Perry 1993). By contrast, bereavement rituals in Mexico today and among Mexican Americans in both rural and urban settings generally follow the orthodox Catholic service (Younoszai 1993). The Day of the Dead is an occasion for celebration in Mexico and much of Central America. Native Americans generally do not publicly or openly express their grief, nor do they discuss death. Within the family, however, members wail and show other outward signs of grieving (Lipson, Dibble, and Minarik 1996). Those who practice Islam typically bury their dead within twenty-four hours and disapprove of cremation. In contrast, many Hindus believe that death is the end of the body but not the soul and that cremation allows the soul to continue to exist (Kamel, Mouton, and McKee 2002).

Less is known about how culture influences the appropriate emotional expression and integration of losses other than death (e.g., divorce, birth of a disabled child, miscarriage or abortion, unemployment, loss of country). What is important to recognize is that persons from culturally diverse groups may chronically grieve significant losses. Refugees and immigrants, for example, may have to deal simultaneously with the loss of homeland, personal belongings, family members, economic status, professional identity, cultural traditions, language, and sense of self. The ongoing, deep-seated nature of such unresolved grief undoubtedly complicates the intensity and duration of the grieving process. In fact, refugees and immigrants may finally seek mental health services years after their move to the United States.

In sum, the cross-cultural variations in grief are not random but arise out of societal and cultural worldviews. The cultural differences in patterns of behavior and social support reflect the culture's expectations of what is healthy and appropriate. Throughout this book, we provide illustrations of cultural differences both within and across cultures. These are only generalizations, however, and undoubtedly there are exceptions. We have tried to avoid stereotyping or overgeneralizing and acknowledge that numerous variations exist within each culture as well as among cultures. For example, any description of Asian American culture must take account of the great diversity within that culture, in which at least thirty distinct cultural groups speak more than one hundred different languages. Latinos also are extremely diverse, encompassing Cubans, Mexicans, Puerto Ricans, Central and South Americans, and the native Mexican American or Chicano populations. Intragroup differences exist not only because of ethnic background variations but also socioeconomic class and education. As another illustration of diversity within ethnic groups, the lifestyle, values, and beliefs of some upper-middle-class African Americans may be closer to those of Caucasians than to those of African Americans in lower socioeconomic groups.

These examples of cultural variations highlight the need for professionals, families, and friends to take account of different cultural lenses, social realities, languages, and vocabulary. To provide bereavement care from a multicultural perspective, we must be aware that the grief of each individual, group, or family is unique. The grieving person constructs his or her reality in the context of his or her culture. Without taking account of this influence, professionals may see disturbances or aberrations when none exist in that cultural context. Regardless of our own cultural background, our own ideas about grief are undoubtedly only some of many useful ways of thinking about it (Rosenblatt 1993, 2001). Throughout this book, especially when we discuss interventions, we draw attention to the importance of taking account of cultural differences. Our goal is to identify some cultural features that distinguish certain communities, with the hope that professionals will be able to address other cultural characteristics when working with ethnic and cultural groups different from their own. But as we note throughout the intervention chapters, there are few empirically based, culturally competent interventions.

Classical Psychoanalytical Perspectives on Grief
Freud

As developed in his *Mourning and Melancholia* (1953, 1957), Freud's psychoanalytic theory was the first major theoretical perspective on grief, and it profoundly shaped professional interventions. His concept of grief work assumed that the primary task is separating, or detaching, from the deceased. In other words, the bereaved must complete the grieving process before beginning new relationships and taking on new challenges. Although it is normal for the bereaved to have an affective fixation to the deceased for a period of time (Freud 1961), if it lasts for too long, it can lead to an abandonment of interest in the present and future and an inability to form new relationships. *Internalization* is the transformation of the bond with the deceased, in which the bereaved internalizes the deceased's image and relates to that internal object as if it were the actual person. Internalization is a preliminary stage to letting go (Freud 1957).

Hypercathexis—encountering an emotionally painful memory of or implicit assumption about a loss—was viewed as painful, intrusive, preoccupying, and thus detrimental to other mental activities. C. S. Lewis described hypercathexis as he struggled with his wife's death: "People get over these things . . . one is ashamed to listen to this advice but it seems for a little while to be making out a good case. Then comes a sudden jab of red hot memory and all this 'common-sense' vanishes like an ant in the mouth of a furnace" (1961:7). According to the psychoanalytic perspective, a grieving individual must sort through internal or mental representations of the lost person, and then the ego must "decathect" from each one in order to reclaim "libido" for new mental activities, relationships, and commitments.

To achieve this separation demands intense psychological input from the mourner, hence the concept of "grief work" as central to Freud's approach. *Grief work* refers to the hard active effort of acknowledging and expressing painful emotions such as guilt, self-reproach, and self-accusation. This effort then frees the bereaved person from his or her attachments, or *cathexis*, to the dead person, inhibitions of becoming a separate person, and conflicts or ambivalence regarding the lost relationship. Because the bereaved has only a limited time and energy to devote to grief work, in order to form new relationships, the connection with the deceased must end. *Decathexis*—or breaking the bonds between the survivors and the deceased—was seen as central to grief work and to other mental activities. The bereaved also must explore early connections of infancy and childhood—the past—before successfully resolving the loss in the present. Detaching and breaking such attachments reorganizes the psychic structure. The bereaved can then recover from a loss within a year or two and return to earlier levels of functioning related to daily routines (Freud 1957; Osterweis, Solomon, and Green 1984). Later psychoanalytic grief work used the word *introjection* to describe a process in which the deceased is held more closely during the early phases of grief and is then given up at the end of the grieving process (Fenechel 1945).

Similar to treating a physical wound, the psychoanalytical perspective views grief work as a healthy process that slowly heals the wound in the psyche or the soul (Engel 1961). Freud believed that time alone does not heal all wounds, that it also takes hard work, time, energy, and courage. He assumed that if a person confronted with loss does not engage in grief work, the wound will fester, and the grief process will become complicated and increase the risk of mental and or physical illness (Leick and Davidsen-Nielsen 1996). Although grief is not a disease, it can be fatal. Recent research has found that major losses can unleash a flood of stress hormones that can stun the heart, causing sudden life-threatening spasms in otherwise healthy individuals (Martikainen and Valkonen 1996; Wittstein et al. 2001). Similarly, the mortality and the suicide rates for older widowers were found to be higher than those for their married counterparts or widows, in part because of higher morbidity rates (Nolen-Hoeksama and Larson 1999). But most widows and widowers do not die of a "broken heart," nor do they suffer long-term physical and mental health risks. Indeed, some bereaved partners find personal growth and newfound skills. The variables affecting the grief process of those who have lost a partner or spouse are discussed more fully in chapters 8, 10, and 12.

The grief work model presupposes a limited amount of time and energy to invest in grief work, hence the importance of "moving on" as quickly as possible to "normal." Freud's individualized model of emotional catharsis, detachment, and full recovery appealed to Western cultural beliefs related to efficiency, autonomy, and independence. Ironically, although Freud maintained that mourning ends within a relatively short time, he maintained attachments to his daughter and grandson for as long as thirty years after they died (Shapiro 2001). Contrary to his widely advanced theoretical perspective, as a parent he was well aware of the long-term nature of grief and ongoing connections to dead children.

Freud's work is frequently criticized for implying that completed grief work represents a cure and for pathologizing nearly all grief reactions. Today, very few practitioners believe in literal libido or the idea that the mental energy invested in representations of one person is necessarily lost to other mental activities, even though elements of the psychoanalytical perspective still may influence practice. In contrast, the social functional and postmodern perspectives emphasize that the goal of grieving is not to disengage completely from memories of lost relationships and bonds with the deceased.

Lindemann and Parke

Freud's concepts were followed by the pioneering work of Eric Lindemann (1944), who studied grief within a medical framework. He viewed acute grief as a syndrome having five psychological and somatic symptoms: somatic distress, preoccupation with thoughts of the deceased, guilt, hostility, and loss of usual patterns of behavior. Grief was thus regarded as a disabling condition, particularly when it was prolonged or delayed and when psychological suffering was manifested in physical problems, mortality, and morbidity. Lindemann maintained that the duration of grief reactions depended on how well the bereaved person performed his or her "grief work." Resolution was "emancipation from the bondage to the deceased," "readjustment to the environment without the deceased," and the ability to form new relationships (1944:143). This separation process encompassed protest, despair, and detachment. The bereaved's personality and the community's sanction and support also influenced the type and severity of the grief reaction. But Lindemann believed that with effective management and treatment, severe psychosomatic and/or medical problems stemming from distorted grief could be avoided, ameliorated, or eliminated. Although he recognized the bereaved person's uniqueness and special needs, Lindemann suggested that the grief reaction could be managed in eight to ten interviews over four to six weeks. Grief that lasted longer than this was considered to be distorted or, in Lindemann's terms, pathological.

C. M. Parkes, another pioneer grief researcher, also was strongly influenced by Freud's concept of grief work. Parkes believed that if bereaved persons were able to "work through" and express their feelings, they could achieve resolution within a relatively short time. He identified two elements influencing bereavement:

1. Stigma of the person "tainted by death," with others often avoiding the bereaved person or feeling uncomfortable in his or her presence.
2. Deprivation owing to the absence of love and security provided by the dead person.

Because such views of grief were based on clinical observations and psychotherapy, they often overlooked larger social and cultural forces or interpersonal interactions in the grief process. Both Lindemann and Parkes also considered loss in terms of lost objective relations, which required that the grieving person reorganize his or her internal object world. Nevertheless, the psychodynamic approach, represented by Freud, Lindemann, and Parkes, had a significant impact on theory and practice. For example, the conceptualization of grief as a stressful life event requiring coping skills developed out of the psychodynamic framework, as discussed in chapter 3 (Folkman 2001; Pearlin 1989; Stroebe and Stroebe 1987).

Loss is a life-changing event that forever alters the shape and outlook of our lives. Therefore, we should not look at it as an event that we must "get over" as quickly as possible but as a process that takes time and patience (Silverman and Klass 1996). Unfortunately, well-meaning professionals and friends may indicate that "grief is taking too long" or that a bereaved person should "keep busy, go out, meet new people, have another child, join a singles' group." Such expectations emerge from our human desire to be assured or perceived by others that "we are fine." In addition, we often put on an exterior appearance that will keep others at an emotional distance and avoid the discomfort we might cause them by talking about our grief. Regardless of how we approach our losses, grief tends to be exhausting, consuming extensive emotional and physical energy. In that sense,

all grieving is hard work, even if it does not fit into the grief work model proposed by the early grief theorists.

Despite numerous critiques of grief work, it continues to affect present-day
practice interventions related to loss (Rosenblatt 2001; Stroebe 1992; Worden
2002). Because of its dominance, it is important to understand the grief work
approach and to make use of those parts that seem helpful, as well as later perspectives, such as the postmodern view of the importance of ongoing bonds
with the deceased.

Bowlby

Freud and Lindemann failed to recognize fully the importance of the prior
specific relationship, especially the extent of the attachment. When studying
bereavement, attachment theory is useful as a way of thinking about what is
"broken" or "lost" when a family member or friend dies, leaves, or disappears
from our lives and of identifying individual differences in intense emotional
reactions to loss. The role of attachment or security emerged in John Bowlby's
research on the effects of losing their mother on children's later psychopathology and delinquency, in which he used the concept of attachment to explain the
psychological impact of loss (1960, 1969). According to Bowlby, attachment is a
protective biological mechanism that serves to ensure the survival of the individual species, and it derives from the basic need for security and safety.

Adult attachment bonds are derived from the same emotional system underlying child attachment (Main, Kaplan, and Cassidy 1985; Weiss 1993). In both,
there is a numbing focus of attention on the lost figure through vigilance or a
yearning to recover that figure; restlessness, disorganization, intense distress,
and despair; protest at the separation and loss of security; and reorganization,
including the importance of talking to the deceased (Bowlby 1980). A close
family death disrupts attachment security and elicits an adult version of the
infant's response to attachment threat or loss (Parkes, Stevenson-Hinde, and
Marris 1991; Weiss 1993). Clinging, crying, and angry coercion in grieving
adults represent an effort to restore the attachment bond. The parents' grief
over a child's death, in particular, is conceptualized as a disruption of attachments, creating a similarity between grief in adults (who perceive themselves as
the protectors of their families) and separation distress in children (who are the
protected figures). Attachment in parental grief may emerge as intense wishes
to protect and soothe the lost child, often accompanied by guilt and helplessness for not having protected the child from pain and death. Attachment bonds
encompass both positive and negative feelings (e.g., a child who is neglected or
abused may still feel emotionally connected to the abuser). In contrast, some

philosophical and religious belief systems, such as Buddhism, regard attachment as a primary cause of suffering. Accordingly, people should develop compassion and seek equanimity if they hope to eliminate suffering (Truitner and Truitner 1993).

An attachment bond is associated with feelings of security and expectations of permanence; in fact, the bond persists even when interrupted by loss and distress. To illustrate, entering a new marriage does not end grieving for the partner who has died, although support and intimacy can be found in the new relationship; nor does having another child resolve the grief for the child who died at birth. That is, it is not the loss of the occupant of a role that gives rise to grief; it is the loss of a particular person. A person's despair thus may continue even when what might seem to be substitute relationships are available.

Because of the role of attachment security for adults, emotional loneliness, unique to a primary attachment such as marriage or a long-term homosexual relationship, cannot be assuaged by social support in the way that social loneliness can be. This is because multiple attachment bonds to other relatives, children, and friends are likely to be embedded in such primary relationships. In other words, a widow or divorcée loses not only her partner but also past relationships with children, extended family, and couple-oriented networks (Van Doorn et al. 1998). In contrast, friendships and relationships with work colleagues can be important but not have a bond of attachment. Bowlby assumed that when these types of relationships ended, distress, but not grief, resulted (Bowlby 1982). Although Bowlby's work reflected the classic model of "resolving grief," he did recognize that the death of a loved one is extremely painful and often underestimated by others. He saw talking about the deceased as a way to eventually "let go" of him or her, and the process of grieving as leading to either the ability to make and maintain other relationships or an inability to do so (Walter 2003).

Parkes (2002) investigated attachment style and bereavement outcomes empirically. Adults who reported having secure attachments to their parents during childhood showed less grief and distress than did those who clung to and demonstrated separation distress with parental figures during childhood. Those who had learned to avoid attachments had difficulty expressing their feelings during bereavement. Understanding how attachment styles affect bereavement outcomes is an area for further research (Richardson 2006).

In both Lindemann's and Bowlby's models, the grief process involves yearning and search, disorganization and reorganization. If the bereaved are able to express their feelings, they can achieve resolution or reorganization. Loss is a transient state that is resolved by developing a coherent narrative about it (or what has been called the "coherence of discourse and mind"), in order to be "normal" or healthy (Hess 1999; Shaver and Tancredy 2001). For example, Bowlby recognized the importance of widows' seeing and speaking with their deceased husbands, a process conducive to their healing. Secure individuals are able to experience and express emotions to a moderate degree, provide a coherent account of their loss-related experiences, and update their "internal working models" of the dead person. Unresolved grief is conceptualized as an inability to think and talk coherently about loss and trauma. According to both Lindemann and Bowlby, intense and prolonged grieving involves self-blame and lowers self-esteem. This is viewed as "pathological" and stems from flaws in a person's emotional development during childhood. In sum, an active ongoing effort of working through the memories and emotions associated with the lost relationship is viewed as necessary to come to terms with the loss and to reduce grief over the long term.

Both Bowlby and Lindemann assumed that grief work was necessary to recover from loss through the review and expression of negative emotions, especially anger and hostility toward what or who was lost. Such "working through" is a cognitive process of confronting a loss, going over the events before and at the time of the loss, focusing on memories, and working toward detachment (Stroebe 1992:2). A later *task model* of grief sees resolution as accepting the reality of the loss, experiencing the pain of grief, adjusting to an environment from which the deceased is missing, and reinvesting emotional energy in another relationship (Worden 2002). The *process* of grief work is regarded as a period of intense distress and inevitable pain, which must be confronted, fully experienced, and "worked through" (Rando 1993; Sanders 1998; Worden 1991). Otherwise, avoiding or minimizing the expression of negative grief-related emotions results in a more intense, protracted bereavement, especially when the relationship has been conflicted.

Postmodern Critiques of Grief Work

Although Freud's perspective that grief work is healthy was widely adopted and almost axiomatic for more than fifty years, the empirical evidence for its benefits is weak (Bonanno and Kaltman 1999; Bonanno and Keltner 1997; Cleiren 1993; Klass 1996; Klass, Silverman, and Nickman 1996; Neimeyer 1998, 2001; Nolen-Hoeksema and Larson 1997; Rubin 1999; Stroebe 1992; Stroebe and Stroebe 1987; Walter 2003; Wortman and Silver 1989, 2001). Critics maintain that confronting negative emotions through grief work, which is often accompanied by intense sadness, can lead to more negative thoughts, depression, and malfunctioning, such as difficulty thinking or completing tasks. In fact, there is little empirical evidence that confrontational strategies are associated with better outcomes than avoidant ones are. Instead, confrontational strategies such as thinking about one's relationship with the loved one or how the loss occurred may create future difficulties, such as preoccupation or excessive rumination (Archer 1999).

The findings are mixed regarding whether grief is always accompanied by intense distress and depression. In reviews of the literature, 30 to 40 percent of bereaved persons showed symptoms of clinical depression, whereas more than 50 percent had only moderate symptoms. Some individuals even showed positive emotions (Wortman and Silver 2001). It appears that most bereaved persons are distressed in the weeks and months following a loss, with symptoms ranging from mild upset to severe anguish, but that only a minority suffers from extreme or clinical levels of depression (Rosenzweig et al. 1997; Wortman and Silver 1989). Yet grief work theorists tend to assume implicitly that something is wrong with a person who does not experience distress or depression. Accordingly, they tend to view the expression of positive emotion—pride, cheerfulness, and good spirits—as a form of denial that may result in a "delayed grief reaction," for example, reactions appearing later that initially were inhibited or minimal (Bowlby 1980; Freud 1957; Sanders 1998). Delayed grief reactions are, however, rare, with estimates as low as 4 percent (Bonanno 2001; Bonanno and Field 2001; Bonanno et al. 1995, 1999; Wortman 2002). In contrast, detachment from grief may lead to a more positive recovery than does a focus on feelings of primarily loss, and in some instances, positive emotions such as smiling are found to be associated with reduced grief at fourteen and twenty-five months (Bonanno 2001; Bonanno and Kaltman 1999; Bonanno et al. 1995; Mendes de Leon, Kasl, and Jacobs 1994; Wortman and Silver 1989). In fact, humor—especially laughing with other people—can be therapeutic in the grief process (Cox 2001). Although Wortman and Silver (1989) maintain that depression and distress are not inevitable and universal responses to grief, Stroebe, van den Bout, and Schut (1994) concluded that distress is a common occurrence and that depression is found more often in bereaved than nonbereaved people. According to Stroebe and his colleagues, empirical studies that show that distress (ranging from mild upset to severe anguish) is common and that depression rates elevated in the bereaved compared with the nonbereaved do not contradict studies concluding that "a reaction of distress and depression is not universal or inevitable" (Wortman and Silver 1989:350). Such apparent discrepancies are explained by factors that may lead to the expression of more negative feelings, such as the closeness and security of the attachment to the deceased, an ambivalent relationship with the deceased, the manner of death (e.g., death of a child by a drunk driver), and the extent to which death shatters previously held beliefs about the bereaved or their world (Cleiren 1993; Fraley and Shaver 1999; Janoff-Bulman 1992; Wortman and Silver 2001). Critiques of grief work contend that distress is not necessary and that failure to experience it does not indicate pathology. But Stroebe and his colleagues (1994) observed that the majority of studies showed that "low distress," not "no distress," tends to be associated with good adjustment. A lack of distress thus may not be problematic but may be attributed to cultural norms governing the expression of emotions or to little or insecure attachment to the deceased (Fraley and Shaver 1999).

Findings are also mixed regarding whether grief work aids adjustment. While Wortman and Silver (1989, 2001) suggest that working through grief can have negative consequences, others contend that there is no evidence that those who "work through" a loss are less successful in resolving their grief than those who do not (Stroebe and Stroebe 1991; Stroebe, van den Bout, and Schut 1994). In other words, some bereaved individuals engage in "grief work," but others "keep busy" without necessarily delaying their grief responses (Richardson, in press). In addition, those who take longer than the normative period of grieving are not necessarily suffering from "chronic or pathological" grief (Wortman and Silver 1989, 2001). Others suggest that it is not the length of time per se that distinguishes normal from abnormal grieving but the quality and quantity of reactions over time (Osterweis, Solomon, and Green 1984). Social constructionists, whom we discuss later, contend that "normal" and "abnormal" grief are social constructs and that professionals' use of them can harm bereaved individuals. The particular grief experience is unique to the individual and is a reconstruction of meaning in the face of challenges to life constructs (Neimeyer 1999, 2001; Neimeyer and Mahoney 1995).

In sum, there is growing agreement that grief is not a single event that we must "get over" as quickly as possible (Silverman and Klass 1996; Wortman 2002; Wortman and Silver 2001). Rather, as a life-changing experience, grief takes time and patience.

Social Functional Approach

The *social functional approach* to emotion is a new theoretical integrative perspective on grief (Bonano and Keltner 1997). It maintains that recovery is most likely when emotions focused on the pain and negative nature of the loss are minimized or regulated and when positive emotions that encompass potential gains are sought or enhanced. The social functional approach sees emotion and grief as occurring at different times. It contends that whereas emotions are ephemeral, lasting a few seconds to several hours and related to simple and proximal appraisals of danger or benefit, grief is an enduring state that may last seven to eight years following a loss. Grief involves a profound evaluation of encompassing and irrevocable loss, a sense that a "piece of me is missing" that envelops the grieving person's identity and cognitive understanding of the world and the future (Schuchter and Zisook 1993). Although longer-term appraisals are part of grieving, many different emotions occur during a single period of grief, including positive emotions related to amusement, humor, happiness, and pride (Bonanno 1997, 2001; Bonanno and Kaltman 1999, 2001). That is, emotions are seen as intimately related to short-term efforts to change or maintain the immediate psychological or physiological state, whereas grieving requires longer-term coping efforts.

From the *social functional* perspective on emotion, focusing on only the negative aspects of the loss impedes functioning and leads to more severe grief. Some data have linked prolonged negative emotion (e.g., anger, hostility, guilt, rage) to greater stress and health problems, depression, disrupted social and personal relationships, pessimism, and hopelessness. Positive emotions, especially laughter and reaching out to others, are associated with improved social relations and evoke positive responses from others (Keltner and Bonanno 1997). One study found that physiological indicators of avoiding the emotional processing of anger, rage, or guilt predicted better adjustment, less depression, and less severe grief at fourteen and twenty-five months and an earlier return to normative functioning. Facial expressions of positive emotions (smiling, laughing) predicted improved functioning over the longer-term course of bereavement. In contrast, facial expressions of anger as participants talked about their loss were strongly associated with increased grief at fourteen and twenty-five months (Bonanno and Kaltman 1999; Keltner and Bonanno 1997). Distraction appears to be useful when it minimizes the amount of information about the distressing loss. Such evidence underlies the social functional perspective minimizing the expression of negative emotions (e.g., anger, rage, betrayal) through distraction in the early months of bereavement. Limited social disclosures of and the continuation of a relationship to the deceased are healthier and lead to a faster recovery than does the expression of primarily negative emotions. In addition, grief is better resolved when bereaved persons try to make sense of their negative experiences by trying to find meaning in the changes in roles and rules of the family system and the boundaries of the social environment.

Later empirical evidence suggests that sharing an emotion and confronting and processing a loss does not necessarily bring emotional relief or recovery (Neimeyer 2000). Accordingly, the expression of primarily negative emotions can reduce a person's contact with some support networks. That is, too much "talking about" may cause listeners to withdraw and lead to less social contact and support (Bonanno and Kaltman 1999). Conversely, social sharing, particularly with those who have experienced similar losses, serves functions other than relief by enhancing interpersonal relationships, social integration, and a sense of community. For example, participation in self-help groups, such as Compassionate Friends for bereaved parents or Widow-to-Widow, may lead to new relationships or to maintaining close, satisfying ones. In contrast to "talking" about grief, writing about painful experiences, especially for those who may not readily disclose their feelings to others, was found to be associated with indicators of well-being, including fewer visits to physicians and improvements in mood. Critiques of the grief work approach acknowledge, however, that the emotional avoidance of loss through alcohol or substance abuse is an exception to the patterns of distraction and denial identified as functional (Bonanno and Field 2001; Wortman and Silver 1989).

A Postmodern Social Constructionist View of Grief

In contrast to the earlier models that conceptualize grieving as severing bonds with the deceased, the postmodern social constructionist approaches view such bonds as resources for enriched functioning in the present (Klass, Silverman, and Nickman 1996; Neimeyer 1998; Rubin 1999; Walter 1996, 2003). Postmodernism acknowledges the multiplicity of perspectives on grief, since each bereaved individual's struggle is uniquely his or her own (Gergen 1994; Neimeyer 1998, 2001). This contrasts with earlier modernist or positivist models implying that the dominant model of grief was a process of detachment characterized by universal symptoms and stages of adaptation. From the postmodern perspective, vacillating between avoiding and engaging in grief work is fundamental to grieving (Neimeyer 1998; Stroebe and Stroebe 1987). For many of us, this means finding and experiencing joy as we work through our sorrow and pain.

These later models point to the reconstruction of a world of meaning as central to the grieving process. The mourning process is viewed as a "crisis of meaning" in which the bereaved copes with thoughts of what might have been and tries to preserve meaning in the face of disruption (Davis 2001; Neimeyer 2000, 2001). Experiencing death or other major losses can validate or invalidate our beliefs and assumptions about life. But loss, especially one that is sudden and unanticipated, can interfere with a bereaved person's ability to rebuild his or her assumptive world. Or bereaved individuals may have no mental constructions to help them with the meaning-making process to incorporate loss into a new worldview (Fleming and Robinson 2001; Richardson, in press).

Most definitions of meaning in the literature contain two concepts: (1) making sense of the loss (e.g., death was predictable in some way and fits the bereaved's perspective on life and religious or spiritual beliefs) and (2) finding benefits from the loss, such as growth in character, a gain in perspective, and a strengthening of relationships (Davis 2001). In fact, these two processes are undoubtedly interrelated, as one way to make sense of a loss is to find benefits from the experience and thus to perceive the world and oneself in positive terms (Fleming and Robinson 2001).

Since grief is a highly personal process, it can be understood only within the ongoing process of "constructing and maintaining our most basic sense of self" (Neimeyer 1998:90; Walter 2003). The death of those we love can greatly alter our sense of who we are, in large part because we create our identities through reflections from others. As a result, the grieving process requires not only relearning a world disrupted by a loss but also constructing a new sense of self. The bereaved need to learn how to act in a world without their loved ones (Attig 2001a, 2001b). This process requires active decision making, rather than passively waiting out the phases of grief. The bereaved person must reconstruct a personal world that "makes sense" and restore a sense of meaning and direction to a life that will be forever transformed (Walter 2003). In effect, the reconstruction of meaning is the central process of grief, for grieving is the act of affirming or reconstructing a personal world of meaning that has been challenged by loss. Those who engage in such a rebuilding process recover more readily than do those who continue to feel adrift and shattered (Neimeyer 1997, 1998, 2001). Feelings are not symptoms or problems requiring treatment but are signals of the development of meaning-making efforts. Bereaved persons return to aspects of their lives by discovering what is nourishing in their daily activities (Neimeyer 1998, 2001). Meaning is restored by telling stories as a way of socially validating their lives in new and existing relationships, and social, community, and cultural groups. Bereaved individuals transform their identities by redefining their connection to the deceased while also maintaining and negotiating relationships with family, friends, and new networks, such as support groups for the bereaved (Neimeyer 1997, 1998:83; Walter 2003). Integration of the loss suggests that it becomes a part of us (Neimeyer 1995).

The postmodern perspective does not envision a "period of letting go"; instead, the relationship with the bereaved is transformed and continued for an indefinite amount of time (Walter 2003). Grief also is not defined as pathological, since each response must be considered in the context of the bereaved's person-ality, relationship to the deceased person, and family background (Hagman 1995, 2001; Walter 2003). In fact, what may have been termed a pathological or problematic response may actually have been an effort to preserve and maintain an attachment to the deceased (Attig 2001a, 2001b; Walter 2003).

In contrast to the classic view of severing bonds with the deceased as central to "recovery," these connections, which become inner representations of the deceased, are changed both cognitively and emotionally while continuing (Klass 1999; Klass, Silverman, and Nickman 1996). Redefining but continuing these bonds is essential to redefining meaning and reconstructing a person's worldview and sense of self. Studies have documented the redefinition of adults' ongoing relationships with the deceased while grieving the loss of a partner or a child (Klass, Silverman, and Nickman 1996; Riches and Dawson 2000; Zisook and Schuchter 1993). These bonds with the deceased are discussed more fully in chapters 4 and 10.

These different views of grief work have implications for social work inter-ventions, which we discuss in more detail in subsequent chapters. Beyond acknowledging that these views conflict, we know too little to claim that we have discovered the best way for people to grieve. We should be skeptical of the universality of a predictable "emotional trajectory" and recognize that adapta-tion is more complex than a movement from disequilibrium to readjustment (Neimeyer and Keesee 1998). In contrast to early theories, a "new wave of grief theory" makes no assumptions about the universality of how we respond to loss (Neimeyer 1998, 2001). This constructionist approach recognizes that no two persons can be assumed to experience similar grief in response to the same loss and that cognitive processes (constructing meaning or rebuilding previously held assumptions) are central (Gilbert 1996). According to this perspective, each person constructs a different phenomenological world and occupies a distinc-tive position in relation to culture, gender, and spirituality (Janoff-Bulman and Berg 1998). Thus it is not surprising that men and women often grieve infertility, and parents often grieve a child's death or a chronic physical or mental illness in markedly different ways. Grieving also is increasingly seen as an active process, with conscious and unconscious choices. Our private grief is linked with others' constraining and enabling responses, with how friends, family, and even strangers react to our loss (Neimeyer and Keesee 1998).

Reconciliation of Theoretical Perspectives

Torill Lindstrom (2002) tried to reconcile some of the conflicting views. He discouraged both traditional grief work that might make bereaved persons force themselves into endlessly repeated ruminations and the opposite idea that people should try to forget their loss at all costs. Instead, his compromise position recognizes that we can have sad emotions without becoming engulfed by them and also be able to stop focusing on our sadness and pain when the grief becomes too burdensome. Thinking about and cognitively sorting out emotions does not mean compulsive grief work. Involvement in ordinary life should be encouraged as much as the bereaved individual can manage, since daily tasks and social encounters are often connected to positive associations and experiences, which can help rebuild the bereaved's life. Consistent with the perspective on grieving as a reconstruction of meaning, interventions should not try to alleviate grief to the point that its benefits disappear. Although they are painful, grief and loss can add meaning and perspective to one's life, "just as shadows give depth to a landscape" (Lindstrom 2002:20; Neimeyer and Keesee 1998).

Proposing a combination of the classic and postmodern paradigms, Simon Rubin (1999) argued that the grief process both disrupted and achieved new levels of functioning and of the quality and nature of the relationship to the deceased and memories of that person. Involvement with the deceased should not replace relationships in the present but instead should complement them to enable current functioning. When the bereaved can establish a more comfortable and open connection with the deceased, resolution is more likely. Resolution is assumed to occur when the memories and thoughts of the deceased are balanced and provide a measure of strength and warmth for the bereaved. Others also refer to a dual process of "holding on" and "letting go" or alternating between loss and restoration, between confrontation and the avoidance of different stressors (Bowlby 1980; Marris 1986; Stroebe and Schut 1999; Stroebe, Schut, and Stroebe 1998; Stroebe and Stroebe 1987). Throughout this book, we show how the bereaved's attempts at making meaning and transforming the relationships with the deceased (and with others) contribute to the ongoing process of grief. We urge the reader to select those parts of these paradigms that fit their experience while remaining open and attuned to their bereaved clients' experiences.

Summary

This review of theories of grief reveals both the consistency and the divergence of views. Most models of grief are derived from either clinical practice or research. The clinical models concentrate on the manifestations and behaviors associated with grief in order to develop interventions and are based on largely individual, psychodynamic views of personality. The research models typically identify variables affecting grief responses, such as personal and family characteristics, other concurrent stressors, social supports, the relationship with the deceased, and the nature of the death. Most theoretical models explain only a few aspects of the grief experience and do not take account of cross-cultural differences. Gaps in these models require longitudinal research, such as understanding the cross-generational nature of loss for the family and the social, cultural, and environmental contexts that influence the grieving process over time.

Conceptualizations of the duration of bereavement were revised many times during the twentieth century. Early clinicians considered the grief response to be long term (Freud 1953, 1955). In the middle of the century, grief was seen as an acute, short-lived crisis (Caplan 1961, 1964; Lindemann 1944). The current thinking is that grief is a long-term process and that most people never return to their previous levels of functioning (Wortman 2002). A "new wave" of grief theory is emerging that recognizes the complexity and cultural diversity in grief and posits that meaning making is central to grieving (Neimeyer 2001:4). With the evolution of both clinical practice and research has come some agreement on general concepts, such as the normalcy of many grief manifestations, but which symptoms and behaviors constitute complicated or "pathological" grieving are still being debated.

2

The Grief Process

THE *grief process* has been conceptualized as *stages, tasks,* and *phases* of grief. Regardless of the particular configuration, grieving involves psychological, spiritual, social, and physiological changes, as discussed in chapter 1. This chapter reviews the major theoretical models related to the stages, tasks, and phases of grief; the definitions of complicated and traumatic grief; and the cultural variations in the grief process, especially related to ongoing bonds with the deceased. Although most of these theories pertain to the major loss of death, they also are relevant to the wide range of other losses discussed throughout this text.

Five Stages of Dying Model

The *five stages of dying model* is widely known and can be applied to both the dying and their survivors, if sometimes inappropriately. Viewing death as the final stage of growth, Kübler-Ross (1969, 1981) identified the *stages* of (1) shock and denial, (2) anger, resentment, and guilt, (3) bargaining, (4) depression, and (5) adjustment/acceptance. Her model implies that the failure to complete any of these stages could result in incomplete healing and is based on her extensive clinical work with the dying, not on survivors dealing with grief. Despite that, these stages are often inappropriately applied to the grief process of the bereaved. Kübler-Ross's perspective, widely criticized for suggesting that individuals must move through these stages, has been empirically rejected, as grief cannot be easily separated into sequential stages. Whether applied to the dying person or the bereaved, grief does not proceed in a linear fashion but reappears again and again to be reworked, with the emotional reactions to death varying greatly (Corr 1993; Kastenbaum 1986b; Klass 1996a, 1999:56; Leick and Davidsen-Nielsen 1996; Neimeyer 1998a, 2001; Walter 2003). Nevertheless, Kübler-Ross's pioneering work continues to influence both research and practice, and

Kastenbaum's (1986b) criticism of it offers some guidelines that can be used for the grief process of those attending to the dying:

- Set aside stages.
- Refrain from suggestions of linear directedness.
- Emphasize description rather than prescribing a "right" way.
- Take into account the totality of the coping person's life.
- Attend to influences from the person's social environment. (Corr 1993)

Later models conceptualize grief as tasks (Bowlby 1980; Worden 1991, 2002), phases, or processes (Rando 1988, 1993). The *process perspective* recognizes the alternating currents of emotion, thought, and behavior through which people move at different rates and perhaps more than once. In addition, when we grieve a loss, typically one in our social networks, we must cope with not only with the immediate loss but also secondary losses. As C. S. Lewis wrote, "Sorrow turns out to be not a state, but a process. It needs not a map but a history. . . . there is something new to be chronicled everyday" (1961:38–39). Although both researchers and clinicians have rejected fixed stages or phases of grief and recognize the wide variations in groupings of frequently occurring reactions, they have not identified any universal experiences. In discussing these models, therefore, we too need to consider cross-cultural variations in the experience of grief.

Grief Tasks Model

The tasks that researchers and clinicians regard as necessary to resolve grief and to heal (e.g., restore functioning and integrate the loss) are

- Accepting the reality of the loss.
- Experiencing the pain of grief.
- Adjusting to an environment in which the deceased is missing or a loved person is absent.
- Withdrawing emotional energy from the past relationship and reinvesting it in other relationships.

According to the *task model*, a person's mourning is complete when he or she has accomplished these tasks (Worden 1982, 1991, 2002).

The *growth-oriented model* has three tasks addressing grief: (1) awareness, (2) acceptance, and (3) reformulation. Shifting from one task to another represents a key turning point in the grief process (Schneider 1984). The concept of tasks of grief continues to be debated, however, with the most recent research finding that grief oscillates in a broad cyclical fashion rather than proceeding through fixed tasks (Bozarth 1994; Rando 1988, 1993; Worden 2002).

Recognizing the importance of transitions to the grief process, Parkes viewed grief as an acute stress response to major life transitions that necessitate readjustment: "a complex time-consuming process in which a person gradually changes his view of the world and the places and habit by means of which he orients and relates to others" (Parkes 1970:465; Parkes 1972a, 1975a; Parkes and Weiss 1983). Here losses are conceptualized as turning points that may become growth points, but only if the pain is worked through by releasing emotions of grief. Such emotions are manifested as "pangs of grief": acute episodes of severe anxiety and psychological pain in which the absent person is strongly missed and of "pining," a persistent and obtrusive wish for the person who is gone, along with preoccupation with thoughts of the deceased. Pining can lead to intense searching behavior in an attempt to recover and reunite with the lost object or person (Parkes 1972a). When such searching fails, the bereaved feels intense psychological pain, separation anxiety, anger, guilt, depression, and aimlessness (Parkes 1970, 1972a). A grieving person may also have physical reactions, such as sleep disturbances, aches and pains, and a loss of energy and appetite (Glick, Weiss, and Parkes 1974).

Phases of Grief Model

Most clinicians and researchers now conceptualize the grief process in phases, although they use different concepts to capture the emotions, thoughts, and behaviors of each phase, as summarized in box 2.1.

Box 2.1 Different Models of Phases of Grief

- Protest, despair, and realization/reorganization (Parkes 1972).
- Avoidance, confrontation, and accommodation (Rando 1988, 1993).
- Integrative or dual-process model (Stroebe et al. 1998).
- Process of mourning (Rando 1988; Stroebe et al. 2001; Weiss 2001; Worden 1991).

According to Parkes (1972a), the phases of grieving are

1. Protest or preoccupation with the loss that includes agitation, tension, and vigilant attentiveness to the possibilities that the lost figure or object may reappear.
2. Despair: numbness and disorganization, withdrawal of attention from everyday life, low moods, and sadness.
3. Realization and reorganization when the death becomes psychologically real.

Grieving is increasingly recognized as an active process, involving conscious and unconscious choices (Bowlby 1980; Parkes 1972a). This process does not have distinct phases; instead, the bereaved person moves back and forth between them over time. Moreover, the phases may not be sequential, with the person's feelings of guilt, anger, fearfulness, and anxiety intermeshed with protest and despair (Weiss 2001).

Researchers generally agree on the following phases of the grieving process (Bozarth 1994; Rando 1988, 1993):

1. *Avoidance* is the phase that encompasses shock, numbness, disbelief, and denial, all of which can function as buffers from the painful reality, especially when first learning of the loss. Other feelings at this phase may be fear, anxiety, and dread, as well as unreality, disorganization, and an inability to comprehend the situation. Bereaved individuals may try to gain some control and understanding by gathering information about what happened and telling and retelling the story. Some people surround themselves with as many people as possible, whereas others prefer to be alone. Others may keep their grief distant by focusing on the tasks to be done, like preparing meals, making financial and funeral arrangements, or caring for children.

2. *Confrontation* is the phase when a person's grief is most intense and he or she really learns or "hears" that the loved one is gone. Common feelings include intense sadness; guilt or blaming others or oneself; helplessness, panic, confusion, and powerlessness ("going crazy" or "being out of one's wits with grief"); the diffused energy of unfocused anger, rage, and despair; a loss of faith; a sense of injustice or disillusionment; and intense sadness.

3. *Accommodation* is the phase when the bereaved person gradually reenters the everyday world, "moves on," and learns to live with the loss.

As we discuss more fully later, terms like *accommodation, integration, adaptation,* and *adjustment to the loss* are more accurate than *resolution* or *recovery,* since loss produces permanent changes and grieving does not have a definitive end. Most people do not find resolution or closure to their grief and do not return to their state before the loss. Some theorists and clinicians prefer the concept of *integration:* the "act of combining into an integral whole" (Murray 2001; Neimeyer 1995, 2001). In fact, the goal is not to return to previous levels of functioning but to learn how to negotiate a meaningful life without the deceased and to integrate each new loss into a new social context and identity (Miller and Omarzu 1998; Rando 1993; Rosenblatt 1993). For example, bereaved parents may assume a new identity of helper to others through groups such as Compassionate Friends. Other bereaved persons acknowledge and find appropriate ways to channel their anger, like the mothers who formed Mothers Against Drunk Driving or parents whose daughters have been sexually assaulted who seek legislation that will lock up sex offenders for a longer time.

Even though the grieving person reaches accommodation or integration, his or her painful feelings may persist for many years, perhaps for the rest of the person's life. A cross-sectional study of bereaved parents who had lost sons in war found that more than a decade later, many were still more anxious and preoccupied with the loss than were a sample of nonbereaved parents who also had lived through the war (Rubin 1996). Research on widows and widowers discovered that some respondents took nearly forty years to be able to "only rarely" experience negative feelings. For most, the painful feelings never faded completely but resurfaced in "aftershocks" many years after the death; they also became more acute around what are considered to be joyous occasions, such as birthdays and holidays, or around significant dates, such as anniversaries of the death. These findings suggest an open-ended model of grief, in which grief is never completely resolved and always is present (Carnelley, Wortman, and Kessler 1999; Eakes, Burke, and Hainsworth 1999; Wortman 2002; Wortman and Silver 1989, 2001).

Integrative and Dual-Process Models

The *integrative theory of bereavement,* based on empirical research and psychodynamic theories, has five phases: shock, awareness of the loss, conservation-withdrawal, healing, and renewal. At the end of the conservation-withdrawal phase, the bereaved individual makes a decision, whether conscious or not, to survive or to remain in perpetual grief. This decision does not, however, mark the end of the grief process, since bereaved people must be motivated to make enormous changes in their lives to reach renewal. It is this inclusion of motivation, although inadequately defined, that differentiates the integrative model from others (Sanders 1989). The integrative model of spousal bereavement, for example, maintains that the bereaved are motivated to express and integrate the painful feelings, continue their relationship with the deceased, and maintain their health and ability to function, including the ability to form new partner relationships (Schuchter and Zisook 1993). Motivation and explicit decision making are thus central to an integrative model of grief.

The *dual-process model* states that most bereaved individuals alternate between approaching and avoiding grief and its associated secondary stressors, for example, between a loss orientation and a restoration orientation, both of which are necessary. During the initial phase of *loss orientation*, we concentrate on dealing with and processing some aspect of the loss experience, yearn for the absent person or object, cry as we confront our emotional reactions, and cling to the past. At this phase, we may also try to derive meaning from the loss but mainly focus on the lost relationship (Stroebe and Schut 1999). This orientation is congruent with attachment theory (Bowlby 1980).

The *restoration orientation* requires adjustment to both the immediate and the secondary losses. We need to learn new routines, master new activities alone, create new traditions and memories, and fulfill new roles and identity as we adjust to the world without the loved person or object. A young widower may suddenly need to assume new roles and identities as single parent, cook, and housekeeper as he tries to create new traditions and memories for his children without their mother. We get used to our loss through repeated exposure and confrontation (e.g., loss orientation) and also through forgetting, distractions, and the necessity of daily routines (e.g., restoration orientation) To illustrate, the young widower may be so busy managing the household that he finds himself surprised by how rarely he thinks of his wife. This back-and-forth process helps people integrate the loss without grieving continuously. These alternating orientations are summarized in table 2.1 (Stroebe and Schut 1999; Stroebe, Schut, and Stroebe 1998).

TABLE 2.1
Integrating a Loss Through Two Orientations

Loss Orientation	Restoration Orientation
Grief work	Attendance to life changes
Intrusion of grief	New activities
Breaking bonds/ties/relocation of the deceased	Distraction from grief
Denial/avoidance of restoration/changes	Denial/avoidance of grief
Holding on to past roles and relationships	New roles/identities/relationships

The phases of grief wax and wane and may coexist with prior responses. What is predictable is that grief is unpredictable, coming in waves and sometimes leaving the bereaved feeling out of control. From the moment the loss takes place, the grieving individual's complex emotions intertwine with his or her accommodation to the loss. As emphasized throughout this book, there is no timetable for grief and no "correct" way to grieve.

R Process Model

The *six R's process of mourning* appears to integrate much of what has been written about grief phases or tasks and provides guidelines for our discussion of loss at different phases of life as well as for possible interventions (Parkes 1972a; Rando 1988; Raphael and Nunn 1988; Stroebe et al. 2001; Weiss 2001; Worden 1991). But this model should not be viewed as directive, since exceptions to each of these phases exist and some people may return to earlier phases even years after the loss. Nevertheless, the R process model, formulated and adapted primarily by Therese Rando (1983, 1988), is useful for both professionals and the bereaved and refers to different types of loss.

Recognizing and Accepting the Reality of the Loss

The first phase of the R process model is *recognizing and accepting the reality of the loss*, which means acknowledging and accepting the truth that the person, place, or object is gone and will not ever return, that the loss is irreversible. Many bereaved individuals initially try to deny the loss. Denial behaviors include gathering extensive facts about the loss, hoping that they will awaken from what seems to be a nightmare, dreaming that the loss has not occurred, believing that the loss can be reversed, or expressing anger at well-wishers, who by their presence visibly symbolize the loss. To illustrate, my husband wrote of "wanting to throw against a wall all the food that had been given to us" because the presence of numerous food baskets symbolized that Chris (our son) had indeed died. Common feelings during this first phase are fear of the unknown and unfamiliar, panic when waking up, unreality ("being out of one's wits"), and feeling overwhelmed. Some survivors feel that they are a different person, wondering whether they are losing their mind, and fear being stuck in this painful crazy state forever (Rando 1988). C. S. Lewis wrote, "No one ever told me that grief felt so like fear. I am not afraid, but the sensation is like being afraid. At other times it feels like being mildly drunk, or concussed. There is a sort of invisible blanket between the world and me. I find it hard to take in what anyone says" (1961:1).

Some survivors feel this fear as pervasive anxiety, describing feeling jumpy, oversensitive, overreactive, and agitated over minor things.

Denial during the initial phase is common but can become what is defined as *complicated grief*, exemplified by keeping a person's possessions "mummified" for years, ready for use when she or he returns, or alternatively, getting rid of all clothes and personal items that would bring the bereaved face to face with the reality of the loss. Preoccupation is common early on and emerges in a variety of ways: as a wish to undo the loss that allows us to be with our loved one if only in our thoughts, holding on to someone or something tightly before saying good-bye and letting go, and fears that we will not be able to remember the person. Such preoccupation can, however, be problematic if it persists and becomes *obsessive rumination*; for example, the bereaved thinks about, searches for, and believes he or she has seen the dead person—nearly all the time. (Rumination is discussed more fully later in relation to complicated or prolonged grief.) Ruminators engage in negative thoughts and behaviors that hold their focus on negative emotions, their causes, and consequences, a process that increases distress (e.g., anger, anxiety) (Davis and Nolen-Hoeksema 2001). Rumination can be especially detrimental if over time the bereaved's preoccupation interferes with their problem-solving ability and capability of taking care of themselves or others, especially their children, and distances them from others (Rando 1988).

Reacting to, Experiencing, and Expressing the Pain of Separation

The second phase of the R model is *reacting to, experiencing, and expressing the pain of separation,* or giving up control, giving way, and abandoning ourselves to the feeling of chaos. After the death of his wife, C. S. Lewis captured the pain of grief that is present no matter how one might try to hide from it:

> Do I hope that if feeling disguises itself as thought I shall feel less. Aren't all these notes the senseless writhing of a man who won't accept the fact that there is nothing we can do with suffering except to suffer it. Who still thinks that there is some device (if only he could find it), which will make pain, not be pain. It doesn't really matter whether you grip the arms of the dentist's chair or let your hands lie in your lap. The drill drills on. (1961:18)

The encounter with chaos and the uncontrollable aspects of existence paradoxically gives us the strength and courage to live (Rando 1983, 1988). In the grief work model described in chapter 1, an active confrontation with the loss—through rage, anger, and the honest expression of sorrow—is widely assumed to be necessary for deliverance from the past, as it requires recognizing all facets of the loss (Harvey 1998; Leick and Davidsen-Neilsen 1996; Rando 1983, 1988).

Accordingly, we cannot integrate our grief by permitting it to remain at a cognitive level or "in our head."

As described in chapter 1, critics of the early "grief work" perspective recognize that people deal with their painful feelings in a wide range of ways, including denial beyond the early phase, the avoidance of memories, or the distraction of work, traveling, "keeping busy," humor, and simply "getting on with their lives" (Bonanno and Kaltman 1999; Weiss 1998). Those who do not engage in intensive "grief work" may believe that they can honor the dead or absent person better by the quality of their continued living than by constantly remembering the past and confronting negative feelings (Tatelbaum 1980). Nevertheless, some "distraction" techniques are clearly not helpful, such as denying that one feels pain, idealizing the dead or absent person, working to the point of neglecting one's health or family, traveling to the point of exhaustion, or using alcohol, drugs, or excessive food to keep from addressing the pain. Some family members may encourage distraction techniques, such as traveling, moving, or "getting away for a while," as if the change in physical location would resolve grief. Grief cannot be covered up by "running away from it" or by a false sense of gaiety, such as pretending on holidays that nothing has changed. Nonetheless, persons who avoid conscious grieving do not necessarily break down—typically with some form of depression—or have to go through the grief process later in life (i.e., delayed grief reaction). In other words, short-term denial and distraction are not necessarily maladaptive in the long run (Stroebe and Schut 1999; Stroebe, Schut, and Stroebe 1998).

As chapter 1 noted, the expression of grief through crying was found to be universal, with the exception of the Balinese. In our society, weeping or crying is "breaking down," which implies that "something is wrong with us" or that we are "not strong." Yet crying affords us a necessary release of intense feelings (Tatelbaum 1980). Shallow weeping is different from deep weeping. Early on, "calling" weeping tends to be shallow as the bereaved tries to hold onto the person or thing that has been lost; his or her breathing is rapid, and crying may not bring relief. Physiologically, this is because the brain and other organs are deprived of necessary oxygen, which interferes with physical and emotional recovery, and the pain becomes lodged tightly in the muscles.

Shortly after the mountain rangers found Chris's body, a grief counselor asked me about my eating, sleeping, and support network. But what made the most difference was her reminder (however simplistic it might appear) to remember to breathe. When we are in shock and grappling with the enormity of our loss, we tend to hold our breath and become tighter and tenser. After I started breathing more deeply and taking in more oxygen, I was able to weep.

Deep weeping occurs when we begin to let go of the loss, and over time we are able to release bodily or muscular tensions, such as the feeling of "being wound as tight as a drum" or "ready to jump out of our skin" (Bowlby 1980; Bozarth 1994; Leick and Davidsen-Nielsen 1996).

Weeping that heals is experienced as a profound sobbing in which, like a baby, we let go of tensions in our body and give way fully to our pain. Bereaved individuals may find that they can fully sob in the privacy of their shower when the water shuts out the sounds or in the dark anonymity of their car. As examples of cross-cultural variations, loud crying is sometimes uncontrollable among Filipinos, particularly when the family gathers to see the body before it is taken to the morgue. By contrast, some Japanese try to control their public expression of emotions, including crying (Klass 1996b; Rosenblatt 2001).

When we dare to give way, the deeper our weeping, the longer lasting the feeling of relief will be. But many of us avoid deep weeping because it means letting go of the lost security and the person who gave meaning to our life (Leick and Davidsen-Neilsen 1996). It can be frightening for an adult to give way and feel once more like a small, insecure, and helpless child. My daughter at age nine expressed this fear when she said that she "was afraid to cry because she thought if she started, she might not ever stop." Not surprisingly, many children do not weep deeply following a death but wait to do so months or even years later. Moreover, their sobbing may be precipitated by something other than the original loss.

Guilt may be expressed in the early phases of grief, especially by grieving parents and those bereaved by suicide and unexpected death. Similar to all expressions of grief, how we talk about our guilt is influenced by interpersonal, personal, situational, cultural, and societal variables. Terms frequently used to describe guilt feelings include *remorseful, regretful, responsible, accountable, at fault, unworthy, wrong, ashamed,* and *blameworthy.* Guilt is a common and expected aspect of grief because human relationships are not perfect. Instead, they contain some mix of positive and negative feelings—regret, self-reproach, blame for not preventing the loss, or a sense of relief after a long period of illness and caregiving. Guilt can be caused by self-accusations, such as a perceived failure to do the right thing for the person who has died, negligence, and exaggerated minor omissions (Lindemann 1944).

Guilt is multifaceted. *Relationship guilt* results from a perceived failure to live up to one's own or society's expectations of our relationship with our loved one or from doing certain things in the relationship.

I still experience pangs of guilt that I was busy working on a book and spent little time with my son the week before he left for Mount McKinley. Not surprisingly, a later dream in which Chris returned contained the dilemma of whether to take a trip with him to a warm climate, as he requested, or meet a book deadline!

Moral guilt results from the belief that the loved one's death is punishment or retribution for violating a moral, religious, or ethical standard.

As I struggled with the question of why my son had to die, I searched my past, fearful that I had caused his death by my failure to attend church regularly, by a minor shoplifting incident when I was teenager, or by my not being a "good enough mother."

In some instances, guilt is profound because there is a direct cause-and-effect relationship between what we did or failed to do, resulting in serious harm to someone else (e.g., causing an accident that kills one's family and others because of driving while intoxicated). *Illegitimate guilt* comes from unrealistic expectations and standards out of proportion to the events (e.g., my son's friends believing that they should have been there on the mountain to save him or prevent his death). Survivors often feel guilty when they first start to enjoy life again, as if they are disloyal to their loved ones by laughing or socializing. Such guilt can stem from beliefs that the young are more worthy and should outlive the old. Survivor guilt is especially common among siblings. When we met our older son at the airport the day after Chris had fallen, his first words were, "It should have been me." *Grief guilt* also may result from our perceived failure to fulfill our own or society's expectations for us to grieve in an appropriate way (i.e., that we are not feeling sad enough). There are few nonverbal cues for our guilt feelings. Unless we express our guilt verbally, friends, family, or counselors may be unaware of it. In any case, intense, unrelenting, and prolonged guilt is outside the parameters of a typical grief response (Miles and Demi 1991).

Reminiscing

Whether alive or dead, who we are and what we have done in our lives reside in others' memories (Rando 1988). Accordingly, the third phase of the R model, *reminiscing*, or telling and retelling memories, is a way to keep our loved one alive. Individuals vary widely over time in their talking about memories, looking at photographs, and sharing stories verbally or in writing. For example, bereaved parents fluctuate between finding comfort or pain in looking at pictures. As the Christian philosopher Nicholas Wolterstorff wrote in *Lament for a Son*:

> Photographs that once evoked the laugher of delighted reminiscence now cause only pain. Why are the photographs of him as a little boy so incredibly hard for me to look at? Why is it easier to look at him as a grownup? . . . so it is with the

memories of him. They all lead into that blackness. All I can do is remember him. I can't experience him. He's only in my memory now, not in my life. Nothing now can happen between us. Everything is sealed tight, shut in the past. (1987:47)

Reminiscence may also be a search for meaning, which may mean accepting reasons that cannot be comprehended and answers that may not exist. What appears to be important to healing is moving from being "haunted by memories" to "gently embracing memories" (Harvey 1998).

Writing, which appears to have a restorative power, may be easier for some survivors than looking at pictures or talking about the deceased. Writing in a journal can be a means of facing our new reality, organizing our chaotic thoughts, and gaining a sense of control in dealing with them. Writing can be a way to complete the last chapter of the deceased's life. Reviewing what we have written— sometimes years later—can also help gauge the progress we have made since the death. Others may write about their anger or guilt, then tear up or burn the paper so that no one can read it. Some bereaved individuals write a letter to their loved one on his or her birthday or holidays and leave it at the grave or next to a photo. Those for whom writing does not come easily may prefer to talk with others about the deceased. Whether through writing or talking, telling the story of the death in some form appears to be central to finding meaning in the loss (Harvey 1996; Rosenblatt 2000a).

Dreaming can also be a means of remembering, experiencing, and working through the emotionally charged loss, even of problem solving. Experiencing our dreams in the present tense—telling them to a friend or writing them down—can provide new meanings, insights, and connections. Although grief dreams may be painful, dream theorists maintain that our dreams do not tell us more than we can bear. In most instances, dreams of the dead person are comforting, although some might be perhaps disquieting and cause anxiety (Bozarth 1994).

Relinquishing Old Attachments

The concept of letting go of one's attachment to the absent person or lost object was central to the early work of Freud, Lindemann, and Parkes (see chapter 1). More recent research, however, has shown that many bereaved individuals maintain their bond with the deceased. Unfortunately, some people convince themselves they will never love again and hold on to past attachments without being able to form new relationships (Leick and Davidsen-Nielsen 1996; Volkan and Zintl 1993). The challenge is to maintain a connection with our loved ones who have died but still hope that we can form new attachments and love other people.

We describe later the ways in which connections with the deceased are maintained. Nearly all clinicians or researchers now agree that the prior attachment/relationship must change, that survivors must find an appropriate place for the dead in their emotional lives—a place that will enable them to go on living effectively in the world. For many, grieving diminishes when there is no longer a need to reactivate the representation of the dead with exaggerated intensity in the course of daily living. Balance—letting go of relationships to some extent but growing from them—is viewed as desirable (Volkan 1985):

> We reopen these relationships, examine them. . . . What is the significance of these relationships? They are not over. They are not finished. They do not end; they are still fresh. The emotions are there and stir us still. In some sense the person is still there, still meaningful, still influential in our lives. These are the people we know as we know no living persons. They are a part of us unchanged for the rest of our lives. These, the dead, teach us the meaning of relationships. They teach us the importance of intensity, passion and vulnerability. They teach us that duration, the number of hours or days or years in relationship, is not the significant dimension. (Brantner 1977:301)

In effect, we must rebuild the present with a new everyday life that contains both what is left and some necessary changes (Leick and Davidsen-Nielsen 1996). Since loss produces permanent change, the bereaved do not return to a "baseline" or earlier state of well-being (Stroebe 2001).

Readjusting and Reinvesting

The last two phases of the R model are closely connected and are frequently referred to as the accommodation, acceptance, adjustment, and integration of the loss as personal growth and benefits. Whether one ever is able to accept a loss or to resolve one's grief is unclear. But one can adapt to the changed situation. The challenge is to integrate what has happened and use it to find or construct meaning and to become fuller and larger in one's being than ever before, even in the face of an apparent diminution of one's life. With accommodation, the bereaved is able to recognize the interplay between life and death, integration and disintegration, and happiness and pain and to live with imperfect reality (Becvar 1997). Everyone who lives suffers, but not all of us learn to live more fully through suffering (Frankl 1959). Suffering itself has no value; it is the use that we make of suffering through our attitudes and actions that has value. As Ann Morrow Lindbergh wrote, "I do not believe that sheer suffering teaches. If suffering alone taught, all the world would be wise since everyone suffers. To suffering must be added mourning, understanding, patience, love, openness and the willingness to remain vulnerable" (1973:35).

An integrative view of loss thus means that to some extent, we must be will-ing to suffer until the end of our life. We must continue to reach out to others, even in our grief and anguish, realizing that we have something to offer. And by giving to others, we gain something (Harvey 1996). "Healthy" grieving results in an ability to remember the importance of a loss, but with a newfound sense of peace rather than searing pain.

More recent researchers and clinicians have identified the benefits of grief or "posttraumatic growth" (Calhoun and Tedeschi 2001; Davis 2001; Frantz, Farrell, and Trolley 2001). Although time alone does not heal, it does give us the oppor-tunity to heal ourselves and "offers us the eternal present of possibility" (Becvar 1988:176). Choice is always present in how we grieve: the choice to endure, to engage in the inevitable conflicts that come after a major loss, to look honestly at ourselves and our lives, to make an assertion with our lives, and to continue to make choices. The ability to choose, which is the essence of human life, can free us over time from the domination of grief (Bowlby 1980; Harvey 1996). It is our choice to use time well and to incorporate past and future into the present moment in order to close old wounds. Through our loss, we can teach ourselves a new way of living, large enough to contain our pain and to transform it into a new kind of power to make us whole (Becvar 1997). If we have actively grieved, we may gen-erally free ourselves to take on new challenges, reinvest our emotions back in living, experience a future with new possibilities, and establish positive relationships (Harvey 1998; Herman 1992; Leick and Davidsen-Nielsen 1996; Rando 1993).

Personal growth and transformation generally differ from adjustment (Attig 2001; Tedeschi, Park, and Calhoun 1998). Many people are able to see value in what has become their reality, put the loss into a less negative perspective, keep connections alive with happy memories rather than through pain, and reinvest in new goals that can structure and give meaning to life and a future with new possibilities—but they can never fully adjust to their loss (Leick and Davidsen-Nielsen 1996). Despite the loss or, in some instances, because of the loss, bereaved individuals can benefit from their pain: they can give energy to their daily life, find freedom from distress, experience pleasure and gratification, be hopeful about the future, and function adequately in their roles as partners, parents, and community members (Harvey 1998; Weiss 1998). Personal growth or transfor-mation requires grieving actively, attempting to understand the loss through self- reflection, searching for meaning to derive some good from the death, and relinquishing ways of viewing the world that were unique to the lost relation-ship (Harvey 1998; Hogan, Morse, and Tason 1996).

Through such active grieving, we can emerge stronger. This strength may be shown in greater self-understanding, empathy, compassion, and altruism toward others. We may become wiser, more mature, more tolerant, and less judgmental. Active grieving often results in greater self-reliance and self-efficacy, expanded relationships and a reordering of priorities, since we now realize the finiteness of life—that death can occur at any time (Hogan and DeSantis 1996; Schaefer and Moos 2001). Some mourners may gain strength from knowing that "nothing can hurt them again" (Bozarth 1994). As Harvey observed, our "losses become a lesson and a gift" (1998:169). Frankl wrote that "people can become wiser by becoming sadder" (1959:88). For some bereaved individuals, confronting their loss and searching for meaning may release prior emotionally deprived patterns so that they may for the first time experience strong genuine emotions. In some instances, this release may produce a new energy, optimism, sense of empowerment, fearlessness toward life, new goals that give meaning, and an ability to be both alone and to enjoy the company of others (Bozarth 1994; Harvey 1998).

As we noted earlier, most of us never achieve closure in our grieving, even though we may appear to "get on" with our lives. Instead, we discover new meanings in loss at various points in our lives, especially at significant transitions such as marriage, the birth of a child, or graduation. Our regrets and horrors about the loss never completely leave our minds and sometimes recur in our thoughts and emotions when we least expect them and are least prepared (Herman 1992). In marked contrast to Lindemann's (1944) view that grief can be resolved in four to six weeks, most clinicians now recognize that that grief will always be present, that "you don't get over it" and that "time does not heal all." But the pain will lessen, and the waves of grief will come less often. We will always be sad when we think of the deceased or absent person, but the pain eventually will lose the wrenching quality it once had. As one widow who also had lost her young adult son observed, "The pain returns, but I can remember the in-between times better" (Leick and Davidsen-Nielsen 1996:38). Survivors need to find an appropriate place for the dead in their emotional lives, a place that will enable them to go on living in the world (Volkan 1985). Regardless of the level and nature of our accommodation to loss, we are forever changed by it and must learn to live without all the answers and to acknowledge the fragility of life and the limits of control (Rando 1983).

Excessive Rumination

Most grief researchers and practitioners agree that the process of experiencing and expressing grief fully should be differentiated from *excessive rumination* or going over and over the same negative thoughts, emotions, and their possible causes and consequences, without taking action to relieve those emotions

(Nolen-Hoeksema 1991, 2001). Rumination is characterized by an inability to put the loss out of one's mind, repeatedly mulling over the events in a set manner, deploring and regretting that the event has happened, blaming oneself, and wondering how one could have prevented it (Stroebe, Van Den Bout, and Schut 1994). Distressingly persistent counterfactuals (i.e., endless "what ifs") are a type of ruminative thought (Davis 2001; Davis and Lehman 1995).

Rumination may prolong distress by drawing people's attention to negative thoughts and memories, thus interfering with their ability to solve problems effectively and impairing their engagement in everyday activities that might increase their sense of control. Rumination has self-perpetuating characteristics, since ruminators lack the motivation to engage in activities that might lift their mood, and it impairs their problem-solving ability. Furthermore, family and friends may be critical of and avoid interacting with ruminators, thereby leaving them feeling even more hopeless, isolated, and prone to believe that they cannot cope alone. Ruminators may remember more negative things about the lost relationship (regrets, guilt, "if onlys") and typically have difficulty engaging in pleasant, distracting activities and making sense of their loss (Nolen-Hoeksema and Larson 1999). In fact, ruminators may contend that they can no longer delude themselves but now see things for how bad they really are. When grieving a death, some ruminators may fear that if they stop persistently and repetitively focusing on the loss, they will lose their ties to the deceased. But bereaved individuals can temporarily forget certain details about the absent person and not lose their connection. Letting go of particular aspects of the absent person or object is not denial but the integration of grief (Klass 1999; Klass, Silverman, and Nickman 1996; Walter 2003).

Why do some people ruminate more than others? Ruminators are found to be neurotic, feel less mastery over their lives, or be less optimistic. They are likely to be beset by multiple negative events around the time of their loss or have a history of uncontrollable events in their lives. People who experience what are considered nonnormative losses (e.g., young parents who lose a child to death or middle-aged adults whose partner dies from a stigmatized illness such as AIDS) may be more apt to ruminate. Those without adequate social supports are more likely to ruminate while at the same time their excessive rumination can drive away support and create conflicts with others (Nolen-Hoeksema and Larson 1999). Individual coping styles, the ability to tolerate painful emotions, and resources for self-care also affect whether a person will move forward or become "stuck" in his or her grief (Holman and Silver 1998).

Complicated Grief

Most of us who grieve can return to full or nearly full functioning, despite periods of prolonged grief that can temporarily impair function and healing. Whether and when grief becomes "complicated" is widely debated but is estimated to occur in about 20 percent of those grieving (Attig 2001a; Harvey 1996; Harvey et al. 2001). The viewpoints and definitions of *complicated* vary widely and have changed over time and across cultures and are likely to continue to change with future research and clinical practice. There is more agreement about the need to understand why some bereaved people grieve "too much" or become "stuck in" their grief, and others emerge strengthened or even transformed by the process, as discussed earlier in connection with active grieving. Yet what is "too much" grieving is unclear.

Complicated grief is defined as the long-term persistence of symptoms of separation distress and feelings of being devastated and traumatized by the death (Jacobs 1999:24). *Complicated grief* was formerly referred to as *traumatic grief*, and even now the terms are sometimes used as though they are interchangeable. However, recent trends in the literature favor the term complicated grief so as to avoid confusion with posttraumatic stress disorder (PTSD), which is not characterized by separation trauma, as traumatic grief is (Jacobs 1999; Ott 2003; Prigerson and Jacobs 2001b; Stroebe et al. 2001). In fact, symptoms of PTSD may exist but not become complicated grief. Since by its nature, all grief is complicated and we do not intend to imply a normative grief process, we find it difficult to discuss complicated grief as a separate phenomenon and sometimes try to avoid using the term. Nevertheless, the concept of complicated grief is used so widely that it is important to try to identify symptoms of it. In fact, the *Diagnostic and Statistical Manual of Mental Disorders* (fifth edition) will probably include "complicated grief" as one of its categories. According to Kenneth Doka (2004), this controversial and important step does recognize that problematic grief exists, but once a category exists, the risk of misdiagnoses increases.

Complicated grief is associated with the presence of conflicted (e.g., markedly angry, ambivalent, abusive) or dependent relationships between the bereaved and the deceased or absent person. Other antecedent variables to complicated grief include prior losses or stressors that were not addressed, mental health problems, and a perceived lack of social support, such as inconsistent parenting (Ott 2003; Silverman, Johnson, and Prigerson 2001; van Doorn et al. 1998). The current concept of adult complicated grief hypothesizes that a person with an insecure, anxious attachment style (i.e., ongoing fears of abandonment, excessive dependency, and unstable attachments) and difficulties in self-regulating affect, goals, values and impulsivity is at risk of developing complicated grief upon the loss of a stabilizing and relatively exclusive relationship (Cohen et al. 2002; Prigerson and Jacobs 2001b). Long-standing dependency needs (retriggered by losing the secure relationship) result in separation anxiety and psychological trauma, which interfere with the adult's ability to grieve.

Three categories of symptoms distinguish persons who experience "complicated" grief:

1. Separation distress, such as being preoccupied with thoughts and upsetting memories of the deceased and longing and continuous searching for the deceased to the point of functional impairment.
2. Traumatic distress, including feelings of disbelief and shock regarding the death, mistrust, anger, guilt, and detachment from others.
3. Somatic symptoms of the deceased (e.g., a son whose father died of stomach cancer may have stomachaches).

The bereaved may engage in actions that promote their own helplessness, withdraw from others, and fail to meet daily demands such as caring for children or going to work.

Criteria for identifying complicated grief did not exist until the Inventory of Complicated Grief (ICG) was compiled, as summarized in box 2.2 (Prigerson and Jacobs 2001b). A cohort sequential study found that the mental health index scores for the complicated grief group were lower and remained low over time. The complicated grief group experienced more additional life stressors, perceived less social support, and achieved less clinically significant changes in their mental health index than did the noncomplicated grief group (Prigerson et al. 1995).

Although physical and mental health problems can develop in any grieving process, they are most likely to occur in instances of complicated grieving. Physical problems may include higher mortality rates (e.g., chronic illness, accidents, and suicide), loss of appetite and weight, excessive eating, depression, increased alcohol and drug consumption, and loss of sexual interest and functioning. Symptoms of psychological distress may include more somatic symptoms, anxiety, depression, insomnia, and, in some instances, self-injury. Because these psychological changes may not evoke a sympathetic response from family or friends, they may in turn intensify the grief reaction (Archer 2001; Prigerson et al. 1997).

As we stated earlier, researchers disagree on the definition of *pathological grief*, its manifestations, its assessment, its prevalence, and its distinction from "normal" grieving (Stroebe et al. 2000). Because each person's response to

Box 2.2 Symptoms of Complicated Grief

- Intrusive thoughts about the deceased.
- Yearning and searching for the deceased.
- Excessive loneliness since the death.
- Purposelessness or feelings of futility about the future.
- A subjective sense of numbness, detachment, or absence of emotional responsiveness.
- Difficulty acknowledging the death (e.g., disbelief).
- Feeling that life is empty or meaningless or that part of oneself has died.
- A shattered worldview (e.g., lost sense of security, trust, or control).
- Harmful behaviors developed as coping mechanisms (e.g., excessive use of drugs and/or alcohol; engagement in violent behavior).
- Excessive irritability, bitterness, and anger related to the death.
- Symptoms lasting at least six months and causing significant functional impairment.

Source: H. G. Prigerson and S. C. Jacobs, Traumatic Grief as a Distinct Disorder: A Rationale, Consensus Criteria and a Preliminary Empirical Test, in *Handbook of Bereavement Research: Consequences, Coping and Care,* edited by M. S. Stroebe, R. O. Hansson, W. Stroebe, and H. Schut (Washington, D.C.: American Psychological Association, 2001), 613–46.

bereavement is unique, what is "normal" must be considered in relation to his or her specific personality, relationship to the deceased person, family, and cultural background (Hagman 2001). The response also depends on the social and cultural context: who is defining what is pathological and what is normal in that person's culture. In addition, research has shown widely varying differences in the incidence of what might be considered pathological or abnormal grief (Murray 2001). Pathological grief is, in effect, an older term for complicated grief.

From our perspective throughout this book, complicated grief is characterized by thoughts of death ("I would be better off dead" or "I should have died with the deceased"), morbid preoccupation with worthlessness, feelings that our assumptive world has been irreparably violated, hallucinatory experiences other than the common experience of hearing the deceased's voice or transiently seeing images of him or her, and repetitious reactions to the trauma (e.g., continuously replaying footage of the planes crashing into the Twin Towers, imagining and going over every detail suffered by a daughter who was raped and murdered). Complicated grief generally is a response to natural disasters, war, rape, terrorism, mutilation, violence, accidents, or a mourner's perception that the death was preventable, especially a child's death (Stroebe, Schut, and Stroebe 1998).

Complicated grief can also be a response to any type of death. In fact, recent theorists contend that all grief is complicated, since people grieve while they relearn a complex world (Attig 2001). For example, one mother shut herself in her room, went out only when her family insisted that she do so, and did not speak the words "My son is dead" for two years. When she was finally able to acknowledge verbally her son's death, she broke down sobbing. Another father abruptly sold his business, moved out of the family home, began to drink heavily, and every day sat in front of the house where his daughter died, watching for any sign of the person whom he believed had killed his daughter, even though the murderer was in prison. Any one of these behaviors by itself might not be considered problematic, but it is the duration, the constellation of a number of dysfunctional, somewhat extreme behaviors, and the ongoing preoccupation that suggest the complicated nature of the grief response.

The early grief theorists (Freud, Lindemann, and Bowlby) assumed that grief became *pathological* when attachments to the deceased were prolonged (i.e., "decathexis," or separation, does not occur). Yet as we pointed out earlier, some presence of our loved one will always exist in our memory, usually at a subconscious level, regardless of how hard we try to break the bond. An effective grieving process does not need to eliminate thoughts of, feelings about, and a sense of connection with a lost love. Rather, healing is likely to involve the development of a respect for this presence while still being able to look positively toward the future without physical interaction with our loved one. The current recognition of the importance of ongoing bonds to the deceased illustrates how behavior that, in accordance with psychoanalytic theories of detachment, was once considered pathological is now seen as normal, healthy, and serving positive functions. Some early research also described the grief process as "reactive depression" (Parkes 1972a), but recent work differentiates normal bereavement from depression.

We thus must be careful about defining any type of grief behavior as pathological, even though some clinicians still use the term. But since bereavement results in a crisis in the meaning by which a person's life is given structure and substance, "pathological grief"—however defined—can sometimes be useful (Hagman 2001). Nevertheless, focusing on complicated or pathological grieving can also obscure some of the positive aspects of the integration of loss related to resilience, as we show in chapter 3. The processes and particular constructions of meaning that lead some bereaved people to a positive integration of grief and others to a problematic integration require further research (Murray 2001).

Sudden or Traumatic Loss

A traumatic loss is typically associated with sudden, unexpected, and sometimes violent circumstances, like an accident, homicide, or suicide (Handsley 2001; Prigerson 2001; Prigerson and Jacobs 2001b). But natural deaths and those with an undetermined cause can also be sudden and traumatic and evoke a complicated traumatic bereavement response, especially when people had no chance to prepare for the death or had a conflictual relationship with the deceased. In other words, traumatic grief, usually following exposure to a horrific or gruesome experience, differs from separation trauma, which causes separation distress (i.e., intrusive, distressing preoccupation with the deceased that includes yearning, longing, or searching). Two assessment tools for traumatic grief are the Traumatic Grief Evaluation of Response to Loss and the Inventory of Traumatic Grief (Prigerson and Jacobs 2001b). Traumatic grief is not typically associated with PTSD (Deranieri, Clements, and Henry 2002).

A sudden loss generally intensifies our grief owing to its shattering of our normal world and the series of concurrent crises and secondary losses (Doka and Davidson 1996, 1998). The Chinese distinguish between a "good death" in which all prescribed rituals are followed and a "bad death" in which they are not. Untimely murder and suicide are considered "bad deaths." The family often does not openly discuss bad deaths because of shame, social taboos, and the fear that the death was caused by bad spirits. The survivors of a bad death tend to dwell on the horrors of hell, not on the possibilities of heaven (Lee 1991). A loss caused by an accident, homicide, natural disaster, or suicide offers no opportunities to say good-bye or to attend to unfinished business. This lack of closure results in intensified feelings of guilt and hopelessness, especially if the deceased suffered physically (Raphael, Minkov, and Dobson 2001).

I obsessed for more than a year about what might have gone through Chris's mind when he realized that he was unable to arrest his fall and whether he was alive when he came to rest at the edge of the crevasse or died during the fall. I read everything I could find on falls, relieved to hear survivors refer to a sense of peacefulness during the fall. Both my husband and I needed to see the ranger's pictures of where Chris was found, even though the image of his crumpled body is now seared in my memory. When I talked with the funeral director in Anchorage about viewing Chris's body, I was thrown off by his response, "Well, we can't tell how he will look until he thaws." The thought of my child frozen, like a piece of meat needing to thaw, was almost unbearable, especially given how many years I, as his mother, devoted to "keeping him warm."

With accidental or homicidal deaths, we may feel more vulnerable and anxious because our world is no longer safe. Survivors may worry obsessively any time a family member is late getting home, imagining the worst. The grieving period following a sudden loss tends to be longer than that with an anticipated loss (Lord 1996). In cases in which the trauma is massive, such as the horrific murder of a whole family on Christmas Eve, survivors are likely to struggle for psychological and physical survival and only later move to deal with both the trauma and its meaning (Raphael, Minkov, and Dobson 2001). Even in instances of major trauma, however, survivors may find *posttraumatic growth*, or positive changes that result from their struggle with the trauma, such as psychological healing and an ability to love and laugh again (Frantz, Farrell, and Trolley 2001). The likelihood and extent of posttraumatic growth appear to vary with the person's particular characteristics, gender, and age (Calhoun and Tedeschi 2001).

Suicide raises additional challenges for survivors. Because suicide carries a stigma in our society, survivors often feel more shame, guilt, and anger, and traditional sources of support from religious institutions, colleagues, and friends may not be offered. Survivors are left with questions about why their loved ones killed themselves and what they could have done to prevent it. Since such questions are unanswerable, the grief process is often prolonged and complicated.

Posttraumatic stress disorder is usually associated with repeated exposure to a particularly horrific or gruesome experience as occurs with violence in wars or inner-city streets). It differs from traumatic grief, which appears to result from a sudden separation from the deceased. Accordingly, PTSD criteria do not include the core symptoms of separation distress, such as yearning or searching for the deceased or loneliness resulting from the loss of the loved one (Prigerston and Jacobs 2001b). The symptoms of PTSD are recurrent distressing recollections or dreams about the event, a sense of the event's occurring again, and intense physiological reactivity or psychological distress in response to reminders of the event. People who have PTSD may or may not experience complicated or traumatic grieving, however. As chapter 4 observes, clinicians first need to address the trauma in situations involving PTSD before they can begin grief interventions with survivors.

We know little about how the unanticipated nature of other types of loss, such as a partner's leaving a relationship without advance warning or the destruction of a home due to natural disaster, affects the grief process. We can surmise from the literature on sudden deaths that the lack of preparation and the possible prevention of the loss are likely to intensify the grief responses, at least in the short term.

Ongoing Bonds with the Deceased

One focus of early grief work was breaking the bond with the deceased. This was believed to be necessary in order to invest in new relationships and behaviors separate from the deceased (Bowlby 1980; Freud 1917; Rando 1984; Raphael 1983). More recent research, however, has determined that constant but changing bonds with the deceased can last for decades and are not associated with poor adjustment. In fact, continued attachments can provide a sense of continuity and facilitate adaptation to the loss (Fraley and Shaver 1999; Klass, Silverman, and Nickman 1996; Weiss 1993). In a study of forty-three bereaved parents of pediatric cancer patients, thirty-eight reported feelings of continued connection (e.g., visions, physical sensations, dreams) with their deceased child. With few exceptions, parents with ongoing connections to their dead child derived psychological benefits from them. These benefits included perceptions of their children's unique qualities; maintenance of their identity as the parents of that child; reassurance, hope, and a sense of peace; better day-to-day management; and tolerance of the uncertainty and ambiguity of life and death. In effect, such attachments represent a shift from a "going on" to an "ongoing" perspective on loss (Fleming and Robinson 2001).

Sensing the presence of the deceased is not the same as searching behavior, since the bereaved person usually does not initiate it. It does not match other search behavior in which people know what they are looking for, and in fact, it may occur years after the loss, when the bereaved person has stopped searching. Such a bond often takes the form of talking with the deceased, typically at the grave, although women have been found to talk to the dead at home (Klass and Walter 2001; Rees 1997). Conversation replaces ritual as the normative way in which the survivor maintains the bond with the dead person (Seale 1998). This also includes talking to others who knew the dead person, especially about parts of their life unknown to the mourner.

Even though my son died six years ago, I always am eager to hear a new story about him (often a story of his adventures that I was lucky not to have known when he was alive!) and am grateful for his friends and acquaintances who continue to contact me to share memories new to me.

Through talking, the bereaved try to complete the person's identity and write the "last chapter" of his or her biography. Even if the stories are not completely true, they serve a memorial function.

The dead—or "social ghosts"—may continue to play a role in our lives (Kaplan 1995). They can help repair our personal identity, providing moral role models for our actions and guidance in making decisions. For instance, we may incorporate virtues of the deceased into our own character or reflect on his or her death to clarify our own values. I often find myself in an "internal dialogue" with Chris, seeking his guidance on decisions related primarily to his little sister. We may identify the deceased as part of our own biography, which provides solace related to moral functioning (Klass 1993, 1996b, 1999b; Marwit and Klass 1988/1989; Normand, Silverman, and Nickman 1996). As his high school adviser said at the memorial service for Chris, "The best way we can remember to him is to 'seek to be as kind as he was,'" a lesson that I try to follow daily. Some parents take on special projects in their child's memory, believing that he or she would have wanted them to do so. Starting a memorial fund in our child's name, being available to other grieving parents, or supporting a cause that our child held dear are ongoing tributes to their lives.

Paranormal or psychic phenomena can be part of ongoing attachments (Becker and Knudson 2003; Riches and Dawson 2000). Grieving parents or siblings, especially adolescents, often seek out and experience after-death contacts, whether through dreams, signs, mediums, or clairvoyant messages. Others may not seek such contact but nevertheless experience it.

Both my other son and a nephew had visits from Chris in their dreams the day after he fell, which is when we think he died. And I continue to have dreams of Chris, particularly when I am in or near the mountains.

Grieving parents often dream about their dead children, hear voices, and smell flowers or have other evocative senses associated with their child's life. Some parents receive messages from the "other side" (however defined by parents) that contain a degree of detail that only the deceased could know. Such communications may provide momentary comfort and reassurance from knowing about the "place" inhabited by the deceased. This is especially the case for survivors who believe that the spirit is primary and the body is secondary and that the spirit acquires another form and goes to heaven or some other place at the time of death. "Messages from the other side" may help us in remembering the life that was lived rather than being fixated on death. But discovering that the child is loved and happy in an afterlife does not necessarily assuage the pain from the death, although it may mitigate it. In addition to after-death communication, psychic phenomena may include premonitions, near-death experiences, and crisis apparitions.

After Chris's death, one of his close friends told us that he had had vivid dreams of Chris dying in the mountains and premonitions of his death for years, often causing him to cry uncontrollably. He had never shared these premonitions with others but always felt that Chris would die at some point on a mountain.

Many people who have after-death experiences are reluctant to talk about them, for fear of being discounted, laughed at, stigmatized, or socially isolated. Since Western cultures do not provide a framework by which to integrate the dead into bereaved's lives, most people do not mention their experiences to others. But studies have found that a significant portion of the population sense the presence of the dead and find this comforting, so it cannot be labeled pathological or even hallucinatory (Klass, Silverman, and Nickman 1996; Stroebe et al. 1992; Walter 1996; Zisook and Schuchter 1993). In sum, we do not know what psychic phenomena are, how they work, or why they work, but we do know that they exist (Blank 1998). Too many survivors have recounted such experiences for them to be discounted.

Cultural Variations in Ongoing Bonds with the Deceased

Cultures vary markedly in their beliefs about the form and meaning of a continuing relationship with the deceased. For the Toraja of Indonesia, the dead communicate with the living through dreams that foretell future prosperity. Since these people grow up knowing about such dreams after death, they eagerly await them. In contrast, Europeans and Americans may feel a connection through a sense of presence, internal conversation, prayers, and dreams but not with any expectation that the dream will foretell future prosperity (Rosenblatt 2001).

Cultures also differ widely regarding the relationship and communication between the living and the dead. Chinese American families often make offerings to the deceased on the first and fifteenth days of the Chinese lunar month to reinforce the bond between the living and their dead ancestors. These offerings are a mode of communication with the dead and remind the living of their continued presence in the family. Since family relationships are believed to continue after death, communication with the dead is possible. These beliefs underlie the importance of ancestor worship and the daily prayers in front of portraits of parents or grandparents in the living room (Klass and Goss 1998). Recognizing the continuity of family relationships after death, Buddhists place a memorial plate in the temple for continued communication purposes. The Hmong believe that when we are born, we are taken from our spirit parents and inducted into the world of living; thus when we die, we must be sent back to the spirit world to be with our ancestors. Accordingly, the souls of the recent dead can cause harm if they are not sent back appropriately.

Given their strong belief in the afterlife and the spirit world, many African Americans acknowledge the deceased's presence at family gatherings (Barrett

1998). Latinos tend to believe that the spirit evolves, beginning at a level of ignorance and moving toward a state of moral perfection. To attain this higher level of "light and understanding," the spirit must be able to detach from Earth, which may be difficult when a person dies prematurely without resolving family conflicts or paying old debts. Similarly, families find it very difficult if they were not present at the death to say good-bye, leaving their loss unresolved. Many Latino families gather for at least seven nights to say a rosary and frequently visit the grave and attend Mass. Because they believe in communication with the dead, they may visit spiritists or mediums when they want to resolve issues with their loved ones, especially when they have dreams about the dead returning to say farewell or deliver a special message. Such a dream is viewed as a sign that the spirit is restless and must communicate before leaving the material world (Garcia-Preto 1991). Native Americans usually do not publicly or openly express or discuss their grief, following rules about how the deceased and the survivors are to be addressed. Hopis are expected to display a positive attitude while grieving, although within the family, members may cry and show other outward signs of grieving (Lipson 1996).

Traditional Judaism affirms personal survival in some form after death, although speculation about the personal form of that survival is usually discouraged. Jewish Americans do not believe in an afterlife, although they may feel a spiritual connection with the deceased. Some Jews' hope for survival is the survival of the people of Israel and their gathering in their historic land. Jewish tradition also speaks of an *olam haba* or "next world," which many believe to be a messianic age here on Earth (Armstrong, personal correspondence, September 2004; Cytron 1993).

Regardless of the particular culture and manifestation of ongoing bonds, friends, relatives, and professionals must be sensitive to the various ways of perceiving and interpreting death and the destination of the deceased (Riches and Dawson 2000). Learning to listen without judging can be powerfully supportive to the bereaved and, in turn, to the listener.

Summary

This chapter supports the concept of the grief process in terms of phases, rather than unilinear stages or tasks; defines excessive rumination, PTSD, and complicated grieving; and recognizes the problem of labeling grief as complicated; differentiates sudden traumatic death and PTSD; provides evidence for ongoing bonds with the deceased; and emphasizes the importance of taking account of cultural variations in the grief process.

3

Resilience and Meaning Making

W<small>HY DO</small> some of us become stuck in grief, with feelings of bitterness and sadness, unable to engage fully with our families and even in life? And why do others of us grow through loss, finding meaning in our new lives and relationships? Writing about the unfairness of death, Rabbi Harold Kushner asked how a Job-like figure in Archibald MacLeish's play *JB* was able to deal with a cold unfair world, in which everything held precious had been destroyed: "Instead of looking outward to churches or to nature for answers, they look inward to their own capacities for loving" (1985:144). Identifying individual and larger factors that affect the outcomes of the grief process can help answer these questions of finding meaning through loss. Two models—the traditional stress and coping models and a newer model of resilience—are useful for understanding different mediating variables and outcomes.

The Stress and Coping Models

The development of stress and coping models followed Freud's and Lindemann's psychodynamic frameworks. Conceptualizations of stressful life events view grief as a major cause of stress and depression as a likely outcome (Pearlin 1989; Shaver and Tancredy 2001). Mediators, such as coping skills, social support, and positive or negative appraisals of the situation, affect how people deal with grief-related stress (Folkman 2001; Folkman and Moskowitz 2000; Pearlin 1982). Adaptive coping strategies, such as accepting feelings of loss; discovering meaning; reorganizing one's identity, social relationships, and daily routines; and reinvesting in new commitments and activities, reduce the negative psychosocial and physical health consequences of bereavement (Stroebe and Schut 2001). In contrast to avoidance, positive appraisal processes (similar to the integrative approach of identifying positives that can emerge from grief) can help

63

us redefine and focus on positive meanings, thus motivating us to try to cope with the stress of grief. This also is similar to Bonanno's (2001b) finding that positive emotions improve bereavement outcomes. Problem-focused coping is directed at managing and changing the problem causing the distress, and emotion-focused coping is oriented to managing the resulting emotions (Folkman 2001; Folkman and Lazarus 1984). Some coping strategies, such as crying, also are symptoms of grief. How bereaved persons cope appears to be more critical to outcomes than personality traits are (Meuser and Marwit 2000). How these complex processes are used during grieving, however, is unclear, and there has been little research on the effectiveness of coping strategies during grief (Stroebe and Schut 2001).

Lazarus and Folkman's stress-coping model has numerous variations. For example, according to Demi (1987, 1989), when we grieve a loss, we move through three crisis periods: numbness and yearning, disorganization, and reorganization. The outcome of each is a potential turning point that may lead to better health and greater maturity or to poorer health and depression (Shaver and Tancredy 2001). The choice depends on both our appraisal of loss and the mediating variables. These variables include our own and our family's developmental stage and the balance of intrapersonal and social cultural resources. Note that Demi's model has not been empirically tested however.

Stroebe and Stroebe's (1987) Deficit Model of Partner Loss applies psychological stress models to partners' bereavement. The demands in this model are the loss of emotional and instrumental support and social identity, and its resources are both intrapersonal and interpersonal. Other mediating variables are concurrent negative life stressors, gender, age, forewarning of the loss, and social support. Some stress and coping models found social supports important mediators to how we respond to loss (Dimond 1981; Maddison and Raphael 1975; Walker, MacBride, and Vachon 1977). Stroebe and Schut (1999) later developed a dual model, or restoration-orientation coping, in which proactive thoughts and actions are associated with planning and goals for the future (for a fuller description of the dual model of grief, see chapter 2).

When it is applied to grief, the stress and coping framework has been criticized for condensing a wide range of emotional reactions into stress alone and for lacking an empirical evaluation of the outcomes. Critics maintain that stress is a much simpler concept than emotion and tells little about the details of previous struggles to adapt to stressors. For example, the emotions of being angry, guilty, or lonely are viewed as more complex than and different from the experience of "stress/nonstress" (Lazarus 1999). Another limitation of the stress and coping framework is its primary focus on individual characteristics and coping processes, without taking account of cultural, social, and community strengths or capacities. Instead, many of the early psychodynamic models assumed a deficit in bereaved individuals; for example, they saw problems with grief as the result of an inability to confront personal feelings, consequences of earlier insecure attachments, or a lack of healthy personal resources developing from earlier bonding experiences.

Based on stress and coping models as well as the theoretical models described in chapter 1, scholars agree on the wide range of mediating factors that affect the grief process: (1) background characteristics (e.g., socioeconomic class, race/ethnicity, gender, and concurrent stressors) and relationships (e.g., that with the deceased); (2) personal capacities (e.g., developmental stage of life, religiosity/spirituality); and (3) social, community, and cultural capacities (e.g., family structure and stability, availability of social support, cultural rituals and norms) (Barry, Kasl, and Prigerson 2002; Carr et al. 2001; Corless, Germino, and Pittman 1994; Richardson and Balaswamy 2001; Stroebe et al. 2001a). Other factors that characterize the loss itself, such as one's relationship with the deceased or absent person, as well as ambivalence and level of attachment in the relationship, also affect bereavement outcomes. When the loss has been caused by death, the nature and type of death (violent, accidental, illness related), forewarning of the death (predictability), and perception of the prevention of and responsibility for the death all are salient factors.

Many of these factors can be conceptualized under a model of resilience, based on social work's historical emphasis on a strengths perspective. We believe that each of us who has suffered loss and found ways to integrate that loss into our lives is, to some extent, resilient. We are active, not passive, that is, acted upon by outside events as we build up a sense of our own resilience and vulnerability over a lifetime. Human beings' capacity for growth and development can last for a lifetime if they embrace, understand, and learn from their experiences. The concept of resilience, rather than deficit, affects interventions with and the types of supports provided to those who are grieving a loss. The resilience framework presented here is not a developed theoretical model but an alternative way of conceptualizing the grieving process that takes account of cultural, community, and social resources and capacities. At this early stage of its formulation, it is a way of organizing one's thinking about grief that offers a wider context than the more individually oriented psychodynamic and stress and coping models.

The early research in the area of resilience identified those factors associated with successful adaptation by children and youth living in high-risk situations due to environmental factors such as poverty and violence. Although most resilience research continues to focus on identifying risk factors and how protective factors moderate psychosocial outcomes in children (Benson 1997; Hawkins et al. 1999; Herrenkohl et al. 2000), resilience as a conceptual framework can also be relevant to understanding how individual, family, community, and cultural capacities can protect people from the disruptions of loss. In presenting this framework as one way to organize and conceptualize the wide range of factors that affect the outcomes of loss, we rely primarily on the work of McCubbin and McCubbin (1993) and Fredriksen-Goldsen (2006).

Resilience Framework

Resilience is defined as the behavioral patterns, functional competence, and cultural capacities that individuals, families, and communities use under adverse circumstances (in this case, loss) and the ability to make adversity (e.g., loss) into a catalyst for growth and development (Fredriksen-Goldsen 2006; Fredriksen-Goldsen and Hooyman 2003). The framework contains the following four factors:

1. Background characteristics (gender, age, race/ethnicity, developmental phase, nature of the relationship, and family structure of both the person grieving and the grieved).
2. Adversity, including the nature of the loss, trauma, and prior losses.
3. Capacities (personal, family, social, cultural, and community resources of the bereaved person).
4. Mental and physical well-being as an outcome (e.g., growth, development, healing, accommodation, or integration of the loss). (Leick and Davidsen-Nielsen 1996; Neimeyer 2001b)

Background Characteristics

Individual background characteristics influence how people confront and integrate loss in their lives, and the following appear to be most salient to the grief process: gender, age, developmental considerations, ethnic minority status and culture, and prior relationship.

GENDER

Gender differences determine how we deal with a wide range of losses over our life (e.g., a partner's separation, divorce, or death) and tend to be most pronounced in parents grieving a child's death. In fact, parents are much more likely to differ in how they grieve than to be similar (Gilbert 1996; Rando 1986, 1991; Raphael 1983; Rosenblatt 2000a). One difference is how publicly, intensely, and long women and men grieve. Women typically grieve longer, express their feel-ings more openly and verbally, generally grow more as a result of the loss, are more likely to turn to others to process their feelings, and are less likely to try to control their emotions (Arbuckle and deVries 1995; Brabant, Forsyth, and McFarlain 1995; Calhoun and Tedeschi 2001; Carroll and Shaefer 1993/1994; Gilbert and Smart 1992; Kavanaugh 1997; Rosenblatt 2000a; Tennen and Affleck 1998; Thomas et al. 1997).

Anne Morrow Lindbergh, grieving the kidnapping and murder of her young son, recognized this: "Women take and conquer sorrow differently from men. They take it willingly, with open arms they blend and merge it into every part of their lives; it is diffused and spread into every fiber, and they build from that and with that. While men take the concentrated bitter dose at one draught and then try to forget—start to work at something objective and entirely separate" (1973:294).

A male partner may feel expected to express emotions and relate to others or act in ways that do not fit for him. For example, a husband who wants to be alone, grieve privately, immerse himself in work, and not talk about certain things may feel pressured by his wife's need for more contact, sharing, and being heard and supported. Conversely, a wife grieving her child may feel emo-tionally abandoned by her husband, needing to fight to have her feelings acknowledged and respected yet not getting the support she needs and desires from her partner.

For the parents of a three-year-old who was kidnapped from a busy grocery store and never found,

> there was no room for anger, no openings. They moved like figures in a quagmire, with no strength for confrontation. Suddenly, their sorrows were separate, insular, and incommunicable. They went their different ways, he with his lists, his daily trudging, she in her armchair, lost to deep, private grief. There was no mutual consolation, no touching, and no love. Their old intimacy, their habitual assump-tion that they were on the same side, was dead. They remained huddled over their separate losses, and unspoken resentments began to grow. (McEwan 1985:22)

This pattern of parents' distancing and pursuit, with death creating a new bond while simultaneously pushing them apart, can increase both conflict and connection between them (Dijkstra and Stroebe 1998; Klass 1997; Rosenblatt 2000a).

Another unanticipated consequence of a child's death is that because of her strong expression of her needs, the mother may emerge emotionally stronger than the father (Calhoun and Tedeschi 2001). According to Rosenblatt, even though the woman may recognize the differences in how each of them grieves, she may insist on her partner's responding to her needs and providing emotional support. In such instances, "the relationship dance becomes changed, with the woman leading and the man watching her feet and following" (2000a:148).

Regardless of the type of loss, women are generally more expressive of their feelings than men are. For example, Chinese American women typically are permitted to wail loudly, but men are generally expected to remain silent and to weep only immediately after a death when all family members gather in the room with the body (Rosenblatt 1993). Compared with men, however, women may need help in rethinking and restructuring their lives and finding new sources of meaning. Another gender-based difference is that women generally use more emotion-focused coping then men do, who tend to use rational problem-solving styles. For example, in searching for things to help with their loss, women may turn to friends and counselors for talking and crying, whereas men often prefer to deal with their grief cognitively and alone, focusing on the tasks to be done (e.g., funeral plans, gathering information about the cause of death in order to "explain" it, making financial arrangements). That is, they may "shelve" their thoughts and feelings in order to meet their immediate obligations. By associating feelings with specific thoughts, men may manage uncomfortable feelings by using various cognitive techniques, such as distracting themselves by "keeping busy" and actively and tangibly taking steps toward the future, like setting up a foundation or funds in memory of their loved one, and, in some instances, bringing a lawsuit against an individual or organization perceived as "causing" the death (Doka 2000a; Miller and Golden 1998; Walter 2003).

After our son died, my husband turned his energy to working to make a used sailboat safe for our older son, Kevin. After he returned from visiting him in New York City for a week, I asked my husband if they had some good talks about Chris. He responded that they never mentioned Chris but focused their energies on remodeling Kevin's new apartment. His goals now were Kevin's future. I said nothing, despite noticing our profoundly different ways of grieving, since I would have felt the need to talk with Kevin about Chris.

Some men may see their loss as a challenging "job"—"I can survive this" or "I can handle this" or "Let's get back to normal" (Martin and Doka 1998). Whether these different comparative coping styles (e.g., women being generally more emotion focused and men more problem focused) can complement each other is crucial, since both styles appear to be essential to dealing with loss over time (Stroebe and Schut 1999). In regard to psychological well-being, women are more likely than men are to admit to feeling anxious and depressed and to seek mental health help during the first year of bereavement. Yet when men do use mental health counseling, they may benefit more from it than women do because it has a greater impact on their ability to express their feelings (Schut et al. 1997; Stroebe et al. 2001a).

In regard to physical health, widowers are more likely to die of cardiac failure during the first year after their wife's death than widows are after their husband's death (Parkes 1996; Stroebe et al. 2001a; Stroebe and Schut 2001). In fact, the overall mortality of bereaved men is higher than that of controlled samples (Archer 1999; Lichenstein, Gatz, and Berg 1998; Stroebe and Stroebe 1993). These differences appear partially due to men's generally having fewer social support networks; they are more likely to have acquaintances and colleagues than close friends with whom they can share their feelings and thus are at greater risk of social isolation (Campbell and Silverman 1996; Sanders 1999).

Assumptions about gender differences have been challenged, however. Two patterns of grieving have been identified as (1) an intuitive one, in which grief is expressed in an affective way and is stereotyped as female, and (2) an instrumental pattern, in which grief is expressed physically or cognitively and is stereotyped as male. A third pattern may be a blending of the two. These patterns are related to, but not determined by, gender (Martin and Doka 2000; Walter 2003). Other researchers suggest that although men have very strong feelings of attachment to the deceased, they are less likely to disclose them (Brabant, Forsyth, and McFarlain 1995). This may result from men's socialization not to cry and their concern that a public display of their feelings can cause concern or discomfort for those who are not used to seeing them express their emotions. How a man grieves can be a way of talking without the words and of "crying without the tears" (Miller and Goldman 1998:21; Walter 2003).

Although men and women tend to grieve differently, neither way is right or wrong—just different—and should be respected as such. Nonetheless, these differences in how grief is expressed, whether or not they are based on gender, are important factors to consider when working with individuals concerning issues of loss. In general, people faced with a loss need opportunities to talk about it, to help make sense out of it, to validate their feelings, and to explore alternative ways of viewing the situation and letting go of negative emotions. Women usually have more opportunities to vent and are more skilled at social contacts that provide these opportunities than men are. Whether women are more resilient than men in their long-term grieving is unclear. What is clear is that differences do exist and can affect a person's resilience, especially through social support mechanisms.

AGE

Adults aged sixty and older are generally better prepared to deal with loss, since losses tend to increase with age and, to some extent, are anticipated. Accordingly, they tend to grieve losses less than younger people do, who may be struggling with "off-time" loss (Lund 1989b; Stroebe et al. 2001a). Younger people have more health impairments, higher mortality rates, and other psychosocial and physical symptoms than older adults do. The extent to which loss is expected as a normal transition in life appears to be an important variable in age-based differences in dealing with loss (Stroebe and Schut 2001). But younger family members may trivialize older adults' losses, viewing them as "normative." The accumulation of loss during a lifetime does not necessarily mitigate the pain of grief and ensure that older adults are better at dealing with it. In fact, in some instances, the accumulation of loss affects an individual's coping capacity (Sanders 1999). Loss in old age is discussed more fully in chapter 12.

DEVELOPMENTAL PHASE OF LIFE

A person's developmental life phase may, but not necessarily, be closely associated with age. Because these phases are so central to the grief response, we have written the chapters of this book to coincide with the developmental considerations and types of loss characteristic of childhood, adolescence, young adulthood, middle adulthood, and old age. Whether or not one views a loss as normative often varies with the life phase. Although when a young adult's child dies, it is usually an infant, the death of an unborn child or infant is not normative for early adulthood, when most young adults are beginning to build their families along with their careers. In contrast, when the parent of a person in late middle age dies, it is increasingly viewed as an "on-time" event but nevertheless can be very painful. By contrast, a parent's death is not normative for a child, but when it does occur, there appear to be typical constellations of developmental issues and behaviors. We hypothesize that a loss that is congruent with the developmental phase probably has fewer and shorter consequences than does one that is incongruent.

ETHNIC MINORITY STATUS AND CULTURE

Ethnicity encompasses culture, values and beliefs, social status, and support systems but not always minority status. For example, Jews are considered an ethnic group, but not a minority or protected group as defined by the federal government (e.g., African Americans, Latinos, American Indians, Asian Americans, and Pacific Islanders). A culture's identity, social support, and rituals influence the growth and well-being or poor physical and mental health of its members.

When associated with fewer educational and economic opportunities, reduced access to health care, poorer health status, and community violence, ethnic minority status dramatically affects the risk of death at an early age. Although these structural factors may not affect the grieving process, they may influence how death is viewed and the nature of the response from families, neighbors, and communities.

The salience of structural factors is illustrated by the power of rituals, symbols, and social support in African American culture. African Americans regard funerals as primary rituals and so their participation in funerals is an important social obligation. When friends, relatives, or neighbors hear of a death, they may spontaneously gather at the home of the bereaved to provide support, without being asked to do so. Expressions of sympathy and condolence are expected and greatly valued as signs of respect of the deceased and the survivors. The more personal the sacrifice of a gift, time, money, or food is, the more highly regarded the offering will be. Accordingly, home-cooked food is of greater value than take-out food from a grocery store. A number of rituals and traditions both honor the dead and strengthen community bonds, such as naming infants after the dead person, passing babies over the caskets of loved ones, pouring libations on the ground for the dead, and acknowledging the presence of the dead at family gatherings. How one participates and conducts oneself during a time of loss and grief can dramatically redefine family ties and relationships. Those who respond according to normative expectations are gathered closer to and more highly regarded by the bereaved, whereas those who fail to respond appropriately are often viewed as additional losses to mourn and grieve (Doka and Davidson 1998).

NATURE OF THE PRIOR RELATIONSHIP

Prior relationships that contain much anger, ambivalence, or dependence are assumed to complicate mourning beyond what is considered to be normative. But more recent studies suggest that instead, stronger bonds and more intense attachments between spouses result in greater psychological distress and that conflictual marriages lead to less grief, especially yearning (Carr et al. 2000). But the type of loss itself cannot gauge the extent of pain. For example, the death of a partner who has been abusive may bring more relief than pain, and a divorce unexpectedly initiated by a dearly loved partner after thirty years of marriage creates mostly pain.

Adversity

The resilience literature defines adversity as a condition of suffering, affliction, or misfortune (Gove and Crutchfield 1993), which also describes loss and grief.

The nature of the loss (e.g., accidental death of a child), trauma, and the accumulation of prior losses help determine the degree of adversity caused by loss. Although adversity affects mental and physical well-being, it is influenced or mediated by capacities, as discussed earlier.

NATURE OF THE LOSS

As described in chapter 1, an accidental or sudden loss typically has more negative repercussions than does one that is "on time" (e.g., a parent's death after a long illness) or anticipated (a divorce that has been carefully planned to minimize disruptions to the children). Rando (1993), for example, found that losses resulting from trauma or random violence are risk factors for complicated mourning (i.e., mourning that exceeds what is considered to be the norm and that defies modest attempts at intervention). Unexpected, accidental, and traumatic deaths, especially if they were perpetrated by trusted others, tend to be the most painful and intense (Jacobs 1993; Ott 2003; Prigerson and Jacobs 2001). The relationship between a sudden death and negative health outcomes is not necessarily clear-cut, though. For example, mediating factors may be internal or external control beliefs, high self-esteem, and age, since sudden death is not as traumatic for older adults as it is for younger adults (Stroebe and Schut 2001). Other studies have found that anticipated deaths that required extensive and lengthy medical care are more difficult for the survivors, who are more likely to become depressed (Carr 2003; Carr et al. 2001). What may explain these differences in outcomes is the bereaved's perceptions of his or her preparedness for a death, with those feeling unprepared more likely to have complicated grief reactions (Barry, Kasl, and Prigerson 2002).

The nature of the death may have a greater impact in the short run than over time. For example, a common assumption is that suicide deaths result in greater adjustment problems, but most studies have found little difference between survivors of suicide and other grieving persons in long-term bereavement outcomes (Carr et al. 2001). Yet survivors' guilt feelings may be most pronounced with suicidal deaths (Stroebe and Schut 2001).

ACCUMULATION OF UNRESOLVED PRIOR LOSSES

Whether a lifetime of other losses prepares people for subsequent losses or depletes their energy and ability to deal with more loss has not been resolved. Past losses can complicate grief by intensifying both the physical and the emotional response to loss (McCandless and Connor 1997). For example, the multiple losses experienced by HIV-AIDS survivors (discussed in chapter 8) are found to increase the likelihood of complicated grief.

Capacities

Capacity is defined as the power or ability to hold, receive, and accommodate, that is, to create the conditions for maximal potential. Capacities are created by the individual, family, culture, and community (Fredriksen-Goldsen 2006; Fredriksen-Goldsen and Hooyman 2003). The concept of capacities is similar to protective factors in the risk and resilience literature (Benson 1997; Hawkins et al. 1999; Herrenkohl et al. 2000; Werner and Smith 1992). Fredriksen-Goldsen (2006) suggests that capacities more accurately capture resilience than do protective factors or moderators, because they directly affect outcomes and protect against or moderate adversity. Capacities are conceptualized as

1. Personal (cognitive ability, mastery or competence, locus of control, tendency to self-blame, religious and spiritual practices, the need for meaning).
2. Cultural (ethnic identity, acculturation/adaptation, rituals surrounding grief and loss).
3. Family, social, and community (family system, family roles, social support, self-help groups for the bereaved, social integration, marital relationship, relationship with the lost person or object).

PERSONAL CAPACITIES

Grieving implies acting rather than remaining passive. The individual level of human agency—the will to do or be something—appears to be important to resilience. Personality factors characteristic of survivors are assertiveness, flexibility to tolerate both closeness to and distance from the deceased, tenacity, optimism, distancing ability, intelligence, group consciousness, and the ability to find meaning and courage in one's life (Leick and Davidsen-Nielsen 1996; Helmreich 1992). In general, however, no obvious patterns have been found between personality and coping with loss (Stroebe et al. 2001a; Stroebe and Schut 2001). Other personal resources are a personal philosophy that can make sense of loss; an ability to acknowledge and express personal feelings; an inner-directed, autonomous identity; and faith in established beliefs that locate the loss in a context that is recognizable to the bereaved (Rosenblatt 2000a).

Spirituality and *religiosity* are aspects of personal capacities that affect the process of grieving a loss. In most cultures, religion is a major area of discourse for dealing with loss and death, life's meaning, morality, fairness, and rituals. Religion provides a way for some people to talk about their loss in detail or to resolve their problems (e.g., it is God's will or part of a supreme being's plan, or this makes sense only if there is a God and everlasting life). Whether in the form of a structured religion or a generalized belief system, spiritual beliefs may be strengthened simply because nothing else helps (Frantz, Farrell, and Trolley 2001). In one study, more than 80 percent of the approximately three hundred adults who had suffered the death of a loved one said that their religious and spiritual beliefs helped them during their grief, with a strengthened belief in the afterlife being a significant benefit of their experience (Frantz, Trolley, and Johll 1996). Similarly, a study of bereaved middle-aged adults found that those with strong spiritual beliefs integrated the death of a loved one more readily than did those without spiritual beliefs (Walsh 2002). But major losses such as death are nonetheless a challenge to religious beliefs and systems. It becomes difficult for the bereaved to sustain their previous definitions of the world. Grieving individuals are often left questioning: "Why did God (however defined) allow this to happen? Why didn't God help? After this, I can't believe there is a loving God." Or they may be angry at a supreme being, and thereby reject or question their prior religious beliefs. When loss threatens our religious foundations, we may struggle with matters of faith, fairness, justice, and the validity of religious teachings. Or we may believe that we are responsible for our terrible loss, wondering whether we have sinned or feeling guilty about what we had or had not prayed for (Rosenblatt 2000a).

The role of religious beliefs in coping with loss is not clear but ranges from being positive, to making no difference, to leading to greater difficulties with adjustment (Stroebe and Schut 2001). For example, religious interpretations may be unacceptable, such as "God loved your son more than you did," and can make us angry and resistant, and can even slow the integration of the loss. The relationship among church attendance, social support (gained through a church or synagogue), and the physical and mental well-being of participants in religious institutions is generally strong, however (Koenig 1997; Koenig and Brooks 2002; Koenig, George, and Peterson 1998; Koenig, McCullough, and Larson 2001; Krause 2003; Nolen-Hoeksema and Larson 1999).

Religiosity appears to be a source of considerable strength for African Americans who view death as part of the natural rhythm of life and believe in life after death. Although their dead ancestors are now in the spirit world, African Americans publicly acknowledge them in their community. Indeed, their belief in an indistinguishable separation between the physical and spiritual world may underlie their expressions of hope, love, and joy at funerals and church services (Doka and Davidson 1998).

Spirituality—a way in which we invest life with meaning—is broader than religion. That is, we can be spiritual without being religious, and perhaps we can be religious without being spiritual (Balk 1999), although Klass (1999b) views religion and spirituality in constant interchange.

Spirituality is not a set of dogmatic beliefs or a state of mind reserved for extraordinary moments; nor is it something that we can possess and attain once and for all. Rather, it is a process, a "way of being in the world," to which we aspire. Traveling this path, we may discover for ourselves that we participate in "creating the person we wish to be and the life we desire to lead" (Becvar 2001:29).

Klass (1999b, 2001b) characterizes a spiritual experience by (1) encountering or merging with a transcendent reality beyond the self; (2) finding a worldview that encompasses a higher intelligence, purpose, or order that gives meaning and order to one's life; and (3) belonging to a community in which the transcendent reality and worldview are validated. Community does not imply religious organization but communion with fellow human beings. An event or experience is spiritual when it is important to us. It could be said that all who grieve are engaged in a spiritual task, since they are asking questions and searching for meaning (Balk and Coor 2001; Doka and Davidson 1998; Neimeyer 2001b). We do not escape from our grief into a spiritual place; instead, the spiritual emerges in our daily coming to terms with the death of a loved one (Klass 1999b). As Attig explained, by relearning the world, we struggle to come to terms with the great mysteries of life in the human condition. We enter into our "spiritual place" within the greater scheme of things (2001b:45).

When faced with a major loss, the world no longer makes sense; there is no comprehensible person-outcome contingency, no guarantee of safety and protection. With our fundamental assumptions shattered, disillusionment and disbelief are pervasive as we struggle with "I never thought it could happen to me. . . . I know that bad things happen but I always thought it won't happen to me," "Why did she have to die?" "Why am I in such pain? And what will happen to me next?" (Doka and Davidson 1998). We may blame ourselves in order to reestablish some semblance of a meaningful universe and minimize the world's randomness. (Think of how often a child blames himself or herself for a parent's death, reviewing every malevolent thought ever held or wish ever made). Or we may engage in counterfactual thoughts (i.e., endless "if onlys"), which may border on rumination (Davis 2001). We may be able to go through the motions of daily tasks so that at least some parts of the world are not random. But we must be able to make meaning of the loss in order to integrate it into our daily lives (Janoff-Bulman and Berg 1998; Neimeyer 2001b). Making meaning may or may not involve religious interpretations but usually moves through a spiritual and cognitive process.

The ability to make or derive meaning from the loss is both an individual, spiritual, and cognitive capacity and a process central to physical and mental

well-being (Neimeyer 2001b). A confrontation with death or some other traumatic life event is an attack on our worldview that gives our life meaning and
structure. Our assumptions about the benevolence and order of the world
become "illusions" with which we must contend. To rebuild our life, we must
again perceive the world and self in positive terms but simultaneously incorporate the loss in our new assumptive world (Fleming and Robinson 2001). In
other words, we must reestablish a meaningful life that includes the deceased's
internal representation and meaning. This need for meaning has been noted
by researchers studying reactions to a wide range of losses and traumas (Davis
2001). Although the reconstruction of meaning is central to the process of
grieving, it cannot begin until the bereaved is ready to explore these issues
(Calhoun and Tedeschi 2001).

Researchers and clinicians have different ideas of what constitutes meaning.
For example, meaning may occur at an emotional level (e.g., a person feels at
one with the universe) (Frankl 1969), or it may mean setting new goals and
purpose or reconstructing a sense of self that incorporates the negative experience (Updegraff and Taylor 2000) or an explanation of the event (Davis and
Nolen-Hoeksema 2001; Davis et al. 2000). What appears to be most important
is that a meaning must be constructed from a loss in a way appropriate to
each person. The ultimate goal is to help the grieving person create a reality
that contains both sadness and joy. Loss marks the end of one life chapter and
signifies the beginning of a new one. Loss has the capacity to open doors to
greater awareness, to enhance sensitivity, and to increase compassion. It may
even lead to greater wisdom (Becvar 2001). This process includes moving from
perceptions of a meaningless, malevolent universe to creating a meaningful life,
not in spite of our loss but because of our loss. In the end, we feel both more
vulnerable and more appreciative. The world is good, we are good, and the world
makes sense, but not always. After faced with a major loss, our representations
of the world and ourselves now allow for misfortune and disaster (Janoff-
Bulman and Berg 1998).

The resilience model states that grieving individuals who can find meaning in
their loss will have a healthier physical and mental well-being. In fact, undesir-
able life events often have positive effects on people's lives and, in some instances,
are turning points transforming their sense of identity or purpose (Antonovsky
1987; Calhoun and Tedeschi 2001; Tedeschi and Calhoun 1995, 1996; Tedeschi,
Park, and Calhoun 1998; Updegraff and Taylor 2000).

Research indicates several ways in which to find meaning through our loss.
We need to change our life's scheme or cognitive representation of our life to be
consistent with the loss experience. This may mean reordering our priorities

(e.g., spending more time with family), reconsidering our lives and what is most important to them (e.g., changing jobs or careers), letting go of some goals and identifying new ones that we can reach despite the loss (e.g., creating meaningful traditions and memories with remaining family members), focusing on areas over which we still have control (e.g., our employment or volunteer work), or adapting our self-image in a positive way that incorporates the loss (I am good at coping, resilient, strong; after this, I can handle anything; nothing else can ever hurt me as much again) (Thompson 1998; Thompson and Janigian 1988). Another option is to modify our perception of the loss by reinterpreting the event more positively. For example, we can choose to change our perspective to include benefits from the loss. These benefits may be growth of character, a gain in perspective (e.g., greater empathy or caring for others), or stronger or new relationships (e.g., the "blessings of friends") (Davis 2001). Or we may benefit from making social comparisons with others who are worse off or have even worse losses. Regardless of how we define meaning, searching for positive meanings—to lessen the loss—is part of moving out of the depths of grief and deciding that life is still worth living (Rosenblatt 2000a).

Creating value and appreciation in our lives is another way of making meaning and finding purpose through the loss. In doing so, we can move from "the world is meaningless" to my life is "full of meaning." Our newfound awareness that terror can strike us at any time promotes a new realization of value and appreciation of even the most mundane events. We recognize that ultimately we do not have control over life's outcomes but that we do have control over our own choices and what matters in our lives. Our choices become the basis for our commitment to benefit others, including future generations, and it is here that meaning and fulfillment lie (Erickson 1963; Janoff-Bulman and Berg 1998; Thompson 1998). Sometimes, however, reasons that cannot be understood or questions that cannot be answered have to be integrated as just that: something that cannot be comprehended but must be accepted and tolerated.

Both storytelling—"narratives" (Rosenblatt 2000a) or the "construction of accounts" (Harvey et al. 2001)—and writing are ways to make meaning of a loss. Both provide a constructive way to release emotions that build up after a loss. Using a story format to explain to others what happened requires both accounting for events to oneself and, more important, sharing the story with others, ideally a close friend. Nonlinear processes of story development can simultaneously encompass identity change, healing, and pain, moving in one direction and then the next. Over time, storytelling can lead to discovering new meaning, experiencing hope, and giving back to others. The centrality of storytelling illustrates that grieving is something people do, not something done to them

(Neimeyer, Keesee, and Fortner 2000). Grief is a dynamic process of constructing new meanings that may last as long as the bereaved does (Harvey et al. 2001).

CULTURAL CAPACITIES

Culture, defined broadly as a set of shared beliefs, values, behavioral norms, and practices that characterize a particular group of people with a common identity, also affects their grief experiences. Ethnic identity highlights the subjective sense of belonging to a group or culture with shared values and beliefs, combined with the significance of that membership (Phinney et al. 2001; Tajfel and Turner 1986). As a two-dimensional process, acculturation illustrates the importance of maintaining one's cultural heritage as well as adapting to the host society and/or dominant culture (Berry 1999; Phinney et al. 2001). The extent to which different ethnic minority groups in American society have been able to retain their cultural values and beliefs regarding death varies with their degree of acculturation and their resources to continue the traditions.

In any culture, both implicit and explicit messages convey whether death is to be considered an uninvited stranger or a welcome guest (Becvar 2001). Whether or not people are conscious of these messages, they affect their response to loss. In Western cultures, for example, pain tends to be seen as something that can and should be avoided, rather than an inescapable part of being human. How messages about grief and loss vary by cultures is described in the following examples.

In Chinese culture, with its influence of Confucianism, Daoism, and Buddhism, death is considered the most significant life transition. Over the past five thousand years, many rituals have evolved to help families deal with death. The funeral is a community affair, a good "send-off" for the deceased to ensure that his or her immortal soul will not live in poverty or hunger. A funeral dinner is held after the procession, where guests come to comfort family members and say good words about the deceased, but not to engage in jokes or happy music. Red envelopes with money and candy are given to guests to rid them of the bad luck associated with going to a funeral.

The Mexican Día de los Muertos, or Day of the Dead, is a time when families and communities exchange memories and commune with the souls of their loved ones, even with the specter of death nearby. The holiday reminds its participants that darkness and light live side by side, that life and death are related and one forms a cycle with the other. Death is viewed as a continuation of life, a transformation without a beginning or end. Similar to a friend of the family, death is even given nicknames, such as "Cry Woman" and "Joker." It is believed that on the Day of the Dead, souls are permitted to visit their living relatives. Because they will be hungry when they arrive, families prepare their loved one's favorite foods to share with them and the rest of the community. Revelers eat candies shaped like skulls, with the names of dead relatives written on them. Special altars decked with candles are constructed as *ofrendas*, or offerings for the dead. But levity still abounds, with altars often adorned with replicas of skeletons engaged in the dead person's hobbies, such as golfing, sunbathing, or car racing. Music, jokes, storytelling, and laughter all are part of the celebration of life. The ancient holiday—as big as or bigger than Christmas for many Mexicans and some Guatemalans—is full of mixed metaphors and quirky juxtapositions. But at its heart are deep spiritual beliefs and an absence of fear. Instead, relatives typically embrace death by celebrating their connection with their deceased loved ones.

African Americans die at a younger age than does the rest of the U.S. population, and they often die suddenly, from a homicide or an accident. Even so, many African Americans do not perceive death as an end but as the beginning of life in another form, a progression or transition to the spiritual world after death. Death is generally accepted as God's will, not as an intrusion or as robbing life of meaning, but as a necessary step to achieve a new life free of pain, suffering, and sorrow. Perhaps these feelings result from African Americans' disadvantages and discrimination throughout history, which have often isolated them in poor, violent communities. Many African Americans accordingly believe that death is not to be feared but should be prepared for throughout life (Opoku 1989).

Since African Americans generally want to provide the "best" for their loved one, great emphasis is placed on the funeral and the expectation that others, including the whole extended family and children, will participate in the rituals and music. Public expressions of grief are encouraged, and the eulogy and music are designed to provoke the release of emotions. Moving spirituals embrace the joy of reuniting with deceased relatives and finally achieving peace. The value placed on open emotional expression, traditional cultural attitudes toward death, the immediate display of family and community support, and strong spirituality may make grieving easier. Nonetheless, although mourners are expected to grieve their loss, they also are expected to "be strong," resourceful, and resilient and to resume their usual functions at home and work. Extended kin, friendship networks, and the church community are African Americans' primary sources of social support, rather than interventions by human service professionals (Hines 1991; Perry 1993). Gender-based differences in African Americans' emotional expressions of grief are not well documented.

Before generalizing about Jewish rituals, it is important to note the number of different schools and interpretations of tradition, including not only Reform,

Conservative, and Orthodox Judaism but also Karaites, Ethiopian Jews, and Samaritans. Many Jews regard suffering as a fundamental dimension of life with a powerful social function. The created world is incomplete, and human beings have the task of finishing the work of creation. Consequently, life can be unpredictable or painful, although on the whole, it is full of potential rather than evil. One suffers because the world is not a perfect place, but even so, the "worst life is better than the best death" (Armstrong, personal correspondence, September 27, 2004; Rubin 1996). Life's pain is not to be borne stoically; instead, one may rail against the unfairness of the world and even God, and the ability to express one's feelings is highly valued. The Holocaust has had multigenerational repercussions for Jewish people, both in regard to survival as a central concern and how loss and death are experienced across generations.

Two values guide grieving for most Jewish Americans: (1) the *kavod hamet*, or the requirement to honor the dead (e.g., a dead body must never be left alone until placed in a grave, and a simple service and burial should take place as soon as possible to be respectful of the corpse; cremation is proscribed), and (2) the *nichum aveline*, or the obligation to comfort mourners (Jonker 1997). Relatives and friends do not customarily visit the mourners during the period between death and burial (*aninut*), but the mitzvah of *halvayat hamet* (participating in the funeral and burial) is traditionally regarded as one of the ten deeds that ensures a person's place in the "world to come" (*olam haba*).

Family members typically participate by filling the grave, a cathartic and symbolic way of laying the dead to rest. After the funeral and burial, all members of the immediate family sit *shivah:* a one-week mourning period marking the deviation from regular living patterns to demonstrate one's grief and to heighten one's awareness of how death disrupts life. Family members are not supposed to leave home or go to work and are to be visited and comforted, with all food and arrangements handled by others. Comforting the mourners (the mitzvah of *nichum*) is considered obligatory. After *shivah*, normal life is gradually resumed and is designed to allow appropriate grieving. For the thirty days immediately after *shivah*, mourners may go back to work but continue to observe other restrictions as a sign of bereavement (known as *sheloshim*, or "thirty" in Hebrew). For example, they will not attend any weddings, dances, parties, or other public amusements during this period. When mourning one's parents, some Jews extend the practice of *sheloshim* for an entire year (Armstrong, personal correspondence, September 27, 2004). Regardless of the type of relationship mourned, the unveiling of the headstone one year after the death marks the completion of formal mourning. Each year, the anniversary of the death is formally remembered by the survivors' lighting a memorial candle, giving to charity, and publicly reciting a memorial prayer in the synagogue (Rosen 1996).

SOCIAL AND ENVIRONMENTAL CAPACITIES

Social resources illustrate the importance of the social and environmental context of the loss and capacities. Individuals faced with loss need social and economic supports to give them time and opportunity to grieve fully. The positive effects of social support on physical and mental health have been extensively documented (Stroebe and Schut 2001a). Similarly, a perception of positive social support is usually identified with a positive adaptation to loss (Rando 1993; Ren et al. 1999). Social support may consist of family, friends, neighbors, acquaintances, and others in the larger community. The link between social support and the integration of loss is complex, as it varies with gender, the support networks' reaction to the loss, the relationship between the provider and the recipient of support, the type of and duration of the loss, and the perception of the victim's responsibility for the loss (Murray 2001).

Existing social networks are sometimes unable or unwilling to provide the support that the grieving person needs, particularly in instances of a child's disability or death. This paradox, which also is associated with death of an adult child or partner, is discussed more fully in chapters 8 and 10. In some interactions, previously helpful networks can become unhelpful. In the face of grief, it becomes apparent which network members are not good listeners, silence any talk about grief, say offensive things, offer unsupportive religious judgments or formulas, or are uncomfortable around the bereaved person (Brabant, Forsyth, and McFarlain 1995; Farnsworth and Allen 1996; Lauterbach 1994; Rosenblatt 2000a). Pretending that the death has not occurred, telling a person how long the grief will last and what he or she must do to "move on and let go," or offering platitudes are typically experienced as aversive and may create rifts in longtime social networks. Just as the bereaved are changed by their grief and must relearn their world after the loss, past relationships also are sorted out, with some being abandoned (Attig 1996, 2001b).

Even when a social support system is functioning well, grieving still is a lonely process. Nicholas Wolterstorff, a Christian philosopher whose son died in a mountain-climbing accident in the Swiss Alps, wrote:

> I have been daily grateful for the friend who remarked that grief isolates. He did not mean only that I, grieving, am isolated from you, happy. He meant also that shared grief isolates the sharers from each other. Though united in that we are

grieving, we grieve differently. . . . I may find it strange that you should be tearful today but dry-eyed yesterday when my tears were yesterday. But my sorrow is not your sorrow. There's something more. I must struggle so hard to retain life that I cannot reach out to you. Nor you to me. The one not grieving must touch us both. It's when people are happy that they say, "Let's get together." (1987:56)

Grief at its most intense generally isolates the bereaved from what they previously enjoyed, whether an activity or a friendship.

Groups of individuals facing similar types of loss are often the most helpful form of support, especially when prior social networks are not helpful. These include groups of divorced or separate parents, the unemployed seeking work, parents who have lost a child (Compassionate Friends), or those faced with loss created through disability and illness (HIV/AIDS, Alzheimer's or other types of dementia, Parkinson's, stroke or cancer survivor groups, groups of parents of children with developmental disabilities or chronic mental illness). Support groups can give their members a vocabulary for talking about their loss, a sense of how alike they are to others facing similar losses, a way to find solutions to practical problems, and contact with people, often strangers, who are more comfortable with their grief than are friends who have suffered similar losses. Support groups can also help with meaning making, such as what to do with pictures of the person lost or how to answer one of the most difficult questions among bereaved parents—how many children they have (Klass 1986/1987, 1988, 1999b). In such instances, support or self-help groups for the bereaved often assume prominence as past relationships fade away.

FAMILY SYSTEMS AND CAPACITIES

Families' differing patterns of grieving and communication affect each member's reaction to the loss (Murray 2001). Family systems and symbolic interactionist theories thus are useful models for conceptualizing the effects of a major loss within the family system as a whole. Events surrounding a death or loss can be normative transitions in the family life cycle that can lead to growth and development or create immediate distress or long-term problems in the family's functioning. Loss disrupts a family's interpersonal strategies for self-definition and emotional control (e.g., the ongoing actions and related meanings from which family members derive a sense of self) and may trigger additional disruptive life events (Rubenstein 1995). Losses can also reverberate across several generations, as noted with Holocaust survivors. To illustrate, all generations are likely to be affected in a family that never openly acknowledges a grandmother's divorce, a great-grandfather's disappearance in World War I, a father's abruptly leaving the home, or an infant's death.

A family's roles and rules are typically disrupted by major loss. Roles refer to the expectations attached to a given position in the family, such as peacemaker, scapegoat, and family star. In our family, my son Chris was the "glue" that held our family together. After his death, no one could fill his role or even attempted to do so. When certain roles are lost, the family often casts about for new actors to partially fill them. Rules refer to the family's unspoken understanding that governs their interactions, including how the family is to grieve. When a family suffers a major loss, the current rules may be inadequate and new rules needed. Families with a wide range of rules are generally more flexible and better able to adapt to the loss. With major losses, families may resort to a closed communication system to protect themselves against the anxiety generated by open discussion (e.g., the rule that no one mentions the deceased's name). Simply helping family members express their feelings, however, does not necessarily ease their emotional integration with one another and the successful integration of their loss, especially since they may be out of phase with the others' grief and judge how others "should" grieve. Developing more effective systems of communication needs to be coupled with helping families reestablish or create functional and emotional roles that restore, or perhaps recreate, the family's equilibrium and strengthen the family unit's ability to meet other life challenges.

In addition to achieving open, effective communication, families face other adaptive tasks: (1) acknowledge the reality and experience of the loss and (2) reorganize the family system to enable investment in other relationships and life pursuits (Shapiro 2001). Both tasks require the family to make meaning of the loss, just as individuals must reconstruct meaning, since reality is socially constructed and people construct meaning through their everyday conversations (Nadeau 2001a). Family members need opportunities to tell and retell their stories of the death and the dead person in order to construct meaning.

Social systems perspectives of grief and loss emphasize the mutually regulating transactions that typically take place among "nested structures." These contain both the stress and the support of family, peer, institutional, community, and cultural relationships and contexts that have been disrupted by grief.

CULTURAL AND COMMUNITY CAPACITIES

The strength and importance of supports vary within and among cultures. For example, the community of the Lakota tribe eats together during the wake and after the funeral, views the body together, and attends the service and burial. At the meal after the burial, the dead person's possessions are given away to those who are present. This practice derives from the Lakotas' belief that nothing of value is obtained apart from the community. Material possessions, of little importance throughout life, are understood to be communally shared. What the community has given to the person in life is returned through the person's life and involvement in the community. Returning the material possessions at death thus completes the life cycle (Brokenleg and Middleton 1993).

When an upper-class Hindu husband in India dies, a formal meeting with his widow is announced in the national newspaper, and those in the community who have any contacts with the deceased or his or her family come to express their condolences. In the twelve days following the death, women friends arrive at 4 p.m. to sit with the widow, talking about her husband, crying, and lending support. But they do not give advice or speak of "shoulds"; rather, their role is to listen, talk, and cry together (Laungani 1997). Unfortunately, especially in Western cultures, people who are uncomfortable and unwilling to be with those who are grieving may drift away from the person faced with loss (Attig 1990).

The resilience model formulated by Fredriksen-Goldsen (2006) sees capacities, whether personal, family, community, or cultural, as interacting with and modifying the relationship between the adversity of loss and well-being. High capacities buffer the impact of loss (serve as moderators) as well as have direct effects on well-being (higher well-being). For example, someone experiencing a loss who has a strong ethnic identity and is well integrated into the community, with extensive positive social networks, generally displays greater psychological and physical well-being. Such supports do not, however, guarantee well-being because of the interaction of personal capacities and background characteristics with environmental capacities. For example, strong networks may not be able to compensate for a lifetime of poverty or discrimination faced by many of our country's ethnic minority groups.

Well-being

The resilience model defines well-being as the absence or lower levels of psychological (e.g., depression, anxiety) and physical (e.g., somatic illness) distress. Well-being in regard to grief has several components: physical health, social functioning, mental health, ongoing connections to the deceased, and integration of the loss to foster personal growth, find purpose in a reconstructed life, and be able to create a new sense of self without the lost person or object. Well-being is not, however, simply the other side of depression or physical illness. A bereaved individual may take pride in new accomplishments and relationships and gain strength from ongoing bonds with the deceased but still may suffer from depression or physical illness (Stroebe et al. 2001a). Well-being is a highly subjective concept, best defined by the bereaved person comparing his or her life and relationships before and after the loss. Accordingly, practitioners need to be careful not to impose their own definitions of well-being on the bereaved.

The extent to which grief and associated depressive symptoms increase the risk of or vulnerability to physical health problems is unclear, partly because of the methodological differences in past research (Hall and Irwin 2001). Some studies find that physiological changes in a person's response to grief lead to an accumulation of wear and tear on the body (Hall and Irwin 2001; Seeman et al. 1997), a decline in cognitive and physical functioning (Seeman et al. 1997), and a greater risk of cardiovascular, infectious, and inflammatory disorders (Musselman, Evans, and Nemeroff 1998). There also is evidence that suppressed grief may affect the neuroendocrine and immune systems, making grieving persons more vulnerable to negative physical and stress-related health consequences (Stroebe et al. 2001a). Mediators that appear to increase physiological risks in the bereaved are younger age, symptoms of stress, and depression. In contrast, physiological resilience following loss is associated with the use of effective strategies to connect with others and the deceased, understanding social support networks, and a healthy lifestyle that includes sleep, exercise, and spirituality (Hall and Irwin 2001).

Summary

The resilience process is referred to throughout this book, especially in discussions of background characteristics and personal, family, social, and cultural capacities that affect the outcomes of loss and grief at each developmental life phase. The bereaved's ability to draw on helpful networks, reject those that no longer are useful, and create new meaningful supports appears to be essential to resilience. We encourage the reader to consider ways to integrate the concept of capacities in their assessments and interventions with bereaved individuals. Regardless of the intensity of the pain or the absence of social supports, human beings are inherently resilient. In fact, Ryff and colleagues (2003) suggested that resilience may be a product of stress and is not additional to the stress. Social work professionals need to assess those capacities conducive to resilience and then build strength-based interventions on them.

Since our grieving varies with family, community, and culture, we should not judge who is grieving "well" or "not well." Grieving well is what "works for the bereaved" and creates positive outcomes: physical and mental well-being, new sources of meaning and satisfaction in life, and new opportunities for the survivors while still maintaining a connection with the deceased.

Resilience is one model for viewing the process of making meaning, achieving mastery, and organizing information in terms of interventions. We encourage you to construct your own working model or guidelines that fit with your experience, knowledge of human behavior across the life span, evidence-based practice, and outcomes. In your assessment and interventions, we hope you will be sensitive to the interaction of domains of background characteristics, family, community and cultural supports, and how you and the client define well-being. As you adapt from and empirically test the resilience model, always place your first priority on listening—really listening—to what the bereaved tell you.

4

Grief and Loss in Childhood

OUR DISCUSSION of grief and loss during childhood addresses children's adaptive processes following three types of losses in the family: death of a parent or sibling, parents' divorce or separation, and adoption or foster care. As difficult and challenging as the grief may be, most children seem to have the capacity over time to deal constructively with a parent's death, divorce, or separation. In fact, in the long run, children may emerge more mature, empathetic, and creative and value relationships more than do many of their peers who have not experienced a major loss (Davies 1999; Oltjenbruns 2001). Yet sadness may lie just below their exterior resilient appearance. Children commonly try to mask their pain through seemingly "normal" behavior, which requires that their family and professionals encourage them to express their feelings.

A parent's death or their divorce or separation is not a single event, stress, or trauma. Instead, it is a loss that reverberates throughout the family and, in some instances, the community and culture. By changing much of what existed before, it shakes a child's basic trust and sense of psychological predictability. Secondary stresses from death or separation—a lower income, adjusting to a babysitter or a parent's working long hours to support the family—also reverberate throughout the family system and across several generations.

Developmental Considerations

Children in early childhood (approximately two through four), middle childhood (five through eight), and late childhood (nine through eleven) grieve differently. The chronological age markers for these developmental stages of childhood vary across studies, and the age groupings in this chapter are only approximate. Cognitive and language capacity, communication styles, developmental tasks, and emotional ability are more important during childhood and adolescence than at any other arbitrary age distinction. In fact, although very young children show grieflike behavior when attachments are broken, their cognitive development is what is most important to their understanding of loss.

Young Childhood: Ages Two Through Four (Preschool Years)

The preschool years are often referred to as the preconceptual stage. Very young children do not have the cognitive capacity to understand the universality and permanence of major losses like death or divorce. Nor do they have the language capability to describe their emotions or to ask for what they need, although by age four, they are able to label emotions, such as "I feel sad because Sally took my toy." When grieving, however, they may assume that others will know what their feelings are and be unable to draw comfort from spoken statements. Conversely, by age three or four, most children are empathetic; that is, they recognize other children's emotional reactions to different situations. By age four or five, most children are able to see a situation from another person's point of view. This allows them to find creative ways to comfort others who are upset; for example, a preschool boy might tell his mother not to cry over his sibling's death because she still has him, and he will take care of her.

Middle Childhood: Ages Five Through Seven or Eight

Children in middle childhood are moving from preoperational (characterized by magical and correlational thinking) to concrete operational thinking (the ability to classify and understand relations) and may still engage in magical, irrational, and nonreversible thought. By this age, however, they tend to be aware of the concepts of irreversibility, nonfunctionality, and universality (Backer, Hannon, and Russell 1994). Overall, they have strong emotions—like intense sadness, anger, and guilt—and personalize external events. Unlike their younger or older siblings, children of this age are less able to distract themselves and to keep their emotions at bay. In contrast to their younger siblings, they directly state and act on their feelings. For example, children at this age may assert that they think they killed their parent through their past negative thoughts or anger or may wish openly that they could die to be with their deceased parent.

Late Childhood: Ages Eight or Nine Through Eleven

Compared with the turbulence of middle childhood, late childhood is a relatively tranquil age. Children's anger typically does not reach the intensity of adolescence nor does their sadness have the overwhelming helplessness characteristic of younger children. As a result, older children generally are able to move ahead after the first few months following a major loss, such as a parent's death or divorce. These gains are largely due to more sophisticated concrete logical-operational thinking and problem-focused coping skills. Such cognitive changes are more conducive to emotional equilibrium and the effective use of defenses against disquieting emotions. Children in late childhood also are more capable of describing their feelings, verbalizing their needs, seeking social support, and beginning to make meaning of their loss, which they may perceive as unjust (Aldwin 1994). They tend to be active in school, sports, and with friends—moving toward new experiences, developing their competence, and rarely expressing grief directly with their peers.

Resilience

Along with a natural maturational sequence of cognition, children's under-standing of the concept of death or divorce/separation, manifestations of grief, and mental and physical well-being vary in accordance with their background characteristics and capacities, which were identified as part of the resilience model in chapter 3, as follows.

Background characteristics refer to socioeconomic and ethnic/minority status and urban/rural location in society. For example, some children living in high-crime neighborhoods are surrounded daily by death: homicide, spousal/partner abuse, gang or school violence, or accidents. Children growing up on farms also see life and death each day, but the nature of death varies widely from what their urban counterparts see. Other children, regardless of their socioeconomic status, may have very limited experience with death, perhaps only of a geographically distant relative or a frail great-grandparent. The constancy of death and vio-lence in the media, however, mean that all children are exposed to violent and sudden deaths more often now than in the past.

Personal capacities refer to the child's age and developmental capacity, sense of identity and self-esteem, problem-solving skills, gender of the child and the deceased/separated parent, nature of the loss, attachment to the parent who has died or is physically/mentally absent, and ability to reattach. For example, a high level of self-esteem may give young children a sense of mastery despite adversity (Kirby and Fraser 1997).

Family capacities encompass parent's love, discipline, and assurance; family rou-tines, structure, and communication patterns; and adult support, nurturance, and continuity (Worden 2002). Having a positive relationship with one parent or another caring adult, who provides a sense of security and problem-solving skills, can help mediate losses (Kirby and Fraser 1997).

Social capacities include peers; other supportive adults such as teachers, mentors, and counselors; and support groups for children grieving similar types of losses. Social support moderates many potential negative outcomes for children grieving the death of a loved one, the divorce of a parent, or being a victim of violence (Garvin, Kalter, and Hansell 1993; Nettles, Mucherah, and Jones 2000).

Cultural capacities include the child's participation in rituals, funeral arrangements, and other customs; and the family's cultural beliefs regarding the deceased's presence and afterlife. In the United States, well-meaning individuals may believe that children should be shielded from the funeral and other rituals (e.g., stay at home with a sitter rather than attend a wake), compared with those in other cultures in which children participate fully in death rituals.

Community capacities to support children are typically schools, religious institutions, after-school programs, grief counseling, and support groups.

Attachment to parents and other caring individuals is a critical component of children's individual or personal capacity. The resilience model incorporates attachment theory to examine the psychological or individual impact of loss on a person's well-being. The particular attachment bond to both parents affects the mourning process experienced after a parent's death, separation, or divorce. Note that attachment is not necessarily the same as closeness, liking, or relationship satisfaction, since it can continue even in abusive or neglectful situations (Shaver and Tancredy 2001). For example, a child may still love an abusive or absent parent.

Bowlby (1969, 1973, 1980) was the first to observe that children's responses to physical separation from their mother resemble the protest, despair, and apathy of bereaved adults. According to Bowlby, grief in children is conceptualized as a form of separation anxiety from their mother. Whether separated from their mother by death or placement in adoption or a foster home, children first react with tears and anger but still remain hopeful that their mother will return. These feelings then turn to despair, alternating with hope. Finally, the memory of the mother's face begins to fade. When a loved one dies, people of all ages have feelings similar to those of children separated from their mother. Bereaved persons are trying to locate who or what has been lost, shifting among periods of anger, yearning, and despair. The intensity of the grief response appears to increase with the strength of the attachment bond or love.

Grieving, irrespective of the nature of the loss, is not ended by replacement of the lost parent (e.g., through remarriage, godparents, or close family friends). The sadness may continue even when what might seem to be positive substitutive relationships are available and supportive. Children often undergo secondary stressors during other changes that imply separation, such as beginning school, going to summer camp, or being left at home when the surviving parent travels. During these transitions, some children may be sad, clinging, and anxious, reactions similar to those associated with the earlier death, divorce, or separation of a parent.

Attachment theory is thus a useful as a way of thinking about what has been "broken" or "lost" when a close relationship ends for a child. It does not imply, however, the psychological separation or the concept of decathexis that characterized early psychoanalytic theories of grief. Instead, most children retain a largely adaptive psychological relationship to the deceased or separated parent (Bowlby 1969, 1973, 1980).

Children younger than five and those in early adolescence (eleven to twelve) generally have the fewest personal capacities to bring to the grief process and therefore are most vulnerable to emotional or behavioral problems (Bowlby 1980; Christ 2000; Fristad et al. 1993). Grieving is not static, however, and personal, social, cultural, and community capacities affect the child's grief process throughout their lives. Children experience and reexperience grief and mature in various domains as they complete new developmental stages, including young adulthood (Edelman 1994; Silverman 1989; Worden 1996). A childhood loss, especially a parent's death, may be regrieved numerous times during the lifetime and can affect the child's decisions and behaviors as an adult. For example, girls whose mother died when they were young often resist "growing up" from fear of what might happen to them when they reach their mother's age at her death. As the bereaved child grows older, the environmental and cultural context for understanding the earlier loss and coming to terms with its impact changes as well (Oltjenbruns 2001).

Childhood Traumatic Grief

Given the growing numbers of children experiencing the death of a loved one in traumatic circumstances such as interpersonal violence, natural disasters, war, and, most recently, the attacks on the World Trade Center and Pentagon, increasing attention has been paid to *traumatic grief* and *posttraumatic stress disorder* (*PTSD*) in children. Traumatic grief, defined as grief resulting from the loss of a loved one in traumatic circumstances, is characterized by trauma-related symptoms interfering with the child's ability to negotiate the bereavement process. However, as is the case with traumatic grief among adults, death from natural anticipated causes also can result in traumatic grief if the child's subjective experience of the death is traumatic, and traumatic symptoms then interfere with his or her grieving of a loved one (Cohen et al. 2002; Elder and Knowles 2002;

Layne et al. 2001b). Such interference occurs in the following ways: intrusive and distressing trauma-related thoughts, memories, and images may be triggered by (1) trauma reminders (e.g., situations, places, people, smells, sights, or sounds reminding the child of the traumatic nature of the death); (2) loss reminders (e.g., thoughts, memories, objects, places, or people reminding the child of the deceased person); or (3) change reminders (situations, people, places, or things reminding the child of changes in his or her living circumstances caused by the traumatic death) (Pynoos 1992). These trauma-related thoughts cause physiological reactions (shaking, pounding heart, headache, dizziness) and extreme psychological distress (fear, horror, helplessness). Children then develop strategies of avoidance and emotional numbing and estrangement. As a result, they may be unable or unwilling to reminisce, feel the pain of the lost relationship, or transform their relationship with the deceased into one of memory, because such tasks require tolerating loss and the reminders of change without the excessive use of avoidance or numbing. Their ability to grieve is disrupted by traumatic intrusion—the horror and fear associated with the death—and the resultant use of avoidance strategies.

These physiological and psychological traits also are characteristic of PTSD. With PTSD, these characteristics may be normative in the weeks immediately following a traumatic death but after a month or more become a cause for concern. Traumatic grief differs from posttraumatic stress in that children may have symptoms of PTSD for a period of time that do not interfere with the process of grieving (box 4.1). Childhood PTSD, similar to the adult form, results from traumatic exposure in which the child experiences, witnesses, or learns about an event that involves actual or threatened death, serious injury, or threat to physical integrity to self and others and in which the child's response is one of intense helplessness, fear, or horror (American Psychiatric Association 2000). Even a child who has not experienced a death or other major loss may develop PTSD.

Variables that may affect whether PTSD symptoms interfere with grieving and thus lead to traumatic grief are the child's past history of trauma or loss, the circumstances surrounding the trauma, and the reactions of significant adults, especially of parents. For example, parents' emotional distress and lack of support are associated with more severe and persistent PTSD symptoms in some cohorts of traumatized children. When such symptoms persist for more than a month and disrupt the child's functioning, they may interfere with grieving (e.g., become traumatic grief). More research is needed on how parents' responses influence the effects of PTSD (Cohen and Mannario 2000; Cohen et al. 2002).

Box 4.1 Symptoms of PTSD in Children

- Recurrent distressing recollections about the event.
- Recurrent distressing dreams of the event.
- A sense of the event's recurring.
- Intense physiological reactivity or psychological distress in response to reminders of the event.
- At least three avoidance or numbing symptoms, such as efforts to avoid thoughts, feelings, or conversations about the event; inability to recall some aspects of the event; decreased interest in normal activities; feeling detached from others; restricted range of affect; and a sense of a foreshortened future.
- At least two hyperarousal symptoms (e.g., sleep disturbance, angry outburst, decreased concentration, or hypervigilance).
- Symptoms persisting for at least a month and causing functional impairment.

Source: Reprinted with permission from the *Diagnostic and Statistical Manual of Mental Disorders*, Copyright 2000, American Psychiatric Association.

Death of a Parent

The death of a parent is probably the most difficult loss for a child. A child's experience of loss from a parent's death is not the same as the loss felt by an adult. In fact, the concepts and language of adult loss are inadequate to capture the feelings of confusion and of being at "a loss for words" of a child who is grieving a parent's death. Even if children have the words to talk about their loss, their flood of feelings tends to be powerful enough to overwhelm any existing conceptual abilities (Harris 1995).

The early research on children and grief was based primarily on retrospective studies of adults, many of whom were in treatment. It therefore is difficult to differentiate what actually occurred from what the adults remembered, and the samples were composed of adults who had a diagnosed emotional or mental disorder. A parent's death thus was assumed to cause psychopathology in later life. Three models were derived from this early research: blunt trauma, shock–aftershock wave, and cascade of events.

The *blunt trauma model* views a parent's death as a single event, a discrete blow "bounded in time, powerful in impact, and more disruptive for children than for adolescents" (Christ 2000:13; Clark, Pynoos, and Gobel 1994). The nature of the event and developmental stage at which it occurred are the critical variables. This relatively simplistic linear approach looked for a specific event in childhood (e.g., a parent's death) to explain adult psychopathology and widely influenced clinical practice related to "resolving" childhood grief (Bowlby 1980; Brown, Harris, and Bifulco 1986; Christ 2000; Finkelstein 1988; Furman 1974; Rutter 1966; Tweed et al. 1989).

The *shock–aftershock wave model* was developed from studies of the relationship between childhood death and adult depression (Bifulco, Brown, and Harris 1987; Brown, Harris, and Bifulco 1986; Christ 2000; Harris, Brown, and Bifulco 1986). The reaction of the surviving parent to the grieving child changes the impact of the death on the child's life and leads to the concept of shock–aftershock. An illustration of shock–aftershock is a mother who never openly grieves nor talks about her husband's death but who, throughout her life, unpredictably lashes out in frustration and anger at her daughter, who physically and emotionally resembles her father.

The *cascade of events model* explains adult psychopathology as a similar process. The "carry forward" of the stress and adversity (i.e., the "cascade" of events) associated with death, which is assumed to be traumatic, heightens the child's vulnerability throughout life, which has cumulative negative effects on his or her self-confidence, trust, and self-esteem. The cascade effects are mediated by the stage of development, the meaning of a parent's death to the child, and subsequent life stressors. This cascade effect applies primarily to death resulting from violence, suicide, or homicide.

These earlier models tended to overlook children's potential resilience after a parent's death (Cerel et al. 1999; Christ 2000; Rutter 1990, 1994). Contrary to these early retrospective studies, more recent research sees bereaved children as comparable to their peers in levels of anxiety and depression approximately one year after a parent's death (Saldinger et al. 1999; Sanchez et al. 1994; Siegel, Raveis, and Karus 1996; Silverman and Worden 1992a; Worden 1996). The death of a parent does not necessarily lead to depression or long-term psychological dysfunction in adolescence or young adulthood, although children often have more problems (social withdrawal, anxiety, social problems, lower self-esteem, and self-efficacy) two years following the death than at one year. This may be because more supports are available in the first year following a death or because children do not absorb fully the reality of the death in the first year. Complicated reactions of disabling grief, which interfere with children's social, physical, and emotional development, are relatively rare (Harris, Brown, and Bifulco 1986; Oltjenbruns 2001; Worden and Silverman 1996).

A child's experience with the death of a parent does, however, differ from that of adults for the following reasons: the feelings of total discontinuity with what previously existed (e.g., a child's world is shattered by a parent's death); terrifying insecurity, since if a loved parent can die, then nothing is safe, predictable or secure; and profound emptiness. Images of the parent as strong or protective may be replaced by even more idealized images of the parent as perfect and the only one who can truly love the child. Along with sadness and anger, children may have "forbidden feelings" of shame and guilt, especially if the death was by suicide or violence; and relief if the parent had been ill for a long time or abusive. A parent's death separates the world into "before and after." In fact, even thirty, forty, or fifty years after the early death of a parent, adults still refer to this as the defining event of their lives. The language that some adults use to describe their experience of losing a parent in childhood is that of catastrophe, devastation, and emptiness, and throughout their lives, they may see the world only in terms of loss, danger, and unpredictability (Harris 1995).

Developmental Considerations and Parental Death

A certain level of cognitive development is needed to understand death because we cannot integrate something we do not understand (Worden 2002). These necessary cognitive concepts include time (e.g., forever), transformation, irreversibility, causality, and concrete operation. Concrete operation appears to develop in children only after the age of seven or eight (Piaget and Inhelder 1969).

INFANTS, TODDLERS, AND PRESCHOOLERS: BIRTH THROUGH AGE FIVE

Infants and toddlers (babies to two-year-olds) experience a sense of "gone-ness" or absence when someone dies. They react to the loss of an attachment figure by sleep disturbance, changes in eating patterns, fussiness, bowel and bladder disturbances, or difficulty being comforted (Emswiler and Emswiler 2000). Preschoolers (three to five years) do not have the cognitive capacity to understand the universality and permanence of death as the cessation of all bodily functions until they enter a more concrete stage of development. They cannot comprehend the word *forever* and often believe that death is reversible. They are likely to talk about death in terms of their parent's waking up and returning, even if they have seen the dead parent in a casket. They may engage in magical thinking and believe that they are powerful enough to influence or reverse the death (Cohen et al. 2002; Emswiler and Emswiler 2000). Perhaps because they do not comprehend the finality of death, they more easily remember and talk about the dead or separated parent than older children do. Lacking the language capacity to describe their emotions, they often express their feelings through nonverbal behavior, drawing a picture of a dead parent or anxiously clinging to the surviving parent when he or she tries to leave, even for a short time. Or they may regress to earlier behavior that includes repression, helplessness, denial, guilt, and magical or wishful thinking that the deceased parent will return (Christ 2000; Oltjenbruns 2001). Because they have not yet learned how to reverse their reasoning process, they may be difficult to convince that they were not responsible for their parent's death. Anxiety, sleeplessness, and mild physical symptoms such as stomachaches, headaches, and exaggerated reactions to normal cuts and bruises are common. Seeing the remaining parent sad and crying upsets most young children. They may startle the distraught parent by asking when he or she will find a "new mom or dad." In fact, they readily shift back and forth between grief, on one hand, and engagement in normal activities, on the other, such as playing outside or visiting a friend's house. The surviving parent may misunderstand such "normal" behavior and question whether the child is grieving appropriately (Christ 2000).

MIDDLE CHILDHOOD: AGES SIX TO NINE

Middle childhood is a difficult time for children grieving a parent's death. Although they may still engage in magical, irrational, and nonreversible thought processes, they usually are aware of the concepts of irreversibility, nonfunctionality, and universality (Backer, Hannon, and Russell 1994). They may be unable to understand and accept, however, logical explanations or reverse erroneous conclusions, such as being the cause of a parent's death or separation. If the death has followed a long illness, they may have felt sad, angry, and rejected during that time. They often readily express their anger about the ill parent's altered ability to function, unable to accept that such changes are due to disease and not rejection. They tend to see death as something tangible or physical (e.g., a spirit angel or ghost) and may externalize or personify death as someone chasing and catching its victims. Because of their strong emotionality and personalization of external events, they may express anger at God or a supreme being and the surviving parent. They may display aggression or other behavioral problems because they do not know how to manage their sadness or anger appropriately. Unlike their younger or older siblings, they are less able to distract themselves and control their emotions.

In contrast to their younger siblings, children in middle childhood say what and act how they feel, openly grieving the loss of the family they had known.

They also talk more openly about communicating with a dead parent or describing their imagined heaven. In some instances, they may state that they want to die to be with the dead parent. Fears about something happening to the surviving parent are intensified (Webb 2002).

When I had to travel out of town in the first year after my husband's death, my daughter Mani, age eight, would cling to me and cry. In one instance, she held on to the car door handle so tightly that two other adults were needed to remove her grip and carry her into the house. She also asked me to phone her as soon as I got safely to my destination, which reflected an active coping style on her part.

Separation anxiety may also show up in a child's wanting to sleep with the surviving parent, a pattern that can provide immediate relief but create long-term difficulties (Christ 2000).

Maturational and social capacities that appear to encourage resilience in children in this middle age range are understanding the death; being able to express their emotions openly, including their own sense of vulnerability and fear of separation; being able to talk about the happy aspects and memories and cherish the dead parent's possessions; and being reassured of the predictability, routine, and structure in family life along with other social supports, even though children may chafe at discipline from the now single parent. Continued reassurance that the surviving children were not responsible for the parent's illness and death also is important (Christ 2000).

LATE CHILDHOOD: AGES NINE THROUGH ELEVEN

Children in late childhood are more capable of describing their feelings, verbalizing their needs, seeking social support, and beginning to make meaning of their loss (Aldwin 1994). They want information to correct misunderstandings and are able to integrate information without becoming overwhelmed and confused. They more readily communicate with others about the facts of their parent's death, although typically with adults other than the surviving parent. With the surviving parent or other adults, they may talk about being strong, brave, and protective and going about their life in a way that the dead parent would have wanted. Since they may express their emotions only sporadically, the surviving parent may misunderstand and think that the child is not grieving. Most children cannot tolerate long periods of intense emotional pain and thus shift back and forth between grieving and engaging in normal activities. Relatives may be shocked by a young child's wanting to go outside and play or an older child's hanging out with friends, but this is actually a healthy response. In fact, it is similar to the dual-process model of bereavement discussed in chapter 1, in which adults alternate between loss and restoration (Stroebe and Schut 1999).

In late childhood, the grieving process tends to be a balance between controlling feelings and reminiscing or actively grieving. For these reasons, carrying out rituals, observing anniversaries, looking at photos, and keeping possessions, clothing, and other special items are important to enable children to reframe their experience over time, reconstructing their relationship with the dead parent and continually revising the deceased's image.

To some extent, having a dead parent may carry a stigma of difference and being an "outsider." If peers tease the grieving older child, school may be more stressful than supportive. Academic problems, anger, hypochondrias, identification with the dead parent, and extreme fear that the other parent will die are likely to arise during late childhood. Grief may be acted out through getting angry, being messy, testing rules, being demanding and critical, and fighting more with siblings and peers. In such instances, parents, teachers, and other significant adults need to be supportive and protective and assure the child that he or she is valued and loved. Such extraordinary efforts are central to maintaining or enhancing the child's self-esteem. Similar to those in middle childhood, older children fear other losses and become anxious if the surviving parent shows any sign of illness or weakness. When Mani was eleven, I developed an allergic cough, which immediately brought her running to me, asking whether I was going to die. No words could reassure her, only the cessation of the cough.

Resilience and the Death of a Parent

Background characteristics and individual capacities that affect children's grief following the death of a parent include knowledge (or not) of the impending death, length of the parent's illness, and the gender of the child and the surviving/custodial parent. It is not clear whether a sudden death is more problematic for children than an anticipated death. In some instances, a period of extended illness that disrupts family functioning may be more difficult than the death itself, resulting in greater anxiety and depression (Christ 2000; Christ et al. 1993; Siegel et al. 1992; Siegel, Raveis, and Karus 1996). Sudden and traumatic death through homicide or an accident, however, may complicate grieving. When death is anticipated, the nature and length of the illness, the parents' patterns of communication, the routine and security they have created for the children, and the parents' presence in their daily lives all affect the intensity of the children's grief. Whether boys or girls have a more difficult time after a parent's death also is not clear (Christ 2000). The deceased parent's gender appears to make a difference, with the loss of a mother worse for most children than the loss of a father. This is due partly to the greater daily life changes and loss of the emotional caregiver role when a mother dies. One study found that the loss of one's mother was associated with greater anxiety, more acting-out behavior, lower self-esteem, and a weaker belief in self-efficacy (Worden 2002).

Events following the death may be at least or even more important predictors for later impairment than is the actual absence of the parent. As conceptualized in the resilience model, the centrality of family, community, cultural, and social capacities to grief outcomes is now widely recognized. In fact, the social context may be more important than individual characteristics. The surviving or custodial parent's functioning level and his or her behavior toward the grieving child are pivotal risk factors (Harris, Brown, and Bifulco 1986; Silverman 2000; Worden 1996, 2002). Inadequate parental care and support are powerful predictors of later difficulties, such as depression (Harris, Brown, and Bifulco 1986; Oltjenbruns 2001). Behavioral or emotional problems that cannot be attributed to the death itself are more likely in instances of parental neglect, depression, or ineffective coping or a conflictual, unhappy, distant relationship between the child and the parent (Christ 2000; Gray 1989; Kranzler, Shafer, and Wasserman 1989; Raveis, Siegel, and Karus 1999; Silverman and Worden 1992a; Worden 1996). Children aged six to eleven show the most disturbances following a death, but their regressive and aggressive behaviors may be efforts to gain adult attention rather than actual grief responses (McCown and Davies 1995; McGowan and Pratt 1985; Oltjenbruns 2001).

The surviving parent can protect the children against the effects of family tragedy and provide anchors for them to use to construct a new view of the world that incorporates the reality of the loss and affects the child's sense of vulnerability. Families who are active problem solvers, find something positive in the painful situation, and minimize the changes and disruptions in daily life can reduce the negative longer-term effects of the children's grieving (Silverman 2000; Worden 1996). Those characteristics associated with fewer difficulties following a parent's death include

- The quality of child care.
- The child's relationship with the surviving parent.
- The parent's warm and comforting presence and an active problem-solving style that also supports the child's competencies.
- The family's stability and cohesiveness.
- Open and shared communication of information about what has happened and encouragement to ask questions and express feelings.
- Adequate income, social support, and opportunities to participate in community, cultural, and religious rituals surrounding the death. (Bowlby 1969, 1973,

1980; Christ 2000; Raveis, Siegel, and Karus 1999; Silverman and Worden 1992b; Tremblay and Israel 1998; Walsh 1998; Worden 1996)

The language that is used to discuss the death can foster either understanding and growth or confusion and misunderstanding. For example, when the surviving parent explains death in terms like "Mom is sleeping peacefully," children may become afraid of falling asleep and then dying. Or when children are told that Grandma died because she was old, they may start to worry and ask about their parents' ages, needing reassurance that they are not so old that they will die. Unfortunately, when explaining death, family and friends often use euphemisms that can unintentionally create misunderstandings, fears, and additional anxieties for children.

Parents must attend to their own mourning in order to be able to be respond to their children's grief and to provide interactions that resonate with the children's feelings, encourage support, and give solace, meaning, and value to their experiences. Unfortunately, some parents are so immersed in their own pain and emotionally exhausted that they are unable, at least initially, to provide the loving structure and open communication that their children need. In some instances, the family environment is disrupted even more by changes in financial circumstances, relocation, or the surviving parent's need to work more hours in order to manage financially (Christ 2000; Christ et al. 1993; Compas et al. 1994; Siegel et al. 1992). At such times, the support of another adult such as a teacher, mentor, counselor, religious figure, or family friend, may compensate for the parent's lack of time, energy, and care.

Culture is a major determinant in how children experience and adapt to loss. How children understand death and the extent to which they participate in culturally based mourning practices, such as the funeral or memorial service or visiting the grave, also affect the outcome of their grief. Western cultures tend to protect young children from participating in such rituals, although research indicates that most children benefit from them.

A grief counselor advised us against having Mani view Chris's body, saying that it would be too upsetting and traumatic for her. Months later, when we visited Alaska, she asked whether we were going to go to the white room where Chris's body was. We suddenly realized that she had been imagining Chris lying in a hospital room all this time. I realize now that her not being allowed to view his body left many more questions and negative images than she would have had if she had come with us to say good-bye to his body before he was cremated.

In contrast, most non-Western cultures encourage children to participate in funerals, in which they have an opportunity to see and touch the body as a final farewell and to be prepared for and supported through the event by trusted adults (Webb 2002; Worden 1996; Young and Papadatou 1997).

Grief Tasks

Regardless of their age or relationship with the dead person, most bereaved children need to move through certain tasks or phases (Worden 1996). As noted in chapter 2, these are not linear, and it is not necessary that a child performs each task before moving to a new one. They should

- Understand that someone has died.
- Face the psychological pain of the loss.
- Be able to cope with the periodic resurgence of pain.
- Invest in new relationships.
- Develop a new sense of identity that includes the experience of the loss.
- Reevaluate their relationship with the person who has been lost.
- Maintain an internal relationship with the person who has died.
- Return to age-appropriate developmental tasks.

Similar to adults whose child dies, most children try to remain connected to the dead parent. They may have numerous questions about where the dead parent is located (e.g., heaven), vividly remember certain details of their interactions with the deceased parent, talk to and feel the deceased's presence, and want to keep some of their parent's belongings. Children connected to the deceased parent appear better able to show their emotional pain, talk with others about the death, and accept support from families and friends (Worden 1996, 2002). In regard to family capacities, the surviving parent plays a central role in contributing to the reconstruction of the dead parent by talking about him or her, providing the child with opportunities to participate in memorializing activities, giving mementos of the dead parent to the child, helping the child find the language to express his or her feelings, and respecting and honoring the child's relationship with the dead parent (Nickman, Silverman, and Normand 1998; Silverman and Nickman 1996; Silverman, Nickman, and Worden 1992). As Silverman, Nickman, and Worden observed, "The emphasis should be on negotiating and renegotiating the meaning of the loss over time, rather than letting go" (1992:502). At a time when children may feel that their lives are out of control, finding areas where they can have some control can be helpful.

When I asked my daughter whether she would like to have a memorial service for her father with just her own friends, she said she wanted to talk to her friends and see what they thought. After getting their support, she and our minister planned the entire service: Mani's standing at the front of the chapel and shar-ing pictures and memories of her dad, the children singing his favorite songs, including "Puff the Magic Dragon," a candlelight circle, and a cake at the end! By being able to make these choices, she gained some control over her life, even though in many ways it had been shattered.

Unfortunately, sometimes the surviving parent, absorbed in his or her own grief, may not be able to give the child the kind of support needed for such meaning making.

As children mature and develop new capacities, they are likely to experience a regrief phenomenon, particularly in regard to intimate relationships that may evoke memories and feelings about the dead parent (Harris 1995). That is, they begin to process the experience of death from a different vantage point than was possible earlier. As described in the resilience framework, they make meaning of the loss. In addition, developmental transitions such as high school or college graduation or marriage may precipitate a resurgence of more intense grief, includ-ing feelings of discontinuity, insecurity, and profound emptiness. Such events make evident once again the reality of the parent's absence (Oltjenbruns 2001).

Death of a Sibling in Childhood

Some studies have found that for children, a sibling's death is more traumatic than a parent's death (McGowan and Pratt 1985; Oltjenbruns 2001). The rea-son may be the length of the sibling relationship, especially if the siblings felt allied against their parents. In one study, children grieving a sibling's death showed significantly more behavioral problems than did children in a standard-ized norm group. These problems included withdrawal, clinging to adults, nightmares, running away, excessive talking, arguing, and hyperactivity. A sib-ling's death may heighten children's sense of vulnerability and inferiority. In addition, for children aged six through eleven who are making the transition to concrete thought, the event and cause of a sibling's death may create confusion, anxiety, and fear about their own safety (McGowan and Pratt 1985; Worden 2002). The parents' emotional availability to and communication with the sur-viving children are critical to their sense of mastery and resilience. Fathers may become emotionally distant, burying themselves in their paid work, and the parents' marital relationship may suffer (Fanos 1996).

Children who are expected to replace or step into the role of the idealized deceased child may have trouble forming their own identity. They typically resent the implicit demand and the subtle message that they, not their sibling, should have died. They may feel guilty and responsible for their sibling's death, particularly if their bereaved parents do not assure them that they were not responsible. Children who were conceived or adopted to "replace" the dead child carry an especially heavy burden throughout their lives (Fanos 1996). Their resentment and anger may intensify when their parents memorialize the dead child, hanging portraits of him or her but not of the other siblings or insisting that the dead child's possessions not be touched. The surviving siblings may interpret such idealization as their not being "good enough."

Losses Associated with Divorce or Separation

The U.S. divorce rate has quadrupled in the past twenty years. Now in more than one-third of American families, the children are being raised by one parent, typically the mother. Indeed, more than one-half of children born in the 1990s are estimated to have spent some time in a single-parent household (Anderson 1999). Children in early childhood appear to be more vulnerable than older children to the emotional and psychological consequences of separation and divorce. This may be because they have difficulty understanding divorce and may believe that the absent parent is no longer a member of the family and that they will not see him or her again. Because of young children's egocentrism, they often feel that the divorce is a result of their own behavior and regard the absent parent's leaving as a rejection and abandonment of them. Other high-risk groups are adolescents, especially girls, and children experiencing a second divorce. In contrast, infants and toddlers seem to have fewer long-term effects, perhaps because they have little memory of both parents living together (Smith 1999).

Children's reactions to divorce are similar to their grief over a parent's death, although the predominant stress and primary affective responses differ. With death, children react with grief and apprehension to the primary stress, the death itself. In divorce, the children's divided loyalties are a major stress, and they feel anger, guilt, and sadness. A study comparing grieving children with a control group found that only those grieving a parent's death scored higher than those struggling with their parents' divorce or separation on measures of uneasiness and negative expectations regarding personal communication, interpersonal inadequacy, and inferiority. And compared with the control group, children experiencing divorce or separation scored significantly higher on scales of somatization, obsessive-compulsive behavior, acting-out behavior, and depression (Christ 2000). Compared with the death of a parent, children of divorced parents may be hurt more by conflict, loss of economic support, and feelings of guilt and rejection. Boys raised by their mothers may be more negatively affected than girls, particularly if the boys do not have male mentors or role models. Support from extended family and community is often compromised by divorce, because of the stigma, anger, and blame associated with it. In addition, the absence of communication in families is more common with divorce than death (Servaty and Hayslip 2001).

Many children have little or no warning that their parents are planning to separate, even though they may be aware of tensions, conflicts, and even domestic violence. Children generally prefer the "known" of their family, no matter how dysfunctional, than the unknown of a "broken home." Their initial response to divorce or separation often is disbelief or denial, feelings that grow stronger when the divorce is not discussed openly. Ignoring what they have been told, children may create fantasies or explanations for their parent's absence: "After they get home from their trip, Dad will be there and he won't ever leave again" or "Mom has gone on a long trip, but I know she will come back to be with all of us." With their world uncertain and unpredictable, children try to explain what has happened and may move relatively quickly to self-blame, feeling that some-how they caused the divorce, or they may ruminate about how they could have stopped it. One boy commented, "It isn't like dying. . . . Dad had a choice and he did not choose me" (Smith 1999:40). They may hope for years that their parents can be united again, even when one parent remarries. In the movie *The Parent Trap*, twelve-year-old twins did everything possible (or even thought to be impossible) to try to bring their parents together again. Denial tends to be followed by a pervasive sadness, loneliness, and yearning for the absent parent. Small children often find it hard to imagine that a parent can care for them when he or she is no longer living with them, since to them, caring means physical contact (Smith 1999). Children also grieve the loss of routine contact with the noncustodial parent, and perhaps with their extended family, security, and routines at school and with friends, as well as their image of the intact family. In addition, they may worry about money and their parents' emotional and physical health (McKay et al. 1999).

Family capacities, especially parental coping and adjustment and the parents' relationship during and after the divorce, are central to how a child reacts to and experiences a divorce. Nevertheless, many parents delay telling their children, especially young children, about their divorce, or may simply say that "Dad has gone on a long trip." While parents may think their children are too young to understand, they need to hear repeatedly that arrangements have been made for their care and safety. Older children may need to know about efforts to save the marriage and to be reassured that they will not be forced to take sides (McKay et al. 1999).

The loss of family supports or capacities is debilitating to those with lower self-esteem. Parents who are feeling stressed, angry, culpable, or guilty about the divorce often underestimate the strength of their children's feelings or, in their own pain, are unable to respond to their children's emotions. In turn, the children may be reluctant to express their feelings, fearing that being outwardly angry or sharing other negative feelings may mean that they will see even less of the noncustodial parent. Consequently, it may be easier for all involved to assume that "he's only a child; he'll soon get over it," or "she's doing fine; she wasn't really that close to her dad, anyway." A parent who is excited about a new relationship or so angry that he or she cannot remember anything positive about the partnership may not share the child's sadness. When parents are not cooperating for their children's sake, the children are more likely to have strong conflicts of loyalty and feelings of loneliness. But they keep their mourning private, painful, and unresolved, fearing that if they talk too openly about their sadness, they will lose the custodial parent as well.

Some children who feel caught between the two parents may feel angry and hopeless and that life is not worth living. Lacking energy and the ability to concentrate, they withdraw from normal activities or have difficulties in school. Others may lose their appetite or not be able to sleep, all the while maintaining a calm exterior, or they may become frozen emotionally. They envy other seemingly happy intact families (Servaty and Hayslip 2001). These issues tend to become more complicated when children move to a new home, community, or school after the divorce or separation or when the noncustodial parent, generally the father, does not see the child regularly (Anthony 1997; Freeman 1984a).

Children often feel anger, anxiety, powerlessness, and a sense of personal failure ("I don't matter or they wouldn't scream at each other in front of me") for a long time before the divorce. This loss of control can be linked to anger or a cover-up for despair and sadness that are felt to be too threatening to express. Anger may also mask a sense of being rejected and not valued: "If they really loved me, they would not have separated." These children may feel that life is unfair because others have ordinary families or that their parents are selfish for doing only what they wanted. Anger is typically expressed in reaction to trivial things but generally lies much deeper, silent, unexpressed, but ever present. When domestic violence is the cause of divorce, they may worry about the abused parent, be anxious that they too may be abused, or wish for revenge. Such children lose their sense of childhood security as they struggle with conflictual feelings of love and fear. In fact, the loss of trust, violence, or the threat of violence may do more long-term damage than the divorce itself (Smith 1999).

Loss and Adoption

Even when an adopted family provides a happy, loving and stable environment, adopted children typically face numerous losses: of their birth parents and their extended families, their communities, and their histories and health information. Although open adoptions are becoming more common, most adopted children do not yet have such connections with their birth families, especially those from other countries. In fact, in addition to their birth parents, international adoptees have also lost their country, culture, and ancestors. In instances of cross-racial adoption, adoptees lose the people who look like them and face a lifetime of difference. Adoptees, especially those who were in institutions or foster care, are in many ways "wounded warriors." Although they had to have been warriors in order to survive, they have been wounded by the many losses and unanswered questions in their lives (Paddock 2001).

The loss of one's mother is hardest. All adopted children, regardless of the age of relinquishment, grieve for their mother, since at some level they were connected with her throughout her pregnancy. Adoptive parents are often not prepared for the endless crying of a grieving child, a crying that no amount of holding and rocking can initially soothe. The birth mother has undoubtedly experienced ambivalence, sadness, and even thoughts of ending the pregnancy or her life, feelings that a near-term fetus may be able to detect and at some level may remember. The trauma of being separated from the birth parent varies with the degree of attachment, but it is universal and needs to be addressed so that the grieving child can begin to bond to the adoptive parent (Rosenberg 1992). Unfortunately, many adoptive parents do not understand this attachment, wondering "how can she miss her mother when she only was with her for a week." Yet the child is grieving the smell, the feel, and the emotions of his or her mother (Paddock 2001).

My four-year-old daughter arrived from India clinging tightly to my husband and refusing to let me hold her for nearly a week. She was very sick and unable to eat, and her dark eyes were wide with both fear and wonderment. For weeks, she was up all night, throwing things in the room, spitting, swearing at us in Telagu (it was probably best that we did not speak Telagu). And then one day, she let me hold her; she started to smile and to laugh. Like many adoptive parents, we sighed with relief and naively thought that the worst was behind us.

Each developmental phase brings new issues of loss related to the adoption, especially around transitional periods such as changing schools or moving to a new home. Birthdays and other special events for adopted children can bring out anger over the birth parent's absence ("If she really loved me, she would remember my birthday and contact me"), leaving both the child and the adoptive parents confused by such sadness and anger during what is supposedly a happy occasion. Children's sense of loss is intensified when they have little or no information about their birth parents or their early years. In some instances, because of either a lack of information about the birth parents or their own ambivalence about the birth relationship, adoptive parents may not provide truthful information or may "shut down" the adopted child's questions, conveying verbally or nonverbally that they are unwelcome.

Adopted children, especially those who do not physically resemble their adoptive parents, may face questions from strangers and acquaintances that highlight their "differentness" even more: "She is so pretty, how could her mother give her up?" or "Do you know anything about her biological parents?" When the adopted parents are asked whether they have any biological children or children of "their own," the adoptee, who is very much biological and their own, experiences yet another negation of who he or she is. Our language of "biological," "real," and "own" can compound the losses experienced by adoptive children.

In the early phases of magical thinking (ages two to three), children come up with their own concrete conclusions regarding adoption. For example, one child who had heard her parents say "that she was put up for adoption," imagined a shelf where she waited for them to come get her (Rosenberg 1992:97). By the time they reach school age, adopted children often develop "family romances" in which their birth parents are the perfect family, unlike their adoptive family that sets rules and disciplines them. They may develop romantic fantasies of having been snatched from idealized birth parents, who are still searching and longing for them. Imagining the perfect parent eases children's normal everyday disappointments in their adoptive parents. The common thread is the loss of the perfect parents and the harsh reality of life with the not-so-perfect parents (Rosenberg 1992). Such fantasies are especially likely to emerge when the children are angry or disappointed with adoptive parents or around special events.

After I say no to my daughter's request for more TV or computer time, I am typically told that I am not her real mother but just some "stupid old stranger who doesn't really understand her."

Children also need to create elaborate rationales for why their parents "gave them up" rather than tarnish their birth parents' perfection. Typically, these explanations blame someone else for the adoption. The issue of abandonment that adopted children confront during school age can leave them feeling inferior, different, and inadequate—perhaps just like their birth parent. In fact, the reality is that adopted children are different; they are the exception in the classroom.

Some adopted children may blame themselves, believing that they were not good enough or their parents would not have given them up for adoption.

School assignments like writing an autobiography or a family history often underscore the adopted children's sense of difference. Indeed, the autobiographies of those children adopted when they were older, from an institution or foster care, can be quite short.

For four consecutive years, grades 3 though 6, my daughter had to write a family history. Each time, she became irritable, resistant, and upset by this assignment, often tearing up her work and throwing it across the room. Her anger is understandable, given that she has no birth family history. I can only reread aloud her mother's letter of relinquishment and tell her as much about her adoptive family history as she can tolerate hearing. In the meantime, I look forward to the day when she does not have such assignments.

When faced with such requirements, adoptees may act out at school. If they make up their family histories, their teachers may reprimand them, adding to their feelings of being different.

The feelings of loss associated with adoption typically surface for adoptees at age eleven, thirteen, and eighteen—before they are launched on their own. Longing for and romanticizing their birth families may be especially intense during these time periods. Some adopted youth during these transitional times express hatred toward themselves and their adoptive parents, think about killing themselves, and experiment with risky behavior. Knowing only half of one's family complicates the normal challenges of late childhood and adolescence, such as developing a self-identity and achieving autonomy and independence from one's family.

Loss and Foster Care

Like adopted children, foster children have to deal with the loss of their birth parents. When the cause is violence, drug abuse, parental death, and/or homelessness, they may not have had a chance to develop meaningful relationships (or attachment) with their biological parents (Hallas 2002). If their parents were deemed unfit by the state to provide care, the children may have been taken suddenly from their homes, with little warning, explanation, or chance to say goodbye. An eighteen-year-old described the night that she, at age eight, and her brother were taken away from their mother and placed in foster care: "It was funny how we were in pain, but the world never stopped for us, it still moved on. I guess you could say it's just like the moon and the stars—you want them to shine forever, but then they disappear and you're left hoping for tomorrow" (Desetta 1996:xv).

Her remembrance from ten years earlier reflects two emotional themes common to most foster children: the pain of separation from family and the stubborn resilience of hope for the future. In addition, foster children may be placed in successive foster homes, never having the chance to connect with another family or to be permanently adopted. In some ways, foster children probably experience chronic grief—living daily with a loss without a sure ending. Their feelings of grief, especially anger, often are not resolved and may lead to their acting out in ways that result in removal from a placement (Russell 2002). An inability to mourn or the lack of support to do so may underlie the seemingly inexplicable behavior of some foster children who do everything in their power to be rejected by family after family (Kagan 1982). In contrast, some foster children are able to bond with their foster families, especially when their foster parents are patient, supportive, caring, and committed to developing a meaningful attachment (Hallas 2002).

With each new placement, foster children grieve the stigma of losing not only their birth family but also their contact with friends and significant others. When they must change schools, they often experience grief and resentment for losing a familiar environment as well as contact with friends from their previous homes, neighborhoods, and schools. Those who have been in residential care may grieve the loss of positive relationships with their care staff. Each phase of development, along with its many relationships, is characterized by discontinuity, with many foster care children suspended in the limbo of substitute care for years, never knowing when this limbo might change (Toth 1997). These losses are generally greater for children of color, who tend to remain in foster care longer and receiver fewer services than do white children. Because there are few African American foster homes for black youths, those who are in transracial placements lose their own culture as well. Accordingly, they must adjust not only to grief and loss but also to racial identity issues (McRoy 1999).

In sum, foster care children must contend with not only the normal developmental issues of separating from family, finding an identity, and coming to terms with adolescence and adulthood but also the loss of home, friends, and schools. In addition, they often undergo these losses for reasons that are beyond their control.

Summary

This chapter reviewed some losses that children may experience: a parent's death or divorce, a sibling's death, adoption, and foster care. Today children around the world are experiencing major losses through war, famine, political terror, forced relocation or immigration, school and community violence, and physical and sexual abuse. Although we cannot address all these childhood losses here, we hope that the resilience model, with its attention to social and cultural capacities, offers a way of organizing information and conceptualizing interventions for other types of loss. The need for positive family capacities during childhood is critical, for without them, children who endure loss are likely to carry more problematic feelings and behaviors into adolescence and young adulthood.

5

Interventions for Grieving Children

THE GRIEF associated with many childhood losses (e.g., relocation, missing toys, death of a pet, unidentified family or community violence, peer snubbing) often is minimized or not acknowledged by adults (Matthews 1999). Most children are incredibly resilient, however, and usually manage to integrate their losses, just as many adults do, without the help of mental health or social service professionals. Children, also like adults, may distract themselves with play, friends, and school in response to profound losses, which may later surface in negative ways. In fact, because children often express their grief in bursts (e.g., crying and then running outside to play with friends), family members may not know how to interpret and support their grieving process. But some children suffering a major bereavement, especially when the loss is not acknowledged or addressed, are at increased risk of "developing psychiatric disorders and may suffer considerable psychological and social difficulties throughout childhood and later in adult life" (Young and Papadatou 1997:197). Human service professionals typically work with children who have had multiple losses and are most at risk of adverse outcomes, and so they must know how to communicate with and support both children experiencing uncomplicated grief and their natural support systems and also how to address children's complicated or traumatic grief.

Grieving children naturally benefit from the compassion of observant adults in their support systems (e.g., parents, teachers, doctors, coaches, scout leaders, neighbors, religious leaders). National efforts to enhance the public's awareness of death and grief have helped people recognize the impact of traumatic and violent death on children, and consequently, the number of referrals for professional intervention has increased (Webb 2000). Parents or other adults may seek help for children from human service professionals in a variety of settings, such as schools, hospitals, hospices, mental health centers, private practice, or child welfare and social service agencies. Most parents find it painful to see their children grieving and may be uncertain about how to respond and whether professional intervention is warranted. Professional help should be considered when the child develops more than one of the following changes if they endure or interfere with the child's usual activities:

• Prolonged depression.
• Extreme difficulty relaxing.
• Less concern about his or her appearance.
• Symptoms affecting the child's physical health.
• Avoidance of any form of social contact or activities and hobbies previously enjoyed.
• Feelings of worthlessness.
• Sleep disturbances (e.g., nightmares, insomnia).
• Difficulties with schoolwork or behavioral problems in school.
• Psychosomatic complaints.
• Eating disruptions or disorders.
• Regressive behaviors. (Grollman 1990; Webb 2000)

The interventions we explore in this chapter include both natural support systems for children with uncomplicated grief (e.g., education for children, communication strategies, literature for parents and children, rituals, support groups), as well as more specialized professional interventions for children with more complicated or traumatic grief (e.g., psychotherapeutic groups, play therapy, family therapy).

Assessment

A multidimensional assessment can determine how to best help a bereaved child and/or his or her family. Like the resilience model, a *tripartite assessment* of a bereaved child looks at (1) his or her individual capacity, (2) factors related to the death, and (3) family, social, and religious/cultural capacity, as shown in figure 5.1 (Webb 2002). This assessment model is a guide for clinicians to explore a child's or adolescent's death-related bereavement that will help set goals and a culturally relevant plan of care (for a more detailed description of additional cultural assessment considerations, see chapter 11). Webb (2002) provides written forms to guide practitioners through these assessments as well as more thorough explanations of each category. For non-death-related losses, the "death-related factors" in figure 5.1 can be modified to include the type of loss (e.g., divorce and whether the child anticipated it, how much marital conflict precipitated the divorce), the child's contact with and relationship with

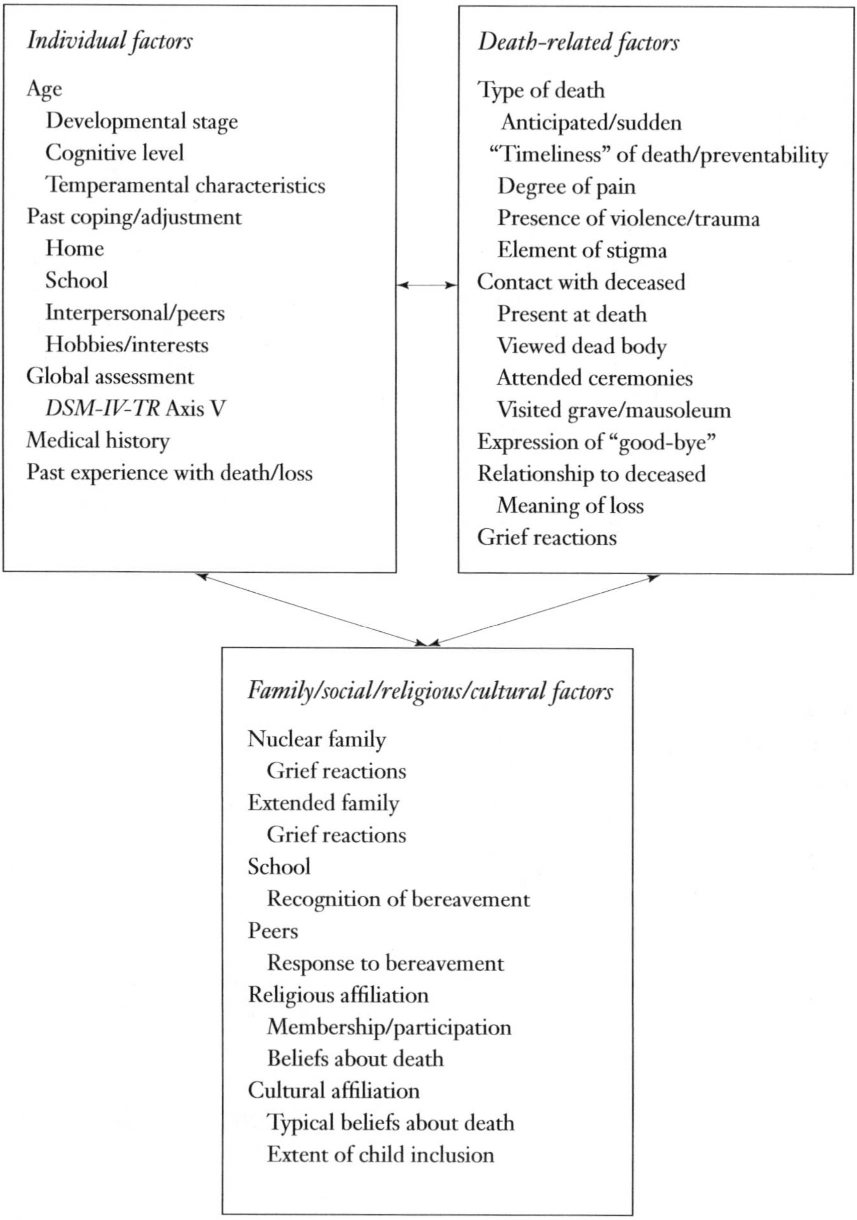

Individual factors

Age
  Developmental stage
  Cognitive level
  Temperamental characteristics
Past coping/adjustment
  Home
  School
  Interpersonal/peers
  Hobbies/interests
Global assessment
  DSM-IV-TR Axis V
Medical history
Past experience with death/loss

Death-related factors

Type of death
  Anticipated/sudden
  "Timeliness" of death/preventability
  Degree of pain
  Presence of violence/trauma
  Element of stigma
Contact with deceased
  Present at death
  Viewed dead body
  Attended ceremonies
  Visited grave/mausoleum
Expression of "good-bye"
Relationship to deceased
  Meaning of loss
  Grief reactions

Family/social/religious/cultural factors

Nuclear family
  Grief reactions
Extended family
  Grief reactions
School
  Recognition of bereavement
Peers
  Response to bereavement
Religious affiliation
  Membership/participation
  Beliefs about death
Cultural affiliation
  Typical beliefs about death
  Extent of child inclusion

FIGURE 5.1. Tripartite assessment of the bereaved child.
Source: N. B. Webb, Assessment of the Bereaved Child, in *Helping Bereaved Children: A Handbook for Practitioners,* edited by N. B. Webb (New York: Guilford Press), 30. Reprinted by permission of Guilford Publications, Inc.

the absent parent (e.g., the quality and frequency of visits with the noncustodial father or mother following a divorce), and expressions of "good-bye" facilitated by the loss (e.g., rituals used to mark the transition from married to divorced parents).

Such assessments are tailored to the situations in which professionals work and to the distinctive needs of children and their families. For example, school social workers planning a support group for children experiencing divorce, illness, or death may place more emphasis on their performance in school, peer relationships, functioning in the school, and relationships with teachers. Child welfare or mental health professionals working with children exposed to violence, trauma, or abuse also should look at their physical health, safety, environmental conditions, posttraumatic stress disorder (PTSD), and traumatic grief (Cohen et al. 2002). Assessments of various contexts often include observations of and/or interviews with the child, parent, or significant others. Primary caregivers are frequently a good source of information about children's bereavement. Interviews with the child's family reveal how family members communicate their reactions to loss and process the events surrounding it.

The following assessment areas are useful to explore with caregivers and other relatives of children bereaved by death:

1. *The child's characteristics.* How old is the child? What are his or her developmental abilities, needs, and temperament?
2. *Details of the loss.* What specifically has occurred? How? Who was present? What did the child see? What was he or she told?
3. *Rituals.* How and to what extent was the child involved in pre- or postdeath rituals (e.g., family meetings, memorial services)?
4. *Caregiving.* Who has been taking care of the child? How has his or her routine changed?
5. *Family support.* Is the family able to support the child materially and emotionally? How are other family members responding to the loss? Are they able to comfort the child when necessary and to show him or her how to display and experience feelings?
6. *Current family functioning.* What are the family's primary needs and concerns? What are their previous experiences with loss, and how have family members coped with past and current losses? How do they give information to the child? What has the child been told? Which of the family's cultural and religious/spiritual beliefs are relevant to the situation? What informal and formal social supports are available to the child and the family? How secure are the family's relationships with and support of the child?

7. *Knowledge of death before the loss.* What were the child's experiences with and understanding of death before the loss?
8. *Understanding of the current loss.* What does the child say about the cause of death? Beliefs about an afterlife?
9. *Grief response and level of functioning.* What are the child's emotional and behavioral reactions to the death? What are his or her manifestations of grief? How does the child's current level of functioning compare with his or her functioning before the death? How well is the child tolerating the emotions of grief? (Masur 1996; Webb 2002)

General Techniques and Interventions

Even though death is an inevitable part of life, many adults, particularly in Western societies, are hesitant to teach children about it. For example, some parents rush to replace the dead goldfish before their children come home from school, thereby missing an opportunity to talk to them about grief, death, family-related beliefs and rituals, and some of life's most important lessons. Professionals therefore should encourage adults to find opportunities to teach children about death as a natural and inevitable fact of life. Box 5.1 gives some examples. Children's films like *The Lion King* or *Bambi* may serve as openings for discussion. Taking advantage of these moments and being open to discussion and expression of

Box 5.1 Teaching Children About Death Through Natural Events

In the fall, I encourage my children to notice the leaves changing color and dropping to the ground. I ask them what they think will happen to the leaves, which leads into a discussion about death and the rebirth that will occur in the spring. When our family cat, George, died, our two children (ages four and seven) were allowed to feel his stiff body and to talk about what had happened to him. They drew pictures or wrote letters to George that could be buried with him. They helped dig and pick the flowers for his grave and were included in every step of the memorial ritual that we planned together. [Betty J. Kramer] feelings will help children face with greater confidence the losses that they are likely to experience in the future.

Literature for Parents and Children About Death, Dying, and Bereavement

Many books are available to help parents talk with their children about death and grief (Emswiler and Emswiler 2000; Fitzgerald 1992; Grollman 1990, 1995; Trozzi and Massimmini 1999). Books that address a wide variety of losses also are available for children of all ages and developmental stages. They both teach concepts and offer ideas for questions and discussion. Box 5.2 lists books for preschool and primary school readers. Parents and professionals should choose those on topics relevant to the child, evaluate the books' suitability, match them to the child's capabilities, and read them to or along with the child (Corr, Nabe, and Corr 2003).

Honest Communication with Children

Children's grief often is complicated when well-meaning adults withhold information or do not talk with them honestly, for their response is strongly influenced by their understanding of the causes and consequences of loss (Baker, Sedney, and Gross 1992). "Good mental health is not the denial of tragedy, but the frank acknowledgement of painful separation. One of the worst difficulties is youngsters' lack of understanding because of adult secrecy" (Grollman 1995:18). Although many adults believe that children are "too young" to understand death, to participate in the rituals that follow death, and to deal with painful situations, children are more likely to become confused and to grieve in isolation when they are excluded from these conversations and events. When not told about a death or other loss, children are likely to be affected by unspoken emotions, make up their own explanations for what is happening around them, misinterpret conversations that they overhear, and feel confusion, guilt, responsibility for the death, and isolation (Schreder 1995). Children excluded from family discussions are denied opportunities to grieve openly with those around them and to learn about life through loss. Instead, clinicians believe that the best way to talk with children is to speak honestly, provide age-appropriate and accurate information, frame explanations within the family's cultural belief system, determine what they want to know, and answer their questions directly (Schreder 1995).

Telling Children About a Death

How children are told of a death can either ease or complicate their bereavement (Servaty-Seib, Peterson, and Spang 2003; Stewart 1999). Professionals

Box 5.2 Books for Children About Death, Dying, and Grief

BOOKS FOR PRESCHOOLERS AND BEGINNING READERS
Deaths of Animals and Pets

R. Biale, *My Pet Died* (1997).
L. K. Brown and M. Brown, *When Dinosaurs Die: A Guide to Understanding Death* (1996).
M. Kantrowitz, *When Violet Died* (1973).
J. Kramer, *A Gift from Rex: Guiding Children Through Life and Loss* (2001).
D. O'Toole, *Aarvy Aardvark Finds Hope* (1988).
C. Rylant, *Dog Heaven* and *Cat Heaven* (1995, 1997).
S. Varley, *Badger's Parting Gifts* (1992).
J. Viorst, *The Tenth Good Thing About Barney* (1971).
H. Wilhelm, *I'll Always Love You* (1985).

Deaths of Siblings, Friends, and Other Children

E. Bunting, *Rudi's Pond* (1999).
A. F. Clardy, *Dusty Was My Friend: Coming to Terms with Loss* (1984).
J. Cohn, *I Had a Friend Named Peter* (1987).
J. Johnson and M. Johnson, *Where's Jess?* (1982).
R. S. Schlitt, *Robert Nathaniel's Tree* (1992).
J. Simon, *This Book Is for All Kids, but Especially My Sister Libby. Libby Died* (2001).
A. B. Weir, *Am I Still a Big Sister?* (1992).

Deaths of Parents, Grandparents, and Other Adults

J. Bartoli, *Nonna* (1975).
C. K. Cohen, *Daddy's Promise* (1997).
J. Czech, *The Garden Angel* (2000).
J. Fassler, *My Grandpa Died Today* (1971).
K. Hesse, *Poppy's Chair* (1993).
J. London and S. Long, *Liplap's Wish* (1994).

continued

M. Mundy, *Sad Isn't Bad: A Good-Grief Guidebook for Kids Dealing with Loss* (1998).

General Topics and Other Death-Related Events

K. L. Carney, *Together We'll Get Through This!* (1997).
D. Fassler and K. McQueen, *What's a Virus Anyway? The Kid's Book About AIDS* (1990).
M. Fox, *Touch Boris* (1994).
S. Greenlee and B. Drath, *When Someone Dies* (1992).
B. Mellonie and R. Ingpen, *Lifetimes: A Beautiful Way to Explain Death to Children* (1983).
M. Shriver, *What's Heaven?* (1999).
J. L. Winsch and P. Keating, *After the Funeral* (1995).

BOOKS FOR PRIMARY SCHOOL READERS
Deaths of Animals, Pets, and in Nature

L. Buscaglia, *The Fall of Freddy the Leaf* (1982).
C. Carrick, *The Accident* (1976).
C. Graeber, *Mustard* (1982).
E. B. White, *Charlotte's Web* (1952).

Deaths of Siblings, Friends, and Other Children

S. Alexander, *Nadia the Willful* (1983).
F. Chin-Yee, *Sam's Story: A Story for Families Surviving Sudden Infant Death Syndrome* (1988).
J. B. Coburn, *Annie and the Sand Dobbies* (1964).
E. Coerr, *Saddako and the Thousand Paper Cranes* (1977).
C. C. Greene, *Beat the Turtle Drum* (1976).
D. B. Smith, *A Taste of Blackberries* (1973).
B. J. Turner and M. Backer, *A Little Bit of Rob* (1996).

Deaths of Parents, Grandparents, and Other Adults

T. A. Barron, *Where Is Grandpa?* (2002).
E. Donnelly, *So Long Grandpa* (1981).
E. Douglas, *Rachel and the Upside Down Heart* (1990).

B. Marshall, *Animal Crackers: A Tender Book About Death and Funerals and Love* (1998).

J. W. McNamara, *My Mom Is Dying: A Child's Diary* (1994).

L. Miles, *The Rag Coat* (1991).

E. S. Powell, *Geranium Morning* (1990).

N. Simon, *We Remember Philip* (1979).

B. W. Tiffault, *A Quilt for Elizabeth* (1992).

R. Whitehead, *The Mother Tree* (1971).

General Topics

C. Arnold, *What We Do When Someone Dies* (1987).

P. Coleman, *Where the Balloons Go* (1996).

E. A. Corley, *Tell Me About Death, Tell Me About Funerals* (1973).

P. Goble, *Beyond the Ridge* (1993).

L. Goldman, *Bart Speaks Out: An Interactive Storybook for Young Children About Suicide* (1997).

L. Van-Si and L. Powers, *Helping Children Heal from Loss: A Keepsake Book of Special Memories* (1994).

Source: Adapted from C. A. Corr, C. M. Nabe, and D. M. Corr, *Death and Dying, Life and Living*, 4th ed. (Belmont, Calif.: Wadsworth, 2003).

may need to help parents with the emotional task of breaking "bad news" to children, especially when the parents are overcome with their own grief or find it difficult to tell them. In some instances, school social workers or counselors may be asked to tell children about a death. Guidelines for breaking bad news to children and teens include the following:

1. Find a quiet and private place to talk to the child and provide a "warning" (e.g., "I have some very sad news for you, Tameka").
2. Sit close to the child while telling him or her the news, and consider using a gentle touch.
3. Provide a brief and accurate description of what happened, using concrete words rather than metaphors that may confuse children. For example, telling a child that "we lost Grandma last night," implies that Grandma may be found, or saying that "your mother is OK now; she is sleeping and at rest"

may be interpreted literally and create tremendous anxiety for the child about going to sleep or offer the hope that his or her mother will wake up and return. In contrast, concrete words like *died* and *death* more accurately convey what has happened, even though some adults are uncomfortable using these words.

4. Be honest with the child, share your own feelings, and if appropriate, let him or her know you, too, are sad or feeling a sense of shock and that it is all right to talk about these reactions.

5. Reassure the child that his or her feelings and reactions are common and normal and that there are no "right" or "wrong" emotions.

6. Sit quietly with the child, allowing time for him or her to take in the news.

7. Respect the child's responses and needs (e.g., to be alone, cry, express anger, scream, or even play or go outside).

8. Reassure the child that someone will take care of him or her. This is especially important when the person who has died was the primary caregiver. (Davies 1999)

Rituals with Bereaved Children

A ritual is defined as "a specific behavior or activity that gives symbolic expression to certain feelings and thoughts of the actor(s) individually or as a group. It may be a habitually repetitive behavior or a one-time occurrence" (Rando 1985:236). In many cultures, rituals are central to helping children with the grief process.

FAMILY-INITIATED RITUALS

Rituals and ceremonies following a death provide an "opportunity for closure and celebration of love and life" (Schreder 1995:209). Children who participate in rituals following a death exhibit less psychological distress in the years following the death than do children who do not (Fristad et al. 2001). Funeral and burial practices and other culturally dictated bereavement rituals may ease the grief experience, provided that children are prepared and given support during the event and follow-up afterward (Corr, Nabe, and Corr 2003; Fristad et al. 2001; Silverman and Worden 1992b). It is helpful to explain rituals to children and ask them whether they want to participate so that they will know what will happen and why such services are held (Corr, Nabe, and Corr 2003). Box 5.3 gives an example of such preparation. During the services, an adult familiar with the rituals in the child's culture should explain what is happening and answer questions. After the services, adults should be available to talk with the child about his or her reactions or feelings and answer questions.

Box 5.3 Preparing a Child to Participate in a Memorial Service

When our seventy-eight-year-old neighbor died suddenly following a fall, our two-and-a-half-year-old son wanted to attend the funeral services. He was very fond of our neighbor and curious about what had happened to him. We explained that according to our belief system, when a person dies, the spirit leaves the body, so without this energy, the body is lifeless. We used the analogy that a glove can move with a hand inside it but that if the hand is removed, the glove will fall to the ground and not be able to move by itself. We explained what he would likely see at the funeral, noting that there would be people crying because they would miss Mr. S. and that the body would lie lifeless in a casket at the front of the room for people to visit one last time before it was buried. We explained that the body would be cold to the touch because it no longer had a spirit to keep it warm or keep the blood flowing, and described other events that would happen. Our son asked many questions and seemed to soak up a great deal of information. He appropriately expressed his sadness through short bursts of tears and then just as easily turned to playing with the neighbor's grandchildren. Although developmental theories suggest that children of this age are incapable of understanding the permanency of death, we were surprised to hear our son explain to his grandmother on the phone that Mr. S. was dead and couldn't live in his house anymore because his spirit had left his body. He seemed to understand, and this initial experience with death and the rituals that followed it laid a foundation that has allowed him to respond to other deaths. [Betty J. Kramer]

PROFESSIONAL-INITIATED RITUALS

Besides funeral rites and other memorial services, children and their families may take part in other culturally appropriate rituals. Be sure to consider the following:

• Rituals should be invented as the child's story of loss is shared; they should not be imposed.

- Rituals usually involve objects that have a symbolic value, such as a candle, letter, song, or picture.
- Rituals should lead to thinking about their implications. After the ritual, it is helpful to discuss the participants' thoughts and feelings. (Doka 2000b)

Examples of helpful activities in ritual ceremonies with children are planting a tree, a flower, or another plant that they may watch growing in memory of the deceased, lighting a candle next to a photograph, drawing a picture, creating a card for a special occasion or for placement in the casket or grave, releasing an ecofriendly helium balloon with a message attached for the deceased, creating a plaque or mural in honor of the deceased, singing a song or writing a poem to recite at a memorial service or on the anniversary of the death, and making a "prayer feather" (a decorated feather with special wishes or thoughts attached to it) and releasing it into the wind (Schreder 1995). In some instances, children may be able to help plan part of the memorial service or, as described in chapter 4, plan a service specifically for their friends.

Rituals may also be created to help children address losses that are not related to death. For example, a ritual could be created to help children and their family members who are going through a divorce. Each person could talk about the strengths of each family member, create a symbolic representation of what the family has and will continue to mean to each of them, discuss how the divorce may change their daily life, and express their love and intentions for the other family members and for the family's future relationships. Music, pictures, or notes written to the noncustodial parent may help children with the transition from married to divorced parents. Creating therapeutic rituals for a wide range of losses is described further in chapter 9.

Acknowledging and Anticipating Triggers of Grief

As their developmental capacities expand, children may "revisit life events and often rework or regrieve a loss" (Ward-Wimmer and Napoli 2000:112). For example, children bereaved by death or divorce may experience a resurgence of grief around special traditional family holidays, anniversaries, or graduation ceremonies, and children who are in foster care or are adopted may mourn again when they enter adolescence (Levine 1988; Schreder 1995). When significant milestones, anniversaries, or holidays draw near, children may become either withdrawn or extremely emotional or engage in unusual behaviors. Anticipating these grief triggers allows adults to prepare and/or respond to activated grief (e.g., touching base with bereaved children at developmental milestones or significant events; being present for but not overwhelming to the child; and being sensitive to the grief that may underlie seemingly inexplicable behavior). A variety of interventions are available to professionals to help children through this regrief experience. For example, the child and/or other family members might perform a ritual to share memories, honor past relationships, and express feelings (e.g., write a letter to the deceased or absent parent, make a cake for the deceased's birthday, draw a picture of favorite memories or reactivated memories).

Primary Communication and Therapeutic Goals

To determine grieving children's needs and create a therapeutic alliance, four goals for communicating with them must be met:

1. Establish a rapport, by meeting the children wherever they are, joining them in their activities, playing alongside them, being comfortable with silence, and being honest with them.
2. Determine the children's developmental level by observing their vocabulary, comprehension, and behavior.
3. Speak to the children at their level, using their vocabulary and taking into consideration their developmental abilities.
4. Form evaluations for your assessment based on the children's statements, body language, and play. (Seager and Spencer 1996)

The main goals in helping bereaved children are (1) ensuring that their family is able to care for them and understands their needs for emotional support and comfort, can provide their daily material needs, and will support their expression of thoughts and feelings regarding the loss; (2) facilitating the mourning process; and (3) preventing the development of complicated grief (Masur 1996). Various professional interventions to meet these goals are described next.

Play and Play Therapy

Children often do not possess the vocabulary necessary to express their feelings and inner conflicts. Play, however, comes naturally to them and allows them to articulate their inner world. They may use dolls, drawings, games, puppets, art supplies, and other media, along with their imagination, to project and act out feelings that may be too powerful or threatening for them to admit to themselves. For example, children who have been abused or who have experienced or witnessed a traumatic event such as a homicide may find it especially difficult to talk about it. The best method of working with these and other bereaved children is to help them process the feelings of grief that they cannot express verbally (Gil 1998). Although extensive formal training is required to become a play therapist, "the basic techniques and concepts of play therapy are accessible to anyone interested in working more effectively with children" (Seager and Spencer 1996:48).

Play therapy is defined as "a helping interaction between a trained adult and a child that seeks to relieve the child's emotional distress through the symbolic communication of play" (Webb 2000:140). The difference between *play* and *play therapy* is the nature of the play "communications" between the child and the therapist (Webb 2000). An adult who understands the symbolic nature of children's play interprets the play activities in a nonthreatening way. For example, Webb described how she validated a child's feelings who repeatedly played the board game Operation during the terminal phase of her mother's progressive decline from cancer. She made comments like "Oh! This poor man; he's had to have so many operations, and he doesn't seem to be getting any better; the doctors keep trying to help him, but he's just getting weaker and weaker! This so upsetting and sad; it's not fair! It's so hard on this family!" (2000:141). In so doing, this therapist echoed back to the child many of the emotions she may have felt.

According to Seager and Spencer (1996), the basic communication techniques of play therapy are drawn from the work of Kottman (1993, 1995) and Kottman and Schaefer (1993): (1) tracking, (2) restating content, (3) reflecting feelings, and (4) encouraging.

Tracking is narrating what a child is doing while playing without naming the toy, object, or action until the child does. *Restating content* is finding a slightly different way to repeat, using similar words, what the child has said during play, in order to help the child feel that he or she is understood and to offer an opportunity to clarify any misunderstandings. *Reflecting feelings* helps build the relationship and may require guessing from the five most frequently expressed feelings (sad, happy, scared, mad, and guilty), based on the child's play behavior and body language. Finally, *encouraging* uses strategies that "convey faith in and acceptance of the child and a positive belief in the child's abilities" (Seager and Spencer 1996:49).

Most children like to draw. As a form of play, it allows them to express unconscious and symbolic experiences and emotions that often are difficult or too painful to talk about directly. Children's drawings may "facilitate communication and enhance understanding of sensory memory" (e.g., what children heard, saw, or felt related to a loss or traumatic death) (Clements, Benasutti, and Henry 2001:14) and may be used for assessment and intervention. Group interventions with bereaved children often have them draw pictures of their family (past and present) and themselves with the deceased or absent parent or sibling. Box 5.4 offers guidelines for the therapeutic use of children's drawings. Although drawing is recommended, to date there has been little research to determine its efficacy in addressing grief symptoms or helping children integrate their losses. Although therapeutic group interventions that integrate play modalities have been successful, studies are needed to demonstrate the conditions and the particular play therapy methods and related techniques that benefit grieving children.

Box 5.4 Practical Tips for Using Drawings with Children

- Consult with or seek the supervision of a registered art therapist.
- Provide introductions and orientation.
- Establish a rapport with the children.
- Create a welcoming, nurturing, nonthreatening, and safe environment.
- When choosing the art media, consider the children's individual needs and the session's structure.
- Select more structured media (e.g., colored pencils, crayons, magic markers, and oil pastels) for lower-functioning children to minimize their frustration.
- Eliminate outside distractions as much as possible.
- Direct the session so as to enhance understanding.
- Avoid hovering over the children.
- Avoid distracting conversations and questions while the children are drawing.
- Convey a genuine interest in the final product.
- Do not make assumptions about or verbal interpretations of their artwork.
- Encourage the children to talk about their drawing, with open-ended questions (e.g., What is the little girl doing? What is the little boy thinking? How do the people in the picture feel? Where are the people in the picture going to go?).

Source: P. T. Clements Jr., K. M. Benasutti, and G. C. Henry, Drawing from Experience: Using Children's Drawings to Facilitate Communication and Understanding with Children Exposed to Sudden Traumatic Deaths, *Journal of Psychosocial Nursing* 39 (2001): 12–20.

CULTURAL CONSIDERATIONS IN PLAY THERAPY

Culturally competent practitioners are "sensitive to and well grounded in knowledge about the sociocultural world that the child comes from" (Martinez and Valdez 1992: 86). Bereaved children of color face issues common to any grieving child but also may be confronted with issues compounded by culture, racism, immigration, and poverty, which practitioners need to consider in both their assessment and interventions (Jackson and Westmoreland 1992). The transactional contextual model of play therapy acknowledges the effects of the social environment and emphasizes empowering the child. Play environments and the materials used in play therapy should reflect the cultural context (Martinez and Valdez 1992). For example, the setting in which children will play should contain culturally diverse artifacts, pictures, and drawings. Play materials should include dolls from different ethnic backgrounds, bilingual and/or culturally diverse children's books, ethnic music that may be played during activities or used therapeutically, culturally relevant games, and maps or globes that provide visual cues for the child to discuss his or her family's place of origin or immigration experience if relevant. Research is needed to develop and test the efficacy of play therapy approaches to address varied losses experienced by children of color and to examine whether the symbolism of a grieving child's play differs across cultures.

Group-Based Interventions
SUPPORT GROUPS

Support groups for bereaved children recognize that parents or other caregivers may be unable to help bereaved children cope effectively with loss and grief (Bacon 1996). The primary aim of such groups is to bring together persons with similar experiences to support and learn from one another. When parents who are overwhelmed by their own grief find it difficult to help their children, children's bereavement support groups may provide surrogate families (Zambelli and DeRosa 1992). Both parents and children can benefit from discovering that they are not the only ones with major losses. Peer relationships that develop in bereavement support groups may help build a child's sense of self-esteem and reduce their sense of isolation in their grief (Bacon 1996). Bereavement support groups for children also can alleviate grief symptoms, depression, and behavioral disturbances (Tonkins and Lambert 1996).

Support groups may take many forms and address a wide variety of losses that may occur in the family (e.g., divorce, death, chronic or terminal illness). The agenda for these groups is determined by the type of loss, the group members' needs, the setting for the group, and the group's goals. In contrast to support groups for adults that are sometimes run by the group members, children's groups require trained leaders who understand the grief process and children's reactions to bereavement and who have the empathy, communication, and group skills to work therapeutically with children. Animals may also be used therapeutically in support groups. The Delta Society provides information about using animals in hospice and bereavement groups.

Task models suggest group-based activities for productive mourning (Bacon 1996). For example, the following are Fox's (1985) proposed group activities appropriate to the four tasks of mourning for children:

1. *Understand and try to make sense out of what is happening or has happened.* Group activities for this task are allowing children to share their personal loss through discussion, drawings, stories, puppets, or another creative medium. Children bereaved by the death of a parent or sibling could illustrate and/or describe the deceased family member, the story of his or her death, the story of the funeral, a picture of the person who has died, and their family's beliefs about what happens to a person after death.

2. *Express emotional or other strong responses to the present or anticipated loss.* Facilitators of support groups offer activities that allow children to express their feelings in ways that do not harm themselves or others and to validate their feelings with the group. Group activities that permit children to express feelings are selecting "feeling" cards or flowers to represent their current mood, sharing music, drawing, role playing or movement, discussing their dreams, sharing the highs and lows of their week, and acting out feeling charades (Bacon 1996).

3. *Commemorate the life that has been lost through formal or informal remembrances.* A common group activity to commemorate the life of the deceased is having children make memory boxes decorated with special items and memories placed inside. Other activities are making memory scrapbooks, decorating a picture frame, and making beeswax candles for the family to light on special occasions (Bacon 1996).

4. *Learn how to continue living and loving.* Facilitators may encourage children to identify others who are important and special to them and helping them examine the changes in their family following the death and to discuss their hopes and dreams for the future (Bacon 1996). Attention to the group's termination is important. Children may want to take a group picture, share contact information, sign memory books, and plan future group reunions if that is possible (Bacon 1996).

Although this task-based model is mainly for groups of children who have experienced a death, it may be adapted to include activities appropriate to other losses. For example, children whose parents have divorced also may benefit from group activities that allow them to understand and make sense of the divorce, express their emotional response to the divorce and its associated losses, commemorate the former family configuration, and learn how to integrate the divorce and reconfigure their relationships to go on living and loving. Support groups for children of divorce are becoming more common at schools and community centers. As is true with persons of any age, a group setting may not appeal to some children, so an individual assessment is necessary to determine its suitability. In addition, various cultural issues need to be considered when designing and implementing groups for children of color and from different ethnic/cultural backgrounds. For example, facilitators should take account of (1) the group's heterogeneity or homogeneity; (2) the child's conceptions, expectations, and needs relevant to the group's structure, process, and experience; (3) the variation in the group members' communication styles; (4) the preparation of children of color for the group; and (5) culturally competent and strength-focused skills and techniques in problem solving (Ho 1992). The rationale of, discussion of, and suggestions for implementing these considerations are beyond the scope of this chapter but can be found in Ho 1992.

Psychotherapeutic and Bereavement Group Interventions

Whereas support groups emphasize informal, mutual support, trained professionals structure the interventions for psychotherapeutic bereavement groups. The goals of these more formal groups vary but usually try to minimize complicated grief reactions, ease symptoms, and enhance psychological well-being. Evidence suggests that preventive therapeutic group interventions for bereaved children can be effective (for a review of the literature, see Schut et al. 2001). For example, an eight-week psychotherapeutic group for seven- to eleven-year-olds bereaved by the death of a parent or sibling was able to reduce depression, overall emotions (sadness, anger, withdrawal, guilt, anxiety, loneliness, and helplessness), and behavioral disturbances. This group provided symbolic modes of communication through play and art projects (e.g., sending off helium balloons in the sky to say "good-bye" to the deceased, drawing pictures of missing aspects of the deceased), discussions, and education (Tonkins and Lambert 1996).

Another study examined the efficacy of a manual-based bereavement group intervention for children following the suicide of a parent or sibling and found less anxiety and fewer depressive symptoms in the children receiving the intervention than in the children not receiving it (Pfeffer et al. 2002). This intervention consisted of ten, ninety-minute psychoeducational and support group sessions for children and their parents. The facilitators used a variety of group-based techniques and activities suitable for the children, such as icebreaking games, activities using stories, expressions of feeling and positive recall, and rituals for ending groups. Group work often uses play techniques to help children process and express their feelings (Neary and Brandon 1997). (For activities that may be used in group work with children, see Smith and Pennells 1995.)

Not all therapeutic group interventions are effective. For example, no differences in grief adjustment, level of anxiety, and classroom behavior were found between elementary school students who participated in eight, thirty-minute bereavement counseling group sessions and students in the control group (Adams 1996). Similarly, Wilson (1995) found no difference between experimental and control groups in grief-induced anxiety and behavioral problems following a time-limited group intervention program for bereaved children. The variability in reported findings may be explained by differences in context, group methods and protocols, type of loss, measurement, outcomes studied, and involvement of caregivers.

Children who lost a parent were found to benefit from groups that met jointly with groups designed for their caregivers (Schoeman and Kreitzman 1997). Joint group sessions provide opportunities for caregivers to (1) acknowledge and express their own grief and anger in relation to the death, (2) discover how children grieve and tolerate the many feelings that children express in relation to the death, and (3) learn how to respond to the anxiety underlying children's requests for information. As a result of these joint meeting groups, "the children and their caregivers begin to grieve together, and can continue to share their feelings after the group has ended" (Schoeman and Kreitzman 1997:245).

Family-Based Interventions
ASSESSMENT

Families often are an important healing resource for grieving children (Rosen 1996). Children of single-parent families, families with same-sex parents, multi-generational families in which the primary caregivers may be grandparents, children in foster care, blended families, and traditional two-parent households all differ in the adversities they face and their capacities for responding to loss. Assessments of families should include the family's social and financial status (e.g., the background factors in the resilience model), the family's gender-based roles, the family's religious and spiritual beliefs, and the child's and family's personal, social, and cultural capacities (Rosen 1996). It is important to understand culturally relevant belief systems, rituals, and expectations regarding mourning in the family (for examples of questions to explore, see chapter 11). Other areas for the assessment of families include family boundaries (i.e., the family's flexibility and openness to others and to new ideas), the family's sense of coherence (i.e., does the family have a coherent image or a way of making meaning that reflects who its members are?), patterns of communication (i.e., how and what information is exchanged and among whom), problem-solving skills, ways of responding to loss, and the extent to which families are centered on parents or children (Silverman 2000). Family members may provide important insights into the child's experiences and also may benefit from a professional's perspectives on the child's reactions and behaviors.

FAMILY THERAPY

The losses experienced by children typically reverberate throughout the family system. Families also face additional challenges in coping with grief when members with different developmental and emotional needs grieve in markedly different ways. In addition to the primary grief reactions to the death of a loved one, children may have secondary grief reactions associated with their parents' grief, such as grief over their parents' preoccupation with the death and thus emotional absence and their "increased fear of losing another attachment figure and to other losses that result from death" (Baker 1997:139). Bereaved parents who are consumed by their own grief may be emotionally labile or preoccupied, inconsistent in their behavior and discipline, and sometimes emotionally vulnerable, making it difficult for them to respond to their children's needs. One of the principal goals of family therapy is minimizing the impact of the parents' grief on children. Parental guidance methods may be used to give emotional support to parents who are themselves grieving, to teach parents about developmental issues that influence their children's experience of grief, to help them plan ways of communicating accurate information about the death and its causes, to understand the child's needs for stability and consistency, and to help them respond to their child's behavioral changes associated with the loss (Baker 1997).

Among the few evaluations of the effectiveness of family therapy for bereaved children are studies showing that family-based programs improve adjustment and reduce depression in both children and their caregivers (Black and Urbanowicz 1987; Carr 2000; Sandler, West, and Baca 1992). Black and Urbanowicz (1987) offered six home-based sessions to children and their family members, two to three months following a parent's death. Their goals were to promote mourning in the children and the surviving parent and to improve communication between them about the death. Family members were invited to talk about the events leading up to the death, to share photographs and mementos, and to express their grief. Play materials appropriate to the children's ages were used to discuss the deceased parent and the children's feelings of grief. At a one-year follow-up, the children in the treatment group exhibited more positive behavior, mood, and health, and the parents had better moods than did those in the control group. Interestingly, the children in the control and treatment groups who cried and talked about the dead parent in the month after their bereavement had fewer and less serious behavioral and emotional problems than did the children who did not cry.

Goals of family therapy typically are identifying the influence of previous losses on the family's current functioning and helping the family understand this influence; encouraging the communication of feelings among family members; "helping the family reorganize its structure following the loss, to reassign important role functions and to restore appropriate generational boundaries"; and "addressing developmental tasks that were not accomplished because of the disruptive influence of the loss, especially the task of helping children to separate and individuate in adolescence" (Baker 1997:143). Family therapists have used Worden's original tasks of mourning to create the following four clinical goals for working with grieving families:

1. Acknowledge the reality of the loss.
2. Put the experience of the loss in context.
3. Reorganize the family system.
4. Reinvest in other relationships and life pursuits. (McGoldrick 1991; Walsh and McGoldrick 1988)

CULTURAL CONSIDERATIONS IN FAMILY THERAPY

Several issues should be considered when engaging culturally diverse populations in family-based interventions. The initial phase is especially important and often challenging when working with ethnically diverse families. Many of these families may (1) have no knowledge of family therapy and sought it only after all other traditional help-seeking attempts have failed; (2) distrust professionals who represent the mainstream society that has oppressed them; (3) regard seeking help from outsiders to be antithetical to their cultural values; (4) view "talk" therapy as incongruent with their cultural norms; and (5) worry about the lack of financial resources to justify family-based therapy (Ho 1992). Therapists need knowledge, skills, and values to address these concerns; to accommodate variations in cultural communication preferences, the perceived role of the therapist, expectations for the relationship, norms regarding privacy and other family cultural norms; and to identify, acknowledge, and validate family strengths throughout the process (Ho 1992). Family therapy as an intervention for bereaved children has not been adequately described or tested to date in a cultural context.

School-Based Interventions

Schools are an important setting for grief interventions, because children's losses, whether in (e.g., school violence) or out of school, may hurt their academic performance. "The general functions of the school social worker include identification, assessment, and resolution of social and emotional difficulties that may interfere with a child's adjustment and achievement in school" (Bluestone 1999:230). School personnel, however, are somewhat limited in how closely involved with a child's personal problems they may be permitted to become. A child requiring intensive psychotherapeutic intervention should be referred outside the school, with the social worker working with the teacher and outside therapist to manage the child's symptoms and providing supportive interventions in school (Zambelli and Clark 1994). Short-term family counseling and parent guidance in the school may be necessary to help children who are struggling with grief. Grief associated with relocation loss following immigration, moves, divorce, and changes in living environments can be addressed through practical strategies by social workers and other school personnel. These strategies include introducing students to the new school through orientation groups, forming peer support systems, helping students maintain contact with their former schools and communities, and working with teachers and parents to broaden their understanding of the children and the effects of divorce or a parent's death on their adjustment to school (Freeman 1984a). Play or art projects may help children in school express and understand their feelings (Bluestone 1999). Art teachers can create ways of helping students remember a classmate, such as making memory books, drawings, collages, and paintings. The effectiveness of school-based interventions has not been evaluated.

Interventions for Children Exposed to Specific Losses
Death of a Pet

Many families own pets and regard them as part of the family (Cain 1985). Thus the strong attachments that children, as well as persons of all ages, have to their pets often lead to strong grief and bereavement responses when they die (Sable 1995). Family members can help children grieve the death of a pet. The books listed in box 5.2 that address the death of animals may be useful to parents, teachers, or other caregivers to help children understand and talk about this loss. There has been little research on which strategies to help children grieving for a pet are best. In any case, ways of supporting children in this process usually include the following:

1. Adapt rituals from those used for human death and encourage children to create their own versions (e.g., formal burial, candle-lighting ceremony, a story written about the pet).
2. Encourage children to participate in ceremonies and allow them to choose the ways in which they would like to be involved.
3. Teach and encourage mourning by providing models for expressing feelings.
4. Help children choose appropriate mementos and photos for a memory box or other special creation.
5. Do not replace the animal too quickly, as this may create resentment or convey the message that "animal life . . . is cheap and replaceable." (Meyers 2002:256)

Responding to Traumatic Events

Children who are exposed to traumatic events, such as witnessing a murder, other forms of intimate or community violence, and catastrophic disasters, may be emotionally traumatized (Burman and Allen-Meares 1994:28). Unless children themselves are the victims of physical or sexual abuse, their psychological and emotional needs and associated grief often go unnoticed or untreated (Black and Kaplan 1988; Davis 1988; Elbow 1982; Wilson et al. 1989). Traumatic experiences are associated with posttraumatic stress disorder (PTSD), depressive disorder, separation anxiety disorder, grief reactions, complicated bereavement, and secondary adversities (Pynoos, Goenjian, and Steinberg 1998). Death from natural causes and various other childhood losses may also result in traumatic grief "if the child's subjective experience of the death [loss] is traumatic and trauma symptoms interfere with grieving" the loss (Cohen et al. 2002:307). The nature of such experiences complicates the treatment and recovery process and necessitates attention to the details and effects of the trauma (Webb 2000). Interventions in situations of trauma that treat children's bereavement only can be ineffective and even harmful (Nader and Pynoos 1993). Several interventions have been proposed to treat children's traumatic grief that rely primarily on group therapy or a combination of group and individual therapy; however, the empirical research documenting the utility of these interventions is very limited (for a review, see Cohen et al. 2002).

CHILDREN EXPOSED TO A PARENT'S HOMICIDE

Abundant anecdotal evidence suggests that for survivors, homicide is often the most distressing form of violent death. Children have both an immediate need for support following the murder of a parent and long-term needs for resolving separation distress and trauma (Rynearson 2001). Children showing complicated grief responses (e.g., phobic behaviors, insomnia and nightmares, fears of safety, school failure, irritability, and social isolation) are often referred for treatment by a responsible caregiver. Individual, family, and group work founded on the development of trust, rapport, and the creation of a safe environment with the therapist is commonly recommended (Burman and Allen-Meares 1994). These interventions use various approaches to grief work for children traumatized by the murder of a parent, including

- Play therapy using symbolic communication techniques (e.g., expressive arts, games, and photographs).
- Cognitive behavioral techniques such as role modeling and observational learning of appropriate behaviors by behavior rehearsal in groups.
- Social skills training in peer groups, open discussion of trauma through symbolic play, fantasy, art, and storytelling, as well as meetings with both the child and the caregiver to enhance understanding and communication among family members.
- Community supports, like education and support groups for parents and big brother/big sister and other mentoring programs.

Studies of the efficacy of these interventions for children bereaved by the murder of a parent are needed.

COMMUNITY-LEVEL INTERVENTIONS

A public mental health approach to address the complex needs of children suffering because of natural disaster, violence, and traumatic bereavement calls for collaborative assessment and intervention on three levels of organizations: (1) governmental and social educational, health, and mental health institutions; (2) school community; and (3) intervention teams (Pynoos, Goenjian, and Steinberg 1998). A clinical triage protocol for any disaster or violent event includes an assessment of children's trauma and loss (objective and subjective), acute difficulties, ongoing adversities, traumatic reminders, and current levels of distress. Collection of this information through screening interviews may help governmental agencies allocate resources for survivors and help clinical intervention teams best define the most vulnerable populations (Pynoos, Goenjian, and Steinberg 1998).

An empirically supported treatment approach, developed by the UCLA Trauma Psychiatry Program, addresses five domains in individual, group, family, classroom, and community intervention settings (Pynoos, Goenjian, and

Steinberg 1998): traumatic experiences, traumatic reminders, bereavement and the interplay of trauma and grief, postdisaster adversities, and developmental impact. These domains may be "addressed though the selective and integrated use of the following therapeutic modalities: (1) psycho educational approaches; (2) social skills training; (3) psychodynamic psychotherapy; (4) cognitive-behavioral therapy; (5) pharmacologic therapies; (6) educational assistance; and (7) remedial interventions to address developmental disruptions" (Pynoos, Goenjian, and Steinberg 1998:202).

Addressing cultural differences is a major premise of treatment and intervention for traumatic grief in children (Nader 1997). School and community interventions must consider culturally differing views of death, attitudes toward mental health response and intervention, styles of approaching a goal, issues of power and authority, views of outsiders, moral issues, and perspectives on victimization. For example, "After shootings on a school ground in Stockton, California, it was essential to perform a ceremony for the removal of angry dead souls before a large population of Vietnamese Buddhist children would return to school" (Nader 1997:164). Much greater attention is needed to implement culturally competent interventions to address traumatic grief in children.

Children in Foster Care

Children who require foster care have almost always been exposed to abuse, neglect, or maltreatment; have been separated from their family of origin; and commonly have experienced uncertainty and chronic forms of loss (Levine 1988; Molin 1990; Silin and Stewart 2003). Children of color may have experienced additional adversities such as the impact of racism on their self-esteem and identity formation, which should be addressed in treating their psychological well-being (Jackson and Westmoreland 1992). Foster parents themselves may need social work support and guidance in order to respond effectively to the child who is grieving while living in their home, to prepare the child for adoption placement, to give permission to the child to bond with a new family, and to address their own grief when the children leave their home (Berman 1986; McFadden 1996). Broad-based training and agency services and supports for foster families can promote family-centered practice with foster-parent families that acknowledge the chronic experiences of loss (McFadden 1996; Urquhart 1989). Interventions for foster families can take place in a variety of settings. For example, school social workers can identify and treat the traumatic losses experienced by children who are removed from their homes and enter foster care (Williams, Fanolis, and Schamess 2001). Innovations in child welfare and other community-based family services are needed to evaluate appropriate interventions to address the profound and pervasive losses experienced by both children in foster care and their birth and foster families. After they have been developed, interventions to address grief among foster children and their families need to be empirically tested.

Abused Children

Many programs and interventions have been established for the concerns and needs of abused children, but they often fail to differentiate adequately among types of maltreatment (e.g., physical, sexual, psychological); have focused on only a few child-centered outcomes, which do not measure grief symptoms (e.g., aggression, developmental deficits, social and interpersonal competence, depression, anxiety, PTSD symptoms, self-esteem); and are limited methodologically (James and Mennen 2001). Because earlier studies of abuse did not include grief symptomatology, little is known about the grief process in children experiencing different forms of maltreatment or how to help them. Clearly, protecting children and preventing abuse is the main goal, and the complex and multidimensional problems associated with abuse require multimodal, ecologically sound approaches. Interventions within this broader framework that specifically address grief reactions precipitated by abuse have yet to be identified and tested. Since play therapy methods are often recommended for work with abused and neglected children in order to permit the expression of painful emotions, play therapy considerations as they relate to issues of loss faced by abused children are briefly explored. But these and other modalities such as cognitive behavioral interventions that have been shown to be effective in treating a variety of other symptoms and problems among abused children (James and Mennen 2001) need to be empirically tested to determine their efficacy in treating grief symptomatology.

Several steps are commonly followed in using play therapy with abused children:

1. Rapport needs to be built with the child, by creating an atmosphere of safety and trust, providing a tour of the therapy room and available toy props and tools, allowing children a range of choices in their play activities, answering questions clearly, being attentive to physical distance, and making few demands.
2. A context for therapy is set by discussing with the parents, when available, what to tell children what they can expect, clarify what the child understands, and inform the parents about how they might be involved as needed.
3. Assessment includes interviewing the child and his or her family and/or caregivers and collecting data through both observation and assessment instruments suited to each situation.

4. Initial goals are set that may offer opportunities for mastery and control, providing a safe environment that fosters feelings of trust and well-being, and identifying, addressing, and achieving closure of the trauma. (Gil 1998)

The actual work of play therapy may be directive or nondirective, depending on the therapist's theoretical orientation. Selecting the appropriate toys is important, making sure that they do not over- or understimulate the child. The toys most commonly used in play therapy are toy telephones, sunglasses, feeling cards, stuffed animals, sand trays and sand miniatures, art materials, nursing bottles, dishes and utensils, medical kits, shields, capes, plastic swords, courtroom replicas, doll houses, miniature family members and animal families, and superheroes and war figures (Gil 1998). The five main categories of toys for a toy room are (1) scary toys (e.g., snakes, rats, plastic monsters, dragons, dinosaurs, alligators), (2) family and nurturing toys (e.g., doll houses, doll families, baby dolls, stuffed toys, rocking chairs), (3) aggressive toys (e.g., punching bags, plastic or rubber knives, tools for pounding such as mallets or hammers, toy soldiers, foam rubber bats); (4) expressive toys (e.g., art supplies, pipe cleaners, egg cartons, newsprint, play dough); and (5) pretend or fantasy toys (e.g., masks, hats, jewelry, purses, doctor kits, puppet theaters, sandboxes, dress-up clothes) (Seager and Spencer 1996). A discussion of the many creative play techniques available for working with bereaved children is beyond the scope of this chapter, but examples and descriptions of play techniques may be found in the following references: Hemmings 1995; Kaduson, Cangelosi, and Schaefer 1997; O'Connor 1991; O'Connor and Schaefer 1994; Schaefer and Cangelosi 1993. Further study is needed to determine the impact of play therapy techniques on the grief experience of abused children.

Summary

This chapter has presented developmentally congruent interventions that may be used with bereaved children, including communication techniques, rituals, play and play therapy, and group-, family-, and school-based interventions. Although these interventions seem to be helpful to children, only a few have been systematically evaluated in treatment outcome studies. There is some evidence that bereavement support groups, psychotherapeutic group interventions, and family-based interventions may help bereaved children. But these studies are in their infancy, and their inconsistent study methodologies, samples, and intervention protocols limit drawing definitive conclusions.

Compared with the many other forms of loss experienced in childhood, most empirical attention has been given to group- and family-based interventions for children who have experienced a death in the family. This chapter offered practice principles and recommended strategies for specific interventions (e.g., play therapy, rituals) and to help children with grief associated with specific losses (e.g., a pet's death, traumatic events, foster care, and child abuse). Nevertheless, we do not know which are the most efficacious. Interventions to meet the needs of children experiencing profound loss must be developed and tested. Interventions by school social workers, child welfare workers, and other human service professionals to address grief associated with childhood violence and trauma are urgently needed. To date, there have been no studies of the cultural congruence of interventions and cultural variation in outcomes, and interventions cannot be assumed to work equally well across populations.

6

Grief and Loss in Adolescence

UNDERSTANDING ADOLESCENTS' experience of loss, like that of children, requires a knowledge of their developmental phases and transitions. Adolescence is a time of paradox: in order to establish emotional connections with others and to work in collective endeavors, adolescents first must separate themselves emotionally from their loved ones. Teenagers' struggles with parents, teachers, other authority figures, and even peers represent their efforts to gain a sense of individuality and competence. By early adulthood they also must acquire a sense of self-coherence so that they can join others, particularly in intimate committed relationships (Balk and Corr 2001). Grief is a time of paradox as well. The bereaved generally must be able to express anger, resentment, and ambivalence before they can reconnect with others. Given teenagers' paradoxical developmental tasks, it is not surprising that their grieving process is complex.

This chapter reviews the primary developmental considerations of adolescence, defined chronologically as roughly ages ten through twenty-two. Although the term *teenager* is used interchangeably with *adolescent*, adolescence actually extends beyond the teenage years into the early twenties. This chapter discusses the losses associated with a parent's death or divorce/separation; the death of a sibling and/or a friend, especially death from suicide or violence; and abortion or miscarriage.

Non-Western cultures generally have distinctive rites or rituals marking the transition to adolescence, such as bar or bat mitzvahs for Jewish teens; indeed, Western cultures' lack of rituals marking the entry to adolescence may underlie some of teens' turbulence. According to a resilience model of development and loss, adolescence is a period when background characteristics and individual capacities are at the forefront. Positive social, family, community, and cultural capacities also are needed as protective factors to ensure a successful transition to young adulthood. Such social supports are especially important when adolescents confront the loneliness and unpredictability of grief.

Developmental Considerations

According to Erik Erikson (1963), individuation and separation are the primary developmental tasks of adolescence. But he constructed his models of adolescent development from samples of white males, so they do not take account of differences in ethnic minority status or gender. For example, girls and adolescents in many non-Western cultures define themselves in relation to others. Although we recognize these differences in gender and culture, we have based our discussion largely on research on the predominant models of adolescent development that focus on individuation. But because of the models' limitations, we encourage readers to be sensitive in their practice to gender and cultural differences among adolescents.

Within Erikson's overarching task, adolescents also need to

- Develop a stable sense of personal identity or self-concept, including a racial and sexual orientation.
- Separate from their family.
- Form appropriate and satisfying relationships with peers.
- Begin to think about their future career choices.

Grieving may create a double crisis in which situational considerations overlay and, to some extent, parallel normal developmental challenges. For bereaved adolescents, experiences involving protest/searching and disorganization/reorganization are often intertwined with the normal developmental tasks of achieving mastery or competence, intimacy, and emotional separation from their parents. At times, it may be unclear which aspects of adolescent grieving emerge from development and which from bereavement (Corr 2000; Corr, Nabe, and Corr 2003). What is clear is that the developmental challenges of adolescence, which are inherently difficult, become even more so when teens are confronted with a major loss.

Early Adolescence: Ages Ten Through Fourteen

Beginning with the onset of puberty, early adolescents begin the shift from concrete operational thinking to formal operational or logical thinking. They learn how to abstract from concrete experiences and to think reflectively. At the same time, they are grappling with the onset of biological sexuality (e.g., "raging hormones"), the physical growth of their bodies, and numerous psycho-social and emotional tasks. One of the main psychosocial challenges is separating emotionally and physically from their parents and other family members and joining a mixed peer group, experimenting with adult behavior and rules, and expanding their geographic territory for experiences (Fleming and Adolph 1986). The mainstream U.S. culture's high value placed on independence and separation from family differs from that of other cultures, such as Asian cultures in which family and community have traditionally been more important than the individual.

Early adolescence is characterized by an unpredictable mix of pulling away from the family, refusing to participate in a family outing, sitting on a parent's lap, screaming at a parent in response to discipline, wanting to be "cool" and hanging out with friends, hugging a parent and expressing love, and being absorbed in instant messaging—all in the span of one hour! Such rapidly fluctuating behavior represents the work of forging an identity. Doing so requires adolescents to regress temporarily to an earlier and more comfortable developmental phase while also forming their own intellectual ideas and identifying with people outside their immediate families as models of behavior and morality. They discover new and powerful emotions when they temporarily resort to childhood anger and fascination with hero figures, and parents and other adult authority figures are left wondering how such tumultuous behavior can eventually produce a mature young adult.

Recent research on the brain identifies physiological causes for some of these inexplicable and intense emotional outbursts. The prefrontal cortex is the most advanced part of the brain, where the most sophisticated of our abilities reside. This part of the brain controls emotions, restrains impulses, and makes rational decisions but in early adolescence has not yet developed. In fact, this part of the brain generally does not develop fully until age twenty (Bradley 2003). Adolescents who alternate between expressing love and hatred toward caregiving parents may, to a certain extent, be unable to control their emotions. Both family members and professionals can benefit from learning more about how structural changes in teenagers' brains may affect their grieving process.

An important developmental task is thus to integrate into a unique self-identity and self-definition this emerging sexuality, desire for self-determination and dependency, and development of cognitive abilities and ethical awareness. For the first time, adolescents get a glimpse of who they are and who they might be and become aware of the dialectic between being and not being (Kastenbaum 1986a). But even though adolescents' sense of the future is sharpened, it rarely includes thoughts of dying or being separated from loved ones. Instead, adolescents tend to view themselves as immortal, especially when compared with the adults in their lives. This belief commonly results in the risk-seeking behavior that terrifies their parents and in higher accident rates than those of other age groups. Because of their feeling of invulnerability, adolescents also vary markedly in their recognition of the potential for loss.

Middle Adolescence: Ages Fifteen Through Seventeen

Middle adolescents begin to organize and integrate their early experiences of separating from their parents, continue to experiment with "possible selves" or alternative self-concepts, and begin to forge a distinctive, mature identity. In some ways, they undergo a second individuation or separation process, fluctuating between independence and dependence in order to achieve competence/mastery/control. They can become personally or individually resourceful by reorganizing the values internalized from their parents, overcoming the egocentrism of childhood and early adolescence, and deciding on future roles and responsibilities (Corr, Nabe, and Corr 2003). A greater distance from their family of origin makes adolescents better able to make long-term commitments to other people and goals. As suggested earlier, the value placed by some cultures on loyalty to one's family of origin can conflict with the mainstream society's pressures to become independent. Middle adolescents' advanced cognitive abilities allow them to take apart ideas, put them back together in new ways, examine both possibilities and realities, and build entire systems of thought. Adolescence is indeed a time of questioning, arguing, and continually debating with peers, parents, and other authority figures. Finally, as adolescents' cognitive abilities develop, so does their moral awareness.

Late Adolescence: Ages Eighteen to Twenty-two

Late adolescence marks the closure of the second individuation process and a shift toward independent thinking, principled reasoning, and awareness of one's own value and legitimation apart from that imposed by society. Another task in late adolescence is the attainment of personal strength by dealing successfully with traumatic life events (Corr, Nabe, and Corr 2003). This typically requires grappling with the meaning of life and death. In doing so, adolescents can emerge with a philosophical, spiritual, and/or religious stance that promotes optimism for the future and a reason to continue living. Their ethics and values are clarified in the dialogues and intense arguments characteristic of adolescence. Even when adolescents engage in high-risk behavior, they still value life. They have completed their physical maturation and are better able to control the surges of their sexual feelings, strong emotions, and newfound adult social skills and abilities.

Achieving intimacy and commitment in sexual and social relations, which involve conflicts between closeness and distance, is a primary challenge of late adolescence. Although U.S. culture does not clearly acknowledge the end of adolescence, as some other cultures do, adolescents' separation from home and financial independence are often thought to mark the shift to young adulthood. Now, however, in most Western societies such financial and familial independence is more difficult to attain, with the growing numbers of late adolescents and young adults who cannot afford to move out of their family's home because of high unemployment and living costs. In addition, some adults remain adolescents developmentally: they are ambivalent about accepting responsibility, forging a separate identity, and sustaining interpersonal intimacy (Balk and Corr 2001). Others are affected by earlier traumatic events, substance abuse, or eating disorders that interfere with their later emotional development.

The phases of adolescent development and the tasks and conflicts associated with each phase suggest some of the issues that bereaved adolescents must confront. One model identifies five issues that adolescents must address cognitively, affectively, and behaviorally:

1. Trusting the predictability of events.
2. Gaining a sense of mastery and control.
3. Forging relationships marked by belonging.
4. Believing the world is fair and just.
5. Developing a confident self-image. (Balk and Corr 2001; Fleming and Adolph 1986)

This model is a useful referent for our later discussion of different types of adolescent loss.

Adolescents' Grief

Adolescents' grief typically is manifested as confusion, crying, feelings of emptiness and/or loneliness, sleep and eating disturbances, and exhaustion. Because of their egocentrism, adolescents are likely to think that their grief is unique and incomprehensible to both themselves and others. As a result, they may express their grief only in short outbursts, or they may try to suppress it because they do not want to be perceived by others as emotionally out of control. The adolescent grieving process usually does not mirror adult mourning but more closely resembles that of childhood. Adolescent bereavement tends to be simultaneously continuous and intermittent, encompassing grief that comes and goes through-out an overall extended process. The grief may become complicated if the adoles-cent has ambivalent relationships with the deceased or other survivors or idealizes the deceased, or if society does not acknowledge the relationship and grief. The intense, somewhat transitory quality of adolescent feelings, the desire to fit in and not be different from peers, or the lack of support from peers or adults may also complicate the grief process. Alternatively, grieving may foster resilience and positive outcomes, such as greater emotional and interpersonal maturity (Corr, Nabe, and Corr 2003).

Resilience

Teenagers bring the following personal, family and community capacities to their grieving process.

BACKGROUND CHARACTERISTICS

Perhaps the most significant background characteristic for adolescents is socio-economic status, which affects the personal and social capacities that they bring to grieving their loss. Low socioeconomic status, for example, is found to account for some of adolescents' long-term problems resulting from their parents' divorce. A history of psychological problems and the amount of economic stress that adolescents experienced earlier in their lives also affects how they deal with the significant losses of a parent's death or a divorce (Buchanan 2000).

PERSONAL CAPACITIES

Expanded *cognitive skills* such as the greater ability to think abstractly, anticipate future events, construct hypotheses, and evaluate consequences affect how ado-lescents, compared with children, deal with loss. Although adolescents some-times demonstrate very poor problem-solving capabilities, these generally are better than children's. For example, if a widowed or divorced parent is unable to manage daily household tasks, adolescents are able to take care of themselves and other family members, even though they may resent having to do so.

Self-concept is a key individual capacity in adolescent bereavement. High self-concept scores are associated with less depression, fear, loneliness, confusion, and intensity of grief; average self-concept scores, with more depression, lone-liness, and anger; and low self-concept scores, with more confusion. Similarly, greater developmental maturity is found to be associated with greater but rela-tively transient psychological distress (Balk 1990; Corr, Nabe, and Corr 2003; Hogan and Greenfield 1991). Most teens are struggling to resolve self-esteem and identity issues associated with gender, sexual orientation, and racial or ethnic identification, with girls especially vulnerable to a loss of self-esteem as they enter adolescence. A major loss thus can interfere with these efforts to achieve self-esteem.

As they confront questions about life and death, some adolescents are able to draw on religiosity and spirituality. In one study, 76 percent of adolescents were found to believe in God; 29 percent believed that they had experienced the presence of God; 42 percent prayed frequently; and 50 percent reported attending religious services in the previous seven days (Gallup and Lindsay 1999). Such spiritual beliefs and practices are found to be associated with positive social behaviors and values (Donahue and Benson 1995).

SOCIAL CAPACITIES

How adults treat adolescents affects both the extent to which they complete necessary developmental challenges as well as how they grieve. Family, community, and cultural capacities differ in the degree of positive and respectful social supports, such as mentors and others who provide constructive learning experiences for mastering adult tasks and achieving personally significant goals. Unfortunately, adolescents' erratic and often aversive behavior can result in adults, especially parents, withdrawing from them. Some parents, particularly those exhausted by grief, may give up on their adolescents, at precisely the time when they most need positive social supports and structures. Without these supports, it is less likely that painful life changes will lead to growth and development.

A strong relationship with at least one parent, positive relationships with siblings, family coherence, and low levels of family conflict can help teens express their opinions and feelings and reduce the likelihood of depression. In some instances, however, it may be adaptive for adolescents to distance themselves from their grieving family. Their ability to return eventually to a relatively stable family appears to be most important (Fleming and Balmer 1996).

The ability to talk with friends about their grief and perceived social support also help determine the outcome of adolescents' bereavement process (Corr, Nabe, and Corr 2003). Schools and peer groups are important sources of support, especially since teens may withdraw from their family or their preoccupied parents may be unable to provide support. Peers, however, may not know what to say or do, which can leave the teen feeling isolated from past sources of support. In such instances, teachers, counselors, religious figures, and other nonparental adults may be able to offset, to some extent, erratic or inadequate parenting and friends' withdrawal or silence.

Death of a Parent

Adolescents face the normal developmental task of cutting parental ties based on relationships of dependence and revising them based on relationships of equality. A parent's death can seriously disrupt this process of emotional emancipation, creating feelings of chaos and uncertainty. Although a major task of adolescence is separation and individuation from parents, a parent's death makes that separation complete, final, irreversible, and frequently sudden and unanticipated. Even while teens are separating, they also need the stability of the parent to come back to periodically, and death ends that stability. As a result, adolescents may feel unsafe and abandoned by a parent's death (Corr, Nabe, and Corr 2003; Tyson-Rawson 1996).

Adolescents also are beginning to struggle with more existential life issues, such as "why me?" or "why do bad things happen to good people?" Feeling that life is unfair to them, they may display anger in their search for meaning (Cohen et al. 2002). In addition, adolescence is a period of intense self-examination, with adolescents often rejecting their parents' controls over their life. When a parent dies, they face the need to try to gain more control over their life just when their emotions appear to be running away from them (Elders 1995). They may test their own mortality through risk-taking behavior or protest the death by withdrawing emotionally (Emswiler and Emswiler 2000). Because the entrance into adolescence and puberty is so disquieting, both professionals and families may have difficulty differentiating grief reactions from those related to developmental changes.

Early adolescents can understand cognitively the full implications of a parent's death but have more difficulty managing their emotions regarding the loss (Christ 2000; Christ, Siegel, and Christ 2002). Adolescents' need to withdraw their emotional investment in their parents directly conflicts with the family's needs for emotional closeness and support as they confront a loss. Early adolescents, particularly, tend to assert their need for privacy, want to avoid disturbing information and feelings, and have an egocentric worldview. In fact, their wish to deny painful feelings can be exhibited as an adamant optimism that everything will be all right, even when their sense of reality has been shattered by a parent's death. Adolescents' emotions tend to become displaced to other situations, with their sometimes exhibiting more sadness over a low grade in school or peer rejection than their parent's absence. Because they understand the permanence of death and, to some degree, its impact on their future, they may develop the profound sadness, sleep and appetite problems, and difficulty concentrating that is typical of adult bereavement. Despite their tendency to deny painful feelings, adolescents often report dreaming about their deceased parent and feeling his or her presence (Christ 2000; Christ, Siegel, and Christ 2002; Cohen et al. 2002).

Adolescents' peer group is typically more important than their family, although it is not necessarily a source of emotional support or a place in which to express painful feelings. Some teens experience more difficulties getting along with peers, especially if their friends are unable or unwilling to discuss the parent's death (Balk and Vesta 1998; Tyson-Rawson 1993). Because of the importance of "fitting in" with the peer group, the sense of difference created by a parent's death can create isolation, even though adolescents long for their friends' support. Simply "hanging out" with their peers can be a source of comfort, however.

In a study of children and youth whose parents had died of cancer, adolescents exhibited more emotional and behavioral problems than did younger children. These problems were varied: mild depression, anxiety, fear, acting out, testing limits, anger, emotional withdrawal, weight gain, stubbornness, and rebellion. In some cases, such problematic behaviors represent an exacerbation of already existing difficulties. In others, they may be a reaction to secondary stressors that develop after a death (e.g., the adolescent's greater responsibility to perform household chores or earn money, a parent's preoccupation with his or her own sadness, or a parent's absence due to employment) (Christ 2000). A parent's death may represent the ultimate unpredictability for adolescents seeking security, which causes even more anxiety and fearfulness (Worden 1996:90).

Older adolescents typically mourn in a more adult manner and are better able to see a death from another's perspective, not just their own. This means that they are generally able to express empathy to the surviving parent and siblings, although this ability to be sensitive to others' needs fluctuates with self-centered or egocentric thinking. Some late adolescents who suffer a major loss may develop deeper and more intimate relationships with peers, having learned what is really important in life. Some may consider themselves more mature than their peers, although this may be compensatory behavior. Others may face more difficulties getting along with their peers as they struggle to gain a sense of belonging now that they are "different" because of a parent's absence (Balk and Coor 2001).

A parent's death can impede the adolescent's developmental task of emotional withdrawal and separation from the family. If in their grief, younger adolescents regress to earlier behavior, the separation process may be slowed. In contrast, an older adolescent may become a surrogate parent to younger siblings and be unable to separate, interfering with the normal developmental tasks to plan for college, employment, and the future. Instead, these adolescents may be fearful about the future, especially when the family's finances have been abruptly reduced or the grieving parent is unable to function effectively. If they feel the need to protect and care for the surviving parent and other siblings, their development will be interrupted, and they will be caught in the role of family caregiver and unable to leave the family home for extended time periods. Such surrogate parenting is found in all cultures but may be more common where adolescent daughters have caregiving responsibilities. Even if adolescents do not become surrogate parents, they still must renegotiate a new relationship with the surviving parent and siblings, and in doing so, they may displace their anger and sadness to the single parent. In addition, how they express their feelings is likely to differ markedly from their parent's grief process. At the same time, they need to alter their relationship with the deceased parent and to find their independence and autonomy in school, work, friendships, peer-group activities, and other activities outside the home.

The family's, community's (e.g., the peer group, teachers, religious figures, and other adults), and culture's social capacities determine an effective grieving process, even as the adolescent may try to push them away. If the people in these social networks do not understand the distinctive developmental tasks of adolescence, they are less likely to support and understand the distinctive ways in which teens express their grief, help them construct a positive memory of the absent parent, and reconfigure family relationships without the other parent's daily presence. As noted earlier, many parents who are enmeshed in their own grief may not have the energy or internal strength to provide such consistent assistance. Other adult family members, counselors, religious institutions, and school and community associations may be able to support the adolescent through this emotionally complicated transition.

Death of a Sibling

The impact of a sibling's death tends to be underestimated by family, friends, and our culture, especially since support systems usually focus on the parent who is grieving the loss of a child. Yet siblings lose both a lifelong companion and a rival, along with a distinctive relationship shared by no other family member. For an adolescent, the death of a sibling can be especially distressful, both psychologically (depression and anxiety are more common among older adolescents) and physiologically (more characteristic of younger adolescents, who may develop a somatic illness, headaches, or health problems after a sibling's death) (Robinson and Mahon 1997). If the adolescent's self-concept is harmed, it can have long-term negative outcomes for his or her self-image, risk-taking sexual behavior, and physical aggression (Perlotto 2001; Worden 1996). The closer the sibling relationship is—the more their life space was shared—the greater the grieving sibling's loss of identity will be. In fact, grief tends to be more intense when the sibling relationship has been either very positive or very negative, for example, conflictual or distant (Riches and Dawson 2000).

Issues of growth, sexual maturation, independence, and identity form the background against which adolescents try to make sense of their sibling's death. Their grief also is affected by the way in which the sibling died (e.g., an anticipated or sudden death or suicide), the quality of the family's relationships and life stage, and the adolescents' own sense of self (Black 1996). Traumatic death is found to have the most negative impact on the surviving siblings. For example, if the sibling was murdered, the surviving siblings are more likely to show symptoms of depression, anxiety, and posttraumatic stress disorder (PTSD) than they are if the death was anticipated (Freeman, Shaffer, and Smith 1996). But regardless of the relationship or nature of the death, siblings are confronted with the stark reality that a life has ended, often abruptly, and with unanticipated and profound questions of meaning (Corr and Corr 1996). The resolution of sibling grief depends to some extent on whether the survivor relied on the deceased sibling for a sense of structure and purpose (Hogan and DeSantis 1996). For some, the deceased sibling may have been their best friend and confidant, the vital link in the family, a role model, or even a surrogate parent. For others, seeking to be different from a sibling may have been central to their self-identity (Fanos 1996). Regardless of the particular role configuration, the special relationship between siblings can never be replaced, even when parents conceive or adopt other children or the surviving children later have their own children. Although bereaved parents may view such grandchildren as "replacements" for their dead child, most surviving young adult siblings deeply miss their brother or sister throughout their life.

Bereaved parents, especially those who have been emotionally depleted and physically exhausted by caring for a sick child, need time alone, even though their surviving children may have even more need for their emotional time and support. These conflicting needs can result in adolescents' feeling abandoned and alone. The family system's ability to provide full access to information and opportunities to share feelings and to make sense of the loss are important to adolescents grieving a sibling's death (Black 1996; Bradach and Jordon 1995; Rubin 1996). Including adolescents in events, explaining to them what is happening, and reassuring them about their role in the death and in the family are crucial. Such communications can come from parents or others who are close to the adolescent, such as grandparents, family friends, or other members of the family support system (Davies 1991, 1993). Perhaps, with good intentions, parents try to shield their adolescent from knowledge and discussion of the death. For example, in cases of terminal illness, some adults may believe that siblings should be shielded from hospital visits, the prognosis, and information about the disease so that they will not be left with recent memories of the ill sibling. But when adolescents do not have accurate information, they tend to replace it with even worse imagined scenarios.

Because of disruptions in the family system and the focus on the grieving parents' well-being, teenage siblings' emotional needs after a death are often unmet. Writer Laura Wexler expressed the psychological absence of her parents, four years after her sister's death:

> It's hard to worry about your own grief when your parents are not parental anymore. My mother, who probably told me when to take my first breath and how long it should last, abruptly withdrew from being an overbearing presence in my life. She never left me completely, but there were enough times when she'd look down and at her feet and say quietly—not in the abrasive voice I grew up hearing—"Laura, I just can't take this right now. I'm lucky if I can get up in the morning." Just as I wanted my old self, my old world back, I wanted a mother I could fight with. (McCracken and Semel 1998:156)

Another sibling observed, "I think I felt more grief at losing my mother than losing my brother. Her hair went from jet black to grey in just one month. It's been twelve years since my brother died and my mother is just coming back" (McCracken and Semel 1998:157). Siblings thus may experience a "double loss"—of the relationship with their dead sibling and that with their parents who are preoccupied and immersed in grief and lack the energy to function as parents to their surviving children (Fanos 1996; McCown and Davies 1995).

Adolescent siblings often become the "forgotten mourners" (Hindmarch 1995) or the "passive spectators" (Rubin 1996). This can be especially problematic, since teenagers typically lack the life experience and insights to know that they can survive this loss (Riches and Dawson 2000). They may feel loneliness, alienation, denial, and confusion combined with anger, detachment, resentment, powerlessness, and rivalry (Brown 1999). Accordingly, they may be reluctant to confront the pain and reflect on what their sibling's death means to them. Adolescents may be embarrassed or uncomfortable about being open with their parents, or they may try to be brave and strong by hiding their own grief to protect their parents or other family members. Likewise, well-meaning parents may try to shelter the sibling from their pain, which can result in adolescents' feeling excluded at a time when they may most want or need to be included. Conspiracies of silence, mutual resentments, guilt, overprotection, or exclusion from information all can increase teenage siblings' vulnerability to later difficulties, including depression (Black 1996). Unfortunately, if grieving adolescents are unable to talk about the sibling's death and its consequences in order to begin to construct its meaning for themselves, they risk "lingering grief" and "unfinished" business going into adulthood and beyond (Lewis and Schonfeld 1994). Surviving siblings may be left with feelings of emptiness and yearning, guilt for surviving and for not protecting their sibling, and anger at their parents' comparing them with the often idealized image of the dead sibling.

Some parents place an intolerable emotional burden on the surviving siblings, keeping them close, and asking them to step into the role of or become like the idealized deceased sibling. This then hinders the siblings' ability to achieve a sense of personal independence, which is an important developmental task in adolescence (Pettle and Britten 1995). The deceased child may be regarded, either implicitly or explicitly, more positively than the living children: idealized, seen as perfect, and memorialized (Fanos 1996). Studies of war deaths have found that parents' positive evaluation, investment, and involvement with dead sons were disproportionately elevated for many years and at considerable cost to their relationships with their other children (Rubin 1996). Adolescents may feel that they can never "be enough" or special in the family when compared unfavorably with the deceased sibling (Davis 1993). Such teens may become "prematurely mature," in which their own grief reactions are subordinated to their increased responsibility for their parents' emotional care and practical household help (Hindmarch 1995; Stahlman 1996). Some bereaved parents, fearing another loss, may become overly protective, even when their children become adults, thus stifling their necessary advance to independence. Ironically, the people on whom children and teens are most likely to depend for successful adaptation to the sibling's death are themselves least emotionally equipped to recognize or deal with the needs of their surviving offspring.

Regardless of age, bereavement is a "social network crisis" and may be even more so for adolescents who are enmeshed in peer groups and preoccupied with school and other support networks outside the family (Hogan and DeSantis 1994). Younger adolescents, not wanting to be seen as different, are less likely to talk about their sibling's death with their peers and are more likely to have problems with forging relationships and achieving a sense of belonging than are older siblings. Not surprisingly, this may increase their vulnerability to psychosomatic symptoms such as headaches and stomach pains. Later adolescents, who tend to be more mature, are less likely to use denial but also may feel more psychological stress, lower self-esteem, more depressive symptoms, and more anger about their sibling's death, especially if he or she was younger (Riches and Dawson 2000).

As noted earlier, the grieving parents' role is pivotal in helping the adolescent siblings' grief process. In instances of undiluted parental grief, in which the parents withdraw into their own loneliness and preoccupation with the lost relationship, teens lose the support of previous family routines. This occurs most often in instances of traumatic death, such as accidents, suicide, or homicide (Bradach and Jordan 1995). When parents are unable to support their surviving children in their open grieving, the children's grief and resentment can create a permanent "wound" in the family (Rubin 1996). Teenagers may be overly concerned with their own health and safety, anxious that they too could cause their parents such pain, and fearful of their parents' death. Families who produce resilient sibling survivors are close, cohesive, and open to differences in one another's grief reactions. They encourage each member to contribute to their collective understanding of how the family as a whole is affected by this loss. Under such conditions, the family members' grief processes are seen as mutually supportive (Riches and Dawson 2000).

When family, community, and cultural capacities support the adolescent siblings' grief in the family's changed configuration, the surviving siblings may discover optimism, maturity, spirituality, and a positive self-identity: all individual capacities inherent in resilience (Case 2001; Hogan and DeSantis 1996). Even when bereaved teens' self-image suffers, and they perceive their conduct and academic performance to be inferior, they still consider themselves to be more mature as a result of this painful experience (Worden 1996). Teens who move through their grief are able to recognize the irreversibility of the loss and realize the need to "get a grip" on their lives. A growing sense of personal control arises when having to "forage" for an identity in the new landscape in which the deceased sibling no longer exists. These challenges may cause a shift from focusing largely on themselves to a greater awareness and appreciation of others (Oltjenbruns 1991). In their search for meaning, adolescents may construct "inner representations" and internal conversations with their deceased sibling, asking for advice, catching up on news, and using this inner representation to guide their behavior. An ability to create this "invisible presence," a sense of spirituality, and a belief that the siblings might one day be reunited also appear to be critical to moving from vulnerability to resilience. Over time, the connection with the deceased sibling changes and capacities develop for new relationships, typically through marriage or parenthood (Hogan and DeSantis 1996).

Divorce of Parents

Divorce, which often occurs when the children reach adolescence, results in multiple losses: those of the family structure, the image of the parents as a couple, the school or home due to relocation, and the parents when they are distracted by financial worries or searching for new lovers or partners. Many teens feel abandoned and ignored during their parents' divorce (Wallerstein, Lewis, and Blakeslee 2000). Adolescents also lose their belief that teenagers should leave their parents, not the other way. Because of teenagers' emerging awareness of the adult world, they may be suddenly propelled into examining their own relationships and wondering on what and whom they can rely and for how long. Enduring their parents' divorce can raise adolescents' anxiety about whether they can make and sustain close relationships in the future and be happy (Smith 1999). Even though teens may acknowledge the problems in their parents' marriage and discuss them with others, adolescents rarely believe that their parents will actually separate, nor do they fully grasp the reality of what a divorce will mean for them. When violence is the cause of the divorce, it often is not discussed with either parent.

Adolescents typically are angry with their parents, especially with the parent who initiated the divorce, which may intensify their developmentally appropriate conflicts with him or her. In response, teens may act even more impulsively, engaging in high-risk behavior, sexual promiscuity, or drug or alcohol abuse as a way to deaden their feelings. If they feel that their parents are disengaged or unpredictable, the adolescents' peer group becomes the main source of their support. Boys are likely to act out, and adolescent girls often react with depression. In addition, girls who have difficulty managing their emotions may move rapidly in and out of sexually promiscuous and perhaps abusive relationships (Hetherington and Kelly 2002; Wallerstein, Lewis, and Blakeslee 2000).

The critical variable in family and social supports appears to be not family structure (one or two parents) but an authoritarian parenting style. Although this may seem contradictory, such a style is characterized by warmth, affection, firmness, parental involvement and supervision, and the children's participation in making rules and decisions. Two-parent families tend to be more authoritarian (e.g., responsive and involved but firm), less permissive, and less neglectful than single-parent families, regardless of social class or ethnic minority status. In many instances, single parents lack the energy, time, and inner strength to maintain a consistent authoritarian style. The less effective parenting found to be characteristic of some single parents is often referred to as *diminished parenting* and can affect the behavior problems often seen in adolescents in the two years following the divorce. This does not mean that single-parent families lack the capacity to maintain a positive parenting style but that they may face structural obstacles in doing so, such as reduced financial resources, long hours at work, and increased stress from managing on their own. Although peers may provide some support, other responsive, involved adult role models can better offset the loss of parental engagement (Avenevoli, Sessa, and Steinberg 1999; Buchanan 2000; Hetherington and Kelly 2002). Conversely, a coercive or punitive parenting style can diminish an adolescent's social competence, resulting in aggression, dependency, and anxiety or withdrawal (Buchanan 2000; Buchanan, Maccoby, and Dornbusch 1996).

Both parents' continued engagement, emotional closeness, and extent of management and control offset some of the disruption created by divorce. The amount of conflict between the parents and how they handle it is another predictor of adolescents' adjustment to divorce. Outcomes of the divorce can be relatively positive for adolescents when a good relationship between parent and child and effective parenting are maintained and when the parents minimize their conflicted interactions so that the children can remain close to both. Opportunities for teens to spend substantial time with both mother and father and the parents being on relatively good terms can also have positive effects.

Death of a Peer or Friend

Although the number of adolescents who have lost a peer through death is estimated to be as high as 90 percent, the grief associated with a friend's death has been rarely studied and may be discounted by others (e.g., disenfranchised grief) (Oltjenbruns 1996). Nearly 74 percent of all deaths of American adolescents are caused by accidents, homicide, or suicide, which are associated with trauma and violence and are, to some extent, preventable (Corr, Nabe, and Corr 2003; Hoyert et al. 2001). In fact, automobile accidents are the main killer of teenage boys, with murder the second leading cause of death. The homicide rate is, furthermore, eight times higher for African American than for Caucasian adolescent males (Doka 1996).

Youth homicide rates are higher in the United States than in any other country. Racial and social class inequities mean that certain adolescent populations are at high risk of homicide, especially African American, Native American, and Latino teens in inner cities, which often are referred to as "war zones" (Corr, Nabe, and Corr 2003; Garbarino and Kostelny 1997). But the dramatic increase in random shootings in schools and other public settings once considered safe now means that all teenagers are at a greater risk of violent death (Doka 2003). One study of urban and suburban youth found that more than 45 percent of them had witnessed a shooting, stabbing, or other serious act of violence during the previous year (O'Keefe 1997). According to a national survey of adolescents, 23 percent reported being both a victim of assault and a witness to violence (Saltzman et al. 2001).

Whether or not they are physically injured by violence, adolescents carry with them lasting emotional scars from having been exposed to chronic threat. It affects not only their development but also their worldview and their capacity to learn, to establish relationships, and to deal with other losses (Groves and Zuckerman 1997; Jenkins and Bell 1997). Even adolescents who are not directly exposed to violence are surrounded by images of violent death in the media, the Internet, advertising, video games, and their communities.

Despite the pervasiveness of violence in U.S. society, most adolescents are not prepared for a peer's death. The nature of homicide, suicide, and accidents means that adolescents often must confront death without any advance warning or time for preparation. What may have seemed to happen only "in those other schools or neighborhoods," on TV, or in the news is now starkly real and personal. There is no time to prepare for the separation or to say good-bye. A friend's sudden death personifies the inability to predict or control the future. Because many adolescents live in the moment, they do not acknowledge personal threats associated with more distant death. But when someone just like them dies, adolescents' fantasies of immortality are suddenly ripped asunder. Not only are they forced to confront the possibility of their own death, but a peer's death also calls into question the logic of the natural order, challenges God's existence, and violates their ideals of fairness, justice, and goodness (Balk and Coor 2001). A friend's death also interferes with the middle adolescent tasks of achieving competence, mastery, and control at a time when they have been enjoying some sense of autonomy (Corr, Nabe, and Corr 2003). Feelings of helplessness and that nothing seems real are common and can be intensified when the relationship contains unfinished business, which is characteristic of most adolescent friendships (Worden 2002).

Teens can be profoundly affected by a peer's death, even if he or she was just an acquaintance or a face in the school hallways, because of its threat to their own mortality. It is terrifying for adolescents to realize that someone their own age, whom they know, can die or, in the case of suicide, choose to die. In addition to their friend's death, another loss is that of the world they knew and trusted, that is, the loss of innocence of their childhood as they are awakened to their own mortality. In addition, the publicity surrounding violent deaths, such as homicides, and the involvement of medical and legal authorities can heighten the unreality and abnormality of the loss (Worden 2002). When death occurs under violent circumstances, adolescents are more likely to have intrusive, distressing memories and emotions, and numbed responsiveness that can disrupt their grieving (Saltzman et al. 2001). Traumatic deaths that people cause or help to bring on themselves or others may have long-term implications for adolescents' developmental tasks of individuation. Their sense of competence and intimacy may be threatened by remorse from carelessness leading to an accidental death, guilt from a perceived failure to prevent a friend's suicide, or anxiety regarding a homicide in their neighborhood (Corr, Nabe, and Corr 2003).

Teenagers often have difficulty talking about a friend's death and hide their anger, distress, and confusion from their parents and other adults. This is most common in male adolescents, who are struggling with when and how to express their feelings and images of "toughness." Guilt is a common reaction to a sudden death, with survivors dwelling on "if only" they had taken some action that might have prevented the death (Worden 2002). Some teens suffer from survivor's guilt, especially if they also were involved in the car accident or the climbing fall and managed to survive. Whereas some adolescents find religion to be helpful, others are angry with God or a supreme being and religious institutions. Nevertheless, as they ask questions and talk about a peer's death, they are performing the spiritual task of making meaning from the loss. Their lives are generally profoundly changed by a friend's death. As with the loss of a parent, bereaved friends may experience secondary losses, such as estrangement from or loss of other friends, and may have difficulties in forming new intimate relationships. The death of a friend is a form of disenfranchised grief, which tends to minimize the loss of a friend compared with that of biological family members (Oltjenbruns 1996). Nevertheless, some teens bereaved by a peer's death reach positive outcomes over time, such as gaining a deeper appreciation of life and improving their problem-solving abilities, communication skills, and emotional strength. One study found that when a friend was lost in war, bereaved adolescents and young adults were actually emotionally healthier than normal nonbereaved individuals, in part because of the meaning that they constructed out of the war-related death (Balk and Coor 2001).

Suicide is the third leading cause of death among adolescents and young adults, after motor vehicle accidents and homicides. In fact, teen suicide rates currently are about three times as high as they were in the 1950s (Riches and Dawson 2000). A peer's death by suicide is especially threatening, because it is self-inflicted and often violent and taps into the adolescent survivors' fears about the future and capacity to manage appropriately young adulthood tasks such as intimacy and self-reliance. It also can interfere with the central developmental task of searching for and achieving a self-identity (Berman and Jones 1995; Martin 2000). Their inability to comprehend the fact of death may be increased by the unexpected, arbitrary, and violent nature of suicide and the lack of a rational explanation. By choosing suicide, the peer has implied that life is not worth living, leaving their friends and acquaintances with a sense of rejection, disillusionment, and perhaps embarrassment.

Because suicide is unnatural and carries a social stigma, it can leave a legacy of shame, regret, reproach, guilt, and damaged self-image for the survivors (Range 1998). Adolescents' initial reaction to a suicide tends to be a mixture of disbelief, denial, anger, fear, relief, repulsion, shame, and guilt. Survivors may feel somehow responsible for not being able to prevent this tragic loss. Their guilt can be profound when teens knew of their peer's suicide plans and did not try to stop him or her (Worden 2002). Grief disrupts their thoughts, feelings, behaviors, and relationships, with adolescents expressing cognitive disorganization, a distortion of reality, and an idealization of the lost peer. They may feel depression, powerlessness, intense rage, a loss of faith in their personal judgment, and a lack of pleasure in their own accomplishments.

Their feelings of futility and aloneness may be intensified by the stigma attached to suicidal death by their family, the larger community, their religion, or their culture. Because of suicide's stigma, adolescents may be less likely to seek informal support or professional help for their grief (Brown 1999; Martin 2000). Teen suicides tend to become public stories, repeated over and over, which can mean that private relationships and personal emotions become public property. If past supportive relationships disappear, survivors become isolated by others' distancing behavior; communications break down when the survivors perceive such silence to be judgmental; and others mistakenly believe that not discussing the suicide is helpful to the surviving teens (Stevenson and Stevenson 1996). Survivors may feel ashamed and believe that others are negatively judging them as somehow responsible, even when they are not. All these reactions may make the grieving process associated with suicide more difficult than that with other types of death (Doka 1996; Martin 2000).

Although they may report significant severity on selected items on the PTSD Reaction Index (Brent et al. 1995; Cohen et al. 2002; Pynoos et al. 1987), the friends of adolescents who commit suicide do not necessarily experience PTSD symptoms, traumatic grief, or functional impairment. But surviving teens may themselves be at risk of suicide, either as a way to punish themselves or to join their friend or because they perceive the death as heroic (Riches and Dawson 2000). The evidence is mixed as to whether teens who are affected by a peer's suicide are more likely to take their own lives than are those who have not known a peer who died from suicide (Centers for Disease Control 1994). Nevertheless, parents, educators, and other helping professions, who typically fear a succession of suicides, may avoid gathering teens together to talk about the suicide for fear of "glorifying" it. This, however, risks creating more silence surrounding the suicide. Since teens often are afraid of their own impulses, survivors may ask, "How do I know that I wouldn't do that?" (Brown 1999; Doka 1996; Martin 2000).

In sum, grief responses to teen suicide, intensified by a strong sense of personal failure, guilt, and lack of control, tend to be prolonged and devastating, and adolescents' emotional development may be delayed compared with their grief with other types of death. With support and structure from family and other community and cultural institutions, teens may again feel hope and refocus on their own life as worth living (Balk and Coor 2001).

Adolescents as Bereaved Parents

Some adolescents face the intense grief of losing a child, whether through abortion, miscarriage, stillbirth, or relinquishment of the child for adoption. Adolescents are more likely to suffer these pregnancy-related losses than other age groups are, with 56 percent of teen pregnancies ending in birth, 30 percent in abortion, and 14 percent in miscarriage (Children's Defense Fund 2001). Adolescent pregnancies also carry more physical risks to mother and infant, including less prenatal care and higher rates of miscarriage, premature delivery, and low birth weight. Adolescent mothers are more likely than their counterparts to drop out of school, be unemployed or underemployed, receive public assistance, and have subsequent pregnancies and lower educational and financial attainment— all factors that reduce teen parents' social and community capacity to deal with loss (Pirog-Good 1995). The invisibility, isolation, and lack of support inherent in most instances of abortion, miscarriage, or relinquishment are another example of disenfranchised grief. Miscarriages and abortions may not be recognized and evoke little support, even from family members. The relinquishment of a child, though morally disapproved by some, may also be rationalized as "better for the young parents and for the child." But such rationalizations also minimize the meaning of the loss for the adolescent parents.

Abortion is the most common pregnancy-related loss in adolescence and the least understood (Gray and Lassance 2003). Because it is elective, abortion differs from other pregnancy-related issues of grief and loss. Adolescent parents have consciously decided, albeit often under stress and pressure, to terminate a pregnancy while they also are experiencing hormonal changes and dealing with issues of identity. They have had to "give something up," and their questions about what it would be like to have a child will never be answered. Instead, they have actively chosen to terminate the pregnancy, rather than being passive and allowing other factors to make the decision for them. The deliberate termination of pregnancy may magnify their sense of loss, especially if they later confront problems of infertility. They lose not only the possibility of having a child but, in many ways, also their innocence. Even when a woman believes that abortion is the only possible course of action, she may nevertheless grieve the loss of the fetus (Gray and Lassance 2003).

Abortion is an unspeakable loss that most women would prefer to forget. Although the initial surface appearance may be feelings of relief, unresolved loss from the abortion, including remorse and regret, the "what ifs" and "if onlys" can gnaw away and surface years later. An unresolved loss is often the result when other supports are unaware of the earlier loss or want it to remain hidden (Gray and Lassance 2003; Worden 2002). In Western cultures, which idealize motherhood, women who have had an abortion may feel especially isolated in their private grieving (Frost and Condon 1996). Our culture does not provide rituals or support to deal with abortion-associated losses. Because of the publicity and moral overtones surrounding abortion in our country, women grieving the loss of a child may also feel like sinners or be ostracized. In contrast, women in New Guinea who have an abortion wear a short mourning veil. In Japan, some women place a *jizo* (guardian deity of children) in a special place in a Buddhist temple ground. Sometimes the mother names the aborted baby and writes a message to it on a wooden prayer plaque. This ritual gives her an outlet for her love, grief, and pain (Gray and Lassance 2003).

In instances of miscarriage, the pregnancy may not be common knowledge, making it difficult for the young parents even to mention the loss to others. When they do, family and friends may react in a matter-of-fact manner. Others may express sympathy but feel that the loss of a child early in the pregnancy is not "real" and expect the young parents to readily resume their daily lives (i.e., return to school). Common responses to stillbirths are self-blame, fears regarding future pregnancies, and a loss of fantasies about the child (Worden 2002). Young parents are particularly vulnerable if they do not receive support (or even recognition of the loss) from family, community, religious, or health care institutions. The lack of support may be intensified if the parents are not married. (The grief associated with miscarriage and stillbirths is discussed further in chapter 8.)

Some adolescent parents make the difficult decision to give up their child for adoption. This decision, which may be made away from family, friends, or the partner's support, is typically marked by oscillation between extremes: approach/ avoidance, uncertainty about what is the right thing to do, stalling to gather strength or to delay the inevitable, hoping for magic, and emotionally shutting down. Denial also is common, for example, an adolescent girl who denies and hides her pregnancy under baggy clothes, even up to the point of birth. In Anna Quindlen's novel *Blessing* (2003), a teenage girl who hid her pregnancy from her parents and boyfriend leaves her daughter on the porch of the richest people in town, hoping that their wealth will ensure a good future for her child, but she later returns to claim the child. Such ambivalence makes young women vulnerable to allowing others to make decisions for them.

The grief of the birth mother, even in open adoptions, includes the multiple losses of daily interaction and family structure; control and security; self-worth, respect, and status; and the acknowledgment that she has given life to a unique human being. The loss experienced by the birth parents in an open adoption is characterized by an orientation to the future and what might have been, marked by an inability to know the fullness of the loss; others' underestimation of the loss; and ongoing grief with each developmental stage of the child. The self-inflicted or voluntary nature of the loss may diminish others' support. In an open adoption, the birth parents are in uncharted, undescribed territory and in a process confounded by moral dimensions. The paradoxical nature of the loss means that while grieving, the birth parents can nevertheless benefit from observing that their child is well cared for and given new opportunities. Gains and losses, satisfaction and sadness, coexist. Nevertheless, regret—the persistence of ambivalence—may hover over this decision throughout the birth mother's life and lead to her further isolation and loss of self-confidence.

Although it is too late to change their decision (to relinquish their child for adoption), adolescents can learn from it and use it in the future for themselves and others who have to make difficult choices. Unfortunately, some birth parents try to undo their decision and minimize their grief by having another child as soon as possible. But the replacement child cannot fill the emptiness created by the one relinquished. An additional emotional risk for the birth parent is choosing to move away from the relinquished child rather than fully embracing the loss (Gritter 2000).

The grief inherent in relinquishment is also complicated by both individual and societal factors. In most instances, Western cultures' social and community capacities are not supportive. Family, colleagues, and even acquaintances usually hold negative images of birth parents (e.g., unloving, self-centered) and may attach a stigma to "out of wedlock birth"; others implicitly convey "how could anyone give up a child?" and disrespectfully label "unloving" birth parents as "different" and dysfunctional. But many birth parents decide to give up their child out of love; in other words, the birth parent is indicating, "I love you so much that I must step away from you" (Gritter 2000:33). Friends and family are usually not aware that the relinquishment decision is generally not made easily or always willingly. Many birth parents may be forced to make such a decision because of external circumstances, such as poverty or youth, but also because of an internal need for what they perceive to be an optimal outcome for themselves and their child (Gritter 2000).

When birth parents feel abandoned or excluded by others, they typically feel low self-worth and self-esteem. Their social capacities are further depleted when family, friends, and the adoptive parents discount and misunderstand them. Some cultures and religious groups label these birth parents as sinners and even pressure them to move away from past social supports, including family. The mother's sorrow at giving up her child may not be acknowledged by other family members or helping professionals (Gritter 2000; Rosenberg 1992). Such feelings of guilt and loneliness may be especially intense for adolescent parents whose child is disabled and who must make the agonizing choice of raising such a child or giving him or her up for adoption (Finnegan 1993).

Regardless of the nature of the child's death or out-of-home placement, the young mother may already have strongly identified with her role as a mother and is greatly affected by the loss of this role. The grief of an adolescent father is often overlooked, especially when the father is absent or is pressured by society to be "strong" (Corr and McNeil 1999). In addition, adolescent parents, who typically have little previous experience with major loss, cannot imagine that others have endured such pain.

Adolescents are apt to think that they are the discoverers of deep and powerful feelings and that no one has ever loved as they have loved. Because love is the other side of the coin of grief, adolescents are highly vulnerable to severe emotional injury. Feeling a mixture of sadness, shame, self-blame, anger, guilt, and loneliness, adolescents often find it difficult to return to the normal world (Corr and McNeil 1999:42).

Adolescents without strong and stable supports are at risk of self-destructive behavior such as drug or alcohol abuse or acting out in socially destructive ways. In any event, the grief over a child's death or relinquishment will be present at some level, however deep, for the rest of their lives. It also will generally be unacknowledged, unsupported, and feared by others, including close family members (Corr and McNeil 1999).

Summary

In Western cultures, adolescence is typically a turbulent time as teens seek to distance themselves from family, try new behaviors and identities, and experiment with sexual and other high-risk behaviors. Most teenagers' worldviews do not include the possibility of the death of a parent, sibling, close friend, or child. Nonetheless, given the violent nature of our society and the risk-seeking behaviors of some adolescents, most are touched by death or divorce in some way. Teenagers' bravado, moodiness, or sullenness may hide the extent to which they are experiencing the pain of loss. They may be especially vulnerable to difficulties in the grief process, since they commonly withdraw from or reject many of the traditional supports of family, religious institutions, teachers, and other mentors. The social capacities of family, community, and culture are critical to supporting teens through the grief process. Fortunately, schools have recognized the importance of grief counseling and crisis interventions in the aftermath of the death of classmates. Community mental health agencies may offer support groups, especially for survivors of suicide and school violence, and parents are more knowledgeable about the importance of their steady presence in adolescents' lives, even when their teens try to push them away. Grief that is not addressed in adolescence will probably surface in young adulthood.

7

Interventions for Grieving Adolescents

ADOLESCENTS' EMOTIONS often are intensified because of the dramatic hormonal changes occurring in their bodies. Common emotional manifestations of grief such as sadness, anger, and guilt may feel overwhelming. Rather than verbally express these feelings, some teens may withdraw, fight, do poorly in school, rebel, run away, use alcohol or other drugs to numb their feelings, be sexually promiscuous, and/or consider suicide. Severe acting out may be a cry for help and should alert social workers and school counselors to determine the underlying causes, which may be related to loss. Furthermore, teens sometimes deliberately test professional helpers, as in the following example: "Shortly before therapy terminated, a family session with Michael and his mother was held. He said to his mother: 'You know, Mom, the other day during my therapy session I did everything I could to get myself kicked out. I was rude and I put my feet on her furniture. But no matter what, she let me stay'" (Bembry and Ericson 1999:187).

Adolescents may resist professional helpers because they perceive them as a threat to their independence. They may be embarrassed or have compelling reasons to hide their feelings of love and pain from peers and/or adults, making it difficult to engage them verbally. The following quotation from an African American male teen living in an inner-city project illustrates how he masked with anger his love for and fear of losing his grandmother in order to protect his self-image:

> One thing I think about almost every night is what it would be like if my grandmother died. Sometimes I have a dream that God calls her name, and I wake up and go upstairs just to see if she's still there. I might act bad around her and get mad at her, but deep down I love my grandmother. It's just that I can't show it. Telling someone that you love them is soft, and if they see you're soft in the projects it's like a shark seeing blood—they're going to attack! (Jones and Newman 1997:55)

The interventions we review in this chapter may help address the challenges of working with teens by drawing on peer supports (e.g., through group work) and using developmentally appropriate nonverbal methods of expression (e.g., using music rather than play as appropriate to younger children).

Practice wisdom dictates that in general, unconditional positive regard, honesty, and empathy are essential to building trust with adolescents. Emotions such as anger or hostility require understanding and compassion. Health and human service professionals should understand the underlying causes of grief-related anger and their function in adolescents' lives. Grieving teens may express anger or hostility because they

- Feel violated or abandoned.
- Are afraid of carrying on alone.
- Are trying to mask their separation anxiety.
- Are trying to protect against other uncomfortable feelings (e.g., guilt, anxiety, unworthiness, and frustration).
- Are assigning blame, which provides a target for their powerful feelings to be expressed.
- Know that something of great value has been taken from them. (Liotta 1996; McKay, Rogers, and McKay 1989)

Validating, normalizing, and not personalizing powerful feelings are considered fundamental to working with bereaved adolescents. As many parents report, meeting their teenagers' anger with anger only serves to heighten hostility and constrain the relationship. Although the use of anger-based techniques for bereaved teens has not been adequately evaluated, numerous texts describe various strategies recommended by human service providers to help adolescents express their anger in ways that will not harm themselves or others (e.g., Fogarty 2000; Goldman 1996, 2000; Perschy 1997). Based on catharsis theory, which promotes the notion that unexpressed anger causes psychological harm and must be released to enhance well-being (Bushman, Baumeister, and Phillips 2001), these techniques are designed to help teens physically express or externalize their anger (e.g., by using a punching bag, gloves, pillow, or foam bat; screaming into a tape recorder or paper bag; tearing up magazines). Although catharsis theory has permeated popular culture and counseling approaches, considerable evidence has discredited this theory (for a review, see Geen and Quanty 1977). Indeed, recent studies suggest that engaging in aggressive activities to express anger may increase rather than decrease anger and aggression (Bushman 2002). Other techniques commonly promoted that may be less likely to fuel anger include verbal or nonverbal forms of expression for individual or group work (e.g., offering narratives or testimony, talking about sources of anger, and writing out feelings of anger and then burning the paper to metaphorically release it) and aerobic exercise or sports. Teenagers may be encouraged to walk briskly or run while they talk about their anger. Goals for professionals treating angry bereaved young people are to (1) offer a more comprehensive and accurate understanding of their loss experience by correcting distorted interpretations that may promote magical thought and harmful anger reactions; (2) help them adjust to the loss by rehearsing more adaptive behavioral responses; (3) help them reduce their expression of harmful anger and encourage more varied emotions of mourning (Fogarty 2000); (4) help them devise a constructive expression of powerlessness; and (5) advocate for teens with parents, teachers, and others in their support network.

Respecting adolescents by allowing them to set the pace and help determine the agenda is essential. Unconventional techniques may be needed for individual and/or group-based work with grieving teens who are especially angry, hostile, or unresponsive. For example, if talking does not seem to work and the teen is inattentive, the social worker may find it useful to stop talking and to write a private note. This may be any friendly and undemanding statement that seems fitting at the time. Similarly, spontaneous and well-placed humor used to gain rapport may help distract a teen who is becoming angry and volatile (Sommers-Flanagan and Sommers-Flanagan 1995). For example, Gilroy (2001) described the therapeutic value of magic tricks as a nonthreatening way to engage adolescents.

Assessment and Treatment of Adolescent Grief-Precipitated Depression

Most adolescents do not feel the need for professional services to cope with their losses. Those who do seek professional assistance tend to have more depressive symptoms (Harrison and Harrington 2001). Certain forms of loss also may put teens at increased risk for major depression. For example, siblings of teens who committed suicide are more likely to have major depression (Brent et al. 1993). Adolescents whose siblings died from cystic fibrosis had more detrimental long-term consequences, including greater anxiety, depression, and guilt, than did younger siblings (Fanos and Nickerson 1991). Helping professionals must, therefore, know how to assess and address depression in adolescents.

The precise diagnostic criteria for a major depressive episode are found in the *Diagnostic and Statistical Manual of Mental Disorders* (4th ed.), but the general symptoms are depressed mood, diminished pleasure in activities, weight loss or gain, difficulty sleeping, energy loss, feelings of worthlessness or guilt, psychomotor agitation or retardation, difficulty concentrating, and recurrent thoughts of death. Practitioners must rule out medical conditions or the effects of substances. Because many of these symptoms are manifestations of grief, the manual suggests that in order to meet the criteria for a major depressive episode, one of the symptoms must persist for longer than two months after the bereavement or be "characterized by marked functional impairment, morbid preoccupation with worthlessness, suicidal ideation, psychotic symptoms, or psychomotor retardation" (American Psychiatric Association 2000:356). Evidence-based treatments of grief-precipitated depression include trauma- or grief-focused group psychotherapy (Layne et al. 2001a), interpersonal psychotherapy (Mufson and Dorta 2000), individual and group cognitive behavior therapy (Moore and Carr 2000), and family therapy (Carr 2000). Surprisingly, there are few or no culture-specific interventions for addressing depression among bereaved youth. Box 7.1 describes how a Native American high school used paradox in a series of "preventive" workshops for depressed adolescents and their friends following three teen suicides.

General Techniques and Interventions
Death Education and Grief Supports in School

Adolescents spend many of their waking hours in school, and there is a reciprocal relationship between school performance and exposure to loss. That is, adolescents exposed to violence, death, and disasters are at greater risk for poor school performance and attendance. Students perceiving little support from classmates and teachers also have higher rates of posttraumatic stress (Dyregrov 2004). Given the growing rates of school violence, including the homicide of students in multiple-victim events (Akiba et al. 2002; Anderson et al. 2001; Shackford 2003) and suicide (Wass 2004), death education and supportive and postvention protocols should, ideally, be in place in every school (Silverman 2000). Death education courses may help adolescents talk about death, dying, and mourning rituals; what to expect when attending a memorial service; and how to cope with losses they may face (Schachter 1991/1992). Unfortunately, a national random survey of 423 public schools revealed that only 11 percent of schools offer a course or unit on death education; 17 percent have a grief education/support program; and 25 percent have suicide prevention and/or intervention programs (Wass, Miller, and Thornton 1990). These percentages may have risen in the past decade with the greater recognition of the importance of preventive and support interventions, yet death education continues to be unavailable to

Box 7.1 The Use of Paradox with Native American Adolescents Bereaved by Suicide

A series of "preventive" workshops were conducted with a group of depressed adolescents in a Native American high school located on a western Indian reservation, following three completed peer suicides.

Assumptions Conveyed Underlying the Intervention

- Native American adolescents may use suffering as a weapon.
- Nobility in death may be exaggerated by these youths (acknowledging the Sioux tradition of a "warrior's death").
- Suicide was not in keeping with the noble warrior tradition.
- Suicide was a white man's tradition (with the exception of the voluntary death of elders).
- All behavior is purposeful.

The Intervention

- Recollections were prompted to help students understand purposeful behavior.
- Questions to prompt recollection included, "What did you do as a child to get what you wanted from your parents? Was there a time as a child that you felt as discouraged as you do now?"
- It was noted that the recollections shared were metaphors for students' current responses.

Reframing the Symptom

- Purpose: To "reframe" the adolescents' "noble notion" of their own death.
- Method: Each student was asked to write his or her own obituary.
- Each obituary was read out loud (anonymously).
- Group discussion followed, and students identified central themes, including themes of "despair, ... the exaggerated notion of nobility, grandiosity," and "self-destruction to heroic proportions."

continued

Prescribing the Symptom (of Depression)

- Purpose: To increase the adolescents' sense of power over the symptom; to give permission to exhibit the symptom rather than repress it (paradoxically putting it to good use); and to "encourage social interest and discourage obsessive, private logic" (190).
- Method: In groups of five to six, adolescents were given the following directive: "You have a friend who is genuinely interested in being depressed but is hopelessly happy. Turn your friend on to depression! Generate a recipe for getting and staying depressed. Your friend is dear to you, and you would do anything for him or her. Give him or her your best shot. Write your strategies on the newsprint, and if you choose to, act out your recipe once you've finished" (188–89).
- The long list of strategies developed by each group was reviewed and discussed.

Facilitator's Observations

"Although it seems absurd and even irreverent, paradoxically, the results have been therapeutic. The first crack of laughter seems to reorient the group and its participants. Quite suddenly, participants take notice of others, and perhaps for the first time in a long time, they demonstrate concern and compassion for someone else. Since participants share a common bond—suffering—they are quick to empathize and identify with their peers, yet their despair seems to have a difficult time prevailing. In some instances the transitions made by youngsters have been so dramatic they border on unbelievable. For example, one extremely attractive but withdrawn young man began his day by assuming a quasi-fetal posture in one corner of the room and finished it as the spokesperson and authority for his group" (189–90).

Source: F. O. Main and J. D. West, Sabotaging Adolescent Depression Through Paradox, Individual Psychology 43 (1987): 185–91.

the majority of students in public schools (Wass 2004). Most school-based grief programs encourage students to share their feelings, answer students' questions about grief, address emotional distress, and provide information about the grief process and how to comfort the bereaved. Crisis intervention, prevention suicide and youth violence, and death education to counteract the pervasiveness of violent death in the media and their potential negative effects to "correct distorted images that glorify or trivialize death" are needed (Wass 2004:301). Many of the interventions described in this chapter are intended for schools. School social workers and counselors may be able to reach many students using group interventions, although they may need to use more than only group interventions for students grieving specific losses, such as the death of a family member, the difficult decisions associated with teen pregnancy, and the traumatic aftermath of teen suicide or school community violence.

Group-Based Interventions

Reducing the sense of isolation common to bereaved teens is one advantage of group-based interventions. Hearing others' experiences helps validate and normalize grief, as illustrated by the following: "I thought my feelings were dumb and was ashamed of them. Then I came to this group and realized that others have the same feelings. When I am with others outside of this group, I feel abnormal. Here I feel more secure. I am a normal grieving person" (Perschy 1989:3, as cited in Perschy 1997:9).

Group therapy may be viewed as less stigmatizing than individual therapy and provide opportunities for teens to learn from others, even if they are reluctant to share actively in a group (Perschy 1997). Adolescents reported the following five benefits of group participation at the Dougy Center, a national bereavement center for youth:

1. Group sharing served to de-pathologize their grief reactions and helped them feel that they were not "going crazy."
2. Group participation helped them feel less alone.
3. Group support helped adolescents realize that others cared about and understood, to some extent, what they were going through.
4. Group sharing provided an opportunity for adolescents to validate intense and difficult feelings.
5. The group's activities helped teens show what they were feeling, both verbally and nonverbally. (Schuurman 2000)

Common objectives for adolescent grief groups include

1. Giving adolescents accurate, appropriate information about the process of grief and how it affects their life.
2. Enabling them, if they are willing, to express their fears, anger, regrets, sadness, desires, and concerns.
3. Helping them address various aspects of grief through specific structured activities.

4. Helping them examine their current support systems and learn how to expand them. This expansion may include finding an appropriate mental health professional.
5. Encouraging them to consult with other group members as well as the leaders as resources in exploring grief-related issues. (Perschy 1997:11)

Although few evaluation studies have specifically tested group models to address adolescent bereavement, a growing body of evidence suggests that group treatment is effective for handling multiple behavioral and emotional concerns with this age group. A meta-analysis of fifty-six outcome studies of group treatment with children and adolescents concluded that group treatment was significantly more effective for youth than for those in wait-list and placebo control groups (Hoag and Burlingame 1997). Several of the outcomes evaluated were those commonly associated with grief, such as depression, anxiety, locus of control, and adjustment to divorce. Further study is needed to test the efficacy of bereavement groups for the wide range of losses experienced by adolescents. Several authors have proposed guidelines and recommendations for forming and structuring adolescent grief groups (e.g., Baxter and Stuart 1999; Johnson 1995; Liotta 1996; Perschy 1997; Schuurman 2000).

As with many other types of intervention at other phases of life, culturally specific group-based bereavement interventions for grieving adolescents have generally not been evaluated. The methods, techniques, and skills recommended for culturally specific group therapy may help social workers design and run groups of culturally diverse adolescents. As described in chapter 5, professionals should consider (1) the group's heterogeneity or homogeneity; (2) the minority youths' conceptions, expectations, and needs relevant to the group's structure, process, and experience; (3) the variation in communication styles that may influence the group's process; (4) the preparation of youth of color for the group; and (5) culturally competent and strength-focused skills and techniques in problem solving (for a discussion of these issues, see Ho 1992).

Expressing Grief Through Music

Based on extensive clinical experience, music therapists and other helping professionals advocate using music to help grieving adolescents (e.g., Bright 1999; Goldman 1996, 2000; Gough 2000; Hinderer 1995; Perschy 1997). The therapeutic use of music has several functions: it serves as a resource to explore feelings (Goldman 2000), facilitates grief work in a nonthreatening environment (Hilliard 2001a), evokes emotions, stimulates memories and discussion, helps in coping, enhances ritualization, and enables teens to share the lost or absent person with others and to feel his or her presence (Gough 2000).

Music enables adolescents to discover and develop more of their emotions and to manage their moods. Whether it is used to get rid of, maintain, or evoke emotions, music nearly always has a big part in adolescents' emotional life (Hakanen 1995:214).

The use of music may be particularly suited to work with children and teens in foster care as a nonthreatening means of exploring difficult emotional and therapeutic issues related to family disruption, abuse, and neglect (Layman, Hussey, and Laing 2002).

The music should speak to the adolescent in a culturally meaningful way. For example, African American adolescents were found to prefer three types of music: rhythm and blues/soul (R and B/soul), rap, and jazz. R and B was associated with grief and anger, whereas rap evoked emotions of excitement and happiness (Hakanen 1995). Practitioners should ask adolescents what kind of music they prefer so that it may have the greatest meaning and impact.

Social workers' and grief counselors' use of music for addressing grief with adolescents is different from the use of *music therapy* with bereaved adolescents. Human service professionals may use the following grief-counseling methods with adolescents:

1. Have teens create a musical self-portrait of songs to describe themselves and/or a musical biography of the deceased that may prompt discussion of the songs' lyrics and themes.
2. Ask teens in individual or group work to bring in music that expresses their feelings or thoughts.
3. Offer music that is relevant to the adolescent's work; for example, if the teen is grieving the death of a friend, rock 'n' roll, hip-hop, or rap all deal with this issue.
4. Encourage adolescents to compile songs that give them comfort and peace.
5. Use complementary techniques like drawing, journaling, photo therapy, painting, creative movement, and dance. (Gough 2000)

In contrast, music therapy is conducted by licensed therapists and may be used in conjunction with such supportive interventions. (Although we cannot describe these methods here, for a comprehensive guide to music therapy, see Wingram, Pederson, and Bonde 2002.)

Although an extensive body of literature documents the ways in which music affects emotional and physical well-being, the therapeutic effects of music therapy, specifically on grieving adolescents, have not been evaluated empirically. Anecdotal and clinical evidence suggests that music helps youth access emotions that are sometimes masked by shock and numbness (Gough 2000), express repressed feelings, and reduce psychiatric symptoms associated with complicated bereavement (Bright 1999). One study reported that young adolescents who participated in music therapy–based bereavement groups had fewer grief symptoms and behavior problems at home than did those in the control group (Hilliard 2001a). More evaluations of music-based interventions with adolescents are needed.

Practical Strategies for Counseling Male Adolescents

The bereavement literature has not evaluated gender-specific interventions. Because male adolescents usually have more difficulty expressing their feelings than female adolescents do, we will highlight strategies for counseling males. Many of the strategies, however, may also be relevant to working with female adolescents, since factors other than gender affect emotional expression. That is, some adolescent males are able to express their feelings, whereas some female teens may try to appear "tough" and not show their emotions. In any case, gender differences in identification, socialization, and acculturation influence the extent to which male youth often contain their grief and limit their expression of feeling (Adams 2001). The following strategies are ways that counselors and other helping professionals use to address the needs of bereaved adolescents, especially young males:

1. Convey interest, caring, trustworthiness, gentleness, persistence, a nonjudgmental attitude, empathy, and flexibility.
2. Respect the adolescents' wish to include significant others in sessions, to provide security, and to make communication easier (e.g., teens may bring a sibling or close friend).
3. Structure the relationship and establish ground rules.
4. Learn about the adolescents' interests and life at home, at school, and in the community, especially their perceptions and interpretations of what has transpired.
5. Demythologize taboos to help males understand that they are not weak or inadequate if they seek assistance or openly express their feelings.
6. Permit them to grieve and express their feelings. For teens, this may require that no one else be present.
7. Ensure confidentiality, and, when appropriate, ask their permission to communicate with or seek their parents' involvement or assistance.
8. Respect their privacy and needs to postpone talking about painful subjects.
9. Help them link thoughts and feelings and encourage their using the phrases *I wish, I feel, I need,* and *I miss.*
10. Help them express their thoughts and feelings through age-appropriate modalities (e.g., acting out feelings through play, music, and drawings).

11. Encourage their recounting of both positive and negative memories.
12. Encourage their reality testing by having them ask family members about the loss.
13. Encourage them to discuss their need to protect others who are grieving and ask them how family secrets pertaining to the loss have affected them.
14. When their thought processes appear to be distorted, help them discuss their beliefs and determine how and when to help them reframe their thoughts.
15. Encourage them to talk about their dreams and visions.
16. Commend their ability to manage their mourning constructively and encourage their continuing activities that help them feel self-sufficient and competent.
17. Urge them to manage their anger constructively (e.g., competitive sports may help boys with destructive tendencies to redirect and diffuse their anger).
18. Suggest ways of talking with their friends about their grief, especially if the friends are teasing them or trying to ignore their grief (e.g., pretending that nothing has happened).
19. Share the loss experiences and constructive grief responses of respected male role models. (Adams 2001:301–2)

Interventions Related to Specific Losses
Death of a Parent or Sibling

Many adolescents have a parent or other family member who has had a long-term serious illness or accident resulting in death. Indeed, because of AIDS alone, 72,000 to 125,000 children and youth have been orphaned in the United States (American Association for World Health 1997; Levine 1995), disproportionately affecting African American families (Parsons and Merrick-Roddy 1996). Interventions for adolescents with a parent with a serious chronic illness like cancer or HIV/AIDS recognize the interdependence and interaction of the family unit and the many ways that these devastating diseases affect families. Health and human service interventions try to support parents through their disease and enhance their coping skills, help them understand and plan for their children's current and future needs, and help children and adolescents adjust to life without their parent (Rotheram-Borus, Stein, and Lin 2001). Evaluations of these interventions found fewer problem behaviors and risk factors for HIV infection among participating teens but did not find any effect on bereavement outcomes (Rotheram-Borus, Stein, and Lin 2001).

One of the few experimental evaluations of a theory-based prevention program for parentally bereaved children and adolescents was designed to modify risk and protective factors believed to influence youth mental health, such as the quality of the relationship between the caregiver and adolescent, the caregiver's mental health, and the young person's exposure to negative events (Sandler et al. 2003). The Family Bereavement Program had conjoint and separate groups for caregivers and adolescents. Caregivers were taught techniques to improve the quality of relationships, provide discipline, challenge negative thoughts, increase the number of positive activities, guide children in problem solving, and reduce children's exposure to negative events (e.g., adult arguments). Adolescents were taught techniques to improve the quality of their relationships, positive coping, coping efficacy, self-esteem, control-related belief, cognitive reframing, problem-solving skills, and the expression of grief. The program was successful in reducing the number of stressful events and improving parenting, coping, and caregiver well-being but helped resolve the problems only for those girls who had higher problem scores in the first place. Although the extent to which this intervention modified grief scores was not evaluated, the results suggest that it is possible to influence risk and protective factors for bereaved adolescents through family-based intervention. Research is needed to replicate this study, evaluate the extent to which it may be effective in community-based service delivery systems, recruit high-risk families, and improve the program's effects for adolescent males (Sandler et al. 2003).

Although there are few evaluations of teen bereavement interventions, practical strategies for supporting adolescents throughout the parent's or sibling's illness and after death come from qualitative investigations of how adolescents experience loss. For example, talking openly about the illness and death appears to be helpful to bereaved teens (Raveis, Siegel, and Karus 1999; Siegel, Raveis, and Karus 1996). Hogan and DeSantis (1994) asked 140 bereaved adolescents what helped or hindered them in coping with and adapting to a sibling's death. Their grief process was facilitated by self-directed stress reduction activities (e.g., exercise, keeping a journal) and support from family members and friends. In contrast, the bereavement process was hindered by intrusive thoughts and feelings of guilt and shame, a sense of loneliness, the surviving parent's distress, insensitivity of support systems, rumors and gossip generated in support systems, and perceptions of the death's unfairness and injustice. These hindrances suggest potential targets for intervention. Such interventions, which are reviewed in this chapter, provide recommendations for addressing the complex feelings and thoughts commonly experienced by adolescents, techniques for helping them feel less alone, and strategies for working with social support systems.

Other recommendations emerging from qualitative research with adolescents stress that during a parent's terminal illness, professionals should promote honest communication, provide factual information, facilitate discussion about feelings and concerns, and help parents understand their children's developmental needs and grief responses, maintain their support network, encourage them to express their feelings and to say good-bye, and be mindful of the demands and expectations being placed on them (Christ, Siegel, and Christ 2002). After a parent's death, it is recommended that the surviving parent encourage the children to select meaningful mementos, actively participate in the memorial service, set limits, provide opportunities for talking about the deceased parent and for grieving, create enjoyable family experiences, make use of the natural supports available to adolescents, and encourage participation in activities that might alleviate their feelings of helplessness (e.g., altruistic volunteer work) (Christ, Siegel, and Christ 2002; Sandler et al. 2003; Silverman, Nickman, and Worden 1995; Worden 1996).

Helping adolescents tell the story of the death is a natural way to initiate the assessment process and may provide emotional relief, facilitate meaning making, encourage family members' empathy toward one another, and offer a way of measuring the progress of treatment as stories are retold over time (Sedney, Baker, and Gross 1994). More generally, telling the story of a loss may be a way for surviving teens to remember the deceased as well as to reconfigure their relationship with him or her. In groups or individual sessions, the leader may ask questions to prompt discussion of the events around each death. Teens may be invited to write their responses to questions about the events and then to share their responses. The following questions may help teens tell their story:

Who died? How did he or she die?
Was it a short or a long time ago?
How did you find out that your loved one died? Who told you?
What was your immediate reaction after hearing of the death?
How do you feel now?
Did you see your loved one after the death?
What was that like for you to see (or not see) your loved one?
Was there a funeral, shivah, or other kind of memorial?
Were you involved in the service?
What parts were really difficult? What parts were less difficult than expected?
What memory of the person who has died makes you feel good?
Who was and is able to support you right now?
What other types of losses have you had in the past? How have you dealt
   with them? (Perschy 1997)

As is true with children, social support helps moderate the grief of teens coping with a family member's death. Adolescents may be encouraged through individual and group work to identify the supports in their life and to understand why a healthy support system is important. Perschy (1997) recommends asking teens (1) to name the people who care about them, including friends, family members, relatives, neighbors, teachers, counselor/mental health professionals, and religious or spiritual persons; (2) to describe the interests that are important to them (e.g., school, church/temple, spirituality, work, sports, and art/crafts) as well as things like their pets or memorabilia (pictures, special items); and (3) to explore strategies that may help strengthen their support network.

Divorce of Parents

Chapter 6 described the many losses that adolescents experience following their parents' divorce. These youth report levels of psychological distress similar to those found in adolescents bereaved by a parent's death (Servaty and Hayslip 2001). Recent evidence suggests that marital conflict, violence, and/or related parenting behaviors before a divorce may affect children's and adolescents' psychological adjustment after the divorce (Kelly 2000). Interventions to address the needs of families following a divorce, which are described in chapter 11, are broadly focused on family-based preventive and postdivorce treatments to support psychological and social adjustment but do not specifically address grief. For example, parent education (teaching parenting skills, conflict resolution and anger management, and strengthening parent–child relationships) is a common strategy for assisting families of divorce (Pedro-Carroll 2001). The usual goals of school group-based interventions for children are reducing isolation, permitting the children to explore their feelings, teaching problem-solving skills, and providing social support, but the effects of these interventions are modest (Grych and Fincham 1992; Lee, Picard, and Blain 1994; Pedro-Carroll 2001). Common goals of psychological and preventive interventions for children and adolescents are dispelling depression, raising self-esteem, resolving home- and school-based behavior problems, and improving relationships (O'Halloran 2000; Wolchik, Sandler, and Millsap 2002). The most effective strategies for these concerns are stress management techniques, social skills training, problem solving, and psychological education (for a review, see O'Halloran 2000). In sum, interventions that may alleviate adolescents' grief associated with divorce have not received much attention. Future studies are needed that move beyond the mere description of general loss and actually measure the grief response. We should find out from adolescents how the manifestations of grief influence them and what their needs are in regard to their losses. We need to understand (1) how adolescents' postdivorce grief affects their social and psychological functioning, (2) cultural and socioeconomic differences of adolescents' postdivorce grief, (3) the efficacy of current intervention models to modify the grief experience, and (4) the most useful specific techniques and interventions for divorce-associated grief.

Teen Pregnancy and Perinatal Death

Adolescents who lose a baby have significant emotional, physical, social, and cognitive grief responses and are at a higher risk for developing depression than their peers (Wheeler and Austin 2000). Although adolescents' perinatal and infant mortality rate is twice as high as that for the adult population (Bright 1987), research on perinatal grief interventions either has focused more on young adult women or has failed to specify age appropriateness. Accordingly, chapter 9 reviews the interventions relevant to perinatal loss. There is little published on developmentally appropriate strategies and few empirical assessment tools or interventions for adolescent mothers facing the difficult decisions and losses associated with pregnancy. In addition, almost nothing has been written about teen fathers' grief.

General practice principles for health and human service professionals working with adolescents bereaved by perinatal death include the following:

1. Reach out and demonstrate caring and concern.
2. Use a broad-based assessment and treatment approach to address losses and other current challenges or concerns in the adolescent's life beyond the pregnancy loss and to identify and overcome barriers presented by significant others. Other key areas for assessment are the parents' attachment to the unborn child, their understanding of the cause of death, their grief responses to the loss, and the availability of support from family members, the father, or friends (for more assessment considerations, see chapter 9).
3. Evaluate for depression and suicide risk.
4. Involve the adolescent in writing a treatment plan to reduce his or her feelings of powerlessness.
5. Use both visual and concrete methods for discovering past and current losses with such tools as an ecomap (a drawing developed jointly by the professional and bereaved parent that uses circles and symbols to portray an individual and his or her family in their social context), a life-history grid (a graphic depiction of significant events in a person's life and/or the "development of significant problems through time" [Sheafor, Horejsi, and Horejsi 2000: 319]), and a written autobiography. (Freeman 1987; Shaefer 1992; Wheeler and Austin 2001)

Specific interventions suggested in the literature but not empirically evaluated are school-based interventions (Shaefer 1992) and counseling for perinatal loss (Chesterton 1996). The proposed school-based intervention (1) assesses the loss, (2) validates the experience of loss, (3) helps the adolescent understand his or her loss and grief response, (4) helps the adolescent develop strategies for grieving and commemorating the loss, and (5) educates others in the adolescent's support systems about providing support (e.g., other school personnel, family) (Shaefer 1992). Studies are needed to test empirically these practice principles as well as other interventions addressing the grief associated with teen pregnancy and perinatal loss. For example, future research might look at how social work professionals in different contexts (e.g., schools, health clinics) try to minimize suffering and maximize the support of teen parents and others who experience perinatal loss, what strategies best help adolescent parents make difficult decisions, and what innovative programs exist and how well are they working.

Suicide

The grief associated with adolescent suicide is profound. Many teens who are bereaved consider suicide, and suicidal adolescents endure tremendous psychological and emotional suffering. One study reported that complicated grief, in particular, dramatically elevated the risk of suicide, even after controlling for major depression and posttraumatic stress disorder (PTSD) (Latham and Prigerson 2004). Human service professionals working with youth should consider suicide prevention and intervention programs for suicidal teens and postvention strategies for adolescents bereaved by the suicides of their peers (Leenaars and Wenckstern 1995).

PREVENTION

Suicide prevention tries to "ameliorate the conditions that lead to suicide" and to educate youth and their gatekeepers (Leenaars and Wenckstern 1995:134). The conditions associated with or that may lead to suicide (i.e., general risk factors and precipitants) are shameful or humiliating experiences, conflict with parents, family violence, sexual or physical assault, completed suicide of a family member or friend, death or other loss of a significant relationship, lack of friendship support or rejection by peers, drug and alcohol abuse, access to firearms, past suicide attempts, current episode of major depression, acculturative stress, and homophobic persecution by others (Bagley and Tremblay 2000; Bridge et al. 1997; Garrison et al. 1993; Gould et al. 2003; Prinstein et al. 2000; Reinherz et al. 1995). These complex conditions and social problems affect large numbers of adolescents and require an ecological approach (i.e., attending to personal, interpersonal, and sociocultural factors and the interactions and transactions between the adolescent and the other systems in his or her social environment) to prevention and intervention efforts for multiple system levels (Ayyash-Abdo 2002).

Social workers, teachers, and other adults who work with adolescents should be able to recognize the signs and symptomatology of emotional instability, self-destructive thoughts, and behaviors that can lead to suicide (table 7.1).

Most prevention programs are based at school and are aimed at (1) helping students identify warning signs of suicide, (2) increasing students' awareness of suicidal behavior, and (3) providing information about mental health resources and how to find them (Kalafat and Elias 1994; Shaffer et al. 1990). The mixed results reported in these studies, stemming in part from their limited focus on providing information, have led to the development of skills-training programs targeted to at-risk students and designed to enhance skills for managing depression, loneliness, anger, problem solving, and social skills. These skills-training programs have shown encouraging results (Berman and Jones 1995; Eggert et al. 1995; Zenere and Lazarus 1997). Other suicide prevention efforts are needed that take into account sociocultural and acculturative stress (Hovey 1998) and sexual orientation (e.g., that try to remove from high school culture the emotional denigration and physical harassment of gay, lesbian, and bisexual youth) (Bagley and Tremblay 2000).

Recent research suggests that communication among youth, their families, and service providers must be improved in order to prevent suicide. For example, in a study of 879 urban youth, only half of those reporting a suicide attempt had spoken with a family member or other adult about their distress, and attempters were more likely than nonattempters to report that they would not go to family members in the future (O'Donnell et al. 2003). An empowerment-based parent education program designed to reduce adolescents' risk factors was found to enhance maternal care (i.e., mother's care of the adolescent was a targeted outcome) and to reduce conflict, substance use, and delinquency (Toumbourou and Gregg 2002). Additional research is needed to test interventions designed to enhance family communication and support and to prevent adolescent suicide.

The media also can be enlisted to prevent suicide contagion. Media professionals may use the guidelines of the Centers for Disease Control (1994) to minimize the negative and potentially contagious effect of publicity about suicide (Ayyash-Abdo 2002). Prevention strategies include presenting information in such a way that (1) does not glorify the person or the suicidal act, (2) describes the act as a result of several events rather than one simple precipitating factor, (3) does not describe in detail the method used, and (4) does not sensationalize

TABLE 7.1
Assessment of Adolescent Suicide

BEHAVIORAL INDICATORS

Previous attempts
Decline in school performance
Giving away prized possessions
Withdrawing from others
Physical fighting with family members
Running away
Violent temper outbursts
Writing a diary about death desirability
Infatuation with death media that glorify death as a solution to life problems in such forms as poetry, drawings, music, or satanic ritual
Extreme risk-taking behaviors
Unresolved past experience with death
Rebellious behavior unusual for the person
Quietly putting affairs in order
Neglect of personal appearance
Increasing use of drugs or alcohol
Sexual promiscuity not typical before

VERBAL INDICATORS
Direct

"I've decided to kill myself."
"I wish I were dead."
"Sometimes she makes me so mad, I feel like killing myself."
"I hate my life and everything about it."
"I just can't go on any longer."
"Life has lost all its meaning for me."
"I've had it, life isn't worth living."

Indirect

"Everyone would be better off without me."
"I just can't deal with this anymore."
"If I don't see you again, thanks for everything."
"I'm not the person I used to be."
"I think I've lived long enough to see what to do."
"Do you know the procedures for donating your eyes after death?"
"I wish I could tell you how important you've been."
"Here, take my [cherished possession]; I won't be needing it soon."

SITUATIONAL INDICATORS

Loss of an important relationship
Loss of an overvalued aspect of life (e.g., not making the team, not getting perfect grades)

Divorce of parents
Violence within the family
Violence with peers
Parent or school overemphasis on achievement
Social isolation from peers
Recent death of a friend
Living away from the family for the first time
Extended physical illness without recovery
Period following a long bout with depression
Suicide in extended family

Affective Indicators

Extreme self-criticism
Apathy
Recent weight loss or gain
Sleeplessness or oversleeping
Loss of pleasure or interest in activities
Lethargy
Becoming easily agitated
Feeling worthless
Feeling hopeless
Easily discouraged
Unable to concentrate or stay on task
Low frustration tolerance
Dwelling on problems
Living in the past
Social withdrawal
Indecisiveness
Focusing on failure
Ideas of self-punishment
Lack of investment in the future
Extreme despondency or euphoria
Lack of goal orientation
Exaggerated fears
Reduced ability to express affection
Feelings of being an undue burden

Source: R. L. Deaton and D. Morgan, *Managing Death Issues in the Schools*, Monograph no. 1 (Helena: Montana Office of Public Instruction, 1992), 27–28.

the death by excessive reporting. Other prevention efforts include changing policy to enforce stricter gun ownership laws (Ayyash-Abdo 2002).

INTERVENTION

Once a suicidal adolescent has been identified, he or she should be contacted immediately to discuss the problems, explore solutions, take action, and arrange follow up. Interventions include "providing immediate crisis response and psychological first aid to reduce and prevent suicidal thoughts and behavior in teens; assessing the level of appropriate intervention; engaging parents and peers; and referring, reintegrating, and monitoring the student returning to the school setting" (Morgan 1995:67). Family members legally responsible for youths should be informed and involved in developing a service plan to reduce the immediate danger. "Supportive confrontation" is a method of empathic interaction that encourages positive action and prevents self-destructive behavior (Morgan 1995:75). Box 7.2 lists the steps and techniques of supportive confrontation. In addition, a written agreement or contract with adolescents, which requires them to promise in writing that they will not harm themselves, is recommended, since teens who have signed a contract find it more difficult to carry out their suicidal plans (Pfeffer 1986; Popenhagen and Qualley 1998).

Other interventions for suicidal adolescents are cognitive behavioral approaches to help them find alternative solutions to problems, defuse black-and-white thinking, and identify positive consequences of solutions (e.g., by having the adolescent explore his or her problems, find alternative solutions, test hypotheses, and resolve conflicts) (Ayyash-Abdo 2002; Trautman 1995); family therapy (Piacentini, Rotheram-Borus, and Cantwell 1995; Rotheram-Borus, Goldstein, and Elkavich 2002); and group therapy (Wood, Trainor, and Rothwell 2001).

POSTVENTION

The New Jersey Adolescent Suicide Prevention Project is a postvention model that was used for the recommendations nationally disseminated by the Centers for Disease Control and Prevention (Underwood and Dunne-Maxim 2000). This model takes a systems perspective that involves the larger community in the crisis management plan and combines crisis intervention strategies, grief theory, and suicide prevention techniques. Note that it has not been extensively evaluated. Specific guidelines and techniques for postvention implementation can be found in the manual *Managing Sudden Traumatic Loss in the* Schools (Underwood and Dunne-Maxim 1997). This model has two stages. The first stage is disseminating accurate information about the death (i.e., to the police or sheriff's department,

Box 7.2 Suicide Intervention: Immediate Supportive Confrontation

- Remove accessibility to the means the person intends to use to kill themselves.
- Always take a positive, affirming approach by emphasizing the persons' most desirable alternatives.
- Always try to sound calm and understanding.
- Use constructive, specific questions to separate and define the person's problems from the confusion surrounding irrational beliefs.
- Help the person understand the situation by focusing on current realities, and firmly dispute inappropriate thoughts and behaviors.
- Offer direct assistance to help the youth develop a plan to address his or her helplessness or hopelessness and regain personal control.
- Coach the student in a step-by-step fashion on specific actions they can use to help themselves. Affirm any level of progress, and continue until the person and you achieve the desired level of success.
- Get a commitment to the initial plan and to continuing communication. Make a contract preferably in writing that she or he will not attempt suicide.
- Assure the person that you and other appropriate helping persons are available to listen and to help should suicidal thoughts and feelings recur.
- Facilitate a program of follow-up and tracking of the person, including documentation of contacts and degree of progress.
- Tell the person that he or she is special and unique and tell them that you want them to live. It is important to reach any suicidal person with direct, human concern for them and their well-being.
- Refer the student to a treatment program if more intervention is needed.

Source: J. D. Morgan, Intervention, in *Planning and Managing Death Issues in the Schools: A Handbook*, edited by R. L. Deaton and W. A. Berkan (Westport, Conn.: Greenwood Press, 1995), 75. Copyright © 1995 by Robert L. Deaton and William A. Berkan. Reproduced with permission of Greenwood Publishing Group, Inc., Westport, Conn.

school superintendent, principals in the local and surrounding schools, religious or other community leaders, president of the school board); asking the crisis team in the school and the community to devise a response strategy; informing all faculty, school staff, and parents; contacting the families of affected students; emptying the dead student's locker and giving the contents to his or her parents; deleting the name of the deceased student from school's mailing list; appointing one media spokesperson; and responding to phone inquiries.

The second stage of this model implements the interventions that may be required during the days following a suicide, such as faculty meetings to support and help the staff respond to students, parents, the media, and their own grief; student crisis stations to provide support for students in organized group sessions and spontaneous meetings based on individual need; debriefing for the crisis team; strategies for media interaction (e.g., using media requests as opportunities to review prevention strategies); funeral planning; and community meetings as necessary. This model pays special attention to media coverage and memorial activities that will minimize contagion behavior. In so doing, it recognizes that "the school community must balance between commemorating the life and not glamorizing the death, especially if it is a result of self-destructive behavior, such as suicide, drug overdose, or a drunk-driving accident" (Underwood and Dunn-Maxim 2000:166). Some evidence suggests that following an adolescent's suicide, talking with students and psychological debriefing may prevent suicide contagion (Poijula, Wahlberg, and Dyregrov 2001).

The grief following a suicide is commonly characterized by intense anger, blame, guilt, shame, and the search for "why?" (Van Dongen 1991; Worden 2002). Evaluation studies have not yet determined how well interventions reduce the grief symptoms of teens coping with such powerful feelings. One evaluation of a manual-based bereavement group intervention for children and teens mourning a relative's suicide found greater reductions in anxiety and depressive symptoms in youth who received the intervention than in those who did not (Pfeffer et al. 2002). This intervention included psychoeducational and supportive interventions for parents and children. Particularly effective group interventions for families and friends of suicide victims address the issue of disenfranchised grief by providing the support of persons who have had similar experiences (Barlow and Morrison 2002).

Trauma

Accidents, homicide, and suicide are the three leading causes of death in adolescents (Hoyert et al. 2001). The sudden, often violent, and perceived preventable nature of these deaths often complicates the bereavement of teen survivors.

Much of the literature on interventions for youth exposed to traumatic loss describes how schools have responded to such events. Box 7.3 is one account of how school personnel helped staff and students following a student's murder by her boyfriend.

Chapter 5 described a public mental health approach to treating children and adolescents after a disaster (Pynoos, Goenjian, and Steinberg 1998). After psycho-educational, supportive, and cognitive behavioral interventions have addressed traumatic experiences and reminders, grief can then be treated. This model's specific therapeutic goals are to

1. Identify grief responses.
2. Teach the nature and course of bereavement.
3. Increase affective tolerance for reminders of the loss.
4. Reconstitute a nontraumatic representation in memory of the deceased.
5. Encourage open reminiscing.
6. Address last memories that stimulate remorse, shame, or guilt.
7. Consider constructive ways to revise mental relationships with the deceased.
8. Examine the influence of the loss of the parent or sibling on current relationships, including those with peers.
9. Promote social skills to talk about the loss, responding to others' comments, and increasing one's capacity for empathy. (Pynoos, Goenjian, and Steinberg 1998)

The Center for Traumatic Stress in Children and Adolescents created a treatment manual for therapists working with children and adolescents bereaved by the September 11, 2001, terrorist attacks on New York City and Washington, D.C. (Cohen et al. 2001). Like the model described in chapter 5 (Pynoos, Goenjian, and Steinberg 1998), the first eight sessions deal with cognitive behavioral therapeutic strategies for treating traumatic bereavement, followed by eight bereavement-focused sessions that introduce the concepts of bereavement and mourning, resolve ambivalent feelings about the deceased, save positive memories of the deceased, redefine the relationship, commit to current relationships, and make meaning of the traumatic loss. Recognizing family members' needs and the primary caregiver's important role, this model combines individual and joint child–parent bereavement-focused sessions. In addition, it looks at cultural factors affecting how symptoms are manifested, along with the traditions and rituals for bereavement. Thus, interventions may be applied "in a manner which respects and benefits from the child's culture and religion" (Cohen et al. 2001:9).

A psychological debriefing may help reduce adolescents' distress after a major disaster (Stallard and Law 1993; Yule and Udwin 1991). Although there have

Box 7.3 Coping with the Trauma of a Violent Death: One School's Response to a Student's Murder

CLASS MEETINGS

Class meetings were held to directly address the facts, minimize rumors, and allow students to share their reactions to the murder. Grief responses were normalized and validated and met with compassion.

PLACES TO GRIEVE

Grieving students were given places in the school where they could grieve with other students.

A MEMORIAL SERVICE

Since the parents of the murdered student did not have a memorial service open to the public, a memorial service conducted in the school gymnasium held after school was perceived to be an important part of the healing process. Cameras and journalists were not allowed at the event.

STUDENT SUPPORT SERVICES IN AND OUT OF SCHOOL

Students were given written information detailing professional and informal supports that would be available to them within the school and in the community. The guidance counselors established a hotline and drop-in center, with the school being open 24 hours a day for five days following the event. Telephone numbers of area outpatient clinics, mental health centers, and emergency services were provided.

BEREAVEMENT COUNSELING FOR STAFF

Bereavement counselors from a local mental health clinic were brought into to talk with staff and provide education and support about their own grief and how to respond to students.

STAFF AND ADMINISTRATIVE PRESENCE

Staff was visible and accessible to students during several days following the event. Class time was given up for discussion of events, and school rules regarding punctuality were relaxed.

THE MEDIA

The school quickly encountered insensitive and unprofessional journalists seeking to sensationalize the story and the emotional response of students. All interviews with journalists were done exclusively by school administrators and guidance counselors after the first day when some journalists handled information from students in ways that left students feeling violated.

MEMORIAL TRIBUTES

Memorial tributes to the student included various memorial scholarships, and the planting of a tree and memorial stone.

Source: Based on J. P. Franson, Coping with the Trauma of a Violent Death, *NASSP Bulletin* 72 (1988): 88–91.

been few studies of interventions to date, Yule (2001) used the emerging evidence, discussions with international experts on disaster interventions, and his own research experience to make the following recommendations for responding to adolescents' exposure to traumatic events and disasters:

1. Schools and community agencies should conduct risk assessments and be prepared for potential disasters.
2. Agencies responsible for adolescents' psychosocial needs after disasters should ensure that staff have experience in helping bereaved children and are adequately trained in appropriate psychosocial debriefing interventions.
3. Primary needs (i.e., for safety, security, health care) must be met before psychosocial intervention is offered.
4. Psychosocial interventions should not be initiated while adolescents are in a state of shock or dissociation.
5. Likewise, group help should not be arranged immediately but, rather, five to ten days after the disaster. Some contact, however, should be made indirectly right away; for example, written materials or appropriate resource pamphlets could be handed out.
6. Individuals trained in group skills and supervision should lead the groups.

7. Schools and agencies should use tried and tested manuals when available.
8. Interventions should not be confined to single sessions.
9. Adolescents should be screened and monitored and referred for additional assistance as indicated.

Community and Gang Violence

Adolescents living in communities afflicted by violence often repeatedly confront traumatic death, resulting in feelings of alienation, despair, and isolation (box 7.4). Indeed, adolescents are two times more likely than adults to be victims of serious violent crime (Saltzman et al. 2001), and those "exposed to violence are at increased risk for a spectrum of adverse psychosocial difficulties and functional impairments" and traumatic grief (Saltzman et al. 2001:291). In a survey of 812 middle school students exposed to trauma, 22 percent were directly exposed to violence, 37 percent had witnessed violence, 58 percent had a close friend or

Box 7.4 Experience of Community and Gang Violence

We live in two different Americas. In the ghetto, our laws are totally different, our language is totally different, and our lives are totally different. I've never felt American, I've only felt African American. . . . It's hard for me to say how I'm an American when I live in a second America—an America that doesn't wave the red, white, and blue flag with fifty stars for fifty states. I live in a community that waves a white flag because we have almost given up. I live in a community where on the walls are the names of fallen comrades of war. . . . Listen to what I'm saying. I know you don't want to hear about the pain and suffering that goes on in "that" part of the city. I know you don't want to hear about the kids getting shot in "that" part of the city. But little do you know that "that" part of the city is your part of the city too. This is our neighborhood, this is our city, and this is our America. This is LeAlan Jones on November 19, 1996. I hope I survive. I hope I survive. I hope I survive. Signing off. Peace.

Source: L. Jones and L. Newman, *Our America: Life and Death on the South Side of Chicago* (New York: Pocket Books, 1997), 199–200.

family member badly hurt or killed in an accident or violent incident, and 7 percent had untreated chronic severe PTSD and comorbid depression from severe trauma or loss experiences (Saltzman et al. 2001).

Group-based interventions with teens exposed to community violence may be helpful. A recent field-trial study of the effectiveness of a school-based trauma- and grief-focused group psychotherapy protocol found that the intervention reduced posttraumatic stress and complicated grief symptoms and improved academic performance (Saltzman et al. 2001). Another pilot study, which evaluated the effects of a ten-week, community-based grief and trauma therapy group for adolescent survivors of homicide, indicated that the group helped reduce PTSD symptoms in inner-city African American adolescent survivors (Salloum, Avery, and McClain 2001). The lack of a control group limits the conclusions that can be drawn from this project, but the study suggests that such interventions should be further tested.

Proposing that the goal of interventions to address gang and community violence be focused on the "secondary victims" of homicidal violence would be negligent. Instead, given the nature and incidence of homicidal violence in socially disadvantaged, urban, nonwhite (i.e., African American and Latino) communities (Barrett 1996), preventive and broader interventions are needed. Recommendations to improve these interventions and the current social policy are as follows:

1. Public education about the problem, treatment, and prevention strategies.
2. Gun control to limit the availability of firearms.
3. Better training of professionals who work with youth.
4. Additional research to evaluate prevention and treatment strategies. (Holinger et al. 1994)

Other recommendations pertain to empowerment strategies of historically disadvantaged communities to protest violence; draw on culturally respected institutional resources (e.g., churches) to lead "educational campaigns and social-ization efforts to discourage propagation of brutality and violence"; involve men in the community to address the issue and provide role models; and educate youth about the risk of lethal confrontation and conflict management skills (Barrett 1996:60). In the long run, the advocacy of social justice policies to ameliorate poverty, address socioeconomic inequities, and reform the correctional system are the most important.

Kids Alive and Loved (KAL) is a grassroots movement founded by Bernadette Leite after the murder of her seventeen-year-old son. Excerpts from an inter-view with her in 1994 describe a process of discovery and her response to the needs of young people exposed to violence. Leite explains that one solution to youth violence is to mobilize

> survivors to offer support to youth who are grieving the violent death of multiple friends and/or family members. Survivors have a deep desire to prevent loss of life and to prevent other families from experiencing the pain of death. Some violence prevention programs focus on taking back the streets. We believe that if we take back our kids, the streets will take care of themselves. (Thomas, Leite, and Duncan 1998:163)

Social workers and other helping professionals must acknowledge and prevent the atrocious conditions in poverty-ridden communities that cause pain and suffering, and work with bereaved families affected by violence to help them heal and confront the local conditions that cause the violence.

Summary

Despite the many interventions for bereaved adolescents, few have been systematically evaluated in treatment outcome studies. This chapter examined issues salient to grief interventions with teens, described developmentally appropriate interventions for this age group, and reviewed interventions and practice principles for the main forms of loss in adolescence. There are several gaps in the descriptions and evaluation studies of interventions for the grief associated with other forms of loss encountered by teens. Examples are grief interventions for adolescents coping with substance abuse, sexual assault, divorce, terminal illness, incarceration, loss associated with immigration, sexual identity, and social alienation. In addition, with the exception of the few studies of youth bereaved by trauma or violence, the bereavement of historically disadvantaged and culturally diverse youth and the most appropriate interventions for their grief have not been explored. Some evidence in intervention studies shows that response and participation rates vary by ethnic minority status (Rotheram-Borus, Stein, and Lin 2001), suggesting that culturally relevant modifications may be needed for ethnic minorities to participate in formal evaluation studies. Because belief systems, manifestations of grief, grief rituals, family roles, and historical experiences all are influenced by culture, social workers and other professionals helping bereaved teens must develop and test culturally competent interventions. Culturally specific methods, techniques, and skills proposed for working with children and adolescents in counseling and therapy (e.g., Ho 1992; Thompson and Rudolph 2000; Vargas and Koss-Chioino 1992) should be adapted and tested in grief interventions.

8

Grief and Loss in Young Adulthood

Young adulthood (defined here as approximately twenty-two to thirty-five years of age) is characterized by an orientation toward the future and anticipation of positive changes: completing college or graduate school, starting and solidifying a career, marrying or committing to a life partner, buying a home, giving birth or adopting children, and forming new friendships. Nevertheless, each of those changes, even when positive, may also bring some losses: moving away from one's family of origin, leaving childhood friends, losing a job, and giving up dreams. Some young adults experience major losses, such as infertility, miscarriage, abortion, or prenatal or perinatal death; death of an infant to sudden infant death syndrome (SIDS); birth of a child with severe disabilities; onset of a physical or mental disability; death of a peer or partner by an accident, AIDS, cancer, or a heart attack; and sexual or physical abuse.

This chapter covers only a few of these losses during young adulthood. But as we discuss loss during young adulthood and then in middle and late adulthood, those characteristics of the grief process found at all ages will become apparent. For example, we begin with young adults' grief over the death of a child in young adulthood and later turn to middle-aged and old adults' grief over the death of an adult child. The focus of this chapter is young parents' grief over the death of a fetus or infant. Similarly, widowhood for a young adult has a different meaning from that of widowhood in middle or old age. Even so, many of the issues faced by grieving partners are similar for all ages. We briefly examine the grief and loss issues associated with interpersonal violence and sexual assault because of the high rates of such trauma in young adulthood, especially for women, as well as how painful feelings associated with earlier childhood abuse can surface in young adulthood.

Developmental Considerations

The main tasks facing young adults are achieving financial independence and stability and establishing autonomy in decision making (Arnett 2000), although these tasks may vary in cultures that place a higher value on the family and community than the mainstream Western cultures do. In most Western cultures, young adults leave home and become responsible for their own housing, get a job or higher education, marry or commit to a significant partnership, raise children and care for others, become more involved in the larger community, and figure out how to spend time with both their family of origin and their newly created family. The decisions made in young adulthood determine much of a person's remaining life in regard to informal relationships, vocation or career, and lifestyle.

According to Erik Erikson's (1968, 1978) theoretical framework, young adulthood is a time when people move from the identity fragmentation, confusion, and exploration characteristic of adolescence into more intimate engagements with significant others. This is the time when young adults try out new relationships and connect with others in new ways while also preserving their individuality. Those who resolve the crisis of intimacy versus isolation are able to experience love. But those who are unable to resolve this problem may feel alienated, disconnected, and alone, unable to form a significant, committed relationship. Marriage, however, may no longer be a salient marker in the transition to young adulthood because of the growing number of young adults who currently live together unmarried, for an increasing number of years, in committed heterosexual and gay/lesbian/transgender relationships. Independent decision making and financial autonomy may be more significant than marriage in marking this transition, although these markers also have become blurred by the current high rates of unemployment and underemployment in our society (Arnett 1998).

Young adults often have to negotiate conflicting, incompatible, or competing life roles and choices. Levinson (1978) described young adulthood as a period in which life structures are in constant motion, evolving as new circumstances unfold. *Life structure* is the result of specific decisions and choices made during life in areas such as relationships, occupation, and childbearing. Levinson suggested that some persons may take up to fifteen years to make the transition to adulthood and to construct a stable adult life structure. Cultural and social capacities (e.g., family support, socioeconomic status, educational opportunities) affect life structure choices by constraining or facilitating opportunities, such as whether or when to marry or to begin or delay childbearing. Major losses during young adulthood, such as a child's or partner's death, can dramatically disrupt the developmental process of constructing a stable adult life structure and completing developmentally appropriate tasks, such as differentiating from one's family of origin. In addition, earlier losses, such as abuse or a parent's early death during childhood, often surface as bitterness, anger, or anxieties in young adulthood. Grief over earlier losses may surface in young adults' dreams, relationships with others, and physical and mental health (Harvey 2000).

Resilience
Background Characteristics

Socioeconomic status and level of education are critical to young adults beginning a career or graduate or professional school. Childhood socioeconomic status is an important mediating factor in young adult transitions. Young adults from higher social-class backgrounds have more opportunities to choose from and more resources with which to negotiate any adversities, whereas low-income and ethnic minority adults have fewer opportunities (Smyer et al. 1998). However, because of current economic conditions, the high rate of unemployment, the high cost of housing, and residential instability, even relatively advantaged young adults have found this transition more difficult. As a result, more young adults are returning to live with their family of origin, even though they are then out of synch with the developmental challenges of mainstream American culture. Conversely, some young adults in some cultures choose to remain living close to one another (e.g., Shoshone families on their tribal land) or to share the same home (e.g., Eastern European three-generation families who share a duplex).

Personal Capacities

The development of an identity, which includes abandoning the adolescent focus on self, becoming self-reliant, and connecting with important others, is integral to positive self-esteem and making adult commitments. Young adults who have been able to define a direction for their lives have more personal resources with which to cope with adversity. Identity development continues throughout adulthood, especially when dealing with various losses.

Compared with adolescents, young adults have more complex abstract cognitive capabilities combined with a greater awareness of personal feelings; that is, they typically are able to see things from several different viewpoints. Young adults generally are solidifying their values and beliefs and developing a moral conscience, as shown in their willingness and ability to take responsibility for others. Spirituality or a focus on what gives meaning, purpose, and direction to one's life is another personal capacity that young adults cultivate, especially when raising their own children.

Social Capacities

Parents' expectations become less salient to young adults, although they may still exert an influence. Being able to turn to parents and other adult role models for advice and support is central to young adults' social capacities. Their expanded social networks may include colleagues, neighbors, friends, parents of their children's friends, and extended family. Neighborhood, community, and friendship supports all affect young adults' decision making and coping with adversity.

Culture

Many young adults want to maintain equilibrium with their family of origin, although the family's expectations of what it means to be a good daughter or son may conflict with others' expectations and create conflicts with their families of origin who are grieving the death of an extended family member. Young adults from other cultures may struggle with their loyalty to their family in the context of mainstream American culture's emphasis on independence. As is true with earlier phases of life, professionals need to recognize and respect how culture may affect developmental considerations as well as reactions to loss.

Prenatal and Perinatal Death and Loss

The worldview of most young adult parents does not include the possibility that a fetus can die. Such deaths, often shrouded in silence or invisible to outsiders, include miscarriage or spontaneous abortion, the naturally occurring loss of a fetus before twenty weeks of gestation; complete abortion, in which the placenta or fetus is surgically removed; and stillbirth in late pregnancy in which either the fetus does not breathe or exhibit a heartbeat or the umbilical chord stops pulsating. It is estimated that 15 to 30 percent of all pregnancies end in miscarriage without a discernible cause, and that stillbirths account for 50 percent of infant mortality just before, during, or just after birth (Worden 2002). In the United States, one in eighty live births is a stillbirth (Gray and Lassance 2003). Generally in stillbirth, labor proceeds immediately and is allowed to occur naturally. But sometimes the pregnancy continues for several days or even weeks following the cessation of movement. With the knowledge that the fetus is already dead, the parents must deal with the anguish of giving birth or having surgery to end the pregnancy. In instances of miscarriage and stillbirth, the mother's emotional state is further taxed by her body, which confirms the reality of having been pregnant and given birth but having nothing to show for it, and by a society that does not appreciate the meaning of the loss (Hebert 1998).

Committed young adult partners usually greet a pregnancy with excitement, family and peer support, and a sense of "being on time" in the developmental tasks of parenting. Thus when such deaths occur, the parents struggle not only with the loss of the child with whom they were forming a bond but also with the loss of the hopes, dreams, and expectations for the child. They may feel as if they have lost part of themselves (Boyle 1997; Gray and Lassance 2003; Rubin and Malkinson 2001). Friends and family may minimize a death due to abortion, miscarriage, or stillbirth, assuming that (1) the unborn child did not have a personality, (2) attachments to an unborn child were never formed, or (3) that the mother is young enough to have another viable pregnancy. A common sentiment may be that "you are young enough to have more children" (e.g., replacement children). In fact, well-intended friends may intensify the loss by encouraging the parents to try for another child right away, without allowing them time to grieve, or by condescendingly assuring a mother who has chosen abortion that she was too young, poor, or inadequate to care for a child.

Another erroneous assumption is that such deaths are less difficult because the parent and newborn have not yet formed a relationship. These assumptions negate the bonds that are often formed throughout pregnancy, especially for the mother. Nowadays, the use of ultrasound imaging promotes bonds for both men and women (Worden 2002). In general, the longer the pregnancy is, and thus the more opportunities for attachment, the greater the grief over a perinatal death will be (Robinson, Baker, and Nackerund 1999). Parents faced with a miscarriage or stillbirth sustain a real loss, and for couples that suffer through numerous miscarriages or stillbirths, the loss is even worse. In such instances, they may also mourn the loss of their fertility or have to change their image of themselves as men or women.

It is important to recognize that in instances of in vitro fertilization, lesbian couples may also have similar grief reactions to a miscarriage or stillbirth. For such couples, a perinatal or infant death is an example of disenfranchised grief; that is, the loss is often discounted, and emotional and cultural supports normally available to other grievers are often not available. Regardless of the parents' sexual orientation, miscarriages in general are often treated as a socially negated loss. Because of the general lack of support, parents may not even tell others about the miscarriage, thereby making their grief even more invisible. Women who have several miscarriages tend to feel isolated from and envious of other mothers, assuming that all other women are able to give birth easily. Or friends and family members may be unaware of or uncomfortable with the loss, often asking intrusive questions about when the parents plan to start a family or why they are waiting so long. They may indicate that this unnatural event should be forgotten as soon as possible. Such discomfort and insensitivity can slow the parents' adaptation to the loss and heighten tensions between them.

Although social workers and other health care professionals may discount the significance of stillbirths, there now is greater recognition of the importance of holding, seeing, and naming the stillborn child and conducting a burial. Such practices can help parents realize their loss and assimilate it into their lives (Rubin and Malkinson 2001). But sometimes health care providers do not realize the importance of parents' connecting with their infant and whisk the child away or swaddle the child's body tightly so as not to let any imperfections show. Seeing the fetus or stillborn child can help some parents focus on the reality of the loss, say good-bye to the child, and begin to deal with their grief, although not all parents will choose to do so (Worden 2002). Chapter 9 presents conflicting evidence on the effectiveness of such interventions to help parents bond with their dead child.

When a baby dies through miscarriage or stillbirth, the parents' reactions tend to be similar to those of other mourners: shock, numbness, disbelief, emotional and cognitive resistance to the reality of the death, anger, bewilderment, guilt, depression, yearning, and somatization (Hebert 1998; Rosenblatt 2000a). However, some feelings, especially fears, self-blame, isolation, hopelessness, and guilt, tend to be intensified, especially when the mother feels responsible for her baby's stillbirth (Worden 2002). Fears of infertility, of the impact of the loss on the marriage, and of being a failure as a parent are common. Parents may struggle with issues of meaning: Why did this happen to them? Will it happen again? There is a tendency to blame oneself (What did I do wrong during the pregnancy?) or one's partner (Why did he or she insist that we wait so long before starting a family?). Similar to other forms of bereavement, people who experience a prenatal or perinatal loss say that they never get over it; instead, they learn to live with it (Hebert 1998).

Cultures vary in how they respond to perinatal death. For example, Muslims regard a perinatal death as being as significant and meaningful as the loss of someone later in life and treat the fetus with dignity and respect. The death is regarded as the will of Allah, and his decision is seen as just. Since the fetus is accorded a moral, legal, and spiritual value, bereavement practices and procedures tend to be similar to those for deceased children and adults. The officially accepted bereavement period is three days, when other family members and the community cater to the bereaved parents. Rituals include sharing prayers, reading from the Qur'an and talking about the baby and his or her life in the hereafter (Hebert 1998; Saleh and Kerr 1996). Such differences highlight the importance of social workers using culturally competent interactions with bereaved young parents.

Sudden Infant Death Syndrome

Sudden infant death syndrome takes the lives of seven thousand to ten thousand infants each year, most frequently of infants two to six months old. In instances of SIDS death, the parents' guilt feelings may be intensified by the lack of any scientific and objective reasons for the death, which can cast suspicion on the grieving parents (Worden 2002). Typically, the baby is healthy, without any apparent illness or distress before dying; the parent may wake in the morning to find that the child has died during the night. The causes and pathogenesis of SIDS are not fully known, although conflicting recommendations for preventing it abound, which can leave parents feeling even more confused, inadequate, and responsible for not following "expert" advice such as "turning the child," playing background music in the room, or not abusing substances. These feelings are often exacerbated by the legal system, since investigations of SIDS deaths are required.

The sense of loss is also worsened by the fact that the baby appeared to be healthy and thriving and then died without any warning. Compared with mothers grieving the death of a baby from causes other than SIDS, mothers recently bereaved by SIDS are found to have greater anxiety, a more negative perception of the world, and less resilience (Boyle 2003; Rubin and Malkinson 2001). Such anxiety may stem from the fact that others may imply that she was negligent and thus responsible for her child's death to SIDS, even though she could not have prevented it. Not surprisingly, all these factors place tremendous stress on the relationship of parents who are struggling with sadness, anger, and guilt (Worden 2002).

Abortion or Relinquishing a Child to Adoption

Abortion or relinquishing a child to adoption are two other types of child-related loss for young adults, although some may experience such losses earlier in adolescence, as discussed in chapter 6. The loss either may be current or may emerge from choices made earlier in life as a teenager without a committed partner (for a discussion of the grief associated with abortion and adoption relinquishment in late adolescence, see chapter 6). Mothers in their twenties or early thirties who earlier chose abortion but now are unable to carry a child to term are confronted with an earlier decision that they may have tried to bury and that is now tinged with regret and self blame (Worden 2002). As with most losses in life, they cannot simply put these earlier losses "out of their minds."

Birth mothers who chose in adolescence or young adulthood to give their child to an adoptive family may grieve for their unknown child until they die. If they felt that a partner or family forced them to relinquish the child, trauma and rage may later make their regret even worse (Haight et al. 2002). If extended family and friends did not have an opportunity to know the newborn, they may not share in the parents' grief or even acknowledge that it exists. When support systems learn about the relinquishment, they may treat the birth as something not to be discussed or even recognized and regard the young mother as unloving and uncaring, thereby creating another instance of disenfranchised grief. Relinquishment often is a family secret, hidden from view but heavy in the birth mother's heart. The birth mother is left with unanswered questions, which vary in salience during her life: Where is her child? Is he or she well cared for? Might she see him or her in a crowd? Would she recognize the child? What if she eventually found her child? Could her child be angry with her? Nonetheless, she may feel unable to express her thoughts and questions to anyone, even if she is later in a committed partner relationship.

Feelings of regret and guilt are especially complicated when parents must give up their children because of abuse, neglect, or incarceration. In such instances, they may face the complexities of trying to sustain a relationship with their child (e.g., incarcerated mothers) while having their behavior monitored and assessed during their visits. Social workers and other human service professionals need to recognize the grief of mothers who have voluntarily or involuntarily given up a child. Too often, the public blames the mother, labeling her as unloving or inadequate, while not knowing the full story—the class, cultural, religious, or racial disparities—behind her behavior.

Adoptive and foster parents also often grieve the loss of a hoped-for child or relationship. Most adoptive families now live with the knowledge that the adopted child may choose to seek out his or her birth mother. Despite their cognitive preparation for this loss, they may nevertheless feel abandoned, unappreciated, or even resented. Foster parents grieve continuously, especially if they want to adopt the child and are unable to do so, usually because of events beyond their control (Edelstein, Burge, and Waterman 2001). Yet professionals, pressured by competing demands from various systems, often overlook such grief.

Birth of a Child with Disabilities

Parents who give birth to a child who is less than "perfect" and not their fantasized child—one with developmental disabilities or other severe impairments such as muscular dystrophy, cystic fibrosis, or spinal bifida—struggle with their shattered dreams. They have some of the grief reactions associated with the death of a baby: shock; disbelief (why me?); despair; fear; anger at life, God or a supreme being, themselves, or their partner; and guilt over what they did wrong to create a child with disabilities. Some parents feel so depressed and desperate that they wish themselves or their child dead. Thoughts of killing themselves or the baby or leaving the baby somewhere else intensify parents' feelings of being "bad" and of being alone, as one mother admitted:

> When the overwhelming nature of the situation became apparent, I felt it was a "no-win" situation. I felt that if Hollie's life was to be so hard and so "missing" that it wasn't perhaps worth it for her to live. I wanted at one time for us to be together because I loved her so much that the only way we could be (together) was in death. We could still stay together that way as mother and child in peace. (Finnegan 1993:21)

Informed about the baby before his wife was, a father confessed, "I was so devastated that I came close to suffocating the baby before they told my wife" (Finnegan 1993:12).

Another young father's statement partially captures the intensity of grief over the birth of a child with disabilities: "Imagine the deepest darkest abyss seething with feelings of worthlessness, hopelessness, helplessness, anger, self-derision, and irrationality. Now magnify that a thousand times and you might get close to how it really feels" (Finnegan 1993:11).

The parents' grief is so intense in part because our cultural expectation is that the months of waiting during pregnancy will culminate in a joyful event. Most childbirth classes, child-rearing books, and the popular press rarely allude to anything other than the "perfect family," although fear of something going wrong during pregnancy often lies just below the surface, especially for mothers. Parents typically receive the news of their child's disability in the strange sur-roundings of a hospital and at a time when they are physically and emotionally exhausted. Health care professionals may insensitively deliver this devastating news right way and hurriedly present complex information when the parents are highly distraught, thereby creating further isolation at a time when support is most needed. They may feel alone in both gathering information and facing decisions regarding their child's care. A particularly difficult situation is when through the result of prenatal testing, parents receive the news that their baby is disabled and are then faced with the agonizing option of abortion, often without professional or family support. In such instances, they grieve a child whom they dearly anticipated but to whom they could not give birth.

The grieving process associated with the birth of a child with disabilities is complicated by the parents' grieving the death of the "expected" baby while at the same time trying to accept the "imperfect" baby. Even though they have the joy of being able to hold and love their baby, their life is suddenly and drastically changed. At the same time, parents may feel overwhelmed by the need to make major decisions within a relatively short time, such as whether to take the child home or consider foster care, adoption, or institutionalization. Even though most parents make their decision based on what will be best for their child, when they acknowledge their own limitations in caring for a child with disabilities, they tend to fear criticism and ostracism in explaining their decision to others. One couple wrote to their friends and family about the decision to give up their disabled child for adoption:

> The decision we have made has not been easy. It is the most painful choice that we have ever had to make. . . . We finally realized that our decision could only be made based on our current life situation. . . . Letting go took courage that we did not know we had. We do love our son and hope that the life that we have chosen for him will grant him the ability to achieve to his fullest and that his parents will give him the opportunities that we felt incapable of. (Finnegan 1993:123)

Parents who choose adoption for a child with a disability often grieve two losses: that of the child they expected and did not get and that of the child to whom they gave birth and "gave away."

With adoption, the fact that the child is living with another family can make integrating the loss more difficult. Paradoxically, parents who lost a child to miscarriage or stillbirth but chose an adoption plan before the child's death have been found to accept the death better than did those who faced the "letting go" required in giving up the child. It is a paradox because death is final, whereas relinquishing a child with disabilities to adoption has no "end," even if the choice is voluntary (Finnegan 1993). The first birthday is often especially difficult, since parents relive the pain and sorrow surrounding the birth, which they had anticipated to be a joyous event. Because they chose to relinquish their child, they may also feel a double sense of isolation: from friends who have never lost a child and from those who have suffered the pain of giving birth to a child with disabilities but are raising the child (Finnegan 1993). They may feel envious or resentful when watching other seemingly "intact" families, especially those who disapprove of their choice.

The birth of a child with disabilities leads to a type of *chronic sorrow*. As noted in chapter 1, the concept of chronic sorrow represents a paradigm shift by recasting as normal what was previously considered pathological and by encompassing grief that has no end point but varies in intensity over the parents' lifetime. Unlike grieving the death of a child who will forever be absent, chronic sorrow is living with unending loss and irreparable wounds. At the same time, the grieving parents must be able to mobilize all their resources, energy, and courage to cope with this loss that will be with them until either they or the child dies. The essence of chronic sorrow is the discrepancy between what is perceived as reality and what continues to be dreamed of. The loss is continuing, since the source of the loss is ever present; that is, the loss is a living loss (Roos 2002). In chronic sorrow, the affected person deals with inevitable and necessary losses entailed in living as well as with the continuing presence of an individual who may not be fully grieved and whose absence may not be fully accepted (Viorst 1986).

When parents give up a child with disabilities for adoption, chronic sorrow permeates the adoption circle of birth parents, adoptive parents, and adoptee. Giving one's child, whether or not disabled, to another family, inevitably leaves both the birth and adoptive parent(s) with unanswered questions and the paradox of simultaneous joy and sorrow. The birth parents that chose relinquishment have feelings of loss, the empty place at the table, and the memories of the "last year" when the pregnancy meant hopes and dreams of a future baby; they must cope with the loss of their child, no matter that he or she was not perfect. Both the birth parents and child may dream of finding each other one day. Even though they chose to adopt a child with disabilities, the adoptive family may struggle with the loss of their dreams for a healthy child who looks like them. At the same time, the adoptive family may be threatened by the adopted child's yearning for and perhaps seeking his or her birth family.

The parents of severely impaired children live each day with the source of their grief. Since the source of the loss is always present, chronic sorrow is about year after year of living with the inevitability of loss, of negotiating reality demands required by the loss, and of contending with ongoing and resurgent grief reactions. Fantasy is central to chronic sorrow: what could have been or what should have been (and maybe will be, after all). To some extent, the parents' responses resemble the grief over a child's death: shock, numbness, denial, and disbelief. At first, denial is necessary; otherwise the shock would be so overwhelming that the child would not be cared for. Parents feel anger and a sense of unfairness; guilt, especially by the mother, at what they might have done to prevent the disability; and "doctor shopping" in search of a cure, a new treatment, or a medication, even turning toward "quackery" in their hope to "fix things." To some extent, the parents of children with severe disabilities must preserve hope, for to do otherwise would make it impossible to wake each day to twenty-four-hour caregiving demands. Although their lives have not been destroyed, they have been dramatically reshaped by the daily reality of having a child to care for who will never grow up as they imagined. Unlike the parents of a child who has died, the parents of severely impaired children cannot fully integrate their loss, since their child continues to live and requires infinitely more care than do other children (Roos 2002). Even in instances of less severe learning disabilities, the daily reminder of the loss intensifies the chronic sorrow of parents, who often blame themselves for the learning difficulties; they have to readjust continually to changes in expectations and an inability to predict behavior according to expectations of a normative outcome (Vigilante 1983).

With the death of a child, social support systems mobilize. With the birth of a child with severe disabilities, support systems may disappear, not knowing what to say or do or even fearful that the disability may in some way be "catching." In addition, a child with disabilities may not be recognized socially, as if she or he does not exist (Roos 2002). Accordingly, parents may start to isolate themselves, reducing their engagement with earlier social networks that fail to acknowledge the continuing loss, and turning instead to support groups of parents with similar challenges. Parents feel the loss of self and others as their world revolves around the needs of their child with disabilities.

As with a child's death, parents never return to the life they had before the birth of their disabled child. Similarly, the birth of such a child can severely strain the parents' relationship, with their blaming each other for the child's "genetic defect," disagreeing about decisions about care alternatives, and being out of synch in their grieving process. The stigma surrounding children with disabilities also may disrupt the family (Roos 2002). It is not unusual for one parent to be left with caring for the child twenty-four hours a day, gradually using up their financial and internal resources. In regard to the concept of resilience, when family or community supports fail to relieve their burdens, the parents' personal capacities are gradually depleted.

Many parents are able to begin a new life together and move on, yet always with a sadness that becomes part of them. Life returns to a "new" normal (Finnegan 1993), with most parents eventually giving birth to another baby. Four themes emerged from a review of sixty books written by parents who had a child with a severe chronic illness or injury: (1) a realistic appraisal of disability, (2) the extraordinary demands made on families, (3) extraordinary emotional stress, and (4) resolution. Resolution does not refer to the end of parental grieving but instead reflects a judgment: whether to remain bitter and angry or to move toward an "unimagined life" in which meaning, empathy, and love emerge (Parkes 1972). Pearl Buck, an acclaimed novelist, captured the choices she made, along with the meaning derived from caring for her severely retarded daughter:

We learn as much from sorrow as we do from joy, as much from illness as from health, from handicap as from advantage—and indeed perhaps more. Not out of fullness has the human soul always reached its highest, but often out of deprivation. This is not to say that sorrow is better than happiness, illness better than health, poverty better than richness. Had I been given the choice, I would a thousand times over have chosen my child sound, a whole, a normal woman today, living a woman's life. I miss eternally the person she cannot be. I am not resigned and never will be. Resignation is something still and dead, an inactive acceptance that bears no fruit. On the contrary, I rebel against the unknown fate that fell upon her somewhere and stopped her growth. Such things ought not to be, and because it has happened to me and because I know what this sorrow is I devote myself and my child to the work of doing all we can to prevent such suffering for others. (1950:57–58)

Buck articulated the persistent fantasy, the gap between her fantasy and her child's abilities, and her determination to make a difference in the world.

Onset of Disability or Chronic Illness in Young Adulthood

Young adults who are severely disabled also experience a type of chronic sorrow, from knowing that their loss will never end, as well as continuous feelings of anger, isolation, sadness, and jealousy of those who can live outside their physical selves. Such life-altering injuries are most likely in adolescence and young adulthood, when young people engage in riskier behavior, especially before they have children.

Although he was not a young adult when he broke his neck while riding a horse, Christopher Reeve, an actor, articulated feelings of grief that may be shared by young adults with a physical disability. He agreed that the unpredictability of his sorrow was the most difficult:

I was told by so many experts . . . that as time went by not only would I become more stable physically but also I would become well adjusted psychologically to my condition. I have found exactly the opposite to be true. . . . Psychologically, I fear I have established a workable baseline; I have my down days, but I haven't been incapacitated by them. This doesn't mean, though, that I accept paralysis or that I'm at peace with it. The sensory deprivation hurts the most. . . . The physical world is still very meaningful to me; I have not been able to detach myself from it and live entirely in my mind. I'm jealous when some talks about a recent skiing vacation, when friends embrace each other, or even when Will plays hockey in the driveway with someone else. (1999:274)

Despite his national visibility, fame, and wealth, Christopher Reeve experienced the social stigma and the disenfranchised grief of someone who was now markedly "different."

Chronic illness or disability in young adulthood violates long-term scripts for the way that life is supposed to be. Assumptions about the world as a benign place are shattered, and the grieving process requires making new and more realistic assumptions (Janoff-Bulman 1992). The now ill or disabled young adult must form new relationships with others, his or her body, and lifestyle. Adults with a brain injury, typically due to an automobile accident, face the loss of purpose, personality, intellectual capacity, sexual function, and capacity to love (Chwalisz 1998). A brain injury can profoundly change a family's interaction and emotional dynamics, especially since the brain-injured young adult is unable to show affection or emotion. Social support is critical to negotiating new assumptions and interpersonal relationships. Unfortunately, however, partners and other family members, embarrassed and uncomfortable by these changes, may pull away from their loved one coping with chronic illness or injury, only adding to his or her many losses (Harvey 2000).

Death of a Partner

In young adulthood, a partner's death is an off-time event, unanticipated and not normative. When we are in our late twenties, we do not expect our partner to die. In fact, young adults and their friends often have had little experience with death and have few guidelines for how to act. Regardless of age or the nature of the death, a partner's death requires that the bereaved "relearn" himself or herself (Campbell and Silverman 1996; Carverhill 1997; Neimeyer 2001a; Walter 2003). The grieving partner confronts questions of "Who am I now?" or "How were those aspects of myself affected, shaped by, and perhaps dependent on my partner who died?" He or she must learn again how to be and act in the world without a partner (Attig 2001b:40–41). Survivors face questions of how their relationship with their deceased partner has shifted, how the loss has changed their life, and what new meanings they have discovered (Walter 2003).

Young Widows and Widowers

Because widowhood under the age of fifty is nonnormative, less is known about young widows and widowers than about those older than fifty. Although age by itself is not a determining factor in grief, death of a partner for young adults tends to be more distressing than for older persons (Lopata 1996; Neugarten and Hagestad 1976; Roach and Kitson 1989). In addition, gender differences in widows' and widowers' well-being are more pronounced in younger than in older adults. According to Levinson, "For young widows, the death of a spouse places them in a category out of synch with their developmental life stage," which can increase their sense of loneliness and difference from their peers (1997:278). Such "off-time" events may have secondary consequences, such as the lack of peer support, role models for grieving, and previous experience with the death of loved ones. Peers may withdraw from the young widow, feeling uncomfortable about including her in activities with their own husbands and perhaps perceiving a young widow as a threat to their own relatively new relationship. In addition, issues faced by couples may seem frivolous and trite to a young widow. At the same time, the young widow may be struggling to raise young children (DeGiulio1992; Shaffer 1993; Walter 2003).

Regardless of age, sexual orientation, or marital status, both widows and widowers have the following issues: loneliness and isolation, an identity shift from "we" to "I," changing relationships, anger, responsibility for oneself, and the handling of rituals and marker events such as anniversaries of the death (Walter 1996). Widows and widowers generally experience five reactions to their loss:

1. Intense emotional and mental reactions to the death (e.g., shock, pain, anger, and guilt).
2. Emotional pain and strong emotional reactions to stimuli that trigger the grief, such as photographs, clothing, various activities, anniversaries, and birthdays.
3. A continuing relationship with the dead partner, including memories, dreams, rituals, and contact through conversation.
4. Changes in functioning, such as withdrawal from social settings and loss of work motivation and interest.
5. Changes in relationships with family, friends, and romantic partners. (Bowlby 1980; Klass 1996a; Lopata 1996; Neimeyer 1998a; Rubin 1999; Schuchter 1986; Schuchter and Zisook 1993)

Young widows and widowers have two kinds of loneliness: (1) the loss of daily shared routines and private moments, of family holidays, and of sexual intimacy; and (2) "no longer being the single most important person in someone's life, nor having a significant other who shares important experiences" (Yalom and Vinogradov 1988:435–36). In effect, the surviving partner must deal with the loss of the "mirror" aspect of his or her relationship, in which one partner can reinforce the positive self-image of the other. The loss of this "mirror" can create secondary losses, such as the loss of the sense of being important, special, beautiful, loved, or even lovable. As a grieving wife complained, "I no longer feel special to anyone" (Walter 1996:74). Bereaved partners must adopt the self-image of a single person as well as readjust to a single person's life.

Most bereaved partners also experience anger, ambivalence, and hostility toward their deceased partner who has abandoned them, even while they try to retain and internalize the positive aspects of their relationship. These feelings may be aggravated by society's tendency to sanctify persons who die young; in other words, their death is seen as more tragic than the death of an older person. A partner's death in young adulthood also raises issues concerning one's own mortality and the recognition that survivors are the only ones ultimately responsible for their life and happiness. "Reconstructed memory"—learning to deal with emotions from the past along with developing new attachments and feelings and changing one's social identity—is a continuing process that generally lasts for the rest of a bereaved partner's life (Kauffman 1994b; Lopata 1996; Schuchter 1986).

The challenges faced by young widows or widowers may push them into searching for new ways to meet their unfilled internal needs and to make interpersonal changes, including a new committed relationship (Levinson 1997). Early bereavement forces young adults to identify and clarify their values and alter their commitments to previously established long-term goals. This may entail changing careers and seeking new ways of being with themselves and others (Shaffer 1993). Young widows' grief may give them opportunities to make positive shifts in their life perspectives, with "a theme of metamorphosis and rebirth." If their husband strongly influenced their ways of living (e.g., as "just a wife"), young widows may now be free to try out new behaviors and life options. Because early widowhood "challenges women's internal assumptive world, a system of beliefs one has about life" (DiGiulio 1992: 99), they may place less emphasis on surface appearances and the approval of friends and family. Such a transformation may be related to the youth of the women experiencing such deep suffering and loss. In fact, young widows may be more resilient than older widows. Loss at an earlier age may enable them to remake their lives and "start over" in a way that is fuller and more complete than previously possible and might seem unrealistic to an older widow. In such instances, young widows gain personal autonomy, an enlarged capacity for caring, a greater appreciation of human relationships, and a strong sense of the preciousness of life (Shaffer 1993:122). In sum, the loss of a partner at a young age appears to initiate a transition that affects a young woman's life in far-reaching ways, such as how she recreates meaning in her life (Weenolsen 1988).

Young widowers may also realize such long-term gains and shifts in priorities, especially if they relied on their wives as central to their life and their sense of identity. If their wife was the primary caregiver for their children, they may be forced to reevaluate the meaning of work to them, because of the daily demands of raising children and managing a household. A young widower may need to relearn his sense of himself and renegotiate his relationship with himself (Campbell and Silverman 1996; Carverhill 1997). Some young widows may have an "I can do it myself" attitude and avoid showing their grief publicly or in front of their children. This may derive from men's being socialized to be strong and to assume the role of "protector" of family members. For men, action may be a way to begin the grieving process and move toward healing (Golden and Miller 1998). Along with this "just do it" stance, young widowers appear more likely to create a memorial for their deceased wife and to try to integrate their personal loss into their professional lives (Walter 2003). Despite their tendency to be more private and autonomous than young widows, widowers are more likely to remarry, and sooner, than widows are (Lister 1991; Walter 2003). Both younger widows and widowers experience changes in their relationships with in-laws, extended family, and friendship networks and have problems with dating, often because of loyalty to the deceased partner. The idea of loving someone else evokes a wide range of feelings, from a signal of healing and readiness to move forward to a sense of betrayal of the marriage, as if loving someone else invalidates the love for the deceased partner (Walter 2003).

The loss of a heterosexual partner in a relationship in which the couple has been cohabiting is another form of disenfranchised grief that is not or cannot be openly acknowledged, publicly mourned, or socially supported (Doka 1989d, 2002a). The closeness of nonrelative relationships in our society is often not understood or appreciated. Because such relationships are defined by society as not legitimate, feelings of grief, especially guilt and anger, often are greater (Walter 2003). Social support is often limited both at the time of and following the death, without defined transitional roles for the survivor. There may be little formal recognition that the lover or cohabiting partner is bereaved, few personnel policies to provide time off from work, and often little sympathy (Doka 1987). When others negate the pain of grief, the survivor's sense of identity is deeply affected. Because of this lack of social sanctioning and support, bereaved partners of nontraditional relationships may become alienated from their family, friends, religious institutions, and colleagues. Like gay and lesbian partners, the surviving partner may face financial and legal barriers, but they may not have the community and friendship networks or capacities that bereaved gays and lesbians may have. In addition, persons in nontraditional heterosexual relationships may disenfranchise themselves by failing to acknowledge and recognize their grief. The person himself or herself, not others, causes the intensified grief, often out of shame and embarrassment (Kauffman 1989, 2002).

Death of a Partner or Friend from AIDS

Although our discussion focuses on gay men, the incidence of AIDS in others, such as African American women, is growing. Regardless of the community affected, traditional theories of loss, which focus on the individual, overlook the experience of multiple losses by an entire community (Dworkin and Kaufer 1995; Walter 2003). The losses associated with AIDS affect not only individuals but also social networks and communities: coworkers, acquaintances, friends, and role models. It is loss not only of an "other" but also of a collective. Survivors usually know hundreds of friends who have died from AIDS, with the onset of mourning one loss often overlapping with the end stage of grieving another. At times, they may feel as if they are watching a rehearsal of their own death.

Survivors live through the cumulative impact of numerous deaths and losses, a toll that includes hours of worry, countless hospital and hospice visits, and actual and contemplated suicides. This cumulative survivor experience has been likened to one leaving a permanent psychological mark or death imprint (Niederland 1971; Nord 1997). The multiple losses encompass a sense of personal history, feelings of safety and positive self-esteem, future, hope and interest in life, community, celebration, and sexual freedom (Nord 1997). Nearly every aspect of AIDS survivors' lives is imprinted with death, with the grieving continuous. For many gay men, "death is less an event than an environment" (Sullivan 1990:19). Fresh losses remind survivors of the previous losses. Survivors talk about the fact that these AIDS-related losses will continue into an interminable future, with little hope that "things will get better" (Nord 1997). The dying process is especially prolonged in instances of early diagnosis of AIDS, a "continuous process which begins the moment that you half consciously accept the probability that you are about to lose someone very close to you: this process may not end until years later, even many years later" (Shernoff 1998:xvii). Fortunately, with new prescription drugs, AIDS is beginning to resemble a chronic illness rather than an immediately life-threatening one, although the long-term effectiveness of the drugs is unknown, and new strains of the HIV virus are emerging.

Those outside the gay community may discredit the cumulative impact of the loss endured. The stigmatization of AIDS compounds the sense of endless or chronic loss. The family members of survivors often are unable, because of their own hostility, shame, and ambivalence, to provide the support so desperately needed. The losses associated with AIDS are another example of disenfranchised grief, a result of both social strictures and stigma and also of the bereaved's reactions of shame, denial, alienation, and withdrawal. Given the multitude of losses over an extended time period, it is not surprising that AIDS survivors are at high risk of complicated grief. Survivor grief is common, with a preoccupation with "why him" and "why not me?" This may be characterized by denial and trying to carry on as if nothing happened, which later may be manifested in somatic symptoms, depression, sleep disturbances, excessive or inappropriate shame or guilt, suicidal thoughts, substance abuse, and a global state of anxiety about "who will be next" (Hintze et al. 1994; Lippmann, James, and Frierson 1993; Martin 1988; Odets 1994; Shrader 1992). The accumulation of numerous losses with delayed grief can traumatize some survivors (Nord 1997; Walter 2003).

Death of a Gay or Lesbian Partner from Other Causes

Although most bereavement research on the loss of a partner in young adulthood has focused on AIDS survivors, some gay and lesbian partners or cohabitating heterosexual couples have partners who die in young adulthood for reasons other than HIV/AIDS. Nevertheless, before AIDS, few young or middle-aged gay men knew widowed gay men and, because of their youth, had only limited experience with death and support resources.

Unfortunately, there has been little research on bereaved gay and lesbian partners, especially those of color. Wide variations in homosexual relationships combined with a lack of research require that social workers should be careful not to oversimplify the complexities of gay, lesbian, and transgendered persons' experiences with death (Walter 2003). What is clear is that our society's homophobia tends to make grieving difficult and complicated, especially when family and friends minimize the magnitude of the loss. Blatant examples of this tendency to minimize the loss are when gay men or lesbians are denied family and medical leave to care for their dying partner; end-of-life decision making; bereavement leave to attend their lover's funeral, memorial service, and other rituals; or any inheritance when there is not a will.

Because the research on widowed gay men and lesbians usually focuses separately on either widows or widowers, we report first the findings for widowed gay men and then for lesbians. But many of the issues are probably similar for both gay men and lesbians. As with other types of loss, attention to individual and cultural differences in lesbian and gay communities is critical.

Gay Widowers

Homophobic reactions of scorn, ostracism, fear, or blame compound the grief of gay men and increase the likelihood of shame (Schwartzberg 1996; Shernoff 1998). Although the surviving partners are, in effect, widowed, they generally do not receive the social support and caring from family and community accorded

to heterosexual widowed persons. To some extent, being a gay widower parallels the coming-out process of accepting and embracing one's homosexuality.
How well the man has accepted a gay identity determines how he handles the
loss of his partner and whether he can develop a positive, integrated identity as
a gay widower (Shernoff 1998). Strong family, community, and cultural capacities are central to these processes.

The absence of compassionate responses from friends, family, and coworkers
can produce shame in some gay widowers, which may result in their denial of the
enormity of the loss and what the deceased man meant to him. Gay widowers
often suffer from depression, made worse by the sense that their life has lost its
meaning (Schwartzberg 1996). Underlying questions in instances of severe
depression are, "How can I live in such pain?" and, in moments of meaninglessness, "Why bother living, what's the point?" (Shernoff 1998). Gay widowers
who are able to rediscover and recreate meaning in their profoundly changed
lives learn to live with their loss. Although many bereaved gay men have disenfranchised grief, those who have openly shared their sexual orientation tend to
have more supportive networks than do those who have pretended that their
lover is "only a roommate" (Schwartzberg 1996; Shernoff 1998).

Similar to heterosexual widowers, gay widowers report connecting with the
deceased so that he remains as part of their life, maintaining active relationships
through memory, and feeling guided by and experiencing the deceased's presence
(Richards 1999). A pattern of transforming the relationship with the deceased
through formal and informal memorials appears to be similar for both heterosexual and homosexual bereaved partners (Rubin 1999; Walter 1996).

Lesbian Widows

The unpredictability of community and family responses during bereavement
is also a source of stress and fear for lesbian women who have lost their partner.
In fact, bereaved lesbians are referred to as the "silent grievers," who typically
have expected to enjoy companionship and affection while growing old with a
long-term partner (Jones 1985). Grieving lesbians often encounter hurtful or
unhelpful family responses, especially when their relationship was not accepted.
Such reactions can prolong and intensify the normal emotions of denial, anger,
and guilt (Walter 2003). For some lesbians, the death of a partner may be the first
time the larger community becomes aware of their relationship. By contrast,
families are found to be helpful if never formally told about the relationship,
but the lesbian daughter assumed that they knew (Deevey 1997). This appears
to contrast with the experience of gay partners, for whom those who have
been more open may receive more support from their family. These seemingly

contradictory findings, however, are based on relatively small samples of bereaved gays and lesbians and thus should be interpreted cautiously. Unfortunately, many bereaved lesbians still face legal and financial discrimination from the larger community and their partner's family and may even not be permitted to participate in funeral or memorial rituals. Because of their youth, they often have no experience with death and with locating resources to support their grieving process.

Because many lesbians strive for an equitable division of tasks, they may not have to learn as many new tasks or find their daily lives as disrupted as do wives in heterosexual couples (Deevey 1997; Walter 2003). The most common goal of a bereaved lesbian partner is incorporating some of her dead partner's positive qualities in herself (Jones 1985). Although keeping memories close is a source of comfort, this can interfere with new relationships, creating issues of loyalty in one's struggle over dating and new relationships.

We turn now to a brief discussion of the losses inherent in abuse or interpersonal violence. A full discussion of the complex grief and loss issues entailed by abuse is impossible, but by raising these issues, we hope to foster the reader's awareness of and sensitivity to them.

Physical and Sexual Abuse

Although all trauma involves loss (e.g., the loss of one's old assumptive world), not all grief involves trauma. But there are similarities between the grief caused by the death of a loved one and the trauma of surviving childhood sexual abuse (Fleming and Belanger 2001). In addition, repercussions from the losses entailed by physical and sexual abuse/assault interfere with the developmental tasks of young adulthood, or the losses may be the direct effects of sexual or physical trauma experienced in young adulthood. Seeking protection and care and fearing abandonment and exploitation, young adult survivors may be at risk of repeated victimization—rape, sexual harassment, battering—throughout their adult life. Indeed, childhood sexual abuse has been found to be associated with a greater risk of sexual assault in adulthood (Chew 1998; Coxell and King 2002; Fleming and Belanger 2001; Harvey 2000; Herman 1992; Krahe 2001). Approximately one in four adult women is a survivor of childhood sexual (contact) abuse, and the rates increase when adult victimization is included. Women who have been revictimized tend to have more problems in the areas such as intimacy and trust and to consider suicide more often than do women who had never been sexually assaulted or those who have never been victimized (DePrince and Freyd 2002; Naugle et al. 2002).

Childhood sexual or physical abuse causes numerous losses: the loss of innocence, childhood, and trust in and protection of the adult world, which may be carried into young adulthood and perhaps beyond. Survivors lose the internal psychological structures of a self securely attached to others, and those who have been physically harmed lose their sense of bodily integrity. Children's fundamental right to be able to trust those who care for them is broken when they are sexually victimized. They must mourn the loss of this basic trust and the belief in a good parent. When they lose important people in their lives (e.g., adults whom they should have been able to trust), they face a void in their social relationships. They must grieve not only for what was lost but also for what was never theirs to lose: a childhood that was stolen from them. Similar to the grief process associated with death, the attachment to the deceased or perpetrator affects the nature and dynamics of grieving childhood abuse (Fleming and Belanger 2001).

Survivors may resist mourning as a way of denying victory or more power to the perpetrator. If previously they have been unable to talk about the trauma, which is surrounded by an atmosphere of secrecy, they may become imprisoned by their feelings at the time of the trauma. The resulting loneliness and isolation throughout their life consequently may be far more damaging than the actual event (Goldman 2001). Some research, for example, has found that an avoidant and emotionally suppressed style of coping was associated with poorer long-term outcomes (Fleming and Belanger 2001; Leitenberg, Greenwald, and Cado 1992). Chronic grief ("losing what we have") resulting from childhood abuse is characterized by reliving the experience and revictimization. Stagnation and avoidance indicate a delayed grief process, and acceptance and growth ("becoming who we are rather than having what we have lost") represents an integration of the losses entailed in childhood sexual abuse (Fleming and Belanger 2001; Fleming and Robinson 1991).

Survivors of childhood abuse report an overwhelming sense of helplessness, because of the unpredictability of the violence, the loss of social supports, and the sense of secrecy and shame surrounding sexual abuse (Fleming and Belanger 2001). Abused children are isolated from other family members as well as from the wider social world. They have discovered that not only is the most powerful adult in their world dangerous but that other adults who are responsible for their care have not protected them. Abandonment by the other parent, usually the mother who does not believe the child or discounts the abuse even years later, is often resented more in adulthood than the abuse itself (Herman 1992).

When survivors of childhood mistreatment confront other types of loss in young adulthood, they usually are more vulnerable and exhibit intense—and sometimes complicated—grief (Clark, Cole, and Enzle 1990; Fleming and Belanger 2001). Confronted with feelings of abandonment and the need to reclaim trust, young adult survivors encounter new conflicts and challenges at each new phase of their life. Most survivors of childhood abuse have problems related to trust, autonomy, and initiative, which can dramatically interfere with the early adulthood tasks of establishing independence and intimacy. Understanding the long-term impacts of childhood abuse can help make sense of previously unexplainable behaviors such as worthlessness, hopelessness, and anger; difficulty forming and maintaining stable relationships; sleep disturbances; and physical/somatic symptoms. Not surprisingly, survivors have higher rates of PTSD symptoms in young adulthood, such as periods during which memory of the trauma is unavailable. Such memory impairment tends to occur when the perpetrator of abuse was a caregiver (DePrince and Freyd 2002).

Reliving or recounting the childhood trauma may plunge survivors into profound grief. But as with other forms of loss, telling the story is important in order to rebuild a sense of self and to live in the present, to develop meaning, and to pursue goals (Chew 1998; Gil 1988; Leahy, Pretty, and Tenenbaum 2003). Coming to terms with the traumatic past is necessary to becoming the person he or she wants to be. Reconciling with and forgiving oneself, reconnecting with others, and recognizing commonality among other survivors of childhood trauma are part of the healing process. The customary rituals of mourning are generally not available to provide consolation, however, since so many of these losses are invisible or unrecognized (Herman 1992). Nonetheless, many survivors of childhood abuse report no long-term effects from earlier assaults. The reasons may be individual and social capacities: strong supportive relationships, maternal support, and a positive self-concept and secure attachments (Constable 1994).

Young adult men are exposed to more traumatic violent events than women are, but women are more likely to be sexually assaulted, especially raped. Grief reactions extend to anger, despair, hopelessness, shame, anxiety, depression, and fear (Petrak 2002). Women's higher rate of sexual assault also is associated with a higher risk of PTSD than is exposure to physical violence or other forms of trauma. Women also regard comparable events as more threatening (e.g., involving more terror, horror, or helplessness) than do men. Women are approximately twice as likely to develop PTSD at some point in their lives, and PTSD is more chronic in women than in men. The high risk for PTSD associated with being female begins in adolescence and continues throughout young adulthood and into middle adulthood (Norris, Foster, and Weisshaar 2002; Petrak 2002). Symptoms of PTSD in young adulthood are disassociation, flashbacks, hypervigilance, exaggerated startle response, sleep disorders, nausea, inability to concentrate, diminished interest in significant activities, disbelief, taking crazy risks, and sense of a foreshortened future (Benedict 1994). This greater risk for PTSD is partly a result of women's greater tendency toward self-blame and helplessness, to have low self-esteem and to hold more negative views of themselves, and to view the world as more unpredictable and dangerous than male trauma victims do (Tolin and Foa 2002). Another factor that increases this risk is society's tendency to blame the victim of sexual assault, making the woman question whether the violence was her fault. Such guilt is vividly described in Alice Seebolt's *Lucky*, a memoir of her being raped as a college freshman.

Family, community, and cultural capacities affect the outcome of sexual assault or abuse in young adulthood. These social capacities are crucial to rebuilding trust and feeling safe and protected. A supportive response from others can mitigate the impact of the event, and a hostile or negative response may exacerbate the survivor's sense of shame and guilt and compound the damage. Unfortunately, many victims of rape are more likely to encounter a negative response from others than a supportive one (Petrak 2002). For survivors of sexual assault who feel isolated and abandoned, their sense of self can be rebuilt only in connection with others (Herman 1992).

Summary

Major losses during young adulthood are generally unanticipated and "off time," making the bereaved out of sync with peers who are married, enjoying healthy children, and looking forward to the future. Young adults often have no life experiences or perspectives to help them in the meaning-making process when they suffer a major loss such as the death of an infant, birth of a child with long-term disabilities, death of a partner, or sexual assault. Their family, community, and cultural capacities may not be as strong and extensive as those of middle-aged and older adults. Given the nonnormative nature of their losses, their limited life experience, and their fewer social capacities, young adults often feel very alone and different in their grief process, feelings that they will carry into middle and late adulthood. But if they are able to integrate these losses, they may be more resilient in midlife and old age than many of their peers are.

9

Interventions for Grieving Young Adults

YOUNG ADULTHOOD in Western societies is characterized by the drive to establish and maintain intimate and mature relationships, become financially independent of parents, start a family, pursue an occupation, and choose a lifestyle. Issues of sexuality and intimacy are important as well. Young adults typically have multiple demands associated with family life, finances, home ownership, and career advancement. For the privileged, it is generally a time of good health, vitality, and hope. For less privileged young adults in our society, however, it is increasingly a time of unemployment or underemployment, chronic illness, or violence. Young adults' losses are often unanticipated or sudden, may constitute disenfranchised grief and interfere with developmental tasks, and thus may complicate their grief. Parents' grief resulting from infertility, abortion, miscarriage, stillbirth, SIDS, birth of a child with developmental disabilities, and abuse or domestic violence all interfere with the hopes and dreams of establishing a family and intimate relationships. AIDS-related deaths and widowhood, in particular, may violate a young person's sense of justice, hope, and expectations for the future (e.g., a long life) and can be especially challenging.

This chapter concentrates on interventions that are based on the family and draw on the strengths of social support systems. We also look at the recently developed Web-based supports, which appear to be popular with this age group. Healing rituals address the many forms of disenfranchised grief reported by young adults, and we review the empirical support for these interventions.

Intervention Models

Research has documented that although it is psychologically painful, grief "is a normal process reflecting both the strengths and value of human attachments and the capacity to adapt to loss and adversity" and that "there can be *no justification for routine intervention* for bereaved persons . . . because grief is not a disease" (Raphael, Minkov, and Dobson 2001:587, italics in original). Human service professionals, especially social workers, commonly work with more vulnerable populations at risk of complicated bereavement. They recognize and are trained to assess the many and varied personal, social, and cultural capacities available to adults and their families that often are critical determinants of well-being. The extent to which these capacities are compromised often determine the need for professional intervention. Social workers and other helping professionals have an ethical responsibility to do no harm, to help bereaved persons to use the resources available to them, and to offer interventions for specific needs.

The *spectrum of interventions model,* which was originally developed for mental health (Mrazek and Haggerty 1994) has been adapted for working with the bereaved. The adapted model includes grief-related complications and risk and protective factors to determine the most appropriate services. These interventions are

1. *Preventive interventions* to reduce risk, increase protective factors, and modify potential adverse outcomes (e.g., education about and support for "normal" bereavement for at-risk populations).
2. *Preventive interventions for people with a higher risk of an adverse outcome,* who are identified (e.g., through crisis intervention, leader-guided, or self-help groups that use psychotherapeutic principles for bereaved widows and parents) as more vulnerable to developing bereavement-related complications or another morbidity.
3. *Early intervention* (e.g., grief counseling, trained widow-to-widow programs, guided mourning) *for complicated grief* that is targeted toward persons showing great bereavement-related distress.
4. *Psychotherapeutic and other treatments to address complicated grief and bereavement.* These include conditions such as posttraumatic stress disorder (PTSD), bereavement-related depression, and anxiety disorders. Each requires different intervention modalities, such as cognitive-behavioral and interpersonal psychotherapy, therapeutic leave-taking rituals, guided mourning, or antidepressants appropriate to depression. (Raphael, Minkov, and Dobson 2001)

The empirical support for many of these interventions is reviewed in this and the following chapters on adulthood.

General Techniques and Interventions
Social Support

Social support is a critical determinant of grief adjustment for people of all ages (Sanders 1999; Vachon and Stylianos 1988). Unfortunately, society's discomfort with grief often diminishes the support available to bereaved persons (Brabant, Forsyth, and McFarlain 1995; Dixon et al. 2001). The relationship between less available social support and more physical and psychological health problems stemming from bereavement is strong and extensively documented (Dixon et al. 2002; Gass 1987; Lennon, Martin, and Dean 1990; Windholz, Marmar, and Horowitz 1985). When they are confronted with a significant loss, changes in social support may exaggerate young adults' sense of loneliness and despair and make it more difficult for them to manage life's seemingly mundane tasks. Many feel that no one else could possibly understand their pain and wonder whether they will ever be able to engage fully in life again. Seeing others who have endured, survived, and emerged from similar significant losses may give them hope, however.

SUPPORT GROUPS

Support groups have numerous advantages for addressing an individual person's grief, including being less costly, because they can treat at one time several people with similar types of loss. The benefits of bereavement support groups, used alone or with other interventions, have been documented in several studies with a range of populations (Goodkin et al. 1999, 2001; Marmar et al. 1988). Their advantages are that a group's participants usually (1) feel less alone when they can share their grief; (2) feel validated when others legitimize their experiences; (3) receive information about their loss; (4) learn strategies for coping with their loss; (5) have role models who offer different ways of solving problems; (6) have an opportunity to express their feelings, thoughts, and grief response; and (7) may be able to help others (Lund 1999; Pesek 2002; Silverman 1995; Spiegel and Yalom 1978). Because support groups aim to enfranchise grievers who are disenfranchised, they can be especially useful for losses that occur during young adulthood (Pesek 2002). As we noted in the introduction, disenfranchised grief results when society fails to recognize, legitimize, or respond to a person's loss. This occurs with many forms of prenatal and perinatal death in which others fail to acknowledge the significance of the loss, with abuse that is invisible to others, and with illnesses like AIDS that are stigmatized by society. Several national support groups are available to address specific losses that often lead to disenfranchised grief, including Compassionate Friends, Candle Lighters, Empty Arms, Begin Again, Widow-to-Widow Program, the Omega Project, and Parents Without Partners. In addition, hospice programs and many hospitals offer grief therapy or support groups.

Not all adults find support groups comfortable and helpful. Some may experience logistical barriers to accessing groups or find it difficult to express grief publicly or with strangers. In general, persons of color and males are underrepresented in support groups. Sharing emotions, thoughts, and experiences in a public forum may be culturally difficult for some people. Regardless of cultural differences, men may be less drawn to interventions that focus on expressing emotion. Referrals to support groups should therefore consider needs, preferences, and timing. Prospective participants need to feel that they are ready to join a group and that this form of support would be useful to them. Young adults, or adults of any age, may resent premature suggestions that they join a support group while their grief is still new, especially when they are experiencing shock, numbness, and disbelief.

WEB-BASED SUPPORT GROUPS AND ONLINE INTERVENTIONS

Young adults use the Internet to find online discussion forums, information sites (Aitken 2002; Sofka 1997), and support groups (Colón 2001; Zinn, Simon, and Orme 1997). Computer-based support interventions, which have become popular in recent years, provide emotional and informational support for young adults and their families (Shaw et al. 2000; Zinn, Simon, and Orme 1997). Users report that online support groups offer convenience and an opportunity to gain knowledge, share experiences, provide support, help others, and minimize costs (Bacon, Condon, and Fernsler 2000; Shaw et al. 2000; Zinn, Simon, and Orme 1997). The impact of computer-based support interventions may be largest for underserved populations who do not usually use more formal supports (Gustafson et al. 2001, 2002). Even though the "digital divide" has been shrinking for many groups, gender, rural residence, socioeconomic status, disability, age, and ethnic minority status still may limit access to such support and need to be considered by advocates of online communication (Czaja and Lee 2001; Emiliani 2001; Lowe, Krahn, and Sosteric 2003; Wilson, Wallin, and Reiser 2003).

There are few systematic evaluations of online support groups and their effectiveness. Although such groups can offer substantial benefits, practitioners should also be mindful of their potential for harm, particularly when designing groups for persons with significant pain and emotional vulnerability. A qualitative analysis of the messages exchanged in three Internet self-help support groups identified numerous examples of online practices that could be harmful to (1) individuals (e.g., misunderstandings, excessive dependence, online emotional distress, loss of anonymity/confidentiality, and barriers to external therapeutic expertise), (2) external dyadic relationships (e.g., displaced aggression, emotional intensity, and premature intimacy), and (3) the group (e.g., infiltration and hidden identities and technological failure/complexity) (Waldron, Lavitt, and Kelley 2000). Given the growing demand for online services, social workers should design strategies to minimize and address harm and risks, reduce barriers to access, and test and disseminate findings regarding service utilization and bereavement outcomes.

THERAPEUTIC BEREAVEMENT GROUPS

Potential benefits, clinical experiences, and approaches to creating and implementing grief and bereavement groups for a variety of young adult losses have been documented (e.g., Buell 1989; Gray, Zide, and Wilker 2000; Hatton and Valente 1981; Kulic 2003; Maasen 1998; Moss 2001, 2002; Robak 1991; Soricelli 1985). The features and processes that all these groups follow are (1) discussing group norms, (2) introducing the participants, (3) describing their personal loss and bereavement, (4) sharing pictures and anecdotes, (5) examining the grief process, (6) discussing relevant topics, and (7) terminating (Cook and Dworkin 1992).

The efficacy of bereavement group interventions with adults, including young adults, is mixed. Widows of suicide victims who participated in a bereavement group intervention had low overall depression and psychological distress, and high social adjustment. But without a control group to allow for comparison, it is uncertain whether the intervention was responsible for the changes observed (Constantino, Sekula, and Rubinstein 2001). Adult daughters who participated in a bereavement group following their mother's death reported less depression than did the daughters in a control group. But the scores on a grief test of the treatment group and a control group were not significantly different (Archer 2001). Another study found no marked differences in the mourning and mental health of bereaved spouses enrolled in brief group therapy treatment groups compared with those in control groups after a follow-up one year later (Lieberman and Yalom 1992). A review of the efficacy of group bereavement interventions revealed that persons participating in bereavement group interventions improved compared with those in control groups. But problems with past research limited conclusions regarding the efficacy of the groups and help explain the variability in study findings (Sharpnack 2001). These problems were too small groups, limited measurements, a tendency to use depression as the primary outcome, a lack of random assignment, eclectic theoretical orientations, and a lack of information reported in studies and heterogeneous groups. Although persons participating in bereavement group treatment often praise the group process (Maasen 1998; Yalom and Vinogradov 1988), further research is needed to identify which populations are most likely to benefit from group interventions and to determine the group's efficacy.

FAMILY-BASED INTERVENTIONS

Families are the most significant social group in which grief is experienced, and their capacities to manage major losses vary. Informal supports provide practical

help in managing daily tasks, such as meals, child care, and funeral arrangements, especially in the early days following a death. As noted throughout this
text, death and many other forms of loss commonly lead to secondary losses that
further affect family life and well-being. Families may experience adversities
resulting from changes in their members' income, time, roles, and emotional
availability. Most families, however, are resilient, and members find strategies
to support one another and adapt to their loss. Assessments of families at
high risk of complicated bereavement, however, may help identify those most
needing family therapy (Kissane, Bloch, and McKenzie 1997). Family conflict,
cohesion, mutual support, and communication are important predictors of
bereavement outcomes that should be considered in assessment (Kissane, Bloch,
and McKenzie 1997; Nelson and Frantz 1996; Silverman and Weiner 1995). The
genogram, for example, is a useful exploratory and visual tool for organizing a
family history, tracking the history of illness and previous losses, family relationships, and dates of critical events in the family (Rosen 1998). As described
more fully in chapter 11, listening to bereaved families tell "the story" of their
loss may be used as an assessment device, an initial intervention, and a gauge of
treatment progress (Sedney, Baker, and Gross 1994).

Professionals should collaborate with families to understand "their distinctive
experience of social and cultural factors that form the ecology of a family's grief
experience" (E. R. Shapiro 1996:316). It is important for social workers and
other human service professionals to understand how families construe death and
assign meaning to it, since this influences how they will grieve (Nadeau 2001b).
Cultural considerations for individual- and family-based interventions are (1)
culturally relevant assessment components; (2) questions relevant to beliefs about
illness and supports; (3) questions about care of the body after death, beliefs,
and rituals; (4) questions about grief and mourning expectations; and (5) guidelines for working with interpreters. To facilitate developmental outcomes in
family bereavement while recognizing grief in a sociocultural context, professionals should (1) work with grieving families to examine the fit between their
particular circumstances and the bereavement expectations of their community
and culture; (2) consider family, extended kin, family of choice, and fictive kin as
resources; and (3) when applicable, appreciate the spiritual and psychological
continuity between the living and the dead (E. R. Shapiro 1995, 1996).

Multiple goals are involved when working with families. Assisting them to
establish "stable, shared emotional regulation" and introducing support for
continuity, stability, and cohesion may help families integrate experiences and
adapt to changes (Shapiro 2001:319). As discussed in chapter 5, family therapists
have modified Worden's tasks of mourning into four clinical goals: (1) share

acknowledgment of the loss, (2) share the experience of the loss and put it into context, (3) reorganize the family system, and (4) reinvest in other relationships and life pursuits (McGoldrick 1991). Evaluation studies are needed to test the efficacy for and cultural relevance of this model to young adults. Interventions for individuals have not been evaluated as extensively as family-based grief interventions have, and the few findings have been contradictory (Kissane and Bloch 1994). As noted in chapter 5, family-based interventions may be particularly helpful to families with young children and teens, and several studies have documented positive outcomes (Black and Urbanowicz 1987; Carr 2000; Sandler, West, and Baca 1992). Further research is needed to better identify the families most likely to benefit from family-based interventions and to design and test appropriate interventions for various kinds of losses. Emerging models of family grief therapy that focus on increasing family cohesiveness, improving communication, and resolving conflicts in culturally appropriate ways require further elaboration and testing (e.g., Kissane et al. 1998).

HEALING RITUALS

Ritual is defined as a "joint activity given to ceremony, involving two or more persons, endowed with special emotion and often sacred meaning, focused around a clearly defined set of social objects, and when performed confers upon its participants a special sense of the sacred and out of the ordinary" (Denzin 1974:272). It involves highly symbolic acts that confer transcendental significance and meaning on certain life events or experiences" (Doka 2002c:135). In U.S. culture, the funeral or memorial service, which addresses the religious, spiritual, and cultural needs of the persons involved, is the most common death ritual (Doka 2002c) and is believed to serve several functions and benefits:

- Help in expressing grief while offering a structure to contain the grief.
- Confirm the reality of the death.
- Stimulate memories of the deceased.
- Offer culturally meaningful structured activities for the bereaved.
- Provide social support, reaffirming the new identities of the bereaved and reincorporating them into the larger community.
- Reaffirm the social order with reminders of the reality of death and the continuity of the community.
- Serve as a rite of passage providing for the final disposition of the body. (Rando 1984; Romanoff and Terenzio 1998)

Rituals and other mourning practices are carried out in a cultural context (Kagawa-Singer 1998). Because the U.S. population is becoming increasingly diverse, health and human service professionals must learn about the dying and death rituals and community services of different cultures. For example, like those of many non-Western societies, traditional Hmong funeral rituals and customs are quite elaborate and are performed over long periods of time (Bliatout 1993; Rosenblatt 2001). Human service professionals thus may be asked to help their Hmong clients find funeral homes that are able and willing to accommodate these lengthy rituals. Social workers should be aware of non-Christian rituals, such as those rooted in Buddhism, that provide spiritual help for the dying and allow the bereaved to continue their bond with the deceased, provide comfort, and help integrate the loss (Klass 2001a; Pang and Lam 2002). One classic text, *The Tibetan Book of the Living and Dying*, is a valuable resource that describes the beliefs and extensive pre- and postdeath rituals and other practices essential to Tibetan Buddhist practitioners (Rinpoche 1994).

Rituals are not always available to the bereaved. In cases of disenfranchised grief, persons are often denied the rights of ritual. Persons with developmental disabilities or gay or lesbian bereaved partners may be discouraged or excluded from participating in funeral rituals. In other instances, rituals may not exist. For example, there are no traditional rituals for young women grieving the loss of a child following an abortion, miscarriage, or adoption, or for families undergoing a divorce. But clinicians now are paying more attention to the potential therapeutic value of ritual to address disenfranchised and other forms of grief (Cook and Dworkin 1992; Sanders 1989; Wyrostok 1995), and resources are available to help professionals create rituals for the bereaved (e.g., Becvar 2001; Mayo 2001; Rando 1993). Social workers, therapists, and other professionals can help the bereaved use their own strengths, resources, and needs to design culturally meaningful therapeutic rituals. These rituals can articulate continuity, transition, reconciliation, and/or affirmation (for further description of these rituals, see Doka 2002c). Table 9.1 describes the steps for creating therapeutic rituals for grief that may be adapted to individuals, families, and groups for their own rituals for a wide variety of losses (Rando 1993).

A few cautionary statements are in order:

1. Since rituals are not for everyone, it is important to determine the suitability of the ritual for each family or individual.
2. Rituals can evoke powerful emotions, so they should allow time for preparation and processing and should be culturally relevant to the mourners.
3. Most of the research evaluating the therapeutic role of rituals has centered on funerals or is anecdotal. (Fristad et al. 2001; Richards, Wrubel, and Folkman 2000)

TABLE 9.1
Rando's Steps in Creating Therapeutic Bereavement Rituals

1. Assess: The bereaved's (a) psychological, behavioral, social, physical, cultural, spiritual, and generational characteristics; (b) prior life experience; (c) psychosocial support; (d) loss characteristics; (e) place in mourning process and associated conflicts.

2. Determine the focus and purpose: What is the ultimate goal of the ritual? To facilitate uncomplicated grief? To address complicated grief?

3. Specify the message to be conveyed: To give symbolic expression to feelings and thoughts, identify the embodying message where possible (e.g., to express anger or love, to say good-bye, to facilitate expressions of regret, memories).

4. Choose the ritual type:

   Transition rituals: Mark major life transitions (e.g., marriage/divorce, birth, death); involving changes in self-image, roles, relationships; helpful for difficulties in letting go of the past.

   Continuity rituals: Confirm life stability and help persons adjust to change, define relationships, and provide security and protection; these include acts of greeting or farewell (e.g., shaking hands) and collective ritualistic activities coinciding with natural changes experienced by the family (e.g., the family dinner or holidays), which demonstrate that the deceased maintains a place in the mourner's life.

5. Choose the ritual elements:

   Who is involved? Who will be included? Who is the focus of the ritual directed to?

   Symbols used: What symbols hold meaning and will help meet the purpose of the ritual? Examples of symbolic tools include music, invocation, silence, incense, candles.

   Symbolic acts: What symbolic acts are consistent with the ritual purpose and mourner characteristics? Examples of symbolic acts include burning written letters, scattering ashes.

   Characteristics: What characteristics will make the ritual personally meaningful and therapeutic? Considerations include (a) an appropriate emotional distance; (b) degree of rigidity/flexibility given to the mourner; (c) amount of repetition; (d) degree of multidimensionality (e.g., involving sensation, various activities); (e) complexity; (f) completeness; and the (g) blend of closed (i.e., prescribed acts) and open parts (i.e., improvisation).

6. Create the context: Determine the ritual's location and atmosphere as well as whether other persons will be present.

7. Prepare the mourner: Consider timing, motivation, and orientation of mourners to the ritual.

8. Implement the ritual: See Rando (1993) for detailed description of leave-taking rituals that include three phases: preparatory, reorganization, and finalization.

9. Process the ritual: Provide opportunity to explore the impact of the ritual upon the mourner during and after the ritual.

10. Reevaluate and redecide: Evaluate with the mourner the effectiveness of the ritual and determine if further rituals are necessary to achieve established goals.

Source: T. A. Rando, *Treatment of Complicated Mourning* (Champaign, Ill.: Research Press, 1993), 318–31.

Efficacy studies of the effects of rituals for multiple forms of loss are long overdue.

Interventions for Specific Losses
Perinatal Death and Other Losses

Perinatal death refers to miscarriage, therapeutic abortion, stillbirth, and infant death shortly after birth (Moscarello 1989). Domains to consider when assessing a loss related to perinatal death or adoption include but are not limited to the following:

1. Sociocultural (i.e., communication patterns, family dynamics, beliefs about rites of passage and appropriate behavior, traditions and rituals important to the family).
2. Spiritual (i.e., belief in a higher being, religious needs, or spiritual distress).
3. Psychological (e.g., grief experience, cognitive understanding of what has transpired, or emotions).
4. Developmental (e.g., how the loss may affect family members' developmental needs and tasks).
5. Physiological (e.g., medications that may dull perception of events, health problems, fatigue from difficult labor, or pain from cesarean section). (Brown 1993)

Understanding the meaning of the loss to the mother, father, and family is an important and unique component of the assessment. For example, depending on the nature of the baby's death and the family's personal capacities and belief systems, they may regard the death as the loss of a possession, a dream, a symbol (e.g., a symbol of independence), a new life relationship, or a relief. The social and cultural capacities available to the individuals and family are important to determine because of the relationships between depressive symptoms and social support, marital relationship, and family conflict (Stirtzinger et al. 1999).

Abortion

The grief and mental health challenges associated with induced abortion have been well documented. Therapeutic interventions for these women and their families are still only descriptive. Clinicians have examined hospital-based programs, self-help support groups (Brown 1992, Speckhard 1997), and culturally and spiritually congruent rituals (Klass and Heath 1997; McAll and Wilson 1987); health and human service professionals who view abortion as a traumatic loss advocate marital counseling and therapy (Bagarozzi 1994) and standard, trauma-based treatment (Speckhard 1997). Qualitative studies of women who

Box 9.1 The Lived Experience of Induced Abortion

- Shock and not knowing what to do about the pregnancy.
- Confusion and conflict in deciding whether to have an abortion or not.
- Loss and depression after making the decision.
- Fear and worry when facing the operation.
- Relief and grief after the abortion.
- Worry about the recovery.
- Mitigating personal sense of guilt by self-persuasion in a religious way.

Source: B. Lee and Y. Yang, The Lived Experience of Unmarried Women Who Underwent Induced Abortion During the First Trimester, *Journal of Nursing Research* 8 (2000): 459.

have had an abortion may help professionals develop interventions to meet their needs. For example, box 9.1 details the results of a phenomenological study identifying seven themes in unmarried women's experience of induced abortion (Lee and Yang 2000). Each theme points to clinical interventions appropriate to the different phases, such as emotional and informational support and problem solving, as well as strategies to address guilt, depression, and worry. Qualitative data from a pilot study suggest that spiritual group interventions may reduce levels of shame and avoidance among women with postabortion grief (Layer et al. 2004). These and other interventions need to be developed and tested further.

Miscarriage

Miscarriage is often experienced as a form of disenfranchised grief, which limits the support available to these women and their partners. Supportive interventions include acknowledging and validating the loss. The meaning of the loss to the woman and her partner influence their mourning process (Marker and Ogden 2003). Research documenting the similarities and differences in couples' grief reactions following a miscarriage suggests that while both men and women grieve such losses, their feelings vary in type, intensity, and duration (Abbound and Liamputtong 2003; Beutel et al. 1996). Accordingly, interventions should help couples understand and support each other. Methodological problems of evaluating interventions for miscarriage limit empirical support for their efficacy.

For example, although there is anecdotal evidence for the benefit of follow-up care and individual or group supportive interventions for parents, there have been no controlled intervention studies (Lee and Slade 1996); outcome measures are often inadequate (e.g., focus on parents' satisfaction [Lasker and Toedter 1994]); and many studies do not distinguish among various pregnancy losses (DiMarco, Menke, and McNamara 2001; Lasker and Toedter 1994). In addition, little attention has been paid to culturally competent interventions. African American women who had a miscarriage or another prenatal and postnatal loss used inner resources for self-help strategies to manage their personal reactions, others' responses, memories of the baby, and subsequent pregnancies (Van and Meleis 2003). Their responses suggest a need for a framework of intervention that supports cultural capacities or strengths.

Stillbirth and Neonatal Death

An assessment of parental grief after a serious perinatal diagnosis or death should consider risk factors like the degree of emotional or financial personal investment in the pregnancy (e.g., multiple in vitro fertilizations), prolonged infertility, mother's age, medical explanation for the death, delayed diagnosis, previous losses, and/or preventable nature of the death (Ashton and Ashton 2000). It is now well documented that fathers as well as mothers are greatly affected by stillbirth and neonatal death. Fathers often feel pressured to protect their partners but find this difficult to do when they themselves are distressed. Bereaved fathers need grief support immediately after a stillbirth or neonatal death and report appreciating the tokens of remembrance that they receive in the hospital (e.g., photos, hand and footprints, a lock of hair, and identification wrist bands) (Kitson 2002).

Standard protocols call for empathic communication, understanding, and interdisciplinary team member support, since these may influence the parents' adjustment following a stillbirth or neonatal death (Caelli, Downie, and Letendre 2002). The parents' satisfaction with the hospital staff's support and comfort was associated with less depression and greater psychological well-being (Murray and Callan 1988). Bereaved parents reported an immediate need for hospital-based intervention and posthospital follow-up by social workers, nurses, and physicians that provided a compassionate response to their grief (Davis, Stewart, and Harmon 1988). A randomized trial of a counseling intervention found little support for routine counseling for all couples but suggested that those who seek counseling might adjust better (Lilford et al. 1994).

Increasingly, hospital staffs are encouraging parents to participate in the direct care of their critically ill infants until the time of death and after. Although parents are often urged to bond with their deceased infant, some recent evidence suggests that such practices may not always be beneficial. For example, one study reported that women who had held their stillborn infant become more depressed than did those who only saw their infant, and women who had seen their stillborn infant were more anxious and had more symptoms of PTSD than did those who had not (Hughes et al. 2002). This study suggests that practice guidelines stating that failing to see and hold the dead child can have adverse effects on parents' mourning may not be justified. Further examination of the context and conditions under which more negative outcomes are experienced, with attention to the intensity and form of support, preparation, and follow-up care provided to parents, is needed. In the meantime, more efforts to explore the parents' wishes and preferences and to talk to them about possible consequences would allow them to make more informed choices regarding their bonding with their dead baby.

Hospital programs to help families bereaved by perinatal deaths generally draw on the skills of nurses, social workers, medical personnel, and/or pastoral counselors. Social workers often offer supportive grief counseling and essential information, such as the details of burial procedures and hospital regulations (Pauw 1991). It is standard hospital practice to give information packets to families regarding autopsies, funeral or cremation options, the nature and expressions of grief and mourning, responses to reactions of friends and relatives, help for siblings, and decisions regarding another pregnancy (Leming and Dickinson 2002; Pauw 1991). According to anecdotal evidence, parents find that bereavement support groups help them feel less alone, learn from others, and normalize their experience (Reilly-Smorawski, Armstrong, and Catlin 2002). A grief intervention program that trained social workers and psychologists to give information and support to parents, affirm the baby's existence, encourage the parents to express their grief and mourn, and notify the parents' social networks was found to reduce the parents' distress, particularly those at high risk of complicated grief (Murray et al. 2000). How well such interventions meet the needs of ethnically diverse bereaved parents has not been tested. A better understanding of the cultural and ethnic factors that influence bereavement at all levels would help determine culturally competent interventions (Herbert 2000).

Sudden Infant Death Syndrome

The grief associated with SIDS is often complicated by tremendous guilt and a sense of responsibility shrouding the unknown cause of this syndrome and is even more devastating for families when they are interrogated by the police. There have been no controlled studies of interventions for SIDS-associated grief. Accordingly, we have reviewed some general-practice principles of clinicians based on their practice wisdom and research on families' needs and perceptions of what is helpful.

Health care and social service providers can help parents adjust to a SIDS
death by providing accurate medical information and empathic support (Caelli,
Downie, and Letendre 2002). SIDS counselors advocate strategies that remove
some of the mystery surrounding the diagnosis, including carefully reviewing
any known medical information and sharing the autopsy report with bereaved
parents (Kotch and Cohen 1985). Professionals need crisis intervention skills,
along with knowledge of the family dynamics and the effects of trauma on family life in order to respond effectively to families grieving a SIDS-related death
(Dyregrov 2001). Given siblings' needs and behavioral upsets, guidance should
be provided immediately following a SIDS death to enable the bereaved parents
to recognize, understand, and respond to their children's grief reactions (McClain
and Shaefer 1996).

Research on parents surviving a SIDS death suggests the usefulness of the
following techniques:

- Providing information on medical causes when it is available; otherwise helping parents answer the question of why the death occurred.
- Addressing the common feeling of guilt reported by bereaved parents and
  other family members.
- Allowing persons to retell their "account of the story" and gently helping
  them understand that given the circumstances, the individual "probably did
  all that he or she could for the baby."
- Listening and asking questions rather than making comments.
- Assessing and addressing irrational and suicidal thoughts.
- Providing information and linkages to available supports and resources.
- Targeting supportive strategies to parents, grandparents, and siblings. (DeFrain
  1991:228)

Given the documentation of gender differences in grief reactions and the
negative impact of SIDS on the marital relationship, it is important to address
both partners and to help them understand each other's feelings (Oliver 1999).
For example,

1. Encourage the parents, both individually and together, to talk about their
   bereavement and the impact of the loss on their relationship.
2. Give the couple information about gender differences in bereavement and
   coping and about the difficulties that many parents encounter after a perinatal or SIDS loss.

3. Encourage each parent to explore the difficulties that he or she may have in adapting to the other's needs.

4. Help the parents view each other's behavior from a more informed perspective and correct misinterpretations and faulty attributions about each other's behavior.

5. Educate the parents about the destructive power of blaming, as well as helping them refute the unrealistic and inaccurate thinking that often accompanies blaming.

6. Help the parents not lose sight of shared goals, values, and all that they continue to appreciate about their life together (Wing et al. 2001:70–71).

7. Acknowledge the distinctive needs of gay and lesbian parents who may experience discrimination and legal barriers in social and health care systems.

Adoption

The profound losses experienced by birth mothers (De Simone 1996; Henry 1999), adoptive families, and children (Berman and Bufferd 1986) have been well documented. It is thus surprising that there are no intervention studies of adoption-related grief. However, "open adoption" has been proposed to minimize this loss through opportunities to maintain a connection between the birth mother and the adopted child (Silverstein and Roszia 1999). Contradicting this assumption, however, Blanton and Deschner (1990) found that continued information about a relinquished child was associated with more grief symptoms in birth mothers. Greater grief was found in birth mothers who felt guilt or shame or were coerced into an adoption. These findings suggest that supporting the birth mother through a discussion of thoughts and feelings and how the relinquishment decision was made may be helpful (De Simone 1996). Although various family treatment and counseling techniques have been proposed, they have not yet been evaluated. These include

1. Assessment tools such as genograms, ecomaps, and family-history taking that use adoptive and birth family information to heighten, in a nonthreatening way, the family's awareness of prior losses, unconscious patterns, and emotional distance.

2. Role-playing to explore family members' feelings about adoption.

3. Sculpting in which the family members arrange themselves to show physically their emotional relationships to one another.

4. Family drawings to illustrate perceptions of family members.

5. Reframing, to redefine problems with a more positive perspective.

6. Circular questioning to highlight differences and interconnectedness of family members.

7. Information (e.g., about developmental needs). (Berman and Bufferd 1986)

Strategies to help adoptive families must be created and tested.

Developmental Disabilities

Issues related to developmental disabilities and loss may surface in different ways in young adulthood. Young adults may experience the loss of giving birth to a child with developmental disabilities. Or young adults with developmental disabilities may face multiple losses at a time when their peer group is graduating, leaving home, forming intimate relationships, and finding employment. In fact, losses for persons with developmental disabilities may worsen during young adulthood because of the association of young adulthood with increasing independence and opportunities. This chapter briefly addresses strategies to support both the parents of children with disabilities and bereaved young adults with developmental disabilities.

PARENTS OF CHILDREN WITH DISABILITIES

As noted in chapter 1, chronic sorrow, defined as "a pervasive sadness that is permanent, periodic, and progressive in nature" and observed in several studies of parents of children with chronic illness or disabilities, suggests a need to support these families (for a review, see Burke et al. 1992:231). Parents of children with developmental disabilities may grieve many times: at the time of initial diagnosis, the age at which the child should begin walking or talking, occasions when siblings surpass the child or when alternative placement is considered; entry into school; management of crises such as behavior problems; onset of puberty; celebration of the twenty-first birthday; and when guardianship is sought (Batshaw 2001; Burke et al. 1992).

Parents of children with disabilities have described their struggles with grief and depression, difficulties obtaining services, negative experiences with health care providers, and concerns about the future (Strauss and Munton 1985). Supportive interventions for these families should address the following basic needs:

1. Information about the child's condition, developmental expectations, and early referrals to developmental programs.
2. Positive feedback about the child's development and the parents' contributions to his or her development.
3. Acknowledgment and validation of the parents' grief.
4. Sensitive and empathic counseling to address thoughts, feelings, and worries.
5. Referrals and linkages to community agencies or support programs to meet their needs.

Research on providing clear information about the diagnosis and prognosis found that it "was more harmful for a mother to hope for a recovery, only to have her hopes shattered, than to expect the worst and be continually delighted by the child's unexpected progress" (Milo 1997:472). Although there are no efficacy studies of support groups and other interventions for parents of children with disabilities, qualitative research suggests that parents in support groups feel validated and emotionally supported and are able to find meaning in their common experiences (Milo 1997). A growing body of literature and Internet resources on parenting children with disabilities is available for parents wanting written information. Box 9.2 lists the authors and titles of several texts that may be helpful.

Given the cultural variability in the meanings of disability, preparation for dealing with a disability, and the family members' capacities and competing needs

Box 9.2 Texts for Parents of Children with Special Needs or Disabilities

M. L. Batshaw, *When Your Child Has a Disability: The Complete Sourcebook of Daily and Medical Care* (2001).

L. Dwight, *We Can Do It!* (1998).

S. I. Greenspan and S. Wieder, with R. Simons, *The Child with Special Needs: Encouraging Intellectual and Emotional Growth* (1998).

E. M. Hallowell, *When You Worry About the Child You Love: Emotional and Learning Problems Children* (1996).

L. Hickman, *Living in My Skin: An Insider's View of Life with a Special Needs Child* (2000).

R. Pierangelo and R. Jacoby, *Parents' Complete Special-Education Guide: Tips, Techniques, and Materials for Helping Your Child Succeed in School and Life* (1996).

B. Santelli, F. S. Poyadue, and J. L. Young, *The Parent to Parent Handbook: Connecting Families of Children with Special Needs* (2001).

M. Segal, with W. Masi and R. Leiderman, *In Time and with Love: Caring for Infants and Toddlers with Special Needs*, 2nd ed. (2001).

R. Simons, *After the Tears: Parents Talk About Raising a Child with a Disability* (1987).

and ethics (for a review, see Banks 2003), culturally competent assessment and interventions must be developed to support families of children with disabilities.

YOUNG ADULTS WITH DEVELOPMENTAL DISABILITIES

Few interventions have been tested for helping young adults with developmental disabilities who are grieving multiple losses as their peers become independent. Suggested practice principles, however, are (1) being honest and inclusive, (2) listening and being available, (3) facilitating nonverbal rituals, (4) respecting photos and other mementos, (5) minimizing change, (6) avoiding assessment of skills, (7) assisting searching behavior, (8) supporting the observance of anniversaries, and (9) seeking consultation if behavioral changes persist (Hollins 1995, as cited in Stoddart and McDonnell 1999). The first step in any intervention is for professionals and family members to acknowledge the disenfranchised grief of many young adults with developmental disabilities.

Luchterhand and Murphy's (1998) text uses the four tasks of grieving identified by Worden (1982) to examine more than one hundred strategies that practitioners may use to support persons with developmental disabilities. These strategies are organized by type of activity, along with detailed illustrations for providing information and for appropriately using creative arts, music, outdoor and physical activities, religious/spiritual practices, and ritual/tradition. Luchterhand and Murphy strongly believe that these "adults should participate as full citizens in the community. They then cannot be denied the opportunities to learn about life and death events that affect them intimately. To do so would be to not allow them the full range of human experiences" (1998:28).

Grief interventions should assess and address several risk factors that contribute to complicated grief in persons with developmental disabilities. These include (1) a lack of general information about the death and knowledge of a loved one's illness or death, since individuals with developmental disabilities have traditionally been denied such information; (2) dependence on caregivers who die, which may be perceived as more traumatic than for other young adults; (3) exclusion from rituals; (4) overprotectiveness that excludes the person from information, involvement, and opportunities to express grief; (5) family conflict; (6) lack of supports; and (7) isolation from family. Systems-level interventions to address these problems include information and education about loss and grief, inclusion in rituals, facilitation of appropriate control, mediation of family conflict, helping developmentally disabled adults become independent, and enhancing support systems and positive family interaction through individual or group work (Stoddart and McDonnell 1999). Preliminary outcome evaluations of bereavement group therapy for persons with intellectual disabilities designed to address several of these issues reported no change in anxiety or knowledge of death/bereavement issues but did find less depression (Stoddart, Burke, and Temple 2002). The small sample size and lack of a control group limit the conclusions that may be drawn from this study, however. A case report further described how young adults with developmental disabilities participating in a bereavement group expressed their feelings about and sensitivity to other group members (Rothenberg 1994). Control studies are needed to evaluate the individual and group approaches suggested in the literature.

Sexual or Physical Abuse

It is widely acknowledged that the various forms of abuse (i.e., sexual assault, physical or sexual abuse, domestic violence) are accompanied by immense suffering. Appropriately so, the principal clinical focus on helping abused women, particularly those in chronically abusive relationships, has been on attending to their "safety" and, more recently, the treatment of associated trauma (DePorto 2003). Human service professionals treating the traumatic nature of physical and sexual abuse may fail to recognize the associated grief and varied losses accompanying assault. Indeed, surprisingly little research has measured this grief or documented the presence of complicated or traumatic grief in women who have been sexually or physically abused. It has been suggested that "all trauma involves loss (e.g., in its most pervasive sense, loss of one's old assumptive world)" (Fleming and Bélanger 2001:311), and now the link between grief and recovery from trauma in situations involving interpersonal violence and abuse is being studied. The following quotation illustrates the connection between grief and recovery from the trauma of abuse reported by a young adult survivor of incest:

> After she had calmly told me about the nights when her father would rape her and then leave her alone in a locked room, I, being shocked by her steady voice, asked her, "But what does your past mean to you now?" and she replied as even as before, "Oh no. I can't say that." To the question "Why?" she answered, "Because that would mean I would have to realize all that I have lost." (Fleming and Bélanger 2001:312)

Family and other forms of interpersonal violence and the conditions underlying various types of abuse are quite complex. Accordingly, prevention initiatives (e.g., building skills in communication and coping, working toward gender equality, changing social values) and treatment efforts (e.g., counseling and psychotherapy for persons who have been assaulted, and anger management, social skills training, psychoeducational groups and psychotherapy for perpetrators of violence) generally do not emphasize the grief experience (for a review, see Enns 2002). Similarly, the most commonly employed interventions for sexual assault in young adulthood (e.g., prolonged exposure, anxiety management training, cognitive-processing therapy, and cognitive behavioral therapy) can reduce the negative psychological effects of rape, especially depression and PTSD (for a review, see Neville and Heppner 2002). But how much they alleviate grief is unknown. Support groups could help battered women identify the losses and personal grief reactions associated with domestic violence (Varvaro 1991), and community healing rituals for survivors of rape have been found to intensify the expression of feelings and to enhance a sense of support among women (Galambos 2001). Efficacy studies are needed to evaluate the impact of these and other interventions for grief associated with various forms of abuse.

An innovative solution-focused approach to crisis intervention that emphasizes the abused person's strengths has been proposed for a variety of situations involving loss (e.g., domestic violence, divorce, harassment, and relationship issues). This approach has not yet been evaluated in regard to the grief process and outcomes of physical and mental well-being (Greene et al. 1996). Table 9.2 lists the necessary steps and accompanying questions and techniques in solution-focused interventions. This model is similar to the resilience model because it emphasizes the importance of drawing on the abused person's personal and social capacities. It also is appealing, given the immediate needs (e.g., crisis nature of abuse) and psychological adversities (e.g., focus on solutions rather than self-blame) of persons who are abused in adulthood. Research is needed to determine who is most likely to benefit from a solution-focused approach and how it might affect the grief experience (e.g., prevent complicated grief) and critical outcomes.

Persons with HIV/AIDS

The stigma, multiple loss, and suffering that accompany HIV/AIDS often complicate grief. Accordingly, the loss is characterized by disenfranchised grief as well as the bereavement overload of many affected members of vulnerable and marginalized communities (Mallinson 1999). Considerations for supporting persons with HIV/AIDS and their significant others include attending to a safe environment, privacy, social support, multiple losses, and needs at all system levels (Mallinson 1999). Anticipatory grief is a salient experience in many forms of chronic illness, including HIV/AIDS, between both the person with the illness and his or her family members and caregivers (Kamya 2000; Walker et al. 1996). Grieving tasks through various phases of illness are acquiring information, identifying and expressing emotions, completing unfinished business, communicating with family, involving the caregivers in treatment plans, accepting

TABLE 9.2
Solution-Focused Approach to Crisis Intervention

Step	Description	Techniques and Example Questions
1. Joining.	Engage the clients and establish a positive working relationship. Determine their safety needs.	Skills include actively listening, identifying, and reflecting the clients' feelings (i.e., empathy); offering support and acceptance; and tracking, matching, and mirroring clients' nonverbal communication.
2. Defining "problems" (i.e., concerns identified by client).	Help clients describe their primary concerns.	Use the words *issues* or *concerns* rather than *problems*. *What kinds of concerns are you having now?* Choose your words carefully to reinforce an internal locus of control (e.g., do not ask, *What brings you here today*, which reinforces an external locus of control). Help clients prioritize their concerns: *You have mentioned several concerns you are having now. Whenever possible, I find it helpful to work on one at a time. Which of the concerns you just mentioned do you want to focus on first in our work together?*
3. Setting goals.	Goals describe how clients will feel, think, or behave differently, and they should set them. Goals represent a future reality that does not contain the presenting problems.	If the client states a goal in negative terms (e.g., *I want to feel less pain* or *I don't want to be depressed*), help him or her reframe it as a positive goal (e.g., *What do you want to be feeling instead?*). Encourage more detailed description. The "Miracle Question": *Suppose that after our meeting today, you go home and go to bed. While you are sleeping, a miracle happens and your issue is suddenly dealt with, like magic. The concern is gone. Because you were sleeping, you don't know that a miracle happened, but when you wake up tomorrow morning, you will be different. How will you know a miracle has happened? What will be the first small sign that tells you that a miracle has happened and that the issue is resolved?* (Berg and Miller 1992:359, as cited in Greene et al. 1996).

continued

TABLE 9.2

Step	Description	Techniques and Example Questions
4. Identifying solutions.	Help clients devise strategies to reach their goals, based on their strengths and capacities.	Use exception questions about past successes to identify solutions, and scaling questions (e.g., *rank this concern and goal on a 1 to 10 scale with a 1 as the worst possible outcome and 10 as the most desirable outcome*), to help clients quantify and evaluate their progress.
5. Developing and implementing an action plan.	Create tasks or homework that draw on thoughts, feelings, and behavior that clients have used in the past or are using now.	Formula First Session Task: *Between now and the next time we meet, we[I] would like you to observe, so that you can describe . . . what happens . . . that you want to continue to have happen* (de Shazer 1985:137, as cited in Greene et al. 1996). Have clients keep track of current successes and predict behaviors that they can control. Invite clients to pretend that the miracle has happened and to do everything they would do if the miracle had happened.
6. Termination and follow-up.	Review goals, assess readiness for termination, and anticipate future setbacks.	Use scaling questions to invite clients to assess their progress and to anticipate setbacks. Seek permission to follow up at future date to see how they are doing.

Source: G. J. Greene, M. Y. Lee, R. Trask, and J. Rheinscheld, Client Strengths and Crisis Intervention: A Solution-Focused Approach, *Crisis Intervention* 3 (1996): 43–46.

caregivers' needs and new roles, and saying good-bye in ways that are satisfactory to the persons involved (Walker et al. 1996). Near the end of life, social workers usually help adults and family members or partners deal with advanced directives, plan for the care of surviving children when applicable, articulate wishes regarding funerals and memorial services and care at the end of life, and prepare for death (Shernoff 1999).

Not surprisingly, given the social stigma and isolation associated with HIV/ AIDS, support groups are widely cited as a needed and appropriate intervention for AIDS-related bereavement. Monahan (1994) reviewed in detail the components necessary for effective support groups for this population. How these groups are designed varies widely, but they usually offer education, companionship, social support, and information about the grief process, the common challenges associated with death from AIDS, and the distinctive features of AIDS bereavement. Many earlier support group studies, which reported benefits from addressing AIDS-related bereavement, suffered from methodological limitations, such as the absence of a control group (Sikkema et al. 1995). Evidence is mounting, however, that the support group model may be a powerful intervention for grief and physical and psychological well-being (for a review, see Goodkin et al. 2001). For example, a support group intervention was found to significantly reduce distress and grief symptoms in a sample of HIV-1 seropositive and seronegative males, compared with the control group (Goodkin et al. 1999). Interestingly, the reduction of stress was not as great for African American and Latinos as it was for European Americans, suggesting that ethnicity-specific modifications are needed. A pilot study of a bereavement support group intervention for HIV-1 infected women found less grief and more positive life events, social support, and active coping (Goodkin et al. 2001).

Young Widows and Widowers

Widowed persons of all ages usually manage their grief without professional intervention (Lund 1989a). But young widows who seek treatment often report feeling "pressured to get on with living" (Lawrence 1992:67). Societal and developmental tasks and responsibilities and the fact that widowhood in young adulthood is an "off-time" event may increase this sense of pressure. For example, single-parent widows experience changes in their roles and responsibilities, loneliness, parenting stress, and the additional challenges associated with the grieving process, employment, child care, dating, and remarriage (Gass-Sternas 1995). Supportive community-based interventions to help widows with children through this transition are needed. Social workers may ask their local hospice organizations to determine the availability of support programs for young widows and widowers.

Most bereavement interventions for spouses or partners are directed at older adults or do not distinguish age in their evaluations. Support group interventions specifically for young adults that are reported in the literature are descriptive rather than evaluative (e.g., Lawrence 1992). Chapter 13 describes in detail the state of the science relevant to grief interventions for widows and widowers, such as mutual support programs, including those for gay and lesbian partners; brief dynamic psychotherapy or counseling; vocal expression sessions; mutual-aid support groups; crisis intervention at the individual, family, or group level; and peer counseling programs.

Summary

Both risk and protective factors and the extent of bereavement complications in young adulthood are important considerations for targeting the most appropriate interventions for losses associated with perinatal death, developmental disabilities, sexual or physical abuse, HIV/AIDS, and widowhood. We reviewed the developmentally congruent interventions that are more commonly used with bereaved young adults, including various support-, group-, family-, and Web-based online interventions, and the intentional use of therapeutic ritual. Although many interventions have been used with young adults, relatively few have been systematically evaluated in treatment outcome studies, and methodological problems limit the validity of the conclusions.

For many of the losses of young adults reviewed in this chapter, interventions have remained at a purely descriptive level or have not yet been proposed. Investigations documenting cultural variability in loss and grief emphasize the need for culturally competent interventions, but few studies have evaluated their effectiveness (Goodkin et al. 1999, 2001; Van and Meleis 2003). Although we presented practice principles and recommended strategies for young adults with loss, additional research is needed to test their efficacy.

10

Grief and Loss in Middle Adulthood

MIDDLE ADULTHOOD is often marked by great losses such as divorce, fewer career opportunities, estrangement from or the death of an adolescent or young adult child, caring for elders with a chronic illness or adult children with a chronic mental illness, and the death of older parents. This chapter considers the grief and losses from the death of an adolescent or young adult child, divorce, caring for a child with chronic mental disabilities, caring for older relatives, and the death of a parent. The death of a child when the parent is in middle adulthood is considered to be one of the most devastating losses. Many of middle-aged parents' grief reactions parallel those of younger or older parents who face the unimaginable death of a child, whom they believed would outlive them. We discuss midlife grief in the context of developmental considerations and a resilience framework.

Developmental Considerations

Middle adulthood—or midlife—is commonly defined as the period between the ages of forty-five and sixty-five, although some researchers contend that this age range is too wide, that the beginning and later phases of middle adulthood have very different age-related changes (Staudinger and Buck 2001). What is more important than chronological age, however, is how losses may be complicated by the developmental challenges typical of middle age: recognizing our mortality, adjusting to age-related changes (e.g., declines in energy, vision, hearing), redefining our postparenting roles, accepting that we have reached the peak of our career, abandoning earlier dreams, coping with disruptions of marital or partner relationships, and taking responsibility for children, parents, and community. Any discussion of middle adulthood must also include the biological aging processes, subjective perceptions of aging, social roles, and historical, generational, and cultural changes.

Erikson (1950) defined the primary challenge of middle adulthood as *generativity*, the ability to transcend personal interests to provide care and concern for future generations through leadership, mentoring, creativity, and guidance. Those who are unable to contribute to future generations or community well-being often become self-absorbed and stagnate. The cultural expectation in the United States is that adults will become more generative in midlife, with the opportunities for generative behavior varying by gender, socioeconomic class, and ethnic minority status (McAdams and de St. Aubin 1998). According to Levinson (1977), one of the developmental challenges of middle adulthood is finding balance in one's life, when middle-aged adults often pay more attention to previously neglected aspects of their lives, like work, family, friendships, or voluntarism. Others view midlife as a tie between the balance of developmental gains (e.g., self-esteem, emotional maturity) and losses (e.g., reduced energy, changes in physical appearance, greater risk of chronic illness) (Staudinger and Buck 2001). Some adults become stagnant in middle age or get out of synch with their partners and peers; others seek to improve their lives through divorce, separation, career changes, or relocation. For increasing numbers, middle age can be a time of creative growth, especially when adult children become financially independent. Nevertheless, the current economic conditions in the United States, especially the cuts in health care and pension benefits, mean that many low-income and working-class midlife adults will not have the choices that their more affluent baby-boomer peers had. How adults experience their midlife also varies with their culture.

Although middle age is commonly referred to as a "crisis," most adults' midlife transition is relatively calm, determined in part by individual perceptions of responses to developmental events (Corr, Nabe, and Corr 2003; Sterns and Huyck 2001). Middle-aged adults typically conserve and draw on previously established personal, social, and cultural capacities. They can dwell on what is past and gone or renew their appreciation of life, find a new self-understanding, and decide how to live the reminder of their life. In any case, most middle-aged adults are keenly aware that their life is half over and that their time left is limited and so become more selective about how they spend their time and resources.

Resilience
Background Characteristics

In midlife, men in our society are typically at the peak of their career and may have the most financial resources to handle different types of loss, such as caring for older parents. Women who have remained at home to care for children may reenter the labor market at midlife. But as more men and women pursue second and third careers or face divorce, unemployment, or the loss of anticipated retirement income, middle adulthood can also be a time of sharply reduced financial resources. Women's financial capacities vary depending on whether their employment has been interrupted by caregiving responsibilities, including past care for children and current care for older parents or grandparents, and by the fact that women generally earn less than men and have less access to health and retirement benefits. Many middle-aged ethnic minorities also face inequities in financial resources.

Personal Capacities

Declining energy is one of the most noticeable changes in middle adulthood, even for adults who are in good physical and mental health. In addition, some adults become less mobile and less active, and some develop a chronic illness. Their rates of functional disability and death rise, particularly due to cancer. African American males have the highest death rates, mainly attributable to accidents, homicides, and HIV/AIDS. The intellectual function of most adults in middle adulthood does not decline, although they worry a great deal about occasional lapses in short-term memory as a sign of dementia.

Personality traits are generally stable in middle adulthood, although men in most cultures begin to exhibit behaviors that are stereotypically assumed to be feminine (e.g., greater nurturance and affiliation), and women acquire characteristics that are stereotypically viewed as male (e.g., greater decisiveness, action orientation, and assertiveness), perhaps due to changes in levels of sex hormones (Borysenko 1996; Havighurst, Neugarten, and Tobin 1968; Neugarten and Gutmann 1968). Many adults in middle adulthood seek ways to enrich the personal meaning of their lives, so spirituality and meaning making, though not necessarily religious affiliation, often become central to their well-being.

Social Capacities

Middle-aged adults usually have several social roles (Antonucci, Akiyama, and Merline 2001). Women, who are more apt to take care of relatives and to have more friendships throughout their life than men do, have the largest and most diverse social networks of any life phase. With the increase in multigenerational families, they often are the middle generation, a phenomenon sometimes referred to as the "sandwich generation" or "women in the middle," who are responsible for both younger and older dependent family members (Brody 1990, 2004). Although women generally have strong friendship networks, family caregiving demands across several generations may necessitate having few close friends with whom they can share intimacy instead of having many acquaintances (Sherman, deVries, and Lansford 2000). Having a close friend, who can serve as a confidante, is often associated with well-being (McQuaide 1998; Vaillant 1998). Middle adulthood is also a time of extensive community capacities, such as participating in employment, neighborhood activities, voluntary associations, and volunteer work (Antonucci, Akiyama, and Merline 2001). How these community resources respond to middle-aged adults' losses affects the outcome of their grief.

Death of an Adolescent or a Young Adult Child

Regardless of age, it is common wisdom, supported by research, that a child's death is the greatest loss a person can suffer (Riches and Dawson 2000; Rubin and Malkinson 2001). Although some early research suggested that a partner's death is more stressful, more recent research has confirmed that a child's death results in more intense, persistent grief and depression than does the death of a partner, parent, or sibling (Nolen-Hoeksema and Larson 1999; Stroebe and Schut 2001a). Their child's death is an awful truth that seems unreal to parents, who often feel as if part of them has been cut off (Kauffman 1994a; Klass 1996a, 1999b, 2001b). Nearly all bereaved parents experience a searing, wrenching pain, almost a physical pain. A science journalist whose eighteen-year-old son was killed in a train wreck while he was returning to college, wrote: "With reality comes pain, and the pain, when it comes, is stunning. The pain is actually physical, mostly in your stomach and chest. Your chest feels crushed and you can't seem to catch your breath. I remember feeling pinned like a butterfly, or somehow eviscerated" (McCracken and Semel 1998:53).

Nine years after the death of her son, McCracken acknowledged: "These days we hardly ever cry. . . . It's not, as I once feared, that we've finally damaged our eyes. We've just learned to live with the pain. That is, like a shadow, it goes where we go. Friends say they don't know how we do it, live this way. Is there a choice? we ask" (McCracken and Semel 1998:104).

The intensity of pain is partly due to the unnatural order of things, since parents expect their children to outlive them. A child's death shakes parents' belief in the order of the universe; life is no longer natural, sequential, and expected. Illusions about the fairness of life are shattered. Parents have also lost one of their hopes for immortality. When young or midlife adults are confronted with the reality that they will die, they can assure themselves that one of the ways that they will live on is through their children. Parents hope that their children will live out their lives, fulfill their dreams, and, in doing so, carry on the parents' life after their death. A young adult child's death thus breaks the progression of genealogical immortality (Klass 1999b).

Most parents define their primary role as protecting their children: being responsible for their health and safety, investing in their education, and providing for other opportunities. Although the physical tasks of child care diminish with time, even when adult children have left home many parents still feel psychologically responsible, wondering and worrying about their child's well-being. A child's death, for which parents somehow feel at fault, thus threatens parents' self-worth and their very reason for existing. They now question the meaning of even daily tasks, since the meaning of parenthood derives from caring for the child (Klass 1999b).

Attachment in parental grief often is manifested as intense wishes to protect and soothe the deceased child, accompanied by guilt and helplessness for not having successfully protected the child from pain and death. Even if the young adult child has physically left home, as a primary object of attachment, he or she is not replaced by other attachment figures (Archer 1999; Stroebe and Schut 2001a). A wide range of emotions accompanies the parent–child bond over the life cycle: love, cooperation, competition, hope, disappointment, anger, and ambivalence. The significance of this bond varies throughout life and does not end with the child's death (Klass, Silverman, and Nickman 1996). But a child's death ends the world in which parents have lived (Brice 1991a, 1991b).

Parents look forward to their children's accomplishments—birthdays, graduations, marriages, and births of grandchildren. Although they also struggle with their maturing children's efforts to assert their independence and autonomy, they know that this is part of the natural order of raising a family. A child's death thus destroys the assumptions parents make about themselves and the world (Gilbert and Smart 1992). Part of the parents' life energy dies, shaking their personalities to their very roots (Rubin 1993; Rubin and Malkinson 2001). With a child's death, parents experience an irreparable loss, because the child is an extension of themselves (Benedek 1959, 1975; Klass 1999b). The moment of the child's death becomes a dividing point between one set of possible futures and another, one era and another; some bereaved parents describe a sense of being "like most parents and not being like them" or drawing a line between when the family was happy and when it was not. As a bereaved father noted: "If grief is resolved, why do we still feel a sense of loss on anniversaries and holidays, and even when we least expect it? Why do we feel a lump in our throat even six years after the loss? It is because healing does not mean forgetting and because moving on with life does not mean that we don't take a part of our lost love with us" (Klass 1999b:30).

A child's death is always present for the parents. Although the pain and suffering usually diminish, they never disappear completely.

The death of friends and other family members during our lifetime can force us to question the meaning of our lives or to feel that our lives have lost all meaning. This is intensified with a child's death, when parents may question their past, present, and future (Cochran and Claspell 1987; Klass 1996a, 1997). Parents face a loss of the future in regard to not only their child but also their identity, roles, parent–child companionship, activities, and love. The death of a young adult child is especially complex, because parents have invested so much time, love, energy, and money in him or her. An adult child represents a foundation on which parents have built their lives and reflects their investment and genetic, reproductive value. They have lost a legacy. In addition, middle-aged parents may have reached a time in their life when they begin to relate to their child as an adult with a unique personality. This transforms their loss into a combination of a lost actual relationship and a lost potential relationship.

A child's death also means the loss of the parent in the child, for he or she represents the genes, personality, values, and other characteristics passed on by the parents. A child's death ends their relationship with a living child, an anticipated future with the child, and relationships with others linked to the child, such as the parents of classmates or teammates. Some parents say that "part of me died with my child's death," a part that was loved, innocent, and optimistic. Parents grieve the loss of their own immortality, the expectation that they will live on through their child after they have died (Klass 1999b). As Crider wrote about the death of his only child in an apartment fire at age twenty-one: "In addition to his only child, his fatherhood and all that it meant has vanished. He has no daughter or son to care for and no lineage going out from him into the future. He still has a lingering fatherly pride and love, but the object of it is gone, and he stands on a severed branch of the family tree" (1996:27).

Paradoxically, parents continue to live while part of themselves and their identity die. The indifference to so much of what used to matter, the absence of positive feelings, and the continuing sense of loss make the metaphor of "part of the self dying" apt to some parents (Rosenblatt 2001). Bereaved parents describe a sense of "going through the motions," of feeling detached from the experience and not attuned to what is going on outside or inside them (Hogan, Morse, and Tason 1996).

Parents also refer to an emptiness or holes in their roles, relationships, and family. Gordon Livingston, a psychiatrist and writer, wrote after the deaths of his two sons: "The hole in my life left by their death is beyond filling. It is a void stretching into whatever future I have left . . . the loss of my sons has brought me to the edge of an abyss. I stare into it and seek only darkness. I would fill it with faith, but whatever belief I had in a just universe has been undone" (McCracken and Semel 1998:53).

Having another child does not end grieving for the child who died. It is not the loss of a role occupant that gives rise to the grief; it is the loss of a particular person.

Many parents who lose a child—regardless of age—feel guilty, lapsing into futile conjectures of "what we should have done that we didn't do" or "what we did do that caused this terrible punishment." They also may need to come to terms with the guilt from what they now perceive to be less than adequate parenting (Klass 1996a, 1999b). With the loss of a partner or parent, adults feel abandoned, but with the loss of a child, parents feel guilty for having failed him or her (Weiss 2001), and even the guilt has little connection to reality.

Searching for explanations for Chris's death, I found myself feeling responsible because we had moved to the Northwest for my job; if we had stayed in the Midwest, he might not have become a climber and might still be alive!

Parents may engage in "endless what ifs," wondering what they or someone else could have done to make a difference and prevent the death: What if I had insisted that Chris attend his brother's college graduation rather than going mountain guiding; what if he had returned home a week earlier when he had taken an ill client to base camp; what if he was not such a caring, responsive human being who rushed to help a client; what if he had not unhooked his rope; what if . . .

To some degree, the "what ifs" are a way to continue taking care of the dead child by continuing to think about what would have been best for him or her. Guilt and blame, often heavy and enduring, are a measure of how much parents lose when a child dies, and confirmation that the child's death was significant to the parents. For example, death caused by a car accident, especially if the parents survived, is characterized by a pervasive, overwhelming, and persistent sense of guilt (Murphy et al. 1998; Rando 1993; Rubin 1993, 1996; Shalev 1991). Unfortunately, focusing on guilt and "what ifs" can stall parents' grief. They must acknowledge that the question "why" cannot be answered; they must stop wondering and asking questions, because there is no adequate reason or explanation for the child's death (Brice 1989, 1991a).

The process of questioning is about meaning making on a spiritual journey; it is not just a psychological process. In every culture, being a parent is linked with central spiritual truths, and rituals are performed to connect a child's birth with transcendent reality. For example, in India, the new mother blesses the family water supply by placing her hands on the family water pots. Her symbolic extension of fertility stresses the creative powers of the female. Jewish boys are circumcised as a sign given to Abraham of the covenant between God and Israel. Christians baptize their children as a sign of God's grace. The first words whispered into a Muslim child's ears are "There is no god but God," which are also the last words a person hears before dying (Klass 1997:306). From the parents' point of view, the bond with their child symbolizes their larger bond with transcendent reality. When their child dies, they lose that sacred connection, and so they face the spiritual task of reestablishing or creating new connections.

The parents' anchors in life—their sense of connection with transcendent reality, the stories and rituals by which they make sense of the world, and the community in which they are embedded—must be rearranged to include the fact that their child has died (Klass 1999b). The immortal and unchangeable reality that bereaved parents know beyond space and time does not change the awful truth that their children were all too mortal. Nonetheless, this transcendent reality can bring solace, or consolation, in the face of irreparable loss (Klass 1999b:23).

Parents choose the path they will follow through the questions they ask and where they seek answers (Rosenblatt 2001). They may search for positive aspects of the child's death, such as the "child has been freed from terrible things," the child could have suffered more or been in a vegetative state, or the child lived life fully. As noted in chapter 3 on resilience, as parents search for meaning, their internal capacities become stronger; they learn what is important in their lives and may become more empathic and caring. Others may become more confident, for having survived the worst possible thing that could happen to them, nothing else could hurt them or be worse. As grieving parents learn to live in a new world, they figure out how to be themselves in a family and a community in a way that makes life meaningful. They learn to grow in those parts of themselves that did not die with the child (Klass 1988:30). As their internal capacities strengthen, their physical and mental well-being may improve as well.

The impact of a child's death lasts for a lifetime, although its meaning continues to change (Klass 1988; Neimeyer 2000).For the rest of their lives, parents continually reevaluate what they have lost and how they have been changed (Silverman and Klass 1996; Stroebe et al. 1992). In Klass's study of support groups for bereaved parents, one mother wrote: "Being a bereaved parent will always be a part of our lives—it just won't be the most important or only part" (1999b: 30).

Middle-aged and older parents whose child died earlier in life, perhaps as infants, continue to grapple with the meaning of death and to be affected by it decades later. They are likely to fear that their deceased child will die forever when they die, since the child's inner representation in the parent will be lost (Malkinson and Bar-Tur 1999). Confronting loss, traversing grief and acute mourning, and reorganizing relationships with the living and dead are tasks for parents that have a sharp beginning but literally no end as long as they live (Ben-Israel Reuveni 1999).

Some midlife and older adults may also have to cope with a grandchild's death, although less is known about its impact. One study found that their feelings were similar to those with a child's death (Fry 1997). Grandparents may also try to be "strong" to protect their adult child and control their grief, especially when interacting with their adult children (Rando 1986). In such instances, grandparents may play an invisible, behind-the-scene role, with their own pain overlooked by others. Issues related to grandparents' caregiving roles are discussed more fully in chapter 12.

Parental Styles of Grieving the Death of an Adolescent or a Young Adult

There are four different parental styles of grieving the death of an adult child:

1. Rejecting a normal living style.
2. Engaging in the culture of a normal life by keeping busy.
3. Rejecting the "normal" and finding new meaning and new support from others who share the same experience.
4. Rejecting the "normal" and searching alone for meanings to explain both the death and the different world it has produced.

Parents may fluctuate among these styles over time or simultaneously engage in all of them as they try to recreate meaning in their lives (Riches and Dawson 2000). These different styles have no value or weight. Instead, the reader is encouraged to use them as guidelines for their professional assessments, interventions, and interactions with bereaved parents. These styles may also apply to bereaved young adult parents, although they were developed from research on middle-aged parents.

1. EXCLUSION FROM NORMAL LIVING

Bereaved parents can decide to go on or not, a choice that in middle age may seem especially difficult. Parents who have a deep urge to be with the child combined with a strong wish to end the pain often consider suicide. The death of another family member by means of suicide or self-neglect after a child's death can be viewed as a statement that the child's death has made life not worth living (Riches and Dawson 2000). Or the grieving parent may choose a symbolic death through emotional isolation. After his dad's death, my older son observed that "Dad died for all us the day that Chris died." Bereaved parents may wish that they would never wake up, because each awakening to a new day reminds them that their child is dead. Deep depression and suicidal thoughts are ways of saying that the loss is so vast, has laid one so low, and the accompanying feelings are so devastating that life may not be worth continuing (Rosenblatt 2001).

When parents choose to keep on living, they nevertheless may be socially and emotionally isolated, feeling marginal and utterly alone. Parents may feel vulnerable, overwhelmed by a sense of dread, terror, and a loss of control or "going mad." They may fear that life can never return to normal. Such feelings of chaos tend to be more intense when the death is unexpected (an accident) or under difficult circumstances that carry a social stigma (homicide, suicide, or AIDS) (Lang and Gottlieb 1993; Lehman et al. 1989; Stroebe 1994). Even when surrounded by family and friends, parents may feel more alone than ever before in their lives or may "build a wall" to keep others at a distance, fearing that intimacy with others may bring even more pain (Martinson and Neelon 1994:23). The devastating feelings that engulf parents are so great that others who do not share them appear to be distant and uncaring (Hogan, Morse, and Tason 1996). The desire to maintain social relationships other than those linked to the dead child may wane or disappear entirely. One mother rationalized her withdrawal by claiming that "it's easier to stay away. Sooner or later, you find the only thing you have to hold on to is yourself" (Riches and Dawson 2000:109). In other instances, friends and family, picking up signs of discomfort and sensing the chasm between themselves and the grieving parents, may drop out of the parents' lives.

Most grieving parents have experienced the "sharp left turn" phenomenon in which a former friend or associate sees the grieving parent in a grocery store or shopping mall and suddenly turns around to avoid interacting with the parent.

Parents may unwittingly widen the chasm between themselves and others through their own discomfort at how others might react to their loss (Rosenblatt 2001). Such distancing behavior also represents others' uneasiness about what to say and do and their fear that if a friend's child can die, then it can happen to them as well. It is almost as if the loss could be catching, especially for parents of a young adult who has committed suicide. Bereaved parents and those close to them are no longer protected by the illusion that death happens only to other people (Klass 1999b). As a result, encounters with familiar people and the first return to commonplace settings, such as one's job, can be overwhelming. Well-meaning friends who try to impose a religious explanation on the death that does not fit the parents' understandings may make the situation even worse (Gilbert 1996, 1997).

Accordingly, bereaved parents may feel that the child and his or her death no longer have a social reality when others stop mentioning the child's name in their presence or imply that the pain is not as great as it is (e.g., well-meaning inquiries about "how are you doing" may implicitly convey "well, it's about time that you got over this"). Learning to travel on different paths and to become a different person confirms that some past relationships are no longer valid (Attig 1996).

As we stated in chapter 6, bereaved parents may also isolate themselves from their families and, in turn, become physically absent and indifferent to their surroundings, their surviving loved ones, and their own health. Their capacity to respond to others' needs, especially those of siblings, is an emotional hurdle for some. The erratic parental contact and support characteristic of undiluted grief is especially hard on surviving siblings (Walker 1993). Author Mary Semel recognized the negative impact of her withdrawal from normal life but felt powerless to change it in the first months following her son's death:

> Not only has Hilary had to cope with losing her brother but also with losing her parents as she knew them. Overnight we were transformed to agonized zombies clinging to life by our fingernails. . . . She was afraid that I would kill myself. She definitely thought that I was too distraught to drive. And I know for a fact that there were times she thought it might be better to be the one who was dead than the one who survived and had to cope with the aftermath. (McCracken and Semel 1998:136)

Resenting the lack of interest shown in them, siblings alternate between distancing themselves from their grieving parents (e.g., going out with friends) and trying to protect them (e.g., staying home to make sure their parents are OK). Parents may misinterpret such confusing responses, especially in younger siblings, as the child's not caring (Frydman-Helfant 1994; Riches and Dawson 2000; Rubin 1999).

When Chris died, we relied on friends and videos to occupy our seven-year-old daughter for more than a month—way too long to be good for her. She withdrew into the videos, watching the same ones over and over, while we wondered why she did not show more visible signs of grief. We knew that we should be attending more to her needs and encouraging her to express her feelings. But given our own grief and limited energy, we did all we could do. I have learned to tell myself that "we did the best that we could do, given the enormity of the loss." At that phase of my grief, I saw no way back, no way forward—only an endless stretch of days without Chris.

Ironically, some parents feel that their emotional distance is protecting their surviving children, by keeping them away from their parents' pain and irritability.

For middle-aged and older parents experiencing age-associated declines in energy, grief is not only emotionally and physically draining but also associated with a loss of stamina and less ability to engage with others or with "normal" life tasks. How can parents engage in "normal" everyday tasks when nothing about a life without their child is normal? As Semel observed after her sixteen-year-old son's death,

> I used to wake up eager to start the day. Not anymore, not since Allie was killed. Sometimes Allie's death is the first thought that comes to mind when I wake up; other times it's not. . . . My thoughts travel to the future, which stretches ahead, a barren vista of grief. What can I do to make my life tolerable after this? Whatever I plan, whatever I do, Allie will always be dead. I will live the rest of my life looking backwards. I cannot bear to contemplate this for long. So I come back to today. How will I navigate the grief until I can return to the anesthesia of sleep? And tomorrow I'll start all over again. (McCracken and Semel 1998:51)

Especially in the early phases of grief, many parents are unable to temper their thoughts of the loss with returning to the concerns of everyday life. Just the act of dressing each day, fixing modest meals, and doing the minimum number of household tasks can be physically taxing and overwhelming. For bereaved parents, getting out of the bed in the morning may be the greatest act of courage (Schiff 1986). Bereaved parents may also cut themselves off from everyday activities that previously had brought enjoyment, such as listening to the news or reading the paper. When the worst thing that could happen has happened, all comforting illusions are gone. Feeling powerless, parents realize that there is nothing that they can do to change the fact that their adolescent or young adult child is dead. What occurs in the larger world seems inconsequential in the face of the worst loss.

Parents are more likely to withdraw from normal living when they are struggling with unfinished business, especially past interpersonal conflicts, with their dead child. Their loneliness may come from deep regret, frustration, or even anger. In their preoccupation with the child's absence, they focus on lost opportunities for resolving conflicts, overcoming resentments, or fulfilling obligations (Riches and Dawson 2000). They also may fear that they will be unable to hold onto memories of their child unless they cling to their grief. Feeling the pain is a way to keep their child's presence alive. Letting go of pain and starting to enjoy themselves may feel like letting go of the child.

2. THE CULTURE OF EVERYDAY LIFE

Focusing on daily tasks—moving on, keeping busy, trying to return to "normal," and distracting oneself from grief—can provide meaning in everyday life. Life still has to go on—work still has to be done, money earned, other children raised. Parents who have been bereaved in the past but believe that there are other things to live for, including surviving children, are better able to maintain everyday relationships than are those who have never faced life's arbitrariness (Powell 1995). This "keeping busy" style is congruent with the benefits from taking time off from grief in the dual-process model of grief described in chapter 2 (Stroebe and Schut 1995). Contrary to the early grief work theories discussed in chapter 1, facing the loss and then temporarily avoiding painful introspections through other activities ("restoration orientation") may lead to a more successful adaptation than does focusing only on distressing thoughts ("loss orientation"). In this dual-process model, parents must still address painful feelings about their child's death. But they have good days as well as bad ones, moments of hope for the future along with times when nothing seems worthwhile, and they swing between the two extremes over time.

Reinvesting in life and social relationships provides a sense of connection and validation from others. In fact, grieving parents who have many social relationships (e.g., social capacity) are more likely to be resilient than are those who have only a few relationships. The reason may be that their personal identity has not relied exclusively on the role of parent (Forte, Barrett, and Campbell 1996). Employment and volunteering—being of value to others—are sources of connectedness, purpose for one's days, and self-esteem.

Parents who try to engage in the "normal" try to manage their grieving in public, with grief as a backstage emotion. But even those who try to resume a normal life are periodically interrupted by feelings of loneliness. Lonesomeness resurfaces for many years in the midst of busy lives and apparently normal relationships (Rosenblatt 1996). Such loneliness may be triggered by anniversary events, seeing a certain person, or being in a particular environment.

For me, loneliness is often greatest when I am surrounded by married parents, cheering on my daughter's soccer team, celebrating her eighth-grade graduation, or attending my son's first New York City art opening. At such times, the absence of Chris and my husband Gene is more real than the presence of others. But this sense of feeling alone when surrounded by others is gradually diminishing over time.

As many of us know, being alone and feeling lonely are different; that is, we can feel lonely even when surrounded by hundreds of other people. Managing grief in public can be exhausting and isolating. For some parents, employment can be a temporary refuge where they can engage in "normal" tasks and relationships. But their return home is often marked by surges of emotion (Klass 1999b).

For months after I went back to work, I could make it through a day at work—and even be productive—but as soon as I walked outside into the darkness, I would cry all the way home. I recognized that I could only hold it together in public for just so long.

Most parents who readily (or too quickly, as defined by others) return to work find that they must eventually take time to deal with their grief directly. Admittedly, economic issues often necessitate an early return to work; in fact, when to return to work is typically not the employee's choice. By trying to gain some control over their shattered lives, parents may engage in behaviors that to outsiders seem bizarre, such as buying things they do not need, redecorating or remodeling the house, or starting a major new project.

Several months after Chris's death, I decided to have my kitchen remodeled, justifying it to others and myself by "if I can't accomplish anything else these days, at least I can handle these relatively minor decisions." I also hoped that it would create a sense of accomplishment for me, since so much of my day was consumed by grieving. The kitchen remodeling was a task I could focus on for short periods of time, a distraction, but it brought no meaning to my life or assuaged my loss in any way. Looking back, this behavior now seems crazy to me—a desperate attempt to feel in charge.

To outsiders, such projects may appear to be strange behaviors, especially if the bereaved parents are unable to afford them financially. But activity can provide a temporary sense of control and of moving forward. Other parents may be able to feel in control by clinging to the dead child's belongings to remind them of his or her physical presence. Some try to gain control by not changing the child's room or creating shrines to their child in the bedroom. To friends and other family members, such behavior may appear irrational and become a source of conflict.

3. NEW MEANINGS AND SUPPORT

Parents often find that past support systems no longer work for them. In fact, they may avoid potentially helpful social situations, through either a fear of losing emotional control or their sense of exasperation with what now seem to be "trivial" conversations. Alternatively, if previous supports pressure them to be "normal" and "fine," parents may feel the stigma of bereavement or that they are "socially significant different." As a result, bereaved parents often seek out those who really understand and have "really been there." "Being there" means sharing with the parent in such a way that the reality of the deceased child and of the pain is not the parent's alone (Klass 1996a, 1999b).

Not surprisingly, support groups composed of others who endure such pain each day may become more important than past friendships to many bereaved parents. If parents have become isolated from past supports, they may be able to feel less alone and find a way back to living through the subculture of bereavement. They develop a relational bond with others who can better understand the pain of their loss (Riches and Dawson 2000; Wheeler 1994). Whether through Compassionate Friends or other parent support groups, bereaved parents may form new relationships with others who have lost a child. A central message of the bereaved parents' self-help process is that the best way to heal grief is to help others. For example, the credo of the Compassionate Friends support groups is

> We reach out to each other with love, with understanding and with hope. Our children have died at all ages and from many different causes, but our love for our children unites us. . . . Whatever pain we bring to this gathering of The Compassionate Friends, it is pain we will share just as we share with each other our love for our children. (Klass 1999b:37)

This credo illustrates the importance of community with other bereaved parents in their bonds to their dead children as way to reduce feelings of being alone.

Adhering to the resilience model, parents who participate in such groups generally draw on and enhance their community capacities. Being able to talk with others about their child is a way to "write the last chapter" of their parent–child relationship. Some parents form or join advocacy organizations related to the cause of their children's death (The Million Mom's March Against Guns or Mothers Against Drunk Driving). Joining such collective efforts can impose an external "expert" validation of what parents experience, publicly acknowledge their continuing pain and bond to the child, and foster a sense of self as active rather than powerless (Rosenblatt 2001). Parents are not "letting go" but are findings ways to "hold on" to their child in light of their physical absence, a process recognized by postmodern theorists, as discussed in chapter 1 (Klass 1996a, 1997, 1999b; Neimeyer 2000, 2001a, 2001b; Walter 2003). Parents who fear that attending to other daily matters might mean forgetting or abandoning their child may need to continually retell the story of their child's death, share pictures, and participate in rituals performed by many support groups.

Others connect with their child by transforming the lost physical relationship into an abstract one that can be held on to and continues to affect the parent's identity (Klass 1996b; Rosenblatt 1996). For most parents, the belief that death is an end to the child's existence in every way is intolerable. Instead, they develop and internalize ongoing bonds with the dead child, as described in chapter 2. In their continuing bonds, parents no longer have an external relationship with their child as a physical being. Rather, they form an "inner representation" of their child, on whom they can call in difficult times as a source of comfort. Such inner representations are not simply pictures, ideas, or feelings; instead, they are thematic memories of the child and emotional states associated with him or her—in effect, an experience of who the child was to the parent when alive and who the child continues to be now. In such continuing bonds, parents are who they were with their children when alive, and their children are again the living children who once were with the parents. Conversations with the child can continue when he or she is still a part of a parent (Klass 1999b; Stroebe et al. 1996).

In the early days of their grieving, many parents describe feeling their child's presence, seeing, hearing, smelling, touching, or talking to their child. They may dream intensely about their child and feel the child's continuing active influence on their thoughts or events. Some parents even internalize characteristics or virtues of the dead (Klass 1999b).

My connection to Chris feels strongest when I take on physical challenges, even risks (e.g., jumping off a high rock into the ocean, swimming farther or longer, rafting the Colorado River that he so loved, or pushing myself to hike farther and longer), and fully experience physical, creative, and inquisitive courage similar to what he daily exhibited.

Such connections, similar to other spiritual experiences, encompass a sense of the uncanny, mystery, wonder, and awe (Riches and Dawson 1998). The interactions within such continuing bonds are not simply an objective presence, since the meaning is strongly personal; nor is it only subjective or "in the head." The intense meanings felt by parents in the bond with their child have no rational proof (Klass 1999b).

Some parents are comforted by envisioning that the child is no longer suffering but instead is in a safe, warm place with relatives or age peers who "have gone before them." Through their belief in life beyond this physical world, many parents are able to find ways to contemplate their child's life with warmth and affection rather than with an overwhelming sense of dread (Rosenblatt 2001). This occurs through a variety of ways: a spiritual search through clairvoyants or channelers to communicate with the child's spirit, more conventional religious movements, continuous storytelling to place the circumstances of death in the context of life as a whole, or personal faith in a place where the child can be pictured as nurtured by others (Walter 1996). Parents may include the dead child's pictures on family portraits taken after his or her death or consciously evoke the child's memory on significant occasions, like holidays, birthdays, and other family gatherings. Many parents still affirm their religious beliefs even while questioning why God or a supreme being allowed the child to die. Some feel intense anger, and others believe that a supreme being is communicating with them to find peace, meaning, and perspective. Or they may search for signs from a supreme being. Through these varied spiritual processes, the dead child comes to exist as a presence in his or her parents' minds, lives, and conversations. Contrary to early grief work's emphasis on separation and detachment, continuing bonds with the dead child are often resources for creative, healthy living (Klass, Silverman, and Nickerman 1996).

Indeed, middle-aged and older parents may perceive the deceased child as more accessible and real than their other children who have moved away from home. One mother articulated the two different realities as "our children have left home. We are at home with him (the deceased child), he is there with us" (Rubin and Malkinson 2001:230). Like this mother, many parents feel that their relationship with their dead child is the closest one they ever had (Ben-Israel Reuveni 1999). They act to keep the child's memory alive through anniversaries, visits to the grave, and memorials to the child as a way to transform the relationship with him or her into something more. Birthdays and other holidays are no longer a reason to celebrate per se, but to honor, commemorate, endure, observe, or just get through them. Because religious holidays are so closely identified with love, parents may feel a child's loss most acutely then and need to figure out what they can endure compared with when their family was "whole." When I was booking our flights to Hawaii the first Christmas after Chris's death, my travel agent assured me that Hawaii is typically full of grieving persons, all of whom are trying to escape their pain. Others create memorial funds in their child's name through educational, sports, or religious institutions or community organizations related to the child's interests or nature of death. Grief is thus not a progression from preoccupation with the dead child to reattachment to the living; it is an oscillation between the demands of living and the continuing perceptions of the deceased.

4. PERSONAL RECONSTRUCTION

Bereaved parents cannot escape the religious and spiritual aspects of death because their child is one of the bonds they have with sacred reality. In other words, there is something in the parents' bond with the dead child that is similar to their bond with larger realities (Klass 1999b). A child's death, particularly that of an only child, presents the kind of suffering and challenge that can create an existential crisis—a search for the meaning of human existence (Talbot 1997:45). Some parents face this crisis by retreating into solitude, which is different from isolation. Solitude can be a basis for introspection, reflection, and interaction with ideas; a self-evaluation; a way of rethinking the nature of the world; and a healthy response to those who pressure parents to get over their grief quickly. C. S. Lewis wrote, "Just as being in love can make the world look different through heightening our awareness, so too that stage of being in grief can make things look different. With grief though it is more the ability to see 'into' or 'behind' things" (1963:47).

Most grieving parents are able to appreciate new aspects of the world and find a personal way back and a new way forward for their lives. Parents' suffering and highly personal exploration of the significance of the death can act as a catalyst for a fundamental review of life's meanings and their role and purpose in it. In the process, their identity can be transformed (Attig 1996).

In their journey of growth and change, other parents "take stock" of their lives—their careers, their friendships, and the way they spend their time. Although they remember their links with the past, they may reevaluate previous social connections, retaining only those that recognize their tremendous loss. They reexamine their normal roles and familial relationships (Rando 1991) and learn to be more discriminating about whom they allow to influence them. They have a greater sense of compassion and wonderment at the fragile but precious nature of life (Kaplan 1995).

When I returned to work, I had much less patience for the small irritants and hassles of academic life. Yet I also became more focused and effective in many of my interactions. I feared nothing, since having experienced the worst thing that could happen to me, I felt that no one or nothing could hurt me again.

Parents discover that friends and family are most helpful when they accept that the pain is irreparable and choose to be there in pain with the parents; they are able to remember the child and allow him or her to be part of their lives just as the child remains part of the parents' world. Such friends paradoxically realize that nothing they can "do" will take away the parents' pain. By just being present, they are able to be part of their healing.

I am fortunate that several parents of Chris's high school friends recognize even now how important it is for me to be able to talk about Chris. They share their memories freely, have his pictures on their refrigerators, and indicate that they, too, think of him often. These are the friends with whom I still walk.

Over time, some bereaved parents may feel less egocentric and more self-assured, emotionally mature, and powerful. For some, grief can be a source of creativity. The death and life of their child gives meaning to their own subsequent choices and decisions, ensuring that "no voice is ever wholly lost" (Kaplan 1995:124).

Fortunately, the human organism is resilient. Humans have been coming to terms with children's deaths since we began as a species, a reality hard to remember during the early days of searing, gut-wrenching pain. In some other societies, especially those devastated by war, the death of adolescent or young adult children is common. In fact, accommodation to parental grief seems hard-wired into our psyche and our communities. In a supportive social context, parents are able to integrate their grief, even though the journey is time-consuming and fluctuates between good and bad days (Klass 1999b).

Death of an Adult Child and the Marital/Partner Relationship

Nearly all parents have to renegotiate their marital/partner relationship after a child's death, regardless of their different grieving styles. Just as the death of a child modifies parents' relationships with friends and relatives, it alters their relationship with each other. Paradoxically, parents' bereavement over a child's death can drive apart those who would normally be expected to give support, isolating them from their most intimate relationships. This is referred to as *intimate loneliness:* parents needing each other's support but finding it hard to ask for and give it (Riches and Dawson 2000). A complicating factor is that intimacy is about not only trust and openness but also hearing another's intensely held but sometimes widely differing perceptions of reality. When pain is so acute, it is often hard to truly hear and accept such different views. Immediately after the death, any talk between parents is likely to degenerate into incoherence and tears. The sheer mention of former joys and memories can plunge them into despair because they realize those joys are gone forever.

To construct new realities and reconstruct old ones, parents must have some grounding for their thinking, feeling, acting, relating, deciding, and talking. Such grounding comes out of language, but few parents start with a language adequate to deal with a child's death. The parents studied by Rosenblatt (2001) struggled to develop shared narratives, or ways of talking about the child's death and the aftermath in order to make sense of what happened. They encountered uncertainties in doing so, since they sensed the marital/partner relationship no longer was a trusted, solid place for grounding realities about the death. Even when parents are able to communicate with each other about their dead child, grief is still a "very individual journey" and creates barriers to sharing warmer memories (Martinson 1991). Disagreements between partners are inevitable, since each parent's narrative of the death is really an account of the self in relationship to the child, the partner, and all else. Because they are different selves, parents never have quite the same story to tell (Riches and Dawson 1996b; Sedney, Baker, and Gross 1994). Each wants to communicate where he or she was when their child died, describe the cause of death, and ask what was wrong and right and who or what had a role in causing the death (Cochran and Claspell 1987; Rosenblatt 2001). In constructing their stories, parents frequently form different perceptions of how the death has changed their relationship.

Questions about the marital/partner relationship reinforce uncertainties that arise from the death about how the couple lived their life and what the right things to do were. Inevitably their narratives about the death move to talk about emotional distance from the other parent and the possibility of separation or divorce. Although referring to separation or divorce is a way of saying how diffi-cult things are, talk about emotional distance does not necessarily lead to divorce.

Many parents have been misinformed that the divorce rate for bereaved par-ents is as high as 80 percent. Although a child's death gererally does not result in divorce, increased marital strain is common and may become serious enough to lead to divorce (Schwab 1998).

Because so many of our friends are professional helpers, they warned my husband and me early and repeatedly about the importance of putting energy into our marriage. But when we barely had the energy to get up each morning and get through the demands of each day, working hard on our marriage seemed overwhelming.

Fear of divorce gives some parents a reason to work even harder to stay together, review their original marital vows as sacred, and emerge as a stronger unit. Agreeing that their child's death is the most tragic loss imaginable, they choose not to lose each other as well. Death can create a new bond between parents even while it pushes them apart. But for some, closeness is not about a higher level of love, communication, and understanding but more about desperate, hurting, needy partners who would be much better off and happier if their child were still alive and they were not compelled to be as close as a couple (Dijkstra and Stroebe 1998; Klass 1986/1987). Their joint grief is a constant, unrelieved aggravation that can drive them apart or leave them clinging to each other.

In many instances, the strains on parents' heterosexual relationship are caused by gender differences in grieving, as discussed in chapter 3. Less is known about grieving gay or lesbian parents, although the roles in such relationships tend to be less distinct and rigid (Walter 2003). The extent to which parents support, listen to, and are sensitive to each other's needs may reflect different perspec-tives on the meaning of "being there." Intimacy in committed relationships re-lates to sharing another's intensely held but sometimes conflicting worldviews. Since each partner experiences loss differently, they may not be able to bridge communication differences. Variations in grieving appear to be key factors in divorce and are intensified if parents come from different cultural backgrounds. Mothers appear to grieve more intensely and longer, cry more, and be more immersed in their grief, in part because their maternal role usually has been more practically and emotionally central than the father's (Duncombe and Marsden1993; Schwab 1998). They may regard their partner as unfeeling when he does not cry or quickly returns to work outside the home. The father is more likely to want to get life back to normal, to "get this over with," and to convey to the mother that she should "shape up" (Schwab 1998). Although these patterns are identified in the grief literature, it is important to acknowledge that in some partnerships, the man is more expressive than the woman, who may seek distraction in employment or household responsibilities.

Gender differences also apply to sexual intimacy and contact, which typically decline immediately after a child's death. The mother's energy and motivation may be so low that she has no interest in sex. For some parents, sexuality is associated with how the child was conceived and a pleasure inconsistent with grief. When parents do touch each other or engage in sexual intercourse, it either can be a bittersweet sense of shared loss or can provide emotional release (Gottlieb, Lang, and Amsel 1996; Hagemeister and Rosenblatt 1997; Schwab 1992). In general, grieving makes partners emotionally unavailable, especially when the child was a primary link between them.

A child's death is not necessarily the cause of the high incidence of divorce in midlife and older bereaved adults. Given the length of most marriages involving adolescents or young adult children, prior problems may worsen with a child's death. Not surprisingly, parents who report a high level of marital satisfaction before the child's death have less marital conflict after a child's death (Moos 1995). In addition, marital distress and communication problems do not necessarily lead to a breakdown. Parents may feel distance, irritation, and even anger with each other but are able to regain emotional intimacy or even increase it over time. Although parents' differences are typically defined in terms of gender, some may be due more to variations in roles, informal networks outside the family, and degree of social connectedness than to gender per se (Schwab 1998). To understand the effects of gender on grief outcomes, more research is needed on same-sex partners grieving the death of an adult child.

When parents do divorce after a child's death, they lose a unique connection to their shared knowledge and memories of the child and each other's feelings toward the child. As a widow, I long to be able to share childhood memories with my husband, the only other person who had been a parent to Chris and could talk about his life and death from that shared perspective. With the divorce or death of the other parent, we lose the one person who could remember details unlikely to be remembered by others (Gilbert 1996; Thuen 1997). The loss of a child is so great that the additional loss of a partner is often felt to be unbearable. To lose a partner is to lose more of the child who died (Rosenblatt 2001).

In sum, parents are more likely to remain together when they accept each other's distinct grieving styles without judgment, permit space in the relationship, place a high value on the family for support and nurturance, and use professional and social networks outside their immediate supports.

Impact of an Adult Child's Death on the Family

A child's death can disrupt and destroy family relationships, routines, communication patterns, identities, shape, and structure. The extent of this disruption varies with the dead child's role in the family. Since a child's death calls into question the point of many family activities, roles, and responsibilities, it threatens family myths and thus can damage family networks (Becvar 2000; Byng-Hal 1979, 1998; Roger 1991). Over time, stories and memories shared by the family gain the status of "legends," acting as a set of symbols through which the family knows it members and represents itself collectively to others. Theorists who recognize the importance of family storytelling, narratives, and myths maintain that the process of story making is central to integrating a child's death. Families need to create a new "myth" that accounts for the death and its consequences. The family thus can be a crucial healing resource if it can share responses and feelings in an open, uncritical way (Nadeau 1998; Rosen 1996; Rosenblatt 1994).

Unfortunately, many families are unable to create new stories and interactions that reflect their reactions. Instead, the family members' different subcultures lead to particular attitudes, expectations, and beliefs about death and "appropriate" responses that can create destructive misunderstandings, particularly for teenagers. The family "project" (e.g., communicating and living together) may lose its meaning, with home seeming bleak and desolate. Older siblings may find it too painful to return home during vacations or college breaks. Although some members may try to stay away from home as much as possible, others may not want to leave home (Riches and Dawson 2000).

Changes to family routines precipitated by a child's death require not only the construction of new stories, myths, memories, and identities but also the negotiation of new roles and relationships. Family relationships have to shuffle around the void left by the dead child.

My son Kevin wrote a song for Chris's memorial service that captured many of his attributes that held our family together: he was the "glue," the fun one, the one who wore "big shoes" to be filled. Over time, the three of us have found new ways to create this glue.

Past internal working models used (e.g., "If we just love our children enough, we can keep them safe; if we are good people, nothing bad will happen to us") and worldviews that once explained what is happening within the family are no longer workable and may create pain. Each member's reaction to the death is affected by differences in his or her social position in the family and other social networks (Rosenblatt 2001). In addition, their grief responses are influenced by age, gender, peer groupings, culture, and subcultures. Since each family member may not be able to reconcile these differences in grieving, the result can be misunderstanding, a sense of resentment, and isolation (Riches and Dawson 2000).

Middle-aged adults may feel chronic sorrow, which was discussed in chapter 8 in regard to parents of children with disabilities, when a young adult child is missing in military action, is kidnapped, or has run away from home. Without a body to grieve, family members remain in limbo, often for many years. Hope may ebb and flow, with parents continuously searching for their missing child, fearful of leaving home in case they might miss a phone call, yet trying to "move on" and bring some structure into their lives. When parents are out of synch with each other during this process (e.g., one parent spends every waking moment hunting for the child, and the other is resigned to the child's permanent absence), their relationship can be severely strained.

Divorce

The divorce rate in midlife is high, rising after fifteen to eighteen years of marriage/partnership (when children reach adolescence), and again after twenty-five to twenty-eight years, when couples are dealing with an empty nest and redefining their parental roles (P. Shapiro 1996). Contrary to the common image of men's marital dissatisfaction and perhaps adultery in middle age, men at midlife report more marital satisfaction than women do, and most divorces are initiated by women (Antonucci and Akiyama 1997; Carter and McGoldrick 1999).

In some instances, divorce may be even more traumatic than death, since death represents a clear ending to a relationship, whereas divorce remains a potential end—albeit an increasingly likely one—but not a certainty (Doka 1989b). Divorce lacks death's finality and universality. In many ways, death is "cleaner" because the source of pain—the partner—is no longer present in one's life. The ambiguous feelings of grief brought by the death of a marriage usually are a mixture of shock, denial, hurt, abandonment, anger, bitterness, panic, hatred, and even relief or excitement (Harvey 2000; McKay et al. 1999). Whereas the finality of death forces the griever to confront the pain, the initiator of a divorce may struggle with guilt and ambivalence beyond the actual divorce, especially when the divorce hurts the children involved. The other member of the divorce or separation must deal with feelings of powerlessness, anger, hostility, and rejection, which can hurt self-esteem, and he or she is likely to engage in self-pity and self-blaming and may experience physical symptoms such as insomnia, trembling, nausea, and diarrhea (McKay et al. 1999). Divorcing couples lose the innocence that they brought to their marital vows and expectations, and in doing so they may lose their self-esteem, sense of control, feelings of interpersonal competence, and hope in life. They also must relinquish their dream of what they thought their lives would be and deal with the daily reality that is at odds with those dreams. Even in deteriorated or conflicted relationships, the partners may still be strongly attached, especially if they have been together since they were young (Harvey 2000).

Two other personal capacity factors make divorce grief worse than death grief: the more pervasive presence of decision-making behavior in divorce grief and differences in how much choice or control one has over divorce versus death. In addition, the decision to separate or divorce is not necessarily the last one that partners must make; they also must make decisions about the disposition of property and possessions, parental rights, living arrangements, and financial obligations. In addition, one partner may still cling to the hope of reconciliation. Throughout this process, fault is assigned and negotiated. Unlike widowhood, divorce is an event tailor-made for feeling bad about oneself. Unlike death, the loss of one's partner through divorce does not necessarily bring other family members' support and understanding. The absence of cultural and societal rituals marking the death of a marriage is another difference in divorce-related grief. There are few culturally accepted postdivorce rituals to aid socialization into a new role, although some adults are inventing their own to help them with this transition (e.g., inviting close friends to mark the day the divorce is finalized). Partners who are mourning the death of their relationship must learn to abandon the dreams entailed in their being together, relinquish past parenting roles, and accept new ones (e.g., that of a single mom or dad), adjust to the changes in finances, reestablish physical and emotional intimacy with someone else, and try to preserve their sense of self.

In the resilience model, mediating variables underlying the disproportionate intensity of grief from divorce are the degree of social support, presence or absence of children, remarriage, and the roles of the divorcing partners. The most significant mediating variable is whether a partner was active or passive in the separation (Doka 1989d). The partner who initiated the separation or divorce is less likely to grieve, which may be partly because he or she anticipated, prepared for, and grieved in advance.

Divorce intensifies grief at two levels: the individual's capacities in how he or she responds to the divorce itself and the environment's (e.g., family, community, and culture) response to the divorcing individual. Since one or both divorcing partners have chosen to divorce, they may be ostracized socially and lose some family and community capacities. Social networks—including those of the family of origin, the family of the former partner, and married friends and acquaintances—may withdraw or take sides. Mothers who are not granted child custody or choose not to be the custodial parent usually feel ostracized by others as they struggle with their grief, sadness, anger, guilt, and loneliness (Babcock 1997). In-law relationships typically weaken after divorce, unless the grandparents are committed to remaining involved with their grandchildren. Widows are more likely to receive the support of friends and family than are divorced women (Doka 1989c). Divorce does not end a relationship but merely changes it, with volatility, anger, and resentment characterizing the new relationship (Weiss 1974). In addition, the divorcing couple may lose the support of their community, especially that of religious institutions that disapprove of divorce.

Caring for a Young Adult Child with a Chronic Mental Illness

The grief of parents caring for a young adult child with a chronic mental illness (e.g., schizophrenia, depression, bipolar disorder, and obsessive-compulsive disorder are the most common) is another form of disenfranchised grief, a psychosocial loss that is not openly acknowledged by professionals or friends, publicly mourned or socially supported (Doka 1989a; Eakes 1995). In a given year, an estimated 22.1 percent of the population aged eighteen and older suffer from a diagnosable mental disorder. Although major disorders can develop at any age, the average age at onset for depression, bipolar disorder, and schizophrenia is the early to mid-twenties, often resulting in disability throughout adulthood (National Institute of Mental Health 2004). Given this incidence in early adulthood, middle-aged parents who anticipated launching their young adult child, whether through college, graduate school, or employment, may suddenly be faced with a chronic mental illness in their child. Their grief response may initially parallel that of parents whose adult child has died: avoidance and denial, anger, guilt, blaming of self and others, and, over time, the reorganization of their lives, belief systems, and self-perception to incorporate the loss. Guilt may be especially intense as parents struggle with what they might have done to prevent the onset of a disease whose cause and course are not well understood. In fact, professionals in traditional mental health settings, who are insensitive to grief and loss issues, may inadvertently imply that the family, especially the mother, is somehow partly responsible for their child's mental illness (MacGregor 1994). In addition, these feelings are often worsened by the stigma of mental illness.

The parents of young adults with a chronic mental illness grieve the loss of their child's personality, potential, family role, and hoped-for future. In fact, they may mourn the physical loss of their child if he or she joins the chronically mentally ill homeless on the streets. They also must grapple with other losses, such as self-esteem and a sense of competence as a parent; hope, dreams, and pleasure in an adult child's success; family's and friends' support; and control, normalcy, and predictability. Their own plans for enjoying an empty nest and being freed from child-rearing responsibilities are thwarted. Because the loss with mental illness is largely psychosocial rather than physical, the community often does not accept the family's loss or provide social or religious rituals or other forms of social support.

Similar to parents of a child born with physical disabilities, parents of a young adult child with chronic mental illness experience chronic sorrow or never-ending sadness. They are dealing with a child who is alive but different, and their energies are often absorbed in a demanding, frustrating, and frightening care situation, which increases their feelings of ambivalence and interferes with their mourning. They also struggle with anger about their never-ending care-giving responsibilities and the difficulties of negotiating with health and mental health care providers and systems (Eakes 1995). Chronic sorrow is most likely to develop in the face of hopelessness regarding progress and when the condition is seen as permanent (Shannon 1996). Parents live with the memories of a once healthy child (and family) and the daily reality of his or her progressive decline and disruption to once "normal" lives. They oscillate between their loss and caring for the source of their loss. Under these conditions, the final phase of grief—the reinvestment of energy in other relationships—may not be possible (MacGregor 1994). In fact, one study found that parents with schizophrenic adult children had more chronic grief than did parents with an adult child who died or was dramatically changed by a head injury (Atkinson 1994). Lacking support from friends, family, or professionals, parents of a young adult with chronic mental illness often feel alone and isolated in silence, especially given the stigma and shame surrounding mental illness. Parents may feel that they are wrongly held responsible for their child's illness, or they may realize, at some level, that they did contribute to the illness. Those who are able to come to terms with their responsibilities and integrate their grief generally are able to construct some positive meaning out of the illness experience, such as active involvement in education and advocacy organizations or working to change policies related to chronic mental illness (Shannon 1996).

Caring for Older Relatives

Family members, primarily women, provide an estimated 80 percent of the care needed by older relatives in home- and community-based settings (Doty et al.

2005). Families offer emotional support and help with instrumental activities (e.g., transportation, meal preparation, shopping), personal care (e.g., bathing, feeding and dressing), and negotiating with agencies for services. The caregivers of older persons are primarily adult children (an estimated 42 percent), followed by partners or spouses (an estimated 25 percent) (National Academy on an Aging Society 2000).

Given the increases in life expectancy and in multigenerational families, caring for older relatives—parents, parents-in-law, grandparents, or other relatives—is becoming normative in midlife, with most middle-aged adults deeply involved with their aging parents. Parent care has become a predictable and nearly universal experience throughout the life course, but many adults are not adequately prepared for it. Although it is often referred to as a "role reversal," an adult child never becomes a parent's parent. Instead, caregiving means letting go of outmoded patterns in order to meet current family needs and grieving our parent or other relatives as we once knew them (McLeod 2001). Furthermore, our sense of loss is intensified as we watch the loss of health, mobility, and personality of our loved ones: "The skein of my life began to unravel, dangling without form or future. So it was that I assumed care of my parents, safeguarding them and keeping them together, to return as best I could the full measure of love they had given me" (McLeod 1999:27).

Nonetheless, most of us are not taught how to learn new ways of being with our older relatives or ill partner: "Caring for a parent throws open the door to our past and demands that we look at it squarely. The past cannot be changed; the future is ours to create. . . . We are testing new limits, learning broader ways of being in the world" (McLeod 1999:72).

Nor do losses associated with caregiving end at death, as family differences related to wills, estate sales, and appropriate memorials may exacerbate the grief and loss. Caregiving typically entails more losses for women than for men, since women comprise over 70 percent of family caregivers to chronically ill elders; in fact, over 50 percent of all women provide such care at some point in the life course (Administration on Aging 2003). Adult children, especially daughters, are the primary caregivers for older widowed women and older unmarried men, and they are the secondary caregivers when the partner of an older person is still alive and able to provide care (Neal, Ingersoll-Dayton, and Starrels 1997). In fact, today the average woman can expect to spend more years caring for an older family member (eighteen years) than for her children (seventeen years).

The concept of a "sandwiched generation" refers to midlife men and women who are faced with the competing responsibilities of caring for parents and children, including young adult children who may have returned home because of economic or other pressures. "Women in the middle" may thus be juggling extensive family responsibilities along with employment and their own age-related transitions. They are more likely than men to give up employment, which results in a loss of income (both current and retirement) and a source of identity and self-esteem: "It is culturally expected to care for a parent in the home, yet it is viewed as women's work, and we don't value that very much in our society. Society thinks 'it's just an old person,' and 'it's just a woman.' So there are no benefits—no unemployment insurance, no vacations. It's insulting, and yet this is important work" (McLeod 1999:36).

Major stressors stem from continuing, multiple losses of a loved one, a relationship and companionship, lifestyle and security, predictability and autonomy, social status and financial security, and family cohesion. Feelings of being isolated and disconnected from others, overwhelmed, out of control, inadequate, and fearful of the unpredictability of the future are the most stressful (McLeod 1999; Moen, Erickson, and Dempster-McClain 2000; Tennstedt 1999). Daughters and daughters-in-law have more emotional stress than sons do, even when men and women are performing similar tasks during similar time periods. Women tend to report more depression, anxiety, and psychiatric symptoms and less life satisfaction than their male counterparts do (Gonyea 2006; Putney and Bengtson 2001). Other losses are time for family, friends, self, and leisure. As one caregiver observed, "By definition, caregiving does not affect your life; it becomes your life. Outside activities disappear. In eight years, I have been to the movies three times" (McLeod 1999:81).

Grief may be manifested as guilt for not doing more, anger and resentment of the care role, self-neglect, burnout or compassion fatigue, depression, and physical and mental health problems (National Academy on an Aging Society 2000; Ory et al. 1999; Prescop et al. 1999; Tennstedt 1999; Vitaliano et al. 1997).

Middle-aged adults caring for older relatives with dementia suffer the greatest losses, because they typically must tolerate an ambiguous, unpredictable situation for long periods of time. Such caregivers often refer to a loved one's dying twice: first the psychological death of the person whom they knew and loved and then the actual physical death. This can result in multiple waves of grief (Epple 2002). The prolonged stress of caring for a loved one with dementia can create a sense of desperation from not being able to control a difficult situation. This chronic sorrow or "long good-bye" can negatively affect caregivers' physical and mental health. In some instances, the grief over lost opportunities and the lost parent–child relationship is misdiagnosed as clinical depression (Meuser and Marwit 2001; Mittelman 2002). It is important to differentiate grief from depression and to be alert to warning signs of depression, such as sleep disturbances, change in appetite, greater use of medication or alcohol, marked changes in mood, physical health problems, chronic fatigue, or rough handling of the older care recipient for more than two weeks (Lustbader and Hooyman 1994). Professionals need to encourage self-care as a way to prevent or minimize some of the stresses from the long-term care of an older parent.

Adult caregivers may, however, also gain satisfaction, a sense of meaning, preservation of values and ideals, and pride from being able to give back to those who once cared for them (Sherrell, Buckwalter, and Morhardt 2001). According to the resilience model, such positive outcomes usually are associated with strong social supports, a high communal orientation (e.g., better able to seek and receive others' support), close family relationships, and cultural values and beliefs regarding filial support (Almberg, Grafstroem, and Winblad 2000; Farkas and Hines 1997; Kramer 1997). For example, some caregivers of color are found to have a strong belief in their responsibility to care for their parents; turn to prayer, faith, and religion more readily; and feel less stress and sense of loss than Caucasian caregivers do (Aranda and Knight 1997; Connell and Gibson 1997). Middle-aged African American daughters have been found to be more realistic about their caregiving limits and resultant losses, including accepting nursing home care when necessary, than younger caregivers are (Groger and Mayberry 2001). Nevertheless, most caregivers grieve numerous losses throughout their life, although they may be unaware of this grief dynamic, which lies just below the surface of their sadness, anger, or exhaustion. Their grief, like those of others in relatively invisible roles in our society, is disenfranchised by others' lack of recognition. Even just having their grief named and acknowledged may give them strength to keep on caring.

When I was speaking at a caregiving conference in Tigard, Oregon, I was moved by the story of a woman in her early forties who was caring for her mother-in-law with Alzheimer's disease, her eleven-year-old daughter, and her eight-year-old son. She had given up a rewarding career, and her other in-laws, who had no children, provided only financial assistance, refusing to help out by giving her respite or time off. Her husband worked two jobs, and although he was supportive of her, he was rarely present to provide help. Caring for her mother-in-law dominated her life, and she had little time to attend her children's special events or sports. Her son had had to give up his room for his grandmother, and her daughter complained about how her mother had no time for her. In the two years of caring for her mother-in-law, she had not had a day just for herself. When she learned about state-funded respite services, she started to sob, recognizing how much she had been grieving the loss of time for herself and her children.

Even though grief is a normal response to loss, not every loss gives rise to grief. After many years of a difficult parent–child relationship, some caregivers may be providing care only because no other viable options exist (Sanders and Corley 2003). For young-old children (fifty-five to sixty-five years) caring for oldest-old parents (over age eighty-five), the bonds of attachment may be weak, especially if past familial patterns were characterized by disruption, neglect, or separation. Other caregivers may suppress, compartmentalize, or refuse to acknowledge their grief.

Death of a Parent

Almost 75 percent of all persons who die in the United States are at least sixty-five years old; of them, 33 percent are over age eighty-five (Moss, Moss, and Hansson 2001). The death of both parents is a milestone that approximately 75 percent of adults are likely to have passed through by age sixty-two (Becvar 2001). Given increased life expectancy and thus the likelihood of living beyond age sixty-five, a midlife adult experiencing a parent's death is a normative or "on- time" loss. In most instances, the parent has been ill and his or her death may be anticipated, although adult children may nevertheless fluctuate between holding on and letting go of their relationship with their parent. Nevertheless, a parent's death, no matter how predictable or expected, may cause great grief, which is generally not anticipated (Becvar 2001; Harvey 2000).

No matter how well adult children may have prepared emotionally for a parent's death and engaged in participatory mourning, it can be a life-changing event (Lund 1989a). As Harvey commented (2000), a parent's death may shake up an adult child's life in such a way that the child feels that he or she no longer has an anchor. Our beliefs about our parents' invincibility and immortality are shattered. In addition, when both our parents die and we become orphans, we become aware of our own mortality and may lose our primary source of unconditional love. We are no longer somebody's child, and our primary connection with the past is gone. Becoming a member of the oldest generation can be a life-altering event, requiring the creation of a new relationship with the world and others in it. Grief over the loss of our first parent also may resurface when the second parent dies (Becvar 2001). Regardless of our age, nearly all of us have a sense that we are our parents' children and that our parents are a haven of security for us. (This may not be the case for adults who were abused, neglected, or abandoned in their youth and may feel little emotional connection to their parents.)

As children, we believed our mother would be with us forever. When she dies, we find it hard to believe that something that seemed to be forever has suddenly been terminated. In general, midlife adults who had a history of conflicts, regrets, and unfinished business with a parent, especially their mother, have more difficulties with the grief process. With the loss of the parental buffer shielding the adult child's eventual death, adult children also become more aware of their own mortality and time left to live (Lutovich 2002; Scharlach 1991; Scharlach and Fredriksen 1993).

Because of the often close connection between mothers and daughters, middle-aged daughters may feel intense grief over their mother's death, the loss of the key player in their childhood (Lutovich 2002). Their mothers may have been the last connection with the family home and the focal point for siblings and other relatives. Since fathers are likely to have died first, daughters often become orphans when their mother dies. Daughters also may become aware that they are aging and likely to die in a way similar to that of their mothers. Traumatic grief is less common in daughters who anticipated the death and were no longer dependent on their mother (Scharlach 1991). Daughters often talk about maintaining a connection with their mother and create a story about themselves in relation to their mothers. Their mother's death represents to African American daughters not only the physical loss of their mother but also their mother's fundamental link with family, the role of consistent nurturer and helper, and the root of the family and the black community (Smith 1998).

Adult children may be allowed little time to grieve their parent's death, because a parent's death in midlife is an "on-time" event and because of ageism in our culture (e.g., the death of an older person is assumed to be less tragic than that of a younger person because he or she would die soon anyway). Accordingly, fewer funeral rituals generally mark the death of older persons (Moss, Moss, and Hansson 2001). Bereaved adult children are typically expected to return to the workplace or assume other responsibilities shortly after their parent's death.

The death of an older parent has a different meaning for each surviving child based on his or her past relationship with the parent and his or her own past losses. Even in middle-aged and older siblings, themes such as parental favoritism and rivalry persist well after the death (Nadeau 1998). Reactions to a parent's death vary to some extent by gender, with bereaved sons emphasizing themes of control, action, thinking, and privacy and bereaved daughters focusing on the loss of relationship, social support, and the expression and sharing of emotions (Martin and Doka 1998; Moss, Rubenstein, and Moss 1997). The parent–child bond tends to endure after the parent's death and gives meaning to the loss. Although sadness represents a recognition of the reality of the loss, it also holds on to thoughts of the deceased (Moss, Moss, and Hansson 2001; Moss, Resch, and Moss 1997). The death of a parent tends to be more complex when business is left unresolved and when the parent has not lived to enjoy milestones with grandchildren. Another factor that may complicate the bereavement process is the degree of stress experienced by the adult child before the parent's death. For example, children who have been primary caregivers, especially for parents with dementia, usually are more emotionally upset and have more health problems and stronger active and symbolic ties to the parent after the parent dies (Moss, Moss, and Hansson 1997).

Summary

Middle adulthood, when we shift away from our youth and toward old age, is typically a time of both gains and losses. For those who have the economic, social, and personal resources, it can be a period of growth, freedom, and creativity. Regardless of our own capacities, however, we are likely to face the death and divorce of friends or adult children, caregiving for young adults with disabilities or for older family members, and the death of our parents. We also begin to feel the cumulative effects of multiple losses from earlier phases of our life. As the resilience model suggests, the impact of these losses can be mediated by strong social supports and the ability to find personal meaning through one's grief.

11

Interventions for Grieving Midlife Adults

ADULTS IN middle age (or what is typically referred to as midlife) commonly "encounter a substantial range of life events, moving through significant physical, emotional, sociocultural, and family changes" (Juntunen and Atkinson 2002:297), which offer both challenges and rewards. These life events often constitute major transitions associated with attending to aging parents, adapting to divorce or other marital/partner changes, grieving the death of a young adult child, relating to grown children, and adopting new family-related roles (Kogan and Vacha-Haase 2002). In addition, adults in midlife are more likely to die than young adults are, with cancer and heart disease accounting for approximately 60 percent of all deaths in middle age (Corr, Nabe, and Corr 2003). As middle-aged persons confront changes in their physical appearance, failing health, declining energy, or own or others' death, they often become more aware of their own mortality, reappraise their priorities, and search for a meaning to their life. If negotiated well, these events and experiences can result in personal or professional growth, an enriched spiritual life, and an integration of undeveloped dimensions of personality (Jung 1971); or they may have less positive outcomes, such as bitterness or depression (Jacques 1965). Social workers, who are familiar with the common transitions, challenges, and potential losses, along with middle-aged adults' strengths and capacities, may be able to validate and "normalize" these experiences, support their adaptation to new roles, and, when asked by their clients, help them search for meaning.

Most persons in midlife who confront normative or other losses do not require long-term professional "intervention." Indeed, mounting evidence suggests that interventions for adults experiencing uncomplicated grief "cannot be regarded as beneficial in terms of diminishing grief-related symptoms" (Hansson and Stroebe 2003; Jordan and Neimeyer 2003; Neimeyer 2000; Schut et al. 2001:731). For these midlife adults, especially in the early phases of grief, social workers and other human service professionals may be most effective "by providing support to natural helpers," such as family, neighbors, friends, and "members of familiar religious, social, or business groups" (Hansson and Stroebe 2003:519–20; Schut et al. 2001). Remember that particularly for many death-related losses, family, friends, neighbors, and colleagues are generally available to provide food, support, and help with daily tasks immediately following the death. It is after these informal supports begin to return to their "normal" lives and the bereaved are alone with the silence in the house that they begin to feel the impact of their loss. We need to educate one another about the ongoing need for support (for acute or chronic loss) and the desire of many bereaved people to talk about their loss and to encourage family and friends to maintain contact over the months (or years) to follow. Phone calls, thoughtful notes or cards, and visits may lessen the bereaved's isolation. For midlife adults who are at risk of or are experiencing complicated or traumatic grief, psychotherapeutic interventions may be beneficial (Jacobs and Prigerson 2000; Jordan and Neimeyer 2003).

Assessment

The assessment of bereaved adults explores the following domains:

1. Emotional (e.g., range of emotional reactions, affect).
2. Cognitive (e.g., perceptions of the loss, thoughts related to the loss, presence of "flashbacks").
3. Behavioral (e.g., seeking behaviors, social isolation, potential to harm self or others).
4. Physical (e.g., appetite changes, quality of sleep, substance use).
5. Spiritual (e.g., questioning previously held beliefs, evidence of shattered assumptions). (Rando 1993)

As chapter 9 states, assessment helps determine the intensity of the intervention that will best match the need or risk. High-risk factors to consider in an assessment include one or more of the following: limited social support, history or immediate evidence of difficulty in responding to the loss, situational stressors (e.g., financial distress, compromised health, multiple loss), ambivalent or conflicted relationship with the object of the loss, major depression or personality disorder, inability to acknowledge the loss, extreme anger or anxiety, and a very high degree of dependence on the loss object (Glass, Cluxton, and Rancour 2001; Walsh-Burke 2000). Other high-risk mourners are men (especially older and isolated males) whose wives have died, mothers whose children have died, and survivors of sudden or violent traumatizing losses (e.g., suicide, homicide, accidental death, terrorist attacks, and warfare) (Jordan and Neimeyer 2003). A risk assessment for grief or bereavement is one way of ensuring that the appropriate services will be offered. Less intensive interventions for persons at low risk of complicated grief include longer-term follow-up phone calls, information and referral, or support and psychoeducational groups. More intensive interventions for persons at high risk or with complicated grief are grief counseling or therapy (Walsh-Burke 2000).

The assessment of complicated grief itself is important, given its higher incidence of serious, even life-threatening physical and mental health consequences (Brody 2004). As chapter 2 explains, persons with complicated grief often have persistent symptoms of separation distress, traumatic distress, and somatic illness. Potential indicators of complicated grief are deep unrelieved depression; intense and prolonged grief or pangs of emotion; self- or other destructive behavior; excessive use of alcohol and/or drugs; excessive irritability, bitterness, and anger related to the loss; distressing yearnings; a shattered worldview (e.g., lost sense of trust, control, or security); feelings of futility about the future; recurrent disturbing images; a feeling of being excessively alone and empty; and intrusive thoughts about and preoccupation with thoughts of the loss experience (Corless 2001; Horowitz et al. 1997; Prigerson and Jacobs 2001b).

The empirical literature does not consistently distinguish between interventions for complicated grief and those for uncomplicated grief. The evidence suggests, however, that adults with complicated grief responses are more likely to benefit from professional intervention that moves beyond purely support- or resource-based approaches (Rowa-Dewar 2002). The intense suffering and discomfort of complicated grief often compel individuals to seek professional help, or family members or friends may seek help for the bereaved. In all situations, interventions must be tailored to the needs and concerns and cultural values, beliefs, and preferences of the individual or family. Rando (1993) described formal therapeutic approaches to complicated mourning, such as psychotherapy, regrief therapy, and other behavior, cognitive, and social therapies designed to help modify troubling behaviors, thoughts, or feelings.

Cultural Considerations

An understanding of midlife adults' cultural values, beliefs, strengths, needs, and preferences is critical to the development of culturally congruent interventions for them. Cultural clashes in grief-related customs and rituals in health care or other settings occur when professionals do not recognize the natural responses and culturally determined rituals of the bereaved families with whom they work (for examples, see Irish, Lundquist, and Nelsen 1993). For example, finding the most appropriate place to die is very important to Hmong families. According to Hmong cultural beliefs in the role and functions of spirits, persons must not die in the home of persons not related spiritually or by blood (e.g., members of another clan). To do so is believed to unleash the anger of the house spirits, who may withdraw their protection from the home owner's family, causing illness or misfortune (Bliatout 1993).

Box 11.1 presents considerations for cultural assessment that pertain to loss and bereavement. Cultural variability in the manifestations of grief is well established. As chapter 1 points out, a grief reaction considered normative in one cultural group may be viewed as unusual by another. Level of acculturation, acculturative stress, and historical/cultural losses also undoubtedly influence the grief experience and have implications for intervention. For example, many Native American clients or their family members have experienced trauma related to being put in a boarding school or feel the effects of generations of trauma that may exacerbate current losses (Weaver and Yellow Horse Brave Heart 1999). Interpreters may be needed for recent immigrants and refugees who have experienced violence, war, and forced removal from their countries. Working with interpreters can make it difficult, however, to understand the nuances of communication relevant to bereavement. Several guidelines for working with interpreters are available (see Amodeo, Grigg-Saito, and Robb 1997; Rothschild 1998).

According to the resilience model, the personal, cultural, social, and environmental capacities available to the bereaved should be considered when looking for sources of support and strength that may help integrate a loss. Social workers helping families facing a member's life-threatening illness must take into account the dying person and family members' beliefs regarding the causes of the illness as well as their beliefs and rituals associated with caring for the body after death. Box 11.1 lists questions relevant to each of these issues.

Telling "the Story" of the Loss

A good way of beginning the assessment is to listen to "the story" of the loss. Telling "the story" may offer emotional relief, help meaning making, bring people together, and provide a way to gauge the progress of treatment as the stories are retold over time (Sedney, Baker, and Gross 1994). The "story" of a death may be elicited by encouraging family members to talk about how the person died, details surrounding the circumstances of the death, the sequence of events leading up to it, how and when each family member learned of the death, and the family members' experiences and reactions at the time (Sedney, Baker, and Gross 1994). Their answers may reveal their cultural beliefs and

Box 11.1 Considerations for Cultural Assessment

SUGGESTIONS FOR PREPARING FOR CROSS-CULTURAL ASSESSMENT AND COMMUNICATION

- Step out of your own cultural frame of reference as you seek to become more culturally competent.
- Do your homework before making direct contact with cultural groups you anticipate working with.
- If possible, talk to knowledgeable others from the same cultural group.
- Never generalize or stereotype ethnic beliefs, values, customs, or rituals.
- Try to understand and anticipate variation in communication patterns and expressions of grief.
- Try to learn from the individuals or family members you are trying to help.
- Approach patients with humility and caution while recognizing that "insiders" have more immediate, subtle, and critical knowledge of their own experiences than anyone else does.
- Use open-ended questions, and encourage the client to tell his or her own story.
- Recognize potential cultural conflicts, and respect choices and decisions.
- Understand cultural norms regarding truth telling that may influence a family wanting to withhold the truth about a terminal illness.
- Never predetermine, judge, or hold expectations about what clients or families "ought to do or feel."
- Identify and use the cultural capacities, strengths, and resources of the individual, family, and community.
- Determine, identify, and/or develop culturally competent interventions appropriate to needs identified.
- Use and train qualified interpreters (see the guidelines on p. 277).

ASSESSMENT COMPONENTS TO CONSIDER

Reactions to loss	Level of acculturation	Religion/spirituality
Manifestations of grief	Acculturative stress	Social and other supports
Determinants of grief	Cultural history	Family dynamics
Grieving rituals	Historical losses	Intergenerational relationships

continued

Mourning style	Interpretation of illness	Financial resources
Values and beliefs	Meaning of the loss	Strengths
Personality	Psychiatric history	

QUESTIONS RELEVANT TO ILLNESS BELIEFS AND SUPPORTS

- How do you define the illness?
- What do you call the illness?
- What do you think caused the illness?
- Why do you think it started when it did?
- What do you think your illness does to you (how does it work)?
- How severe is your illness; will it have a long or short course?
- What are the chief problems for you because of your condition?
- What do you fear most?
- What can improve your/their condition?
- Who can help or support you/them?
- How does religion or spirituality help you/them?
- What happens to your spirit when you are sick?
- Are there any ceremonies or rituals usually performed for this illness?
- What do you or your family need at this time?
- How can I/we help you?
- Are there community healers, shamans, or others who are needed to help this condition?

QUESTIONS RELEVANT TO CARE OF THE BODY AFTER DEATH, BELIEFS, AND RITUALS

- Are there any subjects that are not discussed in your family and culture?
- How long is the body kept in the house after death, and what are the household rituals?
- What happens when the body leaves the house, and what rituals are involved?
- How is the body finally disposed; what happens to the remains?
- What are the community events after the body disposal? Who is invited?
- What ceremonies and rituals are performed, and who is involved?
- What are the barriers that you or others in your cultural group have faced in performing rituals relevant to care of the body following a death in the United States?

- How is death valued in your culture?
- What happens when someone dies? Is there a spirit that leaves the body?
- Where does a person's spirit go when he or she dies?
- What obligations do the living continue to owe the deceased, or do the deceased owe to the living?

Questions Relevant to Grief and Mourning Expectations

- How do people in your family and culture commonly express grief?
- What are the cultural expectations of mourners and those who would help?
- How openly and how long do people normally grieve?
- What should people wear, and what colors are important?
- When and with whom is it appropriate to express emotions?
- Who is expected to show emotion, and who is not?
- How are outsiders to express their solidarity with family members?
- What are the barriers that you or others in your cultural group have grieving in the United States?
- Who tends to be the support system for the grieving? (Who supports you?)
- What is considered acceptable and unacceptable grieving in your family?
- When does the mourning period end?
- What periodic rituals exist, and how long do they last?
- What is an outsider's appropriate response to the periodic rituals?

Guidelines for Working with Interpreters

- Use qualified interpreters, rather than children, relatives, or friends of the interviewee.
- Conduct a preinterview meeting with the interpreter to clarify goals and roles.
- Establish a good working relationship with the interpreter.
- Allow enough time for the interpreted session.
- Make sure the interpreter is acceptable to the interviewee.
- Address yourself to the interviewee, not to the interpreter.
- Communicate only what you want all present to hear.
- Use words, not gestures, to convey your meaning.

continued

- Speak clearly and in a regular tone of voice.
- Avoid jargon and technical terms.
- Keep utterances and questions concise, pausing to permit time for inter-
  pretation.
- Ask one question at a time.
- Expect the interpreter to interrupt when necessary for clarification and
  to take notes.
- Be prepared to repeat yourself in different words if your message is not
  understood.
- Conduct a brief postinterview meeting with the interpreter.

Sources: M. Amodeo, D. Grigg-Saito, and N. Robb, Working with Foreign Lan-
guage Interpreters: Guidelines for Substance Abuse Clinicians and Human Service
Practitioners, *Alcoholism Treatment Quarterly* 154 (1997): 75–87; V. Baez and K. A.
Oltjenbruns, Diversity Within Diversity: Strategies for Developing Insight Among
Professionals, in *Meeting the Needs of Our Clients Creatively: The Impact of Art and
Culture on Caregiving*, edited by J. D. Morgan (Amityville, N.Y.: Baywood, 2000),
49–66; K. L. Braun, J. H. Pietsch, and P. L. Blanchette, eds., *Cultural Issues in End-
of Life Decision Making* (Thousand Oaks, Calif.: Sage, 2000); S. B. Dowd, V. L.
Poole, R. Davidhizar, and J. N. Giger, Death, Dying, and Grief in a Transcultural
Context: Application of the Giger and Davidhizar Assessment Model, *Hospice
Journal* 13 (1998): 33–47; R. M. Huff and M. V. Kline, *Promoting Health in Multi-
cultural Populations: A Handbook for Practitioners* (Thousand Oaks, Calif.: Sage,
1999); D. P. Irish, K. F. Lundquist, and V. J. Nelsen, eds., *Ethnic Variations in Dying,
Death, and Grief: Diversity in Universality* (Washington, D.C.: Taylor & Francis,
1993); D. Klass and R. E. Goss, Asian Ways of Grief, in *Living with Grief: Who We
Are and How We Grieve*, edited by K. J. Doka and J. D. Davidson (Philadelphia:
Brunner/Mazel, 1998), 13–26; R. M. Nakamura, *Health in America: A Multicultural
Perspective* (Boston: Allyn & Bacon, 1999); E. G. Pask, Culture: Caring and
Curing in the Changing Health Scene, in *Meeting the Needs of Our Clients Creatively:
The Impact of Art and Culture on Caregiving*, edited by J. D. Morgan (Amityville,
N.Y.: Baywood, 2000), 67–76.

meaning systems. In addition, in their various explanations of "the story," helping
professionals often hear hints of anger, regret, guilt, blame, and responsibility
for the death (which might suggest more complicated grief reactions) and
detect differences among family members in their exposure to the death. Each
version of the story can provide additional details that other family members
did not know or misunderstood, thereby enhancing the empathy and awareness

of all (Sedney, Baker, and Gross 1994). Given that all losses have their own unique story, "telling the story" of one's loss is an assessment tool not limited to death. In fact, storytelling is an important cultural resource (Cross 2003; Shapiro 1998), and women often process their various losses by telling their stories to others (Gibson and Myers 2000).

General Techniques and Interventions
Grief Counseling and Therapy

Grief counseling and grief therapy are not always distinguished clearly. *Grief counseling* refers to "the facilitation through counseling of the process (tasks) of . . . uncomplicated grieving to alleviate suffering and help bereaved individuals to adjust well" (Stroebe et al. 2001:10). It generally involves one-to-one, family, or group interventions designed to encourage the expression of feelings and to support those seeking help for their bereavement-related distress. *Grief therapy* refers to processes used by highly trained professionals involving "specialized techniques of intervention" to address more traumatic, complicated, or chronic grief (Stroebe et al. 2001:10; Worden 2002). Because the vast majority of social workers are more likely to offer grief counseling rather than grief therapy to individuals and families confronting the many and varied losses described in this text, this book concentrates on grief counseling.

Reviews of the published bereavement outcome research reveal conceptual and methodological limitations that constrain our understanding of the effectiveness of grief counseling and therapy and, in fact, often do not distinguish between the two (Allumbaugh and Hoyt 1999; Neimeyer 2000). Interventions may work better for adults who seek help on their own, as opposed to being recruited into intervention studies (Allumbaugh and Hoyt 1999), and may be more effective for people who are younger and who have more complicated or traumatic grief reactions (Neimeyer 2000). Most of the evaluative studies used generic measures of health, depression, and anxiety (rather than measuring the grief), and the effects by type of intervention were not distinguished (Allumbaugh and Hoyt 1999; Neimeyer 2000). Box 11.2 highlights recommendations for grief counselors that stem from an analysis of several empirical reviews of the literature on grief counseling.

Although their goals may vary, many counseling theories focus on reestablishing hope in the bereaved and helping them search for meaning (Cutcliffe 1998; Nadeau 2001a; Neimeyer 2000). As noted throughout this text, many different forms of loss, particularly those that are sudden and elicit a traumatic response, precipitate a search for meaning. Neimeyer (2000) recommends that counselors

Box 11.2 Recommendations for Grief Counselors Given Current Empirical Evidence

- Do not assume that grief counseling benefits all; adopt a critical attitude toward methods.
- Customize interventions to the individual mourner's particular gender, personality, background, resources, and expressed needs.
- Tailor the intervention's content and process to the individual's or target group's expressed need and problems.
- Make careful assessments to make more informed judgments about the most appropriate intervention methods.
- Give thought to the appropriate timing of interventions, recognizing that most persons integrate their loss without intervention.
- In early contacts with newly bereaved adults, offer general support, establish relationships, and provide psychological education, but do not push mourners into clinical treatment.
- Concentrate on identifying and engaging high-risk mourners.
- Recognize that counseling provided later in the bereavement trajectory may be more beneficial.
- Avoid arbitrary cutoffs (e.g., one year) for programmatic bereavement care services, and consider less frequent but longer-term contacts with bereavement caregivers.

Source: J. R. Jordan and R. A. Neimeyer, Does Grief Counseling Work? *Death Studies* 27 (2003): 765–86.

working with clients who are looking for significance in the loss should facilitate this process, but he cautions that it should not be instigated unless it is undertaken spontaneously by the bereaved. Persons adjust better who use cognitive behavioral strategies, such as attributing a personal meaning to loss, promoting good health, and looking for the predominant themes of distress resulting from their loss (Powers and Wampold 1994).

Deriving meaning from the loss is central to many bereaved persons and is often the focus of grief counseling and therapy (Neimeyer 1998b, 2001a). Three types of questions and examples that counselors may use to facilitate meaning reconstruction are the following:

1. *Entry-level* questions to explore the "experiential world of the client's grieving."
   a. What experiences of death or loss would you like to explore?
   b. What do you remember about how you responded to the event at the time?
   c. How did your feelings about it change over time?
   d. How did others in your life respond to the loss and your reactions to it?
   e. What was the most painful part of the experience to you?
2. *Explanation-level* questions "to extend these preliminary questions into greater concern with meaning."
   a. How did you make sense of the death or loss at the time?
   b. How do you interpret the loss now?
   c. What philosophical or spiritual beliefs contributed to your adjustment to this loss? How were they affected by it?
3. *Elaboration-level* questions "to promote broader perspective taking regarding the loss."
   a. How has this experience affected your sense of priorities?
   b. How has this experience affected your view of yourself or your world?
   c. What lessons about loving has this person or this loss taught you?
   d. How would your life be different if this person had lived or this loss had not occurred?
   e. Are there any steps that you could take that would be helpful or healing now? (Neimeyer 1998b:166–69)

A variety of grief-counseling models have emerged, but few have been validated empirically. A widely adopted task-based model of grief counseling, described in chapter 2 (Worden 2002), is based on the following ten guiding principles. Not all persons will benefit from this model, however, because it was derived from the grief work hypothesis and encourages bereaved persons to confront their loss and express their feelings. An assessment of the individual and family, including exploration of their needs, goals, and intervention preferences, is necessary to determine the usefulness of this task-based model.

1. *Help the bereaved person actualize the loss.* To help him or her have "a more complete awareness of the loss" (Worden 2002:56), practitioners may invite the bereaved person to "tell the story" of the loss as described earlier or engage in activities such as visiting the grave site. A sense of unreality of the loss may create difficulty for the bereaved and be more important in certain situations (e.g., when a person is reported missing in action, when the body of someone

killed is too mutilated to view during a memorial service, or when the body has not been found). Finding tangible evidence to review with the bereaved (e.g., photographs kept by hospitals of stillborn babies previously not viewed by the client) may be an important initial task in counseling.

2. *Help the bereaved to express his or her feelings.* Anger, guilt, anxiety, helplessness, and sadness are unrecognized or unexpressed feelings commonly associated with grief. The discomfort with these feelings often prompts a referral for counseling. Empathic listening, guided questioning, normalization of feelings, and the use of various counseling techniques may help clients identify and express these feelings.

3. *Help the bereaved person live without the deceased.* The bereaved person may need assistance with making decisions, solving problems, and adopting new roles related to living without the deceased. Older widows may need to learn new tasks that were previously performed by their partner. Because exercising good judgment during acute grief is often difficult and change may be accompanied by additional loss, bereaved persons are often advised to refrain from making major life-changing decisions (e.g., moving, selling property, changing careers, adopting children). Many well-meaning adult children may advise their middle-aged parent to move closer to them following a partner's death, but this may create additional losses of friends and lifestyle and only complicate his or her grief.

4. *Help find meaning in the loss.* Finding meaning in the loss is often an important task for the bereaved person. Meaning may be found in his or her belief systems, religious or spiritual convictions, lessons learned, or activities precipitated by the loss (e.g., preventing further tragedies through public education or fundraising for related causes).

5. *Help with the emotional relocation of the deceased.* Bereaved clients need to "find a new place in their life for the lost loved one, a place that will allow the survivor to move forward with life and form new relationships" (Worden 2002:64). By internalizing the relationship with the deceased, they may continue to feel connected with the deceased while also developing meaningful ties to the living.

6. *Provide time to grieve.* Grief takes time, indeed may never end, and may be triggered by critical marker events (e.g., anniversaries, holidays). It is important to help clients understand the often recurring nature of grief, to encourage patience with it, and to allow for expressions of grief as they arise.

7. *Interpret "normal" behavior.* The emotional, physical, cognitive, behavioral, or spiritual manifestations of grief may feel overwhelming to bereaved persons,

who feel that something is seriously wrong with them. Providing information about these common responses can help normalize their grief.

8. *Allow for individual differences.* The variability in how individuals grieve may cause confusion or discomfort among family members who have different grief experiences and needs. Counselors must respect the many and varied ways that grief is experienced and expressed and help family members and other professionals understand, accept, and appreciate these differences.

9. *Examine defenses and coping styles.* Certain forms of responding to loss, such as the excessive use of alcohol or drugs, may "intensify the experience of grief and depression and impair the bereavement process" (Worden 2002:67). Exploring with clients what they have found most difficult, how they have responded to their loss, and what has been most and least helpful enable them to identify strategies that they may wish to modify. For example, when I (Betty J. Kramer) asked one woman how she coped with her grief associated with her husband's illness, she replied, "Oh that's easy, whenever I give him his haldol, I take one too." I was then able to explore with her the extent to which this was helping her, the potential long-term consequences of taking his medication, and a variety of other adaptive coping strategies that might be more helpful.

10. *Recognize difficult problems that require special intervention.* Health and human service providers are ethically obligated to refer persons who have needs that exceed their skills. Referring bereaved individuals to a qualified grief therapist or medical professional may be necessary in a variety of situations. For example, persons who have developed phobias, self-destructive impulses, clinical depression, or physical symptoms that parallel the symptoms of the deceased may need to be referred for therapy.

Grief-Counseling Techniques

Box 11.3 summarizes a variety of widely adopted techniques for grief counseling. Because not all these interventions have been evaluated extensively, we encourage practitioners to test them further and document their efficacy. Many of these counseling techniques are for alleviating a sense of regret and addressing "unfinished business," such as the empty chair technique, guided imagery, role-playing, and letter writing. The use of journals, metaphors, and homework exercises are discussed next.

Journals are used to process and record thoughts and feelings and how they change over time (Ashton and Ashton 2000; Corless 2001). Many personal narratives and descriptions of how writing helped integrate one's grief and loss are

Box 11.3 Examples of Counseling Intervention Techniques

- *Writing:* Have the bereaved write a letter or a series of letters to the deceased (or loss object) expressing their thoughts and feelings. This may provide an opportunity to take care of "unfinished business" by experiencing things they have not had the opportunity to do so previously.
- *Empty chair with or without a picture:* Have the bereaved imagine that the deceased is sitting across from them in an empty chair. Encourage them to express their feelings. A picture of the deceased may be placed on the chair.
- *Cognitive restructuring:* Help the bereaved identify their thoughts and talk and reality-test them for overgeneralization or accuracy.
- *Role-playing:* Role-play with the bereaved various situations that will allow them to build their skills, address fears, lessen uncertainty in future situations they are preparing for, or express feelings to the deceased or others.
- *Guided imagery:* Help the bereaved imagine the deceased or recreate situations in their mind's eye that they may imagine experiencing or responding to.
- *Journal writing:* Have the bereaved write a letter, keep a journal, or write poetry to express their thoughts or feelings.
- *Drawing:* Although more commonly used with children, facilitated expression through drawing with adults may be helpful to reflect their feelings and promote discussion.
- *Role change analysis:* Help the bereaved identify role changes and help them develop the skills needed to address secondary losses (e.g., learning how to balance a checkbook, cook).
- *Listening:* Help the bereaved tell the story of their loss by listening receptively.
- *Memory book:* Encourage individuals or families to create memory books that include stories about family events, photos, poems, drawings, or other memorabilia. This activity facilitates reminiscence and provides a concrete keepsake.

- *Use of symbols:* Have the bereaved bring items to share that hold symbolic meaning (e.g., photos, letters, audio or video tapes, jewelry).
- *Metaphors:* Encourage clients to share their own metaphors of their loss or suggest ones that seem appropriate to their experience of loss.
- *Meaning reconstruction interview:* Ask questions to the bereaved to elicit an understanding of the loss and the meanings and interpretations of the loss from the client's perspective.

Sources: I. B. Corless, Bereavement, in *Textbook of Palliative Nursing,* edited by B. R. Ferreu and D. Coyle (New York: Oxford University Press, 2001), 352–62; R. A. Neimeyer, *Lessons of Loss: A Guide to Coping* (New York: McGraw-Hill, 1998); J. W. Worden, *Grief Counseling and Grief Therapy: A Handbook for Mental Health Practitioners,* 3rd ed. (New York: Springer, 2002).

available (Henderson 2001). The evidence suggests that persons who write about their traumatic experiences have fewer doctor visits, fewer illnesses, less time off from work, and a more positive outlook (Sobel 1997). People who find it particularly difficult to discuss or disclose their painful memories with others may use journals to record and process their experiences. The extensive literature indicates that talking or writing about one's thoughts and feelings regarding traumatic events may improve psychological and physical health, which may be attributed to a person's ability to integrate such experiences coherently (for a review, see Pennebaker 1989). More recent empirical evidence contradicts such assertions, however. For example, an evaluation of writing revealing bereaved spouses' emotions found no difference between the control and the experimental group in bereavement distress or number of doctor visits (Pennebaker and Beall 1986; Stroebe et al. 2002). The researchers tested and found no differential effect for bereaved persons exposed to an unexpected loss who had previously shared their feelings or who had felt a need to reveal their emotions. The authors concluded that while writing and other forms of emotional expression may be helpful, there is not enough evidence to suggest that it will speed up the grief process for uncomplicated bereavement (Stroebe et al. 2002). Since writing is a commonly used self-help strategy and grief-counseling technique, evaluation studies are needed to explore further the use of journaling in various contexts and in response to different losses. Certain questions need to be answered. Who is most likely to benefit from keeping a journal or writing about loss? Do writing-based interventions make a difference for persons with complicated bereavement? What kinds of loss are best suited to keeping a journal? What impact does a journal have on well-being and the grief process of different populations? How, in what context, and with what populations is keeping a journal likely to be most beneficial? What journal techniques are most effective?

Keeping a journal as a counseling technique can include daily journal entries, dream journals exploring dreams, and other forms of personal expression through writing. Bereavement therapists advise attention to the "goodness of fit," appropriate timing, privacy needs, and implementation of this or any other counseling technique that may evoke an intense emotional response (Neimeyer 1998b:148). General guidelines for bereaved adults interested in keeping a daily journal are the following:

1. Focus on the most significant or upsetting losses, as these are likely to yield the greatest benefit.
2. Write what you have discussed least adequately with others to allow opportunity for expression.
3. Record your deepest thoughts and feelings, with attention to explicit accounts of the event and your reactions, to allow a more balanced approach to the processing of the loss experienced.
4. Abandon any concern about neatness, grammar, spelling, penmanship, and accuracy.
5. Schedule a transitional activity following the writing before jumping back into other life responsibilities. This allows a "buffer period" should you need time to process emotions that surface. (Neimeyer 1998b:145–46)

Metaphors are images or symbolic representations of experiences or constructs that hold meaning for individuals, families, or communities (Schwartz-Borden 1992). Metaphors and metaphoric stories of loss provide and express symbolically and culturally relevant meaning, beyond concrete descriptions (Cross 2003). They are especially helpful when "literal words fail us in conveying our unique sense of loss" (Neimeyer 1998b:172). As a counseling technique, human service professionals may suggest metaphors to help clients understand variation in the grief experience and process and normalize their experience. Common metaphors used to represent grief are

• The *onion* with its many layers that as they are peeled away reveal a core of growth within.
• *Waves* that ebb and flow, whose power comes and goes, that may be difficult to ride, may sometimes knock us over, but may be ridden to shore.

- *Walls* or *hurdles* that are sometimes thin, sometimes thick, and may change their diameter and distancing over time and may need to be scaled or jumped to get to the other side.
- *Canal locks* that fill to the brim with emotion, requiring that gates must be opened to release feelings to facilitate movement and equilibrium, coming to yet another lock where the process may be repeated.
- The *wound* that initially is open, raw, and painful; it requires cleansing and care to protect it from further damage yet may nevertheless leave a permanent scar and may take longer than a physical wound to heal.
- The *roller coaster* with its twists and turns and ups and downs that make it difficult to see what's ahead, leaving one with a sense of danger; however once on the ride, it is more dangerous to jump off than to ride it out. (Cairns, Thompson, and Wainwright 2000:334)

Health and human service providers may also help adults express their sense of loss metaphorically by asking them to describe their grief as an image or object (Neimeyer 1998b). Bereaved parents have described feeling that a part of themselves is missing, as exemplified by a father who stated, "It is like I lost my right arm, but I am learning to live as a one-armed man" (Klass and Marwit 1988/1989:41). Metaphors may provide a way of exploring the many meanings and implications of that experience. For example, we could ask this father how living with one arm differs from living with two arms, and what it means symbolically. Neimeyer (1998b) suggested asking about changes and movement in the client's metaphor and offered an example of a woman who described her grief as a constriction around her throat and chest, experienced as an invisible boa constrictor that was suffocating her. She was encouraged to practice deep breathing and to focus on loosening the grip around her, which she found helpful. Metaphoric images may be elicited in individual or group work and may evolve into stories to document changes in the loss experience over time.

Homework exercises between counseling sessions are therapeutic tasks for grieving adults to work on between and before planned counseling encounters; to practice processing, problem analysis, self-management, and contemplative skills; and to give them a historical documentation of their thoughts and feelings (Rich 2001). Some traditional and contemporary counseling approaches have bereaved adults work on carefully designed and agreed-upon outside activities that are intended to lead to attitudinal, behavioral, or emotional changes (Corey 2005). These activities must be relevant to the individual's or family's needs, goals, strengths, and preferences. Human service professionals can use several of the available grief-counseling homework manuals to find the appropriate activities (e.g., Mannino 1997; Mayo 2001; Rich 2001). For example, one of these manuals is a practice planner with ready-to-copy homework assignments to help grieving adults better understand the grief process and their personal grief response, express their feelings, identify and track their behaviors, explore meaning making, reminisce, address unfinished business, make decisions, solve problems, and recognize supports (Rich 2001).

Homework assignments should be introduced in ways that the client does not feel are demeaning. For example, some persons may resent being given "homework." Human service professionals' rationale for assigning homework should be consistent with the bereaved adult's goals, objectives, and preferences. Guidelines for between-session "homework" are

1. Assign work in collaboration with the grieving adults, building on their ideas, preferences, and needs.
2. Respect their "resistance" to homework suggestions or the challenges in carrying them out. Assume that there is a good reason for their hesitation and try to understand their reaction.
3. Respect their privacy by allowing them to edit their work and select what they would like to focus on.
4. Bring the homework into the session by asking how the assignment went and have the clients discuss it.
5. Recognize the value of "being" as well as "doing," so you do not preoccupy the bereaved adults with "busy work." (Neimeyer 1998b:129–32)

Cultural Considerations

Current theories of grief have begun to acknowledge the importance of culture-specific meanings (Klass 2001a) and have increasingly recognized the cultural variations in response to bereavement (Al-Adawi and Burjorjee 1997; Oltjenbruns 1998). Nonetheless, culturally specific interventions are essentially absent from the grief and loss literature. As with any form of social work intervention, grief counseling should be guided by the needs, goals, strengths and capacities of the person seeking professional assistance. Health and human service professionals need knowledge of the variation in grief rituals and norms and should be aware of how professional helpers are viewed in that culture (Ellis 1998). A strengths perspective, combined with brief treatment, is one model that addresses the therapeutic needs of culturally diverse clients and is congruent with the resilience model (Chazin, Kaplan, and Terio 2000). By being aware of and respecting the client's positive attributes, aspirations, and resources, the strengths perspective may produce trust, enhance the client's motivation, and be empowering (Saleebey 1992). Brief treatment counseling has the following attributes:

1. Recognition that time is limited and should be used efficiently.
2. Make the bereaved adult's presenting problems the focus of attention.
3. Acknowledge that change often occurs outside counseling and after its termination.
4. Concentrate on the adult's everyday activities and functioning.
5. Help grieving persons identify and use their inherent strengths and resources. (Chazin, Kaplan, and Terio 2000)

Case examples of how these integrated approaches have been used successfully with culturally diverse populations are described by Chazin, Kaplan, and Terio (2000), but these and other interventions need to be empirically tested.

In general, traditional counseling approaches and mental health services have been criticized for emphasizing the dominant American cultural values of individualism, rational and scientific thinking, self-sufficiency, personal responsibility, and the possession of an internal locus of control, which may be incongruent with the experiences and values of many persons of color (Chin 1994; Comas-Diaz and Greene 1994; Constantine, Greer, and Kindaichi 2003; Corey 2001). Approaches that rely largely on individual treatment and verbal exchanges of thoughts and feelings may be ineffectual, intrusive, and/or incongruent with the cultural worldviews of some Asian American, African American, Native American, Latinos, or the many other ethnic minority groups living in the United States (Constantine, Greer, and Kindaichi 2003).

Culturally competent interventions consider the following cultural values, worldviews, and constructs (Constantine, Greer, and Kindaichi 2003):

1. Collectivism refers to value orientations in which persons subjugate their personal goals for the sake of others, recognizing that they are inextricably tied to those around them (Markus and Kitayama 1991).
2. A family and community-interdependent values orientation refers to the importance of kinship ties, family, friends, and community as sources of personal empowerment and concern for others that are found among many in culturally diverse communities (Garrett and Wilbur 1999; Gloria and Rodriguez 2000; Solberg et al. 1994; Utsey, Adams, and Bolden 2000).
3. Acculturation considerations influence the extent to which persons feel (a) comfortable seeking mental health assistance for their distress, (b) culturally mistrust or view professional intervention as stigmatizing, and (c) face language and other barriers to accessing services (Constantine, Chen, and Ceesay 1997; Mori 2000).
4. Spirituality and/or religion are important cultural resources that provide support, determine belief and meaning systems, and help heal the emotional,

physical, and mental health concerns of members of the African American, Latino, Asian American, and Native American communities (Constantine et al. 2000; Garrett and Wilbur 1999; Koss-Chioino 1995; McRae, Thompson, and Cooper 1999; Tan and Dong 2000).

These cultural values, worldviews, and constructs for intervention

1. Place less emphasis on modifying the individual's grief response and therapeutic goals.
2. Attend to the collective goals of the social network or community.
3. Emphasize relational tendencies and strategies.
4. Attend to acculturation status and acculturative stress.
5. Integrate spiritual and religious beliefs and support systems (e.g., working closely with spiritual leaders to develop interventions, or using religious settings as sites of intervention).

An example of a culturally congruent grief intervention that attended to the collective needs of a community is carving a totem pole and then raising it in a ceremony, which residents of Craig, Alaska, did to help the community deal with their suffering associated with multiple social problems (Frankenstein and Brady 1997). This event was initiated by a father after the accidental drug overdose of his young adult son, with social service and other organizational participants helping plan it. Participants described the ways in which this event alleviated their grief at both the individual and community level. Further development and evaluation of innovative and culturally competent interventions are needed to address grief across all forms of loss.

Interventions Related to Specific Losses
Parents of Children with a Life-Threatening Illness

Communication skills are critical to helping parents of children with a life-threatening illness understand the choices facing them. Evidence suggests that these parents' anxiety may greatly limit their ability to integrate information (Eden et al. 1994). Repetition, clarification, written material, simple videos, and taped interviews may help. (For an extensive review of guidelines for end-of-life decision making to help parents and children, see Hinds, Oakes, and Furman 2001.) The decisions made about the care and treatment of their child and the way that families are treated by health care workers may have a great impact on their grieving.

Interventions for working with these families may address the following elements associated with anticipatory mourning:

1. Intellectual (e.g., stress reduction, keeping a journal/writing, reading and talk therapy, cognitive/behavioral interventions).
2. Emotional (e.g., emotional expression, interventions to address depressive symptoms).
3. Physical (e.g., exercise, healthy eating, sleep).
4. Spiritual (e.g., searching for meaning, exploring dreams and spiritual experiences, planning memorials).
5. Social (e.g., bolstering social supports). (Ashton and Ashton 2000)

Social workers should also recognize the financial burdens of families caring for a chronically ill or disabled child and be prepared to offer information about costs and resources, including how the child's death will reduce or eliminate current benefits (Corden, Sloper, and Sainsbury 2002). Because parents may grieve very differently during their child's illness and following the death, it is useful to normalize these responses and to help them communicate, resolve conflicts, make commitments, and cooperate when needed (Ashton and Ashton 2000; Knafl 1996). Preliminary evidence shows that a weekly support group for caregivers of children with HIV can be beneficial, by reducing depression, anxiety, and isolation and helping with anticipatory mourning. But the absence of a control group limits any definitive conclusions (Crandles et al. 1992).

Parents of a Child Who Dies Suddenly

Many parents in midlife are confronted with a child's sudden tragic death, since automobile and other accidents comprise the main cause of death for children, teens, and young adults (Hoyert et al. 2001; Kochanek, Smith, and Anderson 2001). Lack of preparedness for death is associated with complicated grief and major depressive disorder (Barry, Kasl, and Prigerson 2002). Interventions must therefore attend to the potential grief complications resulting from a sudden loss (i.e., that allows no psychological preparation for the death), the perceived prevention of the deaths (e.g., negligence caused by drunk driving), and the potential trauma caused by inappropriate death notification (e.g., an insensitive police officer telephoning the parents with the news) (Deranieri, Clements, and Henry 2002; Lord 1996; Rando 1993). A study of the experiences of parents grieving the traumatic and sudden death of their child revealed that their unanswered questions or misconceptions regarding brain death, organ donation, and their child's medical care worsened their grief. This implies that information provided by hospital and trauma service personnel can alleviate the grieving process (Oliver et al. 2001). Many parents who have had a child die say they need to talk about it over and over as they process different aspects of their loss, to have their personal reactions accepted and believed, and to be with others who have had similar experiences (Lehman et al. 1999). Grassroots organizations like Mothers Against Drunk Driving and Compassionate Friends may offer mutual support and provide an outlet for action (Lord 1996).

In a review of controlled studies of interventions for bereaved parents, Rowa-Dewar (2002) concluded that only those parents with very great distress, who are at higher risk of more complicated grief, and who request help are likely to benefit from professional interventions. This parallels the findings of empirical reviews of other grief and bereavement interventions for adults. A few more recent studies have shown promising intervention results for bereaved mothers grieving the death of an adult child. Those mothers who received a minimum of six Trager therapeutic touch sessions over fourteen weeks with a therapist scored significantly lower on despair, depersonalization, and somatization than did mothers in the control group (Kempson 2000/2001). A ten-week broad-spectrum intervention with problem- and emotion-focused components was offered to bereaved parents four months after the death of their twelve- to twenty-eight-year-old children due to accidents, homicide, or suicide. Evaluations of this intervention revealed the best results for mothers who were most distressed at baseline, with no immediate benefits shown for fathers. This study found intense and prolonged trauma among the majority of parents, confirmed gender differences among bereaved parents, and suggested the need to develop and test alternative interventions for bereaved fathers (Kempson 2000/2001).

Couples who have lost a child through death have different experiences and meanings of the loss and grief responses, disagreements about the "right way" to grieve, and difficulties giving each other support and validation (Gilbert 1997). Interventions to help couples resolve such differences include enhancing their communication (e.g., exchanging information, expressing emotions, listening), reframing conceptual or emotional viewpoints, sharing the loss, directing efforts toward common goals or values, and encouraging flexibility (e.g. acceptance of differences, sensitivity to each other's needs, and role flexibility) (Gilbert 1997). Although treatment models to help partners integrate the death of a child have been proposed (e.g., Figley 1989; Lantz and Lantz 1991), intervention studies have not been conducted to test their efficacy.

Death of a Parent

Although the challenges, developmental tasks, and even the transformative experiences (Pope 2000) for middle-aged adults associated with a parent's death have been identified, research on interventions for such grief has been limited to children and adolescents (e.g., Lohnes and Kalter 1994; Moore and

Carr 2000; Sandler, Ayers, and Wolchik 2003; Sandler, West, and Baca 1992). Integrating the loss of a parent often means confronting the loss of the parent's power or authority, and the reality of one's own mortality (Douglas 1991). It also entails the tasks of

1. Stocktaking (e.g., reviewing the changes caused by the parent's death).
2. Reminiscing about either meaningful or harsh memories (e.g., helping review positive, negative, and ambivalent feelings about the deceased parent).
3. Internalizing (e.g., expressing the meaning of the parent's death, internalizing the parent's values, and meeting the challenge of personal growth). (Dane 1989:77–78)

Research on adult siblings suggests that sharing their reminiscences about the deceased parents may "enable a family to work toward a common reality about the death, to provide mutual support, to finish unfinished business, and together to wrestle with memories and hopes that are at the heart of grief" (Rosenblatt and Elde 1990:209). In another study, midlife adults bereaved by a parent's death found it helpful to talk with others who have had similar losses but felt that their natural support networks often constrained their emotional expression (Scharlach and Fuller-Thomson 1994). Although other interventions reviewed in this book may be used to help midlife adults confronting a parent's death, particularly those at risk for complicated grief, additional research into interventions for this specific loss is needed.

Most adults who experience a parent's death have the capacities to make this transition without professional assistance, but those who are at greater risk of an adverse outcome should be identified. They include adults who rely on their parents for support and even caregiving. For example, a growing number of persons with severe and persistent mental illness depend on their parents for care. A study of 148 persons with serious mental illness found that approximately 22 percent reported experiencing a significant loss, with 66 percent of this figure being the death of one or both parents (Jones et al. 2003). None of the persons in this sample who experienced severe and prolonged grief had received any preparation for a parent's death, which suggests that mental health service providers should find ways to prepare, both emotionally and financially, persons with severe mental illness for a parent's death and offer bereavement counseling. Empirical studies have not evaluated interventions for adults with mental illness bereaved by a parent's death. Pragmatic interventions would help families overcome psychological barriers (e.g., denial, worry, fear) and plan for continuing care management and residential alternatives after the caregiving parent has died (Jones et al. 2003).

Survivors of a Parent Who Commits Suicide

The suicide rate of older white males is higher in the United States than of any other English-speaking country (Pritchard and Baldwin 2002) and of any other age group (Conwell, Duberstein, and Caine 2002). This statistic translates into large numbers of bereaved adult children. Suicide often leaves them with unanswered questions, fantasies of predeath pain or suffering, and extreme changes in the family system, raising the risk for complicated grief reaction (Attig 2001a). Family members or friends who find the body after a suicide may be left with very disturbing images and a greater risk of traumatic grief. Treatments for traumatic grief have used, with promising results, strategies from interpersonal therapy for depression and cognitive behavioral therapy for posttraumatic stress disorder (Shear et al. 2001). Strategies used to reduce grief include imaginal exposure (e.g., reexperiencing the death scene), in vivo exposure (e.g., to previously avoided activities and situations), and interpersonal therapy. Adults who received both forms of treatment had substantially lower scores for complicated grief than did persons receiving interpersonal therapy alone. A randomized controlled trial is currently under way to further evaluate these interventions (Shear et al. 2001).

Adults bereaved by suicide often find it difficult to talk about their experiences and express their needs (Ness and Pfeffer 1990; Provini, Everett, and Pfeffer 2000). Those needs that they do mention cover a variety of psychosocial concerns, such as family relationships, paying bills, physical illness, and psychiatric and bereavement symptoms. A smaller percentage of adults wanted professional therapy and support for extended family members (Provini, Everett, and Pfeffer 2000). These findings point to a need for care management services for practical daily living and survival concerns for some families. Interventions described in the literature for middle-aged adults bereaved by suicide include counseling and therapy (Barlow and Morrison 2002; Dane 1991; Knieper 1999), which, as noted previously, tend to be more effective for persons with complicated grief (Neimeyer 2000), and support and therapeutic groups (Clark and Goldney 1995; Freeman 1991; Knieper 1999), which enhance social support and address the social stigma experienced by many survivors (Rudestam 1992). Knieper (1999) describes the person-centered, cognitive-behavioral therapies and eye movement desensitization and reprocessing (EMDR) treatments used with suicide survivors. Individual and group interventions commonly address stigma, shame, anger, guilt, blame, suicidal thoughts, and "unfinished business," which are common to the grief associated with suicide.

Divorce

Various factors predict well-being of adults and children in the aftermath of divorce:

1. Availability of financial support.
2. Adequacy of the custodial parent's parenting skills, nurturing, and warmth (assuming that the children are still dependent).
3. The noncustodial parent's engagement and emotional support.
4. Availability of social support from family, friends, and others.
5. Absence or containment of parents' conflict.
6. Minimization of additional external stressors. (Pedro-Carroll 2001; Sigelman 1999)

Interventions may be targeted to the losses, challenges, or tasks associated with distinct phases of the divorce (Schwartz and Kaslow 1997).

In the *predivorce phase*, the couple becomes aware of their discontent. This often heightens their anxiety and/or anticipatory grief as they consider a separation. The *during-divorce phase* frequently includes the challenging emotional and logistical tasks associated with legal, economic, and parent–child custody issues, spiritual and religious considerations, and the effects of their divorce on social relationships. The *postdivorce* phase, which begins when the legal process is complete, is a time of restabilization, new challenges, and opportunities. Individuals and family members experience differently the grief associated with these transitions and their attendant losses (Pedro-Carroll 2001).

Preventive interventions directed at adults often try to reduce stress through group support, to enhance competencies, to clarify misunderstandings, and to provide skills for conflict resolution and anger management. Individual and group interventions for adults address individual adjustment, communication skills, financial planning, parenting skills, social support, depression, self-esteem, legal issues, and career planning. Studies addressing depression and overall distress only have reported improvements (Grych and Fincham 1992; Lee, Picard, and Blain 1994). Although the grief and mourning common to divorce have long been recognized, gender differences in how they are manifested were acknowledged more recently (for a review, see Baum 2003). Given the pervasiveness of the loss associated with divorce, it is surprising that intervention studies have not measured grief as an outcome or found strategies to prevent or minimize grief. Questions to be explored are, Do clients want to reduce the grief-related distress associated with divorce? Is the grief associated with divorce amenable to intervention? What interventions for individuals and family members are most likely to integrate this loss, and how would these vary by culture, gender, and age?

Interventions for Family Caregivers
Caring for Older Parents

More and more middle-aged adults are having to care for older parents, and they cannot help but grieve for their parents' failing health, changes in personality associated with Alzheimer's disease and other types of dementia, and disruptions in their own daily life (Farran et al. 1991; Loos and Bowd 1997; Walker et al. 1994a). Helping midlife adults identify those aspects of the parent–child relationship lost to the aging of their parents and providing information about the progression and symptoms of illnesses are fundamental supportive interventions (Kogan and Vacha-Haase 2002). Chapter 13 reviews the limitations of the intervention studies of the caregivers' grief and offers recommendations for supporting family caregivers in mid- and later life.

Caring for Persons with Mental Illness

The family's response to mental illness is characterized by subjective experiences of grief, symbolic loss, chronic sorrow, empathic pain, and the objective burdens of illness symptoms, caregiving demands, stigma, family disruption, and often fragmented service delivery systems (Eakes 1995; Marsh 1999). Their responses are often complicated by disenfranchised grief, lack of community supports, and limited formal services for families (Dixon 1999; MacGregor 1994). Not all ethnic groups consistently report chronic sorrow, but parents who do experience it ask for practical forms of support, honest and timely information (e.g., about what they might expect), involvement in their child's treatment, practical tips for managing the illness, sources of support and respite, and empathic presence and support (Eakes 1995). A three step-intervention model to meet these needs is the following:

1. *Family consultation* to help families determine their particular needs, provide information about available services, and formulate an appropriate family service plan.
2. *Information, skills, and support* delivered through referral to family support and advocacy groups (e.g., National Alliance for the Mentally Ill, support groups), family education (e.g., about the illness, its treatment, caregiving and management issues, the mental health system, and community resources) and psychological education.

3. *Counseling and psychotherapy* that may be beneficial for family members "who desire the privacy and intimacy of a confidential therapeutic relationship or are having difficulty resolving issues of grief, loss, guilt and responsibility." (Marsh 1999:364)

Anecdotal evidence has shown that two innovative peer-taught programs, Building Recovery of Individual Dreams and Goals through Education and Support (BRIDGES), for consumers of mental health services, and the companion Journey of Hope, for family members, can validate the illness-related loss, reduce isolation, and enhance empowerment (Baxter and Diehl 1998). Multifamily group interventions are inexpensive and effective ways to help families with their grief, loss, and other adjustments, although their efficacy has not been documented (Phillips and Corcoran 2000). Ethnically diverse families often encounter significant obstacles (e.g., transportation costs, language barriers) that may hinder their participation in family support group models commonly advocated by mental health practitioners (Eakes 1995; Finley 1998). Finley (1998) offers strategies to consider for developing culturally competent family support group models. Finally, grief therapy has been proposed as a complementary intervention for the loss associated with mental illness (Miller 1996), but it has not been evaluated.

Caring for Persons with Chronic Life-Threatening Illnesses

The information and support needed by adults and their family members who are diagnosed with malignant forms of cancer or other life-threatening illnesses and the ways that social workers and other health care professionals can help them vary with the stage of their illness and/or treatment (Keitel, Kopala, and Potere 2003). Table 11.1 lists the tasks confronting persons in various stages of illness proposed by Doka (1993). It shows that when the diagnosis is made, the family may need information about treatment options, their pros and cons, and insurance benefits; emotional support; and/or individual/family counseling. Adults receiving treatment during the middle and chronic phases of illness are most often distressed by the treatment side effects. Professional helpers can use cognitive and behavioral interventions to help reduce stress, pain, nausea, and fatigue. New techniques such as progressive relaxation techniques, biofeedback, and hypnosis are being used to treat the stress and pain associated with chronic illness, but they have not been rigorously evaluated.

When people no longer respond to treatment, they face the many tasks associated with approaching death. Ideally, health care providers ensure that the person does not die in pain, address potential conflicts and anxieties about death, and help with difficult matters such as estate planning, including provisions for

TABLE 11.1

Doka's Tasks in Life-Threatening Illness

General	Acute	Chronic	Terminal Phase
Responding to the physical fact of the disease.	Understanding the disease.	Managing symptoms and side effects.	Dealing with symptoms, discomfort, pain, and incapacitation.
Taking steps to cope with the reality of the disease.	Maximizing health and lifestyle. Maximizing one's coping strengths and limiting weaknesses. Developing strategies to deal with the issues created by the disease.	Carrying out health regimens. Preventing and managing health crises. Managing stress and examining coping. Maximizing social support and minimizing isolation. Normalizing life in the face of the disease. Dealing with financial concerns.	Managing health procedures and institutional stress. Managing stress and examining coping. Dealing effectively with caregivers. Preparing for death and saying good-bye.
Preserving self-concept and relationships with others in the face of the disease.	Exploring the effect of the diagnosis on a sense of self and others.	Preserving self-concept. Redefining relationships with others throughout the course of the disease.	Preserving self-concept. Preserving appropriate relationships with family and friends.
Dealing with affective and existential/spiritual issues created or reactivated by the disease.	Ventilating feelings and fears. Incorporating the present reality of the diagnosis into sense of past and future.	Ventilating feelings and fears. Finding meaning in suffering, chronicity, and uncertainty.	Ventilating feelings and fears. Finding meaning in life and death.

Source: K. J. Doka, *Living with Life-Threatening Illness* (Lexington, Mass.: Lexington Books, 1993).

child care if relevant, life support, extended and hospice care, and funeral arrangements (Keitel, Kopala, and Potere 2003). Unfortunately, most health care professionals are not trained in the comfort measures needed for quality end-of-life care and focus more on offering aggressive treatment than on minimizing the pain associated with dying (Field and Cassel 1997). Although family members may grieve at any phase of the disease, the grief is often acute at the time of diagnosis and anticipatory near the time of death.

The dying process associated with many chronic illnesses may be long and painful for the individual and his or her relatives and complicated by the financial impact on families (Leming and Dickinson 2002). Family members of hospitalized persons with a terminal illness have asked for greater continuity in social workers' involvement throughout hospital stays, guidance in how to talk to doctors, and social workers' presence when doctors break bad news (Lord and Pockett 1998). Seriously ill persons indicate that it is important at the end of life to be mentally aware, plan for funeral arrangements, not be a burden, help others, and come to peace with God or a supreme being (Steinhauser et al. 2000).

One model of family grief therapy targets families at risk of complicated grief and tries to help the family adjust during palliative care and bereavement by enhancing family functioning (e.g., cohesiveness, conflict resolution and expression of thoughts and feelings), sharing grief, recognizing patterns of relating, and building capacity to explore problems (Kissane et al. 1998). This family therapy has five sequential phases: assessment, identification of relevant issues emerging from the initial phase, focused treatment, consolidation, and ending. The focused treatment affirms progress, solves problems, clarifies and recognizes family patterns, and explores strong emotions (e.g., anger). Common themes covered in therapy are saying good-bye, addressing disappointment or other past issues, managing care, achieving intimacy, practicing cultural and religious traditions, taking care of younger children's needs, defining a good death, and treating grief and suffering. Efficacy studies testing this model are under way (Kissane et al. 1998).

Predeath rituals and ceremonies have the advantage of including the dying person and significant others and may help families facing death (Zulli and Weeks 1997). Examples of useful predeath rituals are keeping a journal (e.g., for the ill persons to express themselves and to provide a record for their survivors), meditating (e.g., to help persons develop mindfulness and inner peace), taking photographs and videos and reviewing them (allows for memory work and life review), taking an inventory of possessions (provides an opportunity to give them away before death), traveling to do or see something important before death), and taking sacraments of communion, anointing, or baptism, which may provide comfort or peace for the person and/or his or her family members (Zulli and Weeks 1997). Research is needed to document how well such rituals help dying persons and their family members integrate their grief.

SPIRITUAL ASSESSMENT AND INTERVENTION

The diagnosis of a serious illness is often accompanied by a sense of shock, may threaten assumptions about life, weaken a person's sense of control, and cause him or her to ask "why?" (Glass, Cluxton, and Rancour 2001). Related spiritual needs include meaning, hope, relatedness, forgiveness, and transcendence (Kemp 2001). It is beyond the scope of this chapter to review the wide variety of spiritual assessment tools and models that may be used in practice (for a more detailed review of tools available, see Taylor 2001). Box 11.4 provides guidelines for exploring spiritual needs suggested by Glass, Cluxton, and Rancour (2001) that may be used through the active dying phase.

The goals of spiritual care during the active dying phase are the following: (1) help finish unfinished business between the dying person and significant others (e.g., expressions of love, regret, forgiveness, and gratitude); (2) promote integrity of the dying person by honoring his or her life (e.g., encourage reminiscences at his or her bedside, recalling the "gifts" bestowed on the family and his or her legacy of values and qualities passed on to survivors); (3) help the family and dying person make meaning from the dying experience; (4) provide comfort by being present and listening; and (5) offer information about bereavement support groups and/or counseling if indicated (Glass, Cluxton, and Rancour 2001:49). Illustrations of how social workers address goals and needs of persons and families more broadly in end-of-life care practice can be found in Dane (2004) and Jacobs (2004). For more discussion of spirituality-related assessment and intervention, see also chapter 13.

Summary

This chapter presented developmental considerations for helping professionals working with adults in midlife, assessment strategies, grief counseling and therapy for bereaved adults, and cultural considerations. The evidence is fairly strong that interventions are more likely to be effective for adults with complicated or traumatic bereavement, and many of the losses reviewed in this chapter are those that place adults at high risk of such complications. Studies of most of the losses in midlife that we reviewed and for which grief is well documented are just beginning to test systematically the proposed intervention models.

Box 11.4 Spiritual Assessment

- Ask about the importance of religious or spiritual traditions and practices.
- Determine the individual's and family's level of hopefulness about the future: "How do you see the future at this time?" "What are you hoping for?" During active phases of dying, reassure the individual and family that they can be hopeful and still acknowledge that death is imminent, moving toward a transcendent hope.
- Explore prior losses and how the individual and family have dealt with crises of faith or meaning: "What helped you get through that?"
- Determine their desire and comfort level in talking about spiritual matters: "Some people need or want to talk about these things, others don't. How is it for you?"
- Assess their desire to speak with a spiritual support person and ask about such persons available to the family (e.g., rabbi, pastor, spiritual adviser, shaman).
- Explore spiritual self-care practices: "How are you taking care of you at this time?" "Are your prayers bringing you comfort and peace?" Offer assistance as needed in developing self-care practices (e.g., meditation, relaxation, prayer).
- Determine primary concerns or fears, "What is concerning you the most at this time?" "What are your worries?"
- Ask about dreams, visions, or unusual experiences (e.g., seeing persons who have died) and their meaning. Normalize these if they are disclosed.
- Determine need, desire, and willingness for family members to engage in forgiveness, to express feelings to one another, and to say their good-byes.
- Explore the need and desire for additional comfort measures in the environment (e.g., soothing music, devotional readings, gazing out a window at nature, or increased quiet).
- Inquire about anticipated needs and preferences at the time of death.

Source: E. Glass, D. Cluxton, and P. Rancour, Principles of Patient and Family Assessment, in *Textbook of Palliative Nursing*, edited by B. F. Ferrell and N. Coyle (New York: Oxford University Press, 2001), 46–49.

Overall, there is a tremendous gap between research and practice related to bereavement interventions. The *Report on Bereavement and Grief Research* concluded that "there are significant disconnects between the information generated by researchers and the information that is being used to guide the provision of services to the bereaved" (Center of the Advancement for Health 2003:72), as evidenced by the limited empirical support for grief intervention for those with uncomplicated bereavement and the potential harm caused by these programs. The current design of interventions may need to be modified to better address the needs of the bereaved and to target those most likely to benefit from them (Ayers and Sandler 2003; Jordan and Neimeyer 2003; Neimeyer 2000; Schut et al. 2001). Finally, interventions for culturally diverse populations have not been developed or tested adequately.

12

Grief and Loss in Old Age

THE FOLLOWING losses in old age appear to do the greatest harm to physical and emotional well-being:

- Death of a partner, sibling, or friend and the cumulative impact of such losses over one's lifetime.
- Being the primary caregiver for grandchildren when their adult parents are unable or unwilling to care for them.
- Caring for a partner or other relative with a chronic illness, particularly dementia.
- Living with a chronic illness or disability.
- Mistreatment.

Normal age-associated changes and developmental issues do not necessarily hinder an older person's ability to function daily but may exacerbate losses entailed by the death of a loved one or by caring for a partner with a chronic illness or disability. Past losses, such as the death of a child when one was a young adult or a middle-aged parent, may surface again in old age.

Developmental Considerations

Old age—the phase of life when one is most apt to die—is typically characterized as a time of loss and detachment, with the focus of some early social gerontological theories solely on loss and disengagement from past roles (Achenbaum and Bengtson 1994; Cumming and Henry 1961). Fortunately, older adults now have more opportunities to be productive and to contribute to society and personal growth, through volunteering, second careers, part-time employment, and lifelong learning. When discussing the developmental considerations of old age, it also is important to take account of the tremendous diversity of the older population, particularly the differences between the young old (age sixty-five to seventy-four), who usually are in good health, and the oldest old (over age eighty-five) who have the highest rate of chronic illness, frailty, poverty, and isolation. How an older adult manages losses and developmental challenges is also affected by culture, ethnic minority status, sexual orientation, and gender.

Some older adults may feel overwhelmed by bereavement and cumulative negative effects from the many losses associated with growing old (Kastenbaum 1969; Norris and Murrell 1990), such as the following:

- Sensory changes (e.g., declines in vision or hearing, joint degeneration).
- Physiological changes (e.g., less energy).
- Changes in health (e.g., loss of mobility and/or independence owing to chronic health conditions or physical disability).
- Death of others (e.g., partner, siblings, friends, children).
- Social or community supports and roles (e.g., loss of the "productive" roles of employment and civic leadership, income, home, ability to drive, social status, and self-esteem, often created by negative societal attitudes).

All these losses may make late-life grief worse, even for older people who are not struggling with a chronic illness or caring for others. For example, the death of a partner or friends may make a person aware of his or her other losses during life. Older adults often face the deaths of partners and friends, of an adult child or the symbolic death of adult children who are unable to be adequate parents, thereby making them the primary caregivers of their grandchildren. In addition, many older people have to deal with cumulative effect of losses created by lifelong inequities of race, social class, sexual orientation, or gender. With the increase in life expectancy comes the growing number of the oldest old (age eighty-five and over), who have likely experienced a lifetime of bereavement, especially for the death of a partner, and who often have limited physical, emotional, and social/community capacities to help them.

Many older adults regard bereavement as a normative process of adaptation to loss. Bereaved older adults describe the continuity of self and shifts in self, continuity and change in the family, and the maintenance and weakening of ties with the deceased. Many older adults have an inner strength (e.g., personal capacities) to adapt to their grief and to reframe their loss (Moss, Moss, and Hansson 2001). Other older people may be at risk of negative secondary consequences from their loss, such as social isolation, especially if they have few ways to express their sadness and their social support system has been weakened. Unfortunately, family members and social and health care providers may assume that loss in old age is "not a big deal" and thus may devalue older mourners and their feelings. For example, after an adult child dies, the younger family members (e.g., the partner, children, or grandchildren of the deceased) are usually viewed as the primary grievers, with the older person's parental grief considered secondary.

The losses associated with normal age-related changes are intensified by ageism or Western societies' tendency to stereotype and minimize the value of older adults. Aging-related losses sometimes have the secondary consequence of limiting a person's choices and options, although active healthy elders are generally able to adjust or moderate their physical activities. Even with less stamina or agility, elders can still enjoy skiing, swimming, hiking, and running; they may just move more slowly or not go as far. As with every phase of the life cycle, aging adults can grow, change, and find meaning and satisfaction in their lives, although the opportunities to do so are often constrained by poverty or ethnic minority status (Goldman and Miller 1995).

According to Erikson, the primary developmental challenge of old age is the achievement of ego integrity versus despair or disgust (Erikson 1963, 1982). This task has also been conceptualized as self-actualization (Maslow 1968) and reconciliation (Birren 1964). All these concepts refer to the developmental work of attaining an inner sense of wholeness. Resolving earlier developmental tasks and coming to terms with one's past help older adults achieve balance and harmony in this wholeness, from a process of introspection, self-reflection, and reminiscence or "life review" (Butler 1963). In this process, they review, evaluate, and perhaps reinterpret past experiences in order to resolve earlier conflicts and to achieve a new sense of meaning, both as an accounting to oneself of one's past life and as a preparation for death (Erikson and Erikson 1981). If older adults cannot do this, despair may be the result. This translates into dissatisfaction with one's life and with insufficient time or energy to change direction or compensate for the ways in which one has lived (Corr, Nabe, and Corr 2003).

The culture, class, and gender biases implicit in Erikson's developmental stages, identified in our discussion of earlier phases of the life span, also apply to older adulthood. Some cultures that accord wisdom and respect to elders (e.g., Native American, Asian American) may be more conducive to achieving ego integrity than the mainstream Western cultures are. In addition, Erikson formulated his tasks for the last stage of life when life expectancy was shorter and older adults made up only a small proportion of the population. Now, however, older adults, faced with the developmental task of achieving ego integrity, often have twenty to thirty years after their retirement to do so.

Resilience

Older adults who have multiple and successive losses during their life may nevertheless display considerable resilience, especially if their community, family, and cultural capacities are strong. In fact the oldest old, especially among ethnic minorities, are often characterized as "hardy survivors."

Personal Capacities

Older adults bring strong personal capacities to confronting loss; for example, most have already learned how to moderate their emotions effectively, such as reappraising negative events to find something positive in them and lowering their goals and standards as a way to handle adversity (Cartensen, Gross, and Fung 1997; Lawton, Windley, and Byerts 1982). Such dampening of emotional responsiveness may also reflect their reconciliation to loss. Older people may be better at finding meaning in their losses and confiding in others (e.g., through reminiscence) than younger adults are (Moss, Moss, and Hansson 2001). Older adults' experiences with loss are undoubtedly influenced by their own proximity to death, their greater spirituality and/or religiosity, and their capacity to find meaning in life (Ramsey and Blieszner 2000). If an adult has achieved peace and comfort with the thought of his or her own death, other losses may not be as devastating as they are for younger people for whom death seems still far away.

The physiological and cognitive functioning and adaptive reserves of older adults, even the healthy old, are reduced, to some extent, by the normal process of aging. But over time, these age-associated changes may increase elders' vulnerability to chronic physical or mental illness. As noted earlier, old people's declining physiological reserves and health tend to affect how they experience and grieve loss.

Social Capacities

Older adult's bereavement takes place amid socially and culturally rooted assumptions about older people. In American society, ageism tends to overlook or devalue the older person's past, current competence and roles, and significance to others (Moss, Moss, and Hansson 2001). Even though most older adults maintain contact with some family members, their social networks often have shrunk as a result of poor health, deaths, and the geographic relocation of family and friends. In some cultures, however, elders are embedded in strong social networks. The respect and support given to Native American elders by younger family members, for example, can enhance their community and cultural capacities in old age.

Although we have focused on individual and social capacities for the physiological and health losses that generally accompany old age, it is important to recognize that older adults are remarkable survivors and usually are able find ways to compensate for age-associated changes.

Death of a Partner

Although it is not useful to quantify the depth of any particular loss or to assign a greater meaning to some losses, some research indicates that the death of a child when one is in either middle or old age is most intensely grieved, followed by a partner's death, and then a parent's death (Middleton et al. 1998). But little difference in grief responses has been found in older adults losing an adult child compared with losing a partner, and some research suggests that in old age, a partner's death is most devastating (Arbuckle and deVries 1995; Holmes and Rahe 1967). One widow in a support group captured this difficulty by her comment: "My husband is just the person I need to help me get through this death."

A partner may die at any phase of the life span, from within the first few months to several decades into a relationship. No matter when a partner dies or under what circumstances, it is stressful, as the surviving partner is forced to shift from "we" to "I." The loss of a partner can deplete personal and social capacities and reduce well-being in old age. Such losses are intensified when a partner's death was preceded by a long or difficult period of caregiving. For example, in the Changing Lives of Older Couples study, although widowers experienced short-term relief after protracted caregiving, those who became socially isolated while providing care suffered long-term consequences from the lack of interpersonal contact (A. Carr 2001; D. Carr 2004; Schulz et al. 2003).

Older adults are more likely to experience the death of a partner than are young or middle-aged adults. In fact, widowhood is viewed as an "expected event" for older women (Martin-Matthews 1996). A partner's death brings the loss of (1) a many-layered relationship, which may encompass best friend, lover, companion, and confidant(e), as well as rituals, traditions, and interdependencies; and (2) a central part of the surviving partner's identity.

As a result, a partner's death often signifies the loss of a shared past and a future of growing older together, traveling during retirement or sitting on a porch reminiscing about a shared life (Cicirelli 2002). Recent studies indicate that the closer the attachments and bonds are between partners, the greater the distress during bereavement (Carr et al. 2000; Richardson 2006). If the bereaved adult had been highly dependent on the deceased partner, he or she must reconstruct a self-concept, since "marriage brings forth a reconstruction of reality, including the reality of the self and the spouse" (Lopata 1996:120). This new self-concept often involves continuing a bond with the deceased partner while it is being reconstructed.

Both men and women cite loneliness and missing their partner as their greatest problem, much greater than managing the practical challenges of daily life (Davidson 1999). Loneliness is most intense among those whose relationship was harmonious (Grimby 1993; Worden 2002). In addition, the social relationships inherent in being a couple are typically disrupted (Lopata 1996: 120; Lund, Caserta, and Dimond 1993). Indeed, accepting the fact of widowhood means realizing that one is now alone. The terms *widow* and *alone* are almost synonymous, at least during the early phases of widowhood (van den Hoonaard 1997). Such loneliness may be intensified by isolation in one's home and the absence of physical and emotional intimacy and touch (Lopata 1996). If the widowed adult depended on his or her partner for certain roles or activities, adjustment will be especially difficult (Parkes 1992).

Not surprisingly, for widowers, a partner's death is more disruptive to everyday activities than it is for widows. Older widows generally need to learn comparatively fewer skills, such as financial management, than do their male counterparts who are unaccustomed to housework and managing social activities and relationships. Past conflicts in long-term marriages may also later affect the grief process (Hilbourne 1999).

Older widows and widowers are more likely than younger adults to become sick or die; to develop weaker immune systems, more chronic conditions, and functional disabilities; to visit physicians more often, be hospitalized, and spend days in nursing homes; and have greater overall health care costs and more depressive symptoms (Goodkin et al. 2001; Hall and Irwin 2001; Laditka and Laditka 2003; Prigerson, Maciejewski, and Rosenheck 2000; Schaefer, Quesenberry, and Wi 1995). Physical symptoms include dry mouth, loss of or increase in appetite, muscle weakness, tightness in the chest, insomnia, and physical exhaustion (Worden 1991). A majority of widowed elders experience a major depression six months after a partner's death; in fact, even four years later, some are more depressed, sad, and lonely than married persons (Carnelley, Wortman, and Kessler 1999; Sonnega 2002). Findings are mixed regarding gender differences in emotional well-being. Gender differences may be most pronounced with how grief is experienced, not in the way men and women respond to the death (Doka 2000a; Walter 2003).

Men are more likely to have physical health problems and to die shortly after the death of their partner than women are. Mortality, including suicide, and morbidity rates are higher among older men within six months of the death of a partner than they are for older widows. This is partly because men generally are not as good at seeking informal support and may have more difficulty expressing their feelings (Campbell and Silverman 1996; Nolen-Hoeksema and Larson 1999; Schulz and Beach 1999). Men describe themselves as feeling sad and numb but try to handle their pain by keeping busy and praying. Although they tend to think about their wives nearly constantly—a pattern that represents strong feelings of attachment—they typically do not share their thoughts with others (Brabant, Forsyth, and Melancon 1992). For men who focused largely on paid work, their wife's death may raise issues of self-identity (Carverhill 1997). Some men may be less effective at developing an identity separate from that with a partner. Not surprisingly, older widowers are more likely to remarry than older widows are.

Recent research has found two patterns of grieving among older adults:

1. Intuitive, in which grief is experienced and expressed in an affective way, stereotyped as female.
2. Instrumental, in which grief is expressed physically or cognitively, labeled as male.
3. A third pattern that blends the preceding two.

Instrumental and emotive patterns of grieving appear to be related to but not determined by gender (Martin and Doka 2000). In other words, both men and women have very strong feelings of attachment, sadness, and loss, but the men in this current cohort of elders may not articulate their needs as openly as the women do. Some men are comfortable, particular among younger cohorts raised after the inception of the women's movement, with a more "feminine mode" of talking about their grief with others (Golden and Miller 1998). But older men generally do not perceive talking about their feelings as safe and fear that a public display of their emotions will cause concern or discomfort to others accustomed to their "strong" image. Instead, they may prefer to express their grief through action rather than interaction with others. They may choose to heal by trying to change the future rather than talking about the past. Because this pattern involves fewer words, it may not be perceived as grief by others, but it is nevertheless emotionally powerful. Using a problem-solving approach, men generally focus on concrete steps, such as reading all they can about an illness or the grief process or setting up a memorial fund in their wife's name. In effect, men's grief can be a form of talking without the words and even a form of "crying without the tears" (Golden and Miller 1998:21). Men's grief may not always be immediately evident, and their need to grieve may even be met with resistance or discomfort by family, friends, or professionals.

These issues suggest the importance of the professional's legitimizing different ways of expressing grief and being careful not to disenfranchise men's more
typical pattern of instrumental grieving and limited strong affective response
(Doka 2000a, 2002b; Moore and Stratton 2002). Talking about the loss, crying
and sharing one's emotions with others are not the only ways to heal (Golden
and Miller 1998; Walter 2003).

Regardless of the particular configuration of symptoms, many bereaved
partners wonder whether they are "normal," especially when they contemplate
ending their own lives. The initial bereavement of older widows may be less
intense than that of younger widows, but the emotional and physical distress
associated with grief is relieved more slowly in older persons. The death of a
spouse of many years tends to result in greater disorganization of roles, commitments, and patterns of an older widowed person's life, compared with that of
younger widows and widowers (Sanders 1993, Stroebe and Stroebe 1987). As
noted earlier, the death of a partner often triggers "cascading effects," with an
elder's grief interacting with or exacerbating other changes, such as a chronic
illness or disability, loss of independence, or involuntary relocation (O'Bryant
and Hansson 1995).

In addition, a partner's death can bring back the sadness associated with an
earlier death of a child. For example, one study discovered that parents who had
lost a son to war as long as thirty-three years earlier described continuing difficulties in coming to terms with their son's death (Rubin 1993, 1996). In another
study, bereaved parents (mean age seventy-seven) were initially more depressed
than were nonbereaved parents after a partner's death, and their depression did
not abate. In addition, the health of bereaved parents after a partner's death
declined more rapidly than among nonbereaved elders (B. DeVries, Lana, and
Falck 1994; H. M. DeVries et al. 1997). The grief process after the death of an
adult child is influenced by cultural factors as well. For example, for Jewish
women, the loss of an adult child often remains more central to their lives than
it does for non-Jewish women, with Jewish women having higher rates of
depression in middle and old age, which may affect how they respond to a partner's death (Goodman et al. 1991; Lesher and Bergey 1988). Other research,
however, suggests that the earlier experience of deaths of other loved ones
makes it easier for a widow to adapt (O'Bryant and Straw 1991). Interpreting
earlier losses as positive—not just experiencing the pain of past loss—appears to
be important to adapting to widowhood (van den Hoonaard 1997).

Fewer social and community supports may be available to older widows and
widowers than to younger bereaved partners, especially if they are the oldest
old who have outlived many friends, colleagues, and even adult children or if

their family is at a geographic distance. Perceptions of support both before and after death may be more important to assessing support satisfaction than objectively measured social network characteristics are (Feld and George 1994). Others may minimize the loss of those among the oldest old, commenting, "He lived a long life" or "She is free from her suffering." Such answers are not helpful to older adults trying to redefine their life in the context of lifelong losses. Women may feel that they have been abandoned and that life is unfair, while men describe feeling guilty and as if they have lost a physical part of themselves (Zonnebelt-Smeenge and DeVries 1998). Whether the grief of older widows and widowers is more intense and longer lasting than that of their younger counterparts is unclear. It probably depends on the quality and length of the relationship, the extent of loneliness after the death and a lifetime of racial, socioeconomic, and gender inequities, which may have impeded the development of internal resources to adapt to loss in later life (Elder, Liker, and Jaworski 1994; Moss, Moss, and Hansson 2001).

Recent research, however, suggests that widowhood may not be as devastating for older women as is commonly assumed. Because of the focus on role loss, how widows redefine who they are while maintaining important parts of their identity has not been studied as extensively (Lopata 1996; Matthews 1991; van den Hoonaard 1997; Vinokur 2002). Some widows recognize how they have changed, calling themselves "new women." They may renegotiate their relations with adult children, friends, and other relatives and give them new meaning. If they had a good relationship with their husband, widows may feel as if their husbands are talking to them, encouraging them to explore new activities and relationships. In addition, when the death was anticipated and the partners were able to talk about their hopes for the surviving partner, older widows may look back on good memories without regret and are more likely to view widowhood as a continuation of the marriage relationship (van den Hoonaard 1997).

Although sudden deaths are assumed to result in more difficult grief than an anticipated death does, time to anticipate is not necessarily helpful. For example, if a dying partner suffered, such as being in pain, the bereaved person will be more prone to depression, guilt, and feelings of helplessness and will recover more slowly (Carr 2001, in press; Carr et al. 2000; Doka 1997; Richardson and Balaswamy 2001). The location of the death—whether a partner dies at home or in a nursing home—also affects bereavement, with less distress if a partner died at home and particularly if the bereaved person was with his or her partner at the moment of death (Bennett and Vidal-Hall 2000; Pritchard, Fisher, and Lynn 1998; Richardson and Balaswamy 2001). Dying in a familiar and comfortable setting may foster feelings of control and mastery and make it easier to talk about death (Carr 2001). Some studies, however, have found that bereaved persons adjusted more quickly when their partners died in a nursing home, perhaps because they had grieved in anticipation when their partner was placed there (Carr et al. 2001; Richardson 2006).

The length of the illness also may affect the grief process, with some studies finding more anxiety and feelings of isolation and alienation in those whose partners died after a prolonged illness. This may result from the extensive caregiving and long exposure to chronic stressors. In instances of protracted death and caregiving, the loss may be more difficult to integrate than a sudden death is (Carr et al. 2001; Richardson 2006; Richardson and Balaswamy 2001). Others suggest that the critical variable is the bereaved person's perceptions of his or her preparedness for the death, with complicated grief reactions more common in those who felt unprepared for their partner's death (Barry, Kasl, and Prigerson 2002). If so, it is not surprising that traumatic reactions are found most often when a partner dies from a violent death, such as an accident, suicide, or homicide (Zisook, Chentsova-Dutton, and Schuchter 1998).

Over time, most widowed adults are able to balance the positive (e.g., involvement with neighbors, meeting new people, dating) and negative aspects (e.g., loneliness, "feeling down") of their lives. In some ways, this is similar to the dual-focus model of bereavement and oscillations between loss orientation and restoration orientation, or confrontation and avoidance of different stressors (Stroebe and Schut 1999). This back-and-forth process makes it easier to integrate the loss without grieving continually and affects well-being both early and later in the bereavement process (Richardson 2006; Richardson and Balaswamy 2001; Stroebe and Schut 1999; Utz, in press). The widowed person's relationship with the deceased thus is transformed, enabling memories to provide a measure of strength, warmth, and solidarity. This ability to incorporate the memory of the deceased into the bereaved's life allows older widowed persons more opportunities to expand their social networks (Rubin 1999). For some women, especially those who have been in an abusive or neglectful relationship, their partner's death may give them newfound freedom and an opportunity to pursue new goals for the remainder of their lives (Lund, Caserta, and Dimond 1993).

Widows may adjust better at first than widowers do, but they face more difficulties over the longer term, especially if they derived their sense of identity from their partner, lack the skills to access social networks outside the family, or face financial hardship. Many widows do not want to remarry, often discovering advantages to living alone (van den Hoonaard 1997; Walter 2003). They may be reluctant to resume a caregiving role and do not want to risk becoming a widow a second or third time. As in the postmodern paradigm of grief, they are able to begin a new life while continuing a relationship with their deceased husband. Widows who do wish to date or remarry face challenges in doing so, because of the stigma in our society attached to being an older women and the smaller pool of partners for women.

Friendships based on couple relationships also change, especially for widows. Friends who still are in couple relationships may desert widows, wanting to avoid a close connection with the widow's emotions, death, and their own partner's mortality. They also may feel awkward with a widow's altered status, especially if they were accustomed to only couple relationships. The norms of reciprocity and sharing inherent in friendships may no longer fit when the configuration of the couple has changed (Lopata 1996). Other women may view a widow as a "threat" to their own relationship. In turn, in our couple-oriented society, widows may feel like a "half person" (van den Hoonaard 1997). Conversely, given the predominance of women in the aging population, many widows form strong social networks with one another and benefit from widow-to-widow support groups.

Disenfranchised grievers—secret lovers; former partners; gay, lesbian, and transgender partners; and others who are rejected by the immediate family— may mourn their loss with only little family or community support. The relationship of some older gays and lesbians may become public only with their partner's death, so they must deal with both their grief and their family members' reaction to their coming out. They thus may have to bury the social aspects of their grief while they struggle alone with their mourning and feelings of ambivalence, guilt, and isolation. In addition, gay and lesbian partners may not have sick leave, hospital visitation rights, bereavement leave, and partner health benefits. In other relationships that are not socially sanctioned, such as that of lover or former partner, the disenfranchised bereaved partner may not be permitted to express grief or even participate in funeral arrangements and the rituals related to the death. At the same time, they may lose access to the extended family that might otherwise support them during their grief.

Death of a Sibling

Sibling relationships represent the one family bond that can last a lifetime. Most persons now will not lose a sibling to death until they are past seventy years of age (Uhlenberg 1996). Although the death of a sibling is common when one is old, it has been researched relatively little. Siblings of an older deceased man or woman, often overlooked as grievers, have another type of disenfranchised grief, as most of the attention during mourning goes to the immediate family (e.g., the partner and children), pushing siblings to the periphery (Moss, Moss, and Hansson 2001).

The sibling relationship in old age is characterized by a shared history, egalitarianism, and increasing closeness, especially among sisters (Connidis 2001). Given their unique relationship and history, siblings usually have very close bonds, whether positive or negative, harmonious or conflictual. As a result, it is not surprising that bereaved siblings rate their own health lower than a bereaved husband or wife does, although how much this represents the siblings' shared genetic inheritance is unclear (Hays, Gold, and Pieper 1997). Accordingly, social supports for the siblings of a deceased brother or sister are limited, although surviving siblings may comfort one another through reminiscence (Walter 1996). Most older adults maintain their ties with their deceased siblings (Moss and Moss 1989).

Death of Friends

The number of friends and colleagues dying as one grows older obviously increases, especially for those whose social networks are composed primarily of age peers, rather than a mix of younger and older persons. In some instances, such as a childhood friendship, a friend may have been a closer confidant(e) than one's partner. Given how much women value friendship, it is not surprising that they express more grief over a friend's death than do their male counterparts, who tend not to have as close friendship networks. Older adults may be less prepared emotionally for a friend's death, especially if it is accidental, than for the deaths of some family members. Lifelong friends share a history of memories and experiences that no one else can ever fully understand. Friends' lives have been intertwined over many years, creating a sense of inseparability. With a friend's death, older adults lose a past that can never be recaptured with anyone else. Nonetheless, friends are typically accorded fewer rights as mourners than even perhaps more distant members of the deceased's family, making this another form of disenfranchised grief (Archer 1999). Indeed, the friend "who was always there for us" is generally not recognized in obituaries or eulogies (Schiff 1986). We know relatively little about the cumulative effects of numerous friends' deaths in old age.

Caregiving

Whether caring for a partner with a chronic illness, an adult child with disabilities, or grandchildren (or great-grandchildren), older adult caregivers undergo numerous losses. The most common form of care provided by older adults is for their partner. Such caregiving appears to be more stressful for wives than for daughters, because wives are more likely to experience losses in marital and family relationships and in social involvement (Matthews and Heidorn 1998; National Academy on an Aging Society 2000; Seltzer and Li 2000).

As we stated in this book's introduction, loss and grief are the price that people pay for love and commitment to one another. Most caregivers choose to care for a loved one, sometimes for nearly a lifetime, because of love and commitment. Such losses can be physical (the loss of a partner to help run the house) or symbolic (the loss of one's identity to the caregiving role) but always result in deprivation of some kind. The caregivers' needs become subordinate to those of the person being cared for, or the caregiving may result in chronic sorrow. As is true of caregiving in middle adulthood, care in old age can also provide rewards, like a chance for greater closeness, intimacy, and pride (Kramer 1997; Langner 1995; McLeod 2001). But the losses often outweigh the gains: the loss of family members as one once knew them, of self-esteem and self-worth; of time, privacy, leisure, and social life; and of income and assets. Nearly all types of caregiving entail the loss of dreams of what one expected, such as travel, intimacy, and new discoveries in retirement; financial security; and sense of justice and fairness in life.

Similar to the experience of middle-aged adults caring for parents with dementia, the losses of caregiving tend to be intensified when caring for a partner with dementia. Family members provide up to 80 percent of the care for relatives with Alzheimer's disease (Epple 2002). Compared with other caregivers, they are at a higher risk of strain; physical and mental health problems, particularly depression; and family conflicts, and they have less time for leisure and for other family members (George and Gwyther 1986; Ory et al. 1999; Schulz et al. 2001). Interviews with caregivers of persons with Alzheimer's revealed four kinds of loss: the loss of social and recreational interaction, control over life events, well-being, and occupation (Loos and Boyd 1997). The loss of recognition by the care recipient and loss of intimacy are especially painful for spouses or partners (Sanders and Corley 2003; Walker and Pomeroy 1996).

The concept of "learning to bend without breaking" refers to the family's need to accommodate to the unpredictability and continuous change inherent in living with a relative with Alzheimer's disease (Gwyther 1998). When victims of Alzheimer's disease are no longer psychologically present or when their personalities have changed so much that new, disruptive behaviors emerge (e.g., emotional and verbal abuse, aggressive or violent behavior), the loss can be profound, and the grief process prolonged for years. Living in a state of "quasi widowhood," caregivers of relatives with dementia refer to their loved one's dying twice: first the psychological death of the person they knew and loved and then the physical death. (Narayn et al. 2001; Ross, Rosenthal, and Dawson 1997; Williams and Moretta 1997). The emotional responses of partners caring for persons with dementia are similar to those for a partner who has died (Rudd, Viney, and Preston 1999). They grieve the loss of their loved one in waves of denial, anger, guilt, resentment, and depression (Epple 2002). Whereas adult children typically express grief as the loss of their relationship with their parent and their loss of opportunities as a result of their caregiving, partners express grief for the loss of the couple's identity and for the ensuing uncertainty and aloneness (Meuser and Marwit 2001).

According to the resilience model, caregivers' stress is affected not only by their own and the recipient's characteristics but also by the family, community, social, and cultural capacities. In addition, women's grief tends to be characterized by despair, anger, loss of control, somatization, guilt, and anxiety, and men's grief is associated with denial. The anxiety expressed by wives stems from the various losses in the relationship and social roles resulting from their husband's dementia, including the loss of the couple's identity as well as uncertainty and aloneness (Gilliland and Fleming 1998; Meuser and Marwit 2001; Rudd, Viney, and Preston 1999).

Spirituality—the personal relationship with God or a supreme being—religious beliefs, and faith are key personal capacities for older adult caregivers, serving as a source of comfort and a coping mechanism (Ramsey and Blieszner 2000; Stolley, Buckwalter, and Koenig 1999). In a qualitative study of spouses caring for persons with dementia, some caregivers reported that because of their faith, they were not grieving (Sanders and Corley 2003). But such responses may also reflect the caregiver's not expressing grief because of the social stigma of doing so.

An important component of social capacities is the availability and utilization of services like respite care, although some caregivers of adults with dementia report that such services increase their stress rather than reduce it. For example, the work of arranging for respite care and convincing their partner to accept a stranger in the home may be greater than the relief gained by a few hours away from their partner (Administration on Aging 2003).

When their partner has dementia, another neurological disorder, a brain injury, or a personality distortion caused by a stroke, older adult caregivers often have chronic sorrow created by the losses of caring for a loved one for a long time without a predictable ending (Burkes and Eakes 1999). Caregivers of a comatose partner often endure the psychological death of their partner years before the physical death. In addition to chronic sorrow, these caregivers may have disenfranchised grief. That is, their friends and family may visit less frequently, not knowing what to say or do, and they may feel that the person whom they love has already died, and yet they have little social support for their grief. Prolonged grieving can hurt the caregiver's physical and mental health (Ahmed 2003; Hamdy et al. 1994; Mace and Rabins 1986).

Long-term ambiguity about the care recipient's place in the family system—whether he or she is "absent or present, dead, or alive"—makes the caregiver's loss even worse (Boss 1999:4), as it creates a sense of loss of mastery and identity, leading to helplessness, hopelessness, and dissonance in the family system and the primary caregiver's life (Boss 1999; Epple 2002). Caregivers may want the actual death to occur while at the same time wanting to maintain a close relationship with their partner for as long as possible (Sanders and Corley 2003). At the mercy of Alzheimer's, caring partners are unable to live normally and may no longer know what normal is. During this grief process, the family members continually redefine and reinterpret their relationship. Each family member's perception of reality affects the meaning of loss and how family boundaries are defined (Dupuis 2002). Given the caregiver's stress and uncertainty, the care recipient's death often brings relief and enhances well-being (Schulz et al. 2001).

Caring for Grandchildren

Grandparents and other extended family members in families of color and in other cultures have traditionally cared for grandchildren (C. Cox 2002; Pruchno 1999), often in addition to parental care or to support young parents while they are employed outside the home. What has changed in the past two decades is the rapid growth in the number of grandparents (or great-grandparents) who are the primary or sole caregivers for grandchildren because their adult sons or daughters are unable or unwilling to provide care. In fact, grandparent-headed households are currently the fastest-growing type in the United States (Wallace 2001). Although some grandparents gain tremendous pride, love, and feelings of being needed from caregiving, they nevertheless face numerous losses, such as

- Retirement time or income that they had anticipated in a child-free old age.
- Dreams of their multigenerational family.
- Friends who pursue their leisure instead of being constrained by child care responsibilities.
- Shame for their adult children's inability to care for their own children.

Regardless of the reasons, most grandparents feel disappointment, shame, and guilt over their apparent failure as parents who produced an adult child who could give up his or her own child. The grandparents may lose their identity and self-esteem as "good parents." In turn, their grandchildren may be embarrassed by having an older relative caring for them and may repeatedly long for their parents, thereby intensifying the grandparents' grief.

To outsiders, grandparent caregivers may be invisible, largely because of their age and gender (e.g., most are women), even though they may be the primary caregivers for most of their grandchild's life. Service systems such as public child welfare, community mental health, and public schools are not equipped to work with grandparents, to offer them legal and financial benefits, or to recognize the losses faced by the grandchild (Wallace 2001). In public, grandparents may try to appear to be the parents, in order to increase the probability of others' support, typically that of younger parents. What can be especially painful is when other family members and peers fail to help out, increasing grandparent caregiver's sense of isolation and loneliness (Szolnoki and Cahn 2003). Their losses are exacerbated by the lack of rewards or public recognition for the hard work of caregiving.

Caring for Adults with Developmental Disabilities

Chapter 8 discussed the chronic sorrow of younger parents caring for children with severe physical impairments. As they age, these parents' grief may grow with anxiety and worry about the future as they wonder who will care for their adult child when they become ill or die. With the longer life expectancy of adults with developmental disabilities, aging parents may be faced with not only the chronic sorrow of providing care but also fears about their child's future well-being. Most older adults with developmental disabilities continue to live in their families' homes, in part because of the few community-based residential care options. Their aging caregivers are out of sync with their peers, since they have not "launched" their children and may have fewer social support networks than do caregivers of parents or partners (Kraus and Seltzer 1993; Smith, Tobin, and Fullmer 1995). In many ways, as parents age and "wear out" from years of caring, they become "depleted caregivers" (Roos 2002:124).

But even as they worry about their adult child's outliving them, a significant number of parents, especially poor and African American families, do not make plans for their child (Heller and Factor 1993). Their failure may reflect denial, partially because talking about dying and transferring care responsibilities to other family members only reminds them of their sorrow. Family discussions about future plans may also provoke siblings' and other family members' past anger, resentment, and grief (Roos 2002). Conversely, when parents do plan financially and establish a trust for their child's care, nondisabled siblings may feel disregarded once more, especially if they have unresolved resentments from the past or are facing financial difficulties. Such family conflicts can be overwhelming to the older caregiver, who then seeks to avoid them by not preparing for the future.

Mistreatment of Older Adults

Although there is little research on grief and loss among older adults who have been mistreated, clinical accounts suggest that elders who are abused or financially exploited by their children may grieve some of the following losses:

• The person they had hoped their child would become.
• Their anticipated security and safety in old age.
• Their feelings of trust.
• Their pride of their own parenting capability.

Most instances of elder abuse are committed by family members (Gaugler, Kane, and Langlois 2000; Wolf 2000). Losses of this sort can damage a person's capacity to trust others and even to trust a self that has proved vulnerable to mistreatment (Weiss 1998). When older adults deny they are being mistreated, they may believe that living with a familiar if abusive situation is preferable to reporting the abuse to others and thus admitting that their child is abusing them. Some older people, unaware of other community-based care options, do not want to reveal their mistreatment for fear of being removed from their home and placed in a nursing home (Bergeron 2000; Wolf 1998; Wolf and Pillemer 1989). If the abuser is arrested, restrained from the home, or abandons the elder, the older adult will suffer the loss of that relationship, no matter how bad it may have been (Quinn and Tomita 1997; Sprecher and Fehr 1998). Abused elders grieve the loss of the family member who was abusive as well as the other losses caused by the mistreatment.

Cultural backgrounds and norms may determine the elder's response to abuse and/or its termination (Brownell 1997). Old people in Korean families, for example, tolerate financial abuse because of the traditional patriarchal property transfer system, in which sons enjoy exclusive family inheritance rights. This system promotes an adult son's financial dependence and occasional exploitation of an older parent (Moon, Tomita, and Jung-Kamei 2001). Cultural differences, however, should not be used to justify abuse. More research is needed on the grief and loss stemming from a family's mistreatment of older adults in different cultures as well as on interventions with elders who have been mistreated.

Loss from Chronic Illness and Pain

Older adults with chronic disabilities lose not only their health and possibly their well-being but sometimes also their individual and social capacities. For example, their self-confidence and concept as an active person is usually destroyed,

and their informal family and community capacities may be altered through losses in personal relationships, employment, social life, and dreams of what their
old age would be. These losses are generally worse for old people placed in
long-term-care facilities, such as assisted living or nursing homes. Restrictions
on their independence, inherent in institutionalization, can harm their mental
health and cause powerful grief responses (Katz and Yelin 2001). Older adults
with chronic disabilities are more likely to have depression, negative thinking,
and perhaps a sense of being misunderstood when others discount their pain.
Depression, in turn, can worsen other conditions, leading to greater cognitive
and physical impairment and the resulting grief (Adamek 2003). Their caregivers,
who are faced with physical, financial, and emotional burdens, may also become
depressed, thereby harming their interpersonal interactions (Kelley 1998).

Similar to the grief associated with death, old persons must acknowledge and
understand their disabilities, feel the pain and react to the loss, and then move
into a new life, often at a long-term-care facility (Rando 1988). When elders move
from being independent to being dependent, from being healthy to having a
chronic condition, from feeling in control to feeling powerless and uncertain
about each day, from feeling attractive and energetic to feeling tired and unde-
sirable, they lose much of themselves, along with their ability to perform
normal daily functions. Because they live with the pain and illness daily, they
cannot return to normal functioning or "get beyond the loss" (Kelley 1998).
With the sense of loss nearly continuous, elders with chronic illness and pain
must mourn their old self and then reconstruct their identity (Lindgren et al.
1992). In doing so, they may be able to discover new strengths, capacities, and
positive meaning and thus create new realities. For example, stroke victims have
been found to suffer greatly as a result of the loss of taken-for-granted freedoms,
abilities, and ways of relating to others. When describing these losses, they use
words like *frustrated, afraid, sad, depressed, embarrassed*, and *loss of self-esteem*. But
over time they are often able to develop a new perspective on life, finding enjoyment and beauty in ordinary things and using phrases such as "fortunate to be
alive" (Pilkington 1999).

Summary

All older adults grieve some types of loss, but some are more resilient than others.
Their resilience may be threatened by chronic illness and pain, reduced social
networks, geographic distance from family, abusive or neglectful family relationships, and limited community participation. Losses characteristic of old
age are the death of an adult child, sibling, friend, or partner; caregiving for a

partner or grandchildren (or great-grandchildren); and living with the risk of abuse or neglect. Even as elders grieve losses, they nevertheless may be able reconstruct their lives to create meaning, self-esteem, and mental well-being. They often find new ways to be involved in their communities and culture, through voluntarism, civic engagement, or care for family members. In doing so, they strengthen their capacities, including their inner capacity to derive life's lessons and meaning from their losses. Such resilience, in turn, enhances their physical and mental well-being.

13

Interventions for Grieving Older Adults

IN CONTRAST to working with persons of other ages, older adults' multiple losses, experiences of ageism, physiological changes, and cohort specific socialization all may present challenges. Even though older adults are more heterogeneous than any other age group, they do share age-related changes. This chapter examines strategies addressing the potential barriers and challenges and developmentally appropriate grief interventions.

Multiple Losses

Many older people face multiple losses, including physical changes (e.g., loss of vision, joint degeneration), health problems (e.g., loss of mobility and/or independence), deaths of others (e.g., partner, siblings, friends, children), and social or environmental losses (e.g., of income, home, productive roles, status). For some, the accumulated losses and depletion of individual and social capacities may complicate their bereavement. For example, old people who have survived their siblings and partner, have become frail, live in an institution, and have few outside social contacts may be at greater risk of social isolation and depression than their healthier counterparts are. In such instances, relationships with social and health care professionals may become a critical social support (Karel et al. 2002). Practitioners should treat these relationships with respect, try to strengthen mutual support networks, and use the elders' internal personal capacities to address their bereavement needs.

Ageism

The effects of ageism leave many older persons suspicious of professional intervention. Old persons may fear that well-meaning professionals will take over their lives and force them to do things they do not want to do (e.g., place them in a nursing home against their wishes). Many experience ageism from health care providers and/or family members when they are treated paternalistically (e.g., they are talked about in the third person) or are not considered for treatment because expectations for later life change, growth, and healing are low (Chinen and Berg-Cross 1994). Therefore, service providers must guard against and oppose institutional and personal ageism, recognize the lifelong potential for growth, be committed to alleviating later-life suffering, be positive, and maximize the older person's decision-making ability and sense of personal control.

Ageism may affect communication in a variety of ways. It may make older people more anxious during their assessment, so conveying respect for them can alleviate their anxiety and improve the assessment and interventions (Karel et al. 2002). Strategies to convey respect include the following:

1. Use surnames and titles unless the older adult asks you to do otherwise.
2. Obtain permission from the older person to include others (e.g., family members) in the interview or to ask others to provide information to the practitioner.
3. Continue to address and include the older person in the conversation when family members are present during an interview.

Physiological Changes Affecting Communication

Common age-related sensory changes; diseases that affect sensory, cognitive, and physical functioning; and normal declines in reaction time may make communication difficult. But rather than automatically assuming that an older person has sensory deficits, professionals should assess him or her for such limitations and make the appropriate accommodations. For example, if an older adult reports better hearing in one ear, the practitioner should sit on that side (box 13.1). Bereaved older adults with serious sensory and other physical impairments that prevent them from leaving their homes must be visited at home.

Cohort Experiences

Cohort-specific socialization and experiences may create communication and mental health service utilization barriers. For example, persons who were born between 1900 and 1930 learned ways of viewing and interacting with health care professionals that influence how they receive current professional encounters: "Socialized to a paternalistic medical system, they often take a passive stance during a medical encounter. They tend to answer only those questions that are asked and to accept physician authority with little questioning or interaction"

Box 13.1 Guidelines for Effective Communication

- Guard against invading the elder's privacy by ensuring that others cannot overhear the conversation and by asking only those questions that are necessary to establishing rapport or addressing the concerns at hand.
- Allow sufficient time for an interview to accommodate changes in reaction time.
- Be positioned near enough to reach out and touch the elder if appropriate.
- Speak clearly and slowly, asking one question at a time.
- Ensure adequate lighting so that the elder may see written materials and nonverbal communication.
- Use large print for written materials to accommodate visual changes.
- Speak directly to the older person so your lip movements can be seen.
- Be comfortable with silence.
- Remain alert to nonverbal communication.

Source: D. G. Blazer, *Emotional Problems in Later Life: Intervention Strategies for Professional Caregivers* (New York: Springer, 1998).

(Karel et al. 2002:33). These age cohorts were socialized differently with respect to the appropriateness of self-expression. They may associate social workers with public welfare, perceive them as less competent than other helping professionals, or attach a stigma to seeing a social worker, in part because of historically negative media portrayals of social work. Accordingly, some older persons do not see the value of talking about their feelings and may have negative views of social and mental health service professionals.

Bereaved older persons, particularly persons of color, typically do not seek professional help (Moore et al. 1996). More commonly, social service providers receive referrals from concerned family members, neighbors, or health care providers about an older person who is neglecting personal needs, isolating himself or herself, or having mental health problems. Cultural differences in instances of racism, historical oppression, and earlier negative encounters with health and social service systems influence older people's help-seeking practices and service utilization and should be considered in initial contacts with bereaved elders.

The Resurgence of Grief in Later Life

Grief from very profound losses that may have been buried or suppressed may resurface in later life. Erikson's (1982; Erikson, Erikson, and Kivnick 1986) developmental theory proposes that individuals in later life try to integrate their life's experience before they die and that failing to do so results in states of despair. Similarly, Butler (1963) suggested that many older adults undergo a naturally occurring life review process. When they were children, today's elders may have been excluded from grief rituals, taught not to express painful feelings, and socialized to pull themselves up with their "boot straps" to cope with life's hard blows. As these earlier memories resurface in their advanced years, the "old-old often enter a final life struggle: to express strong emotions, mend broken relationships, and find a meaning and an identity in order to die with self-respect" (Feil 1999:592). Several of the interventions reviewed in this chapter address this resurgence of grief, including reminiscence and life review, counseling and psychotherapy, and group work. In addition, validation therapy may be used with persons with dementia to validate emotions from prior losses and the internal conflicts that emerge as older adults reexperience or dwell on earlier memories and previously unexpressed grief (Feil 1999). These interventions need to be empirically tested.

When memories revive earlier traumatic experiences, such as those commonly experienced by Holocaust survivors, the client should be assessed for posttraumatic stress disorder (PTSD) and interventions for the trauma and grief. "Sensory triggers," such as moving into a nursing home and being showered (or bathed) by a stranger, may precipitate trauma reactions (Safford 1995). Holocaust survivors have lived their lives in silence, repressing horrifying memories (Shoshan 1989). But in later life, when they confront major life transitions or losses, such as retirement, sudden illness, or the death of family members, their memories may return. They may need to reminisce in order to relate and integrate their difficult past (Schindler, Spiegel, and Malachi 1992).

Aware that most people cannot "comprehend the overwhelming trauma" that the Holocaust survivors experienced, elders may not trust professionals to understand, either. Elders who have a strong faith or religious orientation may be encouraged to seek support from commemorative or other religious holidays or religious leaders of their faith (Schindler, Spiegel, and Malachi 1992). Professionals should recognize and convey the survivors' strengths and coping resources while assessing them for PTSD. Although group treatment may be a useful therapeutic modality for Holocaust survivors and their children (Fogelman 1989; Muller and Barash-Kishon 1998), it has not been adequately tested empirically.

Safford (1995) described various therapeutic interventions and programs for Holocaust survivors, including mixed and tailored interventions, varied therapeutic groups to meet multiple challenges specific to generations and cohorts, short- and long-term groups, mutual support groups, services offered in nonclinical and nonthreatening environments, organized opportunities to give testimony about the Holocaust, crisis intervention, and grief therapy. One group model, with active leader interventions for strengthening interpersonal relationships among the members, tried to help elders achieve a greater sense of ego integrity to facilitate the ongoing mourning process (Muller and Barash-Kishon 1998). When therapeutic strategies are used that allow the topic to be "approached more openly, a process appears to occur that enables the families of survivors to free themselves of the shame and guilt in which they have been enveloped" (Shoshan 1989:207). More studies are needed, however, to evaluate the effectiveness of these and other interventions for grief resurgence.

Assessment

The assessment of bereaved elders, particularly those with cognitive changes, is much more comprehensive than that of persons at other ages. This assessment may cover physical, functional, social, emotional, spiritual, financial, and environmental domains, because interactions among them become more complex with age. For example, normal physiological changes with age may make a person more susceptible to neurological and chemical imbalances caused by sometimes minor modifications (e.g., vitamin deficiencies, changes in medications). Grief may trigger changes that reverberate across these domains. For example, changes in diet (e.g., resulting from a grief-related loss of appetite), in living arrangements (e.g., resulting from a caregiving partner's death), and alcohol or drug consumption may precipitate the development of delirium, a "transient organically based disorder that frequently mimics dementia" (McInnis-Dittrich 2002:120). Unexpressed grief may also be evident in somatic symptoms. (Although a full description of assessment methods and tools for working with older persons is beyond the scope of this chapter, see Emlet et al. 1996; Greene 2000; Kane and Kane 2004; Mouton and Esparaz 2000; Zarit and Zarit 1998.)

When assessing older persons who are grieving a death, watch for the following variables outlined in the resilience model:

1. Factors that influence the progress of the bereavement (e.g.. the nature of the relationship, type of death, type of illness, and ways in which the loss affects daily functioning).

2. The bereaved elder's personal capacities (e.g., ability to manage tasks of daily living, self-esteem, previous experience of loss, religious or spiritual beliefs).
3. Background and social/cultural capacities (e.g., age, income, education, social support, cultural beliefs, rituals, and attitudes toward death and bereavement). (McKiernan 1996)

A multidimensional assessment of grief includes attention to (1) emotional and cognitive experiences, (2) coping, (3) the continuing relationship with the deceased, (4) functioning, (5) social relationships, and (6) identity (Zisook and Schuchter 1996).

Differentiating between depression and bereavement is difficult because of the similarity of the symptoms. Older adults may become depressed in reaction to a loss, have a chronic history of depression, and often experience both depression and grief simultaneously. Elders who are bereaved with depressive symptoms are less likely to present with morbid feelings and preoccupations of worthlessness, which are characteristic of major depression (Chinen and Berg-Cross 1994). Gerontological practitioners should be trained to differentiate between major depressive syndrome and depressive symptoms of uncomplicated bereavement (e.g., Zisook and Schuchter 1996) and to use the variety of assessment instruments to diagnose depression (e.g., Karel et al. 2002). Risk factors for major depressive syndrome in bereaved older spouses or partners are

1. Presence of a major depressive syndrome soon after the loss.
2. Intense symptoms of depression soon after the death.
3. Family history of major depression.
4. Increased alcohol consumption soon after the loss.
5. Poor physical health around the time of the death.
6. The partner's sudden and unexpected death. (Zisook and Schuchter 1993, as cited in Zisook and Schuchter 1996:548)

The genogram and ecomap are useful assessment tools for later-life loss from an ecological perspective, and may complement grief assessment protocols (Freeman 1984b). The genogram maps out family history in regard to quality of relationships, significant family events, roles, communication patterns, and major losses. It may be used for a life review and offers a pictorial representation for the elder and the professional of significant life events, transitions, traumas, and other losses (McGoldrick and Gerson 1985; McGoldrick, Gerson, and Shellenberger 1999). The ecomap is a paper-and-pencil assessment tool that provides a visual representation of the older person's social relationships and interactions. It may be used to help older clients view their situation in a broader social context (Sheafor, Horejsi, and Horejsi 2000). The diagram may help older persons find gaps in their social networks that were affected by, resulted from, or constituted recent losses that may be addressed through supportive interventions. For example, widowhood or relocation may be accompanied by changes in the frequency and nature of social contacts with others. Examining these additional losses may help validate the older person's multiple loss experiences or lead to discussions about possible interventions to enhance supports (e.g., rationalizing peer support, support group referral, or another form of intervention). Several excellent articles and texts describe commonly used tools for assessing grief, (e.g., Gabriel and Kirschling 1989; Neimeyer and Hogan 2001; Tomita and Kitamura 2002) and the development and clinical uses of the genogram and ecomap in practice (Hartman 1978; McGoldrick and Gerson 1985; McGoldrick, Gerson, and Shellenberger 1999; Sheafor, Horejsi and Horejsi 2000; Walsh and McGoldrick 1991).

General Techniques and Interventions
Reminiscence and Life Review

Reminiscence in later life is part of a naturally occurring life review (Butler 1963) and is initiated by an awareness of approaching death and an unconscious desire to resolve and reintegrate past experiences and conflicts. Although reminiscence may occur at any age, "the intensity and emphasis on putting one's life in order are most striking in old age." In fact, studies report that 49 to 84 percent of elders have reviewed their lives or are currently reviewing them (Butler, Lewis, and Sunderland 1998:90). Reminiscence may be prompted by the elder or the practitioner to facilitate therapeutic mourning (Viney, Benjamin. and Preston 1989) and may be used in individual or group settings (Burnside 1994).

Practitioners may also use life review therapy as a more structured and purposive way to facilitate the integration of losses and conserve dignity. Life review therapy is systematic guided reminiscence to help older persons "integrate disparate aspects of the self, to assist with current problem-solving strategies, and to bequeath a legacy" (Molinari 1999:159). Life review goals are to

1. Address the whole range of life cycle events.
2. Enable older clients to review, renew, and evaluate their past experiences.
3. Help elders prepare for death. (Beaver 1991)

Therapy is a supportive process of listening, showing interest, giving reassurance, and expressing feelings and thoughts associated with memories, helped along by cognitive-behavioral techniques (e.g., reframing one's problems and expectations, reevaluating beliefs and thoughts, and assigning homework) (Weiss 1995). The *Life Review Interview Guide* offers a structure and a way to document the life review (Beechem, Anthony, and Kurtz 1998). The *Guide* looks at educational experiences, family history (e.g., deaths, meaningful relationships, changes in family structure), health events (e.g., onset of illness, surgery), social and recreational activities, spiritual development, recognition from others (e.g., awards, honors), and significant economic events (e.g., loss of job, retirement). It also notes strong, conflicted, and tenuous relationships as well as themes of loss relevant to these issues. Props like photographs, personal belongings, memorabilia, audiotapes, and music may be used as well. Human service professionals may help elders and their family members to create an extensive autobiography that includes family albums, scrapbooks, and other memorabilia (Beaver 1991).

The effectiveness of life review therapy and reminiscence in relieving grief has not been tested empirically. Some early evidence, however, suggests empirical support for individual and group-based methods for reducing depressive symptoms (Ashida 2000; Goldwasser, Auerbach, and Harkins 1987; Parsons 1986).

Counseling and Psychotherapy

Supportive counseling is often needed to help elders acquire and use a greater range of social supports, learn new skills (e.g., teach husbands to cook), and normalize and validate the grief process. The principal goals are to (1) provide comfort and support, (2) facilitate mourning and readjustment, and (3) mitigate complicated grief (Young and Black 1997).

Although most older adults do not require counseling, those who are socially isolated and at risk of mental health problems may benefit from professional intervention (McKiernan 1996). Empirical evidence regarding psychotherapy with the bereaved among adults more generally "argues for our selective engagement in grief therapy with those bereaved persons whose grief is traumatic or prolonged" (Neimeyer 2000:555). Prematurely encouraging counseling or therapy may result in the withdrawal of support from natural support systems and should be avoided (Schut et al. 2001).

Given the pervasiveness of loss in old age, it is surprising that few studies have tested the efficacy of different therapy approaches to address complicated bereavement in elders (Zisook and Schuchter 1996). Case reports present anecdotal evidence that psychotherapy (Essa 1986), traumatic grief therapy (Frank et al. 1997), and interpersonal psychotherapy (IPT) (Klarel et al. 2002) may help people adapt to loss and reduce older bereaved adults' distress, although other investigations have reported no therapeutic effects (Beem et al. 1999). A pilot investigation of interventions for adults diagnosed with traumatic grief found fewer grief symptoms and associated anxiety and depression, following the imagined reliving of the death, in vivo exposure to avoided activities and situations, and interpersonal therapy, but this study did not focus on older populations (Shear et al. 2001).

Culturally derived therapeutic techniques suitable for grieving elders have not been studied, and only one study suggests that differential counseling approaches may be useful for bereaved men and women. For example, problem-focused counseling was more beneficial for widows, whereas emotion-focused counseling was more effective for widowers (Schut et al. 1997). Cognitive therapies may be indicated for those whose thoughts dwell on negative evaluations of themselves, the world, and the future following a loss (Malkinson 2001).

A growing body of experimental evidence suggests that behavioral interventions like guided mourning therapy help adults of all ages overcome severe and especially complicated grief reactions (Malkinson 2001; Mawson et al. 1981; Sireling, Cohen, and Marks 1988). The theory of guided mourning is that prolonged and consistent exposure to anxiety-provoking stimuli associated with grief (as opposed to avoiding these stimuli) elicits over time increasingly weaker grief responses. This approach may be particularly helpful for persons with complicated grief responses who have avoided reminders of the loss and the associated grief (McKiernan 1996:177). Consider the following case example:

> Mrs. Feldman was a seventy-eight-year-old woman who had been happily married for forty-eight years until she found her husband John dead from a self-inflicted gun shot. Three years after his death, her grief was still interrupting her appetite, sleep, and concentration. She had lost contact with her friends, dropped out of her church activities, and continued to ruminate obsessively about what she could have done to prevent Joe's death. She was overwhelmed by her anxiety and enduring grief. She avoided memories of the death itself, suppressed expressions of grief to protect her two adult children, and had not visited the grave site. Although the trazodone prescribed by her primary care doctor was helping her sleep, her anxiety and grief continued. She felt too anxious to join a support group but agreed to individual therapy.

Guided mourning with Mrs. Feldman would require an assessment of the domains described earlier in this chapter, with special attention to depression and PTSD, since she was the one to find her husband after his death. She would be given information about grief (the process, indicators of complicated grief), major depression, and the rationale and process for guided mourning therapy. The therapist would create a supportive trusting relationship with Mrs. Feldman. She would be guided to revisit painful events and memories associated with her husband's death, which would allow her to evoke grief responses in a supportive environment (Thyer, Thyer, and Massa 1991). She might be encouraged to do homework assignments, reflect on her life experiences influencing her grief response, visit her husband's grave, and engage in new activities. In sum, Mrs. Feldman's avoidance of grief and reminders of her husband's death, combined with the stigma of the suicide and the resulting loss of support, produced a complicated grief reaction that required professional intervention. In the presence of a supportive, nonjudgmental, and skilled practitioner, she might be able to mourn and integrate her losses, so that she could move on with her life. As similar with earlier phases of the life span, an integrated, dual-process grief model of avoidance/restoration can be effective with older bereaved adults.

Group Work

Group work is used extensively with older persons and their family members in a wide variety of community and institutional settings. Both practitioners and researchers believe that group work with bereaved elders

- Enhances their sense of belonging and affiliation.
- Legitimizes and normalizes their emotions associated with grief.
- Provides chances to express and integrate their experiences.
- Offers opportunities to learn new coping skills from others who have had similar losses.
- Creates a forum for learning and receiving information relevant to the loss and to living beyond it.
- Develops social relationships and supports.
- Allows people to solve their problems with the help of others. (Cohen 1999; Hill, Lund, and Packard 1996; Scharlach and Fuller-Thompson 1994; Thompson 1996; Toseland 1990)

Support groups are particularly useful for grieving elders as a means of strengthening their social support, which often diminishes during bereavement (Goodkin et al. 2001). Social support is vital to physical and psychological well-being in later life and is a powerful predictor of postbereavement psychological adjustment (Gass 1987; Lund, Caserta, and Dimond 1993; Rowe and Kahn 1998; Windholz, Marmar, and Horowitz 1985). One study found that many support group participants, particularly the more depressed, lonely, and stressed, pursued outside social contact with group members, which reduced their loneliness over time (Caserta and Lund 1996).

Support group models vary in accordance with the group's objectives, setting, participants' needs, and sponsor. Some support groups focus on the expression of feelings, whereas others place more emphasis on providing content and/or skills training. Caserta and Lund (1996) used a self-help model in which the leaders acted as facilitators and used Worden's (1982) tasks of grief as the group's objectives. The group helped the participants share and recognize the commonality of their experiences and learn from one another the skills needed to cope with and integrate their grief.

The timing for the optimal therapeutic value of support groups has not been adequately evaluated. Because most bereaved elders require a private period during the acute phases of their grief, support groups may not be as helpful immediately following a death. By contrast, a recent exploratory study of the experiences of a small group of people who participated in bereavement support groups reported that most benefited within the first three months following a death (Picton et al. 2001). An examination of patterns reported in an empirical review of group studies suggests that interventions are most helpful for persons with complicated grief, which is not usually determined immediately (Schut et al. 2001). The timing and extent to which bereaved elders benefit most from group support requires further empirical investigation. (Although a discussion of the strategies for organizing and implementing support groups for the bereaved are beyond the scope of this chapter, see Hughes 1995; Schwab 1986.)

Support groups are widely used for older widows (Caserta and Lund 1996; Constantino 1988; Lund, Caserta, and Dimond 1993), family caregivers (Toseland and Rossiter 1989; Walker et al. 1994b), and persons bereaved by specific forms of loss such as a partner dying of cancer (Picton et al. 2001) or suicide (Clark and Goldney 1995; Renaud 1995). Several impediments and gender biases inherent in the support group model and other services help explain why research has failed to find a treatment effect for bereaved widowers participating in mutual help groups (Kaye 2002; Tudiver et al. 1992). Group interventions have focused on female Caucasian populations and have been methodologically flawed. Thus conclusions about the efficacy of support groups for bereaved adults have not been empirically established (for critical reviews of the literature, see Kato and Mann 1999; Schut et al. 2001). There is some evidence, however, that widows at risk of complicated bereavement may benefit from self-help groups (Constantino 1988; Liebermann and Videka-Sherman 1986; Vachon et al. 1980).

Some elders who were raised to "keep family business within the family" may be uncomfortable in a support group. The idea of sharing their feelings and information about their family with strangers would violate long-held norms. Men may be more reluctant than women to share personal matters with others. In addition, some elders from cultures that place a high value on the family's privacy are less likely to participate in support groups. Another barrier to support group participation is transportation, especially if the elder no longer drives or lives in a rural area with little public transit.

Grief and Bereavement in Older Men

Grief responses are strongly influenced by a person's social and cultural background, especially his or her gender-based norms and expectations. Men (and women) respond to major losses in the ways that they are taught and expected to behave. Thus when faced with profound losses and challenging emotions, older men often guard their feelings, remain silent, mourn by themselves or keep their grief "secret," take physical or legal action, feel anger and aggression, or become immersed in activity (Staudacher 1991). It is important not to stereotype older men's grief responses and to recognize the wide variation in how men experience and process losses (Miller and Golden 1998). It also is useful to recognize the ways in which socialization and others' expectations may hinder or facilitate the older male's personal style of grieving (Kramer 2000). The tendency to promote emotional expression as the basis for most bereavement interventions suggests a potential gender and cultural bias toward women and Caucasians and a class bias toward those with higher education and income.

There "is now a reasonably sound body of evidence to support the conclusion that men suffer more severe health consequences from partner loss than women" (Stroebe and Schut 2001:360). Reviews of the literature reveal higher mortality rates and psychological distress in widowers compared with married men than in widows compared with married women (Stroebe 1998; Stroebe and Stroebe 1983). Identifying and treating psychological distress among older males becomes challenging, given barriers to mental health and social service utilization. (For guidelines for assessment and clinical applications for working with men coping with loss, see Doka and Martin 2001; Rankin 2001.) Although interventions specifically for older bereaved men have not yet been explicitly tested, box 13.2 describes Kramer's (2000) practice guidelines for developing and/or modifying interventions.

Spiritually Attentive Interventions

Older people facing their own or another's death generally try to understand the meaning of life and wonder what will happen at the time of death. They may seek answers to these questions in their religious beliefs or sense of spirituality, defined as the "search for transcendence, meaning, and connectedness beyond the self" (Sherwood 1998:81).

Religion and spirituality provide "a source of great comfort and encouragement when elders are faced with overwhelming challenges" and "offer a cognitive

Box 13.2 Practice Guidelines for Addressing Grief in Older Men

- Reflect on your own expectations of male expressions of grief, and remain open to their distinctive experience.
- Demonstrate understanding, compassion, and acceptance.
- Assess loss history and prior and current coping responses.
- Individually tailor your approach with consideration of their type of loss, grief response, needs, cultural beliefs, customs, rituals, and values.
- Provide education about grief symptoms and process. Use metaphors and analogies that provide nonthreatening symbolic representations of the grief experience (e.g., likening grief to battle fatigue, amputation, and internal wounds that require hospitalization).
- Aid expression of thoughts and feelings using open-ended inquiries with language that is compatible with their perception of the male role (e.g., inquire about "thoughts," "reactions," or "responses," as opposed to "feelings," unless he uses "feeling" words).
- Understand and work with the grieving process (e.g., recognize the protective function of shock and numbness, help explore strategies for venting anger, help men adjust to the changed environment by teaching new skills following the death of a partner, and help them find new meaningful activities).
- Facilitate action (e.g., taking an active, problem-solving approach in individual and group sessions; recommending self-help or other pertinent literature; looking through photo albums, reading or keeping a journal; putting together a memory book; building a coffin or constructing an urn; adopting advocacy roles; providing testimonies).
- Bolster social support, contact, and activity (e.g., one-to-one support from other widowers, education of family members about the importance of social support as a buffer against the harmful impact of bereavement for older men).
- Attend to practical needs (e.g., concerns about finances, funeral arrangements, unfinished business, or legal planning).
- Encourage continuity to prevent any other major changes that may introduce new losses (e.g., moves).

- Inquire about substances used to mask grief and discuss the potentially damaging effects of alcohol and drugs.
- Encourage physical activity (e.g., aerobic exercise as an outlet for anger and aggression and for treatment of depression, organized sports to enhance companionship and support).

Source: B. J. Kramer, Grief and Bereavement in Older Men, *Geriatric Care Management Journal* 10 (2000): 17–23.

framework for elders to accept painful events as part of the rhythm of life" (McInnis-Dittrich 2002:258). As chapters 1 and 3 point out, the importance of spirituality and religion varies widely among different ethnic groups. For example, the African American community has a long history of religious traditions, with the church often central to both religious and secular social supports (Levin and Taylor 1997; Stolley and Koenig 1997). Spirituality or religious beliefs should be considered when assessing and treating culturally diverse groups of elders, or any elders to whom spirituality or religion is important (Idler 2002; Koenig and Brooks 2002; Koenig, McCullough, and Larson 2001; Krause 2003; Walsh et al. 2002). Spiritual beliefs underlie some bereaved elders' search for meaning and determine how they view their relationship with the deceased, explain the death, and experience hope for the future (Goldsworthy and Coyle 1999). One study, for example, found that gay male caregivers with a strong sense of spirituality were better able to enter into and work through their grief (Richards, Acree, and Folkman 1999). Their spirituality, which remained with them after their partner's death, shortened their healing and made it more peaceful. The documented relationships between spirituality and well-being suggest that clinicians and other professionals would do well to use spiritual supports when counseling bereaved older adults.

Assessment tools such as the spiritual genogram and time line visually depict a person's spiritual and/or religious upbringing and belief systems (McInnis-Dittrich 2002). A spiritual genogram is an adaptation of the family genogram; it can be used to map the evolution of a person's familial, religious, or spiritual identification, which may affect his or her current belief systems and experiences. The spiritual time line, which is a linear depiction of a person's spiritual development, may help elders ponder spiritual and religious beliefs that inform their current experience with loss or thoughts about facing their own mortality (Bullis

1996). A person's spiritual history may also be assessed with Puchalski's (2000) FICA assessment tool. The questions used to guide the interview using the FICA acronym are as follows:

F: *Faith or beliefs* (Do you consider yourself a religious or spiritual person? What is your faith? Which of your activities give meaning to your life?)

I: *Importance and influence* (How does your faith influence how you take care of yourself? How do your beliefs influence your current experience? Are your faith and beliefs important to your life?)

C: *Community* (Do you belong to a religious or spiritual community? Does it support you? How? Is there a person or group of people who are really important to you?)

A: *Address* (How would you like other care providers and me to address these issues in working with you?)

These assessment tools may lead to discussions that help the human service professional understand needs and potential interventions and may help older people identify unfinished business and explore their thoughts, expectations, and beliefs about grief, death, dying, and afterlife.

Service professionals may want to work closely with religious and spiritual leaders in churches, synagogues, mosques, temples, and other communities who can provide additional sources of support for bereaved older adults or who might know elders in need of professional assistance. One pastoral care intervention related to grief was found to reduce depression scores of continuing care retirement community residents (Baker 2000). The faith community is well positioned to refer people with mental health problems, including complicated bereavement, if they are aware of the available resources (Brat 2001).

Interventions for Specific Losses
Spousal/Partner Bereavement

In reviewing the empirical literature on spousal bereavement, Lund (1989a) concluded that although bereavement is a stressful process, many spouses are quite resilient and do not want or need intervention services. The most difficult adjustments are loneliness and learning the tasks associated with daily living (e.g., skills previously carried out by one's partner).

Interventions with widows and widowers include brief dynamic psychotherapy or counseling; mutual-aid support groups; crisis intervention at the individual, family, or group level; and peer-counseling programs (for reviews, see Kato and Mann 1999; Potocky 1993; Schut et al. 2001). Other interventions are

- Reminiscence to help widows and widowers share their memories.
- Healing rituals to facilitate expressions of continuity, transition, or reconciliation (for further description, see chapter 9 and Doka 2002c).
- Financial and life-skills planning to prepare for the future. (Chinen and Berg-Cross 1994)

Some evidence suggests that mutual support programs, such as Widow-to-Widow, have therapeutic effects, particularly for those with much distress (Lieberman and Videka-Sherman 1986; Vachon et al. 1980). Although supportive interventions such as support groups may help relieve a widowed person's profound loneliness (Lund, Caserta, and Dimond 1993), some evaluative studies report no difference between treatment and control groups, as well as sometimes potentially harmful effects (Schut et al. 2001). Interventions that are merely described in the literature (e.g., the prevention intervention program detailed by Raveis 1999) and those that have demonstrated potential therapeutic effects but whose design precludes valid scientific evaluation (e.g., Constantino, Sekula, and Rubinstein 2001; Marmar et al. 1988; Segal et al. 1999; Stewart et al. 2001) need to be tested.

Suicide

Elders who attempt suicide are usually experiencing hopelessness, despair, and suffering, and many are driven to do so from the many losses they have already endured. Their suicide makes the bereavement of the surviving family members even more difficult. Thus, preventing suicide is the most important goal in working with at-risk elders. Box 13.3 lists factors for assessing suicide risk in older persons.

COLLABORATION WITH PRIMARY CARE PHYSICIANS

The majority of older persons who commit suicide, many of whom have recently been bereaved, saw their health care providers a few months before their suicide, and more than 33 percent, within a week of their death (Alexopoulos et al. 1999). Educating primary care physicians about risk factors has shown some promise in preventing suicide by ensuring that depression is assessed and treated (Conwell 1997). Social service professionals should thus work with physicians and other health care providers to ensure adequate assessment, referral, prevention, and treatment of depression and suicide.

RESTRICTING AVAILABILITY TO LETHAL MEANS

Health care and social service providers should ask about the older person's access to weapons and then try to negotiate their removal from the house.

Box 13.3 Suicide Assessment

RISK FACTORS

1. Demographic Factors
   a. Gender. Eighty-four percent of all later-life suicides are committed by men (Surgeon General 2003). Women make more attempts but are less successful than men. They also tend to display indirect life-threatening behavior and use more passive forms of suicide (Osgood, Brant, and Lipman 1989).
   b. Ethnicity and age. Suicide rates are highest among white men over age eighty-five (National Institute of Mental Health 2003).
2. Ego-Weakening Factors (Richman 1996) / Stressful Life Events (Conwell 1997)
   a. Chronic physical illness and pain (Richman 1996). Illnesses associated with suicide include cancers, diseases of the central nervous system, peptic ulcers, cardiopulmonary complications, rheumatoid arthritis, urogenital disease (Conwell 1997), congestive heart failure, chronic obstructive lung disease, and seizure disorders (Juurlink et al. 2004).
   b. Depression, anxiety, or other affective disorders (Conwell, Duberstein, and Caine 2002; Juurlink et al. 2004).
3. Social Factors (Waern, Rubenwotz, and Wihelmson 2003)
   a. Isolation (e.g., limited contact with others, living alone).
   b. Alienation (e.g., having few or no friends).
4. Dynamic Factors
   a. Loss, bereavement, and complicated grief (Szanto et al. 1997).
   b. Alcoholism and drug abuse (Waern 2003).
   c. History of suicidal behavior in the self and in family members (Conwell 1997; Richman 1996).
5. Clinical Factors and Communication (Richman 1996)
   a. Giving away prized possessions.
   b. Verbal and nonverbal expressions of hopelessness, despair, and suicidal intent.
   c. Hints of a plan (e.g., storing up medication or buying a gun, verbal statements that others will not have to worry about him or her for long).
6. Family Factors (Waern et al. 2003)
   a. Family conflict
   b. Severe disturbances in response to separation and loss.
   c. Role and behavior disturbances.

The quantities and potential toxicities of prescribed medications, other drugs, and alcohol that may be used in an overdose should be determined as well (Conwell 1997).

IDENTIFICATION AND ASSESSMENT OF DEPRESSION

The assessment and treatment of depression in later life is critical, given the high incidence of depressive and organic disorders in elders who attempt suicide (Osvath, Fekete, and Voeroes 2002). Chapter 7 gave the criteria of the *Diagnostic and Statistical Manual of Mental Disorders* (DSM-IV-TR; American Psychiatric Association 2000) for a major depressive episode. A growing body of research has pointed to differences in older adults' presentation of symptoms (for a review, see Caine et al. 1994). They include more prominent somatic symptoms, fewer ideational symptoms (e.g., guilt), and a lower prevalence of dysphoria. Examples of commonly used assessment tools for evaluating late-life depression can be found in Karel et al. (2002).

TREATMENT OF DEPRESSION IN LATER LIFE

The most promising approach in working with suicidal individuals with depressive disorders is to treat the depression aggressively (Kasl-Godley, Gatz, and Fiske 1998:215): "Major depression, as opposed to uncomplicated grief, is a serious disorder that warrants clinical attention. To fail to treat major depressive episodes is to expose individuals to unnecessarily prolonged suffering, dysfunction, and despair" (Zisook and Schuchter 2001:785). Unfortunately, many depressions are never detected and treated. One study investigating the incidence and treatment of depression in 543 older suicide completers revealed that 87 percent received no treatment for their depression; that those who were treated were given medications that were lethal in overdose (e.g., tricyclics), as opposed to safer serotonin reuptake inhibitors; and that those seeing their general practitioner were less likely to be treated with antidepressants than were those seeing a psychiatrist (Duckworth and McBride 1996).

Zisook and Schuchter (2001) provide an excellent review and critique of interventions for treating major depression associated with bereavement. Some of the best validated approaches are mutual support interventions, group work, psychotherapy, guided mourning, and cognitive-behavioral approaches. Zisook and Schucter reported on the most efficacious medications for treating late-life depression and recommended an integrative treatment "that maximizes support, education, cognitive and interpersonal techniques, psychodynamic principles, grief-specific strategies, bright light, exercise, and cutting edge medication management" to maximize treatment success (2001:791).

SUPPORTIVE SERVICES

A pilot test of telephone assessment and support services helped reduce suicide risk in older adults. The users of a telephone help line and emergency response service had lower rates of suicide deaths than nonusers did (De-Leo, Buona, and Dwyer 2002). Persons who were targeted as being at increased risk of suicide and received a telephone intervention had better social contacts, fewer depressive symptoms, and fewer unmet needs at an eight-month observation (Morrow-Howell, Becker- Kemppainen, and Judy 1998). Hinrichsen observed that "family/ interpersonal factors are the best longitudinal predictors of recovery and relapse from depression as well as of subsequent suicide attempt[s]" and proposed inter-personal psychotherapy as a useful form of treatment (1995:991).

Strategies for assessing and targeting culturally competent interventions for treating depression and suicide in later life need to be developed and evaluated, given the high percentage of completed suicides of ethnic minorities in some areas of the country. For example, older Cuban American males in Florida had a rate of suicide 1.67 times higher that of older non-Cuban Americans in that state (Llorente et al. 1996). A culturally modified version of rational emotive behavior therapy (REBT) was used with a suicidal older African American male to reduce depressive symptoms and suicide risk (Sapp, McNeely, and Torres 1998). The adapted model emphasizes African American men's preferred communication styles, such as active-direct counseling, which involves "challenging clients, as opposed to approaches that exclusively stress empathic listening," and recognizing external oppressive barriers (e.g., discrimination and racism). Although the authors recommend REBT as a culturally appropriate end-of-life intervention for African American and Latino elders who usually score higher on external locus of control, its effectiveness with bereaved elders of color should be formally tested.

Dementia

Elders with dementia have multiple losses that affect all domains of life. Compared with the large body of literature addressing the impacts of dementia on family caregivers, surprisingly little has been said about the predictors of well-being in persons with dementia and interventions for their grief or grief resurgence. Support groups for newly diagnosed persons with Alzheimer's disease are one way of addressing their grief and loss, but there is no empirical evidence documenting their utility (Yale 1989). Individual and group validation therapy is suggested as a way to help older adults with dementia resolve earlier conflicts before their death. Validation principles indicate that persons late in life "return to the past to heal themselves" and that the bottled-up and painful feelings that surface during this process are relieved when validated by compassionate others (Feil 1999:595). Feil (1993, 1999) provides a full description of validation techniques for four phases of grief resolution and for group validation.

Family Caregiving in Later Life

The losses of family members caring for older adults with chronic impairments and the fluctuations in their grief over time have been extensively documented and were discussed in chapter 11 (Bass, Bowman, and Noelker 1991; Farran et al. 1991; Loos and Bowd 1997; Meuser and Marwit 2001; Mullan 1992; Ponder and Pomeroy 1996; Rudd, Viney, and Preston 1999; Walker et al. 1994a). Interventions for caregivers have been oriented to reducing stress, burden, and depression and increasing self-efficacy through support groups (Kaasalainen, Craig, and Wells 2000; Toseland and Rossiter 1989, Toseland, Rossiter, and Labrecque 1989), respite care (Zarit et al. 1998), stress management techniques (Ducharme and Trudeau 2002; Horton-Deutsch et al. 2002), home environment interventions (Gitlin et al. 2001), and psychoeducational (Gallagher-Thompson et al. 2000; Stolley, Reed, and Buckwalter 2002; Walker et al. 1994b) and educational approaches (Kuhn and Mendes-de-Leon 2001).

Practical recommendations for working with grieving caregivers are providing information (e.g., about the disease process, community resources, and the grief process), supporting the expression of feelings, encouraging communication with others (e.g., other family members and the care recipient), and seeking support (Walker and Pomeroy 1996). Using Rando's (1984) three-phase grief process model of anticipatory grief, Liken and Collins (1993) made recommendations for facilitating pre- and postdeath grief for family caregivers of elders with dementia. Before death, interventions emphasize validating the caregivers' efforts, understanding the difficulty of acknowledging the disease, identifying future sources of support, providing information about the disease when they are ready ("avoidance phase"), helping with intense feelings, providing information about the grief process, reminiscing, providing respite resources, and encouraging replenishment activities ("confrontation phase"). After death, interventions emphasize being available to talk, maintaining contact, and providing information about the grief process ("avoidance phase"), inviting the caregivers to talk about their relative, encouraging the use of other supports, sharing information about the grieving process, linking the caregivers with bereavement supports, encouraging self-care ("confrontation phase"), allowing the caregivers to tell their story, developing ways to keep memories alive, helping anticipate difficult times (e.g., holidays), identifying ways to gain perspective on their experience (e.g., journal writing), and being alert to signs of depression ("reestablishment phase") (Liken and Collins 1993:23, 25).

In addition to the growing number of elders caring for elders, more and more grandparents are taking over the care of their grandchildren (Fuller-Thomson, Minkler, and Driver 1997; Szinovacz, DeViney, and Atkinson 1999). The most common reasons that grandparents become their grandchildren's primary care-givers are the children's parents' substance abuse (Joslin and Brouard 1995; Minkler and Roe 1993); child abuse, neglect, or abandonment (Jendrek 1994); incarceration (Dressel and Barnhill 1994); divorce (Cherlin and Furstenberg 1986); AIDS (Burnette 1997; Joslin and Brouard 1995); and the parents' death (Jendrek 1994). Culturally congruent practical interventions and financial pol-icies to support these elders and their grandchildren and attend to their losses need to be developed and tested.

Life Transitions
RETIREMENT

Although acknowledged as a major life transition for many older adults, the gerontological literature has not discussed the grief associated with retirement-related losses. Many adults regard retirement as an exciting transition, one that is planned for and eagerly anticipated. For others, though, retirement may pre-cipitate or be accompanied by losses. For example, many family caregivers are forced to retire from jobs that they enjoy or need for income in order to provide care. They may lose social connections with others. If their sense of self is closely tied to their employment, they may feel a loss of identity. Forced retirements are particularly difficult, because older adults have no control over a decision that directly affects their retirement income and lifestyle. The literature tends to concentrate on planning retirement and smoothing the transition, but it does not describe or evaluate specific interventions for postretirement difficulties (Sterns and Gray 1999; Tinsley and Bigler 2002).

RELOCATION

Declining health and subsequent relocation may lead to multiple disruptions and "be accompanied by grieving and a feeling of powerlessness" (Choi 1996:340). Many older adults view being placed in a nursing home as a death sentence and have much higher rates of depression than do noninstitutionalized elders (Nelson 2001). Institutionalization often "engenders a great sense of loss and grief" in family members that is rarely acknowledged and addressed during the transition (Greenfield 1984:15). Nursing homes have very few grief and bereavement ser-vices (Murphy, Hanarahan, and Luchins 1997; Research Dissemination Core

2002). Although few publications address clinical interventions for nursing home residents and their family members, Drysdale, Nelson, and Wineman (1993) discuss a four-session supportive-educational family group program for relatives of institutionalized residents. Several sessions offer opportunities for the participants to express their feelings. This program has not been formally evaluated, however. Remnet (1989) described practical strategies that long-term care facility administrators and staff may use to ease residents' relocation. Examples are learning about the new residents, being aware of factors that precipitated the move, individualizing the admission process, allowing for incremental moves, encouraging personalization of space (e.g., furniture, pictures), and respecting personal space and privacy. Interventions for grief associated with transitions in living arrangements, such as counseling, group interventions, and reminiscence, should be tested to determine whether they minimize the grief and distress associated with relocation.

Grief and Approaching Death

Anticipatory mourning and grief are fundamental to the end of life (Corr and Corr 2000; Meagher and Quinn 2000). Personal characteristics (e.g., gender, mental health, fears of death), quality of interpersonal communication and relationships, socioeconomic and environmental factors (e.g., financial resources, access to medical care), and specific illness characteristics all influence how an older person may respond to approaching death (Rando 1984).

The primary needs commonly are (1) preserving a sense of self (e.g., affirming one's identity and value); (2) participating in decisions about one's own life; (3) being reassured that one's life has value (e.g. demonstrating respect, maximizing quality of life); and (4) receiving appropriate and adequate health care. Many deaths in later life result from acute, unpredictable, and sudden crises associated with advanced chronic disease that give older adults little time to say good-bye to their families. Deaths that occur in acute care settings such as intensive care units may plunge individuals and their families into crisis, characterized by shock and confusion (Holmes-Garrett 1989). These deaths are often accompanied by complex technological interventions that may prolong the patient's suffering and inhibit communication, making it especially difficult for family members.

Elders with chronic illness enrolled in hospice or other palliative care programs receive interdisciplinary care that attends to their psychological, emotional, spiritual, and physical needs; minimizes suffering; and more routinely addresses issues of grief and bereavement. Hospice's bereavement services, such as grief education, support groups, and individual counseling, are offered to family members as well. In addition to these more traditional forms of intervention, music therapy may help older patients and families in hospice care to cope with grief, pain and anxiety, disorientation, lack of meaning, and hopelessness (Hilliard 2001b; West 1994).

Family members caring for elders with advanced chronic disease must make critical medical decisions and carry out most treatment recommendations at the end of life (Hauser and Kramer 2004). Indeed, 96 percent of primary caregivers of people at the end of life are family members (Emanuel et al. 1999). Family members facing end-of-life decisions or the impending death of an older family member may have emotional and psychological issues as well as physical, social, and financial costs. Human service professionals must determine the family's structure, roles, relationships, cultural values and beliefs, strengths, emotional responses, understanding of illness, and socioeconomic factors and resources in order to identify the most pressing needs and most appropriate interventions (for a detailed discussion of assessment domains, see Blacker and Jordan 2004).

The most common interventions that social workers and other human service professionals use to support elders and their family members at the end of life are referrals for resources and planning for care needs, family conferencing, and other team interventions to prepare families for caregiving responsibilities; and family counseling and therapy to provide support and to adapt to their changing roles (Taylor-Brown et al. 2001). Although these interventions, particularly as they might affect grief, have not been evaluated, some evidence suggests the importance of professional communication. One study found bereavement outcomes were significantly influenced by the communication and quality of information offered to family members while the elder was still living (Main 2000). Bereavement therapists recommend open communication among family members, although cultural variations in belief systems that do not permit discussion or awareness of death should be recognized (Ersek et al. 1998).

Communication often centers on important decisions regarding the elder's care, which may be influenced by the family members' anticipatory mourning. For example, those who have been involved in the care may already have grieved and thus be more prepared for the death than those geographically far away who arrive only when the older person is close to death. Long-term or current family conflicts make communication more difficult (Kramer and Pierre 2003). Families facing difficult decisions regarding the withdrawal of life supports may feel guilty and need to be supported. They should be encouraged to talk about the elder's preferences; resolve conflicts; understand the pros, cons, and likely outcomes of these decisions; and provide emotional support and comfort (Keenan et al. 2000; Prendergast and Puntillo 2002).

Interventions may be required to address anticipatory grief and to help family members with "unfinished business with the dying patient" (Rando 1984:356). Anticipatory and current losses should be discussed with both the elder and his or her family members. Clinical approaches to the anticipatory mourning of family members of persons near the end of life are detailed extensively in Rando 2000. Examples are providing appropriate information, helping families achieve homeostatic balance following changes in roles, normalizing grief responses, engaging the family in a life review, helping plan for the future, and facilitating communication. Guided imagery is another method for addressing anticipatory grief. Although the effectiveness of guided imagery with the bereaved has not been evaluated, earlier research suggests that guided imagery may help dying elders and their families work through their grief, stimulate communication, envision future events that might trigger pleasant memories, reduce stress and pain, relieve depression, and increase a sense of control (for a review of the literature, see Turkoski and Lance 1996). Guided imagery should be used carefully and not without training in assessment and implementation methods.

Summary

This chapter presented developmentally congruent interventions used with grieving elders, such as reminiscence, life review, group work, counseling, and spiritually attentive interventions, although only a few have been systematically evaluated in treatment outcome studies. Guided mourning counseling approaches and mutual support programs (e.g., Widow-to-Widow Program) appear to have the most extensive empirical support for older persons with great distress and complicated grief. Interventions for bereaved spouses or partners have received the most empirical attention. Although we presented practice principles and recommended strategies for persons with grief associated with dementia, family caregiving, major life transitions (e.g., retirement, relocation), acute and long-term care, and grief resurgence, we do not have enough evidence to name the most efficacious interventions.

Interventions for several other forms of grief and loss reported in later life are strikingly absent. For example, is there a link between elder abuse and grief? If so, what are the best interventions for this social problem? How should we help elders with losses and grief associated with divorce and family discord or conflict? What innovative strategies should we use for older grandparent caregivers who grieve the plight of their children who have drug addictions or who are incarcerated, while simultaneously coping with their own health problems and the care of their grandchildren? What interventions would be most effective for older immigrants grieving for their lost home (Casado and Leung 2001)? Some elders with strong attachments to their companion animals (Sable 1995) and those who are forced to have their pet euthanized may grieve more deeply following their pet's death than they do after the deaths of other friends or relatives (Meyers 2002; Schmall and Pratt 1986). Yet there is little guidance in the literature regarding optimal strategies to address elders' pet bereavement.

With the exception of the descriptive study by Sapp, McNeely, and Torres (1998), the literature identifies no aging specific interventions for grieving persons of color. Many of the theories on which interventions are based may not be relevant to persons of color. For example, Erikson's theory and developmental crisis of integrity versus despair in later life may not pertain to older African Americans or other ethnic groups who, as a result of discrimination and racism, are less likely to believe that they had control over their earlier lives or who are preoccupied with daily survival (Sapp, McNeely, and Torres 1998). The poor and persons of color are less likely to avail themselves of services such as hospice that would offer them interdisciplinary palliative care and bereavement support for family members (Jackson et al. 2000). Alternative and innovative interventions in care delivery are needed to allow persons of color greater access to bereavement support.

14

Professional Self-Awareness and Self-Care

THIS TEXT has examined a range of losses experienced across the life span and ways in which human service and health care professionals may use developmental and cultural considerations in their approaches to helping clients of all ages in their grieving. Caring professionals may be deeply moved and challenged by the pain they experience through their empathy, and suppressed feelings about their own losses and fears of loss may emerge. In addition, social work practitioners often face many organizational and institutional demands and barriers, so they need self-awareness and self-care strategies both to help their clients and to enable themselves to continue to do this highly demanding work. This chapter describes some the satisfactions and challenges of working with the bereaved and suggests organizational and personal self-care strategies.

The Gifts and Challenges of Working with the Bereaved

Professionals who work with the dying and the bereaved commonly report feeling privileged and finding meaning and satisfaction in their work (Becvar 2003). Social workers learn from the bereaved about the inescapable reality of loss and also how to grapple with existential questions of meaning as they accompany their clients through this process (Calhoun and Tedeschi 2001). One bereavement counselor summarized professional rewards and growth as follows:

> We have the satisfaction of doing meaningful work; we see clients reclaim themselves and their lives; we gain wisdom; and we have endless opportunities to learn about the deeper recesses of the human heart, our own included. Many of us become especially sensitive to the fleeting nature and preciousness of life, and of how things are always in transition. The insight that change is the norm, that nothing ever stays the same, can enhance our ability to savor the sweet moments in our own lives ("This is wonderful, and it is temporary") as well as to withstand

the periods of loss and inner desolation that we inevitably encounter ("This is horrible, and it is also temporary"). This heightened awareness and enlarged perspective accompany one's ongoing development as a psychotherapist. (Gamble 2002:347)

The potential gifts inherent in working with those of all ages enduring profound or traumatic losses are nonetheless accompanied by numerous challenges. Furthermore, the multiple losses, particularly if traumatic or sudden, that practitioners encounter in various professional contexts may profoundly influence and test their beliefs and assumptions about the world (Wilson and Lindy 1994). It is especially difficult for social work professionals to encounter painful, emotionally wrenching experiences when they feel inadequately prepared to respond effectively, and this seems to be the norm (Leff, Chan, and Walizer 1991). Several studies have documented human service professionals' inadequate bereavement training. Courses on the broad topic of death education in social work programs are general electives taken by fewer than 25 percent of students (Dickinson, Sumner, and Frederick 1992). In addition, 22 percent of hospice social workers reported that they had had no prior training or courses on grief issues (Kovacs and Bronstein 1999). On average, in their final year of training, social work graduate students feel only "a little" or "somewhat" prepared to respond to clients and families who are grieving or dying (Kramer 1998). Only 31 percent of 390 respondents in a national survey of health care social workers agreed that the grief, loss, and death content of their social work programs adequately prepared them for postgraduate employment (Csikai and Raymer 2002). The content available to faculty and students in the most commonly used social work textbooks also does not cover current theories of grief or evidence-based interventions for multiple forms of loss (Kramer, Pacourek, and Hovland-Scafe 2003). It is our hope that this textbook will provide a valuable resource to begin remedying these gaps in training and educational tools. Box 14.1 describes some of the challenges most frequently associated with professionals' exposure to loss and grief.

Regularly confronting particular forms of loss places some practitioners at greater risk of professional distress. For example, service providers working with families of persons who have committed suicide often have traumatic and complicated grief. This may emerge as self-doubt and uncertainty, anxiety at work, and avoidance of other clients perceived as being at risk of suicide (Fox and Cooper 1998; Linke, Wojciak, and Day 2000; Valente and Saunders 2002). The grief of service providers working with persons with HIV/AIDS (Oliver and Dykeman 2003) and in hospice and palliative care (Vachon 2000) is well

Box 14.1 Common Challenges for Professionals Working with the Bereaved

- Experiencing overload from exposure to multiple loss when working continually with those who have experienced traumatic events or with those who die.
- Helping someone integrate a loss that resembles a personal or dreaded experience of our own.
- Addressing difficult processes of transference and countertransference, when the client reacts unexpectedly toward us, or we to the client because of unacknowledged emotions.
- Helping someone with a grief that is so far outside our own experience that it seems incomprehensible to us or is emotionally difficult to bear.
- Addressing ethical dilemmas that surface in care of the dying and the bereaved.
- Addressing family conflicts related to differential grief responses.
- Experiencing feelings of inadequacy when we cannot help alleviate suffering.

Source: R. Bright, *Grief and Powerlessness: Helping People Regain Control of Their Lives* (London: Kingsley, 1996), 165–67.

documented. Other related occupational hazards associated with bereavement care are chronic bereavement, vicarious traumatization, compassion fatigue, and burnout.

Chronic bereavement refers to multiple losses and "includes the effects of chronic anticipatory, and unresolved grief, as well as the compounding effects of experiencing several episodes of grief concurrently" (Cho and Cassidy 1994:275). It is most often seen in professionals who work directly with the dying and their family members and who thus may be confronting loss more often than they would in other service settings. End-of-life care professionals often experience loss as ongoing and pervasive. While meeting the emotionally intense needs of the dying and their families with anticipatory grief, these professionals often develop personally meaningful relationships, which result in incontrovertible losses following the patient's death (Larson 2000). Chronic bereavement also is difficult for service providers when it is disenfranchised (Kaplan 2000). This may happen when their work environments fail to recognize, normalize, accept, or acknowledge their bereavement response. When confronted with many losses in a short period of time, practitioners may not have an opportunity to process their own grief adequately. If this is combined with the organization's and the practitioner's lack of awareness and acknowledgment of grief, it may make it impossible for him or her to continue in this line of work. For example, a student enrolled in my (Kramer) grief course said that she signed up for the class because she was completely overwhelmed by her field placement in a hospital where she had been working with dying children. The many deaths in a short period of time, combined with the lack of institutional supports to acknowledge and facilitate her grief, made it difficult for her to function. She needed much self-reflection, education about grief, opportunities to express her grief through therapeutic ritual, and support from her field supervisor to work effectively. Unfortunately, such supports are not always available to practitioners who face heavy workloads and service cutbacks.

Compassion fatigue describes the convergence of secondary traumatic stress and cumulative stress or burnout, which is most prevalent among professionals, family members, and associates of trauma survivors (Figley 1995, 2002; Gentry, Baranowsky, and Dunning 2002). Persons with previous exposure to personal trauma are more vulnerable to compassion fatigue (Solomon 1990), which applies to human service workers, the majority of whom have had early-life traumas and problems with their family of origin (e.g., child abuse, sexual assault, domestic violence, alcohol and drug problems) that influenced their career choice (Black, Jeffreys, and Hartley 1993; Russel et al. 1993; Sellers and Hunter, in press). The following symptoms of compassion fatigue are similar to those of primary traumatic stress disorder, with the exception that the traumatizing event is not experienced directly by those emotionally affected by the trauma (Figley 1995, 2002):

1. *Cognitive* (e.g., lack of concentration, apathy, disorientation, preoccupation with trauma).
2. *Emotional* (e.g., powerlessness, anxiety, guilt, anger, numbness, fear, sadness).
3. *Behavioral* (e.g., impatience, irritability, withdrawal, sleep disturbance, nightmares, hypervigilance).
4. *Spiritual* (e.g., questioning the meaning of life, loss of purpose, pervasive hopelessness, loss of faith).

5. *Personal relations* (e.g., mistrust, decreased intimacy, overprotection, intolerance, increased interpersonal conflicts).
6. *Somatic* (e.g., shock, sweating, rapid heartbeat, breathing difficulties, dizziness, greater number and intensity of medical maladies).
7. *Work performance* (e.g., low morale, low motivation, avoidance of tasks, staff conflicts, irritability, obsession about details). (Unpublished study by Pelkowitz 1997, as cited in Figley 2002)

Programs to help professionals feel more empowered in their professional and personal lives treat the deleterious effects of compassion fatigue. An example is the Accelerated Recovery Program (ARP), designed to reduce the intensity, frequency, and duration of symptoms in professionals who encounter trauma in their work (Gentry, Baranowsky, and Dunning 2002). Its components are

• Individualized assessment.
• Anxiety management (i.e., participants are taught anxiety and stress reduction strategies).
• Narratives (i.e., telling "the story").
• Exposure or resolution of secondary traumatic stress (i.e., using "exposure" methods common to treatment of PTSD).
• Cognitive restructuring (i.e., helping participants examine their beliefs, change automatic thoughts, and facilitate self-care).
• PATHWAYS (i.e., an aftercare component that focuses on a sense of personal commitment to wellness). (Gentry, Baranowsky, and Dunning 2002:130–31)

Preliminary testing suggests that this model may reduce compassion fatigue symptoms and enhance empowerment (Gentry, Baranowsky, and Dunning 2002). In general, balance, boundaries, organizational support, and self-care are critical to the prevention of compassion fatigue (Cerney 1995; Yassen 1995).

Vicarious traumatization (VT) is defined as "the negative transformation in a helper's inner experience that takes place as a result of deep empathic engagement with traumatized clients coupled with a sense of professional responsibility to help" (Saakvitne et al. 2000, as cited in Gamble 2002:349–50). Many of the losses reviewed in this text that are commonly confronted by social workers (e.g., child abuse, domestic violence, homicide, assault, suicide, gang violence) put them at risk for VT. Table 14.1 lists professional self-care considerations for VT related awareness, balance, and connection to others, as proposed by Gamble (2002).

TABLE 14.1
Vicarious Traumatization: Self-Care Approaches

AWARENESS

Recognize signs of vicarious traumatization.

Cultivate mindfulness in daily activities, thoughts, and feelings rather than distracting yourself or tuning out.

Discuss changes noticed by others.

Avoid substances that numb or alter awareness.

Make efforts to slow the pace of your activities.

Consider meditation or other forms of contemplation.

BALANCE

Modify work experiences to reduce exposure to trauma in your caseload.

Develop greater variety in clinical roles.

Be more aware of restoration and growth themes in clients' experiences.

Set limits on availability and create realistic boundaries for therapeutic work (i.e., be alert to rescue tendencies).

Set realistic expectations and develop priorities for balancing your personal and professional lives.

CONNECTION

Identify and cultivate a relationship with a confidant to address your work experiences and responses.

Consider holding workplace weekly meetings to discuss your experiences of VT and countertransference.

Consider joining a peer support group outside work.

Implement agency policies to support peer consultation.

Source: Based on S. J. Gamble, Self-Care for Bereavement Counselors, in *Helping Bereaved Children: A Handbook for Practitioners,* edited by N. B. Webb (New York: Guilford Press, 2002), 355–57.

Burnout refers to physical, emotional, and psychological exhaustion accompanied by a sense of demoralization and diminished caring, creativity, and personal accomplishment (Iacovides, Fountoulakis, and Kaprinis 2003; Larson 2000; Maslach 1982). It is a strong predictor of job turnover for social service and mental health providers (Mor Barak, Nissly, and Levin 2001). Determinants of burnout include

1. *Personal* (e.g., psychological well-being at time of hiring and ways of coping; Koeske and Kirk 1995; Poulin and Walter 1993).

2. *Organizational* (e.g., workload, role conflict, role ambiguity, wages, supervisory supports; Barber and Iwai 1996; Poulin and Walter 1993; Siefert, Jayaratne, and Chess 1991).

3. *Client* factors (e.g., number of deaths experienced, extent of trauma exposure; Baird and Jenkins 2003; Mueller 1995; Poulin and Walter 1993).

Next we describe the need for self-awareness and review individual and organizational strategies to prevent, alleviate, and address burnout and the challenges facing professionals who work with the bereaved. (A more detailed discussion of burnout prevention and self-care strategies may be found in Baker 2003; Morrissette 2001; Skovholt 2001.)

Self-Awareness

As human service professionals, we must be mindful of our own personal losses and grief: "Only when we are comfortable grieving our own losses and confronting our closeness and distance from potential loss can we help our clients with the overwhelming grief in their own lives" (Katz and Genevay 2002:328–29).

Most professional codes of ethics require practitioners to recognize personal conflicts, problems, and emotional needs and how they may influence their work with clients (Corey, Corey, and Callanan 2003). The social work profession has long acknowledged the need for disciplined awareness in the "conscious use of self" and personal qualities as potential resources in helping relationships (Compton and Galaway 1999; Imre 1982, Miley, O'Melia, and DuBois 2004). Personal experiences and the extent to which we have integrated them may hurt or help our practice with clients.

Personal Loss, Beliefs, and Experience with Grief

Social workers and other human service professionals bring with them their own history of loss and personal way of grieving that "can either enhance the therapeutic process or impede it" (Cook and Dworkin 1992:171). Many therapists have written about the ways that their intimate losses have influenced their personal and professional lives (Morrison 1996; Rappaport 2000). Indeed, most social workers who work with the dying, in child welfare, in domestic violence, and many other specific contexts associated with grief, are drawn to do so because of their personal experiences with similar losses (Black, Jeffreys, and Hartley 1993; Kovacs and Bronstein 1999; Sellers and Hunter, in press). Evidence suggests that professionals' personal exposure to loss also may influence where they direct their attention and how they intervene. For example, professionals who themselves have been bereaved by homicide focus more on the emotional pain of their clients' bereavement and offer more time to them than do those who have not had this experience (Hatton 2003).

The bereaved clients' grief often stimulates strong feelings about the practitioner's previous or feared losses (e.g., existential anxiety regarding one's own death or that of family members) (Lamers 2002; Worden 2002). An examination of their own history with loss thus would give professionals a better understanding of (1) the grief process; (2) things to say or not to say and resources available to the bereaved; (3) remaining conflicts or difficulties from earlier losses; and (4) an appraisal of the kinds of situations that they can address adequately (Worden 2002). Social workers should determine how they first learned about grief in their personal lives, the extent to which they as children were respected and included in grief rituals, what messages they were taught about grief, and how they grieve their own losses. Other questions that professionals might ask themselves are

- To what extent was my grief acknowledged, accepted, and expressed in my family of origin?
- Were certain responses not allowed, discouraged, or even punished?
- To what extent did my family acknowledge and allow themselves to grieve?
- How willing were they to use self-care strategies for their personal grief?

Unless practitioners answer these questions, it will be difficult for them to help their clients address feelings that they themselves avoid. Self-awareness should be an ongoing process of monitoring one's personal reactions to one's bereaved clients' losses and grief responses and asking the following questions:

How comfortable are you in the presence of intense emotion, such as anger or profound despair?

Which losses are most difficult for you to hear about?

How do you feel when you hear others describe the circumstances of their loss, especially if it contains elements of trauma or violence?

In what ways do your clients' losses remind you of your own losses or potential losses, and what do you do with these feelings?

To what extent are you grieving your own losses, and how are you processing your own grief?

How much have you thought about your own mortality and that of those you care about? (Cook and Dworkin 1992:170)

Countertransference and Grief

Human service and mental health professions influenced by psychoanalytic theory (Freud 1910; Gabbard 1999) acknowledge the importance of counter-transference. *Countertransference* is broadly defined as the personal reactions (i.e., emotions, feelings, statements, and behavior) elicited in the professional relationship, directed toward the client and stemming from the professional's previous experiences (Corey 2001). Although countertransference can be beneficial (e.g., feelings of warmth for one's own family members may be projected to the client), "destructive countertransference occurs when a counselor's own needs or unresolved personal conflicts become entangled in the therapeutic relationship, obstructing or destroying a sense of objectivity" (Corey, Corey, and Callanan 2003:49).

Various ethical issues surface when the professional's ability to work with bereaved clients is obstructed by the following countertransference reactions:

1. *Being overprotective,* by treating clients as fragile, trying to take their pain away or steering them away from painful material that you subconsciously wish to avoid.
2. *Treating clients benignly* and superficially to preclude expressions of anger that might be uncomfortable for you.
3. *Rejecting a client* and creating distance in certain situations.
4. *Needing constant reinforcement and approval,* responding in ways that will elicit approval rather than what is therapeutically indicated.
5. *Seeing yourself in your clients* to the extent that you lose objectivity, are unable to distinguish your own feelings, or react to traits in clients that you dislike in yourself. (Corey, Corey, and Callanan 2003:50–51)

In sum, disciplined self-awareness is necessary to ensure that we respond to the needs of our clients and not our own. Each of us is responsible for getting the help we need to process our own experiences and professional reactions.

Self-Care Strategies

Human service professionals who work with the bereaved require continuous self-reflection, awareness, and vigilance in order to prevent and address the many challenges faced in practice. Self-care is an individual process tailored to one's needs, beliefs, interests, lifestyle, and spirituality. Accordingly, we describe various strategies that practitioners can use to create their own plans for self-care.

We recommend further development and evaluation of personal and organizational strategies to prevent and treat chronic bereavement, compassion fatigue, vicarious traumatization, and burnout in various human service contexts.

Table 14.2 offers an assessment tool showing a variety of strategies relevant to five primary dimensions of self-care. Practitioners are encouraged to use it on their own or in consultation with coworkers, supervisors, or personal therapists to review the current state and adequacy of their own self-care.

Physical Self-Care

We all know that our physical and our psychological well-being are linked. Taking care of our physical bodies through exercise, good nutrition, medical attention, and other self-care practices keeps us limber, relieves physical aches and pains resulting from tension, minimizes physical discomfort, maintains health, and prevents disease (Rowe and Kahn 1998). Physical activity is an effective intervention for mental health problems, with strong evidence for a causal link between physical activity and a decrease in depression (Mutrie 2000), anxiety, stress, tension, and fatigue (Plante 1993). Exercise and massage release toxins that build up in our bodies when we are exposed to stress (Holmes 1993), and endorphins released during vigorous exercise often make us feel tranquil and peaceful. Professionals who are also balancing multiple caregiving roles (e.g., those of mother, social worker, volunteer, and daughter) may greatly benefit from the therapeutic effects of massage or other healing modalities. Other self-care techniques that affect the physical body and may have other benefits (e.g., psychological and emotional well-being) are stress reduction strategies like diaphragmatic breathing, progressive muscle relaxation, autogenic relaxation (i.e., repeating scripted phrases to reflect the sensations of a relaxed body), and yoga (Olson 1997).

Psychological Self-Care

The link among thoughts, perceptions, and cognitions and well-being also is well established and is the basis for efficacious cognitive therapies. Practitioners should take time to gain perspective and to see the bigger picture of their lives and to reflect on their thoughts, beliefs, and experiences in order to protect their psychological well-being. Students, therapists, and other helping practitioners can use personal therapy to enhance their self-awareness, self-understanding, and psychological growth related to loss or other needs, as well as to complement professional training (Holzman, Searight, and Hughes 1996; Pope and Tabachnick 1994). Keeping a journal, reflecting, minimizing stressors, expanding our interests, having realistic expectations of ourselves, and approaching life

TABLE 14.2
Personal Assessment of Self-Care Strategies

How frequently do you do the following? 1. Often 2. Sometimes 3. Rarely 4. Never.

Physical Self-Care	Psychological Self-Care	Emotional Self-Care	Spiritual Self-Care	Workplace or Professional Self-Care
Eat regularly	Take day trips or minivacations	Spend time with others whose company you enjoy	Make time for reflection	Take time to eat lunch
Eat healthily	Turn off the phones. Make time for reflection	Stay in contact with important people in your life	Spend time in nature	Take time to chat with coworkers
Exercise			Find a spiritual connection/ community	Make quiet time to complete tasks
Get regular medical care	Have your own counseling or therapy	Give yourself affirmations, praise yourself	Be open to inspiration	Identify rewarding projects or tasks
Get medical care when needed	Write in a journal	Love yourself	Cherish your hope and optimism	Set limits with clients and colleagues
Take time off when sick	Read literature that is unrelated to work	Reread favorite books, review favorite movies	Be aware of nonmaterial objects	Balance your caseload so no one day or part of day is "too much"
Get enough sleep	Do something at which you are not expert or in charge	Identify comforting activities, objects, people, relationships, and seek them out	Try at times not to be in charge or the expert	
Get massages				
Dance, swim, walk, run, play sports, or do other physical activities you enjoy	Attempt to minimize stress in your life		Be open to not knowing	Arrange your work space so it is comfortable and comforting
Allow yourself to be sexual with yourself or a partner	Listen to your thoughts, beliefs, attitudes, and feelings	Allow yourself to cry	Identify what is meaningful to you and its place in your life	Get regular supervision or consultation
Wear clothes you like	Let others know different aspects of you	Find things that make you laugh	Meditate	Negotiate for your needs (pay raise, benefits)
Take vacations	Engage your intelligence in a new area	Express your outrage in social action, letters, donations, marches	Pray	Have a peer support group
	Practice receiving from others	Play with children	Sing	Develop a nontrauma area of your work
	Be curious		Spend time with children	Strive for balance in work life and play
	Say "no" to extras		Experience "awe"	
			Contribute to causes in which you believe	
			Read inspirational literature	
			Be mindful of your interior	

Source: Adapted from K. W. Saakvitne, S. Gamble, L. A. Pearlman, and B. Tabor Lev, *Risking Connection: A Training Curriculum for Working with Survivors of Childhood Abuse* (Baltimore: Sidran Institute Press, 2000), 168–69. Used by permission of the publisher.

openly and with curiosity are strategies for psychological self-care (Pritchett and Lucas 1997).

Emotional Self-Care

Common emotional self-care strategies are cultivating a sense of self-compassion, expressing one's emotional responses to and grief associated with this work, forming relationships with those who provide nourishment and support, engaging in activities to replenish one's sense of humor, and affirming one's contributions. Activities and experiences that elicit pleasurable emotions such as love, gratitude, happiness, joy, and peace enrich and bring balance to life. In fact, increasing the number of pleasant events in one's life has been found to alleviate depression when combined with other cognitive behavioral strategies (Zarit and Zarit 1998).

Spiritual Self-Care

"When we see meaning in life, we are able to endure suffering" (Barnes 1994:20). Victor Frankl witnessed incomprehensible suffering in the Nazi death camps. In *Man's Search for Meaning* (1959), he concluded that people's ability to make or find meaning in their experience was the single most important determinant of their actual survival. As social workers confronting grief in our professional and personal lives, we can make or find meaning in the conditions that give rise to suffering.

In our experience, social workers and other human service professionals who work with those who are dying, bereaved, or traumatized and who do so with boundless energy and joy are those who have confronted their own mortality and find meaning and purpose in life. These remarkable practitioners find personal satisfaction in their work, view their own losses as an opportunity for personal growth, and approach their own suffering with reverence and gratitude:

> You may even come to feel mysteriously grateful toward your suffering, because it gives you such an opportunity of working through it and transforming it. Without it you would never have been able to discover that hidden in the nature and depths of suffering is a treasure of bliss. The times when you are suffering can be those when you are most open, and where you are extremely vulnerable can be where your greatest strength really lies. (Sogyal 1992:316)

Clinicians have written about the benefits encountered in honoring the spiritual nature of their work (Collins 1999):

> Seeing our work from a spiritual perspective does not mean "preaching" or trying to convert our clients to any system of belief. Rather, it is about tuning in to what

is universal about a client's experience, continually developing our compassion and self-compassion, working with issues of forgiveness as they arise for our clients, staying open to influences that are not "scientific" and rational, and being grateful for signs of hope and healing, even when they are small. To honor the spiritual depth of our work, we can arrange our offices so that they are sacred spaces—with artifacts and pictures of the beautiful natural world, with reminders of people who have given us wise counsel, with objects that connect us to thoughts of healing, and with books that have given us inspiration. (Gamble 2002:359)

Other strategies to facilitate spiritual self-care are spending time in nature, learning to meditate, creating peaceful home and work environments (e.g., using nature, music, or sounds like that of a bubbling rock fountain), initiating a formal association with a religious or spiritual group, reading literature that teaches spiritual practices or inspiring biographies of spiritual leaders, allotting time to engage in our chosen spiritual practices, sharing our experiences with others, and keeping a spiritual journal or diary (Olson 1997).

Workplace or Professional Self-Care

Organizational factors and the availability of supportive workplace policies affect workers' stress and satisfaction (Foster and Davidson 1995). Strategies that administrators may use to promote self-care are providing places for private meetings, empathic supervision, time to attend funerals and memorials to facilitate grieving, staff retreats, adequate vacation time, and flexibility in schedules (Becvar 2003; Riordan and Saltzer 1992). Encouraging staff to care for themselves sends a powerful message that in itself may ease stress. Social workers generally benefit by using supervision time wisely (e.g., sharing the burden of cases in supervisory sessions), seeking backup and relief from colleagues for cases too difficult to bear, taking breaks when needed, and balancing their exposure to grief in regard to caseload and other work responsibilities (e.g., supplementing direct-service bereavement interventions with community education and outreach activities) (Cook and Dworkin 1992; Dershimer 1990). Practitioners contending with role overload (i.e., when there is just too much to do) may need to set limits and prioritize their demands.

Summary

Most social work professionals are regularly confronted with grief and suffering in their practice, which may stimulate their own fears, memories, and emotional reactions. The tremendous suffering associated with varied and multiple forms of loss commonly addressed in practice by human service professionals put them at risk for chronic bereavement, compassion fatigue, vicarious traumatization, and burnout. While fundamental to helping relationships, empathy may enlarge the practitioner's own grief response. Disciplined self-awareness, compassion, and the conscious use of self are essential to ensure that the bereaved's needs are being addressed and that practitioners are getting the necessary help to process their own experiences. Self-care practices, which include physical, psychological, emotional, spiritual, and workplace strategies, may help prevent and address the many challenges confronting human service and health care professionals and enhance their fulfillment and satisfaction in practice with the bereaved.

Concluding Thoughts

JUST AS this book represented a blending of the personal and professional for us as authors, we hope that it will be useful to you, the reader, in both your personal and professional lives. Life is accompanied by continuous loss, although not all loss gives way to grief that requires professional intervention. Instead, as shown throughout this book, most human beings, at every age, are remarkably resilient. They use their internal, family, community, and cultural capacities to deal with life's hardships. In many instances, these informal social supports, sometimes reinforced by professional support, help the bereaved move through the shock, numbness, and despair of grief to the integration of the loss into their lives.

When a person's individual and informal capacities are depleted by several large losses, whether through age, chronic illness, poverty, or historical disadvantage, professionals need knowledge, skills, and values to assess his or her needs and develop culturally competent interventions. Similarly, when grief is traumatic or becomes complicated, interfering with the bereaved person's ability to function, professional interventions are essential. We presented the resilience model as one way of conceptualizing strategies that build on the bereaved person's strengths and capacities and foster physical and mental well-being. This conceptual model needs further development, testing and evaluation, however, which we encourage you to do as you assess the grieving person's strengths and implement interventions.

We began the book with a review of the major theoretical perspectives on grief, the grief process, and critiques of traditional concepts like "grief work." Our review highlighted the widely different opinions about the importance of "working through" grief, some of which may not seem to fit with practice wisdom. Our experience, however, suggests that bereaved individuals do need to actively address loss in order to integrate it into their lives. A common cliché is that "time heals," yet time alone does not heal. Hard work also is needed.

Perhaps what is most important is that we as professionals not attach value to the form of such "work." For some persons, burying themselves in their job or taking on a major project may be the best way for them to deal with their grief, at least at that particular time. For others, the "work" consists of attending support groups, talking with friends, reading, keeping a journal, storytelling, and perhaps seeking professional intervention. We do know, however, that certain ways of dealing with grief can be destructive to bereaved persons and/or their families, such as trying to escape it through drugs, alcohol, an affair, or violence. Rather than adhering to a fixed model of "grief work," professionals need to be alert to risk factors that may be harmful to physical health and mental health. Recognizing that there is no right or wrong way to grieve, we must work with bereaved individuals to build their capacities and reduce their risk of complicated grief.

Another theme throughout this book is the developmental considerations at each phase of life that affect our individual and social capacities and thus the way in which we grieve. Whether a loss is "on or off" time according to each life phase also can affect how we mourn. Across the life span, similar issues emerge, such as the importance of informal social support, societal and cultural norms and expectations, whether the grief is recognized by others or disenfranchised, and the role of spirituality and ongoing bonds with the deceased. Variations in gender, culture, ethnic minority status, socioeconomic class, and sexual orientation have been noted throughout, with the caveat that exceptions to such generalizations exist. We have reiterated the need for professionals to be culturally competent in their assessment and interventions. At this point, we know far too little about what strategies are most effective with different ethnic minority populations, immigrants, and gay/lesbian and bisexual populations.

Our review of individual, family, group, and community-level interventions repeatedly emphasized the need for more rigorous testing of interventions with bereaved individuals of all ages. We know the most about the efficacy of interventions with children and widowed adults, much less about those for adolescence and young and middle adulthood. In addition, more is known about the effectiveness of group interventions, especially support groups, than about other levels of intervention. While repeatedly emphasizing the need for more empirical testing of interventions, we also recognize the complexities of doing so, especially the ethical problems. The ethical issues of control groups is a challenge facing social science researchers in general, but particularly for those studying loss and grief.

When we began the book, we had not planned a chapter on self-care. However, as we wrote about the various types of loss and appropriate interventions, the professional stress of working with the bereaved became apparent. Since the evidence-based literature related to self-care is even more limited, you need to decide what self-care strategies fit with your own capacities, values, and lifestyle.

A primary motivation for writing this book was the absence in the social work literature of evidence-based interventions for addressing loss and grief across the life span. This contrasts markedly with the numerous books on grief in other disciplines, such as psychology or psychiatry, and with the wide range of self-help books available in any bookstore. Writing this book has been a profound and humbling experience for both of us. In the end, we hope that we have given you a beginning template for working effectively with the bereaved, with resources to turn to, and with critical issues to consider.

REFERENCES

Abbound, L. N., and P. Liamputtong. 2003. Pregnancy Loss: What It Means to Women Who Miscarry and Their Partners. *Social Work in Health Care* 363:37–62.

Achenbaum, W. A., and V. C. Bengtson. 1994. Re-engaging the Disengagement Theory of Aging: Or the History and Assessment of Theory Development in Gerontology. *The Gerontologist* 34:756–63.

Adamek, M. 2003. Late Life Depression in Nursing Home Residents: Social Work Opportunities to Prevent, Educate and Alleviate. In *Social Work and Health Care in an Aging Society*, edited by B. Berkman and L. Harootyan, 15–48. New York: Springer.

Adams, D. 2001. The Grief of Male Children and Adolescents and Ways to Help Them Cope. In *Men Coping with Grief*, edited by D. A. Lund, 273–308. Amityville, N.Y.: Baywood.

Adams, K. N. 1996. Bereavement Counseling Groups with Elementary School Students. *Dissertation Abstracts International*, Section A: *Humanities and Social Sciences* 56.

Administration on Aging, National Association of State Units on Aging. 2003. *The Aging Network Implements the National Family Caregiver Support Program*. Washington, D.C.: U.S. Administration on Aging.

Ahmed, I. 2003. Coping with the Burden of Caregiving. Paper presented at the Conference on Aging and Diversity, University of Hawaii, Honolulu, June.

Aitken, A. 2002. Webwatch. Internet Resources for Work with Bereaved Parents. *Bereavement Care* 213:45.

Akiba, M., G. K. LeTendre, D. P. Baker, and B. Goesling. 2002. Student Victimization: National and School System Effects on School Violence in 37 Nations. *American Educational Research Journal* 39:829–53.

Al-Adawi, S., and R. Burjorjee. 1997. Mu-Ghayeb: A Culture-Specific Response to Bereavement in Oman. *International Journal of Social Psychiatry* 43:144–51.

Aldwin, C. M. 1994. *Stress, Coping and Development: An Integrative Perspective*. New York: Guilford Press.

Alexopoulos, G. S., M. L. Bruce, J. Hull, J. Sirey, and T. Kakuma. 1999. Clinical Determinants of Suicidal Ideation and Behavior in Geriatric Depression. *Archives of General Psychiatry* 56:1048–53.

Allumbaugh, D. L., and W. T. Hoyt. 1999. Effectiveness of Grief Therapy: A Meta-Analysis. *Journal of Counseling Psychology* 46:370–80.

Almberg, B., M. Grafstroem, and B. Winblad 2000. Caregivers of Relatives with Dementia: Experiences Encompassing Social Support and Bereavement. *Aging and Mental Health* 4:82–89.

American Association for World Health. 1997. *The 1997 World AIDS Day Resource Book.* Washington, D.C.: American Association for World Health.

American Psychiatric Association. 2000. *Diagnostic and Statistical Manual of Mental Disorders.* 4th ed. Washington, D.C.: American Psychiatric Association.

Amodeo, M., D. Grigg-Saito, and N. Robb. 1997. Working with Foreign Language Interpreters: Guidelines for Substance Abuse Clinicians and Human Service Practitioners. *Alcoholism Treatment Quarterly* 154:75–87.

Anderson, C. 1999. Single-Parent Families: Strengths, Vulnerabilities and Interventions. In *The Expanded Family Life Cycle: Individual, Family and Social Perspectives,* 3rd ed., edited by B. Carter and M. McGoldrick, 399–416. Boston: Allyn & Bacon.

Anderson, M., J. Kaufman, T. R. Simon, L. Barrios, L. Paulozzi, G. Ryan, R. Hammond, W. Modzelski, T. Feucht, and L. Potter. 2001. School-Associated Violent Deaths in the United States, 1994–1999. *Journal of the American Medical Association* 286:2690–702.

Anthony, K. H. 1997. Bitter Homes and Gardens: The Meanings of Home to Families of Divorce. *Journal of Architectural and Planning Research* 141:1–19.

Antonovsky, A. 1987. *Unraveling the Mystery of Health.* San Francisco: Jossey-Bass.

Antonucci, T., and H. Akiyama. 1997. Concern with Others at Midlife: Care, Comfort or Compromise? In *Multiple Paths of Midlife Development,* edited by M. Lachman and J. James, 145–69. Chicago: University of Chicago Press.

Antonucci, T., H. Akiyama, and A. Merline. 2001. Dynamics of Social Relationships in Midlife. In *Handbook of Midlife Development,* edited by M. Lachman, 571–98. New York: Wiley.

Aranda, M and B. G. Knight 1997. The Influence of Ethnicity and Culture on the Caregiver Stress and Coping Process: A Sociocultural Review and Analysis. *The Gerontologist.* 37:342–54.

Arbuckle, N. W., and B. de Vries. 1995. The Long-Term Effects of Later Life Spousal and Parental Bereavement on Personal Functioning. *The Gerontologist* 35:637–47.

Archer, J. 1999. *The Nature of Grief: The Evolution and Psychology of Reactions to Loss.* New York: Routledge.

Archer, V. 2001. Adult Daughters and Mother Loss: The Impact of Bereavement Groups. *Dissertation Abstracts International,* Section A: *Humanities and Social Sciences* 62:770.

Arnett, J. J. 1998. Learning to Stand Alone: The Contemporary American Transition to Adulthood in Cultural and Historical Context. *Human Development* 41:295–97.

Arnett, J. J. 2000. Emerging Adulthood: A Theory of Development from the Late Teens Through the Twenties. *American Psychologist* 55:469–80.

Ashida, S. 2000. The Effect of Reminiscence Music Therapy Sessions on Changes in Depressive Symptoms in Elderly Persons with Dementia. *Journal of Music Therapy* 37:170–82.

Ashton, J., and D. Ashton. 2000. Dealing with the Chronic/Terminal Illness or Disability of a Child: Anticipatory Mourning. In *Clinical Dimensions of Anticipatory Mourning: Theory and Practice in Working with the Dying, Their Loved Ones, and Their Caregivers,* edited by T. A. Rando, 415–54. Champaign, Ill.: Research Press.

Atkinson, S. D. 1994. Grieving and Loss in Parents with a Schizophrenic Child. *American Journal of Psychiatry* 151:1137–39.

Attig, T. 1990. Relearning the World: On the Phenomenology of Grieving. *Journal of the British Society for Phenomenology* 21:53–66.

Attig, T. 1996. *How We Grieve: Relearning the World.* New York: Oxford University Press.

Attig, T. 2001a. Relearning the World: Always Complicated, Sometimes More Than Others. In *Complicated Grieving and Bereavement: Understanding and Treating People Experiencing Loss,* edited by G. Cox, R. Bendiksen, and R. Stevenson, 7–19. Amityville, N.Y.: Baywood.

Attig, T. 2001b. Relearning the World: Making and Finding Meanings. In *Meaning Reconstruction and the Experience of Loss,* edited by R. A. Neimeyer, 33–54. Washington, D.C.: American Psychological Association.

Avenevoli, S., F. M. Sessa, and L. Steinberg. 1999. Family Structure, Parenting Practices and Adolescent Adjustment: An Ecological Examination. In *Coping with Divorce, Single Parenting and Remarriage: A Risk and Resiliency Perspective,* edited by M. Hetherington, 65–92. Mahwah, N.J.: Erlbaum.

Ayers, T., and I. Sandler. 2003. Bereavement, Childhood. In *Encyclopedia of Primary Prevention and Health Promotion,* edited by T. P. Gullotta and M. Bloom, 213–20. New York: Plenum.

Ayyash-Abdo, H. 2002. Adolescent Suicide: An Ecological Approach. *Psychology in the Schools* 39:459–75.

Babcock, G. M. 1997. Stigma, Identity Dissonance and the Nonresidential Mother. *Journal of Divorce and Remarriage* 28:139–56.

Backer, B., R. Hannon, and N. Russell. 1994. *Death and Dying: Understanding and Care.* 2nd ed. Albany, N.Y.: Delmar.

Bacon, E. S., E. H. Condon, and J. I. Fernsler. 2000. Young Widows' Experience with an Internet Self-Help Group. *Journal of Psychosocial Nursing and Mental Health Services* 38:24–33.

Bacon, J. B. 1996. Support Groups for Bereaved Children. In *Handbook of Childhood Death and Bereavement,* edited by C. A. Corr, and D. M. Corr. New York: Springer.

Baez, V., and K. A. Oltjenbruns. 2000. Diversity Within Diversity: Strategies for Developing Insight Among Professionals. In *Meeting the Needs of Our Clients Creatively: The Impact of Art and Culture on Caregiving,* edited by J. D. Morgan, 49–66. Amityville, N.Y.: Baywood.

Bagarozzi, D. A. 1994. Identification, Assessment and Treatment of Women Suffering from Post Traumatic Stress After Abortion. *Journal of Family Psychotherapy* 53:25–54.

Bagley, C., and P. Tremblay. 2000. Elevated Rates of Suicidal Behavior in Gay, Lesbian, and Bisexual Youth. *Crisis* 2:111–17.

Baird, S., and S. R. Jenkins. 2003. Vicarious Traumatization, Secondary Traumatic Stress, and Burnout in Sexual Assault and Domestic Violence Agency Staff. *Violence and Victims* 18:71–86.

Baker, D. C. 2000. The Investigation of Pastoral Care Interventions as a Treatment for

Depression Among Continuing Care Retirement Community Residents. *Journal of Religious Gerontology* 12:63–85.

Baker, E. K. 2003. *Caring for Ourselves: A Therapist's Guide to Personal and Professional Well-being*. Washington, D.C.: American Psychological Association.

Baker, J. E. 1997. Minimizing the Impact of Parental Grief on Children: Parent and Family Interventions. In *Death and Trauma: The Traumatology of Grieving*, edited by C. R. Figley, B. E. Bride, and N. Mazza, 139–57. Philadelphia: Taylor & Francis.

Baker, J. E., J. A. Sedney, and E. Gross. 1992. Psychological Tasks for Bereaved Children. *American Journal of Orthopsychiatry* 62:105–16.

Balk, D. E. 1990. The Self-Concepts of Bereaved Adolescents: Sibling Death and Its Aftermath. *Journal of Adolescent Research* 5:112–32.

Balk, D. E. 1999. Bereavement and Spiritual Change. *Death Studies* 23:485–93.

Balk, D. E., and C. A. Corr. 2001. Bereavement During Adolescence: A Review of Research. In *Handbook of Bereavement Research: Consequences, Coping and Care*, edited by M. S. Stroebe, R. O. Hansson, W. Stroebe, and H. Schut, 199–218. Washington, D.C.: American Psychological Association.

Balk, D. E., and L. C. Vesta. 1998. Psychological Development During Four Years of Bereavement: A Case Study. *Death Studies* 22:3–21.

Banks, M. E. 2003. Disability in the Family: A Life Span Perspective. *Cultural Diversity and Ethnic Minority Psychology* 9:367–84.

Barber, C. E., and M. Iwai. 1996. Role Conflict and Role Ambiguity as Predictors of Burnout Among Staff Caring for Older Dementia Patients. *Journal of Gerontological Social Work* 26:101–16.

Barlow, C. A., and H. Morrison. 2002. Survivors of Suicide: Emerging Counseling Strategies. *Journal of Psychosocial Nursing* 40:28–39.

Barnes, R. C. 1994. Finding Meaning in Unavoidable Suffering. *International Forum for Logotherapy* 17:20–26.

Barrett, R. K. 1996. Adolescence, Homicidal Violence, and Death. In *Handbook of Adolescent Death and Bereavement*, edited by C. A. Corr, and D. E. Balk, 45–64. New York: Springer.

Barrett, R. K. 1998. Sociocultural Considerations for Working with Blacks Experiencing Loss and Grief. In *Living with Grief: Who We Are and How We Grieve*, edited by K. Doka and J. Davidson, 83–96. Philadelphia: Brunner/Mazel.

Barry, L. C., S. V. Kasl, and H. G. Prigerson. 2002. Psychiatric Disorders Among Bereaved Persons: The Role of Perceived Circumstances of Death and Preparedness for Death. *American Journal of Geriatric Psychiatry* 10:447–57.

Bass, D. M., K. Bowman, and L. S. Noelker. 1991. The Influence of Caregiving and Bereavement Support on Adjusting to an Older Relative's Death. *The Gerontologist* 31:32–42.

Batshaw, M. L. 2001. *When Your Child Has a Disability: The Complete Sourcebook of Daily and Medical Care*. Baltimore: Brookes.

Baum, N. 2003. The Male Way of Mourning Divorce: When, What, and How. *Clinical Social Work Journal* 31:37–50.

Baxter, E. A., and S. Diehl. 1998. Emotional Stages: Consumers and Family Members Recovering from the Trauma of Mental Illness. *Psychiatric Rehabilitation Journal* 21:349–55.

Baxter, G., and W. Stuart. 1999. *Death and the Adolescent: A Resource Handbook for Bereavement Support Groups in Schools.* Toronto: University of Toronto Press.

Beaver, M. L. 1991. Life Review/Reminiscent Therapy. In *Serving the Elderly: Skills for Practice,* edited by P. K. H. Kim, 67–88. New York: Aldine.

Becvar, D. S. 1997. *Soul Healing: A Spiritual Orientation in Counseling and Therapy.* New York: Basic Books.

Becvar, D. S. 2000. Families Experiencing Death, Dying and Bereavement. In *The Handbook of Family Development and Intervention,* edited by W. C. Nichols, D. S. Becvar, and A. Y. Napier, 453–70. New York: Wiley.

Becvar, D. S. 2001. *In the Presence of Grief: Helping Family Members Resolve Death, Dying and Bereavement Issues.* New York: Guilford Press.

Becvar, D. S. 2003. The Impact on the Family Therapist of a Focus on Death, Dying, and Bereavement. *Journal of Marriage and Family Therapy* 29:469–77.

Becvar, D. S., and R. Becvar. 1988. *Family Therapy: A Systemic Integration.* Boston: Allyn & Bacon.

Beechem, M. H., C. Anthony, and J. Kurtz. 1998. A Life Review Interview Guide: A Structured Systems Approach to Information Gathering. *International Journal of Aging and Human Development* 46:25–44.

Beem, E. E., H. Hooijkaas, M. H. P. D. Cleiren, H. A. W. Schut, B. Garssen, M. A. Croon, L. Jabaaij, K. Goodkin, H. Wind, and M. J. De Vries. 1999. The Immunological and Psychological Effects of Bereavement: Does Grief Counseling Really Make a Difference? A Pilot Study. *Psychiatry Research* 85:81–93.

Bembry, J. X., and C. Ericson. 1999. Therapeutic Termination with the Early Adolescent Who Has Experienced Multiple Losses. *Child and Adolescent Social Work Journal* 16:177–89.

Benedek, T. 1959. Parenthood as a Developmental Phase. *American Psychoanalytic Association Journal* 7:389–417.

Benedek, T. 1975. Discussion of Parenthood as a Developmental Phase. *Journal of the American Psychoanalytic Association* 23:154–65.

Benedict, H. 1994. *Recovery: How to Survive Sexual Assault for Women, Men, Teenagers and Their Families.* New York: Columbia University Press.

Ben-Israel Reuveni, O. 1999. The Effect of Time on the Adjustment of War Bereaved Parents: Functioning, Relationship and Marital Adjustment. Master's thesis, University of Haifa.

Bennett, K. M., and S. Vidal-Hall. 2000. Narratives of Death: A Qualitative Study of Widowhood in Women in Later Life. *Ageing and Society* 20:413–28.

Benoliel, J. Q. 1994. Death and Dying as a Field of Inquiry. In *Dying, Death and Bereavement:*

Theoretical Perspectives and Other Ways of Knowing, edited by I. B. Corless, B. B. Germino, and M. Pittman, 3–14. Boston: Jones and Barlett.

Benson, P. 1997. *All Kids Are Our Kids*. San Francisco: Jossey-Bass.

Bergeron, R. 2000. Serving the Needs of Elder Abuse Victims. *Policy and Practice of Public Human Services* 58:40–45.

Berman, A. L., and D. A. Jones. 1995. Suicide Prevention in Adolescents Age 12–18. *Suicide and Life-Threatening Behavior* 25:143–54.

Berman, L. C. 1986. Foster Parents as a Resource in Preparing Children for Placement. *Adoption and Fostering* 10:40–43.

Berman, L. C., and R. K. Bufferd. 1986. Family Treatment to Address Loss in Adoptive Families. *Social Casework: Journal of Contemporary Social Work* 67:3–11.

Berry, J. W. 1999. *Cultures in Contact: Acculturation and Change*. Allahabad: Pant Social Science Institute.

Beutel, M., H. Willner, R. Deckardt, M. von Rad, and H. Weiner. 1996. Similarities and Differences in Couples' Grief Reactions Following a Miscarriage: Results from a Longitudinal Study. *Journal of Psychosomatic Research* 40:245–53.

Bifulco, A., G. Brown, and T. Harris. 1987. Childhood Loss of Parent, Lack of Adequate Parental Care and Adult Depression: A Replication. *Social Psychology* 16:187–97.

Birren, J. E. 1964. *The Psychology of Aging*. Englewood Cliffs, N.J.: Prentice-Hall.

Black, D. 1996. Childhood Bereavement. *British Medical Journal* 31:1496.

Black, D., and T. Kaplan. 1988. Father Kills Mother: Issues and Problems Encountered by a Child Psychiatric Team. *British Journal of Psychiatry* 15:624–30.

Black, D., and M. Urbanowicz. 1987. Family Intervention with Bereaved Children. *Journal of Child Psychology and Psychiatry* 28:467–76.

Black, P., D. Jeffreys, and E. Hartley. 1993. Personal History of Psychosocial Trauma in the Early Life of Social Work and Business Students. *Journal of Social Work Education* 29:171–80.

Blacker, S., and A. R. Jordan. 2004. Working with Families Facing Life-Threatening Illness in the Medical Setting. In *Living with Dying: A Handbook for End-of-Life Healthcare Practitioners*, edited by J. Berzoff and P. R. Silverman, 548–70. New York: Columbia University Press.

Blanton, T. L., and J. Deschner. 1990. Biological Mothers' Grief: The Post Adoptive Experience in Open Versus Confidential Adoption. *Child Welfare* 69:525–35.

Blazer, D. G. 1998. *Emotional Problems in Later Life: Intervention Strategies for Professional Caregivers*. New York: Springer.

Bliatout, B. T. 1993. Hmong Death Customs: Traditional and Acculturated. In *Ethnic Variations in Dying, Death, and Grief: Diversity in Universality*, edited by D. Irish, K. Lundquist, and V. Nelsen, 79–100. Washington, D.C.: Taylor & Francis.

Bluestone, J. 1999. School-Based Peer Therapy to Facilitate Mourning in Latency-Age Children Following Sudden Parental Death. In *Play Therapy with Children in Crisis: Individual, Group, and Family Treatment*, edited by N. B. Webb, 225–51. New York: Guildford Press.

Bonnano, G. A. 2001a. The Crucial Importance of Empirical Evidence in the Development of Bereavement Theory: A Reply to Archer. *Psychological Bulletin* 12:561–64.

Bonnano, G. A. 2001b. Grief and Emotion: A Social-Functional Perspective. In *Handbook of Bereavement Research: Consequences, Coping and Care*, edited by M. Stroebe, R. O. Hansson, W. Stroebe, and H. Schut, 493–515. Washington, D.C.: American Psychological Association.

Bonanno, G. A., and N. Field. 2001. Examining the Delayed Grief Hypothesis Across Five Years of Bereavement. *American Behavioral Scientist* 44:798–816.

Bonanno, G. A., and S. Kaltman. 1999. The Self-Regulation of Grief: Toward an Integrative Perspective on Bereavement. *Psychological Bulletin* 12:760–76.

Bonanno, G. A., and S. Kaltman. 2001. The Varieties of Grief Experience. *Clinical Psychology Review* 21:705–34.

Bonanno, G. A., and D. Keltner. 1997. Facial Expressions of Emotion and the Course of Conjugal Bereavement. *Journal of Abnormal Psychology* 106:126–37.

Bonanno, G. A., D. Keltner, A. Holen, and J. Horowitz. 1995. When Avoiding Unpleasant Emotions Might Not Be Such a Bad Thing. *Journal of Personality and Social Psychology* 69:975–89.

Bonanno, G. A., H. Znoj, H. I. Siddique, and M. J. Horowitz. 1999. Verbal-Autonomic Dissociation and Adaptation to Midlife Conjugal Loss: A Follow-up at 25 Months. *Cognitive Therapy and Research* 23:605–24.

Borysenko, J. 1996. *A Woman's Book of Life: The Biology, Psychology and Spirituality of the Feminine Life Cycle*. New York: Riverhead Books.

Boss, P. 1999. *Ambiguous Loss*. Cambridge, Mass.: Harvard University Press.

Bowlby, J. 1960. Grief and Mourning in Infancy and Early Childhood. *Psychoanalytic Study of the Child* 15:9–52.

Bowlby, J. 1969. *Attachment*. Vol. 1 of *Attachment and Loss*. New York: Basic Books.

Bowlby, J. 1973. *Separation, Anxiety and Anger*. Vol. 2 of *Attachment and Loss*. New York: Basic Books.

Bowlby, J. 1980. *Loss, Sadness and Depression*. Vol. 3 of *Attachment and Loss*. New York: Basic Books.

Bowlby, J. 1982. Attachment and Loss: Retrospect and Prospect. *American Journal of Orthopsychiatry* 52:664–78.

Boyle, F. M. 1997. *Mothers Bereaved by Stillbirth, Neonatal Death or Sudden Infant Death Syndrome*. Sydney: Ashgate.

Bozarth, A. 1994. *Life Is Goodbye, Life Is Hello: Grieving Well Through All Kinds of Loss*. Minneapolis: CompCare Publications.

Brabant, S., C. J. Forsyth, and G. McFarlain. 1995. Life After the Death of a Child: Initial and Long Term Support from Others. *Omega* 31:67–85.

Brabant, S., C. J. Forsyth, and G. McFarlain. 1997. The Impact of the Death of a Child on Meaning and Purpose in Life. *Journal of Personal and Interpersonal Loss* 2:255–66.

Bradach, K. M., and J. R. Jordon. 1995. Long-Term Effects of a Family History of Traumatic Death on Adolescent Individuation. *Death Studies* 19:315–36.

Bradley, M. J. 2003. *Yes, Your Teen Is Crazy: Loving Your Kid Without Losing Your Mind.* Gig Harbor, Wash.: Harbor Press.

Brat, P. 2001. Aging, Mental Health and the Faith Community. *Journal of Religious Gerontology* 13:45–54.

Braun, K. L., J. H. Pietsch, and P. L. Blanchette, eds. 2000. *Cultural Issues in End-of-Life Decision Making.* Thousand Oaks, Calif.: Sage.

Brent, D. A., J. A. Perper, G. Moritz, L. Liotus, D. Richardson, R. Canobbio, J. Schweers, and C. Roth. 1995a. Posttraumatic Stress Disorder in Peers of Adolescent Suicide Victims: Predisposing Factors and Phenomenology. *Journal of the American Academy of Child and Adolescent Psychiatry* 38:672–79.

Brent, D. A., J. A. Perper, G. Moritz, L. Liotos, J. Schweers, C. Roth, L. Balach, and C. Allman. 1993. Psychiatric Impact of the Loss of an Adolescent Sibling to Suicide. *Journal of Affective Disorders* 28:249–56.

Brice, C. W. 1989. The Relational Essence of Maternal Mourning: An Existential-Psychoanalytic Perspective. *Humanistic Psychologist* 17:22–40.

Brice, C. W. 1991a. Paradoxes of Maternal Mourning. *Psychiatry* 54:1–12.

Brice, C. W. 1991b. What Forever Means: An Empirical Existential-Phenomenological Investigation of Maternal Mourning. *Journal of Phenomenological Psychology* 22:16–38.

Bridge, J. A., D. A. Brent, B. A. Johnson, and J. Connolly. 1997. Familial Aggregation of Psychiatric Disorders in a Community Sample of Adolescents. *Journal of the American Academy of Child and Adolescent Psychiatry* 36:628–37.

Bright, P. D. 1987. Adolescent Pregnancy and Loss. *Maternal Child Nursing Journal* 16:1–12.

Bright, R. 1996. *Grief and Powerlessness: Helping People Regain Control of Their Lives.* London: Kingsley.

Bright, R. 1999. Music Therapy in Grief Resolution. *Bulletin of the Menninger Clinic* 63:481–98.

Brody, E. 1990. *Women in the Middle: Their Parent Care Years.* New York: Springer

Brody, E. 2004. *Women in the Middle: Their Parent Care Years.* 2nd ed. New York: Springer.

Brokenleg, M., and D. Middleton. 1993. Native Americans: Adapting Yet Retaining. In *Ethnic Variations in Dying, Death and Grief,* edited by D. P. Irish, K. F. Lundquist, and V. J. Nelsen, 101–12. Washington, D.C.: Taylor & Francis.

Brown, C. 1999. *Lamb in Love.* New York: Bantam Books.

Brown, E. W. 1999. Teen-age Suicide: A National Tragedy. *Medical Update,* August 1.

Brown, G., T. Harris, and A. Bifulco. 1986. Long-Term Effects of Early Loss of Parent. In *Depression in Young People,* edited by M. Rutter, C. Izard, and P. Read, 251–96. New York: Guildford Press.

Brown, Y. 1992. The Crisis of Pregnancy Loss: A Team Approach to Support. *Birth* 19:82–91.

Brown, Y. 1993. Perinatal Loss: A Framework for Practice. *Health Care for Women International* 14:469–79.

Brownell, P. 1997. The Application of the Culturagram in Cross-Cultural Practice with Elder Abuse Victims. *Journal of Elder Abuse and Neglect* 9:19–33.

Buchanan, C. M. 2000. The Impact of Divorce on Adjustment During Adolescence. In *Resilience Across Contexts: Family, Work, Culture and Community*, edited by R. Taylor and M. Wang, 179–216. Mahwah, N.J.: Erlbaum.

Buchanan, C. M., E. E. Maccoby, and S. M. Dornbusch. 1996. *Adolescents After Divorce*. Cambridge, Mass.: Harvard University Press.

Buck, P. 1950. *The Child Who Never Grew*. New York: Day.

Buell, J. S. 1989. Bereavement Groups in the Hospice Program. *Hospice Journal* 5:107–18.

Bullis, R. K. 1996. *Spirituality in Social Work Practice*. Washington, D.C.: Taylor & Francis.

Burke, M. L., and G. G. Eakes. 1999. Milestones of Chronic Sorrow: Perspectives of Chronically Ill and Bereaved Persons and Family Caregivers. *Journal of Family Nursing* 16:4–7.

Burke, M. L., M. A. Hainsworth, G. G. Eakes, and C. L. Lindgren. 1992. Current Knowledge and Research on Chronic Sorrow: A Foundation for Inquiry. *Death Studies* 16:231–45.

Burman, S., and P. Allen-Meares. 1994. Neglected Victims of Murder: Children's Witness to Parental Homicide. *Social Work* 39:28–34.

Burnette, D. 1997. Grandmother Caregivers in Inner-City Latino Families: A Descriptive Profile and Informal Social Supports. *Journal of Multicultural Social Work* 5:121–37.

Burnside, I. 1994. Reminiscence Group Therapy. In *Working with Older Adults: Group Process and Techniques*, 3rd ed., edited by I. Burnside and M. G. Schmidt, 163–78. Boston: Jones and Bartlett.

Bushman, B. J. 2002. Does Venting Anger Feed or Extinguish the Flame? Catharsis, Rumination, Distraction, Anger and Aggressive Responding. *Personality and Social Psychology Bulletin* 28:724–31.

Bushman, B. J., R. F. Baumeister, and C. M. Phillips. 2001. Do People Aggress to Improve Their Mood? Catharsis Beliefs, Affect Regulation Opportunity, and Aggressive Responding. *Journal of Personality and Social Psychology* 81:17–32.

Butler, R. N. 1963. The Life Review: An Interpretation of Reminiscence in the Aged. *Psychiatry* 26:65–76.

Butler, R. N., M. I. Lewis, and T. Sunderland. 1998. *Aging and Mental Health: Positive Psychosocial and Biomedical Approaches*. 5th ed. Boston: Allyn & Bacon.

Byng-Hal, J. 1979. Re-editing Family Mythology During Family Therapy. *Journal of Family Therapy* 1:103–16.

Byng-Hal, J. 1998. Evolving Ideas About Narrative: Re-editing the Re-editing of Family Mythology. *Journal of Family Therapy* 20:133–41.

Caelli, K., J. Downie, and A. Letendre. 2002. Parents' Experiences of Midwife-Managed Care Following the Loss of a Baby in a Previous Pregnancy. *Journal of Advanced Nursing* 39:127–36.

Cain, A. O. 1985. Pets as Family Members. In *Pets in the Family*, edited by M. B. Sussman, 5–10. New York: Haworth Press.

Caine, E. D., J. M. Lyness, D. A., King, and B. A. Connors. 1994. Clinical and Etiological Heterogeneity of Mood Disorders in Elderly Patients. In *Diagnosis and Treatment of*

Depression in Late Life: Results of the NIH Consensus Development Conference, edited by L. S. Schneider, C. F. Reynolds, B. D. Lebowitz, and A. J. Friedhoff, 23–53. Washington, D.C.: American Psychiatric Press.

Cairns, M., M. Thompson, and W. Wainwright. 2000. *Transitions in Dying and Bereavement: A Psychosocial Guide for Hospice and Palliative Care*. Baltimore: Health Professions Press.

Calhoun, L. G., and R. G. Tedeschi. 2001. Posttraumatic Growth: The Positive Lessons of Loss. In *Meaning Reconstruction and the Experience of Loss*, edited by R. A. Neimeyer, 157–72. Washington, D.C.: American Psychological Association.

Campbell, S., and P. Silverman. 1996. *Widower: When Men Are Left Alone*. Amityville, N.Y.: Baywood.

Caplan, G. 1961. *An Approach to Community Mental Health*. New York: Basic Books.

Caplan, G. 1964. *Principles of Preventive Psychiatry*. New York: Basic Books.

Carnelley, K. B., C. B. Wortman, and R. C. Kessler. 1999. The Impact of Widowhood on Depression: Findings from a Prospective Survey. *Psychiatric Medicine* 29:1111–23.

Carr, A. 2000. Evidence-Based Practice in Family Therapy and Systemic Consultation: I: Child-Focused Problems. *Journal of Family Therapy* 22:29–60.

Carr, A. 2001. *What Works with Children and Adolescents? A Critical Review of Psychological Interventions with Children, Adolescents and Their Families*. Florence, Ky.: Taylor & Francis/Routledge.

Carr, D. 2003. A Good Death for Whom? Quality of Spouse's Death and Psychological Distress Among Older Widowed Persons. *Journal of Health and Social Behavior* 44:215–32.

Carr, D. 2004. Gender, Preloss Martial Dependence and Older Adults' Adjustment to Widowhood. *Journal of Marriage and the Family* 66:220–35.

Carr, D. In press. A Good Death for Whom? Quality of Spouse's Death and Psychological Distress Among Older Widowed Persons. *Journal of Health and Social Behavior*.

Carr, D., J. House, R. Kessler, R. Nesse, J. Sonnega, and C. Worman. 2000. Marital Quality and Psychological Adjustment to Widowhood Among Older Adults: A Longitudinal Analysis. *Journals of Gerontology* 55B:S197–207.

Carr, D., J. House, C. Wortman, R. Nesse, and R. Kessler. 2001. Psychological Adjustment to Sudden and Anticipated Spousal Loss Among Older Widowed Persons. *Journals of Gerontology* 56B:S237–48.

Carroll, R., and S. Shaefer. 1993/1994. Similarities and Differences in Spouses Coping with SIDS. *Omega* 28:273–84.

Cartensen, L. L., J. J. Gross, and H. H. Fung. 1997. The Social Context of Emotional Experience. *Annual Review of Gerontology and Geriatrics* 17:325–52.

Carter, B., and M. McGoldrick. 1999. The Divorce Cycle: A Major Variation in the American Family Life Cycle. In *The Expanded Family Life Cycle: Individual, Family and Social Perspectives*, 3rd ed., edited by B. Carter and M. McGoldrick, 273–380. Boston: Allyn & Bacon.

Carverhill, P. 1997. Bereaved Men: How Therapists Can Help. *Psychotherapy in Private Practice* 16:1–20.

Casado, B. L., and P. Leung. 2001. Migratory Grief and Depression Among Elderly Chinese American Immigrants. *Journal of Gerontological Social Work* 36:5–26.

Case, J. L. 2001. Coping Strategies, Family Membership Loss and Ego Identity Status Among Late Adolescent Females. *Dissertation Abstracts International*, Section A: *Humanities and Social Sciences* 61:4190.

Caserta, M. S., and D. A. Lund. 1996. Beyond Bereavement Support Group Meetings: Exploring Outside Social Contacts Among the Members. *Death Studies* 20:537–56.

Center for the Advancement of Health. 2003. *Report on Bereavement and Grief Research*. Washington, D.C.: Center for the Advancement of Health. Available at: http://www.cfah.org/pdfs/griefreport.pdf.

Centers for Disease Control and Prevention. 1994. Suicide Contagion and the Reporting of Suicide: Recommendations from a National Workshop. *Morbidity and Mortality Weekly Report* 42:13–18.

Cerel, J., M. Fristed, E. Weller, and R. Weller. 1999. Suicide-Bereaved Children and Adolescents: A Controlled Longitudinal Examination. *Journal of the American Academy of Child and Adolescent Psychiatry* 38:672–79.

Cerney, M. A. 1995. Treating the "Heroic Theaters." In *Compassion Fatigue: Coping with Secondary Traumatic Stress Disorder in Those Who Treat the Traumatized*, edited by C. R Figley, 131–49. New York: Brunner/Mazel.

Chazin, R., S. Kaplan, and S. Terio. 2000. The Strengths Perspective in Brief Treatment with Culturally Diverse Clients. *Crisis Intervention* 6:41–50.

Cherlin, A. J., and F. F. Furstenberg Jr. 1986. *The New American Grandparent: A Place in the Family, a Life Apart*. New York: Basic Books.

Chesterton, D. 1996. Bereavement Counseling: Stillbirth and the Adolescent. *Modern Midwife* 6:30–33.

Chew, J. 1998. *Women Survivors of Childhood Sexual Abuse: Healing Through Group Work*. New York: Haworth Press.

Children's Defense Fund. 2001. *The State of America's Children, 2001*. Washington, D.C.: Children's Defense Fund.

Chin, J. L. 1994. Psychodynamic Approaches. In *Women of Color*, edited by L. Comas-Diaz and B. Greene, 194–222. New York: Guilford Press.

Chinen, R. T., and L. Berg-Cross. 1994. Assessment and Treatment of Depression and Loss in the Elderly. In *Innovations in Clinical Practice: A Sourcebook*, edited by L. VandeCreek, S. Knapp, and T. L. Jackson, vol. 13, 151–66. Sarasota, Fla.: Professional Resource Press.

Cho, C., and D. E. Cassidy. 1994. Parallel Processes for Workers and Their Clients in Chronic Bereavement Resulting from HIV. *Death Studies* 18:273–92.

Choi, N. G. 1996. Older Persons Who Move: Reasons and Health Consequences. *Journal of Applied Gerontology* 15:325–44.

Christ, G. H. 2000. *Healing Children's Grief: Surviving a Parent's Death from Cancer*. New York: Oxford University Press.

Christ, G. H., K. Siegel, and A. E. Christ. 2002. Adolescent Grief: "It Never Really Hit

Me . . . Until It Actually Happened." *Journal of the American Medical Association* 288:1269–79.

Christ, G. H., K. Siegel, B. Freund, D. Langosch, S. Henderson, D. Sperber, and L. Weinstein. 1993. Impact of Parental Terminal Cancer on Latency-Age Children. *American Journal Orthopsychiatry* 63:417–25.

Christ, G. H., K. Siegel, F. Mesagno, and D. Langosch. 1991. A Preventive Intervention Program for Bereaved Children: Problems in Implementation. *American Journal of Orthopsychiatry* 61:417–25.

Chwalisz, K. 1998. Brain Injury: A Tapestry of Loss. In *Perspectives on Loss: A Sourcebook*, edited by J. H. Harvey, 189–200. Philadelphia: Brunner/Mazel.

Cicirelli, V. 2002. *Older Adults' Views on Death*. New York: Springer.

Clark, D., R. Pynoos, and A. Gobel. 1994. Mechanisms and Processes of Adolescent Bereavement. In *Stress, Risk and Resilience in Children and Adolescents: Processes, Mechanisms and Interventions*, edited by N. G. R. Haggard, M. Rutter, and L. Sheerod, 100–146. Cambridge: Cambridge University Press.

Clark, G. T., G. Cole, and S. Enzle. 1990. Complicated Grief Reactions in Women Who Are Sexually Abused in Childhood. *Journal of Psychosocial Oncology* 8:87–97.

Clark, S. E., and R. D. Goldney. 1995. Grief Reactions and Recovery in a Support Group for People Bereaved by Suicide. *Crisis* 16:27–33.

Cleiren, M. 1993. *Bereavement and Adaptation: A Comparative Study of the Aftermath of Death*. Philadelphia: Hemisphere.

Clements, P. T., Jr., K. M. Benasutti, and G. C. Henry. 2001. Drawing from Experience: Using Children's Drawings to Facilitate Communication and Understanding with Children Exposed to Sudden Traumatic Deaths. *Journal of Psychosocial Nursing* 39:12–20.

Cochran, L., and E. Claspell. 1987. *The Meaning of Grief: A Dramaturgical Approach to Understanding Emotion*. Westport, Conn.: Greenwood Press.

Cohen, J. A., T. Greenberg, S. Padlo, C. Shipley, A. P. Mannarino, E. Deblinger, and K. Stubenbort. 2001. *Cognitive Behavioral Therapy for Traumatic Bereavement in Children Treatment Manual*. Pittsburgh: Center for Traumatic Stress in Children and Adolescents.

Cohen, J. A., and A. P. Mannarino. 2000. Predictors of Treatment Outcome in Sexually Abused Children. *Child Abuse and Neglect* 24:983–94.

Cohen, J. A., A. P. Mannarino, T. Greenberg, S. Padlo, and C. Shipley. 2002. Childhood Traumatic Grief: Concepts and Controversies. *Trauma, Violence, and Abuse* 3:307–27.

Cohen, M. A. 1999. Bereavement Groups with the Elderly. *Journal of Psychotherapy in Independent Practice* 1:33–41.

Collins, B. J. 1999. Some Thoughts on Avoiding Vicarious Traumatization. *Treating Abuse Today* 9:40–41.

Colón, Y. 2001. Online Bereavement Support. *Innovations in End-of-Life Care* 3. Available at: www.edu.org/lastacts.

Comas-Diaz, L., and B. Greene. 1994. Gender and Ethnicity in the Healing Process. In *Women of Color*, edited by L. Comas-Diaz and B. Greene, 185–93. New York: Guilford Press.

Compas, B., N. Worsham, J. Epping-Jordan, D. Howell, K. Grant, G. Mireault, and V. Malcarne. 1994. When Mom or Dad Has Cancer: Markers of Psychological Distress in Cancer Patients, Spouses, and Children. *Health Psychology* 13:507–15.

Compton, B. R., and B. Galaway. 1999. *Social Work Processes*. 6th ed. Pacific Grove, Calif.: Brooks/Cole.

Connell, C. M., and G. D. Gibson. 1997. Racial, Ethnic and Cultural Differences in Dementia Caregiving. Review and Analysis. *The Gerontologist* 37:355–64.

Connidis, I. A. 2001. *Family Ties and Aging*. Thousand Oaks, Calif.: Sage.

Constable, D. A. 1994. The Process of Recovery for Adult Survivors of Childhood Sexual Abuse: A Grounded Theory Study. *Dissertation Abstracts International*, Section B: *The Sciences and Engineering* 56.

Constantine, M. G., E. C. Chen, and P. Ceesay. 1997. Intake Concerns of Racial and Ethnic Minority Students at a University Counseling Center: Implications for Developmental Programming and Outreach. *Journal of Multicultural Counseling and Development* 25:210–18.

Constantine, M. G., T. M. Greer, and M. K. Kindaichi. 2003. Theoretical and Cultural Considerations in Counseling Women of Color. In *Handbook of Counseling Women*, edited by M. Kopala and M. A. Keitel, 40–52. Thousand Oaks, Calif.: Sage.

Constantine, M. G., E. L. Lewis, L. C. Conner, and D. Sanchez. 2000. Addressing Spiritual and Religious Issues in Counseling African Americans: Implications for Counselors in Training and Practice. *Counseling and Values* 45:28–38.

Constantino, R. E. 1988. Comparison of Two Group Interventions for the Bereaved. *IMAGE: Journal of Nursing Scholarship* 20:83–87.

Constantino, R. E., L. K. Sekula, and E. N. Rubinstein. 2001. Group Intervention for Widowed Survivors of Suicide. *Suicide and Life-Threatening Behavior* 31:428–41.

Conwell, Y. 1997. Management of Suicidal Behavior in the Elderly. *Psychiatric Clinics of North America* 20:667–83.

Conwell, Y., P. R. Duberstein, and E. D. Caine. 2002. Risk Factors for Suicide in Later Life. *Biological Psychiatry* 52:193–204.

Cook, A. S., and D. S. Dworkin. 1992. *Helping the Bereaved: Therapeutic Interventions for Children, Adolescents, and Adults*. New York: Basic Books.

Cook, A. S., and K. A. Oltjenbruns. 1998. *Dying and Grieving: Lifespan and Family Perspectives*. 2nd ed. Fort Worth, Tex.: Harcourt Brace.

Corden, A., P. Sloper, and R. Sainsbury. 2002. Financial Effects for Families After the Death of a Disabled or Chronically Ill Child: A Neglected Dimension of Bereavement. *Child: Care, Health and Development* 28:199–204.

Corey, G. 2001. *Theory and Practice of Counseling and Psychotherapy*. Belmont, Calif.: Brooks/Cole.

Corey, G. 2005. *Theory and Practice of Counseling and Psychotherapy*. 7th ed. Belmont, Calif.: Wadsworth/Thomson Learning.

Corey, G., M. S. Corey, and P. Callanan. 2003. *Issues and Ethics in the Helping Professions*. 6th ed. Pacific Grove, Calif.: Brooks/Cole.

Corless, I. B. 2001. Bereavement. In *Textbook of Palliative Nursing*, edited by B. R. Ferreu and D. Coyle, 352–62. New York: Oxford University Press.

Corless, I. B., B. B. Germino, and M. A. Pittman. 1994. *Dying, Death and Bereavement: Theoretical Perspectives and Other Ways of Knowing*. Boston: Jones and Bartlett.

Corr, C. A. 2000. What We Know About Grieving Children and Adolescents. In *Living with Grief: Children, Adolescents and Loss*, edited by K. J. Doka, 295–314. Washington, D.C.: Hospice Foundation of America.

Corr, C. A., and D. M. Corr. 1996. *Handbook of Childhood Death and Bereavement*. New York: Springer.

Corr, C. A., and D. M. Corr. 2000. Anticipatory Mourning and Coping with Dying: Similarities, Differences, and Suggested Guidelines for Helpers. In *Clinical Dimensions of Anticipatory Mourning: Theory and Practice in Working with the Dying, Their Loved Ones, and Their Caregivers*, edited by T. A. Rando, 223–51. Champaign, Ill.: Research Press.

Corr, C. A., and J. N. McNeil, eds. 1999. *Adolescence and Death*. New York: Springer.

Corr, C. A., C. M. Nabe, and D. M. Corr. 2003. *Death and Dying, Life and Living*. 4th ed. Belmont, Calif.: Wadsworth.

Cowles, K. V. 1996. Cultural Perspectives of Grief: An Expanded Concept of Analysis. *Journal of Advanced Nursing* 23:287–94.

Cox, C. 2002. Empowering African American Custodial Grandparents. *Social Work* 47:262–67.

Cox, G. R. 2001. Dying and Bereaved Children and the Arts, Humor and Music. In *Complicated Grieving and Bereavement: Understanding and Treating People Experiencing Loss*, edited by R. G. Cox, R. A. Bendiksen and R. G. Stevenson, 303–16. Amityville, N.Y.: Baywood.

Coxell, A. W., and M. B. King. 2002. Gender, Sexual Orientation and Sexual Assault. In *The Trauma of Sexual Assault: Treatment, Prevention and Practice*, edited by J. Petrak and B. Hedge, 45–68. New York: Wiley.

Crandles, S., A. Sussman, M. Berthaud, and A. Sunderland. 1992. Development of a Weekly Support Group for Caregivers of Children with HIV Disease. *AIDS Care* 4:339–51.

Crider, T. 1996. *Give Sorrow Words: A Father's Passage Through Grief*. Chapel Hill, N.C.: Algonquin Books.

Cross, T. L. 2003. Culture as a Resource for Mental Health. *Cultural Diversity and Ethnic Minority Psychology* 9:354–59.

Csikai, E. L., and M. Raymer. 2002. The Social Work End-of-Life Care Educational Program SWEEP: A National Initiative. Paper presented at the Project on Death in America Annual Social Work Leader's Research Retreat. Lake Tahoe, Calif., July.

Cumming, E., and W. E. Henry. 1961. *Growing Old*. New York: Basic Books.

Cutcliffe, J. R. 1998. Hope, Counseling, and Complicated Bereavement Reactions. *Journal of Advanced Nursing* 28:760.

Cytron, B. D. 1993. To Honor the Dead and Comfort the Mourners: Traditions in Judaism. In *Ethnic Variations in Dying, Death and Grief: Diversity in Universality*, edited by

D. P. Irish, K.F. Lundquist, and V. J. Nelsen, 113–25. Washington, D.C.: Taylor & Francis.

Czaja, S. J., and C. C. Lee. 2001. The Internet and Older Adults: Design Challenges and Opportunities. In *Communication, Technology and Aging: Opportunities and Challenges for the Future*, edited by N. Charness and D. C. Parks, 60–78. New York: Springer.

Dane, B. O. 1989. Middle-Aged Adults Mourning the Death of a Parent. *Journal of Gerontological Social Work* 14:75–89.

Dane, B. O. 1991. Counseling Bereaved Middle Aged Children: Parental Suicide Survivors. *Clinical Social Work Journal* 19:35–48.

Dane, B. O. 2004. Integrating Spirituality and Religion. In *Living with Dying: A Handbook for End-of-Life Healthcare Practitioners*, edited by J. Berzoff and P. R. Silverman, 424–38. New York: Columbia University Press.

Davidson, K. 1999. *Gender, Age and Widowhood: How Older Widows and Widowers Differently Realign Their Lives*. Guilford: University of Surrey.

Davies, B. 1991. Long-Term Outcomes of Adolescent Sibling Bereavement. *Journal of Adolescent Research* 6:83–96.

Davies, B. 1994. Sibling Bereavement Research: State of the Art. In *A Challenge for Living: Dying, Death and Bereavement*, edited by J. B. Corless, B. B. Germino, and M. Pittman, 173–201. Boston: Jones and Bartlett.

Davies, B. 1999. *Shadow in the Sun: The Experience of Sibling Bereavement in Childhood*. Philadelphia: Brunner/Mazel.

Davis, C. G. 2001. The Tormented and the Transformed: Understanding Responses to Loss and Trauma. In *Meaning Reconstruction and the Experience of Loss*, edited by R. A. Neimeyer, 137–55. Washington, D.C.: American Psychological Association.

Davis, C. G., and D. R. Lehman. 1995. Counterfactual Thinking and Coping with Traumatic Life Events. In *What Might Have Been: The Social Psychology of Counterfactual Thinking*, edited by N. J. Roese and J. M. Olson, 353–74. Mahwah, N.J.: Erlbaum.

Davis, C. G., and S. Nolen-Hoeksema. 2001. Loss and Meaning: How Do People Make Sense of Loss. *American Behavioral Scientist* 44:726–41.

Davis, C. G., C. B. Wortman, D. R. Lehman, and R. C. Silver. 2000. Searching for Meaning in Loss: Are Clinical Assumptions Correct? *Death Studies* 24:497–540.

Davis, D. L., M. Stewart, and R. J. Harmon. 1988. Perinatal Loss: Providing Emotional Support for Bereaved Parents. *Birth* 14:242–46.

Davis, K. 1988. Interparental Violence: The Children as Victims. *Issues in Comprehensive Pediatric Nursing* 11:291–302.

Deaton, R. L., and D. Morgan. 1992. *Managing Death Issues in the Schools*. Monograph no. 1. Helena: Montana Office of Public Instruction.

Deevey, S. 1997. Bereavement Experiences in Lesbian Kinship Networks in Ohio. Ph.D. diss., Ohio State University.

DeFrain, J. 1991. Learning About Grief from Normal Families: SIDS, Stillbirth, and Miscarriage. *Journal of Marital and Family Therapy* 17:215–32.

De-Leo, D., M. D. Buona, and J. Dwyer. 2002. Suicide Among the Elderly: The Long-Term Impact of a Telephone Support and Assessment Intervention in Northern Italy. *British Journal of Psychiatry* 181:226–29.

Demi, A. S. 1987. Hospice Bereavement Programs: Trends and Issues. In *Hospice: The Nursing Perspective*, edited by S. Schraff, 131–51. New York: National League for Nursing.

Demi, A. S. 1989. Death of a Spouse. In *Midlife Loss: Coping Strategies*, edited by R. Kalish, 218–48. Newbury Park, Calif.: Sage.

Denzin, N. K. 1974. The Methodological Implications of Symbolic Interactionism for the Study of Deviance. *British Journal of Sociology* 25:269–82.

DePorto, D. 2003. Battered Women and Separation Abuse: A Treatment Approach Based on "Knowing." In *Handbook of Counseling Women*, edited by M. Kopala and M. A. Keitel, 279–306. Thousand Oaks, Calif.: Sage.

DePrince, A. P., and J. J. Freyd. 2002. The Intersection of Gender and Betrayal in Trauma. In *Gender and PTSD*, edited by R. Kimerling, P. Ouimette, and J. Wolfe, 98–116. New York: Guilford Press.

Deranieri, J. I., P. T. Clements Jr., and G. C. Henry. 2002. Assessment and Intervention After Sudden Traumatic Death. *Journal of Psychosocial Nursing* 40:30–37.

Dershimer, R. 1990. *Counseling the Bereaved*. New York: Pergamon Press.

Desetta, A. 1996. *The Heart Knows Something Different: Teenage Voices from the Foster Care System*. New York: Persea Books.

De Simone, M. 1996. Birth Mother Loss: Contributing Factors to Unresolved Grief. *Clinical Social Work Journal* 24:65–76.

DeVries, B., R. D. Lana, and V. T. Falck. 1994. Parental Bereavement over the Life Course: A Theoretical Intersection and Empirical View. *Omega* 29:47–69.

DeVries, H. M., D. W. Hamilton, S. Lovett, and D. Gallagher-Thompson. 1997. Patterns of Coping Preferences for Male and Female Caregivers of Frail Older Adults. *Psychology and Aging* 12:263–67.

Dickinson, G. E., E. D. Sumner, and L. M. Frederick. 1992. Death Education in Selected Health Professions. *Death Studies* 16:281–89.

DiGuilio, J. F. 1992. Early Widowhood: An Atypical Transition. *Journal of Mental Health Counseling* 14:97–109.

Dijkstra, I. C., and M. S. Stroebe. 1998. The Impact of a Child's Death on Parents: A Myth Not Yet Disproved? *Journal of Family Studies* 4:187–99.

DiMarco, M., E. M. Menke, and T. McNamara. 2001. Evaluating a Support Group for Perinatal Loss. *American Journal of Maternal/Child Nursing* 26:135–40.

Dimond, M. 1981. Bereavement and the Elderly: A Critical Review with Implications for Nursing Practice and Research. *Journal of Advanced Nursing* 6:461–70.

Dixon, D., S. Cruess, K. Kilbourn, N. Klimas, M. A. Fletcher, G. Ironson, A. Baum, N. Schneiderman, and M. H. Antoni. 2001. Social Support Mediates Loneliness and Human Herpes Virus Type 6 HHV-6 Antibody Titers. *Journal of Applied Social Psychology* 31:1111–32.

Dixon, L. 1999. Providing Services to Families of Persons with Schizophrenia: Present and Future. *Journal of Mental Health Policy and Economics* 2:3–8.

Doka, K. J. 1987. Silent Sorrow: Grief and the Loss of Significant Others. *Death Studies* 11:455–69.

Doka, K. J. 1989a. Death, Loss, and Disenfranchised Grief. In *Disenfranchised Grief— Recognizing Hidden Sorrow*, edited by K. J. Doka, 13–23. Lexington, Mass.: Lexington Books.

Doka, K. J., ed. 1989b. *Disenfranchised Grief—Recognizing Hidden Sorrow*. Lexington, Mass.: Lexington Books.

Doka, K. J. 1989c. A Later Loss: The Grief of Ex-Spouses. In *Disenfranchised Grief— Recognizing Hidden Sorrow*, edited by K. J. Doka, 103–13. Lexington, Mass.: Lexington Books.

Doka, K. J. 1989d. The Left Lover: Grief in Extramarital Affairs and Cohabitation. In *Disenfranchised Grief—Recognizing Hidden Sorrow*, edited by K. J. Doka, 67–76. Lexington, Mass.: Lexington Books.

Doka, K. J. 1993. *Living with Life-Threatening Illness*. Lexington, Mass.: Lexington Books.

Doka, K. J. 1997. When Illness Is Prolonged: Implications for Grief. In *Living with Grief: When Illness Is Prolonged*, edited by K. J. Doka, 5–15. Washington, D.C.: Hospice Foundation of America.

Doka, K. J. 2000a. *Men Don't Cry . . . Women Do: Transcending Gender Stereotypes of Grief*. Philadelphia: Brunner/Mazel.

Doka, K. J. 2000b. *Using Ritual with Children and Adolescents*. In *Living with Grief: Children, Adolescents, and Loss*, edited by K. J. Doka, 153–59. Washington, D.C.: Hospice Foundation of America.

Doka, K. J. 2002a. Introduction to *Disenfranchised Grief: New Directions, Challenges and Strategies for Practice*, edited by K. J. Doka, 323–36. Champaign, Ill: Research Press.

Doka, K. J. 2002b. *Living with Grief: Loss in Later Life*. Washington, D.C.: Hospice Foundation of America.

Doka, K. J. 2002c. The Role of Ritual in the Treatment of Disenfranchised Grief. In *Disenfranchised Grief: New Directions, Challenges, and Strategies for Practice*, edited by K. J. Doka, 135–47. Champaign, Ill.: Research Press.

Doka, K. J. 2003. *Living with Grief: Coping with Public Tragedy*. Washington, D.C.: Hospice Foundation of America.

Doka, K. J. 2004. Interview. Available at: http://www.hospicefoundation.org/publications/doka5.htm. Accessed September 8, 2004.

Doka, K. J., and J. D. Davidson. 1996. *Living with Grief After Sudden Loss*. Washington, D.C.: Hospice Foundation of America.

Doka, K. J., and J. D. Davidson. 1998. Who We Are, How We Grieve. In *Living with Grief: Who We Are and How We Grieve*, edited by K. J. Doka and J. D. Davidson, 1–5. Philadelphia: Brunner/Mazel.

Doka, K. J., and T. Martin. 2001. Take It Like a Man: Masculine Response to Loss. In *Men Coping with Grief*, edited by D. A. Lund, 37–47. Amityville, N.Y.: Baywood.

Donahue, M. J., and P. L. Benson. 1995. Religion and the Well-being of Adolescents. *Journal of Social Issues* 51:145–61.

Doty, P. J., R. Stone, M. E. Jackson, and J. L. Drabek. 2005. Informal Caregiving. In *The Continuum of Long Term Care*, 3rd ed., edited by C. J. Evashivick, 139–52. Albany, N.Y.: Delmar.

Douglas, J. 1991. Patterns of Change Following Parent Death in Midlife Adults. *Omega* 22:123–37.

Dowd, S. B., V. L. Poole, R. Davidhizar, and J. N. Giger. 1998. Death, Dying, and Grief in a Transcultural Context: Application of the Giger and Davidhizar Assessment Model. *Hospice Journal* 13:33–47.

Dressel, P. L., and S. K. Barnhill. 1994. Reframing Gerontological Thought and Practices: The Case of Grandmothers with Daughters in Prison. *The Gerontologist* 34:685–91.

Drysdale, A. E., C. F. Nelson, and N. M. Wineman. 1993. Families Need Help Too: Group Treatment for Families of Nursing Home Residents. *Clinical Nurse Specialist* 7:130–34.

Ducharme, F., and D. Trudeau. 2002. Qualitative Evaluation of a Stress Management Intervention for Elderly Caregivers at Home: A Constructivist Approach. *Issues in Mental Health Nursing* 23:691–713.

Duckworth, G., and H. McBride. 1996. Suicide in Old Age: A Tragedy of Neglect. *Canadian Journal of Psychiatry* 41:217–22.

Duncombe, J., and D. Marsden. 1993. Love and Intimacy: The Gender Division of Emotion and "Emotion Work." *Sociology* 2:221–41.

Dupuis, S. 2002. Understanding Ambiguous Loss in the Context of Dementia Care: Adult Children's Perspective. *Journal of Gerontological Social Work* 37:93–114.

Dworkin, J., and D. Kaufer. 1995. Social Services and Bereavement in the Gay and Lesbian Community. In *HIV Disease: Lesbians, Gays and the Social Services*, edited by G. Lloyd and M. A. Kuszelewicz, 41–60. New York: Harrington Park Press.

Dyregrov, A. 2001. Early Intervention—A Family Perspective. *Advances in Mind-Body Medicine* 17:168–74.

Dyregrov, A. 2004. Educational Consequences of Loss and Trauma. *Educational and Child Psychology* 21:77–84.

Eakes, G. G. 1995. Chronic Sorrow: The Lived Experience of Parents of Chronically Mentally Ill Individuals. *Archives of Psychiatric Nursing* 9:77–84.

Eakes, G. G., M. L. Burke, and M. A. Hainsworth. 1998. Middle-Range Theory of Chronic Sorrow. *Journal of Gerontological Nursing Scholarship* 30:179–84.

Edelman, B. 1994. Interpersonal Relationships. *Annual Review of Psychology* 45:89–113.

Edelstein, S., D. Burge, and J. Waterman. 2001. Helping Foster Parents Cope with Separation, Loss and Grief. *Child Welfare* 80:5–25.

Eden, O. B., I. Black, G. A. MacKinlay, and A. E. Emery. 1994. Communication with Parents of Children with Cancer. *Palliative Medicine* 8:105–14.

Eggert, L. L., E. A. Thompson, J. R. Herring, and L. J. Nicholas. 1995. Reducing Suicide Potential Among High-Risk Youth: Tests of a School-Based Prevention Program. *Suicide and Life-Threatening Behavior* 25:276–96.

Elbow, M. 1982. Children of Violent Marriages: The Forgotten Victims. *Social Casework: Journal of Contemporary Social Work* 63:465–71.

Elder, G. H., Jr., J. K. Liker, and B. J. Jaworski. 1994. Hardship in Lives: Depression Influences from the 1930s to Old Age in Postwar America. In *Life Span Developmental Psychology: Historical and Generational Effects*, edited by K. A. McCluskey and H. W. Reese, 161–201. Orlando, Fla.: Academic Press.

Elder, S. L., and D. Knowles. 2002. Suicide in the Family. In *Helping Bereaved Children*, edited by N. B. Webb, 128–48. New York: Guilford Press.

Elders, M. A. 1995. Theory and Present Thinking in Bereavement. *Issues in Psychoanalytic Psychology* 17:67–83.

Ellis, R. R. 1998. Multicultural Grief Counseling. In *Living with Grief: Who We Are; How We Grieve*, edited by K. J. Doka and J. D. Davidson, 248–60. Washington, D.C.: Hospice Foundation of America.

Emanuel, E. J., L. Fairclough, J. Slutsman, H. Alpert, D. Baldwin, and L. L. Emanuel. 1999. Assistance from Family Members, Friends, Paid Care Givers, and Volunteers in the Care of Terminally Ill Patients. *New England Journal of Medicine* 341:956–63.

Emiliani, P. L. 2001. Special Needs and Enabling Technologies: An Evolving Approach to Accessibility. In *User Interfaces for All: Concepts, Methods, and Tools*, edited by C. Stephanidis, 97–113. Mahwah, N.J.: Erlbaum.

Emlet, C. A., J. L. Crabtree, V. A. Condon, and L. A. Treml. 1996. *In-Home Assessment of Older Adults: An Interdisciplinary Approach*. Gaithersburg, Md.: Aspen.

Emswiler, M. A., and J. P. Emswiler. 2000. *Guiding Your Child Through Grief*. New York: Bantam Books.

Engel, G. 1961. Is Grief a Disease: A Challenge for Medical Research? *Psychosomatic Medicine* 23:18–27.

Enns, C. Z. 2002. Prevention and Treatment of Family Violence. In *Counseling Across the Lifespan: Prevention and Treatment*, edited by C. L. Juntenen and D. R. Atkinson, 279–95. Thousand Oaks, Calif.: Sage.

Epple, D. 2002. Senile Dementia of the Alzheimer's type. *Clinical Social Work Journal* 30:95–109.

Erikson, E. H. 1950. *Childhood and Society*. New York: Norton.

Erikson, E. H. 1963. *Childhood and Society*. 2nd ed. New York: Norton.

Erikson, E. H. 1968. *Identity: Youth and Crisis*. New York: Norton.

Erikson, E. H. 1978. *Adulthood*. New York: Norton.

Erikson, E. H. 1982. *The Life Cycle Completed: A Review*. New York: Norton.

Erikson, E. H., and J. M. Erikson. 1981. On Generativity and Identity: From a Conversation with Erik and Joan Erikson. *Harvard Educational Review* 51:249–69.

Erikson, E. H., J. M. Erikson, and H. Q. Kivnick. 1986. *Vital Involvement in Old Age*. New York: Norton.

Ersek, M., M. Kagawa-Singer, D. Barnes, L. Blackhall, and B. A. Koenig. 1998. Multicultural Considerations in the Use of Advance Directives. *Oncology Nursing Forum* 25:1683–90.

Essa, M. 1986. Grief as a Crisis: Psychotherapeutic Interventions with Elderly Bereaved. *American Journal of Psychotherapy* 40:243–51.

Fanos, J. H. 1996. *Sibling Loss.* Mahwah, N.J.: Erlbaum.

Fanos, J. H., and B. G. Nickerson. 1991. Long-Term Effects of Sibling Death During Adolescence. *Journal of Adolescent Research* 6:70–82.

Farkas, J. I., and C. I. Hines. 1997. The Influence of Caregiving and Employment on the Voluntary Activities of Midlife and Older Women. *Journals of Gerontology* 52B:S180–89.

Farnsworth, E. B., and K. R. Allen. 1996. Mother's Bereavement: Experiences of Marginalization, Stories of Change. *Family Relations* 45:360–67.

Farran, C. J., E. Keane-Hagerty, S. Salloway, S. Kupferer, and C. S. Wilkin. 1991. Finding Meaning: An Alternative Paradigm for Alzheimer's Disease Family Caregivers. *The Gerontologist* 31:483–89.

Feil, N. 1993. *The Validation Breakthrough: Simple Techniques for Communication with People with Alzheimer's-Type Dementia.* Baltimore: Health Professions Press.

Feil, N. 1999. Current Concepts and Techniques in Validation Therapy. In *Handbook of Counseling and Psychotherapy with Older Adults,* edited by M. Duffy, 590–613. New York: Wiley.

Feld, S., and L. K. George. 1994. Moderating Effects of Prior Social Resources on the Hospitalizations of Elders Who Become Widowed. *Journal of Aging and Health* 6:275–95.

Fenechel, O. 1945. *Psychoanalytic Theory of Neurosis:* New York: Psychoanalytic Association.

Field, M. J., and C. K. Cassel, eds. 1997. *Approaching Death: Improving Care at the End of Life.* Washington, D.C.: National Academy Press.

Figley, C. R. 1989. *Helping Traumatized Families.* San Francisco: Jossey-Bass.

Figley, C. R. 1995. Compassion Fatigue as a Secondary Traumatic Stress Disorder: An Overview. In *Compassion Fatigue: Coping with Secondary Traumatic Stress Disorder in Those Who Treat the Traumatized,* edited by C. R. Figley, 1–20. New York: Brunner/Mazel.

Figley, C. R. 2002. Introduction to *Treating Compassion Fatigue,* edited by C. R. Figley, 1–16. New York: Routledge.

Finkelstein, H. 1988. The Long-Term Effects of Early Parent Death. *Journal of Clinical Psychology* 44:3–9.

Finley, L. Y. 1998. The Cultural Context: Families Coping with Severe Mental Illness. *Psychiatric Rehabilitation Journal* 21:230–40.

Finnegan, J. 1993. *Shattered Dreams—Lonely Choices: Birth Parents of Babies with Disabilities Talk About Adoption.* Westport, Conn.: Bergin and Garvey.

Fitzgerald, H. 1992. *The Grieving Child: A Parent's Guide.* New York: Simon and Schuster.

Fleming, S. J., and R. Adolph. 1986. Helping Bereaved Adolescents: Needs and Responses. In *Adolescence and Death,* edited by C. A. Corr and J. N. McNeil, 139–54. New York: Springer.

Fleming, S. J., and L. E. Balmer. 1996. Bereavement in Adolescence. In *Handbook of Adolescent Death and Bereavement,* edited by C. C. Corr and D.E. Balk, 139–54. New York: Springer.

Fleming, S. J., and S. K. Bélanger. 2001. Trauma, Grief and Surviving Childhood Sexual Abuse. In *Meaning Reconstruction and the Experience of Loss*, edited by R. A. Neimeyer, 311–30. Washington, D.C.: American Psychological Association.

Fleming, S. J., and P. J. Robinson. 1991. The Application of Cognitive Therapy to the Bereaved. In *The Challenge of Cognitive Therapy: Applications to Nontraditional Populations*, edited by T. M. Vallis, J. L. Howes, and P. C. Miller, 135–58. New York: Plenum.

Fleming, S. J., and P. J. Robinson. 2001. Grief and Cognitive Behavioral Therapy: The Reconstruction of Meaning. In *Handbook of Bereavement Research: Consequences, Coping and Care*, edited by M. S. Stroebe, R. O. Hansson, W. Stroebe, and H. Schut, 647–69. Washington, D.C.: American Psychological Association.

Fogarty, J. A. 2000. *The Magical Thoughts of Grieving Children: Treating Children with Complicated Mourning and Advice for Parents*. Amityville, N.Y.: Baywood.

Fogelman, E. 1989. Group Treatment as a Therapeutic Modality for Generations of the Holocaust. In *Psychotherapy with Holocaust Survivors and Their Families*, edited by P. Marcus and A. Rosenberg, 119–33. New York: Praeger.

Folkman, S. 2001. Revised Coping Theory and the Process of Bereavement. In *Handbook of Bereavement Research: Consequences, Coping and Care*, edited by M. S. Stroebe, R. O. Hansson, W. Stroebe, and H. Schut, 563–84. Washington, D.C.: American Psychological Association.

Folkman, D., and R. Lazarus. 1984. *Stress, Appraisal, and Coping*. New York: Springer.

Folkman, S., and J. T. Moskowitz. 2000. Positive Affect and the Other Side of Coping. *American Psychologist* 55:647–54.

Forte, J. A., A. V. Barrett, and M. H. Campbell. 1996. Patterns of Social Connectedness and Shared Grief Work: A Symbolic Interactionist Perspective. *Social Work with Groups* 19:29–51.

Foster, Z., and K. Davidson. 1995. Satisfactions and Stresses for the Social Worker. In *A Challenge for Living: Dying, Death, and Bereavement*, edited by I. B. Corless, B. B. Germino, and M. A. Pittman, 285–300. Boston: Jones and Bartlett.

Fox, R., and M. Cooper. 1998. The Effects of Suicide on the Private Practitioner: A Professional and Personal Perspective. *Clinical Social Work Journal* 171:55–64.

Fox, S. S. 1985. *Good Grief: Helping Groups of Children When a Friend Dies*. Boston: New England Association for the Education of Young Children.

Fraley, R. C., and P. R. Shaver. 1999. Loss and Bereavement: Attachment Theory and Recent Controversies Concerning "Grief Work" and the Nature of Detachment. In *Handbook of Attachment: Theory, Research and Clinical Applications*, edited by J. S. Cassidy and P. R. Shaver, 735–59. New York: Guilford Press.

Frank, E., H. G. Prigerson, M. K. Shear, and C. F. Reynolds III. 1997. Phenomenology and Treatment of Bereavement-Related Distress in the Elderly. *International Clinical Psychopharmacology* 12 (suppl. 7):S25–29.

Frankenstein, E., producer and director, and L. Brady. 1997. *Carved from the Heart* (video). Hohokus, N.J.: New Day Films.

Frankl, V. E. 1959. *Man's Search for Meaning*. Revised and updated. New York: Simon and Schuster.

Franson, J. P. 1988. Coping with the Trauma of a Violent Death. *NASSP Bulletin* 72:88–91.

Frantz, T. T., M. M. Farrell, and B. C. Trolley. 2001. Positive Outcomes of Losing a Loved One. In *Meaning Reconstruction and the Experience of Loss*, edited by R. A. Neimeyer, 191–212. Washington, D.C.: American Psychological Association.

Frantz, T. T., B. C. Trolley, and M. P. Johll. 1996. Religious Aspects of Bereavement. *Pastoral Psychology* 44:151–63.

Fredriksen-Goldsen, K. I. 2006. Caregiving and Resiliency: Predictors of Well-being. *Journal of Family Relations*.

Fredriksen-Goldsen, K. I., and N. R. Hooyman. 2003. Multigenerational Health, Development and Equality. Concept paper, University of Washington School of Social Work.

Freeman, E. M. 1984a. Loss and Grief in Children: Implications for School Social Workers. *Social Work in Education* 6:241–58.

Freeman, E. M. 1984b. Multiple Losses in the Elderly: An Ecological Approach. *Social Casework: Journal of Contemporary Social Work* 65:287–96.

Freeman, E. M. 1987. Interaction of Pregnancy, Loss, and Developmental Issues in Adolescents. *Social Casework: Journal of Contemporary Social Work* 68:38–46.

Freeman, L., D. Shaffer, and H. Smith. 1996. Neglected Victims of Homicide: The Needs of Young Siblings of Murder Victims. *American Journal of Orthopsychiatry* 66:337–45.

Freeman, S. J. 1991. Group Facilitation of the Grieving Process with Those Bereaved by Suicide. *Journal of Counseling and Development* 69:328–31.

Freud, S. 1910. The Future Prospects of Psychoanalytic Therapy. In *Collected Papers of Sigmund Freud*, edited by E. Jones, vol. 2, 285–96. New York: Basic Books.

Freud, S. 1917. *The Complete Psychological Works*. London: Hogarth Press.

Freud, S. 1953. Totem and Taboo. In *The Standard Edition of the Complete Psychological Works of Sigmund Freud*, vol. 13, 18–74. London: Hogarth Press.

Freud, S. 1955. Case Histories. In *The Standard Edition of the Complete Psychological Works of Sigmund Freud*, vol. 2, 22–181. London: Hogarth Press.

Freud, S. 1957. Mourning and Melancholia. In *The Standard Edition of the Complete Psychological Works of Sigmund Freud*, vol. 14, 243–58. London: Hogarth Press.

Freud, S. 1961. *Letters of Sigmund Freud*. New York: Basic Books.

Fristad, M. A., J. Cerel, M. Goldman, E. B. Weller, and R. A. Weller. 2001. The Role of Ritual in Children's Bereavement. *Omega* 42:321–39.

Fristad, M. A., R. Jedel, R. Weller, and E. Weller. 1993. Psychosocial Functioning in Children After the Death of a Parent. *American Journal of Psychiatry* 150:511–13.

Frost, M., and J. T. Condon. 1996. The Psychological Sequelae of Miscarriage: A Critical Review of the Literature. *Australian and New Zealand Journal of Psychiatry* 30:54–62.

Fry, P. S. 1997. Grandparents' Reactions to the Death of a Grandchild: An Exploratory Factor Analysis. *Omega* 35:119–40.

Frydman-Helfant, S. 1994. Sibling Bereavement. Master's thesis, University of Haifa.

Fuller-Thomson, E., M. Minkler, and D. Driver. 1997. A Profile of Grandparents Raising Grandchildren in the United States. *The Gerontologist* 37:406–11.

Furman, E. 1974. *A Child's Parent Dies: Studies in Childhood Bereavement*. New Haven, Conn.: Yale University Press.

Gabbard, G. O. 1999. An Overview of Countertransference: Theory and Technique. In *Countertransference Issues in Psychiatric Treatment*, edited by G. O. Gabbard, 1–25. Washington, D.C.: American Psychiatric Press.

Gabriel, R. M., and J. M. Kirschling. 1989. Assessing Grief Among the Bereaved Elderly: A Review of Existing Measures. *Hospice Journal* 5:29–54.

Galambos, C. 2001. Community Healing Rituals for Survivors of Rape. *Smith College Studies in Social Work* 71:441–57.

Gallagher-Thompson, D., S. Lovett, J. Rose, C. McKibbin, D. Coon, A. Futterman, and L. W. Thompson. 2000. Impact of Psychoeducational Interventions on Distressed Family Caregivers. *Journal of Clinical Geropsychology* 6:91–110.

Gallup, G., Jr., and D. M. Lindsay. 1999. *Surveying the Religious Landscape: Trends in U.S. Beliefs*. Harrisburg, Pa.: Morehouse.

Gamble, S. J. 2002. Self-Care for Bereavement Counselors. In *Helping Bereaved Children: A Handbook for Practitioners*, edited by N. B. Webb, 346–62. New York: Guilford Press.

Garbarino, J., and K. Kostelny. 1997. What Children Can Tell Us About Living in a War Zone. In *Children in a Violent Society*, edited by J. D. Osofsky, 32–41. New York: Guilford Press.

Garcia-Preto, N. 1991. Puerto Rican Families. In *Living Beyond Loss*, edited by F. M. Walsh and M. McCormick, 192–200. New York: Norton.

Garrett, M. T., and M. P. Wilbur. 1999. Does the Worm Live in the Ground? Reflections on Native American Spirituality. *Journal of Multicultural Counseling and Development* 27:193–206.

Garrison, C. Z., R. E. McKeown, R. F. Valois, and M. L. Vincent. 1993. Aggression, Substance Use, and Suicidal Behaviors in High School Students. *American Journal of Public Health* 83:179–84.

Garvin, V., N. Kalter, and J. Hansell. 1993. Divorced Women: Factors Contributing to Resiliency and Vulnerability. *Journal of Divorce and Remarriage* 21:21–39.

Gass, K. A. 1987. The Health of Conjugally Bereaved Older Widows: The Role of Appraisal. *Research in Nursing and Health* 10:39–47.

Gass-Sternas, K. A. 1995. Single Parent Widows: Stressors, Appraisal, Coping, Resources, Grieving Responses, and Health. *Marriage and Family Review* 20:411–45.

Gaugler, J. E., R. A. Kane, and J. Langlois. 2000. Assessment of Family Caregivers of Older Adults. In *Assessing Older Persons: Measures, Meaning and Practical Applications*, edited by R. L. Kane and R. A. Kane, 320–59. New York: Oxford University Press.

Geen, R. G., and M. B. Quanty. 1977. The Catharsis of Aggression: An Evaluation of a Hypothesis. In *Advances in Experimental Social Psychology*, edited by L. Berkowitz, vol. 10, 1–37. New York: Academic Press.

Gentry, J. E., A. B. Baranowsky, and K. Dunning. 2002. ARP: The Accelerated Recovery Program ARP for Compassion Fatigue. In *Treating Compassion Fatigue*, edited by C. R. Figley, 123–37. New York: Routledge.

George, L. K., and L. P. Gwyther. 1986. Caregiver Well-being: A Multidimensional Examination of Family Caregivers of Demented Patients. *The Gerontologist* 26:253–59.

Gergen, K. J. 1994. Mind, Text and Society: Self-Memory in Social Context. In *The Remembering Self: Construction and Accuracy in the Self-Narrative*, edited by U. Neisser and R. Fivush, 78–104. Cambridge: Cambridge University Press.

Gibson, D. M., and J. E. Myers. 2000. Gender and Infertility: A Relational Approach to Counseling Women. *Journal of Counseling and Development* 78:400–410.

Gil, E. 1988. *Treatment of Adult Survivors of Childhood Abuse*. San Francisco: Launch Press.

Gil, E. 1998. *Essentials of Play Therapy with Abused Children: Video Manual*. New York: Guilford Press.

Gilbert, K. R. 1996. "We've Had the Same Loss, Why Don't We Have the Same Grief?" Loss and Differential Grief in Families. *Death Studies* 20:269–83.

Gilbert, K. R. 1997. Couple Coping with the Death of a Child. In *Death and Trauma: The Traumatology of Grieving*, edited by C. R. Figley, B. E. Bride, and N. Mazza, 101–21. Philadelphia: Taylor & Francis.

Gilbert, K. R., and L. S. Smart. 1992. *Coping with Infant or Fetal Loss: The Couple's Healing Process*. New York: Brunner/Mazel.

Gilliland, G., and S. Fleming. 1998. A Comparison of Spousal Anticipatory Grief and Conventional Grief. *Death Studies* 22:541–70.

Gilroy, B. D. 2001. Using Magic Therapeutically with Children. In *101 More Favorite Play Therapy Techniques*, edited by H. G. Kaduson, and C. E. Schaefer, 429–38. Northvale, N.J.: Aronson.

Gitlin, L. N., M. Corcoran, L. Winter, A. Boyce, and W. W. Hauck. 2001. A Randomized, Controlled Trial of a Home Environmental Intervention: Effect on Efficacy and Upset in Caregivers and on Daily Function of Persons with Dementia. *The Gerontologist* 41:4–14.

Glass, E., D. Cluxton, and P. Rancour. 2001. Principles of Patient and Family Assessment. In *Textbook of Palliative Nursing*, edited by B. F. Ferrell and N. Coyle, 37–50. New York: Oxford University Press.

Gloria, A. M., and E. R. Rodriguez. 2000. Counseling Latino University Students: Psychosociocultural Issues for Consideration. *Journal of Counseling and Development* 78:145–54.

Goldman, L. 1996. *Breaking the Silence: A Guide to Helping Children with Complicated Grief: Suicide, Homicide, AIDS, Violence, and Abuse*. Washington, D.C.: Accelerated Development.

Goldman, L. 2000. *Life and Loss: A Guide to Help Grieving Children*. 2nd ed. Philadelphia: Accelerated Development.

Goldman, L. 2001. *Breaking the Silence: A Guide to Helping Children with Complicated Grief: Suicide, Homicide, AIDS, Violence and Abuse*. 2nd ed. New York: Taylor & Francis.

Goldman, T., and J. Miller. 1995. *When a Man Faces Grief: A Man You Know Is Grieving*. Fort Wayne, Ind.: Willowgreen Press.

Goldwasser, A. N., S. M. Auerbach, and S. W. Harkins. 1987. Cognitive, Affective, and Behavioral Effects of Reminiscence Group Therapy on Demented Elderly. *International Journal of Aging and Human Development* 10:555–57.

Goldworthy, R., and A. Coyle. 1999. Spiritual Beliefs and the Search for Meaning Among Older Adults Following Partner Loss. *Mortality* 4:21–41.

Gonyea, J. 2006. Midlife, Multigenerational Bonds, and Caregiving. In *Caregiving: Science to Practice*, edited by R. Talley. New York: Oxford University Press.

Goodkin, K., T. T. Baldewicz, N. T. Blaney, D. Asthana, M. Kumar, P. Shapshak, B. Leeds, J. E. Burkhalter, D. Rigg, M. D. Tyll, J. Cohen, and W. L. Zheng. 2001. Physiological Effects of Bereavement and Bereavement Support Group Interventions. In *Handbook of Bereavement Research: Consequences, Coping and Care*, edited by M. S. Stroebe, R. O. Hansson, W. Stroebe, and H. Schut, 671–703. Washington, D.C.: American Psychological Association.

Goodkin, K., N. T. Blaney, D. J. Feaster, T. Baldewicz, J. E. Burkhalter, and B. Leeds. 1999. A Randomized Controlled Trial of a Bereavement Support Group Intervention in Human Immunodeficiency Virus Type 1 Seropositive and Seronegative Homosexual Men. *Archives of General Psychiatry* 55:52–59.

Goodman, M., R. L. Rubenstein, B. B. Alexander, and M. Luborsky. 1991. Cultural Differences Among Elderly Women in Coping with the Death of an Adult Child. *Journals of Gerontology* 46B:S321–29.

Gottlieb, L. N., A. Lang, and R. Amsel 1996. The Long-Term Effects of Grief on Marital Intimacy Following an Infant's Death. *Omega* 33:1–19.

Gough, M. 2000. Smashing Pumpkins and Blind Melons: Using Popular Music to Help Grieving Adolescents. In *Meeting the Needs of Our Clients Creatively: The Impact of Art and Culture on Caregiving*, edited by J. D. Morgan, 151–65. Amityville, N.Y.: Baywood.

Gould, M. S., T. Greenberg, D. M. Velting, and D. Shaffer. 2003. Youth Suicide Risk and Prevention Interventions: A Review of the Past 10 Years. *Journal of the American Academy of Child and Adolescent Psychiatry* 42:386–405.

Gray, K., and A. Lassance. 2003. *Grieving Reproductive Loss: The Healing Process*. Amityville, N.Y.: Baywood.

Gray, R. 1989. Adolescents' Perceptions of Social Support After the Death of a Parent. *Journal of Psychosocial Oncology* 73:127–44.

Gray, S. W., M. R. Zide, and H. Wilker. 2000. Using the Solution Focused Brief Therapy Model with Bereavement Groups in Rural Communities: Resiliency at Its Best. *Hospice Journal* 15:13–30.

Greene, G. J., M. Y. Lee, R. Trask, and J. Rheinscheld. 1996. Client Strengths and Crisis Intervention: A Solution-Focused Approach. *Crisis Intervention* 3:43–63.

Greene, R. 2000. Assessment and Functional Age. In *Social Work with the Aged and Their Families*, edited by R. Greene, 51–67. New York: Aldine.

Greenfield, W. L. 1984. Disruption and Reintegration: Dealing with Familial Response to Nursing Home Placement. *Journal of Gerontological Social Work* 8:15–21.

Grimby, A., 1993. Bereavement Among Elderly People: Grief Reactions, Post-Bereavement Hallucinations and Quality of Life. *Acta Psychiatrica Scandinavica* 87:72–80.

Gritter, J. L. 2000. *Life Givers: Framing the Birthparent Experience in Open Adoption.* Washington, D.C.: Child Welfare League of America.

Groger, L., and P. Mayberry. 2001. Caring Too Much: Cultural Lag in African American's Perceptions of Filial Responsibilities. *Journal of Cross-Cultural Gerontology* 16:21–39.

Grollman, E. A. 1990. *Talking About Death: A Dialogue Between Parent and Child.* Boston: Beacon Press.

Grollman, E. A. 1995. Grieving Children: Can We Answer Their Questions. In *Children Mourning: Mourning Children,* edited by K. J. Doka, 17–27. Washington, D.C.: Hospice Foundation of America.

Groves, B. M., and B. Zuckerman. 1997. Interventions with Parents and Caregivers of Children Who Are Exposed to Violence. In *Children in a Violent Society,* edited by J. D. Osofsky, 183–201. New York: Guilford Press.

Grych, J. H., and F. D. Fincham. 1992. Interventions for Children of Divorce: Toward Greater Integration of Research and Action. *Psychological Bulletin* 111:434–54.

Gustafson, D. H., R. P. Hawkins, E. W. Boberg, F. McTavish, B. Owens, M. Wise, H. Berhe, and S. Pingree. 2002. CHESS: 10 Years of Research and Development in Consumer Health Informatics for Broad Populations, Including the Underserved. *International Journal of Medical Informatics* 65:169–77.

Gustafson, D. H., R. P. Hawkins, S. Pingree, F. McTavish, N. K. Arora, J. Mendenhall, D. F. Cella, and R. C. Serlin. 2001. Effect of Computer Support on Younger Women with Breast Cancer. *Journal of General Internal Medicine* 16:435–45.

Gwyther, L. 1998. Social Issues of the Alzheimer's Patient and Family. *Neurological Clinics* 18:993–1010.

Hagemeister, A. F., and P. C. Rosenblatt. 1997. Grief and the Sexual Relationship of Couples Who Have Experienced a Child's Death. *Death Studies* 21:231–52.

Hagman, G. H. 1995. Mourning: A Review and Reconsideration. *International Journal of Psychoanalysis* 765:909–25.

Hagman, G. H. 2001. Beyond Decathexis: Toward a New Psychoanalytic Understanding and Treatment of Mourning. In *Meaning Reconstruction and the Experience of Loss,* edited by R. A. Neimeyer, 13–32. Washington, D.C.: American Psychological Association.

Haight, W. L., J. E. Black, S. Mangelsdorf, G. Giorgio, L. Tata, S. Schoppe, and M. Szewczyk. 2002. Making Visits Better: The Perspectives of Parents, Foster Parents and Child Welfare Workers. *Child Welfare* 81:173–202.

Hakanen, E. A. 1995. Emotional Use of Music by African American Adolescents. *Howard Journal of Communications* 5:214–22.

Hall, M., and M. Irwin. 2001. Physiological Indices of Functioning in Bereavement.

In *Handbook of Bereavement: Consequences, Coping and Care*, edited by M. S. Stroebe, R. O. Hansson, W. Stroebe, and H. Schut, 473–93. Washington, D.C.: American Psychological Association.

Hallas, D. M. 2002. A Model for Successful Foster Child–Foster Parent Relationships. *Journal of Pediatric Health Care* 16:112–18.

Hamdy, R., J. Turnbull, J. Edwards, and M. Lancaster. 1994. *Alzheimer's Disease: A Handbook for Caregivers*. St. Louis: Mosby.

Hansson, R. O., and M. S. Stroebe. 2003. Grief, Older Adulthood. In *Encyclopedia of Primary Prevention and Health Promotion*, edited by T. P. Gullotta and M. Bloom, 515–21. New York: Plenum.

Harris, M. 1995. *The Loss That Is Forever: The Lifelong Impact of the Early Death of a Mother or Father*. New York: Dutton.

Harris, T., G. Brown, and A. Bifulco. 1986. Loss of Parent in Childhood and Adult Psychiatric Disorder: The Role of Social Class Position and Premarital Pregnancy. *Psychological Medicine* 17:163–83.

Harrison, L., and R. Harrington. 2001. Adolescent's Bereavement Experiences. Prevalence, Association with Depressive Symptoms, and Use of Services. *Journal of Adolescence* 24:159–69.

Hartman, A. 1978. Diagrammatic Assessment of Family Relationships. *Social Casework: Journal of Contemporary Social Work* 59:465–76.

Harvey, J. H. 1996. *Embracing Their Memory: Loss and the Social Psychology of Storytelling*. Boston: Allyn & Bacon.

Harvey, J. H. ed. 1998. *Perspectives on Loss: A Sourcebook*. Philadelphia: Brunner/Mazel.

Harvey, J. H. 2000. *Give Sorrow Words: Perspectives on Loss and Trauma*. Philadelphia: Taylor & Francis.

Harvey, J. H., H. R. Carlson, T. M. Huff, and M. A. Green. 2001. Embracing Memory: The Construction of Accounts of Loss and Hope. In *Meaning Construction and the Experience of Loss*, edited by R. A. Neimeyer, 231–44. Washington, D.C.: American Psychological Association.

Hatton, C. L., and S. M. Valente. 1981. Bereavement Group for Parents Who Suffered a Suicidal Loss of a Child. *Suicide and Life-Threatening Behavior* 11:141–50.

Hatton, R. 2003. Homicide Bereavement Counseling: A Survey of Providers. *Death Studies* 27:427–48.

Hauser, J. M., and B. J. Kramer. 2004. Family Caregivers in Palliative Care. *Clinics in Geriatric Medicine* 20 (special issue on end-of-life-care): 671–88.

Havighurst, R., B. L. Neugarten, and S. Tobin. 1968. Personality and Patterns of Aging. In *Middle Age and Aging*, edited by B. L. Neugarten, 173–77. Chicago: University of Chicago Press.

Hawkins, J. D. R. F. Catalano, R. Kosterman, R. Abbott, and K. G. Hill. 1999. Preventing Adolescent Health-Risk Behaviors by Strengthening Protection During Childhood. *Archives of Pediatrics and Adolescent Medicine* 153:226–34.

Hays, J. C., D. T. Gold, and C. F. Pieper. 1997. Sibling Bereavement in Late Life. *Omega* 35:25–42.

Hebert, M. P. 1998. Perinatal Bereavement in Its Cultural Context. *Death Studies* 22:61–78.

Heller, T., and A. Factor. 1993. Aging Family Caregivers: Support Resources and Changes in Burden and Placement Desire. *American Journal on Mental Retardation* 96:163–76.

Helmreich, W. 1992. *Against All Odds*. New York: Simon and Schuster.

Hemmings, P. 1995. Communicating with Children Through Play. In *Interventions with Bereaved Children*, edited by S. C. Smith and S. M. Pennells, 9–23. London: Kingsley.

Henderson, C. 2001. *Losing Malcolm: A Mother's Journal Through Grief*. Oxford: University Press of Mississippi.

Henry, D. L. 1999. Resilience in Maltreated Children: Implications for Special Needs Adoption. *Child Welfare* 78:519–40.

Herbert, M. P. 2000. Perinatal Bereavement in Its Cultural Context. *Neonatal Intensive Care* 13:38–46.

Herman, J. L. 1992. *Trauma and Recovery: The Aftermath of Violence—From Domestic Abuse to Political Terror*. New York: Basic Books.

Herrenkohl, T. I., E. Magui, K. G. Hill, and R. D. Abbott. 2000. Developmental Risk Factors for Youth Violence. *Journal of Adolescent Health* 26:176–86.

Hess, E. 1999. The Adult Attachment Interview. Historical and Current Perspectives. In *Handbook of Attachment: Theory, Research and Clinical Applications*, edited by J. Cassidy and P. R. Shaver, 395–433. New York: Guilford Press.

Hetherington, E. M., and J. Kelly. 2002. *For Better or for Worse: Divorce Reconsidered*. New York: Norton.

Hilbourne, M. 1999. Living Together Full Time? Middle Class Couples Approaching Retirement. *Aging and Society* 19:161–83.

Hill, R. D., D. Lund, and T. Packard. 1996. Bereavement. In *Treating the Elderly*, edited by J. I. Sheikh, 45–74. San Francisco: Jossey-Bass.

Hilliard, R. E. 2001a. The Effects of Music Therapy–Based Bereavement Groups on Mood and Behavior of Grieving Children: A Pilot Study. *Journal of Music Therapy* 38:291–306.

Hilliard, R. E. 2001b. The Use of Music Therapy in Meeting the Multidimensional Needs of Hospice Patients and Families. *Journal of Palliative Care* 17:161–66.

Hinderer, P. 1995. Music Therapy for Children with Cancer. In *Beyond the Innocence of Childhood: Helping Children and Adolescents Cope with Life-Threatening Illness and Dying*, edited by D. W. Adams and E. J. Deveau, 45–54. Amityville, N.Y.: Baywood.

Hindmarch, C. 1995. Secondary Losses for Siblings. *Child Care, Health and Development* 21:425–31.

Hinds, P. A., L. Oakes, and W. Furman. 2001. End-of-Life Decision Making in Pediatric Oncology. In *Textbook of Palliative Nursing*, edited by B. F. Ferrell and N. Coyle, 450–60. New York: Oxford University Press.

Hines, P. M. 1991. Death and African American Culture. In *Living Beyond Loss*, edited by F. Walsh and M. McGoldrick, 186–92. New York: Norton.

Hinrichsen, G. A. 1995. Treatment Resistant Depression in the Elderly. *International Journal of Geriatric Psychiatry* 10:991–92.

Hintze, J. T., I. Dempler, G. Cappelletty, and W. Frederick. 1994. Death Depression and Death Anxiety in HIV-Infected Males. In *Death Anxiety Handbook: Research, Instrumentation, and Application*, edited by R. A. Neimeyer, 193–200. Washington, D.C.: Taylor & Francis.

Ho, M. K. 1992. *Minority Children and Adolescents in Therapy*. Newbury Park, Calif.: Sage.

Hoag, M. J., and G. M. Burlingame. 1997. Evaluating the Effectiveness of Child and Adolescent Group Treatment: A Meta-Analytic Review. *Journal of Clinical and Child Psychology* 26:234–46.

Hogan, N. S., and L. DeSantis. 1994. Things That Help and Hinder Adolescent Sibling Bereavement. *Western Journal of Nursing Research* 16:132–53.

Hogan, N. S., and L. DeSantis. 1996. Adolescent Sibling Bereavement: Towards a New Theory. In *Handbook of Adolescent Death and Bereavement*, edited by C.A. Corr and D. E. Balk, 173–95. New York: Springer.

Hogan, N. S., and D. B. Greenfield. 1991. Adolescent Sibling Bereavement Symptomatology in a Large Community Sample. *Journal of Adolescent Research* 6:97–112.

Hogan, N. S., J. M. Morse, and M. C. Tason. 1996. Toward an Experiential Theory of Bereavement. *Omega* 33:43–65.

Holinger, P. C., D. Offer, J. T. Barter, and C. C. Bell. 1994. *Suicide and Homicide Among Adolescents*. New York: Guilford Press.

Hollins, S. 1995. Managing Grief Better: People with Developmental Disabilities. *Habilitative Mental Healthcare Newsletter* 14:50–52.

Holmes, D. S. 1993. Aerobic Fitness and the Response to Psychological Stress. In *Exercise Psychology: The Influence of Physical Exercise on Psychological Processes*, edited by P. Seraganian, 39–63. New York: Wiley.

Holmes, T. H., and R. H. Rahe. 1967. The Social Readjustment Scale. *Journal of Psychometric Research* 11:213–18.

Holmes-Garrett, C. 1989. The Crisis of the Forgotten Family: A Single Session Group in the ICU Waiting Room. *Social Work with Groups* 12:141–57.

Holzman, L. A., H. R. Searight, and H. M. Hughes. 1996. Clinical Psychology Graduate Students and Personal Psychotherapy: Results of an Exploratory Study. *Professional Psychology: Research and Practice* 27:98–101.

Horowitz, M. J., B. Siegel, A. Holen, G. A. Bonanno, C. Milbrath, and C. H. Stinson. 1997. Diagnostic Criteria for Complicated Grief Disorder. *American Journal of Psychiatry* 154:904–10.

Horton-Deutsch, S. L., C. J. Farran, E. E. Choi, and L. Fogg. 2002. The PLUS Intervention: A Pilot Test with Caregivers of Depressed Older Adults. *Archives of Psychiatric Nursing* 16:61–71.

Hovey, J. D. 1998. Acculturative Stress, Depression, and Suicidal Ideation Among Mexican-American Adolescents: Implications for the Development of Suicide Prevention Programs in Schools. *Psychological Reports* 83:249–50.

Hoyert, D. L., E. Arias, B. L. Smith, S. L. Murphy, and K. D. Kochanek. 2001. Deaths: Final Data for 1999. In *National Vital Statistics Reports*, vol. 49. Hyattsville, Md.: National Center for Health Statistics.

Huff, R. M., and M. V. Kline. 1999. *Promoting Health in Multicultural Populations: A Handbook for Practitioners*. Thousand Oaks, Calif.: Sage.

Hughes, M. 1995. *Bereavement and Support: Healing in a Group Environment*. Philadelphia: Taylor & Francis.

Hughes, P., P. Turton, E. Hopper, and C. D. H. Evans. 2002. Assessment of Guidelines for Good Practice in Psychosocial Care of Mothers After Stillbirth: A Cohort Study. *Lancet* 360:114–18.

Iacovides, A., K. N. Fountoulakis, and S. Kaprinis. 2003. The Relationship Between Job Stress, Burnout and Clinical Depression. *Journal of Affective Disorders* 75:209–21.

Idler, E. L. 2002. The Many Causal Pathways Linking Religion to Health. *Public Policy and Aging Report* 2:7–12.

Imre, R. W. 1982. *Knowing and Caring: Philosophical Issues in Social Work*. Lanham, Md.: University Press of America.

Irish, D. P., K. F. Lundquist, and V. J. Nelsen, eds. 1993. *Ethnic Variations in Dying, Death, and Grief: Diversity in Universality*. Washington, D.C.: Taylor & Francis.

Jackson, F., S. M. Schim, S. Seely, K. Grunow, and J. Baker. 2000. Barriers to Hospice Care for African Americans: Problems and Solutions. *Journal of Hospice and Palliative Nursing* 2:65–73.

Jackson, H. L., and G. Westmoreland. 1992. Therapeutic Issues for Black Children in Foster Care. In *Working with Culture: Psychotherapeutic Interventions with Ethnic Minority Children and Adolescents*, edited by L. A. Vargas and J. D. Koss-Chioino, 43–62. San Francisco: Jossey-Bass.

Jacobs, S. 1993. *Pathologic Grief*. Washington, D.C.: American Psychiatric Press.

Jacobs, S. 2004. Spirituality and End-of-Life Care Practice for Social Workers. In *Living with Dying: A Handbook for End-of-Life Healthcare Practitioners*, edited by J. Berzoff and P. R. Silverman, 188–205. New York: Columbia University Press.

Jacobs, S., and H. Prigerson. 2000. Psychotherapy of Traumatic Grief: A Review of Evidence for Psychotherapeutic Treatments. *Death Studies* 24:479–95.

Jacques, E. 1965. Death and the Mid-Life Crisis. *International Journal of Psychoanalysis* 46:502–14.

James, S., and J. S. Mennen. 2001. Treatment Outcome Research: How Effective Are Treatments for Abused Children? *Child and Adolescent Social Work Journal* 18:73–95.

Janoff-Bulman, R. 1992. *Shattered Assumptions: Towards a New Psychology of Trauma*. New York: Free Press.

Janoff-Bulman, R., and M. Berg. 1998. Disillusionment and the Creation of Value: From Traumatic Loss to Existential Gains. In *Perspectives on Loss: A Sourcebook*, edited by J. H. Harvey, 35–47. Philadelphia: Brunner/Mazel.

Jendrek, M. P. 1994. Policy Concerns of White Grandparents Who Provide Regular Care to Their Grandchildren. *Journal of Gerontological Social Work* 23:175–200.

Jenkins, E. J. and C. C. Bell. 1997. Exposure and Response to Community Violence Among Children and Adolescents. In *Children in a Violent Society*, edited by J. D. Osofsky, 9–31. New York: Guilford Press.

Johnson, C. 1995. Adolescent Grief Support Groups. In *Beyond the Innocence of Childhood: Helping Children and Adolescents Cope with Death and Bereavement*, edited by D. W. Adams and E. J. Deveau, 229–40. Amityville, N.Y.: Baywood.

Jones, D., J. Harvey, D. Giza, C. Rodican, P. J. Barreira, and C. Macias. 2003. Parental Death in the Lives of People with Serious Mental Illness. *Journal of Loss and Trauma* 8:307–22.

Jones, L. 1985. The Psychological Experience of Bereavement: Lesbian Women's Perceptions of the Response of the Social Network to the Death of a Partner. Ph.D. diss., Boston University.

Jones, L., and L. Newman. 1997. *Our America: Life and Death on the South Side of Chicago*. New York: Pocket Books.

Jonker, G. 1997. The Many Facets of Islam: Death, Dying and Disposal Between Orthodox Rule and Historical Convention. In *Death and Bereavement Across Cultures*, edited by C. M. Parkes, P. Laungani, and B. Young, 147–65. London: Routledge.

Jordan, J. R., and R. A. Neimeyer. 2003. Does Grief Counseling Work? *Death Studies* 27:765–86.

Joslin, D., and A. Brouard. 1995. The Prevalence of Grandmothers as Primary Caregivers in a Poor Pediatric Population. *Journal of Community Health* 20:383–401.

Juarbe, T. C. 1996. The State of Hispanic Health. In *Hispanic Voices: Hispanic Health Educators Speak Out*, edited by G. Torres, 93–113. New York: National League of Nursing.

Jung, C. 1971. The Stages of Life. In *The Portable Jung*, edited by J. Campbell, 3–22. New York: Viking Press.

Juntunen, C. L., and D. R. Atkinson, eds. 2002. *Counseling Across the Lifespan: Prevention and Treatment*. Thousand Oaks, Calif.: Sage.

Juurlink, D. N., N. Herrmann, J. P. Szalai, A. Kopp, and D. A. Redelmeier. 2004. Medical Illness and the Risk of Suicide in the Elderly. *Archives of Internal Medicine* 14:1179–84.

Kaasalainen, S., D. Craig, and D. Wells. 2000. Impact of the Caring for Aging Relatives Group Program: An Evaluation. *Public Health Nursing* 17:169–77.

Kaduson, H. G., D. Cangelosi, and C. Schaefer, eds. 1997. *The Playing Cure: Individualized Play Therapy for Specific Childhood Problems*. New York: Aronson.

Kagan, R. M. 1982. Storytelling and Game Therapy for Children in Placement. *Child Care Quarterly* 11:280–90.

Kagawa-Singer, M. 1998. The Cultural Context of Death Rituals and Mourning Practices. *Oncology Nursing Forum* 2510:1752–55.

Kalafat, J., and M. Elias. 1994. An Evaluation of a School-Based Suicide Awareness Intervention. *Suicide and Life-Threatening Behavior* 22:315–21.

Kamel, H., C. Mouton, and D. McKee. 2002. Culture and Loss. In *Living with Grief: Loss in Later Life*, edited by K. J. Doka, 282–94. Washington, D.C.: Hospice Foundation of America.

Kamya, H. 2000. Bereavement Issues and Spirituality. In *HIV/AIDS at Year 2000: A Sourcebook for Social Workers*, edited by V. J. Lynch, 242–56. Boston: Allyn & Bacon.

Kane, R. A., and R. L. Kane. 2004. *Assessing Older Persons: Measures, Meaning, and Practical Applications*. New York: Oxford University Press.

Kaplan, L. J. 1995. *No Voice Is Ever Wholly Lost*. New York: Simon and Schuster.

Kaplan, L. J. 2000. Toward a Model of Caregiver Grief: Nurses' Experiences of Treating Dying Children. *Omega* 41:187–206.

Karel, M. J., S. Ogland-Hand, M. Gatz, and J. Unutzer. 2002. *Assessing and Treating Late-Life Depression: A Casebook and Resource Guide*. New York: Basic Books.

Kasl-Godley, J. E., M. Gatz, and A. Fiske. 1998. Depression and Depressive Symptoms in Old Age. In *Clinical Geropsychology*, edited by I. H. Nordhus, G. R. VandenBos, S. Berg, and P. Fromholt, 211–17. Washington, D.C.: American Psychological Association.

Kastenbaum, R. J. 1969. Death and Bereavement in Later Life. In *Death and Bereavement*, edited by A. H. Kutscher, 27–54. Springfield, Ill: Thomas.

Kastenbaum, R. J. 1986a. Death in the World of Adolescence. In *Adolescence and Death*, edited by C. A. Corr and J. N. McNeil, 4–15. New York: Springer.

Kastenbaum, R. J. 1986b. *Death, Society, and Human Experience*. 3rd ed. Columbus, Ohio: Merrill.

Kato, P. M., and T. Mann. 1999. A Synthesis of Psychological Interventions for the Bereaved. *Clinical Psychology Review* 19:275–96.

Katz, P. P., and E. H. Yelin. 2001. Activity Loss and the Onset of Depressive Symptoms. *Arthritis and Rheumatism* 44:1194–1202.

Katz, R. S., and B. Genevay. 2002. Our Patients, Our Families, Ourselves: The Impact of the Professional's Emotional Responses on End-of-Life Care. *American Behavioral Scientist* 46:327–39.

Kauffman, J. 1989. Intrapsychic Dimensions of Disenfranchised Grief. In *Disenfranchised Grief: Recognizing Hidden Sorrow*, edited by K. J. Doka, 25–29. New York: Lexington Books.

Kauffman, J. 1994a. Dissociative Functions in the Normal Mourning Process. *Omega* 28:31–38.

Kauffman, J. 1994b. Group Thanatopsis. In *Ring of Fire*, edited by V. Schermer and M. Pines, 149–73. London: Routledge.

Kauffman, J. 2002. The Psychology of Disenfranchised Grief: Liberation, Shame and Self-Disenfranchisement. In *Disenfranchised Grief: New Directions, Challenges and Strategies for Practice*, edited by K. J. Doka, 61–77. Champaign, Ill: Research Press.

Kavanaugh, K. 1997. Gender Differences Among Parents Who Experience the Death of an Infant Weighing Less Than 500 Grams at Birth. *Omega* 35:281–96.

Kawaga-Singer, M. 1998. The Cultural Context of Death Rituals and Mourning Practices. *Oncology Nursing Forum* 25:175–261.

Kaye, L. W. 2002. Service Utilization and Support Provision of Caregiving Men. In *Men as Caregivers: Theory, Research, and Service Implications*, edited by B. J. Kramer and E. H. Thompson Jr., 359–78. New York: Springer.

Keenan, S. P., C. Mawdsley, D. Plotkin, G. K. Webster, and F. Priestap. 2000. Withdrawal of Life Support: How the Family Feels, and Why. *Journal of Palliative Care* 16 (suppl.):S40–44.

Keitel, M. A., M. Kopala, and J. C. Potere. 2003. Helping Women Negotiate the Cancer Experience. In *Handbook of Counseling Women*, edited by M. Kopala and M. A. Keitel, 360–76. Thousand Oaks, Calif.: Sage.

Kelley, P. 1998. Loss Experienced in Chronic Pain and Illness. In *Perspectives on Loss: A Sourcebook*, edited by J. H. Harvey, 201–12. Philadelphia: Brunner/Mazel.

Kelly, J. B. 2000. Children's Adjustment in Conflicted Marriage and Divorce: A Decade Review of Research. *Journal of the American Academy of Child and Adolescent Psychiatry* 39:963–73.

Keltner, D., and G. A. Bonanno. 1997. A Study of Laughter and Disassociation: Distinct Correlates of Laughter and Smiling During Bereavement. *Journal of Personality and Social Psychology* 73:687–702.

Kemp, C. 2001. Spiritual Care Interventions. In *Textbook of Palliative Nursing*, edited by B. F. Ferrell and N. Coyle, 407–14. New York: Oxford University Press.

Kempson, D. A. 2000/2001. Effects of Intentional Touch on Complicated Grief of Bereaved Mothers. *Omega* 42:341–53.

Kirby, L., and M. Fraser. 1997. Risk and Resilience in Childhood. In *Risk and Resiliency in Childhood*, edited by M. Fraser, 10–33. Washington, D.C.: NASW Press.

Kissane, D. W., and S. Bloch. 1994. Family Grief. *British Journal of Psychiatry* 164:728–40.

Kissane, D. W., S. Bloch, and D. McKenzie. 1997. Family Coping and Bereavement Outcome. *Palliative Medicine* 11:191–201.

Kissane, D. W., S. Bloch, M. McKenzie, A. C. McDowall, and R. Nitzan. 1998. Family Grief Therapy: A Preliminary Account of a New Model to Promote Health Family Functioning During Palliative Care and Bereavement. *Psycho-Oncology* 7:14–25.

Kitson, C. 2002. Fathers Experienced Stillbirth as a Waste of Life and Needed to Protect Their Partners and Express Grief in Their Own Way. *Evidence-Based Nursing* 5:61.

Klarel, M. J., S. Ogland-Hand, M. Gatz, and J. Unutzer. 2002. *Assessing and Treating Late-Life Depression: A Casebook and Resource Guide*. New York: Basic Books.

Klass, D. 1986/1987. Marriage and Divorce Among Bereaved Parents Who Experience the Death of a Child. *Omega* 17:237–49.

Klass, D. 1988. *Parental Grief: Solace and Resolution*. New York: Springer.

Klass, D. 1993. Solace and Immorality: Bereaved Parents' Continuing Bond with Their Children. *Death Studies* 17:343–68.

Klass, D. 1996a. The Deceased Child in the Psychic and Social Worlds of Bereaved Parents During the Resolution of Grief. In *Continuing Bonds: New Understandings of Grief*, edited by D. Klass, P. R. Silverman, and S. L. Nickman, 199–216. Washington, D.C.: Taylor & Francis.

Klass, D. 1996b. Grief in an Eastern Culture: Japanese Ancestor Worship. In *Continuing Bonds: New Understandings of Grief*, edited by D. Klass, P. R. Silverman, and S. L. Nickman, 59–72. Washington, D.C.: Taylor & Francis.

Klass, D. 1997. The Deceased Child in the Psychic and Social Worlds of Bereaved Parents During the Resolution of Grief. *Death Studies* 21:147–75.

Klass, D. 1999a. Developing a Cross-Cultural Model of Grief: The State of the Field. *Omega* 293:153–78.

Klass, D. 1999b. *The Spiritual Life of Bereaved Parents*. Philadelphia: Brunner/Mazel.

Klass, D. 2001a. Continuing Bonds in the Resolution of Grief in Japan and North America. *American Behavioral Scientist* 445:742–63.

Klass, D. 2001b. The Inner Representation of the Dead Child in the Psychic and Social Narratives of Bereaved Parents. In *Meaning Reconstruction and the Experience of Loss*, edited by R. A Neimeyer, 77–94. Washington, D.C.: American Psychological Association.

Klass, D., and R. E. Goss. 1998. Asian Ways of Grief. In *Living with Grief: Who We Are and How We Grieve*, edited by K. J. Doka and J. D. Davidson, 13–26. Philadelphia: Brunner/Mazel.

Klass, D., and A. O. Heath. 1997. Grief and Abortion: *Mizuko kuyo*, the Japanese Ritual Resolution. *Omega* 34:1–14.

Klass, D., and S. Marwit. 1988/1989. Toward a Model of Parental Grief. *Omega* 19:31–50.

Klass, D., P. R. Silverman, and S. L. Nickman, eds. 1996. *Continuing Bonds: New Understandings of Grief*. Washington, D.C.: Taylor & Francis.

Klass, D., and T. Walter. 2001. Processes of Grieving: How Bonds Are Continued. In *Handbook of Bereavement*, edited by M. S. Stroebe, R. O. Hansson, W. Stroebe, and H. Schut, 431–48. Washington, D.C.: American Psychological Association.

Knafl, K. 1996. Family Response to Childhood Chronic Illness: Description of Management Styles. *Journal of Pediatric Nursing* 11:315–26.

Knieper, A. J. 1999. The Suicide Survivor's Grief and Recovery. *Suicide and Life-Threatening Behavior* 29:353–63.

Kochanek, K. D., B. L. Smith, and R. N. Anderson. 2001. Deaths: Preliminary Data for 1999. In *National Vital Statistics Reports*, vol. 49. Hyattsville, Md.: National Center for Health Statistics.

Koenig, H. G. 1997. *Is Religion Good for Your Health? Effects of Religion on Mental and Physical Health*. New York: Haworth Press.

Koenig, H. G., and R. G. Brooks. 2002. Religion, Health, and Aging: Implications for Practice and Public Policy. *Public Policy and Aging Report* 12:13–19.

Koenig, H. G., L. K. George, and B. L. Peterson. 1998. Religiosity and Remission of Depression in Medically Ill Older Patients. *American Journal of Psychiatry* 155:536–42.

Koenig, H. G., M. E. McCullough, and D. B. Larson. 2001. *Handbook of Religion and Health*. New York: Oxford University Press.

Koeske, G. F., and S. A. Kirk. 1995. The Effect of Characteristics of Human Service Workers on Subsequent Morale and Turnover. *Administration in Social Work* 19:15–31.

Kogan, L. R., and T. Vacha-Haase. 2002. Supporting Adaptation to New Family Roles in Middle Age. In *Counseling Across the Lifespan: Prevention and Treatment*, edited by C. L. Juntunen and D. R. Atkinson, 299–327. Thousand Oaks, Calif.: Sage.

Koss-Chioino, J. D. 1995. Traditional and Folk Approaches Among Ethnic Minorities.

In *Psychological Interventions and Cultural Diversity*, edited by J. F. Aponte, R. Y. Rivers, and J. Wohl, 145–63. Boston: Allyn & Bacon.

Kotch, J. B., and S. R. Cohen. 1985. SIDS Counselors' Reports of Own and Parents' Reactions to Reviewing the Autopsy Report. *Omega* 16:129–39.

Kottman, T. 1993. *Adlerian Play Therapy Workshop Material*. Waterloo, Iowa: Cedar Valley Hospice.

Kottman, T. 1995. *Partners in Play*. Alexandria, Va.: American Counseling Association.

Kottman, T., and C. Schaefer, eds. 1993. *Play Therapy in Action: A Casebook for Practitioners*. Northvale, N.J.: Aronson.

Kovacs, P. J., and L. Bronstein. 1999. Preparation for Oncology Settings: What Hospice Social Workers Say They Need. *Health and Social Work* 24:57–64.

Krahe, B. 2001. Childhood Sexual Abuse and Revictimization in Adolescence and Childhood. In *Post Traumatic Stress Theory: Research and Application*, edited by J. H. Harvey and B. G. Pauwels, 49–66. Philadelphia: Brunner/Mazel.

Kramer, B. J. 1997. Gain in the Caregiver Experience: Where Are We? What Next? *The Gerontologist* 37:218–32.

Kramer, B. J. 1998. Preparing Social Workers for the Inevitable: A Preliminary Investigation of a Course on Grief, Death and Loss. *Journal of Social Work Education* 342:211–27.

Kramer, B. J. 2000. Grief and Bereavement in Older Men. *Geriatric Care Management Journal* 10:17–23.

Kramer, B. J., L. Pacourek, and C. Hovland-Scafe. 2003. Analysis of End-of-Life Content in Social Work Textbooks. *Journal of Social Work Education* 39:299–320.

Kramer, B. J., and C. C. Pierre. 2003. Family Conflict at the End-of-Life: Lessons Learned from a Model Program for Vulnerable Older Adults. Paper presented at the Gerontological Society of America's Fifty-sixth annual scientific meeting. San Diego, November.

Kranzler, E., D. Shafer, and G. Wasserman. 1989. Early Childhood Bereavement. *Journal of the American Academy of Child and Adolescent Psychiatry* 294:513–20.

Kraus, M. W., and M. M. Seltzer. 1993. Current Well-being and Future Plans of Older Caregiving Mothers. *Irish Journal of Psychology* 60:935–42.

Krause, N. 2003. Religious Meaning and Subjective Well-being in Late Life. *Journals of Gerontology* 58B:S160–70.

Kübler-Ross, E. 1969. *On Death and Dying*. New York: Macmillan.

Kübler-Ross, E. 1981. *Living with Death and Dying*. New York: Macmillan.

Kübler-Ross, E., and D. Kessler. 2001. *Life's Lessons: Two Experts on Death and Dying Tell Us About the Mysteries of Life and Living*. New York: Scribner.

Kuhn, D. R., and C. F. Mendes-de-Leon. 2001. Evaluating an Educational Intervention with Relatives of Persons in the Early Stages of Alzheimer's Disease. *Research on Social Work Practice* 11:531–48.

Kulic, K. R. 2003. An Account of Group Work with Family Members of 9/11. *Journal of Specialists in Group Work* 28:195–98.

Kushner, H. S. 1985. *When Bad Things Happen to Good People*. New York: Avon Books.

Laditka, J. N., and S. B. Laditka. 2003. Increased Hospitalization Risk for Recently Widowed Older Women and Protective Effects of Social Contacts. *Journal of Women and Aging* 15:7–28.

Lamers, W. J., Jr. 2002. Disenfranchised Grief in Caregivers. In *Disenfranchised Grief: New Directions, Challenges, and Strategies for Practice*, edited by K. J. Doka, 181–96. Champaign, Ill.: Research Press.

Lang, A., and L. Gottlieb. 1993. Parental Grief Reactions and Marital Intimacy Following Infant Death. *Death Studies* 17:233–55.

Langner, S. R. 1995. Finding Meaning in Caring for Elderly Relatives: Loss and Personal Growth. *Holistic Nursing Practice* 9:75–84.

Lantz, J., and J. Lantz. 1991. Franklian Treatment with the Traumatized Family. *Journal of Family Psychotherapy* 2:61–72.

Larson, D. G. 2000. Anticipatory Mourning: Challenges for Professional and Volunteer Caregivers. In *Clinical Dimensions of Anticipatory Mourning: Theory and Practice in Working with the Dying, Their Loved Ones, and Their Caregivers*, edited by T. A. Rando, 379–95. Champaign, Ill.: Research Press.

Lasker, J. N., and L. J. Toedter. 1994. Satisfaction with Hospital Care and Intervention After Pregnancy Loss. *Death Studies* 18:14–64.

Latham, A. E., and H. G. Prigerson. 2004. Suicidality and Bereavement: Complicated Grief as Psychiatric Disorder Presenting Greatest Risk for Suicidality. *Suicide and Life-Threatening Behavior* 34:350–62.

Laungani, P. 1997. Death in a Hindu family. In *Death and Bereavement Across Cultures*, edited by C. M. Parkes, P. Laungani, and B. Young, 52–72. London: Routledge.

Lauterbach, S. S. 1994. In Another World: Essences of Mothers' Mourning Experience. In *In Women's Experience*, edited by P. L. Munhall, 233–91. New York: National League for Nursing Press.

Lawrence, L. 1992. "Till Death Do Us Part": The Application of Object Relations Theory to Facilitate Mourning in a Young Widows' Group. *Social Work in Health Care* 16:67–81.

Lawton, M. P., M. H. Kleban, D. Rajagopal, and J. Dean. 1992. Dimensions of Affective Experience in Three Age Groups. *Psychology and Aging* 7:171–84.

Lawton, P., P. G. Windley, and T. O. Byerts. 1982. *Aging and the Environment: Theoretical Approaches*. New York: Springer.

Layer, S., C. Roberts, K. Wild, and J. Walters. 2004. Postabortion Grief: Evaluating the Possible Efficacy of a Spiritual Intervention. *Research on Social Work Practice* 14:344–50.

Layman, D., D. Hussey, and S. Laing. 2002. Foster Care Trends in the United States: Ramifications for Music Therapists. *Music Therapy Perspectives* 20:38–46.

Layne, C. M., R. S. Pynoos, W. R. Saltzman, B. Arslanagic, M. Black, N. Savjak, T. Popvic, E. Durakovic, M. Music, N. Campara, N. Djapo, and R. Houston. 2001a. Trauma/Grief-Focused Group Psychotherapy: School-Based Postwar Intervention with Traumatized Bosnian Adolescents. *Group Dynamics* 5:277–90.

Layne, C. M., N. Savjak, W. R. Saltzman, and R. S. Pynoos. 2001b. UCLB/BYU Expanded Grief Inventory. Unpublished instrument. Provo, Utah: Brigham Young University.

Lazarus, R. 1999. *Stress and Emotion: A New Synthesis*. New York: Springer.

Leahy, T., G. Pretty, and G. Tenenbaum. 2003. Non-Clinically Distressed Adult Survivors. *Professional Psychology: Research and Practice* 34:657–65.

Lee, B., and Y. Yang. 2000. The Lived Experience of Unmarried Women Who Underwent Induced Abortion During the First Trimester. *Journal of Nursing Research* 8:459–69.

Lee, C. M., M. Picard, and M. D. Blain. 1994. A Methodological and Substantive Review of Intervention Outcome Studies for Families Undergoing Divorce. *Journal of Family Psychology* 8:3–15.

Lee, C. M., and P. Slade. 1996. Miscarriage as a Traumatic Event: A Review of the Literature and New Implications for Intervention. *Journal of Psychosomatic Research* 40:235–44.

Lee, E. 1991. Mourning Rituals in Chinese Culture. In *Living Beyond Loss*, edited by F. Walsh and M. McGoldrick, 200–205. New York: Norton.

Leenaars, A. A., and S. Wenckstern. 1995. Helping Lethal Suicidal Adolescents. In *Beyond the Innocence of Childhood: Helping Children and Adolescents Cope with Life-Threatening Illness and Dying*, edited by D. W. Adams and E. J. Deveau, 131–50. Amityville, N.Y.: Baywood.

Leff, P., J. Chan, and E. Walizer. 1991. Self-Understanding and Reaching Out to Sick Children and Their Families: An Ongoing Professional Challenge. *Children's Health Care* 20:230–39.

Lehman, D. R., E. Lang, C. B. Wortman, and S. Sorenson. 1989. Long-Term Effects of Sudden Bereavement: Marital and Parent–Child Relationships and Children's Reactions. *Journal of Family Psychology* 2:344–67.

Lehman, D. R., C. B. Wortman, M. Haring, R. G. Tweed, B. de Vries, A. DeLongis, K. J. Hemphill, and J. H. Ellard. 1999. Recovery from the Perspective of the Bereaved: Personal Assessments of Sources of Distress and Support. In *End of Life Issues: Interdisciplinary and Multidimensional Perspectives*, edited by B. de Vries, 119–44. New York: Springer.

Leick, N., and M. Davidsen-Nielsen. 1996. *Healing Pain: Attachment, Loss and Grief Therapy*. London: Tavistock/Routledge.

Leitenberg, H., E. Greenwald, and S. Cado. 1992. A Retrospective Study of Long-Term Methods of Coping with Having Been Sexually Abused During Childhood. *Child Abuse and Neglect* 16:399–407.

Leming, M. R., and G. E. Dickinson. 2002. *Understanding Dying, Death, and Bereavement*. 5th ed. Belmont, Calif.: Wadsworth/Thompson Learning.

Lennon, M. C., J. L. Martin, and L. Dean. 1990. The Influence of Social Support on AIDS-Related Grief Reaction Among Gay Men. *Social Science and Medicine* 31:477–84.

Lesher, E. C., and K. J. Bergey. 1988. Bereaved Elderly Mothers: Changes in Health, Functional Activities, Family Cohesion and Psychological Well-being. *International Journal of Aging and Human Development* 26:81–90.

Levin, J. S., and R. J. Taylor. 1997. Age Differences in Patterns and Correlates of the Frequency of Prayer. *The Gerontologist* 37:75–88.

Levine, C. 1995. Orphans of the HIV Epidemic: Unmet Needs in Six US Cities. *AIDS Care* 7 (suppl. 1):57–62.

Levine, K. G. 1988. The Placed Child Examines the Quality of Parental Care. *Child Welfare* 67:301–10.

Levinson, D. 1977. The Mid-Life Transition. *Psychiatry* 40:99–112.

Levinson, D. 1978. *The Seasons of a Man's Life*. New York: Knopf.

Lewis, C. S. 1961. *A Grief Observed*. New York: Seabury Press.

Lewis, M., and D. Schonfeld. 1994. Role of Child and Adolescent Psychiatric Consultation and Liaison in Assisting Children and Their Families in Dealing with Death. *Child and Adolescent Psychiatric Clinics of North America* 3:613–27.

Lichtenstein, P., M. Gatz, and S. Berg. 1998. A Twin Study of Mortality After Spousal Bereavement. *Psychological Medicine* 28:635–43.

Lieberman, M. A., and L. Videka-Sherman. 1986. The Impact of Self-Help Groups on the Mental Health of Widows and Widowers. *American Journal of Orthopsychiatry* 56:435–49.

Lieberman, M. A., and I. Yalom. 1992. Brief Group Psychotherapy for the Spousally Bereaved: A Controlled Study. *International Journal of Group Psychotherapy* 42:117–32.

Liken, M. A., and C. E. Collins. 1993. Grieving: Facilitating the Process for Dementia Caregivers. *Journal of Psychosocial Nursing* 31:21–26.

Lilford, R. J., P. Stratton, S. Godsil, and A. Prasad. 1994. A Randomized Trial of Routine Versus Selective Counseling in Perinatal Bereavement from Congenital Disease. *British Journal of Obstetrics and Gynaecology* 101:291–96.

Lindbergh, A. M. 1973. Hour of Gold, Hour of Lead. In *Diaries and Letters of Anne Morrow Lindbergh, 1929–1932*, 274. New York: Harcourt Brace Jovanovich.

Lindemann, G. 1944. Symptomatology and Management of Acute Grief. *American Journal of Psychiatry* 101:141–48.

Lindgren, C. L., M. L. Burke, M. A. Hainsworth, and G. E. Georgene. 1992. Chronic Sorrow: A Lifespan Concept. *Scholarly Inquiry for Nursing Practice: An International Journal* 6:27–42.

Lindstrom, T. C. 2002. It Ain't Necessarily So . . . Challenging Mainstream Thinking About Bereavement. *Family and Community Health* 251:11–21.

Linke, S., J. Wojciak, and S. Day. 2002. The Impact of Suicide on Community Mental Health Teams: Findings and Recommendations. *Psychiatric Bulletin* 26:50–52.

Linna, L. 1987. The Mourning Work of Small Children After the Loss of a Parent Through Divorce. *Psychiatria Fennica* 18:41–51.

Liotta, A. J. 1996. *When Students Grieve: A Guide to Bereavement in the Schools*. Horsham, Pa.: LRP Publications.

Lippmann, S. B., W. A. James, and R. L. Frierson. 1993. AIDS and the Family: Implications for Counseling. *AIDS Care* 5:71–78.

Lipson, J. G., S. L. Dibble, and P. A. Minarik. 1996. *Culture and Nursing Care*. San Francisco: UCSF Nursing Press.

Lister, L. 1991. Men and Grief: A Review of Research. *Smith College Studies in Social Work* 61:220–35.

Llorente, M. D., C. Eisdorfer, D. A. Loewenstein, and Y. A. Zarate. 1996. Suicide Among Hispanic Elderly: Cuban Americans in Dade County, Florida 1990–1993. *Journal of Mental Health and Aging* 2:79–87.

Lohnes, K. L., and N. Kalter. 1994. Prevention Intervention Groups for Parentally Bereaved Children. *Orthopsychiatry* 64:594–603.

Loos, C., and A. Bowd. 1997. Caregivers of Persons with Alzheimer's Disease: Some Neglected Implications of the Experience of Personal Loss and Grief. *Death Studies* 21:501–14.

Lopata, H. 1996. *Current Widowhood: Myths and Realities.* Thousand, Oaks, Calif.: Sage.

Lord, B., and R. Pockett. 1998. Perceptions of Social Work Intervention with Bereaved Clients: Some Implications for Hospital Social Work. *Social Work in Health Care* 27:51–66.

Lord, J. H. 1996. America's Number One Killer: Vehicular Crashes. In *Living with Grief After Sudden Loss: Suicide, Homicide, Accident, Heart Attack, Stroke,* edited by K. J. Doka, 25–39. Washington, D.C.: Hospice Foundation of America.

Lowe, G. S., H. Krahn, and M. Sosteric. 2003. Influence of Socioeconomic Status and Gender on High School Seniors' Use of Computers at Home and at School. *Journal of Educational Research* 49:138–54.

Luchterhand, C., and N. Murphy. 1998. *Helping Adults with Mental Retardation Grieve a Death Loss.* Philadelphia: Taylor & Francis.

Lund, D. A. 1989a. Conclusions About Bereavement in Later Life and Implications for Interventions and Future Research. In *Older Bereaved Spouses: Research with Practical Applications,* edited by D. A. Lund, 217–31. New York: Hemisphere.

Lund, D. A. 1989b. *Older Bereaved Spouses: Research with Practical Applications.* Washington, D.C.: Hemisphere.

Lund, D. A. 1999. Giving and Receiving Help During Late Life Spousal Bereavement. In *Living with Grief: At Work, at School, at Worship,* edited by J. D. Davidson and K. J. Doka, 203–12. Washington, D.C.: Hospice Foundation of America.

Lund, D. A., M. S. Caserta, and M. F. Dimond. 1993. The Course of Spousal Bereavement in Later Life. In *Handbook of Bereavement: Theory, Research and Intervention,* edited by M. S. Stroebe and W. Stroebe, 240–54. Cambridge: Cambridge University Press.

Lustbader, W., and N. R. Hooyman. 1994. *Taking Care of Aging Family Members: A Practical Guide.* New York: Free Press.

Lutovich, D. S. 2002. *Nobody's Child: How Older Women Say Good-bye to Their Mothers.* Amityville, N.Y.: Baywood.

Maasen, T. 1998. Counseling Gay Men with Multiple Loss and Survival Problems: The Bereavement Group as a Transitional Object. *AIDS Care* 10 (suppl. 1):S57–63.

Mace, N. L., and P. V. Rabins. 1986. *The 36-Hour Day.* Baltimore: Johns Hopkins University Press.

MacGregor, P. 1994. Grief: The Unrecognized Parental Response to Mental Illness in a Child. *Social Work* 39:160–66.

Maddison, D., and B. Raphael. 1975. Conjugal Bereavement. In *Bereavement: Its Psychosocial Aspects*, edited by B. Schoenberg, I. Gerger, A. Wiener, A. H. Kutscher, D. Peretz, and A. C. Carr, 26–40. New York: Columbia University Press.

Main, F. O., and J. D. West. 1987. Sabotaging Adolescent Depression Through Paradox. *Individual Psychology* 43:185–91.

Main, J. 2000. Improving Management of Bereavement in General Practice Based on a Survey of Recently Bereaved Subjects in a Single General Practice. *British Journal of General Practice* 50:863–66.

Main, M., N. Kaplan, and J. Cassidy. 1985. Security in Infancy, Childhood and Adulthood: A Move to the Level of Representation. In *Growing Points of Attachment Theory and Research*, edited by I. Bretherton and E. Waters, 66–106. Monographs of the Society for Research in Child Development, serial no. 209, vol. 50. Chicago: University of Chicago Press.

Malkinson, R. 2001. Cognitive-Behavioral Therapy of Grief: A Review and Application. *Research on Social Work Practice* 11:671–98.

Malkinson, R., and L. Bar-Tur. 1999. The Aging of Grief in Israel: A Perspective of Bereaved Parents. *Death Studies* 23:413–31.

Mallinson, R. K. 1999. Grief Work of HIV-Positive Persons and Their Survivors. *Nursing Clinics of North America* 34:163–77.

Mannino, J. D. 1997. *Grieving Days, Healing Days*. Boston: Allyn & Bacon.

Marker, C., and J. Ogden 2003. The Miscarriage Experience: More Than Just a Trigger to Psychological Morbidity? *Psychology and Health* 18:403–15.

Markus, H., and S. Kitayama. 1991. Culture and Self: Implications for Cognition, Emotion and Motivation. *Psychological Review* 98:224–53.

Marmar, C. R., M. J. Horowitz, D. S. Weiss, N. R. Wilner, and N. B. Kaltreider. 1988. A Controlled Trial of Brief Psychotherapy and Mutual-Help Group Treatment of Conjugal Bereavement. *American Journal of Psychiatry* 145:203–9.

Marsh, D. T. 1999. Serious Mental Illness: Opportunities for Family Practitioners. *Family Journal: Counseling and Therapy for Couples and Families* 7:358–66.

Martikainen, P., and T. Valkonen. 1996. Mortality After the Death of a Spouse: Rates and Causes of Death in a Large Finnish Cohort. *American Journal of Public Health* 86:1087–93.

Martin, J. 1988. Psychological Consequences of AIDS-Related Bereavement Among Gay Men. *American Journal of Public Health* 61:856–62.

Martin, T. L. 2000. In the Aftermath: Children and Adolescents as Survivors-Victims of Suicide. In *Living with Grief: Children, Adolescents and Loss*, edited by K. J. Doka, 263–74. Washington, D.C.: Hospice Foundation of America.

Martin, T. L., and K. J. Doka. 1998. Revisiting Masculine Grief. In *Living with Grief: Who We Are, How We Grieve*, edited by K. J. Doka and J. D. Davidson, 133–42. Philadelphia: Brunner/Mazel.

Martin, T. L., and K. J. Doka. 2000. *Men Don't Cry, Women Do*. Philadelphia: Brunner/Mazel.

Martinez, K. J., and D. M. Valdez. 1992. Cultural Considerations in Play Therapy with Hispanic Children. In *Working with Culture: Psychotherapeutic Interventions with Ethnic Minority Children and Adolescents*, edited by L. A. Vargas and J. D. Koss-Chioino, 85–102. San Francisco: Jossey-Bass.

Martin-Matthews, A. 1996. Widowhood and Widowerhood. *Encyclopedia of Gerontology* 2:621–24.

Martinson, I. 1991. Grief Is an Individual Journey: Follow-up of Families Postdeath of a Child with Cancer. In *Children and Death*, edited by D. Papadatou and C. Papadatos, 255–66. New York: Hemisphere.

Martinson, I., and V. Neelon. 1994. Physiological Characteristics of Dying and Death. In *Dying, Death, and Bereavement*, edited by I. Corless, B. Germino, and M. Pittman, 123–34. Boston: Jones and Bartlett.

Marwit, S. J., and D. Klass. 1988/1989. Toward a Model of Parental Grief. *Omega* 19:31–50.

Maslach, C. 1982. *Burnout: The Cost of Caring*. Englewood Cliffs, N.J.: Prentice-Hall.

Maslow, A. 1968. *Toward a Psychology of Being*. 2nd ed. Princeton, N.J.: Van Nostrand.

Masur, C. 1996. Individual Treatment of the Bereaved Child. In *Handbook of Childhood Death and Bereavement*, edited by C. A. Corr and D. M. Corr, 305–21. New York: Springer.

Matthews, J. D. 1999. The Grieving Child in the School Environment. In *Living with Grief: At Work, at School, at Worship*, edited by J. D. Davidson and K. J. Doka, 95–113. Washington, D.C.: Hospice Foundation of America.

Matthews, S. H., and J. Heidorn. 1998. Meeting Filial Responsibilities in Brothers-Only Sibling Groups. *Journals of Gerontology*, 53B:S278–86.

Mawson, D., I. M. Marks, E. Ramm, and R. Stern. 1981. Guided Mourning for Morbid Grief: A Controlled Study. *British Journal of Psychiatry* 138:185–93.

Mayo, P. E. 2001. *The Healing Sorrow Workbook: Rituals for Transforming Grief and Loss*. Oakland, Calif.: New Harbinger.

McAdams, D., and E. de St. Aubin, eds. 1998. *Generativity and Adult Development: How and Why We Care for the Next Generation*. Washington, D.C.: American Psychological Association.

McAll, K., and W. P. Wilson. 1987. Ritual Mourning for Unresolved Grief After Abortion. *Southern Medical Journal* 80:817–21.

McCandless, N., and F. Connor. 1997. Older Women and Grief: A New Direction for Research. *Journal of Women and Aging* 9:85–91.

McClain, M. E., and A. J. M. Shaefer. 1996. Supporting Families After Sudden Infant Death. *Journal of Psychosocial Nursing* 34:30–34.

McCown, D., and B. Davies. 1995. Patterns of Grief in Young Children Following the Death of a Sibling. *Death Studies* 19:41–53.

McCoy, S., T. Pyszcynski, S. Solomon, and J. Greenberg. 2000. Transcending the Self: A

Terror Management Perspective on Successful Aging. In *The Problem of Death Among Older Adults*, edited by A. Toner, 37–61. Washington, D.C.: Taylor & Francis.

McCracken, A., and M. Semel. 1998. *A Broken Heart Still Beats: After Your Child Dies*. New York: Hazelden.

McCubbin, M., and H. McCubbin. 1993. Family Coping with Illness: The Resiliency Model of Family Stress, Adjustment and Adaptation. In *Families, Health, and Illness*, edited by C. Danielson, B. Hamel-Bissell, and P. Winstead-Fry, 21–63. St. Louis: Mosby.

McEwan, I. 1985. *The Child in Time*. Boston: Houghton Mifflin.

McFadden, E. J. 1996. Family-Centered Practice with Foster-Parent Families. *Families in Society* 77:545–58.

McGoldrick, M. 1991. Echoes from the Past: Helping Families Mourn Their Losses. In *Living Beyond Loss: Death in the Family*, edited by F. Walsh and M. McGoldrick, 50–78. New York: Norton.

McGoldrick, M., and R. Gerson. 1985. *Genograms in Family Assessment*. New York: Norton.

McGoldrick, M., R. Gerson, and S. Shellenberger. 1999. *Genograms: Assessment and Intervention*. New York: Norton.

McGowan, D., and D. Pratt. 1985. Impact of Sibling Death on Children's Behavior. *Death Studies* 9:323–35.

McInnis-Dittrich, K. 2002. *Social Work with Elders: A Biopsychosocial Approach to Assessment and Intervention*. Boston: Allyn & Bacon.

McKay, M., P. D. Rogers, J. Blades, and R. Gosse. 1999. *The Divorce Book: A Practical and Compassionate Guide*. Oakland, Calif.: New Harbinger.

McKay, M., P. D. Rogers, and J. McKay. 1989. *When Anger Hurts: Quieting the Storm Within*. Oakland, Calif.: New Harbinger.

McKiernan, F. 1996. Bereavement and Attitudes to Death. In *Handbook of the Clinical Psychology of Ageing*, edited by R. T. Woods, 159–82. New York: Wiley.

McLeod, B. W. 1999. *Caregiving: The Spiritual Journey of Love, Loss and Renewal*. New York: Wiley.

McLeod, B. W. 2001. Self-Care: The Path to Wholeness. In *Caregiving and Loss: Family Needs, Professional Responses*, edited by K. J. Doka, 195–207. Washington, D.C.: Hospice Foundation of America.

McQuaide, S. 1998. Women at Midlife. *Social Work* 43:21–31.

McRae, M. B., D. A. Thompson, and S. Cooper. 1999. Black Churches as Therapeutic Groups. *Journal of Multicultural Counseling and Development* 27:207–20.

McRoy, R. 1999. *Special Needs Adoptions: Practice Issues*. New York: Garland.

Meagher, D. K., and M. Quinn. 2000. Advance Directives and Anticipatory Mourning. In *Clinical Dimensions of Anticipatory Mourning: Theory and Practice in Working with the Dying, Their Loved Ones, and Their Caregivers*, edited by T. A. Rando, 493–510. Champaign, Ill.: Research Press.

Mendes de Leon, C. F., S. V. Kasl, and S. Jacobs. 1994. A Prospective Study of Widowhood and Changes in Symptoms of Depression in a Community Sample of the Elderly. *Psychological Medicine* 24:613–24.

Meuser, T. M., and S. J. Marwit. 2000. An Integrative Model of Personality, Coping and Appraisal for the Prediction of Grief Involvement in Adults. *Omega* 40:375–93.

Meuser, T. M., and S. J. Marwit. 2001. A Comprehensive Stage Sensitive Model of Grief in Dementia Caregiving. *The Gerontologist* 41:658–70.

Meyers, B. 2002. Disenfranchised Grief and the Loss of an Animal Companion. In *Disenfranchised Grief: New Directions, Challenges, and Strategies for Clinical Practice*, edited by K. J. Doka, 251–64. Champaign, Ill.: Research Press.

Middleton, W., B. Raphael, P. Burnett, and N. Martinek. 1998. A Longitudinal Study Comparing Bereavement Phenomena in Recently Bereaved Spouses, Adult Children and Parents. *Australian and New Zealand Journal of Psychiatry* 32:235–41.

Miles, M., and A. Demi. 1991. Guilt in Parents Bereaved by Accident, Suicide, and Chronic Disease. *Omega* 24:203–15.

Miley, K. K., M. O'Melia, and B. L. DuBois. 2004. *Generalist Social Work Practice: An Empowering Approach*. Boston: Allyn & Bacon.

Miller, E. D., and J. Omarzu. 1998. New Directions in Loss Research. In *Perspectives on Loss: A Sourcebook*, edited by J. H. Harvey, 3–20. Philadelphia: Brunner/Mazel.

Miller, F. E. 1996. Grief Therapy for Relatives of Persons with Serious Mental Illness. *Psychiatric Services* 47:633–37.

Miller, J., and T. Goldman. 1998. *When a Man Faces Grief: A Man You Know Is Grieving*. Fort Wayne, Ind.: Willowgreen Press.

Milo, E. M. 1997. Maternal Responses to the Life and Death of a Child with a Developmental Disability: A Story of Hope. *Death Studies* 21:443–76.

Minkler, M., and K. M. Roe. 1993. *Grandmothers as Caregivers: Raising Children of the Crack Cocaine Epidemic*. Newbury Park, Calif.: Sage.

Mittelman, M. S. 2002. Family Caregiving for People with Alzheimer's Disease: Results of the N.Y.U. Spouse Caregiver Intervention Program. *Generations* 3:104–6.

Moen, P., M. A. Erickson, and D. Dempster-McClain. 2000. Social Role Identities Among Older Adults in a Continuing Care Retirement Community. *Research on Aging* 22:559–79.

Molin, R. 1990. Future Anxiety: Clinical Issues of Children in the Latter Phases of Foster Care. *Child and Adolescent Social Work Journal* 7:501–12.

Molinari, V. 1999. Using Reminiscence and Life Review as Natural Therapeutic Strategies in Group Therapy. In *Handbook of Counseling Psychotherapy with Older Adults*, edited by M. Duffy, 154–65. New York: Wiley.

Monahan, J. R. 1994. Developing and Facilitating AIDS Bereavement Support Groups. *Group* 18 (special issue: *The Challenge of AIDS*): 177–85.

Moon, A., S. K. Tomita, and S. Jung-Kamei. 2001. Elder Mistreatment Among Four Asian American Groups: An Exploratory Study on Tolerance, Victim Blaming and Attitudes Toward Third Party Intervention. *Journal of Gerontological Social Work* 36:153–69.

Moore, A. J., and D. C. Stratton. 2002. *Resilient Widowers: Older Men Speak for Themselves.* New York: Springer.

Moore, M. C., L. Browne, E. M. Forte, and D. K. Sherwood. 1996. Mental Health Home Visits for the Elderly. *Perspectives in Psychiatric Care* 322:5–9.

Moore, M. C., and A. Carr. 2000. Depression and Grief. In *What Works with Children and Adolescents? A Critical Review of Psychological Interventions with Children, Adolescents and Their Families,* edited by A. Carr, 203–32. Florence, Ky.: Taylor & Francis/Routledge.

Moos, N. L. 1995. An Integrative Model of Grief. *Death Studies* 194:337–64.

Mor Barak, M. E., J. A. Nissly, and A. Levin. 2001. Antecedents to Retention and Turnover Among Child Welfare, Social Work, and Other Human Service Employees: What Can We Learn from Research? A Review and Meta-analysis. *Social Service Review* 75:625–61.

Morgan, J. D. 1995. Intervention. In *Planning and Managing Death Issues in the Schools: A Handbook,* edited by R. L. Deaton and W. A. Berkan, 67–95. Westport, Conn.: Greenwood Press.

Mori, S. 2000. Addressing the Mental Health Concerns of International Students. *Journal of Counseling and Development* 78:137–44.

Morrison, A. 1996. Trauma and Disruption in the Life of the Analyst. In *The Therapist as a Person,* edited by B. Gerson, 41–54. Mahwah, N.J.: Analytic Press.

Morrissette, P. J. 2001. *Self-Supervision: A Primer for Counselors and Helping Professionals.* New York: Brunner-Routledge.

Morrow-Howell, N., S. Becker-Kemppainen, and L. Judy. 1998. Evaluating an Intervention for the Elderly at Increased Risk of Suicide. *Research on Social Work Practice* 8:28–46.

Moscarello, R. 1989. Perinatal Bereavement Support Service: Three-Year Review. *Journal of Palliative Care* 5:12–18.

Moss, E. 2001. The Ones Left Behind: A Siblings' Bereavement Group. *Group Analysis* 34:395–407.

Moss, E. 2002. Working with Dreams in a Bereavement Therapy Group. *International Journal of Group Psychotherapy* 52:151–70.

Moss, M. S., and S. Z. Moss. 1989. Death of the Very Old. In *Midlife Loss,* edited by R. A. Kalish, 121–45. Newbury Park, Calif.: Sage.

Moss, M. S., S. Z. Moss, and R. O. Hansson. 2001. Bereavement and Old Age. In *Handbook of Bereavement Research: Consequences, Coping and Care,* edited by M. S. Stroebe, R. O. Hansson, W. Stroebe, and H. Schut, 241–60. Washington, D.C.: American Psychological Association.

Moss, M. S., N. Resch, and S. Z. Moss. 1997. The Role of Gender in Middle-Age Children's Responses to Parent Death. *Omega* 35:43–65.

Moss, S. Z., R. L. Rubenstein, and M. S. Moss. 1997. Middle Aged Son's Reactions to Father's Death. *Omega* 34:259–77.

Mouton, C. P., and Y. B. Esparaz. 2000. Ethnicity and Geriatric Assessment. In *Handbook of Geriatric Assessment,* edited by J. J. Gallo, T. Fulmer, G. J. Paveza, and W. Reichel, 13–28. Gaithersburg, Md.: Aspen.

Mrazek, P. J., and R. J. Haggerty, eds. 1994. *Reducing Risk for Mental Disorders: Frontiers for Preventive Intervention Research*. Washington, D.C.: National Academy Press.

Mueller, K. P. 1995. The Relationship Between Social Support and Burnout Among Social Work Caregivers and HIV/AIDS Clients. *Dissertation Abstracts International, Section A: Humanities and Social Sciences* 57:3683.

Mufson, L., and K. P. Dorta. 2000. Interpersonal Psychotherapy for Depressed Adolescents: Theory, Practice, and Research. In *Adolescent Psychiatry: Developmental and Clinical Studies*, edited by A. H. Esman and L. Flaherty, 139–67. Hillsdale, N.J.: Analytic Press.

Mullan, J. 1992. The Bereaved Caregiver: A Prospective Study of Changes in Well-being. *The Gerontologist* 32:673–83.

Muller, U., and R. Barash-Kishon. 1998. Psychodynamic-Supportive Group Therapy Model for Elderly Holocaust Survivors. *International Journal of Group Psychotherapy* 48:461–75.

Murray, J. A. 2001. Loss as a Universal Concept: A Review of the Literature to Identify Common Aspects of Loss in Diverse Situations. *Journal of Loss and Trauma* 6:219–41.

Murray, J. A., and V. J. Callan. 1988. Predicting Adjustment to Perinatal Death. *British Journal of Medical Psychology* 61:237–44.

Murray, J. A., D. J. Terry, J. C. Vance, D. Battistutta, and Y. Connolly. 2000. Effects of a Program of Intervention on Parental Distress Following Infant Death. *Death Studies* 24:275–305.

Murphy, K., P. Hanrahan, and D. Luchins. 1997. A Survey of Grief and Bereavement in Nursing Homes: The Importance of Hospice Grief and Bereavement for the End-Stage Alzheimer's Disease Patient. *Journal of the American Geriatrics Society* 45:1104–7.

Murphy, S. A., L. C. Johnson, K. C. Cain, A. Das Gupta, M. Dimond, J. Lohen, and R. Baugher. 1998. Broad Spectrum Group Treatment for Parents Bereaved by the Violent Deaths of Their 12 to 28 Year Old Children: A Randomized Controlled Trial. *Death Studies* 22:209–85.

Musselman, D. L., D. L. Evans, and C. B. Nemeroff. 1998. The Relationship of Depression to Cardiovascular Disease: Epidemiology, Biology and Treatment. *Archives of General Psychiatry* 55:580–92.

Mutrie, N. 2000. The Relationship Between Physical Activity and Clinically Defined Depression. In *Physical Activity and Psychological Well-being*, edited by S. J. H. Biddle, K. R. Fox, and S. H. Boutcher, 46–62. London: Routledge.

Nadeau, J. W. 1998. *Families Making Sense of Death*. Thousand Oaks, Calif.: Sage.

Nadeau, J. W. 2001a. Family Construction of Meaning. In *Meaning Reconstruction and the Experience of Loss*, edited by R. A. Neimeyer, 95–112. Washington, D.C.: American Psychological Association.

Nadeau, J. W. 2001b. Meaning Making in Family Bereavement: A Family Systems Approach. In *Handbook of Bereavement Research: Consequences, Coping, and Care*, edited by M. S. Stroebe, R. O. Hansson, W. Stroebe, and H. Schut, 329–47. Washington, D.C.: American Psychological Association.

Nader, K. O. 1997. Treating Traumatic Grief in Systems. In *Death and Trauma: The Traumatology of Grieving*, edited by C. R. Figley, B. E, Bride, and N. Mazza, 159–92. Philadelphia: Taylor & Francis.

Nader, K. O., and R. Pynoos. 1993. School Disaster: Planning and Initial Interventions. *Journal of Social Behavior and Personality* 8:299–320.

Nakamura, R. M. 1999. *Health in America: A Multicultural Perspective*. Boston: Allyn & Bacon.

Narayn, S., M. Lewis, J. Tornatore, K. Hepburn, and S. Corcoran-Perry. 2001. Subjective Responses to Caregiving for Spouses with Dementia. *Journal of Gerontological Nursing* 27:19–28.

National Academy on an Aging Society. 2000. *Helping the Elderly with Activity Limitations: Caregiving*, vol. 7. Washington, D.C.: National Academy on an Aging Society.

National Association of State Units on Aging. 2003. *The Aging Network Implements the National Family Caregiver Support Program*. Washington, D.C.: Administration on Aging.

National Institute of Mental Health. 2003. Older Adults: Depression and Suicide Facts. Bethesda, Md.: National Institute of Mental Health. Available at: http://www.nimh .nih.gov/publicat/elderlydepsuicide.cfm.

National Institute of Mental Health. 2004. *The Numbers Count: Mental Disorders in America*. Bethesda, Md.: National Institutes of Health.

Naugle, A. E., H. S. Resnick, M. J. Gray, and R. Acierno. 2002. Treatment for Acute Stress and PTSD Following Rape. In *The Trauma of Sexual Assault: Treatment, Prevention and Practice*, edited by J. Petrak and B. Hedge, 135–66. New York: Wiley.

Neal, M. B., B. Ingersoll-Dayton, and M. E. Starrels. 1997. Gender and Relationship Differences in Caregiving Patterns and Consequences Among Employed Caregivers. *The Gerontologist* 37:804–16.

Neary, M., and G. Brandon. 1997. A Group's Journey Through Separation and Loss: Therapeutic Group Work with Children as a Social Work Intervention. *Group Work* 10:30–40.

Neimeyer, R. A. 1995. An Invitation to Constructivist Psychotherapies. In *Constructivism in Psychotherapy*, edited by R. A. Neimeyer and M. J. Mahoney, 1–8. Washington, D.C.: American Psychological Association.

Neimeyer, R. A. 1997. Meaning Reconstruction and the Experience of Chronic Loss. In *Living with Grief: When Illness Is Prolonged*, edited by K. J. Doka and J. D. Davidson, 159–76. Philadelphia: Taylor & Francis.

Neimeyer, R. A. 1998a. Can There Be a Psychology of Loss? In *Perspectives on Loss: A Sourcebook*, edited by J. H. Harvey, 331–52. Philadelphia: Brunner/Mazel.

Neimeyer, R. A. 1998b. *Lessons of Loss: A Guide to Coping*. New York: McGraw-Hill.

Neimeyer, R. A. 1999. Narrative Strategies in Group Therapy. *Journal of Constructivist Psychology* 12:65–85.

Neimeyer, R. A. 2000. Searching for the Meanings of Meaning: Grief Therapy and the Process of Reconstruction. *Death Studies* 24:541–58.

Neimeyer, R. A., ed. 2001. *Meaning Reconstruction and the Experience of Loss.* Washington, D.C.: American Psychological Association.

Neimeyer, R. A., and N. S. Hogan. 2001. Quantitative or Qualitative? Measurement Issues in the Study of Grief. In *Handbook of Bereavement Research*, edited by M. S. Stroebe, R. O. Hansson, W. Stroebe, and H. Schut, 89–118. Washington, D.C.: American Psychological Association.

Neimeyer, R. A., and N. J. Keesee. 1998. Dimensions of Diversity in the Reconstruction of Meaning. In *Living with Grief: Who We Are, How We Grieve*, edited by K. J. Doka, 223–38. Philadelphia: Brunner/Mazel.

Neimeyer, R. A., N. J. Keesee, and B. V. Fortner. 2000. Loss and Meaning Reconstruction: Propositions and Procedures. In *Traumatic and Non-traumatic Loss and Bereavement*, edited by R. Malkinson, S. Rubin, and E. Wiztum, 197–230. Madison, Conn.: Psychosocial Press.

Neimeyer, R. A., and M. Mahoney, eds. 1995. *Constructivism in Psychotherapy.* Washington, D.C.: American Psychological Association.

Nelson, B., and T. Frantz. 1996. Family Interactions of Suicide Survivors and Survivors of Non-Suicidal Death. *Omega* 33:131–46.

Nelson, J. C. 2001. Diagnosing and Treating Depression in the Elderly. *Journal of Clinical Psychiatry* 62 (suppl. 24):18–22.

Ness, D. E., and C. R. Pfeffer. 1990. Sequelae of Bereavement Resulting from Suicide. *American Journal of Psychiatry* 147:279–85.

Nettles, S., W. Mucherah, and D. Jones. 2000. Understanding Resilience: The Role of Social Resources. *Journal of Education for Students Placed at Risk* 5:47–60.

Neugarten, B., and H. Hagestad. 1976. Age and the Life Course. In *Handbook of Aging and the Social Sciences*, edited by E. Shanas and R. Binstock, 35–55. New York: Van Nostrand Reinhold.

Neugarten, G., and D. Gutmann. 1968. Age-Sex Roles and Personality in Middle Age: A Thematic Apperception Study. In *Middle Age and Aging*, edited by B. L. Neugarten, 58–71. Chicago: University of Chicago Press.

Neville, H. A., and M. J. Heppner. 2002. Prevention and Treatment of Violence Against Women. In *Counseling Across the Lifespan: Prevention and Treatment*, edited by C. L. Juntenen and D. R. Atkinson, 261–77. Thousand Oaks, Calif.: Sage.

Nickman, S. L., P. R. Silverman, and C. Normand. 1998. Children's Construction of a Deceased Parent: The Surviving Parent's Contribution. *American Journal of Orthopsychiatry* 68:126–34.

Niederland, W. G. 1971. Introductory Notes on the Concept, Definition and Range of Psychic Trauma. In *Psychic Traumatization: Aftereffects in Individuals and Communities*, edited by H. G. Krystal and W. G. Niederland, 1–10. Boston: Little Brown.

Nolen-Hoeksema, S. 1991. Responses to Depression and Their Effects on the Duration of Depressive Episodes. *Journal of Abnormal Psychology* 100:569–82.

Nolen-Hoeksema, S., and J. Larson. 1997. Rumination and Psychological Distress Among Bereaved Partners. *Journal of Personality and Social Psychology* 72:855–62.

Nolen-Hoeksema, S., and J. Larson. 1999. *Coping with Loss*. Mahwah, N.J.: Erlbaum.

Nord, D. 1996. Assessing the Negative Effects of Multiple AIDS-Related Losses on the Gay Individual and Community. *Journal of Gay and Lesbian Social Services* 4:1–34.

Nord, D. 1997. *Multiple AIDS-Related Loss: A Handbook for Understanding and Surviving a Perpetual Fall*. Washington, D.C.: Taylor & Francis.

Normand, C. L., P. R. Silverman, and S. L. Nickman. 1996. Bereaved Children's Changing Relationship with the Deceased. In *Continuing Bonds: New Understandings of Grief*, edited by D. Klass, P. R. Silverman and S. L. Nickman, 87–112. Washington, D.C.: Taylor & Francis.

Norris, F. H., J. D. Foster, and D. L. Weisshaar. 2002. The Epidemiology of Sex Differences in PTSD Across Developmental, Societal and Research Contexts. In *Gender and PTSD*, edited by R. Kimerling, P. Ouimette, and J. Wolfe, 3–42. New York: Guilford Press.

Norris, F. H., and S. A. Murrell. 1990. Social Support, Life Events and Stress as Modifiers of Adjustment to Bereavement by Older Adults. *Psychology and Aging* 5:429–36.

O'Bryant, S. L., and R. O. Hansson. 1995. Widowhood. In *Handbook of Aging and the Family*, edited by R. Blieszner and V. H. Bedford, 440–58. Westport, Conn.: Greenwood Press.

O'Bryant, S. L., and L. B. Straw. 1991. Relationship of Previous Divorce and Previous Widowhood to Older Women's Adjustment to Recent Widowhood. *Journal of Divorce and Remarriage* 15:49–67.

O'Connor, K. J. 1991. *The Play Therapy Primer: An Integration of Theories and Techniques*. New York: Wiley.

O'Connor, K. J., and C. E. Schaefer, eds. 1994. *Advances and Innovations*. Vol. 2 of *Handbook of Play Therapy*. New York: Wiley.

Odets, W. 1994. AIDS Education and Harm Reduction for Gay Men: Psychological Approaches for the 21st Century. *AIDS and Public Policy Journal* 9:1–16.

O'Donnell, L., A. Stueve, D. Wardlaw, and C. O'Donnell. 2003. Adolescent Suicidality and Adult Support: The Reach for Health Study of Urban Youth. *American Journal of Health Behavior* 27:633–44.

O'Halloran, M. 2000. Adjustment to Parental Separation and Divorce. In *What Works with Children and Adolescents? A Critical Review of Psychological Interventions with Children, Adolescents and Their Families*, edited by A. Carr, 280–99. Florence, Ky.: Taylor & Francis/Routledge.

O'Keefe, M. 1997. Adolescents' Exposure to Community and School Violence: Prevalence and Behavior Correlates. *Journal of Adolescent Health* 20:368–76.

Oliver, C., and M. Dykeman. 2003. Challenges to HIV Service Provision: The Commonalities for Nurses and Social Workers. *AIDS Care* 15:649–63.

Oliver, L. E. 1999. Effects of a Child's Death on the Marital Relationship: A Review. *Omega* 39:197–227.

Oliver, R. C., J. P. Sturtevant, J. P. Scheetz, and M. E. Fallat. 2001. Beneficial Effects of a Hospital Bereavement Intervention Program After Traumatic Childhood Death. *Journal of Trauma-Injury Infection and Critical Care* 50:440–46.

Olson, M. 1997. *Healing the Dying*. Albany, N.Y.: Delmar.

Oltjenbruns, K. A. 1991. Positive Outcomes of Adolescents' Experience with Grief. *Journal of Adolescent Research* 6:43–55.

Oltjenbruns, K. A. 1996. Death of a Friend During Adolescence: Issues and Impacts. In *Handbook of Adolescent Death and Bereavement*, edited by C. A. Corr and D. E. Balk, 196–215. New York: Springer.

Oltjenbruns, K. A. 1998. Ethnicity and the Grief Response: Mexican American Versus Anglo American College Students. *Death Studies* 22:141–55.

Oltjenbruns, K. A. 2001. Developmental Context of Childhood: Grief and Regrief Phenomena. In *Handbook of Bereavement Research: Consequences, Coping, and Care*, edited by M. S. Stroebe, R. O. Hansson, W. Stroebe, and H. Schut, 186–88. Washington, D.C.: American Psychological Association.

Opoku, K. A. 1989. African Perspectives on Death and Dying. In *Perspectives on Death and Dying: Cross-Cultural and Multi-Disciplinary Views*, edited by A. Berger, P. Badham, and A. H. Kutscher, 14–23. Philadelphia: Charles Press.

Ory, M. G., R. R. Hoffman, Y. Yee, S. L. Tennstedt, and R. Schulz. 1999. Prevalence and Impact of Caregiving: A Detailed Comparison Between Dementia and Non-Dementia Caregivers. *The Gerontologist* 39:177–86.

Osgood, N. J., B. A. Brant, and A. A. Lipman. 1989. Patterns of Suicidal Behavior in Long-Term Care Facilities: A Preliminary Report on an Ongoing Longitudinal Study. *Omega* 19:69–78.

Osterweis, M., F. Solomon, and M. Green. 1984. *Bereavement: Reactions, Consequences, and Care*. Washington D.C.: National Academy Press.

Osvath, P., S. Fekete, and V. Voeroes. 2002. Attempted Suicide in Late Life: Review of Results of Pecs Centre in WHO/Euro Multicentre Study of Suicidal Behavior. *Psychiatria Danubina* 14:3–8.

Ott, C. 2003. The Impact of Complicated Grief on Mental and Physical Health at Various Points in the Bereavement Process. *Death Studies* 27:249–72.

Paddock, D. 2001. The Orphan and the Warrior. Paper presented at Winter Park, Colo., July.

Pang, T. H. C., and C. W. Lam. 2002. The Widowers' Bereavement Process and Death Rituals: Hong Kong Experiences. *Illness, Crisis and Loss* 10:294–303.

Parkes, C. M. 1972. *Bereavement: Studies of Grief in Adult Life*. New York: International University Press.

Parkes, C. M. 1975. Determinants of Outcome Following Bereavement. *Omega* 6:303–23.

Parkes, C. M. 1992. Bereavement and Mental Health in the Elderly. *Reviews in Clinical Gerontology* 2:45–51.

Parkes, C. M. 1996. *Bereavement: Studies of Grief in Adult Life*. 3rd ed. London: Routledge.

Parkes, C. M. 2001. A Historical Overview of the Scientific Study of Bereavement. In *Handbook of Bereavement Research: Consequences, Coping, and Care*, edited by M. S. Stroebe, R. O. Hansson, W. Stroebe, and H. Schut, 25–46. Washington, D.C.: American Psychological Association.

Parkes, C. M. 2002. Grief: Lessons from the Past, Visions for the Future. *Death Studies* 26:367–85.

Parkes, C. M., P. Laungani, and B. Young. 1997. *Death and Bereavement*. London: Routledge.

Parkes, C. M., J. Stevenson-Hinde, and P. Marris. 1991. *Attachment Across the Life Cycle*. London: Routledge.

Parsons, C. I. 1986. Group Reminiscence Therapy and Levels of Depression in the Elderly. *Nurse Practitioner: American Journal of Primary Health Care* 11:68, 70, 75–76.

Parsons, S., and P. Merrick-Roddy. 1996. AIDS Orphans in Louisiana in the Year 2000: The Potential Economic Impact on the Foster Care System. *Journal of the Louisiana State Medical Society* 148:391–98.

Pask, E. G. 2000. Culture: Caring and Curing in the Changing Health Scene. In *Meeting the Needs of Our Clients Creatively: The Impact of Art and Culture on Caregiving*, edited by J. D. Morgan, 67–76. Amityville, N.Y.: Baywood.

Pauw, M. 1991. The Social Worker's Role with a Fetal Demise and Stillbirth. *Health and Social Work* 16:291–97.

Pearlin, L. I. 1982. The Social Contexts of Stress. In *Handbook of Stress: Theoretical and Clinical Aspects*, edited by L. Goldberger and S. Breznitz, 363–79. New York: Free Press.

Pearlin, L. I. 1989. The Sociological Study of Stress. *Journal of Health and Social Behavior* 30:241–56.

Pedro-Carroll, J. 2001. The Promotion of Wellness in Children and Families: Challenges and Opportunities. *American Psychologist* 56:993–1004.

Pennebaker, J. W. 1989. Confessions, Inhibition, and Disease. In *Advances in Experimental Social Psychology*, edited by L. Berkowitz, vol. 22, 211–44. Orlando, Fla.: Academic Press.

Pennebaker, J. W., and S. K. Beall. 1986. Confronting a Traumatic Event: Toward an Understanding of Inhibition and Disease. *Journal of Abnormal Psychology* 95:274–81.

Perlotto, M. J. 2001. Self-Reported Psychopathology and Risk-Taking Behaviors Among Parentally Bereaved Adolescents. Ph.D. diss., Pace University. Available at: http://digitalcommons.pace.edu/dissertations/AAI3011868.

Perry, H. L. 1993. Mourning and Funeral Customs of African Americans. In *Ethnic Variations in Dying, Death and Grief: Diversity in Universality*, edited by D. P. Irish, K. F. Lundquist, and V. J. Nelsen, 51–66. Washington, D.C.: Taylor & Francis.

Perschy, M. K. 1989. Crazy Grief. *To Make the Road Less Lonely*. Newsletter, Winter.

Perschy, M. K. 1997. *Helping Teens Work Through Grief*. Washington, D.C.: Accelerated Development.

Pesek, E. M. 2002. The Role of Support Groups in Disenfranchised Grief. In *Disenfranchised Grief: New Directions, Challenges, and Strategies for Practice*, edited by K. J. Doka, 127–33. Champaign, Ill.: Research Press.

Petrak, J. 2002. The Psychological Impact of Sexual Assault. In *The Trauma of Sexual Assault: Treatment, Prevention and Practice*, edited by J. Petrak and B. Hedge, 19–44. New York: Wiley.

Pettle, S. A., and C. M. Britten. 1995. Talking with Children About Death and Dying. *Child: Care, Health and Development* 21:395–404.

Pfeffer, C. R. 1986. *The Suicidal Child*. New York: Gilford Press.

Pfeffer, C. R., H. Jiang, T. Kakuma, J. Hwang, and M. Metsch. 2002. Group Intervention for Children Bereaved by the Suicide of a Relative. *Journal of the American Academy of Child and Adolescent Psychiatry* 41:505–13.

Phillips, J. H., and J. Corcoran. 2000. Multi-Family Group Interventions with Schizophrenia. *Group Work* 12:45–63.

Phinney, J. S., G. Horenczyk, K. Liebkind, and P. Vedder. 2001. Ethnic Identity, Immigration, and Well-being: An Interactional Perspective. *Journal of Social Issues* 573:493–510.

Piacentini, J. C., M. J. Rotheram-Borus, and C. Cantwell. 1995. Brief Cognitive-Behavioral Family Therapy for Suicidal Adolescents. In *Innovations in Clinical Practice: A Source Book*, edited by L. VandeCreek and S. Knapp, 151–68. Sarasota, Fla.: Professional Resource Press/Professional Resource Exchange.

Piaget, J., and B. Inhelder. 1969. *The Psychology of the Child*. New York: Basic Books.

Picton, C., B. K. Cooper, D. Close, and J. Tobin. 2001. Bereavement Support Groups: Timing of Participation and Reasons for Joining. *Omega* 43:247–58.

Pilkington, F. B. 1999. A Qualitative Study of Life After Stroke. *Journal of Neuroscience Nursing* 31:336–47.

Pirog-Good, M. 1995. The Family Background and Attitudes of Teen Fathers. *Youth and Society* 26:351–76.

Plante, T. G. 1993. Aerobic Exercise in Prevention and Treatment of Psychopathology. In *Exercise Psychology: The Influence of Physical Exercise on Psychological Processes*, edited by P. Seraganian, 358–79. New York: Wiley.

Poijula, S., K. Wahlberg, and A. Dyregrov. 2001. Adolescent Suicide and Suicide Contagion in Three Secondary Schools. *International Journal of Emergency Mental Health* 3:163–68.

Ponder, R. J., and E. G. Pomeroy. 1996. The Grief of Caregivers: How Pervasive Is It? *Journal of Gerontological Social Work* 27:3–21.

Pope, K. S., and B. G. Tabachnick. 1994. Therapists as Patients: A National Survey of Psychologists' Experiences, Problems, and Beliefs. *Professional Psychology: Research and Practice* 25:247–58.

Pope, W. A. 2000. Personal Transformation in Midlife Parental Loss: An Empirical Phenomenological Study. *Dissertation Abstracts International, Section B: The Sciences and Engineering* 61:2798.

Popenhagen, M. P., and R. M. Qualley. 1998. Adolescent Suicide: Detection, Intervention, and Prevention. *Professional School Counseling* 1:30–36.

Potocky, M. 1993. Effective Services for Bereaved Spouses: A Content Analysis of Empirical Literature. *Health and Social Work* 18:288–301.

Poulin, J. E., and C. A. Walter. 1993. Social Worker Burnout: A Longitudinal Study. *Social Work Research and Abstracts* 29:5–11.

Powell, M. 1995. Sudden Infant Death Syndrome: The Subsequent Child. *British Journal of Social Work* 25:227–40.

Powers, L. E., and B. E. Wampold. 1994. Cognitive-Behavioral Factors in Adjustment to Adult Bereavement. *Death Studies* 18:1–24.

Prendergast, T., J., and K. A. Puntillo. 2002. Withdrawal of Life Support: Intensive Caring at the End of Life. *Journal of the American Medical Association* 288:2732–40.

Prescop, K. L., H. H. Dodge, R. K. Morycz, R. M. Schulz, and M. Ganguli. 1999. Elders with Dementia Living in the Community With and Without Caregivers: An Epidemiological Study. *International Psychogeriatrics* 11:235–50.

Prigerson, H. G., A. J. Bierhals, S. V. Kasl, C. F. Reynolds III, M. K. Shear, N. Day, L. C. Beery, J. T. Newsom, and S. Jacobs. 1997. Traumatic Grief as a Risk Factor for Mental and Physical Morbidity. *American Journal of Psychiatry* 154:617–23.

Prigerson, H. G., E. Frank, S. V. Kasl, C. F. Reynolds III, M. B. Anderson, G. S. Zubenko, P. R. Houck, C. J. George, and D. J. Kupfer. 1995. Complicated Grief and Bereavement-Related Depression as Distinct Disorders: Preliminary Empirical Validation in Elderly Bereaved Spouses. *American Journal of Psychiatry* 152:22–30.

Prigerson, H. G., and S. C. Jacobs. 2001. Traumatic Grief as a Distinct Disorder: A Rationale, Consensus Criteria and a Preliminary Empirical Test. In *Handbook of Bereavement Research: Consequences, Coping and Care*, edited by M. S. Stroebe, R. O. Hansson, W. Stroebe, and H. Schut, 613–46. Washington, D.C.: American Psychological Association.

Prigerson, H. G., P. Maciejewski, and R. Rosenheck. 2000. Preliminary Explorations of the Harmful Interactive Effects of Widowhood and Marital Harmony on Health, Health Service Use and Health Care Costs. *The Gerontologist* 40:349–57.

Prinstein, M. J., J. Boergers, A. Spirito, T. Little, and W. L. Grapentine. 2000. Peer Functioning, Family Dysfunction, and Psychological Symptoms in a Risk Factor Model for Adolescent Inpatients' Suicidal Ideation Survey. *Journal of Clinical Child Psychology* 29:392–406.

Pritchard, C., and D. S. Baldwin. 2002. Elder Suicide Rates in Asian and English-Speaking Countries. *ACTA Psychiatrica Scandinavica* 105:271–75.

Pritchard, R., E. Fisher, and J. Lynn. 1998. Influence of Patient Preferences and Local Health System Characteristics on Place of Death. *Journal of the American Geriatrics Society* 46:1242–50.

Pritchett, K. T., and P. M. Lucas. 1997. Grief and Loss. In *Psychiatric-Mental Health Nursing: Adaptation and Growth*, 4th ed., edited by B. S. Johnson, 199–218. New York: Lippincott.

Provini, C., J. R. Everett, and C. R. Pfeffer. 2000. Adults Mourning Suicide: Self-Reported Concerns About Bereavement, Needs for Assistance, and Help-Seeking Behavior. *Death Studies* 24:1–19.

Pruchno, R. 1999. Raising Grandchildren: The Experiences of Black and White Grandmothers. *The Gerontologist* 39:209–21.

Puchalski, C. M. 2000. FICA: A Spiritual Assessment Tool. *Journal of Palliative Care* 3:131.

Putney, N., and V. Bengtson. 2001. Families, Intergenerational Relationships and Kin Keeping in Midlife. In *Handbook of Midlife Development*, edited by M. Lachmann, 528–70. New York: Wiley.

Pynoos, R. S. 1992. Grief and Trauma in Children and Adolescents. *Bereavement Care* 111:2–10.

Pynoos, R. S., C. Frederick, K. Nader, W. Arroyo, A. Steinberg, E. Spencer, F. Nunez, and L. Fairbanks. 1987. Life Threat and Post-Traumatic Stress in School Age Children. *Archives of General Psychiatry* 44:1057–63.

Pynoos, R. S., A. K. Goenjian, and A. M. Steinberg. 1998. A Public Mental Health Approach to the Post Disaster Treatment of Children and Adolescents. *Child and Adolescent Psychiatric Clinic of North America* 7:195–210.

Quesenberry, C. P., and S. Wi. 1995. Mortality Following Conjugal Bereavement and the Effects of a Shared Environment. *American Journal of Epidemiology* 126:1142–52.

Quinn, M. S., and S. K. Tomita. 1997. *Elder Abuse and Neglect: Causes, Diagnosis, and Intervention Strategies.* 2nd ed. New York: Springer.

Raad, S. A. 1998. Grief: A Muslim Perspective. In *Living with Grief: Who We Are, How We Grieve*, edited by K. J. Doka and J. D. Davidson, 47–56. Philadelphia: Brunner/Mazel.

Ramsey, J. L., and R. Blieszner. 2000. Transcending a Lifetime of Losses: The Importance of Spirituality in Old Age. In *Loss and Trauma: General and Close Relationship Perspectives*, edited by J. H. Harvey and E. D. Miller, 225–36. Washington, D.C.: Taylor & Francis.

Rando, T. A. 1983. An Investigation of Grief and Adaptation in Parents Whose Children Have Died from Cancer. *Journal of Pediatric Psychology* 8:3–20.

Rando, T. A. 1984. *Grief, Dying, and Death: Clinical Interventions for Caregivers.* Champaign, Ill.: Research Press.

Rando, T. A. 1985. Creating Therapeutic Rituals in the Psychotherapy of the Bereaved. *Psychotherapy* 22:236–40.

Rando, T. A. 1986. The Unique Issues and Impact of the Death of a Child. In *Parental Loss of a Child*, edited by T. A. Rando, 4–44. Champaign, Ill.: Research Press.

Rando, T. A. 1988. *Grieving: How to Go on Living When Someone You Love Dies.* Lexington, Mass.: Lexington Books.

Rando, T. A. 1991. Parental Adjustment to the Loss of a Child. In *Children and Death*, edited by P. Papadatou and C. Papadotos, 233–54. New York: Hemisphere.

Rando, T. A. 1993. *Treatment of Complicated Mourning.* Champaign, Ill.: Research Press.

Rando, T. A. 1994. Complications in Mourning Traumatic Death. In *Dying, Death, and Bereavement*, edited by I. Corless, B. Germino, and M. Pittman, 253–71. Boston: Jones and Bartlett.

Rando, T. A. 2000. Promoting Healthy Anticipatory Mourning in Intimates of the Life-Threatened or Dying Person. In *Clinical Dimensions of Anticipatory Mourning: Theory and Practice in Working with the Dying, Their Loved Ones, and Their Caregivers*, edited by T. A. Rando, 307–78. Champaign, Ill.: Research Press.

Range, L. 1998. When a Loss Is Due to Suicide: Unique Aspects of Bereavement. In *Perspectives on Loss: A Sourcebook*, edited by J. H. Harvey, 213–20. Philadelphia: Brunner/Mazel.

Rankin, E. D. 2001. Assessment and Treatment of Grief States in Older Males. In *Men Coping with Grief*, edited by D. A. Lund, 229–52. Amityville, N.Y.: Baywood.

Raphael, B. 1983. *The Anatomy of Bereavement*. New York: Basic Books.

Raphael, B., C. Minkov, and M. Dobson. 2001. Psychotherapeutic and Pharmacological Intervention for Bereaved Persons. In *Handbook of Bereavement Research: Consequences, Coping, and Care*, edited by M. S. Stroebe, R. O. Hansson, W. Stroebe, and H. Schut, 587–612. Washington, D.C.: American Psychological Association.

Raphael, B., and K. Nunn. 1988. Counseling the Bereaved. *Journal of Social Issues* 44:191–206.

Rappaport, J. 2000. Traumatic Time: The Therapist's Mourning. *Psychoanalysis and Psychotherapy* 17:55–64.

Raveis, V. H. 1999. Facilitating Older Spouses' Adjustment to Widowhood: A Prevention Intervention Program. *Social Work in Health Care* 29:13–32.

Raveis, V. H., K. Siegel, and D. Karus. 1999. Children's Psychological Distress Following the Death of a Parent. *Journal of Youth and Adolescence* 28:165–80.

Reeve, C. 1999. *Still Me*. New York: Random House.

Reilly-Smorawski, B., A. V. Armstrong, and E. A. Catlin. 2002. Bereavement Support for Couples Following Death of a Baby: Program Development and 14-Year Exit Analysis. *Death Studies* 26:21–37.

Reinherz, H. Z., R. M. Giaconia, A. B. Silverman, A. Friedman, B. Pakiz, A. K. Frost, and E. K. Cohen. 1995. Early Psychosocial Risks for Adolescent Suicidal Ideation and Attempts. *Journal of the American Academy of Child and Adolescent Psychiatry* 34:599–611.

Remnet, V. L. 1989. *Understanding Older Adults: An Experiential Approach to Learning*. Lexington, Mass.: Lexington Books/Heath.

Ren, X. S., K. Skinner, A. Lee, and L. Kazis. 1999. Social Support, Social Selection and Self-Assessed Health Status: Results from the Veterans' Health Study in the United States. *Social Science and Medicine* 12:1721–34.

Renaud, C. 1995. Bereavement After a Suicide: A Model for Support Groups. In *The Impact of Suicide*, edited by B. L. Mishara, 52–63. New York: Springer.

Research Dissemination Core. 2002. *Family Bereavement Support Before and After the Death of a Nursing Home Resident*. Iowa City: University of Iowa Gerontological Nursing Interventions Research Center.

Rich, P. 2001. *Grief Counseling Homework Planner*. New York: Wiley.

Richards, T. A. 1999. Spiritual Aspects of Loss Among Partners of Men with AIDS: Postbereavement Follow-up. *Death Studies* 23:105–27.

Richards, T. A., J. Wrubel, and S. Folkman. 2000. Death Rites in the San Francisco Gay Community: Cultural Developments of the AIDS Epidemic. *Omega* 2:323–34.

Richardson, V. E. 2006. Bereavement in Later Life. In *Gerontological Practice for the Twenty-first Century: A Social Work Perspective*, edited by V. E. Richardson and A. S. Barusch, 264–92. New York: Columbia University Press.

Richardson, V. E. In press. A Dual Process Model of Grief Counseling: Findings from the Changing Lives of Older Couples (CLOC). *Journal of Gerontological Social Work*.

Richardson, V. E., and S. Balaswamy. 2001. Coping with Bereavement Among Elderly Widowers. *Omega* 43:129–44.

Riches, G., and P. Dawson. 1996a. Communities of Feeling: The Culture of Bereaved Parents. *Mortality* 1:143–61.

Riches, G., and P. Dawson. 1996b. "An Intimate Loneliness": Evaluating the Impact of a Child's Death on Parental Self-Identity and Marital Relationships. *Journal of Family Therapy* 18:1–22.

Riches, G., and P. Dawson. 1998. Lost Children, Living Memories: The Role of Photographs in Processes of Grief and Adjustment Among Bereaved Parents. *Death Studies* 22:121–40.

Riches, G., and P. Dawson. 2000. *An Intimate Loneliness: Supporting Bereaved Parents and Siblings.* Philadelphia: Open University Press.

Richman, J. 1996. Psychotherapeutic Approaches to the Depressed and Suicidal Older Person and Family. In *Suicide and Depression in Late Life: Critical Issues in Treatment, Research, and Public Policy,* edited by G. J. Kennedy, 103–17. New York: Wiley.

Rinpoche, S. 1994. *The Tibetan Book of Living and Dying.* New York: HarperCollins.

Riordan, R. J., and S. K. Saltzer. 1992. Burnout Prevention Among Health Care Providers Working with the Terminally Ill: A Literature Review. *Omega* 25:17–24.

Roach, M., and G. Kitson. 1989. Impact of Forewarning on Adjustment to Widowhood and Divorce. In *Older Bereaved Spouses,* edited by D. A. Lund, 185–200. New York: Hemisphere.

Robak, R. 1991. Loss and Bereavement Group in the Treatment of Recovering Addicts. *Death Studies* 15:293–301.

Robinson, L., and M. M. Mahon. 1997. Sibling Bereavement: A Concept Analysis. *Death Studies* 21:477–99.

Robinson, M., L. Baker, and L. Nackerund. 1999. The Relationship of Attachment Theory and Perinatal Loss. *Death Studies* 23:257–70.

Roethke, T. 1966. *The Collected Poems of Theodore Roethke.* London: Faber.

Roger, J. 1991. Family Structures and the Moral Politics of Caring. *Sociological Review* 39:799–822.

Romanoff, B. D., and M. Terenzio. 1998. Rituals and the Grieving Process. *Death Studies* 22:697–711.

Roos, S. 2002. *Chronic Sorrow: A Living Loss.* New York: Brunner-Routledge.

Rosen, E. J. 1996. The Family as Healing Resource. In *Handbook of Childhood Death and Bereavement,* edited by C. A. Corr and D. M. Corr, 223–43. New York: Springer.

Rosen, E. J. 1998. *Families Facing Death: A Guide for Healthcare Professionals and Volunteers.* San Francisco: Jossey-Bass.

Rosenberg, G. H. 1992. *The Adoption Life Cycle.* New York: Free Press.

Rosenblatt, P. C. 1993. Cross-Cultural Variation in the Experience, Expression and Understanding of Grief. In *Ethnic Variations in Dying, Death and Grief,* edited by D. P. Irish, K. F. Lundquist, and V. J. Nelsen, 13–20. Washington, D.C.: Taylor & Francis.

Rosenblatt, P. C. 1994. *Metaphors of Family Systems Theory: Toward New Constructions*. New York: Guilford Press.

Rosenblatt, P. C. 1996. Grief That Does Not End. In *Continuing Bonds: New Understandings of Grief*, edited by D. Klass, P. R. Silverman, and S. L. Nickman, 45–58. Washington, D.C.: Taylor & Francis.

Rosenblatt, P. C. 2000a. *Parent Grief: Narratives of Loss and Relationship*. Philadelphia: Brunner/Mazel.

Rosenblatt, P. C. 2000b. Protective Parenting After the Death of a Child. *Journal of Personal and Interpersonal Loss* 5:343–60.

Rosenblatt, P. C. 2001. A Social Constructionist Perspective on Cultural Differences in Grief. In *Handbook of Bereavement Research: Consequences, Coping, and Care*, edited by M. S. Stroebe, R. O. Hansson, W. Stroebe, and H. Schut, 285–300. Washington, D.C.: American Psychological Association.

Rosenblatt, P. C., and C. Elde. 1990. Shared Reminiscence About a Deceased Parent: Implications for Grief Education and Grief Counseling. *Family Relations* 39:206–10.

Rosenblatt, P. C., R. P. Walsh, and D. A. Jackson. 1976. *Grief and Mourning in Cross-Cultural Perspective*. Washington, D.C.: HRAF Press.

Rosenzweig, A., H. Prigerson, M. D. Miller, and C. F. Reynolds III. 1997. Bereavement and Late-Life Depression: Grief and Its Complications in the Elderly. *Annual Review of Medicine* 48:421–28.

Ross, M. M., C. J. Rosenthal, and P. Dawson. 1997. Patterns of Caregiving Following Institutionalization of Caregiving Husbands. *Canadian Journal of Nursing Research* 29:79–98.

Rothenberg, E. D. 1994. Bereavement Intervention with Vulnerable Populations: A Case Report on Group Work with the Developmentally Disabled. *Social Work with Groups* 17:61–75.

Rotheram-Borus, M. J., A. Goldstein, and A. S. Elkavich. 2002. Treatment of Suicidality: A Family Intervention for Adolescent Suicide Attempters. In *Treating Chronic and Severe Mental Disorders: A Handbook of Empirically Supported Interventions*, edited by S. G. Hofmann and M. C. Tompson, 191–212. New York: Guilford Press.

Rotheram-Borus, M. J., J. A. Stein, and Y. Lin. 2001. Impact of Parent Death and an Intervention on the Adjustment of Adolescents Whose Parents Have HIV/AIDS. *Journal of Consulting and Clinical Psychology* 69:763–73.

Rothschild, S. K. 1998. Cross-Cultural Issues in Primary Care Medicine. *Disease a Month* 44:293–319.

Rowa-Dewar, N. 2002. Do Interventions Make a Difference to Bereaved Parents? A Systematic Review of Controlled Studies. *International Journal of Palliative Nursing* 8:452–57.

Rowe, J. W., and R. L. Kahn. 1998. *Successful Aging*. New York: Pantheon Books.

Rubenstein, R. L. 1995. Narratives of Elder Parental Death: A Structural and Cultural Analysis. *Medical Anthropology Quarterly* 9:258–77.

Rubin, S. S. 1993. The Death of a Child Is Forever: The Life Course Impact of Child Loss. In *Handbook of Bereavement: Theory, Research, and Intervention*, edited by M. S.

Stroebe, W. Stroebe, and R. O. Hansson, 285–99. Cambridge: Cambridge University Press.

Rubin, S. S. 1996. The Wounded Family: Bereaved Parents and the Impact of Adult Child Loss. In *Continuing Bonds: New Understandings of Grief,* edited by D. Klass, P. R. Silverman, and S. L. Nickman, 217–32. Washington, D.C.: Taylor & Francis.

Rubin, S. S. 1999. The Two-Track Model of Bereavement: Overview Retrospect and Prospect. *Death Studies* 23:681–714.

Rubin, S. S., and R. Malkinson. 2001. Parental Response to Child Loss Across the Life Cycle: Clinical and Research Perspectives. In *Handbook of Bereavement Research: Consequences, Coping and Care,* edited by M. S. Stroebe, R. O. Hansson, W. Stroebe, and H. Schut, 219–40. Washington, D.C.: American Psychological Association.

Rubin, S. S., and N. Schecter. 1997. Exploring the Social Construction of Bereavement: Perceptions of Adjustment and Recovery in Bereaved Men. *American Journal of Orthopsychiatry* 672:280.

Rudd, M. G., L. L. Viney, and C. A. Preston. 1999. The Grief Experienced by Spousal Caregivers of Dementia Patients: The Role of Place of Care of Patient and Gender of Caregiver. *International Journal of Aging and Human Development* 48:217–40.

Rudestam, K. E. 1992. Research Contributions to Understanding the Suicide Survivor. *Crisis* 13:41–46.

Russel, R., P. Gill, A. Coyne, and J. Woody. 1993. Dysfunction in the Family of Origin of MSW and Other Graduate Students. *Journal of Social Work Education* 29:121–29.

Russell, P. L. 2002. Attachment and Grief in Foster Children. *Dissertation Abstracts International,* Section B: *The Sciences and Engineering* 63:2601.

Rutter, M. 1966. *Children of Sick Parents.* Oxford: Oxford University Press.

Rutter, M. 1990. Psychosocial Resilience and Protective Factors. In *Risk and Protective Factors in the Development of Psychopathology,* edited by J. Rolf, A. S. Masten, D. Cicchetti, K. H. Neuchterlein, and S. Weintraub, 181–214. Cambridge: Cambridge University Press.

Rutter, M. 1994. Stress Research: Accomplishments and Tasks Ahead. In *Stress, Risk and Resilience in Children and Adolescents,* edited by R. J. Haggerty, L. R. Sherrod, N. Garmezy, and M. Rutter, 354–85. Cambridge: Cambridge University Press.

Ryff, C. D., C. L. M. Keyes, and D. L. Hughes. 2003. Status Inequalities, Perceived Discrimination and Eudemonic Well-being. Do the Challenges of Minority Life Hone Purpose and Growth? *Journal of Health and Social Behavior* 44:275–91.

Rynearson, E. K. 2001. *Retelling Violent Death.* Philadelphia: Brunner-Routledge.

Saakvitne, K. W., S. Gamble, L. A. Pearlman, and B. Tabor Lev. 2000. *Risking Connection: A Training Curriculum for Working with Survivors of Childhood Abuse.* Lutherville, Md.: Sidran Press.

Sable, P. 1995. Pets, Attachment, and Well-being Across the Life Cycle. *Social Work* 40:334–41.

Safford, F. 1995. Aging Stressors for Holocaust Survivors and Their Families. *Journal of Gerontological Social Work* 241:131–53.

Saldinger, A., A. Cain, N. Kalter, and K. Lohmes. 1999. Anticipating Parental Death in Families with Young Children. *American Journal of Orthopsychiatry* 691:39–48.

Saleebey, D., ed. 1992. *The Strengths Perspective in Social Work Practice*. New York: Longman.

Saleh, M., and M. Kerr. 1996. Understanding the Muslim Patient. *Journal of the Society of Obstetricians and Gynecologists of Canada* 18:55–64.

Salloum, A., L. Avery, and R. P. McClain. 2001. Group Psychotherapy for Adolescent Survivors of Homicide Victims: A Pilot Study. *Journal of the American Academy of Child and Adolescent Psychiatry* 40:1261–67.

Saltzman, W. R., R. S. Pynoos, C. M. Layne, A. M. Steinberg, and E. Aisenberg. 2001. Trauma- and Grief-Focused Intervention for Adolescents Exposed to Community Violence: Results of a School-Based Screening and Group Treatment Protocol. *Group Dynamics: Theory, Research, and Practice* 5:291–303.

Sanchez, L., Fristad, M., Weller, R., Weller E., and Moye, J. 1994. Anxiety in Acutely Bereaved Prepubertal Children. *Annals of Clinical Psychiatry* 61:39–42.

Sanders, C. M. 1989. *Grief: The Mourning After. Dealing with Adult Bereavement*. 2nd ed. New York: Wiley.

Sanders, C. M. 1993. Risk Factors in Bereavement Outcome. In *Handbook of Bereavement: Theory, Research and Intervention*, edited by M. S. Stroebe, W. Stroebe, and R. O. Hansson, 256–67. Cambridge: Cambridge University Press.

Sanders, S., and C. S. Corley. 2003. Are They Grieving? A Qualitative Analysis Examining Grief in Caregivers of Individuals with Alzheimer's Disease. *Health and Social Work* 37:37–53.

Sandler, I. N., T. S. Ayers, S. A. Wolchik, J. Tien, O. Kwok, R. A. Haine, et al. 2003. The Family Bereavement Program: Efficacy Evaluation of a Theory-Based prevention Program for Parentally Bereaved Children and Adolescents. *Journal of Consulting and Clinical Psychology* 71:587–600.

Sandler, I. N., S. G. West, and L. Baca. 1992. Linking Empirically Based Theory and Evaluation: The Family Bereavement Program. *American Journal of Community Psychology* 20:491–521.

Sapp, M., R. L. McNeely, and J. B. Torres. 1998. Rational Emotive Behavior Therapy in the Process of Dying: Focus on Aged African Americans and Latinos. *Journal of Human Behavior in the Social Environment* 1:305–21.

Schachter, S. 1991/1992. Adolescent Experiences with the Death of a Peer. *Omega* 24:1–11.

Schaefer, C. E., and D. M. Cangelosi, eds. 1993. *Play Therapy Techniques*. New York: Aronson.

Schaefer, C. E., C. P. Quesenberry, and S. Wi. 1995. Mortality Following Conjugal Bereavement and the Effects of a Shared Environment. *American Journal of Epidemiology* 126:1142–52.

Schaefer, J. A., and R. H. Moos. 2001. Bereavement Experiences and Personal Growth. In *Handbook of Bereavement: Theory, Research and Intervention*, edited by M. S. Stroebe, W. Stroebe, and R. O. Hansson, 145–68. Cambridge: Cambridge University Press.

Scharlach, A. E. 1991. Factors Associated with Filial Grief Following the Death of an Elderly Parent. *American Journal of Orthopsychiatry* 6:307–13.

Scharlach, A. E., and K. I. Fredriksen. 1993. Reactions to the Death of Parent During Midlife. *Omega* 27:301–17.

Scharlach, A. E., and E. Fuller-Thomson. 1994. Coping Strategies Following the Death of an Elderly Parent. *Journal of Gerontological Social Work* 21:85–100.

Schiff, H. S. 1986. *Living Through Mourning*. New York: Viking Penguin.

Schindler, R., C. Spiegel, and E. Malachi. 1992. Silences: Helping Elderly Holocaust Victims Deal with the Past. *International Journal of Aging and Human Development* 35:243–52.

Schmall, V., and C. Pratt. 1986. Special Friends: Elders and Pets. *Generations* 10:44–45.

Schoeman, L. H., and R. Kreitzman. 1997. Death of a Parent: Group Intervention with Bereaved Children and Their Caregivers. *Psychoanalysis and Psychotherapy* 14:221–45.

Schreder, M. 1995. Special Needs of Bereaved Children: Effective Tools for Helping. In *Bereaved Children and Teens: A Support Guide for Parents and Professionals*, edited by E. A. Grollman, 195–211. Boston: Beacon Press.

Schuchter, C. 1986. *Dimensions of Grief: Adjusting to the Death of a Spouse*. San Francisco: Jossey-Bass.

Schuchter, S., and S. Zisook. 1993. The Course of Normal Grief. In *Handbook of Bereavement: Theory, Research and Intervention*, edited by M. Stroebe, W. Stroebe, and R. O. Hansson, 23–43. Cambridge: Cambridge University Press.

Schulz, R., and S. R. Beach. 1999. Caregiving as a Risk Factor for Mortality: The Caregiver Health Effects Study. *Journal of the American Medical Association* 282:2215–19.

Schulz, R., A. Mendelsohn, W. Haley, D. Mahoney, R. Allen, S. Zhang, L. Thompson, and S. Belle. 2003. End of Life Care and the Effects of Bereavement on Family Caregivers of Persons with Dementia. *New England Journal of Medicine* 349:1936–52.

Schut, H., M. S. Stroebe, J. van den bout, and M. de Keijser. 1997. Intervention for the Bereaved: Gender Differences in the Efficacy of Two Counseling Programs. *British Journal of Clinical Psychology* 36:63–72.

Schut, H., M. S. Stroebe, J. van den Bout, and M. Terheggen. 2001. The Efficacy of Bereavement Interventions: Determining Who Benefits. In *Handbook of Bereavement Research*, edited by M. S. Stroebe, R. O. Hansson, W. Stroebe, and H. Schut, 705–37. Washington, D.C.: American Psychological Association.

Schuurman, D. 2000. The Use of Groups with Grieving Children and Adolescents. In *Living with Grief: Children, Adolescents, and Loss*, edited by K. J. Doka, 165–77. Washington, D.C.: Hospice Foundation of America.

Schwab, R. 1986. Support Groups for the Bereaved. *Journal of Specialists in Group Work* 11:100–106.

Schwab, R. 1992. Effects of a Child's Death on the Marital Relationship: A Preliminary Study. *Death Studies* 16:141–54.

Schwab, R. 1998. A Child's Death and Divorce: Dispelling the Myth. *Death Studies* 22:445–68.

Schwartz, L. L., and F. W. Kaslow. 1997. *Painful Partings: Divorce and Its Aftermath*. New York: Wiley.

Schwartzberg, S. 1996. *A Crisis of Meaning: How Gay Men Are Making Sense of AIDS*. Oxford: Oxford University Press.

Schwartz-Borden, G. 1992. Metaphor: Visual Aid in Grief Work. *Omega* 25:239–48.

Seager, K. M., and S. C. Spencer. 1996. Meeting the Bereavement Needs of Kids in Patient/Families—Not Just Playing Around. *Hospice Journal* 11:41–66.

Sedney, M. A., J. E. Baker, and E. Gross. 1994. "The Story" of a Death: Therapeutic Considerations with Bereaved Families. *Journal of Marital and Family Therapy* 20:287–96.

Seeman, T. E., B. H. Singer, J. W. Rowe, R. I. Horwitz, and B. S. McEwen. 1997. Price of Adaptation—Allostatic Load and Its Health Consequences—MacArthur Studies of Successful Aging. *Archives of Internal Medicine* 157:2259–68.

Segal, D. L., J. A. Bogaards, L. A. Becker, and C. Chatman. 1999. Effects of Emotional Expression on Adjustment to Spousal Loss Among Older Adults. *Journal of Mental Health and Aging* 5:297–310.

Sellers, S. L., and A. G. Hunter. In press. Private Pain, Public Choices: Influence of Problems in the Family of Origin on Career Choices Among a Cohort of MSW Students. *Journal of Social Work Education*.

Seltzer, M. M., and M. W. Kraus. 1989. Aging Parents with Adult Mentally Retarded Children: Family Risk Factors and Sources of Support. *American Journal of Mental Retardation* 94:303–12.

Seltzer, M. M., and L. Q. Li. 2000. The Dynamics of Caregiving: Transitions During a Three-Year Prospective Study. *The Gerontologist* 40:165–78.

Servaty, H. L., and B. J. R. Hayslip. 2001. Adjustment to Loss Among Adolescents. *Omega* 43:311–30.

Servaty-Seib, H. L., J. Peterson, and D. Spang. 2003. Notifying Individual Students of a Death Loss: Practical Recommendations for Schools and School Counselors. *Death Studies* 27:167–86.

Shackford, S. 2003. School Violence: A Stimulus for Death Education—A Critical Analysis. *Journal of Loss and Trauma* 8:35–40.

Shaefer, S. J. M. 1992. Adolescent Pregnancy Loss: A School-Based Program. *Journal of School Nursing* 8:6–8, 10, 12–13.

Shaffer, D., A. Garland, M. Gould, P. Fisher, and P. Trautman. 1990. Preventing Teenage Suicide: A Critical Review. In *Annual Progress in Child Psychiatry and Child Development*, edited by S. Chess and M. E. Hertzig, 401–28. Philadelphia: Brunner/Mazel.

Shaffer, S. 1993. Young Widows: Rebuilding Identity and Personal Growth Following Spousal Loss. Ph.D. diss., University of San Francisco.

Shannon, C. 1996. Dealing with Stress: Families and Chronic Illness. In *Handbook of Stress, Medicine and Health*, edited by G. Cooper, 321–38. New York: CRC.

Shapiro, E. R. 1994. *Grief as a Family Process: A Developmental Approach to Clinical Practice.* New York: Guilford Press.

Shapiro, E. R. 1995. Grief in Family and Cultural Context: Learning from Latino Families. *Cultural Diversity and Mental Health* 1:159–76.

Shapiro, E. R. 1996. Family Bereavement and Cultural Diversity: A Social Developmental Perspective. *Family Process* 35:313–32.

Shapiro, E. R. 1998. The Healing Power of Culture Stories: What Writers Can Teach Psychotherapists. *Cultural Diversity and Mental Health* 4:91–101.

Shapiro, E. R. 2001. Grief in Interpersonal Perspective: Theories and Their Implications. In *Handbook of Bereavement Research: Consequences, Coping, and Care,* edited by M. S. Stroebe, R. O. Hansson, W. Stroebe, and H. Schut, 301–28. Washington, D.C.: American Psychological Association.

Shapiro, P. 1996. *My Turn: Women's Search for Self After the Children Leave.* Princeton, N.J.: Peterson.

Sharpnack, J. D. 2001. The Efficacy of Group Bereavement Interventions: An Integrative Review of the Research Literature. *Dissertation Abstracts International,* Section B: *The Sciences and Engineering* 61:6721.

Shaver, P. R., and C. M. Tancredy. 2001. Emotion, Attachment and Bereavement: A Conceptual Commentary. In *Handbook of Bereavement Research: Consequences, Coping, and Care,* edited by M. S. Stroebe, R. O. Hansson, W. Stroebe, and H. Schut, 63–88. Washington, D.C.: American Psychological Association.

Shaw, B. R., F. McTavish, R. Hawkins, D. H. Gustafson, and S. Pingree. 2000. Experiences of Women with Breast Cancer: Exchanging Social Support over the CHESS Computer Network. *Journal of Health Communication* 5:135–59.

Sheafor, B. W., C. R. Horejsi, and G. A. Horejsi. 2000. *Techniques and Guidelines for Social Work Practice.* 5th ed. Boston: Allyn & Bacon.

Shear, M. K., E. Frank, E. Foa, C. Cherry, C. F. Reynolds, J. V. Bilt, and S. Masters. 2001. Traumatic Grief Treatment. *American Journal of Psychiatry* 158:1506–8.

Sherman, A., B. de Vries, and J. Lansford. 2000. Friendship in Childhood and Adulthood: Lessons Across the Lifespan. *International Journal of Aging and Human Development* 51:31–51.

Shernoff, M. 1998. *Gay Widowers: Life After the Death of a Partner.* New York: Harrington Park Press.

Shernoff, M. 1999. Dying Well: Counseling End-Stage Clients with AIDS. In *AIDS and Mental Health Practice: Clinical and Policy Issues,* edited by M. Shernoff, 187–97. New York: Haworth Press.

Sherrel, K., K. Buckwalter, and D. Morhardt. 2001. Negotiating Family Relationships: Dementia Care as a Midlife Developmental Task. *Families in Society* 82:383–92.

Sherwood, D. A. 1998. Spiritual Assessment as a Normal Part of Social Work Practice: Power to Help and Power to Harm. *Social Work and Christianity* 25:80–90.

Shoshan, T. 1989. Mourning and Longing from Generation to Generation. *American Journal of Psychotherapy* 43:193–207.

Shrader, G. N. 1992. A Descriptive Study of the Effects of Continuous Multiple AIDS-Related Losses Among Gay Male Survivors. *Dissertation Abstracts International,* Section A: *Humanities and Social Sciences* 53:5454B.

Sickmund, M., H. Snyder, and E. Poe-Yamagata. 1997. *Juvenile Offenders and Victims: 1997 Update on Violence.* Washington, D.C.: Office of Juvenile Justice and Delinquency Prevention.

Siefert, K., S. Jayaratne, and W. A. Chess. 1991. Job Satisfaction, Burnout, and Turnover in Health Care Social Workers. *Health and Social Work* 16:193–202.

Siegel, K., F. Masagno, D. Karus, G. Christ, G. Banks, and R. Moynihan. 1992. Psychosocial Adjustment of Children with a Terminally Ill Parent. *Journal of the American Academy of Child/Adolescent Psychiatry* 31:327–33.

Siegel, K., V. Raveis, and D. Karus. 1996. Patterns of Communication with Children When a Parent Has Cancer. In *Cancer and the Family*, edited by L. Baider, C. Cooper, and A. DeNour, 109–28. New York: Wiley.

Sigelman, C. K. 1999. *Life-Span Development.* 3rd ed. Pacific Grove, Calif.: Brooks/Cole.

Sikkema, K. J., S. C. Kalichman, J. A. Kelly, and J. J. Koob. 1995. Group Intervention to Improve Coping with AIDS Related Bereavement: Model Development and an Illustrative Clinical Example. *AIDS Care* 7:463–75.

Silin, M. W., and H. M. Stewart. 2003. Mother Bear: A Relational Approach to Child Therapy. *Clinical Social Work Journal* 31:235–47.

Silverman, P. R. 1989. The Impact of Parental Death on College Age Women. *Psychiatric Clinics of North America* 10:387–404.

Silverman, P. R. 1995. Helping the Bereaved Through Social Support and Mutual Help. In *A Challenge for Living: Dying, Death, and Bereavement*, edited by I. B. Coreless, B. B. Germino, and M. A. Pittman, 241–57. Boston: Jones and Bartlett.

Silverman, P. R. 2000. *Never Too Young to Know. Death in Children's Lives.* New York: Oxford University Press.

Silverman, P. R., and D. Klass. 1996. Introduction: What's the Problem? In *Continuing Bonds: New Understandings of Grief*, edited by D. Klass, P. R. Silverman, and S. Nickman, 3–27. Washington, D.C.: Taylor & Francis.

Silverman, P. R., and S. Nickman. 1996. Children's Construction of Their Dead Parents. In *Continuing Bonds: New Understandings of Grief*, edited by D. Klass, P. R. Silverman, and S. Nickman, 73–86. Washington, D.C.: Taylor & Francis.

Silverman, P. R., S. Nickman, and J. W. Worden. 1992. Detachment Revisited: The Child's Reconstruction of a Dead Parent. *American Journal of Orthopsychiatry* 62:494–503.

Silverman, P. R., S. Nickman, and J. W. Worden. 1995. Detachment Revisited. In *Children Mourning, Mourning Children*, edited by K. J. Doka, 131–48. Washington, D.C.: Hospice Foundation of America.

Silverman, P. R., and A. Weiner. 1995. Parent–Child Communication in Bereaved Israeli Families. *Omega* 31:275–93.

Silverman, P. R., and J. W. Worden. 1992a. Children's Reactions in the Early Months After the Death of a Parent. *American Journal of Orthopsychiatry* 62:93–104.

Silverman, P. R., and J. W. Worden. 1992b. Children's Understanding of Funeral Ritual. *Omega* 25:319–31.

Silverstein, D. N., and S. K. Roszia. 1999. Openness: A Critical Component of Special Needs Adoption. *Child Welfare* 78:637–51.

Sireling, L., D. Cohen, and I. Marks. 1988. Guided Mourning for Morbid Grief: A Controlled Replication. *Behavior Therapy* 19:121–32.

Skovholt, T. M. 2001. *The Resilient Practitioner: Burnout Prevention and Self-Care Strategies for Counselors, Therapists, Teachers, and Health Professionals.* Boston: Allyn & Bacon.

Smith, G. C., S. S. Tobin, and E. M. Fullmer. 1995. Assisting Older Families of Adults with Lifelong Disabilities. In *Strengthening Aging Families: Diversity in Practice and Policy,* edited by G. C. Smith, S. S. Tobin, E. A. Robertson-Tchabo, and P. W. Power, 80–98. Thousand Oaks, Calif.: Sage.

Smith, H. 1999. *Children, Feelings and Divorce.* London: Free Association Books.

Smith, S. C., and J. Pennells, eds. 1995. *Interventions with Bereaved Children.* London: Kingsley.

Smith, S. H. 1998. *African American Daughters and Elderly Mothers.* New York: Garland.

Smyer, M., A. Gatz, M. Simi, and L. Pederson. 1998. Childhood Adoption: Long Term Effects in Adulthood. *Psychiatry* 6:191–205.

Sobel, D. S. 1997. The "Write" Way to Cope with Trauma. *Partners in Health Newsletter,* Summer, 23.

Sofka, C. J. 1997. Social Support "Internetworks," Caskets for Dale, and More: Thanatology and the Information Superhighway. *Death Studies* 21:553–74.

Sogyal, R. 1992. *The Tibetan Book of the Living and Dying.* New York: HarperCollins.

Solberg, V. S., S. Ritsma, B. J. Davis, S. P. Tata, and A. Jolly. 1994. Asian-American Students' Severity of Problems and Willingness to Seek Help from University Counseling Centers: Role of Previous Counseling Experience, Gender and Ethnicity. *Journal of Counseling Psychology* 41:245–79.

Solomon, Z. 1990. Does the War End When the Shooting Stops? The Psychological Toll of War. *Journal of Applied Social Psychology* 20:1733–45.

Sommers-Flanagan, J., and R. Sommers-Flanagan. 1995. Rapid Emotional Change Strategies: Enhancing Youth Responsiveness to Cognitive-Behavioral Therapy. *Child and Family Behavior Therapy* 17:11–22.

Sonnega, J. 2002. Survey Evidence of Clinical Wisdom: Special Occasions and Grief in the Elderly Widowed. Lecture, University of Michigan, Ann Arbor.

Soricelli, B. A. 1985. Mourning the Death of a Child: The Family and Group Process. *Social Work* 30:429–34.

Speckhard, A. 1997. Traumatic Death in Pregnancy: The Significance of Meaning and Attachment. In *Death and Trauma: The Traumatology of Grieving,* edited by C. R. Figley, B. E. Bride, and N. Mazza, 67–100. Philadelphia: Taylor & Francis.

Spiegel, D., and I. Yalom. 1978. Support Group for Dying Patients. *International Journal of Group Psychotherapy* 28:233–45.

Sprecher, S., and B. Fehr. 1998. The Dissolution of Close Relationships. In *Perspectives on Loss: A Sourcebook*, edited by J. H. Harvey, 99–112. Philadelphia: Brunner/Mazel.

Stahlman, S. D. 1996. Children and the Death of a Sibling. In *Handbook of Childhood Bereavement*, edited by C. A. Corr and D. Corr, 149–64. New York: Springer.

Stallard, P., and F. Law. 1993. Screening and Psychological Debriefing of Adolescent Survivors of Life-Threatening Events. *British Journal of Psychiatry* 163:660–65.

Staudacher, C. 1991. *Grief: A Guide for Men Surviving the Death of a Loved One: A Resource for Caregivers and Mental Health Professionals*. Oakland, Calif.: New Harbinger.

Staudinger, U., and S. Buck. 2001. A View on Midlife Development from Life-Span Theory. In *Handbook of Midlife Development*, edited by M. Lachman, 3–39. New York: Wiley.

Steinhauser, A. E., N. A. Christakis, E. C. Clipp, M. McNeilly, L. McIntyre, and J. A. Tulsky. 2000. Factors Considered Important at the End of Life by Patients, Family, Physicians, and Other Care Providers. *Journal of the American Medical Association* 284:2476–82.

Sterns, H. L., and J. H. Gray. 1999. Work, Leisure, and Retirement. In *Gerontology: An Interdisciplinary Perspective*, edited by J. C. Cavanaugh and S. K. Whitbourne, 355–90. New York: Oxford University Press.

Sterns, H. L., and M. Hellie Huyck. 2001. The Role of Work in Midlife. In *Handbook of Midlife Development*, edited by M. E. Lachman, 447–86. New York: Wiley.

Stevenson, R. G. 1990. Contemporary Issues of Life and Death. In *Death Education in Canada*, edited by J. D. Morgan, 43–79. London, Ont.: Kings College Press.

Stevenson, R. G., and E. P. Stevenson. 1996. Adolescents and Education About Death, Dying and Bereavement. In *Handbook of Adolescent Death and Bereavement*, edited by C. A. Corr and D. E. Balk, 235–49. New York: Springer.

Stewart, A. E. 1999. Complicated Bereavement and Posttraumatic Stress Disorder Following Fatal Car Crashes: Recommendations for Death Notification. *Death Studies* 23:289–321.

Stewart, M., D. Craig, K. MacPherson, and S. Alexander. 2001. Promoting Positive Affect and Diminishing Loneliness of Widowed Seniors Through a Support Intervention. *Public Health Nursing* 18:54–63.

Stirtzinger, R. M., G. E. Robinson, D. E. Stewart, and E. Ralevski. 1999. Parameters of Grieving in Spontaneous Abortion. *International Journal of Psychiatry in Medicine* 29:235–49.

Stoddart, K. P., L. Burke, and V. Temple. 2002. Outcome Evaluation of Bereavement Groups for Adults with Intellectual Disabilities. *Journal of Applied Research in Intellectual Disabilities* 15:28–35.

Stoddart, K. P., and J. McDonnell. 1999. Addressing Grief and Loss in Adults with Developmental Disabilities. *Journal of Developmental Disabilities* 6:51–65.

Stolley, J. M., K. C. Buckwalter, and H. G. Koenig. 1999. Prayer and Religious Coping for Caregivers of Persons with Alzheimer's Disease and Related Disorders: *American Journal of Alzheimer's Disease* 14:181–91.

Stolley, J. M., and H. Koenig. 1997. Religion/Spirituality and Health Among Elderly African Americans and Hispanics. *Journal of Psychosocial Nursing* 35:32–38.

Stolley, J. M., D. Reed, and K. C. Buckwalter. 2002. Caregiving Appraisal and Interventions Based on the Progressively Lowered Stress Threshold Model. *American Journal of Alzheimer's Disease and Other Dementias* 17:110–20.

Strauss, S. S., and M. Munton. 1985. Common Concerns of Parents with Disabled Children. *Pediatric Nursing* 11:371–75.

Stroebe, M. S. 1992. Coping with Bereavement: A Review of the Grief Work Hypothesis. *Omega* 26:19–42.

Stroebe, M. S. 1994. The Broken Heart Phenomenon: An Examination of the Mortality of Bereavement. *Journal of Community and Applied Social Psychology* 4:47–61.

Stroebe, M. S. 1998. New Directions in Bereavement Research: Exploration of Gender Differences. *Palliative Medicine* 12:5–12.

Stroebe, M. S. 2001. Bereavement Theory and Research: Retrospective and Prospective. *American Behavioral Scientist* 44:854–65.

Stroebe, M. S., M. M. Gergen, K. J. Gergen, and W. Stroebe. 1992. Broken Hearts or Broken Bonds: Love and Death in Historical Perspective. *American Psychologist* 47:1205–12.

Stroebe, M. S., M. M. Gergen, K. J. Gergen, and W. Stroebe. 1996. Broken Hearts or Broken Bonds. In *Continuing Bonds: New Understandings of Grief,* edited by D. Klass, P. Silverman, and S. Nickman, 31–44. Washington, D.C.: Taylor & Francis.

Stroebe, M. S., R. O. Hansson, W. Stroebe, and H. Schut. 2001a. Future Directions for Bereavement Research. In *Handbook of Bereavement Research,* edited by M. S. Stroebe, R. O. Hansson, W. Stroebe, and H. Schut, 741–63. Washington, D.C.: American Psychological Association.

Stroebe, M. S., R. O. Hansson, W. Stroebe, and H. Schut. 2001b. Introduction: Concepts and Issues in Contemporary Research on Bereavement. In *Handbook of Bereavement: Theory, Research, and Intervention,* edited by M. S. Stroebe, R. O. Hansson, W. Stroebe, and H. Schut, 3–22. Cambridge: Cambridge University Press.

Stroebe, M. S., and H. Schut. 1995. The Dual Process Model of Coping with Loss. Paper presented at the International Work Group on Death, Dying and Bereavement, St. Catherine's College, Oxford, June 26–29.

Stroebe, M. S., and H. Schut. 1999. The Dual Process Model of Coping with Bereavement: Rationale and Description. *Death Studies* 23:197–224.

Stroebe, M. S., and H. Schut. 2001a. Models of Coping with Bereavement: A Review. In *Handbook of Bereavement Research,* edited by M. S. Stroebe, R. O. Hansson, W. Stroebe, and H. Schut, 375–404. Washington, D.C.: American Psychological Association.

Stroebe, M. S., and H. Schut. 2001b. Risk Factors in Bereavement Outcome: A Methodological and Empirical Review. In *Handbook of Bereavement Research,* edited by M. S. Stroebe, R. O. Hansson, W. Stroebe, and H. Schut, 349–71. Washington, D.C.: American Psychological Association.

Stroebe, M. S., H. Schut, and W. Stroebe. 1998. Trauma and Grief: A Comparative

Analysis. In *Perspectives on Loss: A Sourcebook*, edited by J. H. Harvey, 81–98. Washington, D.C.: Taylor & Francis.

Stroebe, M. S., and W. Stroebe. 1983. Who Suffers More? Sex Differences in Health Risks of the Widowed. *Psychological Bulletin* 93:297–301.

Stroebe, M. S., and W. Stroebe. 1987. *Bereavement and Health: The Psychological and Physical Consequences of Partner Loss*. Cambridge: Cambridge University Press.

Stroebe, M. S., and W. Stroebe. 1991. Does "Grief Work" Work? *Journal of Consulting and Clinical Psychology* 59:476–82.

Stroebe, M. S., and W. Stroebe. 1993. Determinants of Adjustment to Bereavement in Younger Widows and Widowers. In *Handbook of Bereavement: Theory, Research, and Intervention*, edited by M. S. Stroebe, R. O. Hansson, W. Stroebe, and H. Schut, 208–26. Cambridge: Cambridge University Press.

Stroebe, M. S., W. Stroebe, H. Schut, E. Zech, and J. van den Bout. 2002. Does Disclosure of Emotions Facilitate Recovery from Bereavement? Evidence from Two Prospective Studies. *Journal of Consulting and Clinical Psychology* 70:169–78.

Stroebe, M. S., J. van den Bout, and H. Schut. 1994. Myths and Misconceptions About Bereavement: The Opening of a Debate. *Omega* 29:187–203.

Sullivan, A. 1990. Gay Life, Gay Death: The Siege of a Subculture. *New Republic* December 17, 19.

Surgeon General. 2003. *The Surgeon General's Call to Action to Prevent Suicide, 1999*. Bethesda, Md.: U.S. Department of Health and Human Services. Available at: http://www.surgeongeneral.gov/library/calltoaction/fact2.htm. Accessed May 30, 2003.

Szanto, K., H. Prigerson, P. Houck, L. Ehrenpreis, and C. F. Reynolds III. 1997. Suicidal Ideation in Elderly Bereaved: The Role of Complicated Grief. *Suicide and Life-Threatening Behavior* 27:194–207.

Szinovacz, M. E., S. DeViney, and M. P. Atkinson. 1999. Effects of Surrogate Parenting on Grandparents' Well-being. *Journals of Gerontology* 54B:S376–88.

Szolnoki, J., and K. Cahn. 2003. *African American Kinship Caregivers: Principles for Developing Supportive Programs*. Seattle: University of Washington School of Social Work, Northwest Institute for Children and Families.

Tajfel, H., and J. C. Turner. 1986. The Social Identity Theory of Intergroup Behavior. In *Psychology of Intergroup Relations*, edited by S. Worchel and W. G. Austin, 7–24. Chicago: Nelson-Hall.

Talbot, K. 1997. Mothers Now Childless: Structures of the Life World. *Omega* 36:45–62.

Tan, S. Y., and N. J. Dong. 2000. Psychotherapy with Members of Asian American Churches and Spiritual Traditions. In *Handbook of Psychotherapy and Religious Diversity*, edited by P. S. Richards and A. E. Bergin, 421–44. Washington, D.C.: American Psychological Association.

Tatelbaum, J. 1980. *The Courage to Grieve: Creative Living, Recovery and Growth Through Grief*. New York: Harper & Row.

Taylor, E. J. 2001. Spiritual Assessment. In *Textbook of Palliative Nursing*, edited by B. F. Ferrell and N. Coyle, 397–406. New York: Oxford University Press.

Taylor-Brown, S., S. Blacker, K. Walsh-Burke, G. Christ, and T. Altilio. 2001. *Innovative Practice in Social Work: Care at the End of Life*. Rev. ed. Chicago: Society of Social Work Leadership in Health Care.

Tedeschi, R. G., and L. G. Calhoun. 1995. *Trauma and Transformation: Growing in the Aftermath of Suffering*. Thousand Oaks, Calif.: Sage.

Tedeschi, R. G., and L. G. Calhoun. 1996. The Posttraumatic Growth Inventory: Measuring the Positive Legacy of Trauma. *Journal of Traumatic Stress* 9:455–71.

Tedeschi, R. G., C. L. Park, and L. G. Calhoun. 1998. Post Traumatic Growth: Conceptual Issues. In *Post Traumatic Growth: Positive Changes in the Aftermath of Crisis*, edited by R. G. Tedeschi, C. L. Park, and L. G. Calhoun, 1–22. Mahwah, N.J.: Erlbaum.

Tennen, H., and G. Affleck. 1998. Personality and Transformation in the Face of Adversity. In *Post Traumatic Growth: Positive Change in the Aftermath of Crisis*, edited by R. G. Tedeschi, C. L. Park, and L. G. Calhoun, 65–98. Mahwah, N.J. Erlbaum.

Tennstedt, S. 1999. *Family Caregiving in an Aging Society*. Washington, D.C.: Administration on Aging, Symposium on Caregiving.

Thomas, B., B. Leite, and T. Duncan. 1998. Breaking the Cycle of Violence Among Youth Living in Metropolitan Atlanta: A Case History of Kids Alive and Loved. *Health Education and Behavior* 25:160–74.

Thomas, V., P. Striegel, D. Dudley, J. Wilkins, and D. Gibson. 1997. Parental Grief of a Perinatal Loss: A Comparison of Individual and Relationship Variables. *Journal of Personal and Interpersonal Loss* 2:167–87.

Thompson, C. L., and L. B. Rudolph. 2000. *Counseling Children*. 5th ed. Pacific Grove, Calif.: Brooks/Cole-Thompson Learning.

Thompson, S. C. 1996. Living with Loss: A Bereavement Support Group. *Group Work* 9:5–14.

Thompson, S. C. 1998. Blockades to Finding Meaning and Control. In *Perspectives on Loss: A Sourcebook*, edited by J. H. Harvey, 21–34. Philadelphia: Brunner/Mazel.

Thompson, S. C., and A. Janigian. 1988. Life Schemes: A Framework for Understanding the Search for Meaning. *Journal of Social and Clinical Psychology* 7:260–80.

Thuen, F. 1997. Social Support After the Loss of Child: A Long-Term Perspective. *Scandinavian Journal of Psychology* 38:103–10.

Thyer, B. A., K. Thyer, and S. Massa. 1991. Behavioral Analysis and Therapy in the Field of Gerontology. In *Serving the Elderly: Skills for Practice*, edited by P. K. H. Kim, 117–35. New York: Aldine de Gruyter.

Tinsley, D. J. and M. Bigler. 2002. Facilitating Transitions in Retirement. In *Counseling Across the Lifespan: Prevention and Treatment*, edited by C. L. Juntunen and D. R. Atkinson, 375–97. Thousand Oaks, Calif.: Sage.

Tolin, D. F., and E. B. Foa. 2002. Gender and PTSD: A Cognitive Model. In *Gender and PTSD*, edited by R. Kimerling, P. Ouimette, and J. Wolfe, 76–97. New York: Guilford Press.

Tomita, T., and T. Kitamura. 2002. Clinical and Research Measures of Grief: A Reconsideration. *Comprehensive Psychiatry* 43:95–102.

Tonkins, S. A. M., and M. J. Lambert. 1996. A Treatment Outcome Study of Bereavement Groups for Children. *Child and Adolescent Social Work Journal* 13:3–21.

Toseland, R. W. 1990. *Group Work with Older Adults*. New York: New York University Press.

Toseland, R. W., and C. M. Rossiter. 1989. Group Interventions to Support Family Caregivers: A Review and Analysis. *The Gerontologist* 29:438–48.

Toseland, R. W., C. M. Rossiter, and M. S. Labrecque. 1989. The Effectiveness of Three Group Intervention Strategies to Support Family Caregivers. *American Journal of Orthopsychiatry* 59:420–29.

Tot, C. H. 2003. The Impact of Complicated Grief on Mental and Physical Health at Various Points in the Bereavement Process. *Death Studies* 27:249–72.

Toth, J. 1997. *Orphans of the Living: Stories of American Children in Foster Care*. New York: Simon and Schuster.

Toumbourou, J. W., and M. E. Gregg. 2002. Impact of an Empowerment-Based Parent Education Program on the Reduction of Youth Suicide Risk Factors. *Journal of Adolescent Health* 31:277–85.

Trautman, P. D. 1995. Cognitive Behavior Therapy of Adolescent Suicide Attempters. In *Treatment Approaches with Suicidal Adolescents*, edited by J. K. Zimmerman and G. M. Asnis, 155–73. Oxford: Wiley.

Tremblay, G., and A. Israel. 1998. Children's Adjustment to Parental Death. *Clinical Psychology: Science and Practice* 54:424–38.

Trozzi, M., and K. Massimini. 1999. *Talking with Children About Loss*. New York: Penguin Putnam.

Truitner, K., and N. Truitner. 1993. Death and Dying in Buddhism. In *Ethnic Variations in Dying, Death and Grief. Diversity in Universality*, edited by D. P. Irish, K. F. Lundquist, and V. J. Nelsen, 125–36. Washington, D.C.: Taylor & Francis.

Tudiver, F., J. Hilditch, J. A. Permaul, and D. J. McKendree. 1992. Does Mutual Help Facilitate Newly Bereaved Widowers? Report of a Randomized Controlled Trial. *Evaluation and the Health Professions* 15:147–62.

Turkoski, B., and B. Lance. 1996. The Use of Guided Imagery with Anticipatory Grief. *Home Healthcare Nurse* 14:878–88.

Tweed, J., V. Shoenback, L. George, and D. Blazer. 1989. The Effects of Childhood Parental Death and Divorce on Six-Month History of Anxiety Disorders. *British Journal of Psychiatry* 154:823–28.

Tyson-Rawson, K. J. 1993. College Women and Bereavement: Later Adolescence and Father Death. Ph.D. diss., University of Kansas.

Tyson-Rawson, K. J. 1996. Ambiguity in Adolescent Understanding of Death. In *Handbook of Adolescent Death and Bereavement*, edited by C. A. Corr and D. E. Balk, 155–72. New York: Springer.

Uhlenberg, P. 1996. The Burden of Aging: A Theoretical Framework for Understanding the Shifting Balance of Caregiving and Care Receiving vs. Cohort Ages. *The Gerontologist* 36:761–67.

Underwood, M. M., and K. Dunne-Maxim. 1997. *Managing Sudden Traumatic Loss in the*

Schools. New Brunswick, N.J.: University of Medicine and Dentistry of New Jersey–University Behavioral HealthCare.

Underwood, M. M., and K. Dunne-Maxim. 2000. Responding to Traumatic Death in the School: The New Jersey Model. In *Shocking Violence: Youth Perpetrators and Victims—A Multidisciplinary Perspective,* edited by R. S. Moser and C. E. Frantz, 154–71. Springfield, Ill.: Thomas.

Updegraff, J. A., and S. E. Taylor. 2000. From Vulnerability to Growth: Positive and Negative Effects of Stressful Life Events. In *Loss and Trauma: General and Close Relationship Perspectives,* edited by J. H. Harvey and E. Miller, 3–28. Philadelphia: Brunner-Routledge.

Urquhart, L. R. 1989. Separation and Loss: Assessing the Impacts on Foster Parent Retention. *Child and Adolescent Social Work Journal* 6:193–209.

Utsey, S. O., E. P. Adams, and M. Bolden. 2000. Development and Initial Validation of the Africultural Coping Systems Inventory. *Journal of Black Psychology* 26:194–215.

Utz, R. In press. The Economic and Practical Adjustments to Loss. In *Widowhood in Late Life,* edited by D. Carr, R. Nesse, and C. Wortman. New York: Springer.

Vachon, M. L. S. 2000. Burnout and Symptoms of Stress in Staff Working in Palliative Care. In *Handbook of Psychiatry in Palliative Medicine,* edited by H. M. Chochinov and W. Breitbart, 303–19. New York: Oxford University Press.

Vachon, M. L. S., W. A. L. Lyall, J. Rogers, K. Freedman-Letofsky, and S. J. J. Freeman. 1980. A Controlled Study of Self-Help Intervention for Widows. *American Journal of Psychiatry* 137:1380–84.

Vachon, M. L. S., and S. K. Stylianos. 1988. The Role of Social Support in Bereavement. *Journal of Social Issues* 44:175–90.

Vaillant, G. 1998. Are Social Supports in Late Midlife a Cause or a Result of Successful Physical Aging? *Psychological Medicine* 28:1159–68.

Valente, S. M., and J. M. Saunders. 2002. Nurses' Grief Reactions to a Patient's Suicide. *Perspectives in Psychiatric Care* 38:5–14.

Van, P., and A. L. Meleis. 2003. Coping with Grief After Involuntary Pregnancy Loss: Perspectives of African American Women. *Journal of Obstetric, Gynecologic, and Neonatal Nursing* 32:28–39.

van den Hoonaard, D. K. 1997. *The Widowed Self: The Older Woman's Journey Through Widowhood.* Toronto: Wilfrid Laurier University Press.

Van Dongen, C. J. 1991. Survivors of a Family Member's Suicide: Implications for Practice. *Nurse Practitioners* 16:31–36.

Van Doorn, C., S. V. Kasl, L. Beery, S. C. Jacobs, and H. G. Prigerson. 1998. Qualities of Marriage Associated with Traumatic Grief and Depressive Symptomatology. *Journal of Nervous and Mental Disease* 186:566–73.

Vargas, L. A., and J. D. Koss-Chioino, eds. 1992. *Working with Culture: Psychotherapeutic Interventions with Ethnic Minority Children and Adolescents.* San Francisco: Jossey-Bass.

Varvaro, F. F. 1991. Using a Grief Response Assessment Questionnaire in a Support Group to Assist Battered Women in Their Recovery. *Response* 13:17–20.

Vigilante, F. W. 1983. Working with Families of Learning Disabled Children. *Child Welfare* 62:429–36.

Viney, L. L., Y. N. Benjamin, and C. Preston. 1989. Mourning and Reminiscence: Parallel Psychotherapeutic Processes for Elderly People. *International Journal of Aging and Human Development* 28:239–49.

Vinokur, A. 2002. The Structure and Predictors of Grief Reactions: A Prospective Study of Older Widowed Adults. Lecture, University of Michigan, Ann Arbor.

Viorst, J. 1986. *Necessary Losses*. New York: Ballantine Books.

Vitaliano, P. P., R. Schulz, J. Kiecolt-Glaser, and I. Grant 1997. Research on Physiological and Physical Concomitants of Caregiving: Where Do We Go from Here? *Annals of Behavioral Medicine* 19:117–23.

Waern, M. 2003. Alcohol Dependence and Misuse in Elderly Suicides. *Alcohol and Alcoholism* 38:249–54.

Waern, M., E. Rubenowitz, and K. Wihelmson. 2003. Predictors of Suicide in the Old Elderly. *Gerontology* 49:328–34.

Waldron, V. R., M. Lavitt, and D. Kelley. 2000. The Nature and Prevention of Harm in Technology-Mediated Self-Help Settings: Three Exemplars. *Journal of Technology in Human Services* 17:267–93.

Walker, C. L. 1993. Sibling Bereavement and Grief Responses. *Journal of Pediatric Nursing* 8:325–34.

Walker, K., V. M. MacBride, and M. Vachon. 1977. Social Support Networks and the Crisis of Bereavement. *Social Science Medicine* 11:35–41.

Walker, R. J., and E. C. Pomeroy. 1996. Depression or Grief: The Experience of Caregivers of People with Dementia. *Health and Social Work* 96:247–54.

Walker, R. J., E. C. Pomeroy, J. S. McNeil, and C. Franklin. 1994a. Anticipatory Grief and Alzheimer's Disease: Strategies for Intervention. *Journal of Gerontological Social Work* 22:21–39.

Walker, R. J., E. C. Pomeroy, J. S. McNeil, and C. Franklin. 1994b. A Psychoeducational Model for Caregivers of Persons with Alzheimer's Disease. *Journal of Gerontological Social Work* 22:75–91.

Walker, R. J., E. C. Pomeroy, J. S. McNeil, and C. Franklin. 1996. Anticipatory Grief and AIDS: Strategies for Intervening with Caregivers. *Health and Social Work* 21:49–57.

Wallace, G. 2001. Grandparent Caregivers: Emerging Issues in Elder Law and Social Work Practice. *Journal of Gerontological Social Work* 34:127–34.

Wallerstein, J., J. Lewis, and S. Blakeslee. 2000. *The Unexpected Legacy of Divorce: A 25 Year Landmark Study*. New York: Hyperion.

Walsh, F. 1998. *Strengthening Family Resilience*. New York: Guilford Press.

Walsh, F. 2002. A Family Resilience Framework: Innovative Practice Applications. *Family Relations* 2:130:37.

Walsh, F., and M. McGoldrick. 1988. Loss and the Family Life Cycle. In *Family Transition*, edited by C. Falicov, 311–36. New York: Guilford Press.

Walsh, F., and M. McGoldrick. 1991. *Living Beyond Loss: Death in the Family.* New York: Norton.

Walsh, K., M. King, L. Jones, A. Tookman, and R. Blizard. 2002. Spiritual Beliefs May Affect Outcome of Bereavement: Prospective Study. *British Medical Journal* 32:1551–56.

Walsh-Burke, K. 2000. Matching Bereavement Services to Level of Need. *Hospice Journal* 15:77–86.

Walter, C. A. 2003. *The Loss of a Life Partner.* New York: Columbia University Press.

Walter, T. 1996. A New Model of Grief: Bereavement and Biography. *Mortality* 11:7–27.

Ward-Wimmer, D., and C. Napoli. 2000. Counseling Approaches with Children and Adolescents. In *Living with Grief: Children, Adolescents, and Loss,* edited by K. J. Doka, 109–24. Washington, D.C.: Hospice Foundation of America.

Wass, H. 2004. A Perspective on the Current State of Death Education. *Death Studies* 28:289–308.

Wass, H., M. D. Miller, and G. Thornton. 1990. Death Education and Grief/Suicide Intervention in the Public Schools. *Death Studies* 14:253–68.

Weaver, H. N., and M. Yellow Horse Brave Heart. 1999. Examining Two Facets of American Indian Identity: Exposure to Other Cultures and the Influence of Historical Trauma. *Journal of Human Behavior in the Social Environment* 2:19–33.

Webb, N. B. 2000. Play Therapy to Help Bereaved Children. In *Living with Grief: Children, Adolescents, and Loss,* edited by K. J. Doka, 139–52. Washington, D.C.: Hospice Foundation of America.

Webb, N. B. 2002. Assessment of the Bereaved Child. In *Helping Bereaved Children: A Handbook for Practitioners,* edited by N. B. Webb, 19–42. New York: Guilford Press.

Weenolsen, P. 1988. *Transcendence of Loss over the Life Span.* New York: Hemisphere.

Weiss, J. C. 1995. Cognitive Therapy and Life Review Therapy: Theoretical and Therapeutic Implications for Mental Health Counselors. *Journal of Mental Health Counseling* 17:157–72.

Weiss, R. S. 1974. *Loneliness: The Experience of Emotional and Social Isolation.* Cambridge, Mass.: MIT Press.

Weiss, R. S. 1988. Loss and Recovery. *Journal of Social Issues* 44:37–52.

Weiss, R. S. 1993. Loss and Recovery. In *Handbook of Bereavement: Theory, Research and Intervention,* edited by M. S. Stroebe, R. O. Hansson, W. Stroebe, and H. Schut, 271–84. Washington, D.C.: American Psychological Association.

Weiss, R. S. 1998. Issues in the Study of Grief and Loss. In *Perspectives on Loss: A Sourcebook,* edited by J. H. Harvey, 343–53. Philadelphia: Brunner/Mazel.

Weiss, R. S. 2001. Grief, Bonds and Relationships. In *Handbook of Bereavement: Theory, Research and Intervention,* edited by M. S. Stroebe, R. O. Hansson, W. Stroebe, and H. Schut, 47–62. Washington, D.C.: American Psychological Association.

Weller, R., E. Weller, M. Fristad, and J. Bowes. 1991. Depression in Recently Bereaved Pre-Pubertal Children. *American Journal of Psychiatry* 148:1536–40.

Werner, E., and R. Smith. 1992. *Overcoming the Odds: High-Risk Children from Birth to Adulthood.* Ithaca, N.Y.: Cornell University Press.

West, T. M. 1994. Psychological Issues in Hospice Music Therapy. *Music Therapy Perspectives* 12:117–24.

Wheeler, I. 1994. The Role of Meaning and Purpose in Life in Bereaved Parents Associated with a Self-Help Group: Compassionate Friends. *Omega* 28:261–71.

Wheeler, S. R., and J. Austin. 2000. The Loss Response List: A Tool for Measuring Adolescent Grief Responses. *Death Studies* 24:21–34.

Williams, C., and B. Moretta. 1997. Systematic Understanding of Loss and Grief Related to Alzheimer's Disease. In *Living with Grief When Illness Is Prolonged*, edited by K. J. Doka, 119–32. Washington, D.C.: Hospice Foundation of America.

Williams, S. C., V. Fanolis, and G. Schamess. 2001. Adapting the Pynoos School Based Group Therapy Model for Use with Foster Children: Theoretical and Process Considerations. *Journal of Child and Adolescent Group Therapy* 11:57–76.

Wilson, D. L. 1995. An Outcome Study of a Time-Limited Group Intervention Program for Bereaved Children. *Dissertation Abstracts International*, Section A: *Humanities and Social Sciences* 55:3793.

Wilson, J. P., and J. D. Lindy, eds. 1994. *Countertransference and the Treatment of PTSD.* New York: Guilford Press.

Wilson, K. R., J. S. Wallin, and C. Reiser. 2003. Social Stratification and the Digital Divide. *Social Science Computer Review* 21:133–43.

Wilson, S., S. Cameron, P. Jaffe, and D. Wolfe. 1989. Children Exposed to Wife Abuse: An Intervention Model. *Social Casework: Journal of Contemporary Social Work* 70:180–84.

Windholz, M. J., C. R. Marmar, and J. J. Horowitz. 1985. A Review on the Research in Conjugal Bereavement: Impact on Health and Efficacy of Intervention. *Comprehensive Psychiatry* 26:433–47.

Wing, D., P. Clance, K. Burge-Callaway, and L. Armistead. 2001. Understanding Gender Difference in Bereavement Following the Death of an Infant: Implications for Treatment. *Psychotherapy* 38:60–72.

Wingram, T., I. N. Pederson, and L. O. Bonde. 2002. *A Comprehensive Guide to Music Therapy: Theory, Clinical Practice, Research, and Training.* Philadelphia: Kingsley.

Winston, C.A. 2003. African American Grandmothers Parenting AIDS Orphans: Concomitant Grief and Loss. *American Journal of Orthopsychiatry* 73:91–100.

Wittstein, I., et al. 2005. Neurohumoral Features of Myocardial Stunning Due to Sudden Emotional Stress. *New England Journal of Medicine* 6:539–48.

Wolchik, S. A., I. N. Sandler, and R. E. Millsap. 2002. Six-Year Follow-up of Preventive Interventions for Children of Divorce: A Randomized Controlled Trial. *Journal of the American Medical Association* 288:1874–81.

Wolf, R. S. 1998. Elder Abuse: Ten Years Later. *American Geriatrics Society* 36:758–62.

Wolf, R. S. 2000. The Nature and Scope of Elder Abuse. *Generations* 24:6–12.

Wolf, R. S., and K. Pillemer. 1989. *Helping Elderly Victims: The Reality of Elder Abuse.* New York: Columbia University Press.

Wolterstorff, N. 1987. *Lament for a Son.* Grand Rapids, Mich.: Eerdmans.

Wood, A., G. Trainor, and J. Rothwell. 2001. Randomized Trial of Group Therapy for Repeated Deliberate Self-Harm in Adolescents. *Journal of the American Academy of Child and Adolescent Psychiatry* 40:1246–53.

Worden, J. W. 1982. *Grief Counseling and Grief Therapy: A Handbook for the Mental Health Practitioner.* New York: Springer.

Worden, J. W. 1991. *Grief Counseling and Grief Therapy: A Handbook for the Mental Health Practitioner.* 2nd ed. New York: Springer.

Worden, J. W. 1996. *Children and Grief: When a Parent Dies.* New York: Guilford Press.

Worden, J. W. 2002. *Grief Counseling and Grief Therapy: A Handbook for Mental Health Practitioners.* 3rd ed. New York: Springer.

Worden, J. W., and P. Silverman. 1996. Parental Death and the Adjustment of School-Age Children. *Omega* 332:91–102.

Wortman, C. B. 2002. Changing Lives of Older Couples Study. Available at: http://cloc.isr.umich.edu/index.htm.

Wortman, C. B., and R. C. Silver. 1989. The Myths of Coping with Loss. *Journal of Consulting and Clinical Psychology* 57:349–57.

Wortman, C. B., and R. C. Silver. 2001. The Myths of Coping with Loss Revisited. In *Handbook of Bereavement Research: Consequences, Coping and Care*, edited by M. S. Stroebe, R. O. Hansson, W. Stroebe, and H. Schut, 405–29. Washington, D.C.: American Psychological Association.

Wyrostok, N. 1995. The Ritual as a Psychotherapeutic Intervention. *Psychotherapy* 32:397–404.

Yale, R. 1989. Support Groups for Newly Diagnosed Alzheimer's Clients. *Clinical Gerontology* 8:86–89.

Yalom, I. D., and S. Vinogradov. 1988. Bereavement Groups: Techniques and Themes. *International Journal of Group Psychotherapy* 38:419–46.

Yassen, J. 1995. Preventing Secondary Traumatic Stress Disorder. In *Compassion Fatigue: Coping with Secondary Traumatic Stress Disorder in Those Who Treat the Traumatized*, edited by C. R. Figley, 178–208. New York: Brunner/Mazel.

Young, B., and D. Black. 1997. Bereavement Counseling. In *Psychological Trauma: A Developmental Approach*, edited by D. Black, M. Newman, J. Harris-Hendriks, and G. Mezey, 250–63. Washington, D.C.: Gaskell.

Young, B., and D. Papadatou. 1997. Childhood Death and Bereavement Across Cultures. In *Death and Bereavement Across Cultures*, edited by C. M. Parkes, P. Laungani, and B. Young, 191–205. New York: Routledge.

Younoszai, B. 1993. Mexican American Perspectives Related to Death. In *Ethnic Variations in Dying, Death and Grief: Diversity in Universality*, edited by D. P. Irish, K. F. Lundquist, and V. J. Nelsen, 67–78. Washington, D.C.: Taylor & Francis.

Yule, W. 2001. When Disaster Strikes—The Need to Be "Wise Before the Event": Crisis Intervention with Children. *Advances in Mind–Body Medicine* 17:191–96.

Yule, W., and O. Udwin. 1991. Screening Child Survivors for Post-Traumatic Stress Disorders: Experiences from the "Jupiter" Sinking. *British Journal of Clinical Psychology* 30:131–38.

Zambelli, G. C., and E. J. Clark. 1994. Parentally Bereaved Children: Problems in School Adjustment and Implications for the School Social Worker. *School Social Work Journal* 19:1–15.

Zambelli, G. C., and A. P. DeRosa. 1992. Bereavement Support Groups for School-Age Children: Theory, Intervention, and Case Example. *American Journal of Orthopsychiatry* 62:484–93.

Zarit, S. H., M. A. P. Stephens, A. Townsend, and R. Greene. 1998. Stress Reduction for Family Caregivers: Effects of Adult Day Care Use. *Journals of Gerontology* 53B:S267–77.

Zarit, S. H., and J. M. Zarit. 1998. *Mental Disorders in Older Adults: Fundamentals of Assessment and Treatment.* New York: Guilford Press.

Zenere, F. J., and P. J. Lazarus. 1997. The Decline of Youth Suicidal Behavior in an Urban, Multicultural Public School System Following the Introduction of a Suicide Prevention and Intervention Program. *Suicide and Life-Threatening Behavior* 27:387–403.

Zinn, J., V. Simon, and J. Orme. 1997. From on the Couch to Online: Evaluating Internet Support Groups: A Research Study. *New Technology in the Human Services* 103:2–9.

Zisook, S. S., Y. Chentsova-Dutton, and S. R. Schuchter. 1998. Post-Traumatic Stress Disorder Following Bereavement. *Annals of Clinical Psychiatry* 10:157–63.

Zisook, S. S., and S. R. Schuchter. 1986. The First Four Years of Widowhood. *Psychiatric Annals* 15:288–94.

Zisook, S. S., and S. R. Schuchter. 1993. Major Depression Associated with Widowhood. *American Journal of Geriatric Psychiatry* 1:316–26.

Zisook, S. S., and S. R. Schuchter. 1996. Grief and Bereavement. In *Comprehensive Review of Geriatric Psychiatry: II,* 2nd ed., edited by J. Sadavoy, L. W. Lazarus, L. F. Jarvik, and G. T. Grossberg, 529–62. Washington, D.C.: American Psychiatric Press.

Zisook, S. S., and S. R. Schuchter. 2001. Treatment of the Depression of Bereavement. *American Behavioral Scientist* 44:782–97.

Zonnebelt-Smeenge, S. J., and R. C. DeVries 1998. *Getting to the Other Side of Grief: Overcoming the Loss of a Spouse.* Grand Rapids, Mich.: Baker Books.

Zulli, A. P., and O. D. Weeks. 1997. Healing Rituals: Pathways to Wholeness During Prolonged Illness and Following Death. In *Living with Grief: When Illness Is Prolonged,* edited by K. J. Doka, 177–92. Washington, D.C.: Hospice Foundation of America.

INDEX

Numbers in italics refer to boxes, and numbers in boldface indicate figures and tables.

Foundations of Social Work Knowledge
Frederic G. Reamer, Series Editor

David G. Gil, *Confronting Injustice and Oppression:
Concepts and Strategies for Social Workers*

George Alan Appleby and Jeane W. Anastas, *Not Just a Passing Phase:
Social Work with Gay, Lesbian, and Bisexual People*

Frederic G. Reamer, *Social Work Research and Evaluation Skills*

Pallassana R. Balgopal, *Social Work Practice with Immigrants and Refugees*

Dennis Saleeby, *Human Behavior and Social Environments: A Biopsychosocial Approach*

Frederic G. Reamer, *Tangled Relationships: Managing Boundary
Issues in the Human Services*

Roger A. Lohmann and Nancy L. Lohmann, *Social Administration*

David M. Austin, *Human Services Management: Organizational Leadership in
Social Work Practice*

Roger A. Lohmann and Nancy L. Lohmann, *Social Administration*

Toba Schwaber Kerson, *Boundary Spanning: An Ecological Reinterpretation of
Social Work Practice in Health and Mental Health Systems*

David M. Austin, *Human Services Management: Organizational Leadership in
Social Work Practice*

Anthony M. Maluccio, Barbara A. Pike, and Elizabeth M. Tracy,
Social Work Practice with Families and Children

Joan Shireman, *Critical Issues in Child Welfare*

Stuart A. Kirk, *Mental Disorders in the Social Environment*

Sheila H. Akabas and Paul A. Kurzman, *Social Work and the Workplace*

Frederic G. Reamer, *Social Work Values and Ethics*, Third Edition